SCOTTISH HISTORY SOCIETY

SIXTH SERIES

VOLUME 16

The General Account Book of John Clerk of Penicuik, 1663–1674

The General Account Book of John Clerk of Penicuik, 1663–1674

Edited by
J.R.D. Falconer

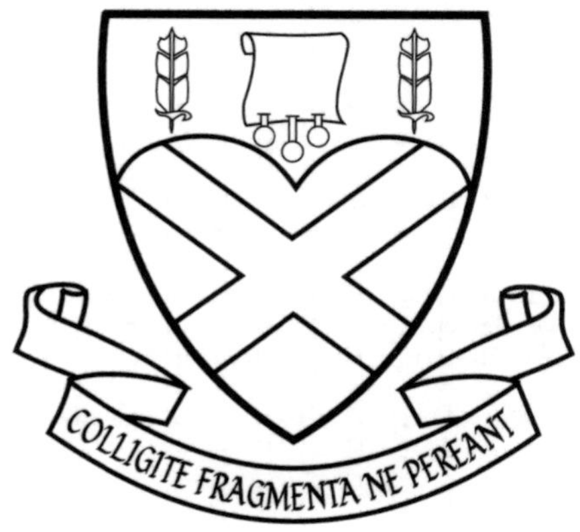
COLLIGITE FRAGMENTA NE PEREANT

SCOTTISH HISTORY SOCIETY
2021

THE BOYDELL PRESS

First published 2021

A Scottish History Society publication
in association with The Boydell Press
an imprint of Boydell & Brewer Ltd
PO Box 9, Woodbridge, Suffolk IP12 3DF, UK

and of Boydell & Brewer Inc.
668 Mt Hope Avenue, Rochester, NY 14620–2731, USA

website: www.boydellandbrewer.com

ISBN 978-0-906245-46-0

A CIP catalogue record for this book is available
from the British Library

Typeset by BBR Design, Sheffield
Printed and bound in Great Britain by TJ Books Limited, Padstow, Cornwall

CONTENTS

ACKNOWLEDGEMENTS

This transcription began as a collaborative project with Ashley Sims, a doctoral student at the University of Alberta. While considerable demands on her time, and the consequences of the COVID-19 pandemic, caused her to be far less involved, it is important to me that I recognise her contributions. Early in the development of this transcription, Ms. Sims played an important role in shaping the proposal and sharing with me her expertise on early modern material culture and trade. I am grateful for all of her assistance in helping to get this project off the ground. A heartfelt thanks also goes to the staff at the National Records of Scotland who provided me exceptional assistance during various trips to Edinburgh. The Office of Research Services at MacEwan University (and the members of various funding committees) provided the necessary financial support that enabled me to travel to Scotland to undertake the research for this work. Dr. John McCallum, Publication Secretary and General Editor, answered all my many email queries, extended his patience, and provided the level and quality of support all academics desire when preparing a manuscript. Of course, this transcription would not have been possible without the support of Sir Robert Clerk Bt. OBE. Sir Robert not only gave his permission to use the Clerk Papers, he actively encouraged the project from the beginning. My sincerest thanks to all of these individuals, and to my colleagues, family, and friends who provided advice, distraction, and encouragement along the way.

Rob Falconer
Grant MacEwan University

INTRODUCTION

In 2013, the Scottish History Society published a letter book belonging to John Clerk, a Scottish merchant who lived and operated in Paris between 1634 and 1646, edited by Siobhan Talbott.[1] Talbott's transcription, and her compelling scholarship on Scottish merchants in Europe, has helped shed light on the world of early modern commercial relationships while providing insights into Clerk's robust trade and banking network and a system built on reputation and trust.[2] Others have focused on Clerk's early years, highlighting his talents as an importer of European art and provider of luxury goods to Scottish elites. Yet, considerably more ink has been spilt examining his progeny; at least one scholar has noted that any interest in Clerk may be due to how he 'points the way to his successors'.[3] Fortunately, Clerk was a prodigious bookkeeper,

1 'The Letter-Book of John Clerk, 1644–45'. *Miscellany of the Scottish History Society* 15, vol. 8, S. Talbott (ed.) (Scottish History Society, 2013), 1–54.

2 S. Talbott, 'Communities on the Continent: Franco-Scottish Network Building in a Comparative European Context, 1560–1685'. *Ecosse et Ses Doubles Ancien Monde Nouveau Monde Old World New World Scotland and Its Doubles* (2010), 21–42; Talbott, 'Beyond "the antiseptic realm of theoretical economic models": New perspectives on Franco-Scottish commerce and the auld alliance in the long seventeenth century'. *Journal of Scottish Historical Studies* 31, no. 2 (2011), 149–168; Talbott, 'British commercial interests on the French Atlantic coast, c.1560–1713'. *Historical Research* 85, no. 229 (2012), 394–409; Talbott, *Conflict, commerce and Franco-Scottish relations, 1560–1713* (London, 2015).

3 I.G. Brown, *Clerks of Penicuik: Portraits of Taste & Talent* (Penicuik, 1987), 7. See also I.G. Brown, 'Sir John Clerk of Penicuik; Aspects of a Virtuoso Life'. University of Cambridge Ph.D. dissertation, 1980; Brown, 'Critick in Antiquity: Sir John Clerk of Penicuik'. *Antiquity* 51, no. 203 (1977), 201; Brown & L. Borley, 'Prelude and pattern: the remarkable Grand Tour of Sir John Clerk of Penicuik (1676–1755) in the 1690s', in L. Borley (ed.), *The Grand Tour and its Influence on Architecture, Artistic Taste and Patronage* (Edinburgh, 2008), 45–71; S. Booth, 'The Early Career of Alexander Runciman and His Relations with Sir James Clerk of Penicuik'. *Journal of the Warburg and Courtauld Institutes* (1969), 332–343; W. Spink, 'Sir John Clerk of Penicuik: Landowner as Designer', in P. Willis (ed.), *Furor Hortensis: Essays on the English Landscape in Honour of H.F. Clarke* (Norwich, VT, 1974), 30–38; A.A. Tait, 'Robert Adam and John Clerk of Eldin'. *Master Drawings* (1978), 53–111; P.R. Backscheider, 'Defoe and the Clerks of Penicuik'. *Modern Philology* 84, no. 4 (1987), 372–381; P. Davidson, 'Herman Boerhaave and John Clerk of Penicuik: friendship and musical collaboration'. *Proceedings of the Royal College of Physicians of Edinburgh* 22, no. 4 (1992), 503–518; S. Cooper, 'Sir John Clerk's garden buildings at Penicuik'. *Architectural Heritage* 13, no. 1 (2002), 47–62; B. Mahon, *The man who changed everything: the life of James Clerk Maxwell* (Chichester, 2004); N. Uglow, 'Antiquity, architecture and country house poetry: Sir John Clerk and the Country Seat'. *North Street Review: Arts and Visual Culture* 13 (2009), 35–45; M.R.F. Williams, 'The inner lives

and his personal and business records contain a wealth of information about his mercantile activities at home and abroad, as well as his extensive social and commercial networks. As his grandson, Sir John Clerk 2nd Bt., noted, Clerk's business acumen can be attested to 'by many of his books which are still in the charter house of Pennicuik [sic]'.[4] The contents that fill Clerk's books and records furnish scholars with an opportunity to build on the work that has already been done examining Clerk's continental business activities.

The manuscript transcribed below provides another window into Clerk's life, blending his world of trade and banking with his life as an improving landlord and financier after he purchased the barony of Penicuik in 1654. This particular account book, which Clerk referred to as a 'book of yeirlie disbursements', begins almost ten years after he 'retired' from trade and started to set down roots in the Scottish countryside.[5] It captures a vast array of household expenditures, including consumables, household durables, his wives' and children's material support, the latter's education, as well as disbursements to labourers, domestic servants, doctors, and various factors operating on behalf of Clerk and his family. Itemised payments to various merchants and craftsmen (both local and from further afield) are common throughout the book, along with summaries and notes on the goods purchased. Such entries suggest the depth and breadth of lowland Scotland's commercial scope in the seventeenth century while assisting the historian in reconstructing Clerk's social and political networks that connected him to many of Scotland's merchants and elite members of society and to those in England and on the Continent. Collectively, the material found in Clerk's records may help facilitate mapping

of early modern travel'. *Historical Journal* 62, no. 2 (2019), 349–373; J. Tildesley, 'The Influence of the Theories of John Clerk of Eldin on British Fleet Tactics, 1782–1805'. *The Mariner's Mirror* 106, no. 2 (2020), 162–174.

4 *Memoirs of the Life of Sir John Clerk of Penicuik: Baronet, Baron of the Exchequer, Extracted by Himself from His Own Journals, 1676–1755*, vol. 12, J. Gray (ed.) (Scottish History Society, 1892), 7. The papers of the Clerk family of Penicuik are extensive, covering business, household, and personal affairs. Currently housed in the National Records of Scotland (NRS), GD18: Papers of Clerk family of Penicuik is an impressive fund comprising approximately 6,458 distinct manuscript collections dating from 1373. There are also a number of related papers in the National Library of Scotland (NLS) as well as a series of uncatalogued papers and objects which have been returned to the Penicuik estate.

5 NRS GD18/2186: General account book (household, personal and estate) of John Clerk of Penicuik and his son, Sir John Clerk of Penicuik, bt (1663–1720). This transcription ends with the death of John Clerk in 1674. Clerk's son, Sir John, maintained the second half of the account book after Clerk's death, with entries made until the early 1720s. The reference mentioned here can be found below, [111]. There are a few earlier household account books for the period between 1654 and 1663. GD18/2393: 'Account book of John Clerk, merchant in Paris, France, later of Pennycook [sic], including account of payments of the price of the lands and barony of Pennycook [sic]'; GD18/2506 contains specialist accounts but also 'Personal, estate and household accounts, 1656–1662'.

his spending patterns, community relations, employment opportunities, and political networks.[6]

However, the importance of this account book for scholars is not merely to help illuminate aspects of early modern economic history. Perhaps unexpectedly, it also provides the reader with a glimpse into parts of early modern life that often escape documentation or are more difficult to uncover: household life-cycle events; the accomplishments of children; personal afflictions and day-to-day concerns; social exchange; and landlord–tenant relationships. Crucially, Clerk does more than simply note such things. In between listing goods and services acquired for the household, Clerk also recorded his observations on the politics of the county, the regional land market, household-family experiences, and the occasional tensions between his neighbours. As one might expect from such a book, it also helps bring some of the more quotidian aspects of early modern life into the picture. Clerk routinely noted the gifts he gave to his children, friends, servants, and farm labourers, the recipes for ink and medications, the titles of books and types of candies purchased on trips into Edinburgh, and how much the household spent monthly on consumables like eggs, white bread, and beef. Clerk also documented any travel that he, members of his household, or proxies undertook on behalf of the family to procure goods, investigate opportunities (commercial, social, political), and to maintain his relationships. These accounts reveal that he spent a significant amount of time, money, and energy improving his estate during a period where political unrest and social instability made such activities relatively rare.[7] Ultimately, this book of disbursements helps bring to life the Clerk household's day-to-day experience, the family's growing influence on local society, and the manner in which Clerk worked to secure a future for his children, the estate, and his family name. Perhaps more importantly, Clerk's records can contribute to broader inquiries into domestic consumption, the improvement of landed estates, gendered spending patterns, the employment of labour, household priorities, material culture, and identities and consumer behaviour in the last half of the seventeenth century.

Recently, a number of micro-historical studies on seventeenth-century households have altered the way we think about consumption in the early modern period. Challenging an earlier tendency to see increased consumerism as primarily an eighteenth-century phenomenon, Jane Whittle and

[6] I am currently working on a monograph-length study of Clerk examining his transition from merchant to landlord after he purchased the barony of Penicuik. Clerk's merchant and banking networks and their implications for understanding Scottish gentry material culture is also the subject of a current University of Alberta doctoral study being undertaken by Ashley Sims.

[7] I.D. Whyte, *Scotland's Society and Economy in Transition, c.1500–c.1760* (London, 1997), 14; Talbott, 'Letter-Book', 3.

Elizabeth Griffiths' reconstruction of the Le Strange household in early seventeenth-century Norfolk, and Susan Whyman's study of the Verney family of Buckinghamshire between 1660 and 1720, have expanded our conception of both the types of goods and services consumed and the period in which consumption patterns began to change.[8] Clerk's accounts point us to very similar conclusions for Scotland.[9] Like those kept by Alice Le Strange and Joyce Jeffreys, Clerk's accounts reveal household spending priorities, but they also identify producers of goods, providers of services, and networks of interdependencies. Because they also include disbursements for (and commentary on) farm labour, the support he provided to his tenants, land acquisitions, and improvements on all of the lands on his estate, Clerk's entries can also help us understand better the complex nature of tenant society.[10] While no single source is sufficient for illuminating the past, the wide-ranging material found in the transcription below should enable scholars to question more broadly current assumptions about seventeenth-century Scotland and guide them towards a deeper understanding of early modern households, patterns of consumption, material culture, and the relationships central to these aspects of Scottish life.

The knowledge arising from keeping a close account of expenditures, and from cross-referencing entries made in this book with other specialist accounts, enabled Clerk to maintain control over household activities. By reconciling bills, predicting revenue streams, organising expenditure groups, and keeping track of weekly, monthly, and annual financial obligations, Clerk's account book played a large role in his household management. There is some debate around the reliability of early modern account books to provide usable data concerning prices, wages, movement of commodities, or changes in living standards.[11] In this regard, Jason Scott-Warren's argument that 'financial

8 J. Whittle & E. Griffiths, *Consumption and Gender in the Early Seventeenth-Century Household: The World of Alice Le Strange* (Oxford, 2012); S. Whyman, *Sociability and Power in Late-Stuart England: The Cultural Worlds of the Verneys 1660–1720* (Oxford, 1999). To these two outstanding examples can be added Judith Spicksley's impressive edited volume of the *Business and Household Accounts of Joyce Jeffreys: Spinster of Hereford, 1638–1648* (Oxford, 2012). While not a monograph that examines patterns of consumption, Spicksley's introduction and careful transcription of Jeffrey's accounts support many of the conclusions drawn in the other two works.

9 Michael Pearce's Ph.D. thesis examining domestic furnishings in early modern Scotland highlights some of the important changes in consumerism occurring in the seventeenth century. While Pearce's focus is primarily on noble households, he does examine Clerk's role in providing luxury goods to some of Scotland's elites. M. Pearce, 'Vanished comforts: locating roles of domestic furnishings in Scotland, 1500–1650'. University of Dundee Ph.D. thesis, 2016).

10 See, for example, I.D. Whyte & K.A. Whyte, 'Continuity and Change in a Seventeenth-Century Scottish Farming Community', *The Agricultural History Review* 32, no. 2 (1984), 159–169.

11 J. Scott-Warren, 'Early modern bookkeeping and life-writing revisited: accounting for Richard Stonley'. *Past & Present* 230, no. supplemental 11 (2016), 151–170; B.G. Carruthers

accounts may be more valuable to the cultural than the economic historian' is compelling. Like many of the account books kept in merchant households, Clerk's book captures so much more than its rows and columns of figures might first suggest. As a form of early modern life-writing, Clerk's account book is valuable not only for identifying the vast quantity and quality of goods and services the household consumed, and the wide-ranging economic activities in which his household participated, but, perhaps even more so, because Clerk recorded them in a highly personalised manner. Indeed, much of this account book reads like a private diary. In part, this can be explained by the fact that households often kept multiple versions of their private accounts in the form of letter books, waste books, and disbursement books, each one potentially capturing the information differently from the next. While it has been suggested that in elite households the task of keeping disbursement accounts often fell to senior male servants, there is no indication that this was the case in Clerk's household.[12] The detail and nature of the personal commentary within the accounts points to Clerk being the principal author of the book until his health began to fail in the winter of 1673–4; from that point on, one of Clerk's children, likely his son John, maintained the book until 1720.[13] Because of the many gaps, spaces, breaks in chronology throughout the book, not to mention the occasional error Clerk made when recording the information or when he changed his mind about *what* he wanted to record or *how* he wanted that information recorded, it is impossible to trace the development of this account book. While it is unclear the extent to which bookkeeping formed part of Clerk's apprenticeship either before or during his time in Paris, there is growing consensus that accounting was an important aspect of a merchant's education gained either through grammar schools or in an apprenticeship.[14]

Beyond documenting household disbursements, and perhaps to maintain personal solvency, Clerk's intention for keeping *this* particular set of accounts is not entirely clear. The cover page on the original, added in 1733 by Clerk's grandson, suggests that the information contained in the book identifies the household's method of accounting, its methods of management, and the price

& W.N. Espeland, 'Accounting for rationality: Double-entry bookkeeping and the rhetoric of economic rationality'. *American Journal of Sociology* 97, no. 1 (1991), 31–69; E. Tebeaux, 'Visual texts: Format and the evolution of English accounting texts, 1100–1700'. *Journal of Technical Writing and Communication* 30, no. 4 (2000), 307–341.

12 Whittle & Griffiths, *Consumption and Gender*, 9.

13 As I have noted below, the account book was likely paginated sometime after Clerk's lifetime. I have maintained the page numbering as found in the original, but have inserted them in square brackets and placed them at the start of each new page. Any reference to specific pages from the original follows this convention. See below, [167]–.

14 J.R. Edwards, 'Accounting education in Britain during the early modern period'. *Accounting History Review* 21, no. 1 (2011), 37–67, at 41. For the convincing arguments around early modern gentry women being educated in accounting, see R.E. Connor, *Women, Accounting and Narrative: Keeping Books in Eighteenth-Century England* (London, 2004); Spicksley, *Business and Household Accounts of Joyce Jeffreys*, xxv–xxvii.

of goods purchased. Clerk recorded very little of these household activities dispassionately, with any exacting precision, or without adding some context. The general layout of the original does not provide any guidance on whether this set of accounts was intended primarily to reconcile other specialist accounts or personal accounts kept by members of the household. While page numbers hint at a particular sequence, there are gaps in the numbering that occur at different points in the book, blank pages in between pages with full accounts, and pages that contain entries which are out of chronological order. The first nine pages of the book are out of sequence with the rest of the accounts. Likewise, towards the very end of the book, where entries date to the 1710s and 1720s, there are pages dedicated to recording expenses from Clerk's lifetime and entered in his own hand. Some of the entries on these pages replicate, either in full or in part, material recorded elsewhere in the book. Starting on page ten, the bulk of the entries appear in a more chronological order.

Occasionally, Clerk digressed from his typical accounting method to provide reflections on other aspects of his personal and business ventures – moneylending, movement of goods to his clients or from his factors, land disputes with his neighbours. There are also moments when Clerk seems to have forgotten information when he sat down to write in this book, perhaps intending to come back at a later date to insert a name, item, place, or amount in the blank space that he had left reserved. Beyond those instances where he struck out what he had written, there are other indications of dating errors, misnamed individuals, or changes in how he wanted to document an expense. On occasion, Clerk's tallies are inaccurate, unclear, or incomplete. Where this occurs, I have left the errors uncorrected and made note of the discrepancy. Yet, what Clerk chose to record, and the fact that many of the entries and lengthy narrative passages contain such fine detail, require us to value these accounts for what they can tell us about expenditures, prices, available goods, and processes, regardless of his occasional errors and omissions. Perhaps it is owing to such periodic imprecision that Clerk's account book offers as much to the cultural and social historian as it does to the economic historian.

Supporting his grandson's assertion about the prodigious number of books in the family charter house, Clerk makes numerous references to specialist accounts and records that either he, or other members of the household, kept. The family stored most of the important household papers in an iron trunk, each one placed in a linen bag for safekeeping and carefully marked for easy identification. Some of the entries in this book reconcile outstanding receipts, debts, or expenditures. In one entry for the month of October 1671, Clerk alludes to his son, James, not only keeping his own accounts, but also failing to reconcile his expenses as part of the household disbursements that Clerk documented in this book.[15] As has been noted already, Clerk's eldest son, John,

15 See below, [127].

not only maintained separate accounts, he had already begun contributing to this book prior to assuming full responsibility for it in early 1674.[16] The various entries in this book that show disbursements paid out directly by Clerk's first wife, Mary Gray, his second wife, Elizabeth Johnston, their children, or by Clerk on their behalf, also make explicit the fact that members of the family kept separate account of their expenditures. Collectively they point to a level of shared household responsibility and accountability.[17] Outside of the occasional gift or a reference to sums given by Clerk to 'my wyffe' to cover expenses when she travelled, for her to buy items for the children, or for her to pay for goods or services that he had arranged, this book contains very few entries documenting Gray's personal expenses. It is possible that Gray, and later Johnston, maintained separate account books to record expenditures not captured in this household book.[18] In March 1663, Clerk paid slightly more than £2.00 'for a compt booke for my wyffe covert in reid leather'.[19] But, unlike the references Clerk makes to a 'booke covert with parchement whair servants fies is wreatten down', this reference does not provide clues as to the types of expenditure Gray recorded in her own account book.[20] Spicksly, Whittle, and Griffiths have revealed the tremendous insights that can be gained into the gendered nature of consumption and methods of accounting found in books kept by early modern women. Likewise, Cathryn Spence has helped to illuminate the crucial role women played as 'active participants' in early modern Scottish networks of debt and credit while routinely engaging in a wide range of economic activities.[21] Unfortunately, it is unclear whether Mary Gray's account books survived or if they were incorporated into other records; they are not readily identifiable amongst the Clerk Papers. While no doubt it would be a great loss if they have not survived, this book captures some of their economic activities.

★

Despite the voluminous records he left behind, John Clerk of Penicuik (1611–1674) has not garnered the same level of historical interest as his son,

[16] See below, [79].

[17] J. De Vries, 'The industrial revolution and the industrious revolution'. *The Journal of Economic History* 54, no. 2 (1994), 249–270; Whittle & Griffiths, *Consumption and Gender*, Ch. 2 'Household management', 26–48.

[18] Clerk and Johnston were married in Edinburgh in January 1670. Johnston was the daughter of a London-based merchant, John Johnston. While a common name, it is likely that this is the same John Johnston with whom Clerk transacted business in the late 1640s. GD18/2423, 'Letters from John Jhonstoun [Johnston] in London to John Clerk in Paris'. It is interesting to note that Clerk recorded in this book considerably more disbursements on Johnston's behalf than he did for Mary Gray. On the subject of 'housewives' keeping separate accounts, see Whittle & Griffiths, *Consumption and Gender*, 31–33.

[19] See below, [11].

[20] See below, [55], [56], [107], [122], and [163].

[21] C. Spence, *Women, credit, and debt in early modern Scotland* (Manchester, 2016).

grandson, and great-grandson.[22] Yet, the Montrose-born merchant, who by the age of 35 was able to retire from his trade and take up the life of a country gentleman, would at his death leave his family in a position of wealth, influence, and stature that ensured their regional and national ascendance. In his *Memoirs*, Sir John Clerk noted that his grandfather was 'an excellent occonomist' and 'a man of great sense and great application to business'.[23] Echoing this assessment, I.G. Brown argued that Clerk was 'the genius behind the eminence of his line'.[24] At the age of 16, Clerk was apprenticed to an Edinburgh Merchant, James Naismith, and in 1634 he was sent to Paris to continue his training, employed as a factor for another Scottish merchant, John Smith.[25] For the next 12 years, Clerk carved out his own path, establishing a considerable trade in luxury items, and supplying foreign art and goods to an extensive clientele that ranged geographically across Scotland, France, Italy, Spain, and the Netherlands, and socially across the ranks of early modern society.[26] While Clerk made frequent trips back to Scotland to maintain his relationships closer to home, he was always a man on the move, recognising the need to be available to his financiers, clients, and business partners.[27] It is unclear, then, what prompted Clerk to remain in Scotland following a trip home in late summer 1646; by September of that year he was styling himself a 'merchant of Edinburgh'.[28] Having amassed a small fortune of £10,000

22 Clerk's son, Sir John Clerk, 1st Bt. (d. 1722), was an MP for Edinburgh; his even more famous grandson, Sir John Clerk, 2nd Bt. (d. 1755), was a baron of the exchequer of Scotland and commissioner for the Union. John Clerk of Eldin, Clerk's great-grandson, was a founding member of the Royal Society of Edinburgh. On Clerk's descendants, see, for example, P.R. Backscheider, 'Defoe and the Clerks of Penicuik'. *Modern Philology* 84, no. 4 (1987), 372–381; Brown, *The Clerks of Penicuik: Portraits of Taste & Talent*.

23 Gray, *Memoirs*, 7.

24 For more on the second Sir John Clerk, see Brown, 'Sir John Clerk of Penicuik (1676–1755): aspects of a virtuoso life'.

25 NRS, GD18/2357, 13 June 1627. The contract between Clerk and Smith indicates that Clerk remained a 'servitor' to Naismith, that any profits generated during the first year belonged to Smith, and that Clerk was to be employed for a sum of '240 francs'. NRS GD18/2359. For his time in Paris, see J.L. Williams, 'The Import of Art: the taste for northern European goods in Scotland in the seventeenth century', in J. Rodding & L. Heerma van Voss (eds.), *The North Sea Culture (1550–1800): Proceedings of the International Conference held at Leiden 21–22 April 1995* (Hilversum, 1995), 298–323, at 306; Talbott, *Conflict, Commerce and Franco-Scottish Relations*.

26 S. Talbott's work on Clerk's activities in Paris, and as a provider of goods and cash to Scottish elites at home, remains the most comprehensive to date. See, for example, *Conflict, Commerce and Franco-Scottish Relations, 1560–1713*. For biographical information on Clerk, see S. Talbott, 'Clerk, John (1611–1674), merchant and landowner'. *Oxford Dictionary of National Biography* (17 September 2015).

27 Talbott, *Conflict, Commerce and Franco-Scottish Relations*, 84, 93.

28 Talbott, 'Beyond "the antiseptic realm of theoretical economic models"', 165. If Clerk's grandson is to be believed, 'upon some disgust in this country, [Clerk] had an intention to have returned again to France'. Gray, *Memoirs*, 4. There has been some suggestion that Clerk's disgust centred on the political unrest Scotland experienced at the time. See Williams, 'The Import of Art', 321.

sterling while in France, and having established connections with Scottish aristocrats, gentlemen, and a number of highly successful merchants, Clerk chose to 'give over all trade' and take up the role of country gentleman.[29] In 1654, Clerk purchased the barony of Penicuik from the heiresses of the countess of Eglinton where, until his death from 'a kind of palsy' in 1674, he worked tirelessly to build up his family's position in the region.[30]

Despite 'retiring' to Penicuik, Clerk continued to participate in mercantile affairs and banking; his trade networks remained incredibly active and the number of individuals to whom he made loans continued to grow throughout the 1660s and early 1670s. His steadfast relationship with William Kerr, 3rd earl of Lothian underscores the importance of social capital in this period.[31] From the 1640s onwards, Clerk actively fed Kerr's seemingly insatiable appetite for art and luxury goods; he also covered many of the earl's growing debts.[32] His ability to navigate the trying political climate of the mid-seventeenth century paralleled his skilfulness at managing and maintaining relationships with friends and partners who were, at times, at odds with one another. In this regard, the protracted legal battle between Michel Mel and Sir William Gray of Pittendrum stands out. Mel, a Scottish merchant based in Dieppe, was one of Clerk's most active trade partners in France, while Gray was a prominent Edinburgh merchant whose daughter, Mary, Clerk married in 1647.[33] When Gray and Mel fell out in the mid-1640s, Clerk used his influence in the region

29 According to Sir John, his grandfather's wealth would have been considerably more substantial had he not retired to the country. Gray, *Memoirs*, 7.

30 In 1646, Sir John Preston sold the Penicuik estates to Margaret Scott, the countess of Eglinton. At the time, the lands included the town and lands of Penicuik; the tower, mill, and 'dominical lands'; the lands of Newbiggin, Luffness, and Silverburn; Cairnhill; the lands of Dykneuk, Brunstane, Ravenshaugh, Braidwood, Walston, and Auchincorth; the lands of Halls and Leadburn; and the lands of Cuiken. See J. Wilson, *The Annals of Penicuik: Being a History of the Parish and of the Village* (Edinburgh, 1891), 147–149. According to a copy of a renunciation by 'Sir John Prestoun, and James Prestoun, his eldest son, to John Clerk, merchant burgess of Edinburgh', the Prestons maintained an interest in the lands and barony of Penicuik, including an annual rent of 3,200 merks, until August 1654. NRS GD18/174. On Clerk's death, see below, [174], [175]; Gray, *Memoirs*, 7.

31 Brown, *The Clerks of Penicuik: Portraits of Taste & Talent*, 7; R.M.G. Wenley, 'William, third earl of Lothian: covenanter and collector'. *Journal of the History of Collections* 5, no. 1 (1993), 23–41; Talbott, 'Beyond "the antiseptic realm"'; Talbott, *Conflict, Commerce and Franco-Scottish Relations*.

32 For example, NRS GD40/2/18/1/8; NRS GD18/2425; NRS GD18/2499.

33 During the reign of Charles I, Gray was considered to be one of Scotland's wealthiest and most successful merchants. His fortunes took a dramatic turn during the War of the Three Kingdoms. For his association with Montrose, he faced considerable pecuniary penalties and was temporarily imprisoned in Edinburgh Castle. He died in 1648. After his death, Gray's wife, Geils Smith, continued to live in the three-storey house Gray had built off the Grassmarket in Edinburgh in 1622. The house was purchased in 1719 by Lady Stair, widow of the 1st earl of Stair. Smith appears frequently in Clerk's book of disbursements. See also W. Harrison, *Memorable Edinburgh Houses* (Oliphant, Anderson and Ferrier, 1898), 10.

to find a solution that would satisfy both parties, recognising the need to protect both reputation and trust as crucial to being successful in business.[34]

As a businessman, Clerk did not suffer fools gladly. A particularly entertaining example of this can be found near the beginning of Clerk's book where he devotes an entire page to set down a scathing assessment of the questionable business practice of his hind, Walter Stewart.[35] Clerk's contempt for unsound trade deals and price gouging, a person's poor character, or a foolish decision that affected him in some way can also be detected in many of the annotations he provides throughout the book. In reference to one of the 'customers' at the West Port who was trying to overcharge him, Clerk noted that he 'wold not be hard with a baisse fellow for so small a matter'.[36] In what to modern ears may sound like casting profane aspersions, Clerk referred to Thomas Rob as a 'faking rascall' due to his shoddy workmanship and for overstaying his welcome at Newbiggin, where he had been employed to make shoes for the household.[37] James Clerk was on the receiving end of his father's freely given criticisms after he indulged in a new suit of clothes while in London and failed to notify his father of his purchase. The elder Clerk noted this unreconciled transaction by exclaiming that he thought this 'a bold impertinent thriftles baisse trick'.[38] In one of the more lengthy narrative sections in the account book, Clerk documented the events surrounding a land dispute with one of his neighbours, Alexander Gibson. Clerk blamed the 'controversy' on Gibson's tenant, James Portois, a 'covetous crocadaill' who Clerk believed was trying to cheat him out of a section of land on his estate. In recounting a meeting with Gibson to address the matter, Clerk referred to one of Gibson's allies as 'Mr Alexander Gibsone bouffe his brother a friend off his own'.[39]

By the 1660s (at least), Clerk had transformed the family home at Newbiggin into the epicentre of his extensive landholding, trade, and industrial activities. A remarkable feature of Clerk's book is the insight it provides into his extensive network of local tradesmen, artisans, farm labourers, and domestic servants that he employed on a regular basis and the exacting standards to which he held all whose services he contracted.[40] Recent scholarship on consumption in

[34] NRS GD18/2463. Talbott, *Conflict, Commerce and Franco-Scottish Relations*, 44–45. Clerk's continued relationship with both Gray's widow and Mel after retiring to Newbiggin can be seen on a number of the entries below. See, for example, [16], [18], [32], [33].

[35] Below, [6].

[36] Below, [27].

[37] Below, [105]. 'Fakin' or 'faikin' means deceitful or fraudulent.

[38] Below, [127].

[39] The term 'bouffe' can be defined as 'a dull, big, stout person'. Clerk used this term to describe his contempt for Gibson's brother. Below, [125].

[40] On the trades, see, for example, A. Allen, *Building early modern Edinburgh: a social history of craftwork and incorporation* (Edinburgh University Press, 2018); A. Allen, 'Finding the builders: Sources lost and extant for Edinburgh's Incorporation of Mary's Chapel', in *Scottish Archives: The Journal of the Scottish Record Association* 20 (2014); M. Jenkins (ed.), *Building Scotland: Celebrating Scotland's Traditional Building Materials* (Edinburgh, 2010).

this period has rightly reflected on the fact that 'practices', as much as objects, help us to understand better gender differences, urban–rural distinctions, and the more ephemeral aspects of goods and services.[41] In this regard, Clerk's accounts provide a relatively unobstructed view into consumption in a rural gentry household. In addition to the unique curios and domestic furnishings accounted for in this book, Clerk's careful recording of wages paid to, gifts given to, and experiences shared with those who undertook labour on his estate will help scholars to refine our knowledge of this facet of early modern Scottish rural history. Moreover, Clerk's reflections on these individuals help illuminate some of the relationships he developed in the region. For example, the account book shows that Clerk developed a solid, long-standing, working relationship with one John Smith and his wife, often using Smith to run errands and his wife for laundry and weaving services. In one instance, the 'good wife' was unable to remove spots from some linens Clerk had given her to clean. In entering the expense for her service, Clerk noted that 'the 15 ell off lining wes not weell bleitched at all – nor ticht nor cleinlie bot it is no mater – I am sorie I sould have troubled you & thanks you for the pains ye have been at'.[42] One of the more intriguing individuals mentioned in the accounts is John Rob, by all appearances one of Clerk's most trusted servants. The book does not make clear his precise role on the estate, but Clerk entrusted Rob to run a very wide variety of errands, obtaining goods and delivering items and cash on behalf of his master. Appearing in the accounts more than anyone who was not related to Clerk by blood, Rob's service began sometime prior to January 1663 and continued until at least Clerk's death in April 1674.

As early as the late 1650s, Clerk worked to improve and add to the house at Newbiggin. A contract made in 1658 with a 'Wille Gray' to 'sklait' the house at Newbiggin provides details of the expense paid for work on the estate while offering a small glimpse into Clerk's standards:

> The money that I peyit to that decaiving kobling knaive Wille Gray [...] his casting up off thair measuring as apears on the peper markit RP cam only to 6 rudes, 30 ells & ane quarter. So that unworthie knave hath got much more money as his wark cums too. Bot iff it had been weill done I wold have cared the lesse – bot it wes all togither stiked & spilt and rained in very many places. Witness the peper markit KL what hath met with such ane obscene decaiving rascal as he is it had been telling me the double off the money I gave him that I had never seen his theiffs face – let him be hanged & so I let him go.[43]

41 S. Pennell, 'Consumption and consumerism in early modern England'. *The Historical Journal* 42, no. 2 (1999), 555; Whittle & Griffiths, *Consumption and Gender*, 2–3.

42 See below, [161].

43 NRS GD18/1749.

Gray's workmanship clearly did not measure up; this may explain why he does not appear in this account book. After 1663 (and likely before), Clerk regularly employed Andrew Casse and John Mein to slate the houses on the Penicuik estate.[44] Crucially, the material found in the transcription below reveals a tremendous amount of productivity, improvement, and advancement taking place on Clerk's estates during a century known more for its general 'crisis'.[45]

Typical of seventeenth-century gentry households, the Clerk household expended a fair amount to keep the house at Newbiggin well appointed. On top of helping to identify the cost of such goods, the account book draws attention to the quality and variety of beds, 'chyres', cabinets, and marble tables, not to mention all of the necessary fabrics, curtains, cushions, and pillows, acquired for the household. Likewise, there were frequent purchases of silverware, glassware, vases, and ornate frames and clocks to complement the relatively modest, yet status-appropriate furnishings. A nice example of this sort of spending can be found on the 'back cover' of the original manuscript, where Clerk noted the acquisition of a 'fyne chass brod off Indian wood and boxwood wood with 32 box wood chasse men blak and yellow'.[46] The study of consumerism and consumption has relied heavily on surviving inventories to shed light on material culture, particularly household durables, often listed by room to reflect both what had been acquired and how it had been used.[47] But, as many have noted, inventories do not document expenditures or how items were used over time, nor do they capture the full extent of household consumption.[48] One of the most dominant features of this account book is the recording of expenses for textiles and foodstuffs, key areas of household consumption that are very rarely captured by probate inventories. From bustian to bukram, damask to dornock, lace, plaiding, and silk, Clerk spent considerable sums dressing his family. His records also reveal an extensive network of weavers, knitters, tailors, and cordiners who were employed on a regular basis to fashion the household, not to mention the tinkers, coopers, and gold and silver smiths who produced, repaired, or refurbished its material goods.

44 See below, [22], [32], [39], [69].

45 Talbott, *Conflict, Commerce and Franco-Scottish Relations*, 84–93; E.J. Cowan, 'The making of the National Covenant', in J. Morrill (ed.), *The Scottish National Covenant in its British Context* (Edinburgh, 1990), 69–89.

46 See below, [back cover].

47 R. Garrard, 'English probate inventories and their use in studying the significance of the domestic interior, 1570–1700', in Ad Van der Woude and A. Schuurman (eds.), *Probate inventories: a new source for the historical study of wealth, material culture and agricultural development* (Utrecht, 1980), 55–81; L. Weatherill, *Consumer behaviour and material culture in Britain, 1660–1760* (Hove, 1996); Pennell, 'Consumption and consumerism in early modern England', 549–564; For a Scottish example, see Pearce, 'Vanished comforts', 26–32.

48 Whittle & Griffiths, *Consumption and Gender*, 117–118; D. Dean, A. Hann, M. Overton, and J. Whittle, *Production and consumption in English households 1600–1750* (London, 2004); M. Overton, 'Household wealth, indebtedness, and economic growth in early modern England' (2006); Pearce, 'Vanished comforts'.

Sara Pennell's work on the material culture of the kitchen has demonstrated that food, the 'pre-eminent' consumer good, has somewhat inexplicably been underexamined by historians of consumption.[49] Fuel, food, drink, and other consumables share with textiles the bulk of entries in this account book. The range of foodstuffs the Clerk household consumed, beyond the monthly tallies for bread, eggs, and beef, reveals changing tastes, a wider access to domestic and foreign products, and a corresponding adaptation to new styles in preparing, cooking, and serving food and drink. The pages below reveal the variety in the Clerk household diet: cheese, geese, herring, lobster, lamb, mutton, oysters, trout, and veal, all washed down with wines from France, Spain, and Germany. Although it is clear that their diet was heavy on meat, bread, and alcohol, their larders also boasted an array of herbs, sweeteners, and spices, not to mention cakes, candies, and other assorted sweets. Pennell has noted that the shift in nomenclature for kitchen items during the early modern period has complicated 'chronologies of use'.[50] Clerk's account frequently refers to iron and brass pots and pans, seldom distinguishing how they were used. However, while far from being the most valuable goods in the household, the quantity and quality of kitchen utensils and tableware procured by Clerk can draw attention to a much-neglected area of domestic consumption. Likewise, other necessary consumables such as medicines, candles, coal, soap, and water reveal shifts in the use of different types of fuel, cleanliness, and health concerns in this period. Throughout the 1660s, Clerk was purchasing coal from Newhall, Carlops, Clarkingtoun, and Loanhead. Although this particular book of disbursements does not make clear whether Clerk himself invested in coal mining in the region, it is well known that by the 1680s his son had begun exploiting the edge-seams to make the colliery at Loanhead more profitable. Well into the eighteenth century, Clerk's descendants were sought out for their mining expertise.[51]

Matching the improvement on his estate, Clerk spent a great deal of energy and money working for the improvement of his family. Many of the goods and services accounted for in this book reflect Clerk's, and his family's, status as members of the rural gentry. Likewise, they bear out contemporary cultural influences that shaped the Clerk household.[52] In this regard, Clerk's lived experience brought together a diverse set of influences as an urban

49 S. Pennell, 'The material culture of food in early modern England, circa 1650–1750'. University of Oxford Ph.D. thesis, 1997; S. Pennell, '"Pots and Pans History": The material culture of the kitchen in early modern England'. *Journal of Design History* 11, no. 3 (1998), 201–216; J. Thirsk, *Food in Early Modern England: Phases, Fads, Fashions, 1500–1760* (London, 2007).

50 Pennell, 'Pots and Pans', 71.

51 While acknowledging their skills, at least one writer condemned Sir John Clerk and his son for having a low opinion of, and mistrusting, the 'colliers of Loanhead'. See B.F. Duckham, 'Life and Labour in a Scottish Colliery, 1698–1755', *The Scottish Historical Review* 47, no. 144 (1968), 109–128, at 111.

52 On this subject, see Pearce, 'Vanished comforts', 19–25.

merchant and rural landlord, European art broker and Scottish moneylender, devout man of faith and humanist. In some respect, the elite consumption in which he participated reflects these wide-ranging tastes and aspects of his life. The entries in the account book identify considerable amounts provided to family members to acquire household items, to cover expenses incurred while travelling, to maintain their appearance, and to support their leisure activities. While there is little doubt that Clerk recognised the importance of maintaining an appearance appropriate to his station, a number of entries in the account book suggest that he was also often inclined to indulge his family. For example, Clerk spent a considerable sum of money monthly buying 'liquorish', clothes, and 'trifling things' for his children. One less-than-trifling expense Clerk incurred was for a gown and petticoat that he had made for his daughter, Mary, in February 1665 at a cost of £117.[53] Gloves, shoes, suits and dresses, spectacles and watches, guns, canes, swords, napkins, and purses were purchased for daily use; the utility of these items was to some extent practical, but also intended to reflect their possessor's identity.[54]

Clerk's interest in music, art, science, history, and literature can be discerned, in part, from this book of disbursements. Like the mandore he purchased from Paris and had sent to Newbiggin, Clerk routinely disbursed money to acquire new instruments or to repair older ones. The mandore was for George Stewart, a local 'mussitian', whose fee of 'twentie thrie dolors' Clerk paid in March 1669.[55] There is also some indication that Clerk's interest in music possibly extended to investing in his household's musical education and refinement. Over the decade covered in this book, Clerk purchased a number of music books and musical instruments for his home. One area where Clerk has gained considerably more scholarly attention is on his early activities brokering the import of European art to Scotland. Widely believed to be one of Scotland's first art dealers, Clerk imported works for himself but also for his clients.[56] Having kept a separate account of his major art purchases, one 'catalogue of pictures' dated December 1668 identified 70 works by artists like Rembrandt, van Goyen, and van Haarlem. In his book of household disbursements he also

53 See below, [27].

54 B. Lemire, 'Consumerism in preindustrial and early industrial England: the trade in secondhand clothes'. *The Journal of British Studies* 27, no. 1 (1988), 1–24; J. Appleby, 'Consumption in early modern social thought', in J. Brewer (ed.), *Consumption and the World of Goods* Pt II (London, 1993), 162–176; P.D. Glennie & N.J. Thrift, 'Consumers, identities, and consumption spaces in early-modern England'. *Environment and Planning A* 28, no. 1 (1996), 25–45; F. Trentmann, 'Beyond consumerism: new historical perspectives on consumption'. *Journal of Contemporary History* 39, no. 3 (2004), 373–401.

55 See below, [80].

56 Williams, 'The Import of Art'; J. Williams, *Dutch art and Scotland: A reflection of taste* (Edinburgh, 1992); Brown, *The Clerks of Penicuik: Portraits of Taste & Talent*; D. MacMillan, 'Art Trade', in M. Lynch (ed.), *The Oxford companion to Scottish history* (Oxford, 2011), 31–32.

recorded purchases of a few 'pictures' from lesser-known artists like Mungo Hinshaw and Henry Sentinel.[57]

One of Clerk's more regular expenditures was for books for both the household, and for his children away at school. While William Patersone and William Gib received the bulk of Clerk's book-binding business, Clerk employed at least five different binders to provide the household (or his clients) with a variety of reading materials printed and bound using a range of quality paper and leather. For example, bibles purchased for the household cost Clerk anywhere from 14 to 28 shillings for a few copies in octava to £7 for more ornate, 'bound in incarnit Maroquin', versions purchased in 1667.[58] As a number of references in Clerk's account book illustrate, book pricing reflected the quality of paper and binding specifications, as well as typeface and edition of the text. The growing availability of books that were produced for everyday use, and some of a more extraordinary quality, reflects the fact that by the middle of the seventeenth century, book binders and book traders in the principal towns of Scotland were filling a need from nearly all levels of society.[59] By the 1660s, when Clerk was adding to his library at Newbiggin, public demand had grown for Scots vernacular literature, Latin classics, legal treatises, religious texts, almanacs, and science and medical texts. Clerk's interests, and those of his children, can be detected by some of the titles he procured. Craig's *De feudis* and Stair's *Practicks*, works by Horace and Ovid, texts printed in French and in English, copies of Lindsay's *Works*, Flavel's *A Saint Indeed*, and Mill's work examining '*the nature and condition of all sorts of night-walkers*' all complement the numerous bibles, New Testaments, and books of Psalms Clerk acquired or had bound during the last decade of his life.[60]

Clerk also invested in his children's education. From an early age, Clerk's children attended schools in Dalkeith, Prestonpans, and Penicuik.[61] On top of payments for tuition and board, Clerk's accounts draw attention to the additional costs of education, as he was required to supply candles, food, ink, pencils, paper, and bound writing books. It is not entirely clear which books, if any, Clerk's children were required to have available to them as part of their education, but there is some indication that they developed an early

57 For example, [25], [81], [83], [84].

58 See below, [46], [100], [159].

59 A.J. Mann, 'The anatomy of the printed book in early modern Scotland'. *The Scottish Historical Review* 80, no. 210 (2001), 181–200, at 200–201.

60 Where Clerk noted in the account book the title of works he purchased or had bound, I have put the title in italics.

61 See E. Ewan, 'Schooling in the Towns, c.1400–c.1560', in R.D. Anderson, M. Freeman & L. Paterson (eds.), *History of Education in Scotland* (Edinburgh, 2015), 39–56; L. Moore, 'Urban Schooling in Seventeenth- and Eighteenth-century Scotland', in Anderson *et al.*, *History of Education in Scotland*, 79–96.

interest in book collecting.[62] Perhaps the greatest expense for educating his children can be detected in the £220 Clerk paid in 1666 for his eldest son's laureation at the 'colledg [sic] in Edinburgh' and the £600 paid to apprentice another son with the Edinburgh merchant, David Boyd.[63] Beyond the cost of tuition, board, and supplies, Clerk's accounts illustrate the time, energy, and genuine interest he invested in his children by making regular trips to enquire into their well-being when they were away at school. Testament to both her piety and her own interest in education, on her deathbed Mary Gray instructed Clerk to provide for a number of young women of the parish of Penicuik so that they may be 'entered to the school there with'.[64]

While Clerk could be quick with a biting rebuke for those who failed to live up to his standards, he seems to have also been quite free with his affections for his family. Throughout the book he regularly used words like 'loving', 'well-beloved', and 'dear angel' when referring to family members. He also used pet names for his second wife, Elizabeth, and for his son, Robert. The emotional tone Clerk took in his notices of births, baptisms, marriages, and deaths reveals his piety and a very deep devotion to his spouse(s) and children.[65] Between January 1667 and May 1668, in what must have been a very difficult year for the Clerk household, Clerk suffered the loss of his daughter Elizabeth, his wife Mary, and his son Archibald. Apart from noting the expense of drugs and for bringing doctors and apothecaries to Newbiggin during their 'tyme of sicknes', Clerk also documented his grief over the death of his 'dear & weell beloved' family members. The household at Newbiggin fits perfectly the model described by Dingwall, where individuals with means were able to afford visits by qualified physicians and apothecaries.[66] Aside from that tragic year, Clerk routinely sought out the advice of medical practitioners, often bringing them to Newbiggin to attend to the household family when any one of them was suffering from some ailment. Clerk also expended considerable sums procuring 'drogs', purgatives, tonics, and leeches. His disbursements and notes make clear that he suffered regularly from a number of ailments,

[62] J. Bevan, 'Seventeenth-century Students and their Books', in G. Donaldson (ed.), *Four Centuries: Edinburgh University Life, 1583–1983* (Edinburgh, 1983); A.J. Mann, *The Scottish book trade, 1500–1720: print commerce and print control in early modern Scotland: an historiographical survey of the early modern book in Scotland* (Edinburgh, 2000).

[63] See below, [64].

[64] Ibid., [50].

[65] Mary Gray died in 1667. Three years later, Clerk married Elizabeth Johnston in the College Kirk of Edinburgh. According to Sir John's *Memoirs*, Gray and Clerk had a total of sixteen children, though some accounts suggest it was ten – five daughters and five sons. Gray, *Memoirs*, 7; P.B. Deward (ed.), *Burke's Landed Gentry of Great Britain: The Kingdom of Scotland*, 19th edn. vol. 1 (Wilmington, 2001), 228.

[66] H.M. Dingwall, *A history of Scottish medicine: themes and influences* (Edinburgh, 2002), 95.

including intestinal disorders and kidney stones.[67] Beyond what he included in this book, Clerk (and his descendants) kept a separate set of records dedicated to expenditures on medicines and medical advice.[68]

Clerk's personal connection with his family, members of his household, and those within his community can also be gleaned from the numerous gifts he made on festival days or in appreciation for extraordinary services rendered.[69] Whether it was investing in the parish kirk and school in Penicuik, attending wedding feasts, or providing 'support', Clerk's actions reflect the idea espoused by Wrightson and others that the reciprocal nature of local social relations are most obvious in the paternalistic duties shown by its leading members.[70] The entries in Clerk's account book draw the reader into this world, providing us with signposts to Clerk's surroundings, his communities, his networks, and his extensive contribution to the region and to Scotland. To some extent, Clerk's network of trade and financial partners has been well documented. Clerk's accounts show that, long after he had settled in Penicuik, he continued to transact business with a group of trusted merchants based in Edinburgh, London, and Paris. One of his most trusted business partners and confidants was John Anderson, who Clerk often referred to as his 'loving brother'.[71] When Clerk was apprenticed to John Naismith in 1627, it was Anderson who consented to the indenture and paid the apprentice fee of 400 merks.[72] Anderson appears regularly in Clerk's accounts as one of his factors in Edinburgh, but also as someone Clerk could trust with the care of his children. Although Clerk maintained a chamber in Edinburgh, and stayed there regularly, he counted on Anderson to intercede on behalf of his sons during their time at the 'colledge' and when they were apprenticed within the town. There is some indication that Anderson was successful in his own right. Ultimately, it is likely that Anderson's success made him a target for violence and theft. In

67 Beyond what he included in his monthly account book, Clerk (and later his descendants) kept an entire account dedicated to expenditure on medicines and medical advice. NRS GD18/2175: Accounts for Medicines.

68 NRS GD18/2175: Accounts for Medicines.

69 How Clerk fulfilled his role as both householder and laird can be discerned in many of the entries in this account book. See, for example, [92]–[93]. On top of the entries noting gifts given on Handsel Monday, support provided to those on his estate, and routine care for those living under his authority, the pages devoted to documenting the preparations for his sister-in-law's wedding and outlining what was involved in his daughter's tocher stand out. See [124], [155].

70 K. Wrightson, *Mutualities and Obligations: Changing Social Relationships in Early Modern England* (New Haven, 2000), 157–194; S. Hindle, 'Power, Poor Relief, and Social Relations in Holland Fen, c.1600–1800'. *The Historical Journal* 41 no. 1 (1998), 67–96.

71 For example, [104].

72 GD18/2357; GD18/2472: 'Transactions with my brother John Anderson'. Another brother, William, witnessed the indenture. One year earlier, William had been apprenticed to James Allan, an Edinburgh-based merchant. See F.J. Grant (ed.), *The Register of Apprentices of the City of Edinburgh, 1583–1666*, vol. 28 (Scottish Record Society, 1906), 36.

November 1674, Anderson was murdered by John Ramsay, one of his own servants, and George Clerk, one of John Clerk's servants, who, according to the deposition, poisoned Anderson and carried off 'a large gold chain, gold bracelets, a gold ring with a blue stone, two pieces of gold, twelve of silver, and five purse pennies, silver buttons, brooches, and various other articles'.[73]

Eleven months earlier, the book of disbursements makes reference to Clerk's increasingly poor health; by April 1674, he had succumbed to his afflictions. In the lead-up to his death, the entries had already begun to be far more limited in detail and quantity. Following the list of expenses for his funeral, there are a number of blank pages, followed by a single page with only a few short entries for June 1674, and another with only a few random notes for February 1675, before the entries begin again in earnest on the next page starting in early 1683. On the last few pages of the bound original, including the back cover, Clerk had filled the pages with disbursements that date back to various points between 1663 and 1673. I have included them in this transcription. In the pages that follow, the household disbursements of John Clerk of Penicuik between 1663 and 1674 reveal the ongoing the transformation of his family into highly regarded connoisseurs and collectors, patrons of the arts, and contributors to science, technology, and public affairs. Ultimately, their material culture reflects their tastes and talent – what Sir Walter Scott called the 'heritable genius of the family'.[74] This account book offers the reader an opportunity to pull back the curtains, open the cupboards, peer into the closets, and gaze onto the fields of Clerk's estate in order to gain a fuller sense of this 'genius' at work.

[73] D. O'Danachair, *The Newgate Calendar*, vol. 1 (2009), 192–193.

[74] D.O. Forfar, 'Origins of the Clerk (Maxwell) Genius', in *Bulletin of the Institute of Mathematics and its Applications* 28, no. 1/2, 4–16, at 5. Brown quotes the 'contemporary' opinion as 'virtuoso genius of the family' in *Clerks of Penicuik: Portraits of Taste & Talent*, 3.

EDITORIAL CONVENTIONS

In editing Clerk's 'book' I tried to maintain much of the structure and appearance of the original. At various points it reads like a ledger book, a personal diary, or a random set of reminders and notes. In order to preserve the character and spirit of the original I have tried to limit the amount of editorial intervention and, where possible, avoided injecting interpretation that could lead to confusion. First and foremost, this is because *how* Clerk documented his expenses and disbursements, his relationships with family members, clients, and those he employed, reveals a great deal about him and is as important as the information he recorded. Household disbursements form the bulk of the material in this book. Within the body of these accounts, Clerk often grouped together like items, items or services obtained at the same time (or from the same individual), and/or items or services that were purchased for (or by) the same person(s). Typically, though not always, he also provided a more substantive sum of these related expenses in the right-hand margin. For someone of such exacting standards, it is interesting that on occasion Clerk's tallies and sums are inaccurate, unclear, or incomplete. I have transcribed such errors as they occur in the original while indicating the mistake in a footnote.

As this is a personal recording of Clerk's personal disbursements, annotated by its creator, it was likely never intended for a wide audience. Like most early modern private documents, Clerk's book is idiosyncratic in terms of spelling, punctuation, grammar, and syntax. One of the biggest challenges in transcribing the material is the irregularity in Clerk's spelling of words and the overall lack, or inconsistent use, of punctuation. Where I thought it would make the account book more accessible, I have corrected or modernised spelling, regularised capitalisation, and drawn attention to obvious errors or omissions Clerk made. Throughout his accounts, Clerk used em dashes, colons, semi colons, or a full stop to indicate the end of a statement. Alternatively, Clerk used the same marks prior to listing related materials. In general, Clerk's overabundant and desultory use of em dashes and his inconsistent use of punctuation, as well as other grammatical errors, highlights the fact that the book was for personal use only.[1] For the most part, I have made no attempt

[1] Clerk frequently used an em dash to indicate that an entry carried over to the next line, to identify a full stop, or to acknowledge a link between a statement and a list that followed.

to change the sentence structure Clerk used or to add modern punctuation. To do so would alter the overall feel of the original book.

To some extent, Clerk's spelling throughout the original reflects both phonetic and regional pronunciation. He often employed different spellings of names, places, and items; sometimes this occurs in the same entry, on the same page, or alternates from page to page. While this was fairly characteristic of the age, it can be quite confusing for the modern reader. As Judith Spicksley reminds us, spelling was seldom uniform in private documents.[2] Clerk's account book is a marvellous illustration of this fact. A simple example can be found in how Clerk routinely alternated between spelling common forenames like 'John/Jhon' or 'Edowart/Eduart'. While not uncommon in many early modern documents, Clerk also alternated in his use of the letters 'u' and 'w' for names like 'Broun/Brown' and 'Steuart/Stewart'. For the reader, the biggest challenge may be less discerning what Clerk meant, but whether to trust what appears on the pages that follow. Strangely, one of the most consistent aspects of Clerk's book is just how inconsistent he was with his spelling. For those interested in orthography, and to preserve the feel of the original, I have chosen to leave much of Clerk's spelling unmodified, making clear when it was necessary to alter the original so as to prevent any misreading. This is particularly the case for internal use of the letters *u/v/w*. For example, 'tous/tows', 'pound/ pownd', 'duel(t)/dwel(t)', 'herwest/hervest', and 'tour/tow[e]r'. However, I have altered the spelling of such words along modern variations only where the context of the entry did not make clear the meaning of the word. For instance, where Clerk consistently spelled the word 'tower' as 'tour', I changed the spelling to 'tow[e]r' to convey more clearly what Clerk meant.[3] As this example illustrates, Clerk also had a tendency to omit letters when spelling particular words. Clerk often spelled 'hardn' for 'harden' (a type of coarse cloth), 'ons' for 'ones', or 'Grhme' for the surname 'Graham'. Where this occurs, I have noted the error in its first occurrence but then maintained it thereafter. If Clerk's spelling does not obscure the understanding of what he was trying to convey, I have made no attempt to offer a correction. As for any unusual spelling that might suggest a transcription error, I have noted the issue by inserting [sic]. Except as indicated above, where it is obvious that letters or whole words are missing in the original, and the missing letter or word

In those instances, I transcribed the entry maintaining the em dashes as they are found in the original. However, there are many instances where Clerk placed an em dash randomly in between words for no clear purpose. I have chosen to omit these from the transcription to limit confusion arising from such use. I have transcribed each instance where Clerk used an en dash in the original.

2 Spicksley, *The Business and Household Accounts of Joyce Jeffreys*, xv.

3 See below, [17]. Clerk regularly alternated his use of the letters 'u' and 'w' both at the start of words and internally. However, Clerk also had a tendency to resort to phrases or words in French. It is possible that when he spelled the word 'tower' as 'tour' he was using the French spelling of the word.

is clear, they have been added and placed inside square brackets. Where the original was damaged, or words and meaning obscured, or if an omission is less obvious, I have indicated this by placing an ellipsis inside square brackets. Unlike many other contemporary manuscripts, there are only a few instances where a 'thorn' or 'yogh' was used – when they appear in the account book, I have transcribed them as 'th' and 'y' respectively. Thus, for the most part, I have made an effort to only correct an error, modernise the spelling, or indicate a potential issue, if it is apparent that confusion might arise from leaving it in its original form.

Another of Clerk's idiosyncrasies is the fact that he often randomly introduced phrases or words in French. For example, on page [108], Clerk wrote '3 ell off lining to be toys *pour la femme*'. Given his lengthy stay in Paris, such inclusions are not altogether surprising, even if they appear suddenly, and often without context. How and when Clerk chose to capitalise words also appears to have been somewhat arbitrary. As some have noted, by the early seventeenth century shifts were occurring in how writers capitalised words as a way of foregrounding particular nouns.[4] For the most part, I have adopted a modern system of capitalisation, starting each new entry with a capital letter (unless that entry is part of a numbered list), and regularising the use of capital letters at the beginning of names, places, and feast days. In the main body of the accounts, abbreviations have been silently extended. On most pages, Clerk provided notes in the left-hand margin to serve as a reference guide to his main entries and, on occasion, to calculate the major tallies for that page. Clerk's marginalia included names, references to commodities mentioned in an entry, symbols, and the occasional doodle or decorative flourish.[5] With the exception of Clerk's doodles and flourishes, I have transcribed the marginalia as it is found in the original, maintaining Clerk's spelling, use of abbreviations, and order and placement on the page. In large part, this was done to maintain the look and appearance of the original, but also due to the challenges of reproducing early modern handwritten accounts using modern word processing.

Overall, I placed an emphasis on producing an accurate transcription, placing a priority on clarity and consistency over trying to create an exact reproduction. Throughout the account book, Clerk used large curly brackets to group together expenses, activities, and disbursements. Using modern technology to reproduce such brackets accurately, while keeping them in line with any marginalia and sums, was not possible. Instead, I have maintained the groups using tabs and keeping the dot leaders that Clerk used in the original to link an entry to a sum in the margin. In the original, Clerk blocked off

4 M. Görlach, *Introduction to early modern English* (Cambridge, 1991), 40; T. Nevalainen, *Introduction to early modern English* (Oxford, 2006), 36.

5 See Talbott 'The Letter-Book of John Clerk, 1644–45', 12.

sections of entries using partial or full lines. I maintained these separations to keep information together while maintaining the flow and appearance of the original. Consistency is somewhat of a challenge given the number of inaccuracies, alternating spelling, and, on occasion, a breakdown in an otherwise chronological accounting of expenses and events. Where Clerk's tallies are incorrect, or he made a verifiable error when he recorded an amount, or a name, I have noted those errors in a footnote. Such errors remind the reader that this was Clerk's diary of disbursements and notable events that he would have maintained daily, and used regularly, to keep track of his financial and personal affairs. As some of the entries in this account book contain Clerk's editorialisation on people and events, and annotations of disbursements, it seems clear that it was never intended for an audit or any other external use. Quite often, Clerk left a gap in the text where he likely intended to add a name, date, or item that he could not remember at the time of entering the information in the book, or where that information was unknown or temporarily forgotten. I have noted such occurrences with the word 'blank' inserted in square brackets.

To assist readers who may be less familiar with some of the goods Clerk mentions or the places he refers to in the account, I have provided a glossary of terms and place names. The glossary is far from comprehensive, but it illustrates the incredible diversity of goods that Clerk brought into his household and which he made available to his clients in the region. While the account book was bound contemporaneously, it is not clear if Clerk (or his son) added page numbers, or if they were added at a later date. For the most part the page numbers on the original appear in the bottom left-hand corner; but on occasion they can be found higher up the page. For ease of use, I have maintained the original page numbers but have placed them in square brackets at the start of each new page and indicated if an error exists in the original.

Notes on Measures and Currency

Weights, measures, and values figure prominently throughout the account book. Except where indicated, all currency is given in pounds Scots. Clerk was explicit when he valued goods and services in English pounds, French livres, Rex dollars, or Spanish dollars. However, in his final sums he converted their value to pounds Scots. I have maintained the information as Clerk recorded it for every entry where this occurs.[6] Likewise, for the most part, I have maintained Clerk's alternating use of abbreviations for pounds, shillings,

[6] French livres typically divide into shillings (*sous*) and pence (*deniers*), the Spanish dollar, in circulation outside Spain, was valued at 8 *reales* (on the basis of the *real de plata*). The Rex (or Rix) dollar was a silver coin minted in Germany, the Netherlands, and parts of Scandinavia. It was in circulation across much of Northern Europe and used in Scotland during periods when there was a shortage of coin.

and pence. Clerk used *ll* and *lib* to refer to the pound (currency). I have transcribed both as they are found in the original, with the addition of a full stop. However, he also used *lib* to refer to the pound (*avoirdupois*). To avoid confusion, I have replaced *lib* with *lb* when the context makes clear that the reference is to a measure of weight.

Scottish money

1 turnor	2 pennies (d.)
1 grot(e)	4 pennies (d.)
12 pennies (d.)	1 shilling (s.)
20 shillings (s.)	1 pound (ll. or lib.)
13s. 4d. (13/4)	1 merk (two-thirds of a lib.)
12ll. (12 lib.) Scots	1li. (1 lib.) sterling

Scottish weights

16 drops	1 ounce
16 ounces	1 pound (lb)
16 pounds (lb)	1 stone

Scottish dry measures

4 lippies*	1 peck
4 pecks	1 firlot
4 firlots	1 boll

* a lippie was roughly 2.3 litres

Scottish liquid measures

4 gills	1 mutchkin
2 mutchkins	1 chopin
2 chopins	1 pint
8 pints	1 gallon

Scottish lengths

1 ell	roughly 94 centimetres
1 fadom(e)	roughly equal to 1.8 metres

Scottish area

1 rude	roughly 1275 sq. metres

The General Account Book of John Clerk of Penicuik, 1663–1674

[Cover Page]

Book off Accompts
by my Grandfather Mr Jo: Clerk
&
father Sir John Clerk
wherein are severall things remarkable

1 their methodes of accompting
2 their methodes of management
3 the different prices of things

John Clerk 1733

[1]
L'estat des ames fidelles
Apres la mort ~~~~//
par amiraut[1]

Thomas Waterstoun – deacon off the tailyeurs in Leith dwels on;
the shore neir Barne Lindsays land sels good brande – – – ;

[...] Dowglas that some tyme dwelt in Lintoun –; is now a waiter or sercher –
[...] [c]ustoms[2] in Leith he dwels in the fit off the pench[3] mercat – in Mr
[Da]vid Adamstouns turnpyke in leith –[4]

A free conference – touching the present state off England both at home & abroad –
in order to the desinge off France[5] ~~~~~~~~~~~~~~~~~~~~~~~~~~~~~~~~~~~~~~
London printed by E. T: for R: Royston book seller to
The kings most excellent maiestie ~~~~~~~~~~~~~~~~~~

3 May David Maither in the place off Ormistoun – excellent coich maker //
1669 William Williamsone merchant dwels in Ormistoun toun ~~~~~~~//

By unitie small things grow great
By contention great things become small

---

15 off December 1669 Jhon Innes of Struthers dwels in Forres
he is both a nottar & a messinger – & does bussynes in the north –

---

1 – 76re – 1672 – 5 dolors – 14–10–00

[2]

1 The 18 off December 1665 to James Adamsone customer at the West Port
29s. to frie me off a yeirs small customs at the West Port to wit fra the
1 off Januar 1666 – till the 1 off Januar 1667 .... • 01 • 09 • –

2 The 20 off December 1666 – to the said James Adamsone halff a dolor to –
frie me off small customs at the West Port for a yeir to cum to wit
fra the 1 off Januar 1667 till the 1 off Januar 1668 .... • 01 • 09 • –

1 'The estate of the faithful souls after death by Amiraut.' M. Amyraut, *Discours de l'estat des fidèles après la mort* (Saumur, 1646).
2 A portion of the manuscript is obscured by a panel placed over this section.
3 Possibly 'painche' (i.e. tripe).
4 Clerk (or one of his descendants) crossed out what had been written in a number of sections on this page. The words underneath are entirely obscured.
5 *A free conference touching the present state of England at home and abroad; in order to the designs of France* (London, 1668).

3 The 3 off February 1668 – to James Adamsone customer at –
the West Port 29s. for my small customs at the said West –
Port fra the – 1 off January 1668 – to the 1 off Januar 1669 .... • 01 • 09 • –

4 The 26 off January 1669 to James Adamsone customer at –
the West Port 29s. for my small customs at the said West Port –
fra the 1 off Januar 1669 till the 1 off January 1670 .... • 01 • 09 • –
on Teusday[6] the 26 off January 1669 I sent this halff dolor to
him with John Rob seald in a peper...

---

5 on Teusday the 4 off Januar 1670 – sent with Jhon Rob – to be delivert
to James Adamsone customer at the West Port halff a dolor which pays –
my small customs at the said Port fra the 1 – off Januar 1670 till –
the 1 off Januar 1671 yeirs .... • 01 • 09 • –

Jhon Clerk

~~The 28 off September 1669 sold a little gray meir for which I resavet
13ll 6s 8d is – 20 merks –~~ ~~• 13 • 06 • 08~~
~~Munday morning – 13 May 1670 – I resavet payment for the same – is is~~ [sic]
payit ~~7 month – 13 days efter – the payment theroff wes promist that 13 May
1670~~[7]

Turn•over 1. – Newhall:

2. lint——:

[3]

Alexander pennycooke off....... Newhall

---

1 The 12 off Marche 1667 to Alexander Pennycooke off Newhall – 12 silver spoons weying – 13 once 14 drope at 3 lib. 6s. the once is 81 lib. 14s. – which I boght fra Edowart Cleghorne goldsmith the said day – and this wes for making – 2 visits out to Newbiging when my dear & weell beloved dochter Elizabeth Clerk wes seik – who dyed the 27 off January 1667 – being on a Sunday at 6 off the clok att night – & for giving his advysse a little befor off some trifling things anent the childring .... • 81 • 14 • –

81 –14–00
42–10–00
51–17–00
176–01–00

2 The 17 off Agust 1667 to the said Alexander Pennycooke – a silver ball – weying 12 onces and a halff at 3 lib. 8s. the once is – 42–10s. which which [sic] I boght fra William Law goldsmith the said day –& this wes – for comeing to Newbiging 2 or 3 tyms at most with Doctor Cuninghame

6 Clerk consistently spelled Tuesday as 'Teusday' throughout the account book.

7 Unlike on the previous page, the words that Clerk crossed out here are entirely legible in the original. I transcribed them as found.

when my dear & weell beloved bedfellow wes seik who –
departit out off this vaile off miserie on – Wedensday[8] the 17 off Aprill –
1667 about 3 howrs in the morneing .... • 42 • 10 • –

3 The 24 off Jully 1668 to the said Alexander Pennycook – a silver –
cadel coup with a covert – weying – 15 once 4 drope at 3 lib. 8s. the –
once – is 51–17s. which I boght fra Edowart Cleghorne goldsmith –
The said day – and this wes for comeing once or twyse to Newbiging at –
most and giveing his advysse anent some of the childring when –
they had the mezels .... • 51 • 17 • –

4 The 21 September 1669 to the said Alexander Pennycooke off Newhall –
nyne pound 2s. Scots for some phisik & drogs he furnisht to –
Mr John Clerk &c in anno 1669 – I offert him 14 dolors in –
a peper bot he wold have no more – bot the said 9 lib. 2s. which –
he peyit out for drogs .... • 09 • 02 • –

John: Clerk ....

5 Munday the 20 off May 1672 – sent with Archbald Miller at Neuhall to be –
delivert to the Lady Neuhall ~~~~~
1– 2 large suger loaffs in bleu peper .... 2 suger loaffs –
2– 2 great cheise – boght fra Mr. Kope in the Spitels about a
stone the peice .... 2 great cheise –
3 – 2 lesser cheise off our owne great cheise .... 2 lesser cheise –
This wes for some visits he made to George Clerk when he wes sick – some advysse –
he gave me anent the gravell – and a visit he made to Neubiging very late whair
he stayed all night for a fyst the thing they call – the Lady Dauffe tooke in hir

taill – it being all togither foly – & ydlenes to have troubled him on that accompt

John Clerk

6 Thursday – 31 October 1672 – sent with Alexander Clerk – to be delivert to the Lady Newhall eight cheisse markit H – off our own cheise – 4 off the great chessire and 4 off the second chessire – is 8 cheise .... 8 cheise

The [blank] off Februar 1674 sent with John Rob to Edinburgh for Neuhall

1– 2 great old cheis off David Glendinings – at 18 lib. the peice......... 2 cheis

2– 2 cheis off David Glendinings at 8 lib. the peice .... 2 cheis

4 cheis –

[8] Clerk consistently spelled Wednesday as 'Wedensday' throughout the account book.

[4]

Lint — A memor off lint boght since the 16 off

1666 — off October....1666~~~~~//

1 16 off October 1666 Margaret Hopkirk boght at Edinburgh 2 ston off lint –
cost – 10–16–8d. .... • 10 • 16 • 08

10 • 16 • 08 2 In October 1667 Marie Clerk boght – 4 ston and a halff off lint at –
21 • 15 • 00 4 lib. 16s. 8d. the stone .... • 21 • 15 • –

18 • 5 • 06 3 The 30 off December – 1668 Anna Irving boght – 4 ston 4 lb[9] of lint –
23 • 0 • 00 at 4 lib. 6s. the ston .... • 18 • 05 • 06
73 • 17 • 2

4 The 13 off February 1668 – Isobell Gray boght 3 ston off knok lint at –
1668 7 lib. 13s. 4d. the stone .... • 23 • 00 • 00

All above till this 1 off Marche 1669..........73–17–02 .... • 73 • 17 • 02

John: Clerk

Marie 8 October 1669 – 4 ston off bound lint at 4 lib. the ston.......... 16–00–00
Clerk boght 3 ston off knok lint at – 5 lib. 13s. 4d. the ston .... 17–00–00 • 33 • 00 • 00

John: Clerk

Soma off all above till the 8 off October 1669 is .... • 106 • 16 • 06

Jhon Clerk

1670 The 8 off December 1670 to Isobell Gray for –
2 ston off knok lint at – 3–16s. the ston 07–12–00
The 3 off Januar 1671 – sent to Mary Clerk for – 4 ston off knok lint
at – 5 lib. 13s. 4d. the ston .... 22–13–04 • 30 • 05 • 04

1671 The 7 off November 1671 to Isobell Gray for – 6 ston 3 pound off bound lint at – 3–16s. the ston is 24–04–06 booked in November 1671 .... • 24 • 04 • 06

1672 The 11 off November 1672 – to Robert Handesyde – for 6 ston of bound lint at – 4–10s. the ston is 27–00–00
To him – for a pound off bearded tow .... 00–07–06 • 27 • 07 • 06
Booked in November – 1672 ~~~~

1673 The 3 of December 1673 payed to James Hammiltone merchant in the Bow for six stone of bound lint at 4–10s. the stone is .. 27–00–00
to him for four pound of knock lint .... 01–15–00 .... 28–15–00 • 28 • 15 • 00

[5]

L A remark or observation what the tenent cairied off lyme everie yeir – begining – at anno – 1667 .... Lyme

Lyme	1:	in anno – 1667 – the tenents cairied of lyme fra the Carlips	191 laid
	2:	in anno – 1668 – the tenents cairied of lyme fra the Carlips	233 laid
	3:	in anno – 1669 – the tenents cairied of lyme fra the Carlips	230 laid
	4:	in anno – 1670 – the tenents cairied of lyme fra the Carlips	260 laid
	5:	in anno – 1671 – the tents [sic] cairied of lyme fra the Carlips only.....	140 laid
	6:	in anno – 1672 – the tenents cairied of lyme fra the Carlips	[blank]

9 As mentioned in the Introduction, Clerk used ll and lib interchangeably to refer to the pound currency (£) and lib to refer to the pound (avoirdupois). To avoid confusion, I have introduced *lb* for measures and weights. See the Introduction above, p.23.

[6]

Some mementos – triks & pranks done be William Stewart our hynd at his own hand – becaus he thinks himselff too wyse to ask my advysse in things~~~~ *William: Stewart*

1: In anno 1667 – he sold in Dalkeith fare – 2 cows cost – 46 lib. for .... 18 lib.

2: In anno 1669 – he gave 35 lib. for a beld ox wes no better then .... 29 lib.

3: In Athelstoun fare 1669 – he sold a coy in trust at his own hand cost to Thomas Mein: 10ll. 10s. he sold hir for 10ll. 10s. payable in the 1 weik off November 1669 – shoe wes not peyit till the ~

4: In December 1669 – I being at home – William Lawsone cam to buy a cow & a calff – I told I wold not give hir under 18 lib. not the lesse at his own hand he sold hir for – 17 lib. and never speird my advyse therin – I being walking about the doors when he sold hir –

5: The [blank] off [blank] 16 [blank] when the sheep wes comptit thair wes 17 sheep found on the ground by & at over our own nomber – William Stewarts own soume & Jo: Diksons 6 sheip

Some pranks he playd in anno 1670 –

1: Borowed money & boght a blind gray meir powny cost 2 dolors and a halff wes not worth 2 dolors – and keeped all summer on my grasse ~

2: Not the lesse that he had a cow off his own – he boght a cow in trust fra James Portois cost – 22 lib. shoe wes not worth – 15 lib. – and keiped hir 6 or 7 weiks on my grasse befor I knew any thing off it then put hir to Ravens Hauch whair shoe wes all ways on my grasse then he put hir to winter with his brother –

a fyne bargan indeid.

3: He borowed fra Charles Pennycooke in the said summer 1670 – 9 lib. .... 9 lib.

4: At summer I say at Lintoun in summer – 1670 – he boght fra one John Corebie – 20 hogs for which he gave his band for – 40 or 48 lib. – broght them on my feild a long tyme er I knew – then made a fashion in puting them – heir & thair – bot certane they wer most on my feld [sic] ~

When John Hodg wes taking ane ox off his own to a fare he behoved to buy him be the gate – for 19 lib. & gave 6 pence in arles – & John Hodg returnt home agane – when he could not get so much as he had promist for him – he broght home the ox and sent him home to John Hodg agane – he is a very fyne merchant without money.................

[7]

Lining cloth for the usse off the bairns

A memor off lining off divers sorts – delivert for the usse off the bairns since the – 5 off October 1669 – which lining I boght fra divers persons & this is by & attour – the lining cloth – &c wes made within the – howsse of the lint – wes boght – in Edinburgh.................................

1: 5 October 1669 – 4 ell off lining to be Helen & Jennet Clerk hoods at 10s. the ell .... • 02 • 00 • –

2: 5 October 1669 – 2 ell off lining to be Marie Clerk toys at – 14s. the ell.. • 01 • 08 • –

3: 3 December 1669 – 2 ell off lining to be Margaret Clerk napkins at
14s. the ell .... • 01 • 08 • –
The 22 off Marche 1670 delivert to my wyffe for the usse off divers of • 04 • 16 • –
the bairns: – – –

17 ell 1: 4 ell of lining at – 14s. the ell............... 02–16–00
2: 6 ell at – 10s. the ell............................ 03–00–00
3: 3 ell – small lining at 28s. the ell .... 04–04–00 all 13 lib. 12s........ • 13 • 12 • 00
4: 4 ell lining at 18s. the ell...................... 03–12–00 17 ell..................

22 May 1670 delivert to my wyffe for ~~

44 ¾ ell 1: 31 Agust 1669 –12 ell boght fra George Blaikie cost 16s. 6d.
the ell.. 09–18–00
2: 19 June 1668 –10 ell of lining boght fra Ladie Bagillo cost 10s.
the ell.. 05–00–00
3: 27 May 1668 – 14 ell 3 quarters boght fra Ladie Bagillo cost 15s.
the ell.. 11–01–03
4: 31 Agust 1669 – 8 ell boght fra George Blaikie at 14s. 6d. the ell .... 05–16–00 • 31 • 14 • –
44 ell – 3 – quarters –: 31–14–03[10]
5: 20 ell off small hardn – boght fra John Hogens – 30 Marche 1669
cost 7ll. 15s. the skore .... • 07 • 15 • –

17 ell...................... 1– 13–12–00–0
44 ell 3 quarters .... 81 ell 3 quarters – cost 2– 31–15–00–3
04 • 16 20 ell...................... 3– 07–15–00–0... 53–02–03 • 53 • 02 • 03
13 • 12
31 • 14 24 June 1670 *Jo: Clerk*

07 • 15	24 June 1670 – 3 ell off Scots Holland to be Margaret & Agnes Clerks		
04 • 10	2 waist cots at 30s. the ell boght fra the Ladie Bagillo the – 19 June 1668		• 04 • 10 • 00
62 • 07	*John Clerk*; soma off all above on this syde is		• 62 • 07 • –
Agnes	The 8 Jully 1671 to Agnes Clerk for hir usse		
Clerk	1: 3¼ ell off lining to be 6 hoods cost 15s. the ell	02–08–09	
	2: 2 ell off lining to be 8 hand naipkins at 12s. the ell	01–04–00	• 03 • 12 • 09
Helen	29 Agust 1671 delivert for Helen Clarks – usse –		
Clark	1: 3 ell to be Helen Clark [blank] bands at 14s. 6d. the ell	02–03–06	
	2: 3 ell to be hir – 6 toys at – 13s. 6d. the ell	02–00–06	• 04 • 04 • 00
William &	Munday 2 October 1671~~		
Alex^r Clerk	1– 2 ell off Holland to be William & Alexander Clerk bands at –		
	32s. the ell	03–04–00	
	2– 2 ell off lining to be them napkins at 12s. the ell	01–04–00	• 04 • 08 • 00
Wills and	23 October – given 1 ell off lining to be stoks to Wille & Alexander		
Alex^r Clerk	Clerks bands..		• 00 • 10 • 00
Margaret	15 Marche 1672 – given for Margaret Clerks usse ~~~~		
Clerk	1 –: 3 ¾ ell –&		
	3 – ell is 6 ¾ ell cost 14s. the ell	04–14–06	
	2 – 1 ell – 3 quarters lining for napkins at 13s. 4d. the ell....................	01–03–04	
	3– 1 – ell off fyne lining to be hand - cuffs	01–00–00	• 06 • 17 • 10

10 I have transcribed the discrepancy between the tally in the body and the sum in the margin as it is found in the original.

Helen – Clerk	The 5 off September 1672 – given for Helen Clerk hir usse when shoe went to John Brouns schoole in Prestoun pans		
	1– 5 ½ ell off lining to be 4 aprons & 6 hand napkins at – 12s. the ell	03–06–00	
	2– 2 ell off lining to be 6 pair off cuffs at 17s. the ell	01–14–00	
	2– 1 ½ ell off small lining to be 6 bands at 20s. the ell	01–00–00	• 06 • 10 • –
Will. Alexr & Robert Clerks	The 10 off December 1672 given all the lining under mentioned to wit // to Agnes Clerk		
	1– 5 ell of round lining at 6s. the ell – to be Will: Alexander & Robert Clerks 20 napkins	01–10–00	
	2– halff ane ell and a naill off Holland to be Robert Clerk – 8 bands at 32s. the ell	00–18–00	• 02 • 08 • 00
	The said day for Jennet & Katherin Clerks		
Jennet & Katherin Clerks	1– 7 ¼ ell off lining to be them – 8 aprons at 13s. 4d. the ell	04–16–08	
	2– 2 ell 3 ½ quarters to be them 8 pair hand cuffs at a merk the ell	01–18–04	
	3– 4 ½ and a naill – to be them 8 hoods – at 12s. the ell	02–14–00	
	4– 3 ell to be them ... 8 bands at – 20s. the ell	03–00–00	• 12 • 09 • –
	The said day given off for Margaret Clerk		
Margaret Clerk	2 ell to be hand napkins at a merk the ell		• 01 • 06 • 08
	The said day given all for Luckie		
E – J~~~	1– 2 ell to be – pair off hand cuffs – at 20s. the ell	02–00–00	
	2– 7 ell to be – aprons at a merk the ell	04–13–04	• 06 • 13 • 04
	The 20 off June 1673 given all for – Jennet Clerk – when shoe went to –		

Jennet	Prestoun pans to Jo: Brouns schoole to be 4 sarks ~~		
Clerk	1 – 5 ¼ ell of lining at – 12s. the ell	03–03–00	
	2 – 8 ell of lining at – 8s. the ell	03–04–00	• 06 • 07 • –
Jenet	The 23 June 1673 taken all 2 ½ ell to be 6 mutches –& – 6 napkins –		
Clerk	when shoe went to Prestoun pans at 8s. the ell	01–00–00	

[8]
[blank page]

[9]
Accompt off soape boght & delivert for
the usse off the howsse 1670

Soape			Soape
	1:	Thursday the 2 of June 1670 – delivert a firikin of soape	1 firikin
	2:	Teusday – 4 October 1670 – delivert a firikin of Leith soape	1 – firikin
	3:	On Wedensday – the 14 off June 1671 – delivert a firikin off soape – which John Stewart broght out off Leith the said day	1 – firikin
	4:	On Teusday – the 3 off October – delivert ane other firkin of soap 1671–	1 – firikin
	5:	Munday – 27 May 1672 – delivert 1 firikin of soape	1 – firikin

6: Thursday – 10 December – I say Thursday the [...] 1672:

1672 12 off December delivert for the usse of the housse 1 firikin off soape ... 1 – firikin

John Clerk

7: On Wedensday the – 30 off Jully 1673 – delivert for the usse of the housse 1 feirikin [sic] off soape ... 1 – firikin

John Clerk.....

[10]

The accompt off disbursments in the month off January – 1663

Januar 1663

10 to Archbald Andersone for his fie fra Witsonday 1662 till Mertimes 1662 ...		• 06 • 00 • –
To Jhon Rob to give to cause baik a goose ...		• 00 • 16 • –
13 to [blank] customer off small customs at the West Port ...		• 01 • 04 • –
14 – peyit for 7 firlots off meill – at 6ll. the boll ...		• 09 • 10 • –
13 – to David Scot apothecar in full off his compt on his discharge ...		• 01 • 10 • –
Peyit for – *Wallace* – David Lindsay –& *Wallace* bund all in leather ...		• 01 • 16 • –
To Jhon Fergusone cordoner for 1 pair off shoone for my wyffe ...	01–06–00	
For fitting 1 pair off boots for my selff ...	02–03–00	• 03 • 09 • –
For 2 pair off mixt gray wo[r]sted hose boght in Leith ...		• 03 • 14 • –
24 January – to Jhon Ramsay for – 24 fowls at 6s. the peice ...		• 07 • 04 • –
28 January 1663 – to Mr William Dalgardno minister at Pennycooke ~~ 322ll. for a yeirs stipend fra Mertimes 1661 till Mertimes 1662 – for which I have his discharge date the 28 off January 1663 ...		• 322 • 00 • –

	30 January – to Alexander Haistie for – 2 kipper – 48s. – 1 grot for his pains		• 02 • 12 • –
	16 Januar – given my wyffe – 12ll. when shoe went in to sie hir mother when shoe fell and woundit hir head		• 12 • 00 • –
	To Jhon Rob in hansell	00–06–00	
	To Wallace for a skull a creill & mending shoone	01–00–00	• 01 • 06 • –
	To Jhon Reid when he went for herings –& things for Sande for his sicknes		• 00 • 04 • –
	For fresh beiffe in January		• 02 • 10 • –
	For breid in January – 30s.		• 01 • 10 • –
	The end off January 1663 disbursments in January 1663		• 377 • 05 • –

Februar	Disbursments in February – 1663~~~~~~~:	
1663	To William Patersone for a long peper booke for Jhon Clerk	• 00 • 10 • –
	To Piter Maill for a rouch hat for him 03–12 – 2 ell off blak rubons thertoo[11] 24s.	• 04 • 16 • –
	3 February to Elspeth Fermer for – 4000 sklait nails at 10s. 9d. the 100 is	• 21 • 10 • –
	1 rim off wreating peper	• 04 • 04 • –
	To Sir Jhon Skougals man James Skougall – 1 rex–dolor	• 02 • 18 • –

[11] Like other words in this book, Clerk spelled 'thereto' many different ways. When he used the abbreviation 'y^r^too', I expanded it to 'thertoo'. This word was also spelled 'thairto' and 'thar[e]too' in this period, and in other places in the manuscript Clerk spelled the word out fully as 'thertoo' or 'thairtoo'.

	To my wyffe to pay Mary Cooke for weiving a web	• 05 • 02 • –
	1 ell of tartin for a saidle cloth..	• 01 • 02 • –
	For stifting raisings suger candie & measses – &c................................	• 02 • 07 • –
	For binding *Tirens* in octava for Jhon Clerk	• 00 • 10 • –
	To my wyffe at hir being in Edinburgh to pay sum small things..........	• 04 • 04 • –
	To Jhon Clerk to get candle for the colledge..	• 00 • 08 • –
	The 9 off February 1663 to Jhon Cooke locksmith in full of his acompt on his discharge the said day..	• 11 • 13 • 04
	16 February to Jhon Pennycooke maltman for making a steip of malt in – December 1662	• 02 • 18 • –
	To Thomas Whyt our gairner for – 6 mands with handles..................	• 01 • 00 • –
	13 February – to Robert Dewer for his super maill in hervest 1662	• 01 • 04 • –
	And 10s. for a firlot off meill wes goten fra him in December 1662	• 01 • 10 • –
	14 off February for timber caps	• 00 • 10 • –
	To a websters wyffe in Braidwood for weiving secking	• 01 • 07 • 06
	To Jhon Rob for salt 3s. 4d..	• 00 • 03 • 04
	Peyit for 8 fadom off tous to pack up a feather bed...........................	• 00 • 16 • –
Adam Grein	20 of February to Adam Greins wyffe to be given to hir sister John – Smiths relict for a feather bed 1 bolster & 2 cods	• 26 • 13 • 04
	To Abraham Clerk for – 24 knaps for a skring – & a turnt fit for a chandler	• 00 • 15 • –
+	23 Februar to William Naper of Wrights Housses on his discharge ~~ For 4 bols of peys & mashlock at 3–6–8d. the boll.............................	• 13 • 06 • 08
	26 of Februar to Jhon Cooke locksmith on his discharge	• 02 • 04 • –

To Thomas Wedel for severall things he did mak & mend for me	• 04 • 04 • –
To Thomas Whyt gairner for the pryce off 4 bols off oats at – 4ll. 8s. the boll – 17ll. 12s.	• 17 • 12 • –
To the said Thomas Whyt for a reid calff...	• 04 • 10 • –
For breid the said month...	• 01 • 02 • –
The end of February 1663: The disbursments off – Februar 1663	• 139 • 00 • –

[11]

Accompt of disbursments in Marche 1663:

March 1663	2: Robert Urie wreatter – 1000 merks – in full off my band with his recept on the bak theroff which band wes date the 29 off November 1662 I have it lying by me canceld	• 666 • 13 • 04
	3 Marche to Alexander Leslie in full off his accompt on his discharge	• 08 • 08 • –
	3: to A[12] David Scot apothecar in full of his compt on his discharge....	• 06 • 00 • –
	12 packits off cords – 8s. .... 8s.	
	6 packits of fyner cords.......... 12s.	• 01 • 00 • –
	To Mage Wade for – 3 pecks off meill for the bairns..........................	• 01 • 04 • –
	To Jhon Reid who wes – 5 dayes at the mill and kill..........................	• 01 • 04 • –
	To Jhon Rob to get 2 pecks off salt...	• 00 • 06 • 08

12 Rather than the 'a' acting as an indefinite article here, it is more likely that Clerk began to write a different name or the word apothecary before proceeding to write 'David'. As in other places in this book, he did not cross out his mistake.

14 Marche to Jhon Pennycooke to buy a sive and a small ridle............ • 00 • 18 • –
16 Marche to Jhon Rob – to get a quart off comon waters................. • 02 • 00 • –
16 Marche for a compt booke for my wyffe covert with reid leather ... • 02 • 06 • –
18 Marche 1663 – to Donald Tailyeur – merchant in Therso in Caithnes
1 – barel off Caithnes beiff 13–00–00
1 – barel conteining – 36 salt tongs at 5s. the peice 09–00–00
7 – salt geisse at 6s. 8d. the peice .... 02–06–08 • 24 • 06 • 08
To Jhon Ferguson cordoner for fitting my blak boots........................ 02–00–00
1 pair off gray waxt shoone for Jhon Clerk 01–10–00
To his man in drink money .... 00–04–00 • 03 • 14 • –
Adam– 20 Marche to Adam Greins wyffe for:
Grein– 11 ell in on[e] peice......................................
11 ell in ane other peice.................................is – 29 ½ ell off lining
7 ½ ell braider in ane other peice ....cloth at 8s. the ell is ..... • 11 • 16 • –
To Thomas Wedel for making and mending severall things: • 01 • 10 • –
21 Marche to Jhon Cooke on his discharge in full off his accompt....... • 04 • 16 • –
To Jhon Broun for – 2 pen knyves........................ 16s.
For puting a handle on ane other pen knyffe.......... 02s. .... • 00 • 18 • –
To Jhon Scot for sum pouders for the gravel .... • 00 • 18 • –
4 – shod shools at 14s. the peice.. • 02 • 16 • –
12 knops more for the skring .... • 00 • 06 • –
+ 20 Marche to Jhon Armstrang for gairden seids acording to his
compt .... • 02 • 00 • –
23 Marche to William Steill colyier in Neuhall – 9–15s. – for– 39 laid

	off cols at – 5s. the laid..		• 09 • 15 • –
+	28 Februar 1663 – peyit to David Dryburgh – for 6 bols off oats –		
	wes goten fra him for Jhon Reid at 4ll. 8s. the boll		• 26 • 08 • –
+	25 Marche 1663 peyit Robert Adamsone for a yeirs fie – fra Mertimes –		
	1661 till Mertimes 1662 is a yeir ~~~~~~~~~		
	1: in money 20ll.	20–00–00;	
	2: in money – 30s. to buy 2 pair off single sold shoone	01–10–00:	• 21 • 10 • –
	25 Marche – 1 pynt 1 mutchkin and a halff clairet wyne....................		• 01 • 04 • 09
	2 pecks of whyt salt		• 00 • 06 • 08
	28 Marche to George Bell for – 2 kipper		• 01 • 16 • –
	30 Marche to James Blaikie for 4 days wark..		• 00 • 16 • –
	For whyt breid in the month off Marche		• 01 • 15 • –
	The end off Marche – 1663; The disbursments in Marche 1663		• 806 • 12 • 01
Aprill 1663	Accompt of disbursments: in Aprill – 1663~~~~~~~~~~~~~~~~~~		
	As follows ~~~~~~~~~~~~~~~~~~~~~~~~~~~		
	1 Aprill 1663 – peyit James Frizel in the Carlips – 14 laid of cols at 4s.		
	the laid is..		• 02 • 16 •
	2 Aprill to James Steuart for – 1 pynt off lint seid oyll	01–08–00	
	4ll. off whyte lead at 4s. 6d. the pound	00–18–00	• 02 • 06 • –
	2 Aprill sent in with Jhon Rob – adrest to Katherin Gray – 40 merks		
	seald in a packit to give hir mother for Marie Clerks boord – 3 month		• 26 • 13 • 04
+	To mak a pynt off good ink~~~~~~		
	1 pynt earthen pig	00–02–06	
	8 once off gals	00–06–00	

8 once off copres 00–01–00
2 once off pomgranat skins 00–04–00
2 once off gum arabick .... 00–06–00 • 00 • 19 • 06
32 –14 –10: • 32 • 14 • 10

[12]

A part off the disbursments in Aprill on the other syde is .... • 32 • 14 • 10
4 once off whyt suger candie – cost .... • 00 • 05 • –
1 lb 4 once off Hollands gleu cost 6s. the pound .... • 00 • 07 • 06
1 once off sene leaves – cost .... • 00 • 08 • –
2 pound off Scots gleu cost 8s. the pound .... • 00 • 16 • –
8 drop off cantarides – or spanish fleis cost .... • 00 • 05 • –
+ 2 hand plains – cost .... 12s.
1 longer plane montit with walnut trie cost .... 17s. .... • 01 • 09 • –
+ 1 once off levander seid – cost .... 12s.
12 drop off tyme seid cost .... 09s. .... • 01 • 01 • –
11 Aprill to Jhon Cooke in full off his accompt on his discharge .... • 04 • 08 • –
To: Thomas Wedel – for doeing sum small things .... • 00 • 12 • –
4 onces off oyll – off sueit[13] almonds – at 8s. the once – 32s. –
1 glasse to hold it 1s. .... • 01 • 13 • –
For whyt breid .... • 01 • 10 • –

The end of Aprill – 1663. The disbursments in Aprill 1663. • 45 • 09 • 04

Accompt off disbursments in May – 1663 ~~~:

May 1663

To Jhon Robertsone in the Bow for pruns: raisings: feygs – suger candie &c	• 04 • 03 • –
2 vinaigre stroup glasses – to Widow Robertsone for them:	• 00 • 09 • –
1 peper booke bound in leather – of a quair of peper for James Clerk disputations	• 00 • 10 • –
To Jhon Rob to get salt	• 00 • 08 • 08
To Jhon Andersone – which he disbursit for Jhon Clerk ~~~:	
to soll his shoone ... 12s.	
to soll his stokings ... 06s.	
to buy suger when he neidit it ... 06s.	
3 limons ... 04s.	• 01 • 08 • –
To Jhon Fergusone cordoner for my wyffs usse ~~~:	
1 – pair off shoone ... 01–09–00	
1 – pair of orange pantons ... 01–09–09	
to his men in drink money ... 00–04–00	• 03 • 02 • –
+ To James Adamsone plumber – in his own housse in presence off Jhon Tod smith – and his own wyffe – for 2 ston of lead – 6s. sterlin which I resavet fra him the – 16 off Jully 1662 –& wes broght out be Jhon Rob	• 03 • 12 • –
1 once off the extract off reglis for the cold	• 00 • 12 • –

[13] Sweet.

To James Stewart for a barel – whairin wes rose water....... 12s. 4d.
1 barel – whairin wes oyll off tarpentin .... 12s. 4d. .... • 01 • 04 • 08
To Henry Harper for severall glasses – &c. acording to his accompt.... • 04 • 04 • –
To Archbald More on his discharge for a wainscot table with
drawers .... • 24 • 00 • –
To Jhon Cooke locksmith on his discharge .... • 01 • 04 • –
3 pair off bairns gloves .... • 00 • 15 • –
To Jhon Scott merchant for Jhon Clerks cloths – on his discharge –
5 ell off gray cloth at – 6ll. 6s. the ell.. 31–10–00
14 ell off blak rubens at 5s. the ell 03–10–00
5 quarters off reid freis to be a caisse for a gun at 20s. the ell .... 01–05–00 • 36 • 05 • –
+ In – James Wilsons – callit cairle off clay his housse – to Hew Wernard
befor Bailyie Foulerton and on[e] Hamilton Mr Wernards good brother –
for the head off a table off marbre..........4 rex dolors .... • 11 • 12 • –
1 a[l]md sheips skin .... • 00 • 06 • 8
1 yrne frying pan .... • 02 • 03 • –
1 urinel glasse .... • 00 • 06 • –
5 mutchkins off canel – water at 3ll. the pynt.................................. • 03 • 15 • –
5 May to Jhon Rob 2 merks to give his mother for a firlot off meill
wes got for the bairns.. • 01 • 06 • 08
29 May – 5 mutchkins off clairet wyne at 18s. the pynt .... • 01 • 02 • 06
5 May to Isobel Scot to get comon teyking for a bed.......................... • 06 • 00 • –
To Jenet Speir for 6 loch leiches .... • 00 • 09 • –
25 off May to Jhon Ramsay to pay for 2 cows & 2 calffs he boght for us • 46 • 00 • –

15 May for fresh beiff – 18s.	• 00 • 18 • –
4ll. off Deip[14] pruns at 4s. the pound	• 00 • 16 • –
6 May to Patrik Craig for 6 bols off oats at 4ll. 8s. the boll to mak – meill off they wer resavet in the month off Marche 1663	• 26 • 08 • –
To a couper	• 00 • 04 • –
To James Blaikie tailyeur	• 00 • 14 • –
7 May to Jhon Ramsay for – 20 mure fowls........at 6s. the peice	• 06 • 00 • –
15 May to Samuel Young for a boll off whyt salt	• 02 • 13 • 04
27 May – to Jhon Brysone measson for 1 lyge off a swyne	• 01 • 07 • 04
28 May to Jhon Pennycooke malt man for making a steip off malt	• 02 • 18 • –
The disbursments above mentioned in May...1663	• 196 • 16 • 10

196–16–10

[13]

The disbursments in the month off May on the other syde is		• 196 • 16 • 10
+ 22 May to George Nicol tailyeur and his good brother Adam Robertson –		
for 6 days at 12s. a day is – 3–12 – I gave him bot	03–10–00	
to him – for 17 once off balling	00–17–00	
To Adam Robertsone in drink money	00–09–00	• 04 • 16 • –
+ 27 May to Robert Cuninghame webster in Leswaid		
For 17 ell of lining at 4s. the ell	03–08–00	

[14] Dieppe, France.

16 ell off comon teyking at 2s. the ell 01–12–00
To his wyffe for sowing seids & creish 00–06–00
And at first my wyffe gave hir for warping .... 00–12–00 • 05 • 18 • –
For whyt breid in the month off May .... • 01 • 17 • –
Formerlie in this month – when I wes at Edinburgh – my wyffe peyit –
to Robert Cuninghame in Leswaid webster for weiving 75 ell off cloth –
off severall sorts and for other small deus[15] to him .... • 10 • 00 • –
To Mary Clerk to get a thick hood .... • 03 • 06 • –
To Jhon Rob to get divers things for liting .... • 03 • 00 • –
For short breid when Lo: Reg. – wes expected: • 01 • 04 • –
The end off May 1663 — Soma off the disbursments in May 1663 • 226 • 17 • 10

Juny 1663

The accompt off disbursments in Juny 1663
4 Juny – at Jhon Broun his brydel in the Wantonwas .... • 01 • 00 • –
+ 8 Juny to Walter Hamilton when he wes at Neubiging for 7 ell of reid
wutert camlit at 29s. the ell .... • 10 • 03 • –
+ 12 Juny to Archibald [blank] Bagillos man when he broght home
Margaret Clerk – 24s. to mak his voyage and – 6s. to drink is .... • 01 • 10 • –
10 Juny at Jhon Bruntons brydel in Pennycooke .... • 00 • 17 • –
13 Juny 1663 – left with my wyffe – 3ll. to compleit Jennet Crookshanks
fie and – 3ll. shoe got formerlie is 6ll. .... • 06 • 00 • –
13 Juny 1663 left with my wyffe – 12ll. to give Cristian Borthwick
for hir fie fra Witsonday 1662 till Witsonday 1663 12–00–00
And 24s. to buy hir a pair off shoone .... 01–04–00 • 13 • 04 • –

22 Juny – to Jhon Gill for 8 ell and halff a quarter of Scots gray cloth at 24s. the ell .... • 09 • 15 • –

+ 17 Juny 1663 to Adam Grein 10ll. on his discharge off the said date for a termes maill off my chamber fra Mertimes 1662 till Witsonday 1663 which wes the last termes maill I peyit to Adam Grein at Witsonday 1663 when he flitit to his good sisters housse .... • 10 • 00 • –

+ To Hew Mackculloch collector – 56–11–4d. for 2 months cesse which the brewers fell short to pay off excyse on his discharge date – 19 Juny 1663 – and that fra the 1 off November 1662 till the 1 off – November 1663 .... • 56 • 11 • 04

For taking doun and puting up my bed 6s. for carying it fra Widou Robertsons housse to my chamber 4s. – is 10s. .... • 00 • 10 • –

17 Juny to James Melvin for 5 mutchkins off Mallaga seck at 30s. the pynt – 37s. 6d. bot he took fra me bot 3s. sterlin .... • 01 • 16 • –

To John Mure for 4 onces off nitmugs .... • 00 • 18 • –

19 Juny to Elspeth Fermer for – 1000 fleuring nails .... • 04 • 10 • –

For mounting a poik Mary Clerk shewed with worsit strings to hold books .... • 01 • 10 • –

+ To Widow Bell for Jhon Clerks boord 3 months fra the 3 off May 1663 till the 3 off Agust 1663 40–00–00

To buy minores poete 01–04–00

To buy Homers *Iliads* 01–10–00

[15] Dues.

3 Juny to mend his shoone & stokings................. 00–10–00
11 Juny to pay a contribution ordained be
the regent... 00–16–00........... • 44 • 00 • –
24 Juny for girding looms to a couper... • 00 • 18 • –
15 Juny to my wyffe – to pay or doe some small bussynes.................. • 03 • 00 • –

+ 166 – 03 –: A.....disbursments in Juny above is ...... • 166 • 03 • –

+ My wyffe wes broght to bed on Sunday in the efternoone – 31 May 1663:
off a dochter callit Isobel – the first Isobell dyed ~~~~~~~~~

29 May to Walter Hamilton – for 10 pynts 3 mutchkins of seck at 30s.
a pynt .... • 16 • 02 • 06
To Walter Hamiltons wyffe to cause baik short breid .... • 03 • 07 • 06
4 Juny to Bessie Crauford midwyffe 6 rex dolors.............................. • 17 • 08 • –
7 Juny to Jhon Broun schoole master when the chyld wes baptized..... • 01 • 04 • –
Said day to Jhon Broun bedel .... • 00 • 06 • –
For fresh beiff – 24s. .... • 01 • 04 • –
For whyt breid in the month of Juny.. • 03 • 10 • –
1 quart clairet wyne .... • 01 • 16 • –
8 once of confectit orange skins: 18s. – 1 boost of carv[i]e 8s. is.......... • 01 • 06 • –
To Adam Patersone for grasse to horse went in severall tyms............. • 00 • 12 • –

B: 46 – 16 B............. • 46 • 16

[14]

	A: The disbursments off Juny on the other syde is		• 166 • 03 • –
	B: more the disbursments off Juny on the other syde is		• 46 • 16 • –
	All the disbursments in Juny is....		• 212 • 19 • –
	The end off the disbursments in Juny.....................1663 ~~~~~~~~		
Jully	The disbursments in Jully – 1663:		
1663	1 ½ hundreth off fleuring nails at 8s. the 100		• 00 • 12 • –
	To James Stewart for 3 earthen pots		• 00 • 12 • –
	8 fadom off small tows 10s.		• 00 • 10 • –
	For *Clavis Hendrica* for Jhon Clerk....in octava	02–08–00	
	1 peper booke in quarto with clasps to wreat his nots in	01–00–00	• 03 • 08 • –
Adam Greins	The 7 Jully 1663 to Adam Greins wyffe for –		
Wyffe	1 feather bed 1 bolster and 2 cods 18–00–00		
	1 doun bed and 2 doun cods 12–00–00		
	1 dornick table cloth and 12 litle dornick serviettes ... 05–00–00		
	3 brasse hatt pins... 01–00–00 all......		• 36 • 00 • –
	Said day given to hir woman Bessie in drink money when I peyit the 36ll.		• 00 • 12 • –
	14 Jully 1663 to David Boyd readie money in full of ane accompt		• 12 • 10 • –
	15 Jully to Jhon Robertsone in the Bow in full off ane accompt..........		• 04 • 15 • 04
	The said day for womens & bairns shoone		• 07 • 11 • –
	3 ell off whyt fingering at 13s. the ell...		• 01 • 19 • –

for hemp 12–
for stifing............................. 08–
for 1 litle brasse pan.............. 08–
for secking to be a poik .... 06– .... • 01 • 14 • –
22 Jully to William Lorimer for 3 ¼ ell off worsit turk to be
James Clerk a cot at 30s. the ell.. • 04 • 17 • 06
23 Jully to Jhon Lindsay for a cows hyde 6–13–4d. given him 12s.
to cause currie the same is .... 07–05–4d. • 07 • 05 • 04
23 – to Jhon Robisone for 2 pair of shone for Marie & Margaret
Clerks .... • 02 • 02 • –
For a leather bag to James Clerk to keip his books in .... • 00 • 06 • –
25 July to Jhon Cooke in full off ane accompt on his discharge .... • 07 • 03 • 04
24 to Jhon Tod in full off ane accompt on his discharge .... • 05 • 14 • 08
+ 22 to Hew Craig – 11–14–6 in full off ane accompt on his discharge ... • 11 • 14 • 06
23 to Jhon Scot merchant in full off ane accompt on his discharge for
a satyne flourd petticot for Mary Clerk .... • 25 • 06 • 08
22 Jully to Robert Douglas in full off ane accompt on his discharge for
lint &c.. • 13 • 13 • 04
23 to David Boyd in full off ane accompt on his discharge for a worsit ~~~~~~~~
& silk goun to my wyffe &c .... • 19 • 10 • –
23 Jully to Hew Wernard on his discharge for 100 dails & 10 treis
for sleds.. • 49 • 00 • –
17 Jully at the baptisme off Glencorse sone to the nourish .... 58s. –
& to the midwyffe .... 29s. is • 04 • 07 • –

	20 Jully to Mr William Dowglas for a sad gray horse 78ll. 4s. – to his man		• 78 • 04 • –
	To William Leishman for carying 2 pair off virginels out off Edinburgh		• 01 • 03 • –
	To Jhon Rob for salmond trouts & hering		• 00 • 11 •
	For whyt breid in the month off Jully		• 01 • 14 • –
	The end off Jully 1663 All the disbursments in Jully 1663		• 302 • 15 • 08
Agust	disbursments in Agust 1663		
1663	1 Agust 1663 to Archebald Andersone for his fie fra Mertimes 1662 till Witsonday 1663 in money	08–00–00	
	6s. in earnest – 1 merk to buy his shoone	00–19–04	• 08 • 19 • 04
	Ane accompt markit AB for mounting a pad for my wyffe		• 15 • 07 • 06
	To James Lishman cordoner for 1 pair off shoone for my wyffe		• 01 • 11 • –
	For virginell strings		• 00 • 16 • –
	To Jhon Andersone in full off ane accompt he furnisht to Jhon Clerk To buy books &c		• 08 • 03 • –
	To Robert Selkrigs woman in drink money callit Jennet		• 00 • 12 • –
	To Samuel Gilles pour un petit chienne		• 01 • 10 • –
	4 ½ lb off glew at 4s. the pound		• 01 • 16 • –
	3 remnants of blak cloth to help 2 sute off blak cloths		• 11 • 12 • –
	To Jhon Rob smith for 2 rods for my bed in Edinburgh – 4 eyes thertoo and 2 little sheilds		• 01 • 18 • –

1 litle silver dish for canel water weying 1 once 4 drop at 3ll. the
once 03–15–00
For making the same .... 00–18–00 • 04 • 13 • –
+ 18 Agust to Jhon Tait in Preston pans on his discharge for 10 lb off rond
lead shot which I got fra him in anno 1657 .... • 01 • 16 • –
19 Agust to William Hamilton for a dry ware trie and a covert .... • 00 • 12 • –
1 lb 3 once of castel soap – 10s. .... • 00 • 10 • –
For severall lame potts .... • 00 • 16 • –
60–11–10 The disbursments in Agust on this syde .... • 60 • 11 • 10

[15]
A part off the disbursments in Agust 1663 on the other syde is .... • 60 • 11 • 10
22 Agust 1663 to Jhon Cooke for a bordert lock 3 skreu nails
1 sheil with 2 clefs for the large fir presse in the laft .... • 01 • 16 • –
For 4 douzane off peirs .... • 00 • 14 • –
To Alexander Mackie tailyeur in full off his accompt on his discharge
date 27 off Agust for making 2 gouns to Marie & Margaret Clerks and
furnishing thertoo .... • 12 • 00 • –
3 ¼ ell of teyking for bags for wreats........cost .... • 02 • 00 • –
+ 28 Agust 1663 to Jhon Maklurg merchant for halff ane anker
off Rainish[16] wyne – conteining 10 pynts and a chopin at 24s.
the pynt is 21s. sterlin to him for excyse theroff – 12s. and 3s.
to the couper & for carying it to Jhon Stewarts is in all –

	with the trie in which it wes		• 13 • 07 • –
	20 fadom off tows cost – 26s. peyit to Jhon Robisons wyffe – 29 Agust		• 01 • 06 • –
	28 Agust to David Clerk to buy 6 hooks		• 01 • 10 • –
	2 grosse off cullort French breist buttons at 25s. the grosse – boght fra James Gr[a]hame – 29 Agust		• 02 • 10 • –
	To David Scots man for halff ane once off pestilentia pils		• 01 • 00 • –
	14 Agust for herings		• 01 • 13 • –
	24 Agust to Samuel [blank] for 1 boll of salt halff a peck lesse		• 02 • 06 • 06
	To James Blaikie tailyeur		• 00 • 12 • –
	for whyt breid in the month of Agust		• 01 • 14 • –
	The end of Agust 1663 — disbursments in Agust 1663		• 102 • 10 • 04
September 1663	Disbursments in September 1663		
	4 September 1663 – compleited Robert Dewer smith in Pennycooke 58ll. 9s. 2d. – acording to ane accompt for severall wark he wroght fra the 29 off Januar 1662 till the 4 off September 1663		• 59 • 09 • 02
	Given Jhon Rob to get lit	00–05–00	
	25 September to Clerkingtouns man that broght some fruit	00–12–00	
	25 September to Jhon Rob to get beiff	00–18–00	• 01 • 15 • –
	5 mutchkins off waters at 20s. the pynt	01–05–00	• 01 • 05 • –
	19 September 1 pynt and ⅛ of canel water at 3ll. the pynt	03–07–06	• 03 • 07 • 06

[16] Rhenish, i.e. wine from areas around the Rhine River.

26 off September 1663 to Robert Adamsone – ~~~~
1– for his fie fra Mertimes – 1662 till Witsonday 1663........................ 10–00–00
+ 2. to buy a pair of shoone.. 00–15–00
6 quarters of gray at 2 merks the ell .... 02–00–00 • 12 • 15 • –
11 off September to Jhon Rob to get 2 ston off hair 00–16–00
To Pourdie Webster in Ryhill – for weiving...................................... 02–08–00
27 off Agust to my wyffe to pay some small things............................ 03–00–00 • 06 • 04 • –
16 September 1663 to John Simson in Bruntstain for 3 bols & 1 firlot
of beir we got in beirseid tyme 1663 at 6ll. 6s. 8d. the boll is .... • 20 • 11 • 08
15 September given to give Mage Wade to get halff a boll of peis meill
+ half a boll of new oat meill and half a hundreth herings .... • 05 • 02 • –
Fryday the 18 off September 1663 to Robert Cuninghame webster in
Leswaid for wirking 24 ell off dyst stuff – 42s. to his man 3s. 4d.:
my wyffe wantit 3 clevs off cullort worsit being 3 lb wecht for which
they differt & shoe rebated some thing for it – so he went away
discontent – & as he went throgh the clos he took up 3 stons & put up in
his pokit – upon what accompt I knowe not – bot it looked ill favered
Jhon Clerk and his sister [blank] Clerk did sie him take them up .... • 02 • 05 • 04
+ The last off Agust 1663 to Mr Wiliam Dalgarno 161ll. for halff a
yeirs stipend fra Mertimes 1662 till Witsonday 1663 on his discharge
date at Pennycooke the last off Agust 1663 .... • 161 • 00 • –
+ The 22 of September 1663 to Mr Robert Alisone minister at Glencorse
48ll. for a yeirs stipend off Cookeing fra Mertimes 1662: I say fra
Witsonday 1662 till Witsonday 1663 on his discharge date Corsehousse

19 Agust 1663		• 48 • 00 • –
The 25 off September to James Flect merchand in Lanerik for 20 onces		
7 drop off litle old antique silver peices at 59s. the once	60–04–00	
4 pair off wemens gloves at 7s. 6d. the pair..	01–10–00	
1 ½ grosse off threid buttons at 6s. 8d. the grosse	00–10–00	
2 bolts off whyt knitings..	00–12–00	
12 ell off grein worsting..	00–06–00	• 63 • 02 • –
The disbursments off September on this syde.........		• 384 • 16 • 08

[16]

	The disbursments off September – on the other syde is	• 384 • 16 • 08
	For whyt breid in September 1663..	• 01 • 03 • 04
	The end off September 1663 The disbursments of September 1663	• 386 • 00 • –
October	Accompt of disbursments in October – 1663 ~~~~~~~~	
1663	To Jhon Stinsone walker in full of ane accompt on his discharge the 30 of September 1663	• 02 • 13 • 04
	1 October to Alexander Leslie in full of his accompt on his discharge..	• 08 • 06 • –
	2 October to Hew Wernard merchant in full of his accompt on his discharge..	• 59 • 16 • –
	2 October to Dame Geils Smith – 45s. which shoe peyit to William Michel baxter for baiking short breid in anno 1661	• 02 • 05 • –

1 silver whisle with bels & reid corail boght for Mr William Dalgarnos sone .... • 08 • 04 • –
1 rouch hatt with a calico poik for my selff cost .... • 01 • 16 • –
For David Lindsay – 5s. for binding it 6s. to given to Neuhall .... • 00 • 11 • –
2 October to John Cooke for making 1 key – 1 vyel & 1 hartring & mending the lock off the press boght fra Walter Hamilton and for tining 2 handes & sneks – and for 2 neu keipers peyit for all .... • 01 • 05 • –
2 pecks of flour.. • 01 • 04 • –
For beiff at several tymes in the said moneth........................ • 05 • 10 • –
1 lyg of mouton fra Silver burn.. • 00 • 12 • –
for oynions & herings – 7s. .... • 00 • 07 • –
5 October to William Steill for 33 laid of cols at 5s. the laid peyit onlie.. • 07 • 10 • –
Halff a ston of small candle.. • 03 • 08 • –
17 October to William Thomson to pay for a plough 3–6–8 & 4s. is.... • 03 • 10 • 08
26 October to Thomas Whyt for 8 thraive off stroe .... • 04 • 16 • –
27 October given my wyffe – 7 rex dolors to give the good wyffe of Silver burne to buy lint at Bigger fare.. • 20 • 06 • –
21 October to Mr Hew Smith regent......................10 rex dolors ...... • 29 • 00 • –
4 ell off twidle harden for a horse sheit at 5s. the ell........................ • 01 • 00 • –
1 lb off cut tobaco..00–18–00
3 ½ lb off row tobaco at 13s. the pound ....02–04–06 • 03 • 02 • 06
1 glasse bottel with halff a mutchkin off sueit oyll for the gravel......... • 00 • 10 • –
2 pair off gloves .... • 01 • 00 • –

	Halff a lb off hat makers cords		• 00 • 07 • –
	10 knops for my wyffs litle cabinet		• 00 • 07 • 04
	1 hatt for my selff	04–04–00	
	1 hatt for Jhon Clerk	02–08–00	• 06 • 12 • –
	24 October to William Seatoun tailyeur for making & furnishing of a sute of gray cloth clothes for Jhon Clerk on his discharge		• 07 • 02 • 06
	To Jhon Cooke for a bordert lock and 2 keys for the dore goes out to the batlement		• 03 • 15 • –
	1 lb off lint seid oyll	01–06–00	
	1 lb off best head hemp	00–10–00	
	2 lb off rosit	00–04–00	
	1 firlot off great salt	01–10–00	• 03 • 10 • –
	More given Isobel Scot 20s. 8d. – she payit 8 merk for the ston of the lint		• 01 • 08 • –
	1 mutchkin off clairet wyne		• 00 • 03 • 06
	17 October to Adam Gibsone cordoner for 17 days work at 6s. ilk day with his meat		• 05 • 02 • –
	For whyt bread in October:		• 01 • 11 • –
	The end of October 1663	The disbursments in October 1663	• 196 • 03 • 06
November	Accompt off disbursments in November 1663		
	2 November to James Grhame tenent under the laird off Welstain for		
1663	1 ox for Walter Hamilton in part off Jhon Clerk boord	27–00–00	
	1 ox for our self to kill	22–00–00	• 49 • 00 • –

When my Lord Rutherfoord sould have cum for seck 02–12–06
For clairet wyne 01–01–04
3 pair off dovs........................ 00–12–00 • 04 • 05 • 10
4 lb off small candle .... • 00 • 18 • –
4 November – to James Thomson glaisier on his discharge the
said day for glaising the new housse &c .... • 43 • 16 • –
11 November at James Bruntons brydel – to Alexander Etkin in
Pennycooke for ane ox wes kild......................for our self................. • 30 • 00 • –
To him for a boll off peys we got in seid tyme .... • 03 • 12 • –

The disbursments in November above • 131 • 11 • 10

[17]
The disbursments off November 1663 on the other syde is .... • 131 • 11 • 10
13 November – when the bairn Isobel Clerk died –
1 quart off clairet wyne........................ 01–08–00
3 grot loaffs 00–11–00
Halff a pound off cut tobaco – 8s. – 12 pyps 1s. 4d. 00–09–04
To James Sandelands who made the kist 00–12–00
To John Broun for making the graff 00–18–00
+ To Arche Craig to pay for ale tobaco & pyps the night the
bairne dyed 00–13–04
To Helen Patersone for drink efter the buriel........................ 00–16–08

To Helen Patersone for 1 barel off ale wes sent to Arche Craigs .... 02–02–08 • 07 • 11 • –

+ 25 November 1663 to Jonet Lamb for hir fie fra n[17] Witsonday 1663
till Mertimes 1663 – 8ll. and 20s. to buy hir shoone .... • 09 • 00 • –

26 November to Barbara Jons for hir fie fra Witsonday 1663 till Mertimes –
1663 – 7ll. in money – 20s. to buy hir shoone .... • 08 • 00 • –

10 November 1663 – my brother gave my wyffe 12 dolors and 7ll.
shoe got for a ox hyde which shoe imployed at Edinburg as follows is both
togither – 41–16s. 41–16–00

12 November to Walter Hamiltouns wyffe 6–6–8 with ane ox the got cost
27ll. which compleits Jhon Clerks boord – 3 months.......................... 06–06–08

To Mary Cooks goodman for liting the worsit of 2 boord cloths
1–16 and to him for weiving the same 3ll. is 4ll. 16s. it
conteins [blank] off lynth [blank] ell Scots 04–16–00

To Walter Hamilton woman in drink money 00–18–00

2 pair off sheits at 40s. the pair 04–00–00

8 ell off secking for a pallias at 8s. the ell 03–04–00

5lb wecht of stifting bleu and whyt 01–10–00

For half a ston off alme 01–12–00

For feygs raisings and almonds 01–10–00

2 ell of gray serge for a waistcot 50s. the ell 05–00–00

2 ell off linze winze at 16s. the ell 01–12–00

17 It appears that Clerk began to write 'November' before changing his mind and writing 'Witsonday'. The small 'n' appears after 'fra' in the original without being struck out.

6 quarters off grein sey	01–12–00	
1 bolt off lougit whyt knitings	00–15–00	
	32–15–08	
And 9ll. bestowed on silver lace for tails	09–00–04	• 41 • 16 • –
For whyt breid in the month off November		• 01 • 08 • –
The end off November 1663 disbursments in November 1663		• 199 • 06 • 10

December 1663

The disbursments in December 1663 –		
3 December to Archbald Andersone for his fie fra Witsonday 1663 till Mertimes 1663 in money – 9ll. to buy a pair of shoone 16s. is		• 09 • 16 • –
Said day to Isobel Scot for a lyg off muton 10s.		
Said day for fish 06s.		
1 haik for a whill 1 pirne & whorl 08s.		
To James Blaikie tailyeur 13s.		• 01 • 17 • –
3 December sent with Pet Craigs brother in the Towr[18] 9ll. which he gave Walter Hamiltons wyffe to buy & pay for 3 ston of fresh butter		~~~ ~~~ • 09 • 00 • –
1 pynts & 3 quarters of a mutchkin of canel water at 3ll. the pint	03–11–00	
1 pynt off comon waters 20s.	01–00–00	• 04 • 11 • –
7 December 1663 disbursit at Edinburgh for:		
1– to Adam Patersone for corn & stroe wes owing him	01–04–00	
2– 1 lame pot to steip pens in	00–06–00	
3– to Jhon Broun for sharping sheirs & razoirs	00–15–00	
4– to Thomas Wedel for doeing some things	01–08–00	
5– for raisings pruns & rysse	03–00–00	• 06 • 13 • –

6– 1 pair off brasse compasses for Jhon Clerk 00–08–00	
7– 1 pair off large brasse compasses for my selff 01–04–00	
8– to David Boyd for 3 ½ ell off gray serge to be myself	
a sark welicot and 1 pair off hose at 48s. the ell 08–08–00	• 10 • 00 • –
41 – 17 – 00 The disbursement above in December ...	• 41 • 17 • –

[18]

The debursments off December 1663 on the other syde is..................	• 41 • 17 • –
8 December to William Mure candlmaker in full of his accompt	• 27 • 14 • –
9 December to James Grhame servitor to Michel Mel in Deip on	~~~ ~~~
his discharge of 64–16s. Scots in full off ane bill of exchange the said	~~~ ~~~
Mr Mel drew on me for worsit he boght at Rouen & sent my wyffe ...	• 64 • 16 • –
10 December 1663 to Robert Selkrig 12ll. for my chamber maill	~~~ ~~~
fra Witsonday 1663 till Mertimes 1663 on his discharge date the	
10 off December 1663	• 12 • 00 • –
To Archbald More wright in Leith wynd on his discharge in	~~~ ~~~
full off his accompt & all other preseiding the 14 off December	
1663 which discharge is date the 14 off December 1663	• 68 • 15 • 04
15 December 1663 to Jhon Gray smith in North Leith in full off	~~~ ~~~

[18] The Tower of Penicuik. Clerk spells it 'Tour' throughout the original. On the one hand, the internal use of the 'u' instead of a 'w' is fairly common in how Clerk spelled many words. However, as Clerk also had a tendency to resort to phrases or words in French, it is also possible that he was using the French spelling of the word.

his accompt acording to his discharge at the fit theroff and off ~~~ ~~~
all uther accompts preseiding the 15 off December 1663 .... • 94 • 10 • –
15 December 1663 to Jhon Dalgarno merchant in full off his
accompt on his discharge at the fit theroff date 15 December
1663 & all uther compts preseiding the said 15 off December
1663.......................................245–11 .... • 245 • 11 • –
19 December 1663 to Alexander Leslie wreatter in full of
his accompt .... • 04 • 14 • –
+ 19 December 1663 to James Lockhart for a large
broun gelding.....210 merks 133–06–08
To his man in drink in money – 30s. 01–10–00
210 merks is 140ll. I omitted the 10 merks...06–13–04 • 141 • 10 • –
23 December to Jhon Reid to get flour & breid at Dudingstoun .... • 01 • 14 • –
For breid in December.. • 01 • 10 • –

The end off December: disbursments in December 1663 ...... • 704 • 11 • 04
1663

Januar –	1663	• 377 • 05 • –
Februar –	....	• 139 • 00 • –
Marche –	....	• 806 • 12 • 01
Aprill –	....	• 045 • 09 • 04
May –	....	• 226 • 17 • 10
Juny –	....	• 212 • 19 • –
Jully –	....	• 302 • 15 • 08

Agust –	....	• 102 • 10 • 04
September –	....	• 386 • 00 • –
October –	....	• 196 • 03 • 06
November –	....	• 199 • 06 • 10
December –	....	• 704 • 11 • 4
	Soma	•3699 • 10 • 11

The haill disbursments in anno 1663 .... •3699 • 10 • 11

Jhon: Clerk

[19]

disbursments in January 1664 ~~ :

January	Given in hansel to severals		
1664	To Jhon Clerk an auval graven peice of silver worth	06–00–00	
	And a shilling	00–12–00	• 06 • 12 • –
	To James Clerk – 6s.		• 00 • 06 • –
	To Marie Clerk 1 dens[e] thick peice off silver worth........................	01–16–00	
	Given hir mother halff a dolor to give hir	01–09–00	• 03 • 05 • –
	To Margaret Clerk – 1 French teston..		• 01 • 00 • –
	To Elizabeth Clerk – 1 dens thick peice off silver	18 s.	
	1 curious 3s. peice	03 s.	• 01 • 01 • –

To Jhon Rob	00–06–00		
To Robert Adamsone	00–09–00		
To Arche Andersone	00–09–00		
To Jhon Hodg	00–04–06		
To George Reid	00–04–00		
In turnors among the bairns	00–10–00		• 02 • 02 • 06
To Katherine Midltoun dochter to umqull Francis Midltoun			• 02 • 18 • –
			• 17 • 04 • 06
5 January 1664 to David Clerk for his fie fra Witsonday 1663 till Mertimes 1663			
1 in money		13–06–08	
1 pair off double sold shoone		01–09–00	
3 ell off gray cost 26s. 8d. the ell		04–00–00	• 18 • 15 • 08
7 January to Jhon Ramsay for 21 mure fowls at 6s. the peice			• 06 • 06 • –
6 January to William Steill for 40 laid of cols at 5s. the laid			• 10 • 00 • –
Said day for 3 bie skaips			• 01 • 04 • –
1 peck of salt	00–03–04		
1 pirn for a whill	00–02–00		
2 douzan off tobaco pyps	00–04–06		• 00 • 12[19] • 10
On the 11 off January 1664 compleited the peyment of 76ll. 13s. 4d. to Jhon Thomsons wyffe in the Luken housses for nourishing Catherin Clerk fra the 25 off Juny 1662 till Candlmes 1664			• 76 • 13 • 04
			• 94 • 16 • –

	1 small meill sive		• 01 • 16 • –
	To the bairns to pay for ale & eygs		• 00 • 12 • –
	12 January 1664: to William Herris customer at the West Port		• 01 • 04 • –
	2 colt helters – 26s. 8d.		• 01 • 06 • 08
	For mending a saidle and tags thairtoo		• 00 • 12 • –
	1 lb off whyt suger candie		• 01 • 00 • –
	4 lb off raisings at 8s. the lb	01–12–00	
	3 lb off fygs at 6s. the lb	00–18–00	
	2 lb bourdeaux plum dames at 2s. 6d. the lb.	00–05–00	• 02 • 15 • –
17 – 04 – 6	1: musick booke printed at Aberdein		• 01 • 10 • –
18 – 15 – 8	To James Grhame for 2 rim peper at 4ll. the rim		• 08 • 00 • –
94 – 16 – 0	2 teis with bukls befor at 21s. the peice		• 02 • 02 • –
55 – 02 – 4	3 ell off serge to lyne my cot at 44s. the ell		• 06 • 12 • –
185 – 18 – 6	16 January to Robert Selkrigs woman		• 00 • 12 • –
	To Jhon Hamiltoun for 6 suger loaffs weying 20 lb 6 once at 12s. the pound		• 12 • 04 • 06
	18 Januar to Jhon Lourie at the Mill 2–2–8d. for a barel off ale wes sent to Bruntstain at my desyre		• 02 • 02 • 08
	19 January to a couper for girding looms		• 00 • 12 • –
	To James Blaikie – tailyeur .... 12s.		
	for oynions — 3s. for hadocks ...... 07s. .... is ...... 10s.		
	2 pomshons to be tals .... 50s. .... 50s.		• 03 • 12 • –

[19] It appears that Clerk made a mistake when tallying up this section. I have transcribed the tally as found in the original.

For whyt breid in January .... 1664 .... • 01 • 12 • –
For fresh beiff in January – 5 tymes .... • 06 • 17 • 06
• 55 • 02 • 04

The end off January
1664 The disbursments in January 1664 : • 185 • 18 • 06

[20]

Februar 1664 Disbursments in February 1664:

The 12 off February 1664 peyit to Margaret Hopkirk
1: in money 32–00–00
2: more in money for 3 pair off shoone at 24s. the pair 03–12–00
3: formerlie my wyffe gave hir 1 pair off shoone cost .... 01–04–00 • 36 • 16 • –
which is for 2 yeirs service fra Witsonday 1662 till Witsonday 1664
1 February to Jhon Gill for 2 bols and a half off meill....14ll. .... • 14 • 00 • –
For a pynt of reid cullort waters .... • 01 • 10 • –
2 pecks off flour .... 01–04–00 ~~~~ ~~~ ~~~
To pay for the bairns in Pennycooke 00–12–00
For fish .... 00–05–04 • 02 • 01 • 04
13 February to Jhon Pennycooke maltman for 2 bols of malt .... • 15 • 00 • –
+ On Saturday the 27 off February 1664 befor James Blaikie tailyeur & his sone – payit to William Dowglas in Leswaid which we wes resting off fie to his dochter Marioun Douglas 14ll. and 42s. I gave him

	more nor we wes oweing hir is 16 lib. 2s. he promist to send me a discharge off the said 16–02s.	2[20] • 16 • 00 • –
	To Jhon Hamilton in the Bow for a ston off Bourdeaux pruns	• 01 • 12 • –
	1 whyt timber box to hold boutons	• 00 • 10 • –
	For fresh beiff in February	• 04 • 07 • –
	For breid in February – 30s.	• 01 • 10 • –
	18 February to Archebald Craig – 4ll. for a boll off oats wes got fra him – the day that the bairn Isobel Clerk wes buried on	• 04 • 00 • –
	26 off February to Patrik Craig for 6 bols off oats wes got fra him for Jhon Reid at 4ll. 6s. 8d. the boll	• 26 • 00 • –
	26 off Februar to Edouart Adamsone for 3 ston off butter he boght for us at 3–6–8d. the ston	• 10 • 00 • –
	The said day to him 10s. his wyffe peyit for fieing Mage Law & 3s. 4d. shoe gave hir in earnest is	• 00 • 13 • 04
	The end off February 1664 The disbursments in Februar 1664	• 134 • 01 • 08

Marche	Disbursments in Marche 1664 ~~~~~	
1664	The 9 off Marche 1664 my wyffe peyit to David Boyd in full of ane accompt	• 21 • 12 • –
	The 8 off Marche 1664 my wyffe peyit John Scot in full of ane accompt	• 13 • 02 • –

[20] This is how the entry appears in the original – Clerk added the 2 shillings above the error he made when he initially entered 16–00–. He makes this type of correction a few times in the account book.

The 8 off Marche 1664 my wyffe peyit to Agnes Arthur in full of ane compt	• 07 • 08 • 06
The 10 off Marche 1664 to Jhon Robisone in full of ane accompt	• 04 • 08 • 08
On a dinner in Walter Hamiltons to the primer & regent	• 10 • 00 • –
To John Scott for lace to my wyffs petticot & Lizes	• 02 • 18 • –
1 pound 4 once of balling	• 00 • 18 • –
2 ell of stenting	• 00 • 18 • –
2 ell of lining – 16s.	• 00 • 16 • –
Halff ell halff quarter off Holland to be John Clerk bands	• 02 • 04 • –
For ribbens to Lize	• 01• 00 • –
The 2 off Marche 1664 my wyffe peyit to John Carbraith webster in Leswaid for weiving 18 ell off lining at 3s. 4d. the ell – 3 lib. & for weiving 44 ell off harden – 56s. is both 5 lib. 16s.	• 05 • 16 • –
To William Straton in Straton for a boll of seed peys	• 04 • 13 • 04
To Gibe Pennycooke for 8 skuls for lyme kils	• 00 • 12 • –
17 Marche to Samuel Burn for 1 boll off whyt salt	• 02 • 13 • 04
16 Marche 1664 to Wiliam Seaton tailyeur 27–19–8 in full off all accompts on his discharge off the said date	• 27 • 19 • 08
16 Marche 1664 to Charles Maitland in full of ane accompt	• 09 • 06 • –
15 Marche to John Armstrang for seids in full off ane accompt	• 02 • 19 • 06
15 Marche to Walter Hamiltons wyffe in full off ane accompt	• 06 • 08 • –
Fra the 8 off September 1663 till the 23 off Marche 1664 peyit to Robert Dewer smith in Pennycooke for divers wark according to his accompt thereoff..................51–12–4	• 51 • 12 • 04

For salt		• 00 • 06 • 08
To James Blaikie tailyeur and his sone for 3 days wark		• 00 • 13 • 06
29 off Marche to a couper		• 00 • 08 • –
To Alexander Moffat for 2 skaips for sawing corn	12s.	
To John Rob for bringing out half a barel off hering	06s.	• 00 • 18 • –
21 Marche given William Thomson 7 lib. to give Robert Dowglas for a firekin off soap he broght fra Leith the said day.................and 4s. to – himselff to drink.................is		• 07 • 04 • –
26 Marche to Robert Montgomrie cordoner in Trenent for mending shoone & boots & making a pair off shoone 40s. – to him for 1 pair off – shoone for a woman – 22s. is		• 03 • 02 • –
For fresh beiff in Marche	04–07–00	
For whyt breid in Marche	01–09–00	• 05 • 16 • –
The end off Marche 1664: The disbursments in Marche 1664		• 195 • 00 • –
		• 00 • 13 • 06

[21]

Disbursments in Aprill 1664 –

Aprill: 1 Aprill to Walter Hamilton for a warrant he obteined to eat flesh		
1664 in Lent		• 01 • 10 • –
The said day to him for halff a barel of Glasgow herrings		• 07 • 10 • –
5 Aprills to John Ramsay for 20 mure foull fowls – 6 lib.		• 06 • 00 • –
To John Rob for trouts	00–06–00	

	For 2 pecks of flour boght at Dudingstoun	01–08–00	
	To ane Inglish man for 5 glasses	01–01–00	
	To John Tinto for caps	00–16–00	• 03 • 11 • –
	18 Aprill to Thomas Baderstown 50s. to buy 2 bouting cloths		• 02 • 10 • –
	20 Aprill to George Nicol tailyeur in the Water off Leith in full of his compt		• 09 • 08 • –
	1 pynt and halff a mutchkin of canel water at 3ll. the pynt	03–07–06	
	1 pynt & 1 mutchkin off comon waters at 3ll. the pynt	01–05–00	• 04 • 12 • 06
	22 Aprill to John Reid to give the maltman in Clerkingtoun to drink 13s. 4d. and 3s. 4d. to him to drink is		• 00 • 16 • 08
	For whyt breid in Aprill		• 01 • 18 • –
	For fresh beiff in Aprill		• 06 • 19 • –
	The end of Aprill 1664 ~~~~~: The disbursments in Aprill 1664		• 44 • 15 • 02

May	Disbursments in May 1664 ~~:		
1664	To John Lourie in Roslin for severall stanes & stave heads	03–08–00	
	To M: W: to pay for caps	00–12–00	• 04 • 00 • –
	2 May to James Steuart for 4 lame pots		• 00 • 12 • –
	To John Solomon for a hatt and a hare string		• 08 • 02 • –
	To John Broun for the blaid off a knyffe	00–06–00	
	For leaff tobaco	00–09–00	
	1 pound off raisings	00–06–00	• 01 • 01 • –
	4 May to Hary Forrest in full off ane accompt for cloth to be John Clerk cloths and for cloth to be courtins to the fixt bed in my		

chamber .... • 38 • 03 • –
5 May to Isobell Fermer for nails according to the accompt .... • 19 • 05 • –
5 May to John Cooke in full of ane accompt on his discharge .... • 10 • 08 • –
6 May to James Melvin on his discharge according to the accompt for wyne seck – salt tongues & dry fishe .... • 32 • 00 • –
6 May to Thomas Sandelands for a wainscot cabinet with a fitt for Elizabeth Clerk – the yrne work wes my own .... • 20 • 00 • –
To Thomas Wedel for several things............16s. .... • 00 • 16 • –
6 May to Eustin Nisbit for 9 once 8 drope off silk freing for the courtins off the litle fixt bed in my own chamber at 26s. the once .... • 12 • 07 • –
The 3 off May 1664 peyit to Hew Macculloch collector 98–19–10 on his discharge off the said date for a month and a halffs cesse for making up what the excyse fell short off – being – 42–08–6d and for 2 moneths [sic] cesse for compleiting the commissioners money to my Lord President Gilmer & Lord Colingtoun for serveing the last 3 sessions of parliament as commissioners for the shyre being 56–11–04 is both togither 98–19–10.. • 98 • 19 • 10
9 May – to a chaipman for severall small wairs .... • 05 • 01 • –
+ 10 May 1664 to Elspeth Heren byre woman for hir fie fra Mertimes 1663 till Witsonday 1664 in money – 8ll. 1 pair of shoone 24s. is......... • 09 • 04 • –
On Fryday the 13 off May 1664 – drink money given at Barnbougell;
1 to the Steuart 05–16–00
2. to the wright .... 01–09–00.....we wes thair 2 nights
3. to the measson.. 00–12–00.........

4. to James Smith fitman .... 00–12–00.........	• 08 • 09 • –
1 ston of hair for plaister	• 00 • 08 • –
1 firlot off salt –12s. a bonnet for Sande 5s. is – 17s.	• 05 • 17 • –
18 May 1664 to Thomas Sandelands for 2 hurle barrows at 3ll. the peice the yrne work wes my own	• 06 • 12 • –
19 May to Thomas Mackie tailyeur in full of his accompt on his discharge date the 19 off May 1664	• 18 • 05 • –
19 May to Mr William Clerks nourish in drink money	• 02 • 18 • –
19 May to Lilias Reid for a haill peice of stitcht satyne rubens conteining 35 ell Scots......................4 rex dolors	• 11 • 12 • –
21 May to James Wilsone servitor to William Jack saidler for 2 neu sled saidls he broght me the said day at 4 merks the peice to the boy in drink money 2s. is in all	• 05 • 08 • 08
23 May given my brother 6 lib. to buy 20 ell of ribens for John Clerks cloths	• 06 • 00 • –
23 off May to William Steill for 23 laid of cols at 5s. the laid.............	• 05 • 15 • –
7 May – to the malt man in Clerkingtoun for working a making of malt	• 06 • 13 • 04
To a cordoner 10s. to David Clerk to go to the kill – 3s. 4d. to William Thomson when he went for Lizes cabinet – 2s. is	• 00 • 15 • 04
Whyte breid in May	• 01 • 06 • –
Fresh beiff in May	• 06 • 02 • –
To James Blaik –15s. 2 hair tethers 10s. 3 lb butter for saiv – 12s.	• 01 • 17 • –
The end off May 1664 — disbursments in May 1664	• 347 • 17 • 02

Juny 1664

Disbursments in Juny 1664:

7 Juny 1664 to Margaret Law for hir fie fra Mertimes 1663 till Witsonday 1664 in money – 6 –12s. – 1 pair off shoone – 24s. is in all .... • 07 • 16 • –

On Teusday the last of May 1664 I went to the lead hill – out of which – I past throgh Crauford moore to Moffat and cam to Moffat on Wedensday the 1 off Juny at – 11 hours – I stayd 2 ½ days at Moffat Wel[l] during which tyme I drank 9 pynts & 1 chopin off water – I returnt on Saturday the 4 of Juny – & cam to Neubiging that night – John Ramsay wes with me and 2 horse – dureing which tyme it cost me.............................. 15–00–00

For some small things boght at Moffat.. 01–04–00 • 16 • 04 • –

Given my wyffe when I went to Moffat Well – 4ll. 10s. .... • 04 • 10 • –

To Robert Selkrig – 12ll. on his discharge date 24 Juny 1664 for my chamber maill fra Mertimes 1663 till Witsonday 1664........................ • 12 • 00 • –

24 Juny to John Tod for the head of a hammer for countrie wark ...... • 00 • 18 • –

On Thursday 23 Juny 1664 at William Mitchels booth dore befor Walter Hamiltoun peyit to Hew Wernard 12 lib. for 24 old single treis at 10s. the peice which Thomas Sandelands boght fra him for my accompt.... • 12 • 00 • –

Said day to William Patersone for binding 3 French books I got fra Wrights Housses.. • 00 • 18 • –

22 Juny to Nans Turnbull for hir fie fra Mertimes 1663 till – Witsonday 1664.. • 12 • 00 • –

For fresh beiff......................... 11s.

For unguentum allum.............. 04s. .... • 00 • 18 • –

1 mutchkin off oyll.. • 00 • 07 • 06
15 Juny – to John Reid in full of all accompts betuixt me my wyffe
and him.. • 00 • 19 • –
18 Juny to Neuhals meassons.. • 01 • 16 • 08
Last Juny at John Marks brydel .... • 02 • 15 • –
For whyt breid in the month off Juny.. • 00 • 18 • –
The end off Juny – 1664 The disbursments in Juny 1664 • 73 • 17 • 02

Jully 1664

Disbursments in Jully..................1664

2 Jully to George Lin chapman in Intherask for lining cloth grein
worsit and prins.. • 12 • 12 • 06
The 6 off Jully 1664 compleited Robert Adamsone a yeir and a halffs
fie to wit fra Mertimes – 1662 till Witsonday 1664 .... ~~~~ ~~~ ~~~
+ 1. In money – 30ll. is 10ll. ilk halff yeir....is 30–00–00
2. 3 pair of single sold shoone –1 pair ilk half yeir at 15s. a pair is........... 02–05–00
3. 4 ½ ell of gray is 6 quarters ilk halff yeir at 2 merks the ell is .... 06–00–00 • 38 • 05 • –
13 Jully to John Ramsay for 25 mure fowls at 6s. the peice .... • 07 • 10 • –
20 Jully to the Lady Bagillo for a silver salt fat at: weying 14 once
2 drop at 3 lib. the once – I peyit not for the 2 drop........................... • 42 • 00 • –
To Thomas Ramsay for 3 skulls 00–08–00
For herings.. 00–13–00
For beiff.. 00–12–00............ • 01 • 13 • –
26 Jully given my wyffe to doe sum bussynes.................................. • 05 • 18 • –
29 Jully to Thomas Pringle on his discharge off the said date for yrne • 26 • 11 • –

	Said day to John Cooke for a rate for the gairden dore........................	• 01 • 16 • –
	2 once off the oyll off skorpion 00–12–00	
	1 pound off raisings — 6s. 00–06–00	
	To Robert Selkrigs woman in drink money........... 00–12–00............	• 02 • 10 • –
	For breid in the month off Jully	• 01 • 10 • –
	The end off Jully 1664: The disbursments in Jully 1664	• 140 • 05 • 06

Agust	Disbursments in Agust 1664 ~~~~:	
1664:	To Androw Casse sklaitter for sklaiting the litle howse above the 2 ovens on his discharge date the 30 off Jully 1664	• 05 • 16 • –
	To John Broun for making a blaid to ane knyffe & dressing ane old knyffe	• 00 • 09 • –
	7 ¼ ell off Aberdeins stuff for Marie Clerks rydeing cloths at 23s. 6d. the ell..	• 08 • 10 • 06
	To Abraham Clerk .... 20s.	
	6 pigs to big in the garden wall for bourds .... 06s.	• 01 • 06 • –
	6 Agust to Jo: Cooke for a hand & sneck & furnittur for the gairden dore	• 01 • 13 • –
	10 Agust to Alexander Simson for 2 suger loafs weying 5 lb 4 once at 15s. the lb	• 03 • 19 • –
	1 pound and a halff off fyne seallers twyne at 10s. the pound.............	• 00 • 15 • –
	To Ard More for a plank off reid wax of reid wood of a suger box	• 00 • 12 • –
	1 brush a short handlt on[e] to wash the wals.................................	• 00 • 06 • –
	To William Patersone for – in the 2 Acts of Parlament when Midltoun –	

wes commissioner – and the Acts off Parlament when the earle off
Rothes wes commissioner – bound in calff leather .... • 04 • 11 • –
The disbursments above in Agust 1664.......... • 27 • 16 • 06

[23]

Agust 1664

The disbursments on the other syde in Agust 1664 is		• 27 • 16 • 06
1 litle laiglen hande for the meassons	00–06–08	
2 ston off hair to mix amongst plaister	00–14–08	
To the Lady Johnstoun for cairding	00–18–00	
To Helen Patersone for 2 milk laiglens	00–14–00	• 02 • 12 • 08
1 pynt and 1 mutchkin of canel water at 3 lib. the pynt	03–15–00	
1 pynt and 3 quarters off a mutchkin off comon waters at 20s. a pynt	01–03–09	• 04 • 18 • 09
20 Agust to William Park for a corn sled and 2 ston barows		• 01 • 19 • 04
To John Lourie in Roslin for a shaft for catch moudewarts	00–04–00	
To James Broun for giveing the gray meir & hiland [sic] broun horse a drink		• 00 • 15 • –
5 ½ bols of meill boght at Leith fra Barbara Dalgarno at 3ll. 10s. a boll		• 19 • 05 • –
To Margaret Hopekirk for 100 heren and 1 pynt off oyll		• 02 • 00 • –
For whyt breid in Agust		• 01 • 11 • –
The end off Agust 1664 – The disbursments for Agust 1664		• 60 • 18 • 03

September 1664 The disbursments in the month off September 1664..........................

The 5 off September 1664 to Mr Robert Alisone minister at Glencorse – 48 for his stipend for the lands off Cookeing – fra Witsonday 1663 till Witsonday 1664 on his discharge date the 21 off Juny 1664 .... • 48 • 00 • –

The said day to John Melvin – 28 lib. for 21 pynts off seck at 2 merks: the pynt is – 44: I say is 42 merks on his discharge date the 5 September 1664 .... • 28 • 00 • –

The 6 off September 1664 to William Seaton tailyeur – 14 lib. in full off ane accompt on his discharge date the 6 off September 1664......... • 14 • 00 • –

The 6 off September to Alexander Leslie in full off ane accompt on his discharge.. • 09 • 13 • –

The 7 off September 1664 to Thomas Sandelands in full off ane – accompt for timber on his discharge date the 7 off September 1664..... • 148 • 06 • 04

8 once off preserved oranger skins 00–18–00
4 once off confectit ginger 00–10–00
16 drop off saffran 02–08–00
12 douzane off courtin rings tind 00–09–00
5 lb off tobaco at 12s. the lb........................ 03–00–00 • 07 • 05 • –
1 pair off comon gloves for my selff........................ • 00 • 08 • –

To John Robisone for –
1 ½ once off measses at 12s. the once 00–18–00
2 pound of currents 00–18–00
2 pound of Diep pruns........................ 00–06–00

12 once off corsdesitron at 34s. the pound........ 01–05–06
4 pound off great raisings at 7s. 6d. the pound........ 01–10–00 • 04 • 17 • 06
10 September to James Lishman cordoner for 3 pair off shoone .... • 02 • 18 • –
12 September to the laird of Livingstouns gairner .... • 00 • 12 • –
14: to Wille Thomsone to get 5 bols off my good mothers meill at Leith –
at 3 lib. 10s. the boll........ • 17 • 10 • –
2 sives for hon[e]y 00–12–00
Beiff 00–19–00
1 pynt clairet wyne........ 00–16–00........ • 02 • 07 • –
For herens & some other things in harvest –00–00 .... • 03 • 02 • –
19 September – to Hawthordens nourish........ • 01 • 10 • –
For breid in September whyt breid........ • 01 • 10 • –
The end off September 1664; The disbursments in September 1664.. • 289 • 18 • 10

October; The disbursments in October 1664:

1664 6 October to David Pringle in full off ane accompt........ • 04 • 07 • –
5 October to James Lishman cordoner in the Canegate in full
of a compt........ • 06 • 06 • 08
5 October Edowart Cleghorne gold smith for making 8 silver ~~~ ~~~~ ~~~~
spoons weying 16 once and a halff: 6s. for ilk once making is – 4 lib. ~~~~ ~~~~
19s. the silver is my own I say the silver wes my own .... • 04 • 19 • –
8 October – to John Ramsay for – 22 fowls at 6s. the peice........ • 06 • 00 • –
14 dicto – to James Pennycooke to get a boll of great salt........ • 05 • 00 • –
3 pecks off small salt .... • 00 • 10 • 08

3 pynts and 1 chopin off whyt & clairet wyne at 16s. the pynt		• 02 • 16 • –
15 October – 5 mutchkins of canel water at 3 lib. the pynt		• 03 • 15 • –
At 2 severall tyms sent to Barbara Dalgarno – 48s. – to by flour – suger and butter for baiking – 2 pecks of flour in short breid		• 02 • 08 • –
19 October to a couper – 24s.	01–04–00	
The said day for fresh butter	01–00–00	
For fresh beiff – 18s.	00–18–00	
To Isobel Scot for a leyg of mouton	00–12–00	
To Robert Paterson for halff a day in making a trives: For the horse 6s. 8d. with his dinner	00–06–08	• 04 • 00 • 08
The disbursments above in October		• 40 • 03 • –

[24]

The disbursments off October on the other syde is	• 40 • 03 • –
The 31 off October 1664 to John Reid – 21 lib. for his beir & stroe as it stood in the yaird – William Thomson & John Reid said thair wold be 4 bols of it..	~~~~ ~~~~ • 21 • 00 • –
26 off October 1664 – to Bessie Crauford 8 rex dolors – shoe wes 14 days at Neubiging this tyme..	• 23 • 04 • –
27 October – to William Thomson to pay for a barel off tar	• 11 • 06 • 08
29 October to William Steill for 47 laid off cols – whairoff he rebated 4 laid – so peyit him 43 laid at 5s. the laid..	• 10 • 15 • –
29 October – to Mage Wade for beir wes gotten fra hir	• 06 • –: • –

The said day to get fresh beiff in Edinburgh .... • 02 • 01 • 06
31 October – 1 quart off clairet wyne got at the Housse off Mure .... • 01 • 12 • –
31 October – to John Broun – schoolmaster 24s. – & to John Broun
bedel when Robert Clerk wes baptized – 6s. is .... • 01 • 10 • –
For whyt breid in the month off October .... • 02 • 14 • –
The end off October – 1664 The disbursments in October – 1664 • 120 • 06 • 02

November 1664

The disbursments in the month off November – 1664:
1 November to Wille Thomson – 5s. to pay the custom off 2 oxen went
to hallou faire[21] .... • 00 • 05 • –
5 November to James Thomsone glaisier in full off ane accompt on –
this discharge date the – 5 off November 1664 .... • 13 • 01 • –
4 November – to John Gray smith in North Leith in full of ane accompt
19 lib. 10s. on his discharge date the 4 off November 1664 .... • 19 • 10 • –
The 2 off November – to Thomas Sandelands 40 lib. 19s. in full off ane
accompt –& all uther accompts presiding the said day – on his discharge
date the 2 off November 1664 .... • 40 • 19 • –
2 hony sives 00–18–00
To Abrahame Clerk 00–03–04
To Robert Spens spurier 04–07–00
1 lb off cut & dry tobaco 00–18–00
Halff a pound off leaff tobaco 00–06–00
11 boosome shafts 00–11–00
To Adam Patersone for horse hyre 01–10–00

I say for horse charges	00	• 08 • 13 • 04
To John Reid gairner for – 8 thraive of oat stroe		• 02 • 04 • –
To Archebald Andersone the 19 off November for halff a yeirs fie – fra Witsonday 1664 till Mertimes 1664	10–00–00	
For a pair off single sold shoone	00–15–00	• 10 • 15 • –
17 November to Robert Adamsone for halff a yeirs fie fra – Witsonday 1664 till Mertimes 1664	10–00–00	
For 6 quarters off gray at 24s. the ell	01–16–00	
For 1 pair off single sold shoone	00–15–00	• 12 • 11 • –
18 November – to Isobel Brunton for halff a yeirs fie fra Witsonday – 1664 till Mertimes 1664 – 8 lib. for a pair off shoone 24s. is in all		• 09 • 04 • –
15 November to Elspeth Heren – halff a yeirs fie fra Witsonday – 1664 till Mertimes 1664 – 8 lib. 1 pair off shoone – 24s. is in all		• 09 • 04 • –
21 November to Nans Turnbull halff a yeirs fie fra Witsonday 1664 till – Mertimes – 1664 – 12 lib. 1 pair off shoone – 24s. is in all		• 13 • 04 • –
November all above		• 139 • 10 • 04
2 November to drink at the drying & milling 19 bols off oats	00–10–00	
15 November to Androu Hepburne webster for 4 lb of Clidsdaill knok lint	02–02–00	
19 November to get a peck off short breid	01–04–00	• 03 • 16 • –

[21] In Scotland, the Hallowmas fair was held typically on 1 November and lasted for one week. On occasion, it could be held on the second Monday of November.

11 November to Isobel Scot for 3 stone off Scots lint at 5 lib. 10s. the ston	16–10–00	
To hir the said day for a barel off small ale	01–00–00	• 17 • 10 • –
24 off November 1664 to Robert Selkrig 12 lib. on his discharge – date 24 November 1664 for a terms maill of my chamber fra Witsonday 1664 till Mertimes 1664		• 12 • 00 • –
24 November 1664 to James Lishman cordoner in full of ane accompt		• 11 • 10 •
To William Patersone for binding *La Maison Rustique*	00–18–00	
To David Pringle for Alexander Clerk 1½ once off oyll off almonds	00–00–00	
With the glass – 13s. – 2 onces off sirop off pale roses with the glas – 13s.	01–06–00	
1 glasse pynt bottel	00–14–00	
1 brush with a long handle	00–16–00	
4 douzane of corks for bottels	00–12–00	• 04 • 06 • –
1– combe for James Clark	00–05–00	
24 November given John Clerk – 24s. to give Alexander Simsons wemen	01–04–00	
1 pynt and a halff a mutchkin off new whyt wine	01–02–06	
100 chestins –11s.	00–11–00	
To Adam Patersone – staibler	00–08–06	• 03 • 11 • –
192–03–04 The disbursments above in November 1664		• 192 • 03 • 4

[25]

	The disbursments off November on the other syde is	• 192 • 03 • 04
+	To Mr William Wallace shireff depute off Edinburgh – with consent off Patrik Scot off Langshaw – some tyme shireff off Edinburgh – 13 yeirs blanche dewtie off the Halls – being 1 pair off glovs yeirlie estimat to 3 lib. the pair – is – 39 lib. fra anno – 1652 till Mertimes 1664 is – 13 yeirs on thair discharge date the 24 off November 1664.......Patrik Scot is consenter in this discharge	• 39 • 00 • –
	The 19 off November to John Pennycooke maltman – for making – 2 makings off malt:– bot he spilt on[e] off the makings for which my wyffe wold give him – bot halff pryce so I gave him a dolor and – and [sic] a halff	• 04 • 07 • –
	19 November to William Thomsone 22s. to pay for a nights charges off men and horse that went for William Nimmo gairner his plenishing	• 01 • 02 • –
	17 November to Helen Baxter – 29s. and my wyffe gave hir a dolor – who cam out first to be nourish to Robert Clerk	• 04 • 07 • –
	For whyt breid in the month off November – 1664	• 01 • 09 • –
	The end off November 1664; the disbursments in November 1664 is ..	• 242 • 08 • 04
December 1664	The disbursments in December – 1664	
	1 December – 1664 at Alexander Haisties brydel	• 03 • 06 • –
	2 December to William Park in full off ane accompt for timber he – furnished to David Ramsay – James Pennycooke & Archbald Craig....	• 10 • 10 • –

13 December 1664 to William Mure candlemaker in Edinburgh in –
full off ane accompt on his discharge .... • 21 • 14 • –
23 December –1664 – to John Dalgarno in full off ane accompt on –
his discharge off all things preseiding the – said 23 December 1664 ..... • 81 • 01 • 04
+ The 23 off December 1664 to Mungo Hinsha painter for the –
pictur off a ship – done by Wroms painter.........3 dolors .... • 08 • 14 • –
The said day to him – 1 rex dollor – with 3 lib. I gave him –
formerlie is 5 lib. 18s. for painting ane yrne coffer – and –
for culloring in gray oyll cullor a curious cut peice in wood which I
had off John Dowglas .... • 05 • 18 • –
3 pair off stirip leathers 01–16–00
2 whips 01–12–00
2: cordoners knyves .... 00–04–00 • 03 • 12 • –
23 December – to James Lishman cordo[ne]r–
1– for mounting 1 pair off blak boots 02–04–00
2– 1 pair of sols for 1 pair of old gray boots 00–18–00
3– 1 pair off shoone for Alexander Clerk .... 00–16–00 • 03 • 18 • –
To a tinkler for mending a pan 00–04–06
1 litle rubber boght fra James Steuart .... 00–04–00 • 00 • 08 • 06
2 ell of a la mod taffatie to be a skairf for Marie Clark .... • 06 • 00 • –
For bairns gloves and some other small things .... • 02 • 18 • –
2 ell off flourd stuff .... • 02 • 18 • –
6 quarters off hare stuff .... • 02 • 18 • –
1 dolor my wyffe gave to my Lord Registers nourish .... • 02 • 18 • –

And 41s. shoe gave to hir mothers women in drink money	• 02 • 01 • –
To Neuhals woman who broght the burd on a blak fit for Sande	• 01 • 09 • –
For a dinner to Mr Hew Smith and Mr William Cuming	• 04 • 00 • –
1 lairge drinking coich – 36s. – 1 lesser drinking coich – 24s. is	• 03 • 00 • –
For small graith to the bairns at the Craims......................................	• 00 • 14 • –
For beiff for boyling – 12s.	• 00 • 12 • –
1. chopin off clairet wyne – 6s. 8d.	• 00 • 06 • 08
For breid in December – 1664	• 01 • 14 • –
1 pound off skaip Malaga raisins for Sande.......................................	• 00 • 05 • –
The end off December – 1664: disbursments in December 1664	• 170 • 15 • 06

[26]

The disbursments in the yeir off God 1664..

Januar	1664	• 185 • 18 • 06
Februar	....	• 134 • 01 • 08
Marche	....	• 195 • 13 • 06
Aprill	....	• 044 • 15 • 02
May	....	• 347 • 17 • 02
Juny	....	• 073 • 17 • 02

Jully	....	• 140 • 05 • 06
Agust	....	• 060 • 18 • 03
September	....	• 289 • 18 • 10
October	....	• 120 • 06 • 02
November	....	• 242 • 08 • 04
December	....	• 170 • 15 • 06

lib. s. d.

The haill disbursments in anno 1664 •2006 • 15 • 09

John: Clerk ✝

January 1665 Disbursments in January – 1665..

	lib. s.	
To John: Clerk 1 suams in hansel dolor – 36s.	01–16	
To James Clerk 1 dams – 18s. peice..	00–18	
To Marie Clerk 1 French gold croun 6 lib. – and halff a dolor 29s. is..7 lib. 9s.	07–09	
To Margaret Clerk – 1 dams mild 36s. peice..................................	01–16	
To Elizabeth Clerk – halff a dolor queen off swams verie weill coynd..	01–09	
In turnors amongst the rest off the bairns	00–06	
13–14–00	13–14:	• 13 • 14 • –
To John Rob......6s.	00–06	
To Mairion Rob .... 6s.	00–06	

To John Broun bedel 12s. 00–12
To my wyffe to give Thomas Andersone tailyeur.............................. 00–12
To my wyffe to give amongst the men servants 24s. 01–04
3 lib. 03–00 • 03 • 00 • –
To Adam Livingston my brothers man for his hansell....................... ~~ ~~ • 00 • 13 • 04
18 October 1664 peyit for a hatt for James Clerk when he –
went in to Edinburgh to the humanitie classe................................ ~~ ~~ • 02 • 08 • –
1 pynt and 1 mutchkin off strong waters at 30s. the pynt .... ~~ ~~ • 01 • 17 • 06
The 9 off January 1665 – to Androu Cassie sklaitter –: 36 lib.
12s. 8d. acording to his discharge of the said date .... • 36 • 12 • 08
To James Sandelands for 5 pictur frams he made to me off my
own timber .... • 03 • 10 • –
To John Broun cutler......00–04–00 00–04–00
To James Stewart for a litle brasse morter & pistol 01–16–00
2 quair off good peper .... 00–11–00 • 02 • 11 • –
Befor John Dalgarno on the high street in Edinburgh peyit to–
Robert Dowglas for 2 achtin dails off soap – 9 lib. – I told him
we wold send to Leith for them – when we had leasur –&
when the days grew longer .... • 09 • 00 • –
For fresh beiff at – 2 tymes... • 01 • 14 • –
For fish – 8s. – 1 peck off flour – 12s. – onions & hering – 6s. is.......... • 01 • 06 • –
For Abraham Clerk for hecks & pirns... • 00 • 18 • –
For whyt breid in the month of January .... • 01 • 06 • –
The end of January 1665: The disbursments in January – 1665 ..... • 78 • 11 • –

[27]

February 1665

The disbursments in February – 1665 ....

A booke in octava callit *The Night's Search*[22] cost .... • 01 • 12 • –

Halff a pound off dry confectit ginger .... • 01 • 04 • –

The 1 & 7 off Februar to Alexander Simson for 6 suger loafs weying
16 pound and a halff at 16s. the pound .... • 13 • 04 • –

2 Scots chamber pots cost 48s. the peice .... • 04 • 16 • –

3 February to James Grhame for 2 rim off peper at 4 lib. 7s.
the rim .... • 08 • 14 • –

To Alexander Glen for – 2 rim of cut peper at – 4 lib. 13s. the rim...... • 09 • 06 • –

For mounting 2 little coichs ~~ ~~~ ~~~

12 drope off silver off my own at 3 lib. the once 02–05–00

To Piter Nilsone – for the warkmanship .... 02–02–00 • 04 • 07 • –

The 1 off Februar 1665 – to William Herreis old customer at the ~~~ ~~~
West Port – 24s. – he alledgit I wes oweing him for the preseiding – ~~~ ~~~
yeir – bot thair wes no such thing I wold not be hard with a – ~~~ ~~~
baisse fellow – for so small a matter .... • 01 • 04 • –

The 1 off Februar 1665 to Lawrens [blank] new customer –
at the West Port for a yeirs small customs at the West Port fra: ~~~ ~~~
the begining off January 1665 till the end off December 1665 – 24s. ... • 01 • 04 • –

The 13 off Februar 1665 to William Steill – for 71 laid off cols as ~~~ ~~~
he said – bot we fand bot 61 laid on the nick stick so I payit him for
65 laid at 5s. the laid 16–00–00
8 laid of small lyme col at 2s. the laid .... 00–16–00 • 16 • 16 • –

To John Lishman for 37 lib. off heklt lint at 8s. the lib.		• 13 • 07 • –
For a cambridge cailyie and draweing for Margret Clerk		• 02 • 08 • –
To Adam Gibsone souter in Calder		• 02 • 07 • –
1. lyge off bacon	01–04–00	
To Margret Hopkir[k] when shoe went to the mill	00–12–00	
2 pound off soap		00–12–00
4 pound off butter	01–00–00	• 03 • 08 • –
		• 83 • 17 • –
1 once of manna	00–08–00	
26 Februar – to Thomas Baderstouns wyffe in Dudingstoun – which wes oweing hir be James Clerk as shoe said for mending his shoone – & turnors given him to give to the brod	00–12–00	
27 Februar – to Richard Young for 1 pair off cottin gloves for my wyffe	01–10–00	
To James Drysdaill for making a perewick – the hair my own	05–16–00	
To William Patersone for binding *Delrius* in quarto	00–16–00	• 09 • 02 • –
The 28 off February 1665 to Richard Young merchant on his recept theroff 55 lib. for 11 ell off flourd stuff to be Mary Clerk a – goun at – 5 lib. the ell	55–00–00	
4 Marche 1665 to Androu Bruce merchant for – 5 ell and halff – a quarter off flourd stuff to be hir a peticot at 10 lib. the ell	51–05–00	

22 H. Mill, *A Nights Search. Discovering the nature and condition of all sorts of night-walkers; with their associates. As also, the life and death of many of them. Together with divers fearfull and strange accidents, occasioned by such ill livers.* 8 vols. (London, 1640).

The 4 off Marche 1665 to [blank] Mackie tailyeour – in full off his
accompt for making hir goun & peticot.. 11–06–00 • 117 • 11 • –
6 ½ lib of lint at 9s. 6d. the pound 02–19–06
12 ell off whyt worsit.. 00–04–00
To Adam Gibsone cordoner .... 00–13–00 • 03 • 16 • 06
For whyt breid in Februar –1665 .... • 01 • 06 • –

The end of Februar 1665 — The disbursments in – Februar – 1665............. • 215 • 12 • 06

[28]

Marche 1665 Disbursments in Marche – 1665~~~~:
The 1 off Marche 1665 to James Adamsone plumber in full off ane accompt
on his discharge...............11 lib. 10s. .... • 11 • 10 • –
2 Marche 1665 to Archbald More chyre maker in Leith wynd – 15 lib. –
4s. in full off ane accompt on his discharge .... • 15 • 04 • –
12 ell of blitcht lining at – 13s. 4d. the ell.. • 08 • 00 • –
1 pound off leaff tobaco 00–16–00
3 pair gloves – 13s. – 3 pair gloves – 32s. all litle on[e]s is .... 02–05–00 • 03 • 01 • –
1 whaill bon buist 00–05–00
18 ell off satyne ribens for Neuhalls bairns at 4s. 6d. the ell .... 04–01–00 • 04 • 06 • –
For fresh beiff.. 01–10–00
1 skallop steill neidle for Jean Blair 00–04–00

1 pound off raisings .... 00–08–00 • 02 • 02 • –

4 Marche 1665 – given my wyffe 05–18s.–8d. to give to Mary Cooks –
good man webster at the West Port – for weiving several sorts
off cloth .... • 05 • 18 • 08

1 pair off Maroquin shoone for my wyffe –& 1 pair for Mary Clerk of
Maroquin both – 3 lib. 10s. .... • 03 • 10 • –

... The 8 off Marche 1665 as it is mentioned at lynth on a long compt
booke with – 3 clasps on the – 44 page theroff – sent to the Lady – +
Bagillo – 22 lib. – for 16 pynts and a chopin off aqua vite –
at – 26s. 8d. the pynt .... • 22 • 00 • –

The 9 off Marche 1665 to John Hastie litster for liting [...] –
3 ston off yarn for hingings at – 6s. 6d. the pound...........is .... • 16 • 00 • –

9 Marche to my wyffe – 3 lib. ....when I went to Edinburgh.. • 03 • 00 • –

Said day to Wille Thomson to get beiff 01–04–00

More to him to get ane almed skin .... 00–06–00 • 01 • 10 • –

For 6 douzane off larks –1–3s. for oysters – 5s. is .... • 01 • 08 • –

7 Marche 1665 to Archbald Craig in the Towr for 2 bols
off oats wes goten in the end off October 1664 to mak meill off .... • 05 • 16 • –

• 103 • 05 • 08

... The 20 off Marche 1665 to David Fleming for 3 months –
service fra the 16 off November 1664 till the 16 off Februar
1665 – 6 lib. 7s. – which wes and cam too the first halff off
everie thing I promist him for the haill halff yeir................................ • 06 • 07 • –

16 off Marche 1665 – to our gairner William Nimmo:
... 1 : to give the laird off Livingstouns gairner 01–10–00

2: given William Nimmo 10s. to drink with him .... 00–10–00 • 02 • 00 • –
20 Marche 1665 delivert to William Nimmo our gairner –
... 1...to give Sir John Smiths gairner 00–18–00
2...to give Mr John Inglis gairner of Cramond 00–18–00
3...to drink with them both – 12s. 30d. for the horse .... 00–14–06 • 02 • 10 • 06
+ 28 Marche 1665 to my wyffe to give hir brother Mr Alexander Gray
for a sute off old cloths off his which Thomas Andersone got which he
took for 9 lib. in part off peyment of his first halff yeirs fie I peyit him –
9 lib. .... • 09 • 00 • –
1. The 27 off Marche 165: 1665 – peyit to Bessie Bruntoun – hir fie
& bountith – fra Witsonday 1664 till Mertimes 1664 which cam to ..... • 08 • 04 • –
2: The said day – compleited Thomas Andersone his fie fra Witsonday
1664 till Mertimes 1664 which cam in all acording to condition – to ... • 19 • 10 • –
3: The 22 off Marche 1665– compleited John Hodg – 9 lib. in full off all
former fies we wes oweing him till Witsonday 1664 .... • 09 • 00 • –
4: The 6 off December 1664 – 18–10–8d. – for his fie to David Clerk fra
Mertimes 1663 till Witsonday 1664 .... • 18 • 10 • 08
5: The 27 off Marche 1665 – to David Clerk for his fie fra Witsonday
1664 till Mertimes 1664 .... • 18 • 13 • 04
The 28 off Marche 1665 to Thomas Pringle for a ston and
a halff of couter yrne to be a couter at – 44s. the ston .... • 03 • 06 • –
To get fresh beiff .... • 03 • 00 • –
To John Rob for flour .... • 00 • 10 • –
23 Marche – to Androu Hepburn – 12s. when he went for Gavan

Gray – 25 Marche to Gavan Gray when he cam to Neubiging 12s. is .... • 01 • 04 • –
Given at severall tyms to get eygs .... • 00 • 09 • –
For whyt breid in the month off Marche .... • 02 • 02 • –

The end of Marche 1665 — The disbursments in Marche 1665 .... • 207 • 12 • 02

[29]

Aprill 1665

The disbursments in Aprill – 1665 ~~~:

To Alexander Simson on his discharge in full of ane accompt........ • 02 • 07 • –
2 ½ ell off canel cullort cloth at 36s. the ell........ • 04 • 10 • –
For orange wirsit freinzies for the canel cullort cloth bed .... • 03 • 00 • –
1 ell off stenting .... • 00 • 09 • –
1 ½ ell off grein sey at 16s. the ell .... • 01 • 04 • –
Breed 00–04–00
3 lapsters 00–10–00
Oysters 00–04–00
Beeff – 36s. .... 01–16–00........ • 02 • 14 • –
The 4 off Aprill 1665 to Alexander Simsons wyffe – 60 lib. for John and James Clerks boord 3 months fra the 18 off Aprill till the 18 off Jully 1665 .... • 60 • 00 • –
The 5 off April 1665 to John Steuart in the loch 1 rex dolor .... • 02 • 18 • –
To James Steuart for 6 pigs........ • 00 • 17 • –

To William Paterson for binding a booke in quarto in leather .... • 00 • 13 • 04
The 7 off Aprill – to John Armestrange in full off ane accompt for
seeds to the yard..........03–10–08 .... • 03 • 10 • 08
2 lb off leaffe tobaco at 16s. the pound .... • 01 • 12 • –
1 bolt off narow reed knitings .... • 00 • 07 • –
+ On Thursday the 6 off Aprill 1665 to James Thomson – servitor to James
Stewart – 3 lib. for 2 pynts off lintseid oyll at – 30s. the pynt the
which oyll I am to send for when I pleas.. • 03 • 00 • –
7 Aprill 1665 to James Sandelands for making 3 draweing shotls for
my fir presse that stands in my chamber in Edinburgh .... • 01 • 10 • –
AAA.. 30 October 1664[23] to John Dicksone – 6 lib. and 1 merk to by his shoone –
for his fie fra Witsonday 1664 till Mertimes 1664: this sould have been
placed in October 1664 bot wes omitted .... • 06 • 13 • 04
17 Aprill to William Nimmo – to give Livingstouns gairner when he
went for herbs & plants – 12s. to himselff to drink – 6s. 8d. is............ • 00 • 18 • 08
17 Aprill to William Thomson – 10 lib. to give Robert Dowglas for a
barel off herings he went to Leith for the said day .... • 10 • 00 • –
1 boll and a peck off whyt salt .... • 03 • 01 • 04
For fresh beiff – 2 tymes .... • 02 • 19 • –
Given Lize at 2 severall tymes to pay eygs 00–11–00
Given 15s. to pay 9 pynts ale when they went to the mill & kill with
Wrights Housses oats 00–15–00
To John Rob for trouts 00–04–00
To Androu Hepburne webster 00–06–08

To a couper & sive wright .... 00–15–00...........
4 lb off fresh butter at 4s. 8d. the lb........................ 00–18–08........... • 03 • 10 • 04

• 115 • 14 • 08

+ 22 Aprill 1665 peyit to David Dryburgh for ~~~
1– 2 bols of oats: wes got for our horse at 4 merk the boll 05–06–08
2– 6 bols of oats: wes goten for our gairner William Nimmo –
at – 3 lib. the boll.. 18–00–00 • 23 • 06 • 08
23 Aprill to my wyffe to pay for some things 02–02–00
To James Stewart for 4 pigs .... 00–16–00 • 02 • 18 • –
24 April 1665 to John Melvin on his discharge for 21 pynts of seck ~~~~~~~~
cam out in – 2 litle barels – 27 lib. 3s. 4d. .... • 27 • 03 • 04
28 Aprill – to Thomas Mossman chaipman for –:
15 ½ ell of ribens at 3s. the ell.. 02–06–06
1 pair of leather poutches & some laces – 1 peper of pins:
4 thimbles 00–13–00
31 ell of divers cullors rubens at 4s. 8d. the ell .... 07–04–08 • 10 • 04 • 02
22 Aprill for fresh beiff .... • 01 • 00 • 04
30: 29 Aprill to Patrik Craig for 2 bols off meill at 3ll. 16s. the boll ..... • 07 • 12 • –
For whyt breid in the month off Aprill.. • 01 • 16 • –
189 – 15 – 02: The disbursments in Aprill 1665...... • 189 • 15 • 02

The end of Aprill – 1665

[23] In the original the year appears directly above '30 October'.

[30]

May The disbursments in May 1665 ~~~:

1665.. 4 May to George Gordon – for chargeing the e[arl] of Seafort with horning.......... • 01 • 09 • –
For a box of Doctor Andersons pils.......... • 03 • 06 • 08
To Conrad for – 21s. worth of gold & for cuting a gold seall.......... • 02 • 18 • –
5 May to John Clerk to pay James Gray – 1 pair of shoone.......... • 01 • 16 • –
4 May to Isobel Fermer in full of hir accompt for nails & hir discharge preseiding the – 4 off May 1665.......... • 60 • 17 • –
… 6 May to Alexander Leslie wreatter in full of ane accompt.......... • 05 • 06 • –
17 May 1665 to Hew Macculloch – on his discharge of the said date – 42 lib. 8s. 6d. as a month and a halffs cesse – off what the brewers fell short fra – the 1 off November 1664 till the 1 off November 1665.......... • 42 • 08 • 06
15 May 1665 to Robert Selkrig – 12 lib. for the maill of a chamber – fra Mertimes 1664 till Witsonday 1665 – I flitit and left the said chamber at Witsonday 1665.......... • 12 • 00 • –
18 May 1665 to Charles Maitland – on his discharge date the said 18 off May – 14–10s. for a remnant off 7 ½ quarters off sad gray cloth.......... • 14 • 10 • –
Munday 15 May to my wyffe.......... 02–08–00
To Jean Blair to by a hood – 58s. – 1 silver stamp 18s. .... 03–16–00 • 06 • 04 • –
Teusday 16 May for fliting & taking doun & puting up my bed.......... • 01 • 06 • –
15 May to Alexander Simson for some small things for liting my wyffe got.......... • 01 • 03 • 04
17 May to Isobell Davisone for a dornick table cloth – 4 ½ ell long –

	2 ell – 1 ½ quarter braid – 14 lib. 16s.	• 14 • 16 • –
	27 May to William Steill for – 30 laid – off cols..........6 lib. 9s.	• 06 • 09 • –
	29 May – to Walter Hamiltoun – 30s. for a warrant he obteind me fra my – Lord Bellenden treasurer deput – for eating flesh in Lent &c 1665.......	• 01 • 10 • –
	1 pynt & halff a mutchkin off waters at – 20s. the pynt......................	• 01 • 02 • 06
	27 May – for beiff..................13s. –	
	For fish ....06s. –	
	Eygs...................................05s. –	• 01 • 04 • –
	To a couper for girding looms.............................. 16s.	
	For a high kirn to kirn butter in .... 26s. 8d.	• 02 • 02 • 08
	For whyt breid in the month off May 1665	• 01 • 16 • –
	The end off May 1665 ~~: The disbursments in May 1665...........	• 182 • 04 • 08
Juny 1665	The disbursments in Juny 1665 ~~:	
	2 Juny to John Robisone for 20 fadome off tows at 18d the fadome.....	• 01 • 09 • –
	To: Alexander Simsone for – 4 quair of gray peper at 2s. 6d. the quair	• 00 • 10 • –
	15 Juny – 3 lib. of glew at 8s. the pound 01–04–00	
	1 sive for lyme.. 00–10–00	
	1 pig in James Stewarts.. 00–03–00	• 01 • 17 • –
	17 Juny to David Boyd for 1 laist skerff for my wyffe – 9 lib. and for – 1 peice off pink cullort taffatie 6d. riben whairoff Jo: Clark got the half of – the same for his drogit minim sute – 9 lib. is both	• 18 • 00 • –
	1 hatt for John Clerk 8s. sterlin	• 04 • 16 • –

To Mr Charles Lumsden – for gimp laces to the lasses peticots .... • 03 • 15 • 06

17 Juny 1665 – my wyffs wairing at Edinburgh:

1 pair of gray mixt hose boght for Thomas Andersone...................... • 01 • 17 • –
1 pair off wooll cairds 01– 10–00
8 lb off pruns.. 01– 00–00
For reid suger candie 01– 01–00
4 once off whyt suger candie... 00–08–00
1 pound off alme 00–06–00
1 gray bonet for – Sande –& 4 – knynves 01–04–00
1 bolt off reid knitings .... 00–08–00 • 05 • 17 • –
2 ell off reid & whyt dyst stuff: & 6 ½ ell of gimp lace....................... 03–08–00
For taffatie to a laist skerff... 01–12–00
Halff ane ell off taffatie & to drawe it off tiffinie .... 03–00–00 • 08 • 00 • –
To Anna Clerk for 1 sute off ribens: 1 taffatie hood & 1 cambridg band... • 12 • 12 • –
To the ladys wemen in drink money: D: G: S:[24] wemen .... • 01 • 14 • –

Munday 19 Juny 1665 to my wyffe to give Baivlaws nurse – • 30 • 00 • –
& women – in drink money – 1 ½ rex dolor .... • 04 • 07 • –
24 Juny to John Stinsone waker on his discharge off all things preseiding the 24 off Juny 1665 –& in full off his accompt................................. • 27 • 04 • –
27 Juny 2 ell off stenting 15–00–00
6 do[ze]n of mandel buttons for James Clerks drogit cloths.. 12–00–00
Corne to the horse be Tomas Andersone .... 02–00–00 • 01 • 07 • –

20–07–6	For beiff & mouton		• 01 • 12 • –
30–00–0	To my wyffe 35s.		• 01 • 15 • –
38–06–0	And 29s. my wyffe gave on[e] off Baivelaws wemen........		• 01 • 09 • –
88–13–6	And 12s. shoe gave to on[e] off Newhals wemen........		• 00 • 12 • –
	The disbursments in Juny above		• 88 • 13 • 06

[31]

	The disbursments in Juny on the other syde is........		• 88 • 13 • 06
	30 Juny to James Simson in Bruntstain for 2 bols off seid oats wes goten in oatseid tyme at 4 lib. the bol is		• 08 • 00 • –
	30 Juny at Isobel Borthwicks brydel in Roslin........		• 02 • 08 • –
	For whyt breid in the month off Juny........		• 01 • 16 • –
	The end off Juny 1665; The disbursments in June 1665........		• 100 • 17 • 06
Jully 1665	To John Hodg for his fie fra Witsonday 1664 till Witsonday 1665 1 Jully 1665 – in money	07–00–00	
	In money at 2 tymes to b[u]y 2 pair off shoone 28s. 8d.	01–08–08	• 08 • 08 • 08
	The 3 off Jully – to John Dicksone 6 lib. for his fie & 13s. 4d. for his shoone which is half a yeirs fie fra Mertimes 1664 till Witsonday 1665		• 06 • 13 • 04

24 Dame Geils Smith. Dame Geils, sometimes referred to as 'Egidia' or 'Geida' Smith, was the wife of Sir William Gray of Pittendrum and the mother of Clerk's first wife, Mary Gray.

4 Jully 1665 to William Stewart hynd to pay for a seyth....32s. .... • 01 • 12 • –
The 14 Jully 1665 to John Cooke locksmith in the Carey at 16 lib. 17s.
4d. on his discharge in full off all accompts preseiding the said day ..... • 16 • 17 • 04
The 15 off Jully 1665 to John Tod locksmith – 11 lib. 15s. in full off ane
accompt on his discharge off all accompts preseiding the said day .... • 11 • 15 • –
Mr Durhams *Treatise of Scandall*[25] in octava – bound in gray leather ..... • 01 • 08 • –
To Robert Mure for violl pins & some turnt knaps .... • 00 • 18 • –
The 14 Jully 1665 to Alexander Simson for 2 suger loaffs weying
9 lb 6 once at 17s. the pound .... • 07 • 19 • 04
For Mr James Durhams *Treatise off Scandal* in octava in gray leather • 01 • 08 • –
1 quart and 1 mutchkin of oyll at 17s. the pynt .... • 01 • 18 • 04
1 leyg off mouton.. 00–17–07
For hering.. 00–06–00
To a chapman – 8s. – to Androu Hepburn webster 6s. is.................... 00–14–00 • 01 • 17 • 06
To Elspeth Broun that nourisht Robert Clerk 8 months;
1– given her at 3 severall tymes 14–00–00
2– the 19 off Jully 1665 – given hir when shoe went away .... 23–04–00 • 37 • 04 • –
The 18 off Jully 1665 to John Pennycooke Neuhals sone when he went
to France.. ~~~ ~~~
1– a Spanish quadruple in gold.............................. 22 livres
2– 2 French crowns in gold at 5 livres 10s. a peice .... 11 livres........... • 33 • 00 • –
25 Jully to Isobell Pittilock for hir fie fra Mertimes 1664 till Witsonday
1665 – 6 lib. and 24s. for hir shoone is 7 lib. 4s. .... • 07 • 04 • –
5 Jully to William Steuart to by fir teathers – 3 off them .... • 00 • 09 • –

	24 July to a couper....18s.		• 00 • 18 • –
	29 Jully to Margaret Hopekirk for herings shoe peyit.........................	00–04–06	
	and 2s. 6d. shoe gave to a couper	00–02–06	• 00 • 07 • –
	For whyt breid in the month off Jully		• 01 • 12 • –
	The end off Jully 1665 The disbursments in Jully 1665		• 141 • 09 • 06

Agust	The disbursments in Agust 1665	
1665	The 1 off Agust 1665 to Mr Robert Alisone Minister at Glencorse 48 lib. on his discharge for his lands off Co: I say for his stipend off the lands off Cookeing fra Witsonday 1664 till Witsonday 1665	• 48 • 00 • –
	1 Agust to James Steuart for a rose water trie	• 01 • 00 • –
	4 Agust spent at William Simsons brydel	• 03 • 10 • –
	8 Agust to Bessie Bruntoun for hir fie fra Mertimes 1664 till Witsonday 1665 – 8 lib. comprehending hir schoone & all.................	• 08 • 00 • –
	10 Agust to James Lishman cordoner for 2 pair off shoone for 11 yeir old & 2 pair for 12 yeir old is 4 pair at 25s. the pair is	• 05 • 00 • –
	For 4 fadom off a small tow – 8s.	• 00 • 08 • –
	17 Agust to John Nicol for a peice off incarnit louping.....................	• 02 • 08 • –
	The said day to William Seaton tailleur[26] in full off his accompt and on his discharge off all uthers preseiding the 17 off Agust 1665 –11–12–8 for – making & furnishing a sute of minim drogit to Jo: Clerk	• 11 • 12 • 08

[25] J. Durham, *The dying man's testament to the Church of Scotland: or, A treatise concerning scandal* (c.1658).

[26] This is the only time in this account book where Clerk used this spelling of 'tailor'.

18 Agust to David Lindsay for 1 barkit cows hyde	06–00–00	
For currying the same........	00–12–00	
For halff a Scots hyde off sol leather	05–10–00	• 12 • 02 • –
18 Agust to Thomas Wedel for a steill band and tining some small things		• 04 • 02 • –
4 drinking caps – 16s. – 4 shooks – 9s. is		• 01 • 05 • –
19 Agust to David Gray cordoner for 1 pair of shoone for Jo: Clark ...		• 01 • 16 • –
19 Agust to Alexander Simsons wemen in drink money		• 01 • 10 • –
19 Agust to Alexander Simson merchant in full of ane accompt		• 05 • 15 • –
The disbursments above in Agust 1665.....		• 106 • 08 • 10

[32]

The disbursments on the other syde in Agust 1665 is	106–8–10	• 106 • 08 • 10
For fresh beiff severall tyms in this month		• 02 • 05 • –
The 4 off Agust 1665 – to Patrik Galloway at William Simsons brydel 24s. for a firlot off ry[e] William Thomson got fra him about 16 months ago		• 01 • 04 • –
The 31 of Agust spent at James Sandelands brydel........	04–04–00	
+ For fresh beiff and whyt breid &c: wes boght at Ed[inbu]r[gh] for his out going – 3:6.8 Forby mouton we kild off our own	03–08–00	• 07 • 12 • –
For whyt breid in the month off Agust........		• 01 • 10 • –
The 29 Jully 1665 given my wyffe when shoe went to Edinburg [sic] which shoe waired as follows: I say my brother John Andersone gave hir for my accom [sic] 43 lib. Scots		• 43 • 00 • –

Which shoe waired as follows ~		• 161 • 19 • 10
6 ells off braid dornick 20 lib.	20–00–00	
1 large yrne pot 5 lib.	05–00–00	
11 ell off blak and whyt tuftit Holland at 14s. the ell	07–14–00	
9 ell off harden to be James Clerk sarks at 8s. the ell	03–12–00	
2 ½ ell off whyt boustin to be Mary Clerk a waistcot at	03–15–00	
1 blak hatt for Alexander Clerk	00–18–00	
	40–19–00	
	02–01–00	
	43–00–00	

The end off Agust 1665:

The disbursments in Agust 1665........	• 161 • 19 • 10

September 1665

The disbursments in September 1665 ~~~~:

The 6 off Jully to: I say the 6 off September to Alexander Makie tailyeur for making & furnishing Margaret Clerks goun on his discharge		• 07 • 03 • –
The 6 off September to George Smelum merchant on his discharge for 8 ell off stuff for Margaret Clerks goun at 46s. the ell		• 18 • 08 • –
+ To Androu Casse sklaiter on his discharge date the 5 off September for sklaiting the housse off Neubiging being 3 rude at 20 merk the rude is 40 lib. and to his men for thair morning drink & 4 hours 5–11–8 and to his men in drink money – 5 lib. is in all........		• 50 • 11 • 08
is in all –: 50 lib. 11s. 8d.		
2 lame pigs	00–06–08	

3 drinking caps	00–15–00	
7 skoops & 2 caps	00–18–00	
For puting a round end to the silver spoone	00–10–00	
To William Gib for binding *Horace* in folio & 12s. off	00–00–00	
strong peper to it – binding – 16s. 6 sheit off peper 5s. is	01–01–00	
1 high painted sand box	00–09–00	
2 glasse pynt botles	01–00–00	
1 barel	00–06–06	
4 earthen pigs & a brush to wash wals	01–00–00	
4 stand of knaps for naipkins	00–04–06	
1 whyt lame pig	00–03–00	
	06–13–00	• 06 • 13 • –
The 8 off September to my mother in lawe Dame Geils Smith for a marbre table broken in 2 peices a large peice and a lesser peice – 3 dolors – 8 lib. 14s.		• 08 • 14 • –
The 8 off September 1665 left at Doctor Cunninghams housse 1 douzan off knives with yvorie handles in a fyne gilt caisse worth		• 13 • 06 • 08
+ The 5 off September 1665 fied Archibald Gib to be our gairner to him in earnest	00–12–00	
To Androu Jacksone gairner that wisht me to him	00–12–00	
Spent at that tyme Wrights Housses being present	00–17–06	• 02 • 01 • 06
On the 16 off September to William Mossman merchant all above for		• 106 • 17 • 10
1– 4 ell 3 quarters off lining at 24s. the ell	05–14–00	
2– 2 ell off lining at 22s. the ell	02–04–00	

3– 6 ell 3 ½ quarters off lining at 19s. the ell	06–15–04		
4– 36 ell off whyt worsit stringing at 8d. the ell	01–04–00	•	15 • 17 • 04
The 4 off September to William Thomson to buy hooks	01–04–00		
Half a hundredth herings	00–14–00		
2 pecks of small salt	00–07–06		
4 lb off small candle	00–17–04		
To David Dick for plumbs and peirs	01–04–00		
1 pynt off clairet wyne	00–16–00	•	05 • 02 • 10
For fresh beiff in September		•	03 • 04 • –
For whyt breid in September		•	01 • 16 • –
The end of September 1665 The disbursments in September 1665		•	132 • 18 • –

[33]

October 1665

The disbursments in October 1665 ~:

10 October to James Lawe cordoner for 2 pair off bairns shoone	•	02 • 01 • –
The said day to John Hastie litster in full off ane accompt	•	02 • 00 • –
11 October to James Aiton officer to the goldsmiths for bookeing 2 – silver spoons wes stoln fra us.....12s.	•	00 • 12 • –
11 October to [blank] Smith cordoner – 29s. for – 1 pair off shoone Margaret Clerk got fra him	•	01 • 09 • –
11 October to Neuhals nourish in drink money	•	02 • 18 • –

To William Gib for binding a booke in quarto	00–08–00	
For sharping 2 razoirs and 1 pair off sheirs	00–06–00	• 00 • 14 • –
12 October to John Cooke for a bordert lock and 2 keys for the batlement dore off the east jamb – 4 lib. –& for 2 auval rings to my – study dore – 8s. – both		• 04 • 08 • –
13 October to Robert Mure for 12 knaps blak for a cabinet – 4 pair off spektakle caisses – 1 violl stick off reid wood – 1 nut for a violstick..		• 02 • 03 • –
2 litle silver vazes at 3 lib. the once	07–17–06	
For the warkmanship off the same	02–08–00	• 10 • 05 • 06
14 October to Dame Geils Smith for 4 bols off meill at 3 lib. 4s. the boll		• 12 • 16 • –
14 October to John Melvin for 2 pynts off brande wyne		• 02 • 14 • –
4 once off leaffe tobaco		• 00 • 04 • –
The 13 off October to Thomas Sandelands on his discharge in full off ane accompt for 100 dails – 10: knapel and 3 wainscot		• 88 • 06 • –
all above		• 130 • 10 • 06
This 21 October 1665 – my wyffe told me that John Lourie at the mill wes resting – 6 geisse for anno 1663 and 6 geisse for anno 1664 for which 12 geisse the said day John Lourie wes content to quyt a laid off seid oats my wyffe got fra him in oatseid tyme being Marche 1665 estimat to		• 08 • 00 • –
24 October to Helen Patersone for 7 gallons 3 pynts off ale goten at 3 several tyms acording to 42s. 8d. the barel which is 4 gallons which 7 gallons 3 pynts cums to 3–18–8d. and 5s. 10d. the bairns wes resting is.......4–4s. 6d.		• 04 • 04 • 06

24 October to Isobell Scot for 1 lyge off young beiff – 40s. and 56s. for a blak coq and 3 heth hens at 14s. the peice is 2 lib. 16s. is togither		• 04 • 16 • –
1 peck off salt	00–04–00	
To Thomas Scot for casting divets to mend the schoole	00–10–00	
To William Steuart to pay custom of ane ox and a meir at Dalkeith fare	00–06–00	
4 lb off candle	00–17–04	
To Elizabeth Clerk to get whyt threid	00–06–08	
For oynions – 3s. 2 skuls – 4s.	00–07–00	
To Jo: Rob for his horse for going for To: Sandelands	00–08–00	• 02 • 19 • –
2 October 1 chopin off canal water off the best sort		• 02 • 10 • –
7 October sent with John Rob – to Walter Hamiltons wyffe – 17s. for – halff a peck off short breid baiken with sugar		• 00 • 17 • –
3 October to John Broun for making the chylds graffe		• 00 • 18 • –
4 October to Bessie Crauford midwyffe – 5 rex dolors – 14 lib. 10s. and a dolor Baivlaws Lady gave hir is in all – 17–8		• 14 • 10 • –
For fresh beiff in the month off October		• 03 • 16 • –
For whyt breid in the month off October		• 03 • 03 • 04
The end off October 1665 – The disbursments in October 1665		• 176 • 04 • 04

November 1665

The disbursments in November –1665 ......

The 4 off November to William Nimmo gairner for – 5 firlots off beir & 3 bols and a halff off oats is – 4 bols 3 firlots – which grew on his aiker ✝

off land – estimat be Archebald Craig and John Lourie to 18 lib. which –
18 lib. I peyit him the said day .... • 18 • 00 • –
4 November to Mark Herreis cordoner in Mussilburgh for –
14 days wark with his dyet daylie at 7s. in the day 04–18–00
1 litle tand calffs skin 00–13–04
3 pair off timber heils 00–03–00
4 once off roset 00–01–04
Given him a grot to drink .... 00–04–00 • 05 • 19 • 08
+ The 13 off November 1665 peyit to William Park in Outers Hill in –
full off ane accompt which is among the peyit accompts for timber –
the 22 off November 1665 to John Hodg for halff a yeirs fie
fra Witsonday 1665 till Mertimes 1665 .... • 10 • 02 • –
1– in money 04–10–00
2– 12s. for his shoone 00–12–00
3– I ewe lamb worth 30s. .... 01–10–00 • 06 • 12 • –

The disbursments above in November 1665 .... • 40 • 13 • 08

[34]

The disbursments in November on the other syde is .... • 40 • 13 • 08
+ The 22 off November 1665 to David Clark for a yeirs fie –
fra Witsonday 1665 till Mertimes 1665 ....
1– in money 26–13–04
2– for 6 ell off gray at 24s. the ell 07–04–00

3– for 2 pair off shoone – 3 lib.	03–00–00	• 36 • 17 • 04
Given David Clerk 12s. the said day to drink in Pennycooke		• 00 • 12 • –
The 27 November 1665 to Robert Dewer – smith in Pennycooke – 56–10s.–10: in full off ane accompt for divers things he furnisht me fra the 9 off May 1664 till the 17 off September 1665....................		• 56 • 10 • 10
+ The 30 off November 1665 to William Lamb for his fie fra Mertimes I say fra Witsonday 1665 till Mertimes 1665 –		
1– in money – 10 lib.	10–00–00	
2– given him 15s. to buy his shoone...	00–15–00	
3– given him to buy 6 quarters off gray at 24s. the ell	01–16–00	• 12 • 11 • –
1 boll off small salt...		• 02 • 18 • –
4 lb off small candle	00–17–00	
4 douzane off oynions..	00–04–06	
For eygs –& herings..	00–12–06	
For fresh beiff at 2 several tymes...	01–05–00	
To John Dicksone for going to the toun with a letter anent John – Hepburne 6s.: to Alexander Hastie for going with a letter to the earle off Haddingtoun anent John Hepburne 12s.	01–04–00	• 04 • 04 • –
For breid whyt breid in the month off November		• 02 • 00 • –
The 30 November 1665 to Edowart Adamsone – 20 lib. 12s. for a cow – wes kild which wes boght fra Robert Mackmillen be said Edouart Adamsone		• 20 • 12 • –
The end off November 1665: The disbursments in November 1665		• 176 • 18 • 10

December 1665

The disbursments in December 1665 ~~

7 December to Robert Deuer for his mans super meill in hervest........ • 01 • 00 • –

9 December to Jean Robisone for hir fie fra Witsonday 1665
till Mertimes 1665 6ll. pound .... • 06 • 00 • –

The 12 off December 1665 to John Pennycooke maltman for making
2 makings & a halff off malt 2 dolors and a halff........ • 04 • 07 • –

20 December 1665 at Edinburgh

19 ½ ell off harden for horse sheits at 7s. the ell........ • 06 • 16 • 06

20 December 1665 to Walter Hamiltoun for –
1– 4 stone 5 ½ pound off salt butter at 3 lib. the stone........ 13–00–10
2– 1 litle barel in which it wes packit 01–02–00
3– halff a barel off herings........ 05–13–04
4– for cairiage off both fra Glasgow –&c........ 03–04–00 • 23 • 00 • 02

To Robert Mure for making 1 pair off tortle shell spektakle caisses..... 00–04–00
1 pound off cut and dry tobaco 00–18–00
1 load off cols for my chamber 00–10–00
8 once off gals – 7s. – 8 once copres 1s.: 2 once pomgranat skins 4s.:
For to mak ink is – 12s.: for corks for bottels: 2s. is........ 00–14–00 • 02 • 06 • –

To Alexander Simpsone on his discharge date the 21 off December 1665
for my chamber maill a yeir to wit fra Witsonday 1665 that I entert thairtoo –
till Witsonday 1666.....24 lib. .... • 24 • 00 • –

21 December 1665 to Alexander Simpsone for 9 pound off tobaco at
12s. 6d. the pound 05–12–06

1 pound off blak spyce	01–02–00	• 06 • 14 • 06
23 December 1665 to James Crommie weiver in the Canegate for weiving 26 ell and a halff off strypit hingings – 10 quarter broad and almost a halff at 26s. the ell	33–16–00	
For the dying off 10 ½ once off carnation ingrain worsit for – which he tooke as much off ours which wes not ingrain	01–00–00	• 34 • 16 • –
23 December to John Gray smith in Nor Leith – in full off ane accompt for mending a litle yrne chimney– stands in the chimney – off my studie in the litle east jamb..........4 lib. 16s.		• 04 • 16 • –
+ 26 December 1665 to Edowart Cleghorne goldsmith – for 2 once 2 drop off silver to help to mak 4 silver spoons at 3 lib. the once	06–07–06	
For making 4 silver spoons at 12s. the peice	02–08–00	
Thair wes 6 once off silver my own which helpit to mak the said 4 spoons – the said 4 spoons weyed 8 once 2 drop		• 08 • 15 • 06
To James Lishman cordoner the 27 off December for 2 pair off leather – heild pantons for my selff	04–04–00	
4 pound off candle for my chamber	00–17–00	• 05 • 01 • –
27 December 1665 to John Cooke lock smith – in full off ane accompt and all other accompts whatsoever preseiding the 27 December 1665		• 05 • 04 • –
28 December to William Gib for binding – 10 books in 4°, 8°, & 12°		• 03 • 16 • –
The disbursments in December 1665		• 136 • 12 • 08

[blank][27]

John: Melvin

The disbursments in December 1665 on the other syde amounts to..... • 136 • 12 • 08
The 27 off December 1665 to John Melvin merchant – 68 merks for 34
pynts off seck at 2 merks the pynt is –45–6–8d. for which 45–6–8d.
he hath given me his ticket to deliver me the said 34 pynts off good
seck betuixt and the last day off Januar 1666 .... • 45 • 06 • 08
The 11 of Januar 1665 peyit him for 2 barels to hold the seck 2:[28]
48s.:...2–8s. ......
The barels did hold bot 33 pynts –& a chopin: so he rendert
me – a merk bak agane...
28 December 1665 to Barbara Dalgarno F: 43s. 10d. to pay William –
Michel baxter ane accompt – which is in full off all that ever we
wes resting him preseiding the said day... • 02 • 03 • 10
The 28 off December 1665 – to my brother John Andersone for 6 –
suger loaffs weying – 26 pound and a halff at 15s. the pound .... • 19 • 17 • 06
28 December 1665 to James Deans procutor & to his man David
Deans for the charges off a decreit he recovert against Mr William
Dalgarno minister at Machlin – executor confirmit to his umquill
brother John Dalgarno merchant in Edinburgh – for the recovering off
700 lib. Scots – which the said John Dalgarno wes resting me at his
deceas according to the accompt .... • 26 • 16 • –
29 December Fryday at night – to Walter Hamiltoun befor his wyffe 20s.
for – bembies breid – his wyffe causd baik & sent to Neubiging when

	Sr: Ja: Pr: & Ed: Dundas wes at our house off Neubiging..................		• 01 • 00 • –
	30 December 1665 to Alexander Simpsons wemen in drink money.....		• 01 • 04 • –
	23 December 1665 to Alexander Simsone for John –& James Clerks boord 3 month fra the 19 off Januar 1666 till the 19 off Aprill 1666		• 60 • 00 • –
+	19 December 1665 to Mr John Wishart regent for John Clerk his fourth yeir at the colledg 14 dolors..	40–12–00	
	21 December – 1665 to Mr William Cuming for James – Clerks first yeir at the colledge – 8 dolors	23–04–00	
	To the janitur off the colledg for James Clerk	01–10–00	
	To John Clerk to give the janitor on hansel Munday	01–10–00	• 66 • 16 • –
	21 December 1665 to Androu Arbuthnot to learne John Clerk to wreat – 6 lib.		• 06 • 00 • –
	1 chopin off ink – 7s. 6d. – 6 painters pincels – 6s.		• 00 • 13 • 06
	To: Adam Patersone for corne & stroe wes oweing at divers tymes.....		• 01 • 00 • –
+	18 December 1665 to James Adamsone customer at the West Port for small customs – in advance – for a yeir till the 1 off January 1667		• 01 • 09 • –
	18 December 1665 to Thomas Sandelands for 12 days his man John Andersone wroght at Neubiging in helping James Sandelands to mak the rooffe off the litle turnpyke at – 12s. ilk day.........................		• 07 • 04 • –

27 This page follows immediately after [34] in the original.

28 The '2:' in the original was likely an error that Clerk did not cross out. I have transcribed the entry as found.

18 December to David Boyd for – a remnant off cambridge off 3 –
quarters large which my wyffe boght fra his wyffe..................3 lib. .. • 03 • 00 • –
18 December to Dame Geils Smith for 6 firlots off malt we got fra
hir at 4 lib. the boll – 6 lib. – the said day I gave hir – 4 lib. which Helen
Patersone gave me to give hir – for a boll of malt shoe got fra hir .... • 06 • 00 • –
18 December 1665 to my wyffe when I went to Edinburgh the said day
1– to give to those went to the mill... 00–18–00
2– to pay Jean Robisons fie fra Witsonday 1665 till Mertimes 1665 06–02–00
3– to pay Wille Steuart a leyg off beiff .... 01–16–00 • 08 • 16 • –
1 December 1665 to my wyffe to give hir sister Helen for lining
cloth .... • 04 • 05 • –
In December for fresh beiff .... 02–07–00:[29]
For eygs – 4s. – fish 9s. – 4 lb small candle 17s. is .... • 01 • 10 • –
20 December 1665 my wyffe sent in with John Rob to give Mary Cooks
good man for weiving – 17 ell off stuff at 5s. the ell Lizes goun wes made
of it .... • 04 • 05 • –
My brother peyit to John Dow: the 9 off November 1665 – 5 ell 3
quarters off braid whyt fingering – to be the lasses petticots – at 22s.
the ell 6–6s.–6d. which I repeyit to my brother the 19 off December
1665 .... • 06 • 06 • 06
17 November 1665 he gave to my wyffe – 7 lib. which I repeyit him the
19 off December 1665 – thir 2 last articles is a part off a compt off 16–12s.–6d.
I peyit to my brother the 19 off December 1665: which compt I have
by me... • 07 • 00 • –

For breid in December 1665		• 02 • 09 • –
The end off December 1665	The disbursments in December 1665	• 419 • 14 • 08

[blank][30]

The disbursments in the yeir off god – 1665

January	1665	• 78 • 11 • –
Februar	....	• 215 • 12 • 06
Marche	....	• 207 • 12 • 02
Aprill	....	• 189 • 15 • 02
May	....	• 182 • 04 • 08
Juny	....	• 100 • 17 • 06
Jully	....	• 141 • 09 • 06
Agust	....	• 161 • 19 • 10
September	....	• 132 • 18 • –
October	....	• 176 • 04 • 04
November	....	• 176 • 18 • 10
December	....	• 419 • 14 • 08
The haill disbursments in anno	1665	•2183 • 18 • 02

John: Clerk

[29] Clerk did not add this entry to a tally in the margin.
[30] Immediately precedes [35] in the original.

January 1666

The disbursments in January 1666 as follows:

1: to John Clerk 1 – 40s. peice ....

2: to James Clerk...1 – 30s. peice with letters about it 03–10–00

3: to Marie Clerk...2 rex dolors 05–16–00

4: to Margaret Clerk...1 rex dolor 02–08–00

5: to Elizabeth Clerk...1 rex dolor –& 1 curious 15s. peice 03–13–00

6: to Agnes: Clerk–14s. 6d. 00–14–06

13–01–06 • 13 • 01 • 06

1: to James Haliburton 00–13–04

2: to Robert Adamsone 00–09–00

3: to William Lamb 00–09–00

4: to John Dicksone .... 00–09–00 • 02 • 00 • 04

5: to Marie Dowglas .... 00–06–00 • 00 • 00 • 06

2 January 1666 to William Steill in Neuhall for 48 laid off cols – at 5s. the laid .... • 12 • 00 • –

To Robert Thomsone in Cairingtoun for – 3 caps: 1 ridle – 10 ell off worsit – 1 litle horne spoone – for all .... • 01 • 02 • 06

To John Broun bedel in hansell .... 12s.

To John Rob in hansell .... 06s .... • 00 • 18 • –

To John Hodge the ministers man in hansell 00–09–00

To my brothers man Adam Livingstoun in hansell .... 01–04–00 • 01 • 13 • –

+ To [blank] in the water off Leith – 15 January 1666 for making 18 bols off malt 08–00–00

For thair drink 01–04–00
To the men to drink that boght it......................... 00–12–00............ • 09 • 16 • –
25 Januar to Robert Cleghorne candle maker in Dalkeith for 3 ston
off candle at 3 lib. 8s. the stone.. • 10 • 04 • –
23 January to George Bell for 4 kipper.. • 02 • 18 • –
1 peck off salt 00–04–00
5 turnt staff heads 00–12–00
For haiks & pirns 00–06–00
To Alexander Simsons wyffs webster 00–08–00
To ane Inglish man for mending cairds 00–12–00
To Wille Clark pour des oeuffs 00–07–00
To Arche Gib for ale 1 quart .... 00–03–04 • 02 • 12 • 04
6 ½ ell off secking at 10s. the ell................................ 3–05– is 8–15 peyit to
4 ell off stuff at 3s. the ell .... 1–12– William Chancellor
4 ell off stuff at 16s. the ell .... 3–04– the 20 off January 1666 –
Half a pound off balling.. 0–14–............... • 08 • 15 • –
+ 20 January to my wyffe to give Walter Hamiltons nourish & wemen in drink –
money 30s. & 24s. is.. • 02 • 14 • –
For fresh beiff in January 1666.. • 04 • 15 • –
For whyt breid in January 1666 .... • 01 • 13 • –
The end off January: The disbursments in January 1666.... • 74 • 08 • 08
1666;

[35][31]

Februar 1666

The disbursments in February 1666;

14 Februar – to William Gib for binding 5 books in quarto at 9s.
the peice.......... • 02 • 05 • –
2 pair off whyt chiffrons 00–16–00
5 key rings – 9s. 00–09–00
Some cassia fistulla.......... 00–02–06
1 pound off leaff tobaco 00–13–04
To the montubank for drogs 02–00–00
To William Gib for binding 3 books.......... 01–04–00 • 05 • 04 • 10
14 Februar – to James Lishman cordoner for –
1: pair waxt boots for my selff 08–10–00
1: pair off shoone for John Clerk.......... 02–00–00
To his man in drink money – 4s. – 4 ell of taging for boots – 4s. is...... 00–08–00 • 10 • 18 • –
9 Februar to John Dow for 9 ell of serge in – 2 remnants at 45s.
the ell.......... • 20 • 14 • –
9 Februar to William Chancellor for –
10 ell of teyking at 9s. the ell.......... 04–10–00
4 ell of teyking at 14s. 6d. the ell .... 02–18–00 • 07 • 08 • –
+ 9 February to Effie Nisbit for –:
6 ell and 1 quarter off knit Deip freing weying – 30 onces 6 drop at
38s. the once is.......... 57–14–03
48 ell off small freing weying 7 once 10 drope at 30s. the once .... 11–08–09 • 69 • 03 • –
15 Februar – to Jennet Gray for a firekin off blak soap.......... • 10 • 10 • –

Entry	Amount	Margin sum
16 February – to John Gray for 10 ½ ell off drogit at 2 merk the ell.....		• 14 • 00 • –
1 pound off hasting peys to Thomas Wyllie		• 00 • 08 • –
The 16 off Februar: to Alexander Simsons wyffe for:		
1– to a webster for weiving 13 ell off worsit turk at 4s. 6d. the ell......	02–18–06	
2– for poping – 3s. to his man – 2s. is	00–05–00	
3– to a litster for dying the same at 5s. the ell	02–18–00	• 06 • 01 • 06
The 16 off February 1666 – to Robert Douglas for a firkin off spreklt – soap: 11 lib. I gave him the 11 lib. at David Boyds booth–dore he desyrd me to send for it when I pleasd and he sould deliverit........................		• 11 • 00 • –
all above		• 157 • 12 • 04
Teusday – 6 February – to my wyffe when I went to Edinburgh.........	03–00–00	
The said day to hir to send for a boll off salt.......................................	03–00–00	
Given my wyffe 3 lib. to give Marion Johnstoun to buy worsit...........	03–00–00	• 09 • 00 • –
Peyit for 24 ell off secking at 8s. the ell	09–12–00	
.27 27 February to James Frizel for 22 laid off cols at 4s. the laid..............	04–04–00	
For fresh beiff in February	02–01–00	
To John Galbraith webster in Leswaid	00–06–08	
30 January given to pay ale wes got at severall grindings at the mill.....	01–05–00	
2 pecks off salt – 6s. 8d. – 2 pirns – 4s.	00–10–08	
To Wille Clark for knitings – 6s.	00–06–00	• 02 • 08 • 04
1 February 1666 at a court holden in Pennycook	01–02–00[32]	

31 As noted in the original.

32 No sum in the margin for this entry.

24 February to John Broun schoole master for 5 hanks off virginel strings 00–04–02
Deux douzane des oeufs.......pour J: A .... 00–04–00 • 00 • 08 • 02
For breid in the month off February........ • 01 • 19 • –
The end off February 1666: soma off the disbursments in Februar .... • 171 • 07 • 10

Marche 1666

The disbursments in Marche 1666 ....

3 Marche – for registrating my discharg to Hermistoun off 1600 lib. thair being 2 extracts........ • 03 • 06 • 08
Said day to John Tod for 100 small bell nails plane headit .... • 02 • 08 • –
+ Said day – before Hermistoun younger to William Petries widow behind the tow booth for a seck pype – 3–18s. which shoe promist to deliver me betuixt and Witsonday 1666 when it wes emptie .... • 03 • 18 • –
To Adam Patersone for a horse hyre to John Elleis – 16s. and for corne & stroe at severall tymes for our horse – 18s. is .... • 01 • 14 • –
+ 5 Marche 1666 to Bessie Brunton for hir fie fra Witsonday 1665 till Mertimes 1665.......8 lib. .... • 08 • 00 • –
The 10 off Marche 1666 to William Ramage on his discharge acording to Robert Heriots order 57 lib. 12s. for – 32 double treis at 36s. the – peice – which the James Sandelands boght fra the said Robert Heriot for my usse – for custome – 6s. for cairidge to Neubiging – 16 lib. is in all .... • 73 • 18 • –
15 Marche to Lize to give Mage Pennycooke for 1 quarter off Holland • 00 • 15 • –
20 Marche to John Lourie at the mill for 6 bols off oats for our gairner –

Archbald Gib – at 3 lib. 6s. 8d. the boll	• 20 • 00 • –
28 Marche to James Blak for a bol off beir –4–2–6 & 2 thraiv off stroe – 16s. is	• 04 • 18 • 06
22 Marche to James Mark for 3 days wark with his meit	• 00 • 18 • –
119–16–2: The disbursments above in Marche 1666:	• 119 • 16 • 02

[36]

The disbursments on the other syde in Marche 1666.........................		• 119 • 16 • 02
6 Marche to David Hislop for 3 bols off seid oats at 4–6–8d. the boll		• 013 • 06 • 08
15 Marche to a chapman for divers small things	01–10–00	
To Rober[t] Waitch the said day for 7 ½ ell off lining at 14s. 6d. the – ell – 5–8–9 – and 1 pair off leather poutches – 2s. is.........................	05–10–09	
For blak worsit & divers small things..	01–04–00	• 08 • 04 • 09
29 Marche – to Robert Deuer for a boll off oats – 4–6–8d. – 2 pecks of beir – 10s. is 4–16–8d. which compleits his yeirs dewtie for our contrie wark fra Witsonday 1665 till Witsonday 1666...		• 04 • 16 • 08
30 March 1666 – compleited Thomas Andersone – a yeirs fie fra Mertimes 1664 till Witsonday 1665 – 18 lib. and 1 pair off shoons pryce – 30s. is		• 19 • 10 • –
28 Marche to Thomas Mossman –& Alexander Broun chapmen for lining cloth and other small things		• 11 • 12 • 06

31 Marche to George Clark cordoner for 1 ½ days wark .... • 00 • 12 • 04
Given to Elizabeth Clerk at divers tymes to pay for some small
things.. • 01 • 09 • –
For fresh beiff and dovs in this month off Marche.............................. • 04 • 14 • –
For whyt breid in this month off Marche.. • 02 • 05 • 04
The end off Marche 1666: The disbursments in Marche 1666...... • 186 • 07 • 05

Aprill The disbursments in Aprill – 1666 ~~
1666 3 Aprill to my wyffe to give to 2 websters.. 01–04–00
To John Donaldsone broght a letter fra Kimerghein.......................... 00–06–00
To Wrights Housses – 2 taskers .... 00–08–00 • 01 • 18 • –
To William Gib for – 3 *Fathers advysses to a sone*[33] at 14s. –
the peice.. 02–02–00
Thomas A Kempis in Inglish in – blew Maroquin................................ 01–00–00 • 03 • 02 • –
3 Aprill – to James Adamsone in his own housse for – 1 pair off litle cairt
whils wes made at the Abey [sic] hill – 3.....– 10 lib. 10s. .... • 10 • 10 • –
1 timber shoole weell shod.. 01–00–00
17 once off steill hemp 00–19–00
To Alexander Simsone for – 15 fadom off tows at – 2s. the fadom 01–10–00
Some small seids for the garden... 00–06–08
1 pound off cut & dry tobaco .... 01–00–00 • 04 • 15 • 08
4 Aprill to Hew Craig for – 9 pound 5 once bend leather at 19s.
the pound .... • 08 • 14 • –

4 Aprill to my brother John Andersone for – 5 ell off Holland at – 2 dolors the ell – which he peyit out at my wyffs desyre when shoe wes in the toun the 9 off Marche 1666 .... • 29 • 00 • –

Peyit to Walter Hamiltoun the 4 off Aprill 1666 – 8 lib. 8s. for oyll his – brother James Hamiltoun sent fra Glasgow for me – to wit –

1 quart and a chopin off oyll at 3 lib. the pynt 06–15–00

1 glasse botle for holding it 01–04–00

For cairiage fra Glasgow to Edinburgh .... 00–09–00 • 08 • 08 • –

5 Aprill to Walter Hamiltons wyffe for 6 d[ozen] Glasgow tobaco pyps 18s. – for cairiage – 3s. is 01–01–00

To Tomas Wedel for a large brydle bit 02–08–00

To him for 2 strong colt healters .... 01–12–00 • 05 • 01 • –

The – 5 off Aprill 1666 – to John Elleis wreatter and his man – 20–18–08d. – & to Alexander Leslie – 5 lib. 16s. – is 26–14–8d. on thair discharges for wreating 2 charters –& 2 seasings – anent Hermistouns entring me – gratis to the lands off Easter & Wester Revensneuks –& Cairnhill...... • 26 • 14 • 08

• 98 • 03 • 04

7 Aprill to Robert Miller webster for weiving – 15 ell sharp off mixt stuff at .... ~~~~

For all I gave him –3–12s. –& for poping money 3s. 4d. is .... • 03 • 15 • 04

[33] Possibly Patrick Scott's *Omnibus et singulis affording matter profitable for all men, necessarie for every man, alluding to a father's advice or last will to his sonne* (London, 1619). The revised edition was published the following year as *A Father's Advice or Last Will to his Son* (London, 1620). Another possibility is Francis Osborne's *Advice to a son; or, directions for your better conduct through the various and most important encounters of this life* (London, 1656).

The 9 off Aprill 1666 to Margaret Hopekirk for 2 yeirs fie to wit – fra Witsonday 1664 till Witsonday 1666 at 16 lib. in the yeir	32–00–00	
More to hir for – 4 pair off shoone at 2 pair in the yeir fra Witsonday 1664 till Witsonday 1666 – 5 lib.	05–00–00	• 37 • 00 • –
To Adam Patersone for a gryce		• 00 • 13 • 04
12 Aprill to Alexander Dobsone for –		
2 pair off brydle rains & 2 head stails for Jack	02–00–00	
2 long curpls for him	01–06–08	
6 fadom off tows	00–12–00	
To Alexander Gray for 3 short oaken planks	01–16–00	• 05 • 14 • 08
26 – Aprill to David Lindsay – for half a cows hyde		• 02 • 18 • –
28 – Aprill to Nicoll Campbell – for 8 nights Jack wes with him – corne & hay ilk night – 10s. is – 4 lib. –& 36s. – for materials to his tongue –& for – his pains in cureing his tongue –& to his man 9s. is in all		• 06 • 05 • –
To Thomas Wedel for a pair off large stirip yrns		• 01 • 00 • –
To Archebald Gib for binding 5 books in gray leather		• 01 • 12 • –
30 Aprill to John Solomon for a wool ryding hatt for my selff		• 03 • 12 • –
26 Aprill 1666 – to Alexander Simpsone for James Clerks boord fra the 26 off Aprill 1666 till the 26 off Jully 1666		• 30 • 00 • –
5 Aprill – to George Clerk cordoner for halff a blak cows hyde		• 03 • 02 • –
3 Aprill given to buy whyt threid – 6s. 8d. 6 pair of timber heils 6s.		• 00 • 12 • 08
4 pair off dovs at 3s. 4d. the pair		• 00 • 13 • 04
For divers other small disbursments – 2 lib. 18		• 02 • 18 • –
The disbursments above in Aprill 1666		• 197 • 19 • 08

[37]

The disbursments in Aprill 1666 – on the other syde is .... • 197 • 19 • 08

John Clerk wes lowriat[34] on Munday 30 Aprill 1666 in the colledg off Edinburgh: the primers name wes Mr William Colvin his regents name wes Mr John Wishart: he wes borne at Edinburgh – on Saturday morning the 7 off Aprill 1649 betwixt 6 & 7 hours in the morneing and wes 17 yeir old and 23 days when he wes lowriat..............................

Accompt off charges disbursit for John Clerk when he was lowriat which wes on Munday the 30 off Aprill 1666 ....

1 24 Aprill to Adam Rae for 5 ell off blak cloth at 15 lib. the ell .... • 75 • 00 • –

2 30 Aprill to William Lorimer for a pair off pearle cullort silk hose ...... • 15 • 00 • –

3 30 Aprill to Hary Steuart for 2 French peice off blak plane 4d. riben ilk peice conteining – 5 French douzane off els – both peices............. • 29 • 00 • –

4 1 pair off whyt chiffrons .... • 00 • 16 • –

5 1 pair off yellowish triple poyntit cordevans .... • 03 • 00 • –

6 To John Solomon for a hatt... • 06 • 06 • –

129–02–00: • 129 • 02 • –

The 29 off June 1666 to William Seatoun tailyeur for making him – a cullort worsit turk clok and some things he furnisht thairtoo –& for making clok and sute off blak cloth when he wes lowriat –& for some things he furnisht thairtoo according to his accompt thereoff and the said William Seaton his discharge date the 29 June 1666 .... • 34 • 14 • 02

[34] Laureate.

1 Given him to give to the comon purse – 12 dolors .... • 34 • 16 • –

2 Given him to give to the bibliothique – 2 dolors .... • 05 • 16 • –

3 Given him to give Mr John Dunlop keeper of the bibliothique for a testimonie .... • 01 • 10 • –

4 Given him to defray some small charges & expensis the weik befor the lauriation.. • 05 • 16 • –

5 Given him 3 dolors to pay his supper the night he wes louriat......... • 08 • 14 • –

• 56 • 12 • –

1 129–02–00
2 34–14–02
3 56–12–00
220–08–00– John Clerks charges at the lauriation ...... • 220 • 08 • –

For whyt breid in the month off Aprill 1666.................................... • 02 • 05 • –

For fresh meit boyling beoff in the month off Aprill 1666 .... [35] • 05 • 14 • –

197–19–08
220–08–00
007–19–00
426–06–08

The end off Aprill 1666: the disbursments in Aprill 1666.......... • 426 • 06 • 08

May The disbursments in May – 1666 ....

1666 The 4 off May 1666 to William Steill for 40 laid off cols at 5s. the laid

10 lib. the Lady Newhall wes oweing Androu Hepburn webster 6 lib. which William Steill accept it in part off peyment of the said 10 lib. and 4 lib. in money I gave him and I wreat – doun the 6 lib. as resavet fra William Steill in part off peyment off what the said Androu Hepburn wes resting me of his maill being – 15 lib. – fra Mertimes 1664 till Witsonday 1665 so that I peyit to William Steill – 10 lib. for the said 40 laid of cols .... • 10 • 00 • –

5 May to Mistresse Turnor for 5 chopins & halff a mutchkin off anis seid water at 24s. the pint .... • 02 • 18 • 06

8 May to John Thomson measson for cuming twyse [sic] to Newbiging and giveing his – advysse anent what I wes tog [sic] big on the west syde in – anno 1666 .... • 02 • 18 • –

2 grein handlt knyves 6s. 00–06–00

With the said John Thomson – measson 00–04–00

4 May to Arche Gib when he went for flours & herbs – 12s. to drink & 12s. to give Sir John Smiths gairner is........24s. 01–04–00

9 –& 22 off May to Lize Clark – to pay thair expensis in Pennycooke 00–16–00

10 May to Wille Steuart when he went to Leith for wyne – whyte & seck – which we got fra Stephen Bruntfeild in 2 litle barels 00–04–00

15 May to William Austin in Cairingtoun for mending sivs & ridls..... 00–08–06

35 Clerk attempted to correct a mistake he made when entering the totals for bread and beef by using arrows to indicate what should be taken as the correct values. The transcription represents the corrected sums.

7 May to William Davisone couper in Lintoun 00–08–08
3 May – 10s. to give a webster in Edinburgh .... 00–10–00 • 03 • 11 • 02
10 May to Tomas Rob cordoner for – half a hors hyde barkit 01–16–00
1 – shod last – 9s. – 2 other lasts – 10s. is – 19s. .... 00–19–00 • 02 • 15 • –
16 May sent to Edinburgh – for ane other halff horse hyde barkit
cost.........42s. .... • 02 • 02 • –
+ To John Dicksone for his fie fra Witsonday 1665 till Mertimes 1665
14 November 1665 to him to buy his shoone........ 00–13–04
22 May 1666 to him in money – 6 lib. .... 06–00–00 • 06 • 13 • 04
30–18s. ....: The disbursments above in May 1666 is........ • 30 • 18 • –

[38]
The disbursments on the other syde in May – 1666 is 30 –18s. .... • 30 • 18 • –
The 21 off May 1666 to James Thomson glaisen wright – 18–16–6d.
on his discharge off all accompts whatsumever preseidin[g] the said 21
off May 1666 .... • 18 • 16 • 06
13 May 1666 – to William Jack saidler for 2 new sled saidles – 4 lib.
19s. and the 4 stocks off 4 old sled saidles I gave him also – he sweir
I peyit him formerlie all ways – 5 merks for the peice off such
sled saidles........ • 04 • 19 • –
1 once off riffart seid........ 00–04–00
1 pound off raisings 00–08–00
6. fadome off tows........ 00–12–00 • 01 • 04 • –

24 May – to David Lindsay – for halff ane Irish hyde off bend leather weying – 8 lib. – 8 once........at 12s. the pound is........................... • 08 • 14 • –

1 hinging sprent lock to put on the storme dore in my chamber in Edinburgh .... • 00 • 13 • 04

The accompt off moneys when shoe went to Edinburgh the 15 off May 1666 .... • 65 • 04 • 10

1– to John Tailyeur tailyour[36] – for making –& furnishing Marie Clerk canel cullort – wateret mohair gown – 7–12s. 07–12–00

2– to John Dow for 16 ell off twidle to be coverts for the carpit chyrs at 5s. 6d. the ell.. 04–08–00

3– 5 ell off stenting at 7s. the ell 01–15–00

4– to [blank] Smith cordoner for 1 pair off shoone for my wyffe and a pair off shoone for Marie Clerk 03–12–00

5– peyit to a webster in the West Bow for weiving – 45 ell off braid lining at – 3s. 4d. the ell 07–10–00

6– to him for sowing – 8s. to his man 6s. is.................................... 00–14–00

17 May 1666 my wyffe peyit to David Boyds wyffe 2 ell off Holland wes gotten when John Clerk wes louriat at – 3 lib. 16s. the ell 07–12–00

8– 3 bolt off twidlt knitings at 12s. the bolt.................................. 01–16–00

9– 3 ½ ell off ribens for Maries tail band off hir goun....................... 01–04–00

10– 1 ½ ell off lining cloth for lyneing Maries slives & bodies 01–04–00

11– 4 once off threid... 01–04–00

[36] This was a rare occasion where Clerk spelled the word 'tailor' with a y.

12– to Archebald Teinder – 6s. 8d. –& 6s. 8d. to give Robert Fergusone
tailyeur in earnest 00–13–04
13– to George Boswell – webster – 14s. – for warping the strypit
stuff for a skring 00–14–00
14– 1 pound off currents – 10s. 00–10–00
15– for halff a fyne plaid – 9 lib. 6s. – whairoff my wyffe got
for ane plaid off hir own – 5–16s. – rests 03–10–00
my wyffs disbursments .... 43–18–04 • 43 • 18 • 04
30 May to William Stinsone for – 2: I say for 4 earthen pots 00–10–00
2 Juny to Alexander Simsone for 1 lb off raisings my wyffe wes owing:
him and a pound I got my selff the said day 00–16–00
28 May to Robert Thomson creill man for severall small harre –
graith 03–05–08
To Lize Clark to pay for eygs 00–15–00
28 – May to Tom Rob cordoner – for 16 days wark at 6s. 8d. a day ..... 04–16–00 • 10 • 02 • 08
31 May 1666 to James Lishman cordoner in the Cannegate – for 1 pair off
Maroquin shoone –& 1 pair off net[37] leather blak shoone John Clerk got at –
the lauriation – 4 lib. 2s. – 4 .... • 04 • 02 • 04
The penult of May 1666 – to Alexander Ogilvie ane off the collector
deputs off a taxation grantit to his Majestie in Agust 1665 as for the first
terms taxt of the personage off Pennycooke fra Witsonday 1665 till
Witsonday 1666 – acording to his discharge given to me thereoff date the
penult off May 1666............55 lib. 2s. 2d. .... • 55 • 02 • 02
For whyt breid in the month off May 1666 .... • 02 • 06 • –

For fresh beiff in the month off May 1666		• 04 • 13 • 06
The end off May – 1666 –: The disbursments in May 1666.......		• 185 • 09 • 10

Juny... 1666

The disbursments in Juny – 1666 ~~~~:		
1 Juny – to Thomas Sandelands in full off ane accompt on his discharge date the 1 off Juny 1666 – for 60 dails: & cairidge off them to Neubiging –&c..		• 35 • 11 • –
The 11 Juny 1666 – to William Lamb for his fie fra Mertimes – 1665 till Witsonday 1666 – 1. in money	10–00–00	
2. to buy his shoone..	00–15–00	
3. to buy – 6 quarters of gray at 24s. ell..........	01–16–00	• 12 • 11 • –
The 11 June 1666 – to Thomas Andersone when he went away for his yeirs – fie fra Witsonday 1665 till Witsonday 1666 in money	36–00–00	
and – 3 lib. for 2 pair off shoone the said yeirs space	03–00–00	• 39 • 00 • –
12 Juny 1666 – to Helen Ritchie for hir fie fra Mertimes 1665 till Witsonday 1666:		
1– in money – 6 lib.	06–00–00	
2– to hir to by hir shoone – 24s.	01–04–00	• 07 • 04 • –
The 15 June 1666 – to Jenet Lamb for hir fie fra Mertimes 1665 till Witsonday 1666 –		
1 in money..	07–00–00	

[37] Neat.

2 in money to buy hir shoone 01–10–00

3 in money to buy ane ell off lining........ 00–12–00 • 09 • 02 • –

The disbursments above in June 1666 is .... • 103 • 08 • –

[39]

The disbursments in the month off June on the other syde is............ • 103 • 08 • –

The moneys that 10 North Berwick stons cost for the soll off our oven the bigest oven soll: The 21 June 1666 to Wille Stewart our hynd who went for 2 cairtfull off them – 17 lib. Scots to pay a baxter in Leith fra whom Patrik Widerspoons boght them at – 34s. the peice is.............. 17–00–00

22 June to David Lishman cairter for bringing out 3 off them on a cairt with – 2 horse........ 02–09–08

To Wille Stewart at 2 severall tymes to pay the horse charges & his own........ 01–05–04

To Patrik Widerspoons to drink when he boght them........ 00–06–00 • 21 • 01 • –

4 June to Archebald Craig for 7 firlots off seid oats at 3–6–8d. the boll .... • 05 • 16 • 08

1 pynt off vinaigre........ 00–13–04

1 quart of fish oyll – for oylling wooll........ 01–12–00

1 lyg off mouton 00–18–00

To John Rob to pay Alexander Simsone for small liting busyness my wyfe got........ 00–04–02

To Lize Clerk to pay some small expensis........ 00–11–06 • 03 • 19 • –

The 18 off June 1666 – to James Blak for 4 thraive off stroe & 6 shaives • 01 • 14 • –

The 25 June 1666 – to John Ramsay for 9 mure fowls he tooke at my desyre to – Newbatle when my Lords[38] dochter wes married to Smitoun at 8s. the peice .... • 03 • 12 • –

+ The 30 June 1666 – to William Mitchel baxter in Edinburgh on his discharge off the said date in full off all accompts preseiding the said day .... • 04 • 14 • 06

The 27 off June to David Pringle apothecar in full of ane accompt on his discharge.......... • 04 • 08 • –

The 28 off June 1666 – to Archbald More for a douzane off carpit chyrs – on his discharge date the – 28 off June 1666 – 100 lib. .... • 100 • 00 • –

The 28 off June – to David Boyd in full off ane accompt on his discharge.......... • 56 • 16 • 06

The 25 –& 29 off June 1666 – to John Gray off Crichie on his discharges off the said date in full off ane accompt .... • 110 • 02 • –

The 27 June 1666 to my brother John Andersone – which he gave to Marie Clerk to buy 1 ell off Holland and some cambridge bands .... • 06 • 00 • –

27 June to James Clerk –

1– for a hatt.......... 02–06–00

2– to buy buttons to his minim drogit sute .... 00–12–00 • 02 • 18 • –

Pearles off eloquence 00–18–00

[38] William Kerr, 3rd earl of Lothian (1605–1675). For more on Clerk's dealings with the 3rd earl, see Talbott, *Conflict, Commerce and Franco-Scottish relations*; Wenley, 'William, third earl of Lothian'.

To: Cristian [blank] Alexander Simsons woman .... 00–12–00 • 01 • 10 • –
For whyt breid in June – 1666 .... • 01 • 12 • –
The end off June 1666: The disbursments in June 1666........ • 427 • 11 • 09

Jully 1666 The disbursments in Jully – 1666:
2 Jully to my Lord Lothians meassons at Newbatle........ 01–10–00:
Said day at Dalkeith for 400 chirries & a creill 00–16–04:
To William Heriot cordoner for mending shoone 00–10–00:
To Lize for small expensse – 6s. 00–06–00:
To hir to give Arche Gib – for fresh butter 00–12–00:
To a chapman for severall small things........ 00–10–08:
To John Rob for carots –& oynions........ 00–04–00: • 04 • 09 • –
9 Jully to Cristian Potter for 4 ell of round lining at 10s. the ell .... • 02 • 00 • –
28 Jully to John Cooke locksmith in full of ane accompt on his discharge date the said 28 Jully 1666 – off all things whatsoever preseiding the said day .... • 08 • 12 • –
To Stephan Bruntfield merchant on his discharge – date the 22 off Jully 1666 for 1 barrel off hering seck and whyte wyne .... • 29 • 15 • –
The 17 off Jully 1666 – to William Brugh in Dundie merchant on his discharge of the said date – 80 lib for 3000 sklaits to theyk the new howsse be west the great new park .... • 80 • 00 • –
The 8 off June 1666 – to John Mein sklaiter on his discharge – 27 lib. 4s. to pay for the fraught & other charges off the said – 3000 sklaits........ • 27 • 04 • –
25 Jully to my brother John Andersone – 6 lib. which he gave to Marie

Clerk to – buy Holland to be Lize bands		• 06 • 00 • –
To Alexander Andersone for mending a copper pan off a dry seat		• 01 • 13 • 04
To Robert Selkrig for – 2 litle barels		• 01 • 04 • –
To Thomas Wedel for – 12 lib. off glew at 8s. the pound		• 04 • 16 • –
28 Jully – to Robert Broun for the first & second tom[e]s off the *Virtuose off France* bound in gray leather.........6 rex dolors		• 17 • 08 • –
2 pound off pruns	00–10–00	
To Thomas Wedel for tining a crosse sheild –& 70 shorn headit nails	00–07–00	• 00 • 17 • –
To the meassons at the ministers housse	00–12–00	
To Lize to pay out for severall small disbursments	01–01–00	
For 2 fir teathers	00–04–08	
To James Bennet for chirries he broght out off Muslbrugh	00–16–00	
13 Jully to Androw Mackgie couper for girding looms	01–09–00	
20 Jully to Wille Stewart to get 6 firlots off meill at Leith	08–00–00	
The said day to him for his sone that keiped the goods	00–18–00	
To: M: G – at James Sandelands baptizeing off his bairne –18s. – & for hering 5s. 6d. is – 23s 6d.	01–03–06	• 14 • 04 • 02
The disbursments in Jully on this syde is		• 198 • 02 • 06

198–02–6 ~~~~

[40]

The disbursments in the month off Jully on the other syde is .... • 198 • 02 • 06

The 26 off Jully 1666 – to Mr Thomas Baird on[e] off the shireff deputs of Edinburgh 24 lib. on his discharge date the said 26 off Jully 1666 – as the first termes payment off a taxation – imposd be the convention off estats in Agust 1665 which 24 lib. sould have been peyit at Witsonday 1666 – for my 12 pound lands off – Pennycooke the Halls and Cookeing. This is the first termes payment off the said taxation – fra Agust 1665 that it wes imposd till Witsonday 1666 .... • 24 • 00 • –

For severall uther small items & disbursment in Jully.......1666............ • 01 • 14 • 06

For whyt breid in Jully 1666............ • 02 • 03 • –

The end off Jully – 1666 ~~: The disbursments in Jully 1666 .... • 226 • 00 • –

Agust 1666 The disbursments in Agust – 1666............

Saturday – 4 Agust to my wyffe 11 lib. to send to Alisone Troup with hir – dochter Nans Gray – for 39 ½ ell off sad gray mixt 8d. taffatie ribens at 5s. 6d. the ell............ • 11 • 00 • –

\+ The 9 Agust 1666 to Robert Adamsone for his fie fra Witsonday 1665 till – Witsonday 1666 ~~~~

1– in money............ 20–00–00

2– to buy 2 pair of single sold shoone............ 01–10–00

3– to buy 3 ell of gray at 2 merk the ell............ 04–00–00 • 25 • 10 • –

10 Agust to John Thomson to get 6 firlots off Leith meill at 7 merk the boll............ • 07 • 00 • –

	11 Agust for fresh beiff	00–14–00	
	To Charles Campbel for 2 days to help to lay the geists in the barne	00–18–00	
	To George Bell for ale & lintel ale	00–12–06	
	24 Agust to Edouart Adamsone for 2 pecks off hemp seid	01–04–00	
	For 3 ell off harden at 5s. the ell	00–15–00	
	28 off Agust to William Park for ane aller sled	01–02–00	• 05 • 05 • 06
	18 off Agust to John Ramsay for 10 wyld fowls		• 03 • 00 • –
+	24 Agust to Thomas Lyle cairter & his brother Robert Lyle for 16 fadom – large off great tard tows – about 4s. the fadome is		• 03 • 07 • 08
	29 Agust to Elspeth Heren for hir hervest supper meill	15s.–00	
	To the smiths man for his hervest supper meill	18[s.]–00	• 01 • 13 • –
	30 off Agust to Robert Thomsone for bikers. cogs. luges – laces knitings &c		• 04 • 13 • –
	For herings		• 01 • 02 • 08
	To Lize to pay some small compts	00–16–04	
	To hir to give the wyffe in the Towr & Arche Gib for butter & eygs	00–16–08	• 01 • 13 • –
	For whyt breid in the month of Agust		• 01 • 13 • –
	The end off Agust 1666. The disbursments in Agust 1666		• 65 • 17 • 10

September	The disbursments in September – 1666 ~~		
1666	1 September for peirs & plumbs &c. at Lintoun fare		• 02 • 18 • –
+	10: September to George Mark in the lyme stain grein – for girsing a mare stage [sic] off 2 – yeir old in summer 1666 – 40s. & a peck off		

beir – 6s. 8d. is........46s. 8d. .... • 02 • 06 • 08

8 September to Jennet Meurs – in Hurlie Hall for – 1 boll off oats wes goten fra hir the 22 off Marche 1666........ • 03 • 13 • 04

10 September to David Clerk to get in Leith – 3 bols of meill at 3 –14s. the boll .... • 11 • 02 • –

11 September to Edowart Adamsone for 1 lyge off toop mouton........ • 00 • 12 • –

7 September to William Stewart to get – 6 firlots off salt at 4 merk the boll &c........ • 04 • 00 • –

15 September to John Rob for a stone off hair for plaister .... • 00 • 07 • 06

18 off September to Lize to give Arche Gib for butter shoe wes to get fra him – in place off 12s. he got to buy oynions at Edinburgh & did it not – 12s. and 2s. shoe – gave out for Francis Spira is 14s. 00–14–00

19 September to John Rob for 1 pound off pack threid for the staible heather........ 00–12–00

For peirs and plumbs 00–13–04

18 September to Edowart Adamsone for 2 pynts of comon waters...... 01–16–00

Said day to him to give drink and breid to powers off heather for: ~~ ~~ ~~

the stable –& to give 4 pynts off ale to Willam Marshall hird........ 01–03–04 • 04 • 18 • 08

19 September to Helen Patersone – for hering 9s. –& 6s. Lize wes oweing is 15s. – & 20s. for 1 litle barel off ale conteining 15 pynts at – 16d. the pynt 20s. & 15s. is .... • 01 • 15 • –

10 September to Margaret Hopkirk when shoe went to Edinburgh –16–17–6 which shoe waird as follows ~~ ~~

4 staine 5 ½ pound off butter at 3 lib. 6s. the stone 14–07–04

For weying it – 16d. salt to salt it 1s. for carying to the weyhouse 1s. is.......... 00–03–04
5 quarters off linze winze grein to be aprons to the bairns 00–13–04
For short breid & bumbis 00–17–06
For – halff a hundreth hering shoe disbursit at Neubiging 00–10–00
1 pair off litle pomp shoes for litle Robin Clerk .... 00–06–00 • 16 • 17 • 06

48–10–8.... all above disbursit in September 1666 • 48 • 10 • 08

The 12 off September 1666 Thomas Mein – in my name peyit to Mr Robert Alisone minister at the kirk off Glencorse – 48 lib. for my proportion off – his stipend for the lands off Cookeing and that fra Witsonday – 1665 till Witsonday 1666. Thomas Mein delivert me his discharge for the said 48 lib. – date corse housse the 12 off Jully 1666 .... • 48 • 00 • –

The disbursments in September 1666 on this syde is .... • 96 • 10 • 08

[41]

The disbursments on the other syde in September 1666 is.......... • 96 • 10 • 08

24 September 1666 – to Adam Patersone for a grysse John Rob broght out.......... • 00 • 12 • –
Said day to John Elleis woman in drink money – 1 dolor.......... • 02 • 18 • –
1 lb – 2 once off leaff tobaco..........2...... 00–18–
Halff a pound off cut and dry tobaco.......... 00–09– • 01 • 07 • –
6 drop off saffran fra William Lorimers wyffe at 6s. 8d. the drop.......... 01–19–00

Item	Amount	Total
For sharping 2 pair off sheirs	00–02–00	
To James Grhams widow for – 6 ell of tuftit Holland at 24s. the ell	07–04–00	• 09 • 05 • –
3 lb off currents at 9s. the pound	01–07–00	
6 ½ pound off pruns at 5s. the pound	01–12–06	
To John Cooke for puting a boull to a key	00–12–00	• 03 • 11 • 06
26 September to Alexander Simpsone – in full off ane accompt markit –A B– and all former accompts preseiding the said day		• 05 • 03 • 04
2 once off cannel at 15s. the once	01–10–00	
1 once off meisses – 14s.	00–14–00	
8 drop off clovs	00–07–00	
1 once off nut mugs	00–06–00	
3 lb off great raisings at 10s. the pound	01–10–00	• 04 • 07 • –
To John Gedes booke binder – 28 September 1666 –		
1– for binding the *Queen of Fairie* in gray leather	01–00–00	
2– for binding a booke in folio – in parchement with a thin paisboord 3 quair off peper for a style booke for John Clerk	00–13–04	
3– for binding a booke in quarto in parchement with a thin paisse boord for James Clerks nots [sic] – 2 quair	00–06–08	• 02 • 00 • –
To Mr Haigens for 2 New Testaments of a blak letter unbound for the bairns		• 01 • 00 • –
		• 30 • 03 • 10
To Lize Clerk to pay for herings –& eygs		• 00 • 08 • –
For fresh beiff in the month off September 1666		• 03 • 10 • 06

For whyt breid in September – 1666 .... • 02 • 03 • –

The end off September 1666: The disbursments in September 1666 ... • 132 • 16 • –

October 1666:

The disbursments in October – 1666: ~~~~

2 October to a woman for a litle yrne pot with a yrne boull .... • 01 • 00 • –

To a couper in Lintoun for girding severall barels & tubs .... • 01 • 00 • –

3 October 1666 – to George Whyt for theyking the staible over agane with hather – for 7 days wark at 10s. in the day with his meit .... • 03 • 10 • –

16 October to William Stewart our hynd for halff a yeir his dochter Jean – Stewart stayd with us .... • 03 • 12 • –

4 October to Patrik Craig to get a firlot of meill 01–02–00

1 bolt of knitings 00–07–00

17 October to William Stewart to get a firlot of great salt in Leith 02–08–00

To John Rob – 4s. to tak a letter to Nans Turnbull to Nidrie & 6s. to him for making small rash rops for the staible to thyk it with heather is 00–10–00

23 October to William Steuart our hynd for ane yrne pot 01–12–00

To a couper in Lintoun – 5s. ......2s. for sharping – a razoir 00–07–00

To David Clerk – 24 of October –18s. to get 4 lb of small candle 00–18–00

26 October to William Steuart hynd to get 6 firlots off meill in Leith .... 05–17–08 • 13 • 01 • 08

16 of October 1666 – to Margaret Hopkirk to ware at Edinburgh as follows –

1 2 stone of lint 10–16–08

2 To George / Robert Miller[39] webster in the West Bow for weiving
15 ell off small – lining – at 6s. the ell 04–10–00
3 For small things for litting 00–12–00
4 Fresh butter – 9s. – oynions – 5s. – short breid – 12s. is .... 01–06–00 • 17 • 04 • 08

28 of October – to John Dryburgh – 8s. – for casting divets a day to Sande Falcons housse 8s. to Wille Elphistouns wyffe – 4s. for dry rashes to be small rops for soweing the heather – on the staible – to John Lowrie at the mill – 8s. 4d. to give his wyffe for 5 pynts of aill – David Clerk got to the men that tild the land in Pennycooke is in all thir – 3 particullars –
20s. – 4d. 01–00–04
For fresh beiff in October 02–02–00
For whyt breid in October 01–10–00
To Lize Clark for some small disbursments – 8s. 4d. –& 9s. 4d. is.............................. 00–17–08 • 05 • 10 • –

The end off October 1666: The disbursments in October 1666 is ... • 44 • 18 • 08

November The disbursments in November – 1666

1666 6 November – to Walter Hamiltouns wyffe in full of ane accompt markit F.............................. • 11 • 08 • 06

For ane long oaken plank James Sandelands boght for me in Leith to be the large outer gate with all charges belonging thairtoo according to the – particullar accompt yairoff I have by me markit S – 38 lib. 12s. .... • 38 • 12 • –

James Clerk entert home on Wedensday – 24 of October 1666 – John Clerk entert home on Thursday the 1 off November 1666 – to William Hamiltoun merchant his housse in boording – on the 6 off November –

1666 to the said William Hamiltoun – for thair boord for 3 month to cum fra ilk ane of thair entries .... • 66 • 13 • 04

The 6 of November – 1666 to Mr James Pillens regent to James Clerk – who entert to the colledge the second yeir on the 24 of October 1666 – 8 dolors .... • 23 • 04 • –

The disbursments above in November 1666 is.........139–17–10 .... • 139 • 17 • 10

[42]

The disbursments in November – 1666 – mentioned on the other syde is • 139 • 17 • 10

The 6 off November 1666 to Alexander Leslie wreatter to the signet 66 lib. 13s. 4d. Scots – for John Clerk for wreating in his chamber for a yeir to cum .... • 66 • 13 • 04

The said day to John Clerk to spend with the young men in the chamber at his brothering .... • 06 • 00 • –

The 8 off November 1666 – to John Geddes for binding 2 Neu Testaments to the bairns in gray leather with clasps – 16s. – and for binding a booke in quarto off 3 quair off peper for James Clerk to wreat his notes in 7s. is .... • 01 • 03 • –

1 glasse botle 6s. 8d. – 1 chopin and a gill off canel water is 45s. is both .... • 02 • 11 • 08

39 Clerk inserted the name 'Robert Miller' after 'George /' and before 'webster' in the body of the account. The text does not make clear whether Clerk made a mistake by naming 'George' as the webster, or if two men, George and Robert Miller, were hired to weave some small linens.

10 November 1666 – to Robert Brysone for 46 ½ ell off blak rubens ... • 13 • 01 • –
Halff a pound off whyt suger candie .... • 00 • 16 • –
Teusday 13 November 1666 – Archbald Gib our gairner went away to
Edinburgh to dwell – peyit to him as follows:
31 October 1666 – to him 6 lib. the 13 off November 1666 to him 12 lib.
is 18 lib. for his corne which my wyffe boght fra him 18–00–00
Said day to him for a hen wes goten fra him...................................... 00–07–00
Said day to him for 4 mands & 2 litle creils...................................... 00–13–04
Said day to him for some bits off treis & other small things I –
got fra him at Mertimes – 1665 when he entert home........................ 03–10–06 • 22 • 10 • 10

As apears on a booke whair servants fies is wreatten markit on the bak
& brods – 347 – to James Haliburton at severall tymes for a yeirs fie
fra Mertimes 1665 till Mertimes – 1666 – 24 lib. 16s. .... • 24 • 16 • –

Saturday – 17 November 1666 – in a seald letter delivert to Patrik
Widerspoons measson – sent to William Smith clark off Mussilburgh
a fourtie fyve – shilling peice – for ane extra[c]t off the valuation off the
teinds off the paroish off Pennycooke: date the 6 off Marche 1630 ...... • 02 • 05 • –
17 November– to John Reid for a pynt off hony he got at Clarkingtoun • 02 • 00 • –
As apears on a booke whair servants fies is wreatten markit on the bak
& brods – 347– to Robert Adamsone for his halff yeirs fie fra Witsonday
1666 till Mertimes 1666 – 1 in money– 10 lib. for 6 quarters of gray
1–16s. for 1 pair off single sold shoone.................15s. is in all........... • 12 • 11 • –
2 November to a webster in Braidwood for weiving 18 ell
of blanketing.. 01–04–00

5 September to Robert Wood for 2 pecks of pan cratch for the ovens	00–08–00	
Saturday– 17 September to I say – 17 November – 25s. 10d. seald in a peper to give Walter Hamiltons wyffe for a peck of short breid	01–05–10	
19 November to John Thomsone – 6–10s. to give Thomas Robisone – for a boll off malt he got fra him the said day for our usse	06–10–00	
10 November to Lize Clark to pay for divers small disbursments	00–14–08	• 10 • 02 • 06
12 November 1666 – to Elspeth Hendersone midwyffe when Archebald Clerk wes borne 8 rex dolors		• 23 • 04 • –
20 November 1666 – to Margaret Turnbull for hir fie fra Witsonday – 1666 – till Mertimes 1666 – in money 6 lib. for 1 pair off shoone 29s. is in all – 7 lib. 9s.		• 07 • 09 • –
+ 22 November 1666 – to John Broun schoolemaster when Archebald Clerk wes baptized –& to John Brown bedel the said day – 6s. is....30s.		• 01 • 10 • –
4 pound off small candle	00–17–04	
3 cunnings	01–04–00	• 02 • 01 • 04
28 November to John Clerk to buy 1 pair of stokings	02–18–00	
To get a pound off candle – 4s. 6d. for a proclimation – 1s. is	00–05–06	• 03 • 03 • 06
29 November 1666 – to Alexander Simpsone for my chamber maill fra – Witsonday 1666 till Mertimes 1666 – 12 lib. on his discharge date the – 29 off November – 1666	:	• 12 • 00 • –
To Thomas Wedel for a brydle bit	02–10–00	
To Alexander Dobsone for a new pair off brydle rains & head staill	01–00–00	• 03 • 01 • –

For registrating a discharge– off 320 lib. Scots to Largo: as 2 yeirs – anuel [sic] rent off – 4000 merks fra Mertimes 1664 till Mertimes 1666 – thair being – 2 extracts thairoff – each on[e] 33s. 4d.	03–06–08	
To Alexander Leslie for wreating 2 discharges – 1 for Mr Francis Durhame off Largo the other for my Lord Ker	00–12–00	• 03 • 18 • 08
30 November to Walter Hamiltons wyffe for a peck of short breid	01–02–00	
12 once off leaff tobaco	00–14–00	• 01 • 16 • –
29 November to my Lord Ramsays man – for Jacks expense 2 nights –		
1– for 3 new shoone – it wes said wes furnisht to him	00–18–00	
2– for corne & stroe 2 nights	01–00–00	
3– to his man in drink money 1 merk –& a pynt ale is	00–13–04	• 02 • 11 • 04
To John Rob – 16s. for 7 days he wes with me at Edinburgh –& intertaind himselff		• 00 • 16 • –
30 November to Adam Patersone for Jack –& the gray horse his expense		• 02 • 12 • –
For fresh beiff in November 1666		• 02 • 19 • –
For whyt breid in November 1666		• 03 • 00 • –
To Nans Johnstoun for 1 ½ yeir fra Witsonday 1665 till Mertimes 1666 – 24 lib. & for – 3 pair of shoone – 58s. is 26–18s.		• 26 • 18 • –
26 November to Jeans Pillens for a yeirs fie fra Mertimes 1665 till Mertimes 1666		• 27 • 00 • –
The end of November 1666 The disbursments in November 1666		• 428 • 07 • 10

[43]

December 1666

The disbursments in December 1666 ~~~~~~

	To David Clerk to pay drink at the mill – it wes to pay drink and give drnik [sic] money to the man maks the malt at the water off Leith......	00–18–00	
	2 pound off butter	00–10–00	
	1 mure fowll..............................	00–06–00	
	2 douzane off eygs..............................	00–04–00	
	To David Clerk to pay kill –& mill ale..............................	00–10–00	
	To: for – 2 skuls	00–04–00	
	2 cunings – 16s.	00–16–00	
	4 lb off small candle	00–17–00	• 04 • 00 • –
	11 December to John Pennycooke in the Coits – 4 merk for a boll off oats we got fra him for our horse the – 15 off October 1666		• 02 • 13 • 04
	The 17 off December 1666 – peyit to John Lowrie at the mill which we wes resting to him the said day –		
1	For making a steip and a halff off malt – which wes spilt in the drying	04–00–00	
2	6 ½ boll off oats to grind – and 1 boll for our horse at 3 lib. 16s. the boll..............................	28–10–00	
3	6 bols off barley my wyffe got to be malt at 8 merk the boll	32–00–00	• 64 • 10 • –
	The 21 December 1666 – to William Lorimer merchant on his discharge the said day in full off ane accompt for 5 ¼ ell off cloth for John Clerks cloths at 6 lib. 13s. 4d. the ell..............................		• 35 • 00 • –

The 22 off December 1666 – to Thomas Airth for the particullars under wreatten for which he gave me a discharge at the fit off his compt date 22 December 1666 –

1– 23 pynts off seck in 2 rubbers at 33s. 4d. the pynt 38–06–08

2– 10 ½ pynts off brande at 20s. the pynt 10–10–00

3– 2 litle new rubbers at – 24s. the peice .... 01–08–00 • 51 • 04 • 08

The accompt off money peyit out to John Clerk –

13 December my brother gave him a dolor to help his brothering 02–18–00

14 December my brother gave him 7s. sterlin to buy a hatt 04–04–00

22 December given him to give William Hamiltons woman in drink money 00–18–00

Said day to him to give James Clerk to give to the janitur – on hansell Munday .... 01–09–00 • 09 • 09 • –

The 20 off December 1666 to James Adamsone customer at the West Port for my small customs for a yeir to cum fra the 1 off January 1667 till the 1 off January 1668....29s. .... • 01 • 09 • –

22 December 1666 – to Alexander Leslie for wreating a discharge to Hermistoun –& ane other for Coits.. • 01 • 00 • –

25 December 1666 to Patrik Craig for half a boll off oats wes got fra him in December 1665 for our horse 01–06–08

25 December 1666 – more to him the said day 20 merks for 2 ½ bols off meill – my wyffe got fra him the 24 December 1666 at 8 merks the boll .... 13–06–08 • 14 • 13 • –

8 December to John Rob for 2 pirns 00–06–00

10 December to Nans Potter for giving Arche Clerk the pape –
a month 01–16–00
4 lb off small candle 00–16–00
2 pair off cunings at 2 tymes 01–10–06
For fresh beiff at severall tymes 02–07–00
For eygs – 9s. –& oynions 4s. is 13s. 00–13–00
26 December to David Clerk to pay for kill ale and mill ale .... 00–12–00 • 08 • 00 • 06

19 December to William Stewart to pay Robert[40] Cleghorne candle maker in – Dalkeith 48s. in exchange off 3 ston 4 lb off tallon tron wecht with candle .... • 02 • 08 • –

The 17 off December 1666 to David Clerk to pay – Thomas Robisone malt maker in the water off Leith – for making 18 bols off beer in malt
1– to himselff 08–00–00
2– to himselff for drink 01–04–00
3– to give his man in drink money 00–06–00
4– to our own men to drink who broght it to Neubiging .... 00–08–00 • 09 • 18 • –

• 204 • 05 • 06

For whyt breid in December – 1666 01–19–00
28 December to our heynd [sic] William Stewart for a syde off a young hudron 03–02–00

[40] The large space in which the name 'Robert' was inserted, and the noticeable difference in ink, suggests that Clerk, or his son, added it to this entry at a later date.

To him the said day for a firlot off small oats wes goten
For our horse 00–10–00
28 December to Lize Clark for some small disbursments .... 01–16–00 • 07 • 07 • –
The end off December – 1666; The disbursments in December 1666 .. • 211 • 12 • 06

The disbursments in anno 1666 is wreatten ilk months
disbursments on the other syde all amonting to the –
soume off .... 2581–03–03d –

[44]
The disbursments in the yeir off God ~~~ 1666;

January	1666	• 74 • 08 • 00
February	...	• 171 • 07 • 10
Marche	...	• 186 • 07 • 05
Aprill	...	• 426 • 06 • 08
May	...	• 185 • 08 • 10
June	...	• 427 • 11 • –
Jully	...	• 226 • 00 • –
Agust	...	• 065 • 17 • 10
September	...	• 132 • 16 • –
October	...	• 44 • 18 • 08
November	...	• 428 • 07 • 10

lib. s. d.	December ...	• 211 • 12 • 06
2581– 03 – 03		

The haill disbursments in anno 1666................ •2581 • 03 • 03

John: Clerk

[45]

Januar 1667

The disbursments in January – 1667

4 Januar to John Taits dochter – 9–18s. for 4 ston– 15 lb 4 once yrne at 40s. the stone....................		• 09 • 18 • –
4 Januar to John Clerk – 45s. to give to James Allens man for 3 parchements – old wreats relateing to the lands off Pennycooke....................	02–05–00	
12 ell off whyt worsiting at 6d. the ell....................	00–06–00	
4 lb off candle for my chamber....................	00–09–00	
To my wyffe to give David Boyds nourice....................	01–10–00	
To John Cooke locksmith in the Canegate 15 lib. 10s. on his discharge in full off all accompts preseiding the – 5 off January 1667....................	15–10–00	
To William Seatoun tailyeur – on his discharge in full off all accompts preseiding the 10 off January 1667 – 7 lib. 17s	07–17–00	• 27 • 17 • –
To John Hamiltoun for a mutchkin and a gill of brande....................	00–06–04	
To William Hamiltoun – for 4 once off jus de reglis at 32d. the once....................	00–08–00	

To John Donaldsone for carying out a letter to send out – my mourning
cloths 00–08–00
For 5 pair off gloves for the bairns 02–04–00
17 ell off grein florat rubens cost in all 02–08–00
For leaff tobaco .... 00–06–08 • 06 • 01 • –

The 11 off January 1667 to David Boyd for –
3 ell off skarlet bais at 58s. the ell 08–14–00
2 ¼ ell lute string taffatie at 5 lib. the ell – blak .... 11–05–00 • 19 • 19 • –

11 January to John Johnstoun chapman – who dwels at the toun end
off Drumfreis for – 25 ell off secking cloth at 7s. the ell 08–15–00
To William Chanceller for 4 ell off harden at – 5s. the ell .... 01–00–00 • 09 • 15 • –

7 January to my wyffe to give Jean Gray for ane old dornick –
table cloth 05–16–00
To John Clerk to buy a pair off blak hose for John Elleis mourning 02–08–00
To my wyffe when shoe wes in Edinburgh – 5 January 1667 .... 09–06–00 • 17 • 10 • –

The 9 off January 1667 to William Hamiltoun merchant for John &
James Clerks boord – ilk ane off them for 3 month to cum to wit John
Clerks fra the 1 off February 1667 to – the 1 off May 1667– and James
Clerks fra the 24 off January 1667 to the – 24 off Aprill 1667 peyit him
100 merks for them – ilk ane off them 3 month .... • 66 • 13 • 04

Fyne bed plaids boght fra Isobell Seaton

The 11 off January 1667 to Isobell Seatoun spous to Richard Smith
messinger for ~~
10 ell ....
9 ½ ell .... is 19 ½ ell off strypit bed plaids at 15s. the ell 14–12–06

	Entry		Amount	Total
	21 ell off braid strypit bed plaids at 22s. the ell		23–02–00	• 37 • 14 • –
	31 December 1666 to James Fergus tailyeur –			
	1– given him 12s. to buy some things for David Clerks cloths		00–12–00	
	2– given him to tak a pynt ale and a loaffe		00–03–00	
	3– given him to pay Adam Patersone for 2 botls off stroe and halff a peck off oats for the 2 horse		00–06–00	• 01 • 01 • –
	196–08–04~: all above			• 196 • 08 • 04
	The 15 January to Patrik Craig for 4 bols off meill at 4 lib. 16s. the boll			• 19 • 04 • –
	Hansell ~:			
1	To my brothers man Adam Livingstoun	01–04–00		
2	To John Donaldsone Adam Livingstouns man	00–03–04	01–07–04	
3	To Alexander Simpsons woman	00–13–04d.	00–13–04	
4	To John Rob 6s. 8d.		00–06–08	
5	To Margaret Douglas – Robert Douglas dochter		00–04–00	• 02 • 11 • 04
1	To David Clerk		00–18–00	
2	To John Clerk – 12s.		00–12–00	
3	To Archebald Craig		00–09–00	
4	To John Dicksone		00–09–00	
5	To litle James Simpsone		00–06–00	• 02 • 14 • –
1	To our hynd William Stewarts sone & dochter		00–05–00	
2	To George Reid 6s. to Helen Reid 4s. is		00–10–00	
3	To Mr William Hamiltouns man halff a swams dolor		00–18–00	
4	To John Broun bedel in Pennycooke		00–12–00	
5	To John Broun schoolemaster – 1 pair off blak worsit stokings cost		01–16–00	

	Item	Amount	Total
6	To Nans Turnbull 1 thick dams – 36s. peice and a pair off whyt wosted [sic] stokings cost 18s. is	02–14–00	• 06 • 15 • –
	Thir 3 last articles		• 12 • 00 • 04
	15 January rent to Walter Hamiltouns wyffe – 48s. with John Rob for a ham – pertaind to the Lady Bagillo		• 02 • 08 • –
	The disbursments in January 1667 on this syde is		• 229 • 13 • 04

[46]

	Item	Amount	Total
	The disbursments on the other syde in January 1667 is		• 229 • 13 • 04
1	To John Clerk a rex dolor	02–18–00	
2	15 January sent him with John Rob 1 new 3 lib. peice	03–00–00	• 05 • 18 • –
3	To James Clerk 1 new halff croun peice		• 01 • 10 • –
1	To Marie Clerk – 1 fyne Bible bound in incarnit Maroquin	07–00–00	
2	1 pair off gloves cost	00–16–00	
3	1 dams – 36s. peice	01–16–00	• 09 • 12 • –
1	To Margaret Clerk 1 fyne Bible bound in incarnit Maroquin	07–00–00	
2	1 pair off gloves cost	00–16–00	
3	1 dams – 36s. peice	01–16–00	• 09 • 12 • –
1	To Elizabeth Clerk 1 fyne Bible bound in incarnit Maroquin	07–00–00	
2	1 pair off gloves cost	00–16–00	
3	1 new halff croun peice	01–10–00	
4	1 litle gold chain weying – 9 drop wecht at 40 lib. the once	22–10–00	• 31 • 16 • 00
1	To Agnes Clerk 1 painted box with drawers	02–00–00	

2 1 pair off gloves	00–06–00	
3 1 new halff dolor	01–09–00	• 03 • 15 • –
To Marie Douglas – ane ort off a rex dolor		• 00 • 14 • 06
Thir last – 7 – articles is		• 62 • 17 • 06
8 January to John Clerk to buy 1 pair off blak stokings for Jo: Elleis buriel	02–8–00	
To him to get – 1 ½ lb of candle for his chamber	00–7–00	
4 Januar – to William Glower for charging Neutoun Ker with horneing	00–9–00	• 03 • 04 • –
295–14–10 – All the disbursments – in Januar till this last article is		• 295 • 14 • 10
My dar [sic] & weell beloved dochter Elizabeth Clerk – departit out off this vail off miserie on Sunday the 27 off January 1667 to hir eternall rest at six off the clok at night		
To Jame Sandelands – for making hir kist – 1 dolor		• 02 • 18 • –
To Robert Dewar smith for ~~		
1– 6 handles – 2 at everie syde – 1 at the head and ane at the fit	01–16–00	
2– 18 nooke bands at 2s. the peice	01–16–00	
3– 7 skore and ten headit nails for the nooke bands	00–08–04	
4– 14 skrew nails	01–08–00	• 05 • 08 • 04
28 January – to Mr Robert Alisone minister at Glencorse for the – len off a velvit mort cloth – 30s. – to his man 6s. is		• 01 • 16 • –

Item	Amount	Total
To John Broun for making the graph		• 01 • 09 • –
		• 11 • 11 • 04
28 January 1667 – to Patrik Craig in the Towr for – 10 ½ pynts of brande at – 20s. the pynt – Robert Douglas helpit him to buy it		• 10 • 10 • –
1– turkie fowll	02–14–00	
1– bak sey off beiff	00–18–00	
2– pair off cunings	01–08–00	
6 great loafs	01–02–00	
18 rols	00–12–00	• 06 • 14 • –
To a chapman for a ridle and some stringing –& worsting	00–15–02	
To [a]ne other chaipman for – 13 ell off whyt worsiting	00–06–06	
22 January to Edouart Adamsone for a lyg off mouton & 2 lb off butter	01–14–00	
18 January to Jo: Rob 18s. to give Helen [blank] to buy oyll for fyning	01–04–00	
25 January– to Sande Haistie for a bee skaip & mending 2 rushies	00–14–00	• 04 • 13 • 08
For – 2 cuning –& 2 douzane oynions	01–12–00	
To Arche Gib 12s. to drink – for cuming out to brew	00–12–00	
To Mage Wade for a soums – sive	00–03–00	
31 January – to David Clerk – 12s. when he went to mak 48 new – harrow teeth –& to mend 72 old teith [sic] for 6 harrows – is 120 in all	00–12–00	
To George Reid for going ane erand	00–03–00	
For whyt breid in the month off January 1667	01–08–00	• 04 • 00 • –

295–14–10			
11–11–04	The end off January	The disbursments in January	
17–04–00	1667	1667	• 333 • 03 • 10
04–13–08			
04–00–00			
333–03–10:			

[47]

Februar 1667

The disbursments in February 1667 ~~~

Till AB: sould have been placed in the month off January 1667 – bot it is all on[e] thing and a matter indiferent ~ ~ ~		
23 January 1667 for a barkit horse hyde	03–14–00	
For a barkit cows hyde gray and curried	07–08–00	
For halff a barkit cows hyde curried	02–08–00	• 13 • 10 • –
4 once off whyt suger candie	00–10–00	
1 pound off raisings	00–10–00	
8 once off suger – breid	00–12–00	
1 pound off plume dames	00–06–00	
For corne & stroe to divers horse when my weell beloved Elizabeth Clerk wes sick which went to Edinburgh at divers tyms	01–02–00	
3 douzane off tobaco pyps	00–04–06	
2 lb off tobaco	01–04–00	• 04 • 08 • 06
AB; all above		• 17 • 18 • 06

1 Februar to Tom Rob for mending shoone 00–04–00
To Lady Johnstoun – 6s. to William Steuarts wyffe for a lb of
butter 4s. 00–10–00
2 February to a webster in Braidwood for weiving plaiding 01–04–00
4 February – to Nans Potter for a mure fowll – 6s. to Gilbert
Ellots man who broght some drogs fra Newhall 6s. is 00–12–00
9 February – 1 peck off salt 00–04–00
To Alexander Hastie for 2 bee skaips & mending some baskits 00–18–00
To Agnes Clerk to pay eygs wes got fra severall persons .... 00–19–04 • 04 • 11 • 04
11 February to William Stewart for halff a syde off beiff 04–16–00
11 February to James Ramsays wyffe for 35 spyndle off small whyt
worsit – at 5s. the spyndle 06–15–00
9 February to Jo: Pennycooke maltman for a boll off malt 05–00–00
6 February to William Steill for 88 laid off cols at 5s. the laid he
rebated the 8 laid is – 2 laid to the skore – so I peyit him 80 laid –
at 5s. the laid is 20–00–00
+ The 11 off February – to our hynd William Stewart to give Robert
Cleghorne candlemaker in Dalkeith for 6: ston off candle at a dolor
the ston is .... 17–00–00 • 53 • 11 • 00
12 Februar to James Blak for – 21 thraive of beir strae at 4s. the
thraive 04–04
1 stouk off oat stroe to be brechins .... 00–04 .... • 04 • 08 • –
The 13 off February 1667 to Mr William Hamiltoun minister at Penycooke [sic] –
322 lib. as a yeir stipend for my lands lying within the paroish of Penycooke

and that fra Mertimes 1665 till Mertimes 1666 and off 4 lib. for his grasse fra Mertimes 1665 till Mertimes 1666 – is both 326 lib. which is includit in on[e] discharge date the 13 of February 1667		• 326 • 00 • –
406–8–10 –: Thomas Mein ~ ~ all above		• 406 • 08 • 10
The 22 off February 1667 to Thomas Mein for 6 ½ bols off seid oats wes got fra him in Marche 1666 at 5 lib. the boll	32–10–00	
To him the said day for 10 bols off oats wes got fra him in Februar 1667 at 3 lib. 16s. the boll is 38 lib. – 7 bols therof for John Reid his yeirs boll fra Mertimes 1666 till Mertimes 1667 –& 3 bols theroff for our hynd William Stewart – in part of his boll fra Witsonday 1666 till Witsonday 1667	38–00–00	• 70 • 10 • –
26 Februar to James Hamilton chapman in Lesmahego ~ 5 ell of lining at 9s. the ell – 45s. – worsit prins & other small things – 13s. is	02–18–00	
4 ell of lining at 25s. the ell	05–00–00	
2 ½ ell off lining at 17s. the ell	02–02–06	• 10 • 00 • 06
22 Februar to Thomas Rob – for making shoone – 15 days with his dyet at 6s. ilk day – 4 lib. 10s. – 6 pair of timber heils – 6s. – is in all	04–16–00	
To Mage Wade for a peck of salt	00–04–00	
To Alexander Hastie for a caisse to hold ane urinel	00–03–04	
To a couper in Lintoun for girding severall tubs	00–06–08	
19 Februar to Walter Hamiltoun for a lb of tobaco he boght for me	01–04–00	
To Adam Patersone for horse charges severall tyms– 16s. for spindls 2s. 6d.	00–18–06	

To George Irving for – 15 ½ ell off harden at 5s. the ell 03–17–06
For eygs 00–03–00
For fresh beiff at severall tyms 03–10–00
For whyt breid in the month off February .... 01–14–00 • 16 • 17 • –
28 February 1667 to Archbald Craig for a litle cow wes got fra him –
the 19 of November 1666 to slay 15–00–00
The said day to him – 20 merks for Archebald Clerks boord or –
nourishing fra the 8 off December 1666 to the 8 off Marche 1667 .... 13–06–08 • 28 • 06 • 08
The end of February 1667 The disbursments in Februar 1667 ...... • 532 • 03 • –

[48]
Marche The disbursments in Marche 1667 –
1667 7 Marche to William Stewart to get a boll of salt at Prestoun pans 04–01–04
8 Marche to Adam Livingstoun when he broght out a lyg
of Berwick vaill [sic] .... 00–18–00 • 04 • 19 • 04
Disbursments at Edinburgh begun the on Munday the – 11 off Marche
1667 ~[41]
+ The 11 of Marche to James Lishman cordoner for 1 pair of shoone
for Ja: Clerk 01–04–00
1 pair of gloves for a woman – 10s. 00–10–00
To Abraham Clerk for turning some – 1 buttons for drawers of a
cabinet 00–12–00
2 once of suger candie 00–06–00

	2 pound of plume dames	00–12–00	
	8 drop off – Doctor Andersons pills in a box	01–13–04	• 04 • 17 • 04
	The 11 off Marche 1667 to David Scot apothecarie – in full of ane accompt of all things on his discharge preseiding the said 11 of Marche 1667	18–00–00	
	The 15 of the said month of Marche to David Scot in full of acompt on his discharge	01–16–00	• 19 • 16 • –
	The 12 off Marche 1667 to John Gray of Crichie in full of ane accompt on his discharge		
	1– 21 ell of spranged bed plaids at 30s. the ell	31–10–00	
	2– 17 ell of whyt serge at 30s. the ell	25–10–00	• 57 • 00 • –
Newhall 81-14 +	The 12 off Marche 1667 to Edowart Cleghorne goldsmith for 12 silver – spoons weying 23 onces 14 drop – at 3 lib. 6s. the once which I gave to Alexander Pennycooke of Newhall the said day –& got Mr Cleghorns discharge theroff at the fit of the compt theroff	78–16–00	
	The said day to Newhals man in drink money	02–18–00	• 81 • 14 • –
	1 pound off raisings	00–12–00	
	1 pound off fygs	00–10–00	
	4 once of suger candie	00–10–00	
	To James Stewart for – 8 once of manna at 9s. the once	03–12–00	• 05 • 04 • –
	15 Marche to Robert Broun for Craig *de Feoudis* in folio unbound	04–00–00	
	To John Gedis for binding the same in gray leather	01–01–00	

41 Clerk made a mistake here when writing ‘the on Munday the …’.

To him binding 2 books for the bairns in gray leather
Smiths *Sermons* .... 00–12–00 • 05 • 13 • –

15 Marche 1667 to Alexander Leslie for wreating –
1 Disposition & assignation to John Byrs of Coits his band of 5000 lib. 02–13–04
2 For ane assignation to Forwood Ley & Whytbanks band of 1800 lib. principall 00–12–00
3 To William Russel in drink money .... 01–04–00 • 04 • 09 • 04

16 Marche to George Boswell webster for weiving – 12 ell of strypit hingins for a skring at – 12s. the ell – 7 lib. 4s. and 12s. for changeing 5 lib. of sad – cullort worsit with light cullors is in all – 13s. sterling is 7–16s. .... • 07 • 16 • –
4 once off leaf tobaco .... • 00 • 06 • –

The 15 of Marche to John Clerk in full of ane accompt he disbursit for me;
1– he said he peyit to David Boyds wyffe for a mourning hatband for himsel 02–13–04
2– The 2 of February he peyit out for the blew gray horse 00–03–00
3– 16 douzane off braid whyt threid buttons 00–16–00
4– For a string to the silver mounter I lent him 00–10–00
5– For mending his shoone – 6s. 00–06–00
6– 1 pound of hasting peis 00–06–00
7– 15 February – 1 lb raisings –& 1 pound of plum dames 00–15–00
8– 1 pound of candle 00–04–06
9– 1 printed Act of the *Convention of Stats* holden in Januar 1667 .... 00–06–00 • 05 • 19 • 10

A..soma off all above is		• 197 • 14 • 10
The 22 of Marche 1667 to James Blak in Pennycooke for 8 bols off oats – 2 pecks lesse with the stroe at – 5–6s.–8d. the boll is 42 lib. – 1 plough 1 couter and a sock – 5 lib. 10s. – is in all – 47 lib. 10s. – whairof rebated the said day – for 15 hens he wes oweing my wyffe – at 6s. the peece is 4 lib. 10s. – so I peyit him the said – 22 off Marche 1667 – 43 lib. in full off all I wes oweing him..		• 43 • 00 • –
Munday – 11 Marche to my wyffe when I went to Edinburgh...........	03–00–00	
20 Marche to Helen Fergusone when shoe went away........................	02–00–00	
To a chapman for peirling & 2 pair off gloves....................................	00–18–00	
Munday the 11 off Marche to Adame Patersone for a grysse	00–12–00	
3 pair off doves	00–15–00	
At divers tymes given to the bairns to pay for eygs & some other things...	00–15–00	• 08 • 00 • –
30 off Marche to a woman in Clarkingtoun for 32 ell off grein lining at 11s. the ell		• 17 • 12 • –
For beiff in Marche 1667 – fresh beiff – 6–11s.		• 06 • 11 • –
For whyt breid in Marche 1667		• 02 • 07 • –
30 Marche for gairden seids according to the accompt which George Reid & Arche Gib helpit him to buy		• 02 • 15 • –
		• 29 • 07 • –

The end off Marche 1667

The disbursments in Marche 1667......	• 278 • 01 • 10

[49]

Aprill 1667 The disbursments in Aprill 1667 ~~~

2 Aprill to my wyffe to give a websters wyffe in Braidwood for weiving
31 ell off cloth – 6 quarter braid to be courtins .... • 03 • 00 • –

+ 4 Aprill – to David Clerk 16s. 8d. to pay 10 pynts off ale David Clerk
got to wit – 5 pynts for plowers – 4 pynts for drying malt– 1 pynt Sande
gave him – 10 in all .... • 00 • 16 • 08

5 Aprill – when I went to my Lady Lothians buriell to Newbatle
1– to Mr Ro: Prestons gairner 00–06–00
2– to Hawthorndens quariers 00–09–00
3– to Sir John Nicolsons meassons 01–09–00
4– to Sir John Nicolsons gairner 00–12–00
5– spent at Neubatle – 36s. .... 01–16–00 • 04 • 12 • –

Wedensday– 10 Aprill to Doctor Cuninghame when he cam out to sie
my wyffe when shoe had the feaver [sic] – 12 dolors 34–16–00
+ To his man a dolor .... 02–18–00 • 37 • 14 • –

On Fryday 12 Aprill – to Doctor Cuninghame the second visit he made
to sie my wyffe when shoe had the feaver – 5 dolors 14–10–00
To his man the said day – halff a dolor .... 01–09–00 • 15 • 19 • –

Munday 15 Aprill to Walter Hamiltouns wyffe which shoe disbursit –
1. for a chopin off clairet wyne 00–12–00
2. for a pound off plum dames 00–06–00
3. for a powny hen off the Lady Bagillos .... 02–00–00 • 02 • 18 • –

The 15 off Aprill 1667 to John Carbraith webster in Leswaid –

1. for weiving – 20 ell off beir corne at 6s. the ell 06–00–00
2. for weiving – 25 ell off lining at 4s. the ell .... 05–00–00 • 11 • 00 • –
Formerlie my wyffe peyit him a dolor –& on the 15 off Aprill 1667 –
I peyit him 8 lib. 2s. – is both – 11 lib. ....

5 mutchkins off whyt wine 01–10–00
For: stroe – horse corne –& Arche Craigs expenssis severall tyms fra
the 8 off Aprill to the 16 of April 02–04–00
16 Aprill – to Marie Clerk to give Mage Alexander – 18s. –& 3s. to mak
up David Clerks – 24s. at my wyffs desyre is .... 01–01–00 • 04 • 15 • –

A..... + On Teusday the 16 off Aprill to Doctor Cuninghame when he made
the third visit to sie my wyffe – 10 dolors 29–00–00
To his man the said day 1 dolor .... 02–18–00 • 31 • 18 • –

For severall horse hyre & horse meat dureing my wyffs sicknes.......... 06–16–00
4 lb off plums dames 01–04–00
2 ell 3 quarters off stenting...........for blak cloths 01–06–00
some small charges – it cost – J: C 01–01–00
1 pynt off whyt wyne 01–04–00
1 chopin off seck .... 01–04–00 • 12 • 15 • –

6 quarters off lowe for a mourning hatt band at 3 lib. the ell 04–10–00
1 peice off whyt satyne rubens..........3d. braid 08–08–00
1 once off blak silk... 01–04–00
1 long taild button for James Clerks clok 00–05–06
6 ell off Holland for the winding sheet at 4 lib. the ell 24–00–00
1 pair off blak worsit stokings for my selff 02–08–00

Fryday the 19 off Aprill to Edowart Moss Inglish man – for the len off a horse with – 4 horse covert with mourning– 36s. sterlin –& 8d. – more given him; for carying the corps fra Newbiging to Pennycooke

Item	Amount	Total
is	22–00–00	
5 pound off tobaco	03–12–00	
5 douzane off pyps	00–08–00	• 66 • 15 • 06
1 drop off olium – rodium	00–09–00	
For the gray horse charges	00–05–00	
1 pound off currents – 12s.	00–12–00	
1 blak hatt for James Clerk	01–14–00	• 03 • 00 • –
5 douzane off rolls	02–00–00	
6 grot loaffs	01–02–00	
For a lamb	03–00–00	
2 lygs off veill – 3 lib.	03–00–00	
4: bak seys off beiff	08–14–00	
4 turkie fowls	11–00–00	• 28 • 16 • –
To John Broun bedel for making the graffe	02–18–00	
To Archebald Teinder for his service the day off the buriell	04–07–00	
To James Sandelands for making the kist	05–16–00	
For the len of a mort cloth – 30s. to the ministers man of Glencorse 6s.	01–16–00	• 14 • 17 • –
To James Blaikie for himselff & his sone a day	00–10–00	
20 Aprill to Mary Clerk to pay a pair off shoone	01–16–00	
22 Aprill to Helen Patersone for a barell off ale	02–02–08	

23 Aprill to the good wyffe of Silver burne for 1 barel off ale .... 02–02–08 • 06 • 11 • 04

The disbursments above in – Aprill 1667 is .... • 255 • 07 • 06

[50]

Aprill 1667

The disbursments in Aprill 1667 on the other syde is .... • 255 • 07 • 06

On Thursday the – 18 off Aprill 1667 – to Patrik Craig in the Towr – 31 lib. 4s. to – bring the wyne eftermentioned out off Leith– which he did acording to the accompt thairoff which Archebald Campbel in the sope [sic] warke sent me which compt I have lying by me markit ~~~ A B ~~~

1 11 pynts and a chopin off seck at 38s. the pynt 21–17–00

2 11 pynts & a chopin off clairet wyne at – 17s. the pynt .... 09–70–00 • 31 • 04 • –

To Robert Dewer smith in Pennycooke for yrne wark to the kist ~~~

1 8 handles at 8s. the peice 03–04–00

2 24 nooke bands at 2s. the peice 02–08–00

3 16 vyce nails at – 2s. the peice... 01–12–00

4 124 shorne headit nails to put on the nooke bands .... 00–10–00 • 07 • 14 • –

My dear & weell beloved wyffe desyrd me on hir death bed to give what is eftermentioned to severall young on[e]s in the paroish – who wes hir god dochters & desyrd to tell them I mean thair parents to enter them to the schoole ther with –

1 To William Thomsone in Pennycooke for his dochter Mary Thomson 02–18–00

2 To William Clerk in Pennycooke for his dochter Mary Clerk............ 02–18–00

3 To Patrik Craigs dochter in the Towr – Marie Craig 02–18–00
4 To Edouart Adamsons dochter in Silver burne for Mary Adamsone.... 05–16–00 • 14 • 10 • –
The which 5 dolors I delivert to all thair parents within 3 or 4 days ~~
efter the death off my dear & weell beloved wyffe:

The 17 off April 1667 to Robert Hamiltoun younger merchant in Edinburgh –
for 10 ell off blak London cloth at 9 lib. 14s. the ell to be my selff a cot
–& to be John Clerk – a mourning sute & a syde blak mourning clok –
255–07–06 acording to the accompt & his discharge theron – dated the 24 off
31–04–00 Aprill 1667 97–00–00
07–14–00 The 17 off Aprill 1667 to William Lorimer merchant for 4 ½ ell off
14–10–00 blak Yorkshyre cloth to be James Clerk – a mourning sute & clok
122–10–00 at 5–13s. 4d. the ell – according to his accompt & discharge theron –
431–05–06 date the 24.....off Aprill – 1667 .... 25–10–00 • 122 • 10 • –

431–05–06 All above.......... • 431 • 05 • 06

Thursday the 11 of Aprill 1667 – my wyffe gave to 3 off hir childring
to wit –
1 To John Clerk – 1 ring with a rond [sic] diamant cut in fasset cost
120 livres.. • 120 • 00 • –
2 To Mary Clerk – 1 ring with on[e] round diamant cut in fasset – cost
180 livres.. • 180 • 00 • –
3 To Margaret Clerk – 1 ring with on[e] round diamant cut in fasset cost
120 livres.. • 120 • 00 • –
To Marie Clerk 1 litle gold chein – worth 24 lib. Scots........................ • 24 • 00 • –

444–00–0 • 444 • 00 • –

The 24 off Aprill 1667 – I gave the 3 peices of gold under wreatten to John Marie and Margaret Clerks –& desyrd them to esteeme them as iff thair mother had given them – the same – when shoe gave them the 3 rings – which I know shoe wold have done if shoe had rememberit.

1. to John Clerk – a new mild 20s. peice off gold worth 13–00–00
2. to Mary Clerk – a new mild 20s. peice off gold worth.................. 13–00–00
3. to Margaret Clerk – a double ducat with 2 heads on it worth .... 11–00–00 • 37 • 00 • –

And on the said 11 off Aprill 1667 – shoe gave to 2 off hir childring to wit –

444–00–00 1. to James Clerk – a peice of gold coynd be Queen Elizabeth for –
37–00–00 20 merks bot it is a fare wechtie on[e] and is worth at present 15
30–00–00 lib. Scots 15–00–00
511–00–00 2. to Agnes Clerk – a fare peice of gold coynd be King James for ~~~~
20 merks bot it weys 14 gram wecht more nor any other of that
& is worth at present – 15 lib. Scots .... 15–00–00 • 30 • 00 • –

The tokens shoe gave to these five hir childring above mentioned amonts to .... • 511 • 00 •

On Saturday – 27 Aprill – 27 Aprill 1667 – sent with John Rob – seald in a peper to be given to my brother John Andersone which he disbursit for me as follows ~~~~

1 2 ell off blak dutch serge to be 2 pair off hose for my selff at
3 lib. 2s. the ell 06–04–00
2 1 once off blak shewing silk 01–06–08
3 1 once off sad minim shewing silk 01–06–08
4 4 once off blak threid... 00–08–00 • 09 • 05 • 04

Thursday – 25 Aprill – I gave James Fergus money to buy what is under wreatten –

	1	2 pound off balling – at 36s. the pound	03–12–00	
	2	4 ell off stenting at 8s. 6d. the ell	01–14–00	
	3	1 ell off bukrim	00–13–04	
	4	1 weir off blak clasps & eyes for the bairns cloths	00–02–08	
	5	2 once off blak threid	00–03–04	
	6	6 ell off blak worseting for the bairns cot tails	00–04–00	
431–05–06	7	To himselff to get his brak fast	00–03–00	• 06 • 12 • 04
511–00–00	1	To our hynd William Stewart for a syde off a young beast	04–00–00	
09–05–04	2	To him the said day to give to James Marshall – 50s. – for working 10		
06–12–04		days at the fald dyks – 5s. the day with – 2 mails off meit ilk day	02–10–00	
08–13–04	3	1 pynt & halff a mutchkin off whyt wyne	01–07–00	
966–16–06	4	More for horse charges in Aprill 1667	00–16–04	• 08 • 13 • 04
		The disbursments on the other syde and this in Aprill 1667 – is – 966–16–6d.		• 966 • 16 • 06

[51]

April 1667

A memor off some tokens my wyffe gave to hir freinds and desyrd me to give to them – upon Thursday the 11 off Aprill 1667 – which wes the 8th day off hir sicknes – shoe tooke hir sicknes on Thursday the 4th off Aprill 1667 – on which day shoe went to the Towr off Pennycooke – with hir sister Isobell Gray – to see hir youngest sone Archebald –

Clerk: efterward shoe told me shoe fand hirselff very unweell – the said day –: and on Wedensday morning the – 17 off Aprill 1667 – neer 3 off the clok in the morneing – it pleased the almightie God to call hir out off this vale off miserie to hir eternall rest – The Lord hath given –& the Lord hath taken – blessed be the name off the Lord for ever –

I say heer follows the tokens shoe gave to such off hir freinds as wes besdyde hir – and desyrd me to give to some wes absent at Neubiging – Thursday the 11 off April – 1667 ....

1 Shoe gave to hir sister Isobell Gray Walter Hamiltouns wyffe – a double gold souverain worth – 24 lib. Scots 24–00–00

2 Shoe gave to hir sister Isobell Gray to be given be hir to hir howsband Walter Hamiltoun – ane other double souverain off the same worth & wecht – worth 24 lib. .... 24–00–00 • 48 • 00 • –

3 The said day shoe gave to hir sister Helen Gray – a peice off gold with 3 XXX on it off King James the 6 – his coyn: f: coynd for 30s. sterlin – bot it is worth – 20 lib. Scots –& I gave no lesse for it at London in anno– 1650 .... • 20 • 00 • –

4 The said day shoe gave to hir niece Mary Dowglas ~~~
1– a peice off gold worth – 4 lib. 10s. with a rose on it 04–10–00
2– a new French gold croun worth– 5– 10s. .... 05–10–00 • 10 • 00 • –

5 On Teusday at night the 16 off Aprill 1667 which wes the day befor hir death – hir sister Katherin cam out off Duns the said day to sie hir – and at hir desyre I gave to my dochter Marie Clerk – a gold double

souverain worth – 40s. sterlin – the which my dochter gave to the said
Katherin Gray – my wyffs sister the said day.. • 24 • 00 • –

6 And on the said Teusday the – 16 off Aprill 1667 – at my wyffs desyre
I gave to my dochter Mary Clerk – a gold double souverain – worth 24 lib.
Scots – which according to hir mothers desyre shoe gave the said day –
to my wyffs niece Jean Gray dochter to the master off Gray .... • 24 • 00 • –

7 At my wyffs desyre befor hir death ———|| on Fryday the 19 off Aprill
48–00–00 1667 which wes the day on which my wyffe wes buried – efter the buriell
20–00–00 Mr William Gray minister at Duns cam up to Neubiging – and I gave to
10–00–00 my dochter Mary Clerk – which shoe gave to the said Mr William Gray
24–00–00 the said day – a double gold souverain worth 40s. sterlin – and be him to
24–00–00 be given to his wyffe Anna A: Gray – as a small token fra my well
24–00–00 beloved wyffe.. • 24 • 00 • –

32–00–00 The 29 off May 1667 – delivert to John Clerk to give to the parties under
182–00–00 wreatten – which his mother did desyre to give to to [sic] the pairties underwreatten
333–06–08 which he did accordinglie ....

515–06–08 1. to hir brother Mr Alexander Gray 1 – 20s. peice coynd at Oxford
42–10–00 anno 1644.. 13–00–00
557–16–08 2. to Rachel Gray Mr Androw Gray dochter – 2 Hungers[42]
ducats worth 09–00–00
3. to hir sister – Geils Gray – 1 litle Louis worth 5–10:
ane ane other peice off King James the first worth –
4 lib. 10s. is both .... 10–00–00 • 32 • 00 • –

My dear & weell beloved wyffe on hir death bed desyrd me to give as a token fra hir to hir sister Margret Gray the Lady Bagillo – fyve hundreth merks Scots and on the 10 off June 1667 I wreat to hir to cum to Newbiging. The copie off my letter to hir is on the booke whair I wreat the copies of letters. I wreat to divers persons on Teusday at night the 18 off June shoe cam to Newbiging – and on Wedensday the 19 off the said month off June 1667 – at Newbiging befor my twa dochters Mary & Margaret Clerks I did pay and delyver to the said Margaret Gray my dear & weell beloved wyffs sister fyve hundreth merks Scots in these peices under mentioned to wit –

1– 114 rex dolors at 58s. the peice is 330–12–00

2– in Inglish money – 4s. 6d. and 14 turnors 002–14–08

Is fyve hundreth marks Scots inde .... 333–06–8d • 333 • 06 • 08

At Newbiging Wedensday the 19 off June 1667

John: Clerk ....

Newhall 13 Agust 1667 to William Law goldsmith – for a silver salt weying – 12 onces

42–10 and a halff – at 3 lib. 8s. the once is 42 lib. 10s. which I gave to Alexander Pennycooke off Newhall for cuming out 3 tymes with Doctor Cuninghame to visit my dear & weell beloved wyffe the tyme off hir sicknes – who dyed the 17 off Aprill 1667 .... • 42 • 10 • –

557–16–8 This syde amonts to .... • 557 • 16 • 08

[42] Hungarian ducat.

[52][43]

Aprill 1667

The 3 off October 1667 – acording to the desyre off my dear & weell beloved wyffe – I delivert to Isobel Gray relict off umquhill Walter Hamiltoun merchant in Edinburgh – six dolors – to be given to Charles Gray – sone to the deceist master off Gray –& be him to be given to his regent for teaching him – a yeir at the colledge .... • 17 • 08 • –

~~On Teusday morning 22 off October – 1667 Archbald Gib – began to wirk at the heydging and planting betwixt the gairners — housse and the corne yard – and went away on Saturday the 9 off November is – 16 days he wroght for which I gave him – 2 dolors with his meat........ 05–16–00~~

~~To Patrik Dryburgh – for wirking 11 days the said hedging .... 03–10–00~~

~~For 6 quarts off ale I gave them when they wer wirking........ 01–00–00~~

~~For by the help off Alexander Falcon– Alexander Hastie – Willie Clerk –& John Reid & our own men – dureing the doeing off the same .... • 10 • 00 • –~~

~~This sould not have been wreatten heir – I wreat it over agane the month of November~~

The charges peyit out anent the confirmation off my dear & weell beloved bedfellow Mary Gray hir testament dative who – dyed upon the 17 day off Aprill 1667 ....

The 3 off January 1668 to Mr James Deans for presenting a charge off horneing to the commissers for obteining a continouation off a charge off horning till the 10 of February 1668........ • 01 • 09 • –

To the clerk that wreat the continouation on the bill .... • 00 • 12 • –

To the clerk for minuting the desyre off the bill with the deliverance theroff – and for continowing [sic] the same till the 18 off Februar

		1668 – 12s. and 6s. is 18s.		• 00 • 18 • –
		12 February 1668 to comisser Falconers man		• 01 • 09 • –
		The said day to Robert Stark for wreating the act off cautionrie		• 01 • 09 • –
		To James Deans procurator – for his pains in the bussyness	08–14–00	
		To his sone Mr James Deans– a dolor	02–18–00	• 11 • 12 • –
				• 17 • 09 • –
		The 20 off February 1668 disbursit all in on[e] soume to John Smart as follows		
	1	For the edict execution &c	02–18–00	
	2	To commissers for sealling	20–00–00	
	3	For the clerk	21–06–08	
	4	For the fiscall	13–06–08	
	5	To the bishop for the cotta	46–00–00	
	6	Registration	05–16–00	
	7	Messinger & box	01–04–00	
	8	To the lad for doubling	00–12–06	
	9	To John Smart for his pains	02–01–00	
	10	To the fiscall deput	05–16–00	
		Soma	119–00–04	
17–09–00		Which – 119 lib. 4d. I delivert to John Smart all in on[e] soume in James		
119–00–04		Deans chamber on the 20 day off February 1668		• 119 • 00 • 04
136–09–04		*John: Clerk*......		

[43] Despite the month of April being identified in the margins of this page, Clerk's entries are out of sequence. He returns to April on the next page.

The charges off the confirmation off my wyffs testament as is
above mentioned amonts to 136–9–4d. .... • 136 • 09 • 04

John: Clerk.......

17–08–0
136–09–4
153–17–4

This syde amounts to........................ • 153 • 17 • 04

[53]

Aprill 1667

Thir accompts under mentioned with money that I gave John Clerk he – peyit the same – they wer resting when my dear & well beloved bed fellow dyed which wes on Wedensday morning the the [sic] 17 off Aprill 1667 – neer 3 off the clok in the morneing ....

1 The 6 off May 1667 to David Scot apothecar – 44–11–8 in full off ane accompt on his discharge off the said date on the accompt and all other accompts whatsoever preseiding the said – 6 off May 1667 .... • 44 • 11 • 08

2 To Thomas Airth merchant the 7 off May 1667 – 23 lib. for 23 pynts off brande wyne at 20s. the pynt on his discharge date the said 7 off May 1667 .... • 23 • 00 • –

3 To Robert Miller webster in the West Bow the 8 off May 1667 – in full off ane accompt & all other accompts – on his discharge – at the fit theroff date the 8 off May 1667 .... • 05 • 18 • –

4 The 8 off May 1667 to George Broun litster in the Cowgate – 11–18s. in full off all accompts – on his discharge at the fit theroff date the said 8 off May 1667.. • 11 • 18 • –

5 The 6 off May 1667 to John Androw cutler for –
1– 2 penknyffe blaids & 2 silver virols.. 01–04–00
2– 1 blaid for a gray fish skin handle with silver virols...................... 00–07–00
3– for dichting – 3 new lancets – 1 old lancet – 1 straight bistorie ane crooked bistorie – 1 pair off litle sheirs– 1 penknyffe.................... 01–02–00 • 02 • 14 • –

6 The 10 off May 1667 to Isobell Fermer – naill wyffe in full off ane accompt on hir discharge at the fitt theroff and all other accompts preseing the 10 off May 1667.. • 32 • 10 • –

All above on this syde is............... • 120 • 11 • 08

The 15 May 1667– to Robert: 00000 all above ...... ~~~~~

The 17 off May 1667 to Thomas Andersone – 1 dolor with his meat for 13 working days in helping to mak 2 gouns off blak Scots stuff for Mary & Margaret Clerk & the bairns coits – is a grot in the day with his meat –& 6 pence more 02–18–00
The said day to James Blaikie for 7 wark days & his meat in helping to mak the bairns mourning at 4s. a day given him................ 01–09–00 • 04 • 07 • –

Four accompts which John Clerk peyit in Edinburgh – Teusday the 21 off May 1667...................for severall things for the bairns murning [sic] –
1– to Isobell Gray relict off Walter Hamiltoun in full off ane accompt on her discharge 54–00–00

2– to David Hume litster in the Canegate 14–4–6 in full off ane accompt
on his discharge 14–04–06
3– to Lilias Campbell – in full of ane accompt on hir discharge 12–12–00
4– to Mistresse Grhame in full off ane accompt on hir discharge 10–13–00
All thir 4 discharges wes date the 21 off May 1667 .... • 91 • 09 • 06

Accompt of small disbursments John Clerk disbursit in Edinburgh
1– to David Hume for dying 1 pair off silk hose blak 00–18–00
2– to him for dying John Clerks gray clok blak 01–16–00
3– to Adam Livingstoun for dying my fathers blak rouch hatt.......... 00–06–00
4– 2 onces off leaff tobaco 00–04–00
5– to John Fergusone for 2 pair off shoone for my father 04–04–00
6– to Mr Mill for mending a silver mounter I lent to Jo: Clerk 02–00–00
7– to John Fergusone for a pair of blak mourning shoone for
Jo: Clerk 02–00–00
8– to David Boyds wyffe for 1 ½ ell off lowe for myselff at 3 lib.
the ell.. 04–10–00
9– to Thomas Abernethie for making a velvit cap for Jo: Clerk......... 00–10–00
10– for 4 douzane off blak buttons – for a jupe for Jo: Clerk 01–00–00
11– for 1 douzane off small blak buttons– for the said jupe................. 00–02–00
12– to Jo: Dows wyffe for 3 ½ ell off hemp cloth to be Jo: Clerk
drawers at 12s. the ell 00–02–00
13– to Wrights Housses man & Adam Patersone for the gray horse 2
severall days.. 00–12–00

14– for his dinner in John Dows – 2 severall days and some other small expenssis – in all – 25s. 01–05–00

20–11–00: Thir last small disbursments – 20–11s. ..... • 20 • 11 • –

The 13 off June 1667 to David Boyd in full off an accompt on his discharge date
1 the 13 off June 1667 – 36–5s.–4d. for severall things wes goten in Aprill 1667 for Marie & Margaret Clerks mourning.................... 36–05–04

2 The 13 off June 1667 – to Alexander Mackie tailyeur on his discharge off the said date 12–13s.–8d. – for making & furnishing Marie Clerk hir mourneing goun 12–13–08

3 The 13 off June 1667 to John Tailyeur – tailyeur – on his discharge off the said date – 12 lib. 15s. for making & furnishing to Margaret Clerk hir mourneing goun 12–15–00

4 The 14 off June 1667 to William Seatoun tailyeur in full off ane accompt on his discharge off the said date – 16–18–6 for making & furnishing to Jo: Clerk his mourneing cloths 16–18–06

36–5–4
12–13–8
12–15–0
16–18–6
78–12–6

Thir 4 last compts is .... • 78 • 12 • 06

The disbursments in Aprill on this syde is .... • 315 • 11 • 08

[54]

April 1667 To James Blaikie and his sone for working 2 days with thair meet....... • 00 • 16 • –

To Mary Dowglas – 40d. to pay Wille Steuarts wyffe – 2 douzane off eyges – 40d. to pay George Bell a quart ale –& 40d. to give Pyper Johnstoun is .... • 00 • 10 • –

More for horse charges in Aprill 1667 .... • 00 • 16 • 04

24 Aprill 1667 given Mary Clerk to pay ....

1: to Wille Stewart for a syde off veill........ 04–00–00

2: to pay 5 douzane off eygs 00–08–04

3: to give John Reids wyffe for a hen........ 00–07–00 • 04 • 15 • 04

06–17–08 29 Aprill 1667 to William Steill for 31 laid off cols bot he rebated .... • 06 • 17 • 08

07–00–00 3 laid – rests 28 laid at 5s. the laid is – 7 lib. in which is includit 2 laid

22–19–04 which cam the said day .... • 07 • 00 • –

36–17–00 29 Aprill – to John Ramsay for 38 mure fowls at 6s. the peice............ 11–08–00

22–13–04 For whyt breid in the month of Aprill 1667........ 02–09–04

35–00–00 For beiff and w: lamb in the month of Aprill 1667........ 09–02–00 • 22 • 19 • 04

94–10–04 The disbursments above in Aprill 1667 is .... • 36 • 17 • –

22 Aprill 1667 to William Thomsone in Pennycooke –

1– for a boll off peys wes sawn in Pennycooke 04–00–00

2– for 4 bolls of oats wes sawn in Pennycooke at 4–13s.–4d. the boll .... 18–13–04 • 22 • 13 • 04

The 19 off June 1667 – John Clerk peyit to Robert Hamiltoun for 3 ell off blak cloth to be me a short mourning clok at 11 lib. 13s. 4d. the ell –

35 lib. on his discharge at the fit off the accompt date the said 19 off June 1667 .... • 35 • 0 • –

The disbursments in Aprill 1667 on this syde above mentioned is........ • 94 • 10 • 04

The haill disbursments in the month off Aprill 1667 – on the 17 day off the said month off Aprill 1667 my – dear and weell beloved bedfellow dyed at Newbiging – in the said month off Aprill 1667 is also comprehendit – the charges off the confirmation off my dear & weell beloved bedfellows testament ....

1: the disbursments on the first syde in Aprill 1667	• 255 • 07 • 06
2: syde	• 966 • 16 • 06
3: syde	• 557 • 16 • 08
4: syde	• 153 • 17 • 04
5: syde	• 315 • 11 • 08
6: syde	• 094 • 10 • 04
	lib. s. d.
The haill disbursments in Aprill 1667 is – 2344–00–00	•2344 • 00 • 00

John: Clerk

The first and second syde is both onlie	• 966 • 16 • 10
The 3 syde is	• 557 • 16 • 08
The 4 syde is	• 153 • 17 • 04
The 5 syde is	• 315 • 11 • 08
The 6 syde is	• 094 • 10 • 04

The haill disbursments in Aprill 1667 is
2088–12–10.. •2088 • 12 • 10

John: Clerk

[55]

May 1667 The disbursments in May – 1667 ~~~~

The 6 off May 1667 to Robert Dunepaisse for –

1– 3 ell off lining at – 16s. the ell........................ 02–08–00
2– 2 ell – 3 quarters off lining at 10s. the ell.................. 01–07–06
3– 7 ell off lining at – 13s. the ell........................ 04–11–00
4– 3 ell off peirling for the bairns at 4 s. the ell................ 00–12–00
5– 7 blak laces for the bairns cots at – 1s. the peice............ 00–07–00
6– 1 once off whyt threid .... 00–06–06 • 09 • 12 • –

Munday the – 6 off May 1667 – peyit to Thomas Mein which wes sawn
+ in Pennycooke this yeir in oat seid tyme 12 bols off oats gotten at 3
severall tymes at – 4 lib. 13s. 4d. the boll.......................... • 56 • 00 • –

9 May – to John Davisone couper – for 35 girds at – 8d. the peice...... • 01 • 04 • 04

10 May to Jennet Meurs in Hurlie 8 lib. for 2 bols off oats for our
horse.. • 08 • 00 • –

The 13 off May 1667 to George Peacoke in Libertin –

1– for 2 bols of peis we got which grew in Pennycooke in the corne gate –
roume for our horse – on[e] boll off them we got fra his man James Blak –
in Februar 1666 – and the other boll we got fra the said James Blak

.9 – 12 – 0 the 19 off Aprill 1666 – is 2 bols at 4 lib. the boll........................ 08–00–00
56– 00 – 0 2– more to him the said day for – 78 rude off fald dyks he bigit on the
.1 – 04 – 4 feild land belonging to the cornegate roume at 2s. the rude – 16–7–16s. –
.8 – 00 – 0 the said roume fell in our own hand at Mertimes 1666 – so we behoved
.5 – 16 – 0 to pay him– the said fald dyks becaus the said roume fell in our own –
.5 – 16 – 0 hand & the said George Pecoke [sic] did quyt it at Mertimes 1666 –
.5 – .2 – 6 the said George Peacoke mairied Effie Simson relict of umquhll –
0 – 12 – 0 Alexander Etkin – who laboured & possest the said roume off the – –
102 – 2 – 10 corne gate formerlie the said 78 rude off fald dyks at – –
2s. the rude is – 7 lib. 16s. .... 07–16–00 • 15 • 16 • –

Munday the 13 off May 1667 to John [blank] servitor to Sir Robert –
+ Sinclair – 2 dolors when his master cam out the said day to give me
advysse anent my bussynes – which he did gratis –& wold tak no
money at all .... • 05 • 16 • –

The 15 off May 1667 to Robert Dewer smith in Pennycooke ~~
1: for a boll off oats 04–10–00
2: for 2 pecks off beir.. 00–12–06
which compleits his boll fra Witsonday 1666 – till Witsonday
1667 .... • 05 • 02 • 06

The said day to him – 12s. – for laying the plough yrnes that laboured
the corne gate roume in Pennycooke fra Mertimes 1666 till Witsonday
1667 .... • 00 • 12 • –

102 – 02 – 10: The debursments above in May 1667 is .... • 102 • 02 • 10

The 18 off May – 1667 to James Sandelands for a large Scots pistol stokit
with yrne – 7 lib. 10s. with 5 plaits off silver on the ratch theroff – he wes
oweing me – 3 lib. 10s. for a litle fir kist he got fra me – off thick sawn dails
with neuk bands on it – with a lock & key – the said day I gave him 4 lib.
which made 7 libs. 10s. for the said pistol.. 07–10–00
The 29 May 1667 peyit to David Clerk – 26 lib. 12s. in full off all things –
for 9 months service to wit fra Lammes 1666 till Witsonday 1667
as apears on a booke covert with parchement whairin servants fies ar[e] –
wreatten on co: markit on the bak –: 347 on the 1 page theroff .... 26–12–00 • 34 • 02 • –

8 May to John Rob........for 2 voyages extreordinar to Edinburgh....... 00–12–00
11 May to Nans Potter for swingling hards 00–06–00
To Wille Clark for 5 chikens [sic] 08–00–00
4 douzane off eygs.. 06–06–00
1 quart off ale at the Towr...................................... 03–04–00.......... 00–17–10
18 May for trouts – 3s. 4d. to the workmen 4 pynts off ale when they
mendit the sled gate to Hurlie & Bruntstaine is 00–10–00
21 May – to John Reid when he went for some plants & herbs 01–01–04
21 May – to David Clerk 3 pynts off ale – 5s. to give the millers for
drying 12 bols off oats laiking [sic] a firlot– which is to be ground
presentlie 00–05–00
To Arche Craig – 12s. – when he went in for Sir: Ro: Sinclair with 2
horse & 3s. for the horse when he went in for Jean Pillens 00–15–00

Thir last small disbursments is .... 04–11–02 • 04 • 11 • 02

102 – 2 – 10	For fresh beiff and a syde off a lambe in the month off May	10–17–06	
34 – 2 – 0	For whyt breid in the month off May	01–03–08	• 12 • 01 • 02
. 4 – 11 – 2	The end off May –1667; The disbursments in May 1667		• 152 • 17 • 02
11 –01 – 2:			
152 –17 – 2			

[56]

June ~ The disbursments in June – 1667 ~~~~~~~~;

1667 At Neubiging Wedensday the 29 off May 1667 – to John Lowrie at the mill of Pennycooke – 3 lib. 6s. 8d. to pay – James Blak for muck he boght fra him for my usse to lay – on the beir land in a roume off Pennycooke callit the corn gate 03–06–08

To James Fergus tailyeur for his fie fra Witsonday 1666 till Witsonday 1667 for all 36 lib. 36–00–00

This I peyit to him the 1 off June 1667...

The 1 off June 1667 to Mage Alexander byre woman for hir fie fra ~~Wit~~ Mertimes 1666 till Witsonday 1667 .... 08–10–00 • 47 • 06 • 08

The 1 off June 1667 – to Nans Turnbull – for half a yeirs fie fra Mertimes 1666 till Witsonday 1667 – 1 – in money 12 lib. – 30s. to buy hir shoone – 01–10 – and 20s. I gave hir more nor condition is in all – 14–10 .... 14 –10–00

The 31 off May 1667 to Alexander Simpsone – 12 lib. for my chamber mail fra Mertimes 1666 till Witsonday 1667 – on his discharge date – 31 May 1667 .... 12–00–00 • 26 • 10 • –

The 1 off June 1667 to Hew Macculloch – 83–12–06d. Scots as 3 months cesse for – January – February & Marche 1667 – imposed be the convention off estats in January 1667 on his discharge date the said – 1 off June 1667 .... • 83 • 12 • 06

3 June 1667 – John: Clerk disbursit at Edinburgh ~~~ ~~~ ~~~:
1– a pound off ginger 00–08–00
2– 1 pynt off vinaigre 00–13–04
3– 1 a pound off stiffing 00–06–00
4– his expensis in the toun .... 00–18–00 • 02 • 05 • 04

As appears on a booke covert with parchement market on the bak – 347– whair servants fies is wreatten on the 10 page theroff – it apears that on the 4 off June 1667 I peyit to James Simsone in Bruntstaine – as much money –
+ as made James Simpsone sone to umquhill John Simpsone in Westaine – 7 lib. 14s. for a yeirs fie for being – hird fra Witsonday 1666 till Witsonday 1667 .... • 07 • 14 • –

As appears on a booke covert with parchement market on the bak 347 on the 18 page theroff – peyit to John Dicksone – hird – a yeir and a half yeirs fie fra Mertimes 1665 till Witsonday 1667 in fie and all that he can clame [sic] or crave preseiding Witsonday 1667 – 18 lib. 1s. which compleited him – 24 lib. 1s. as a yeir and a halffs – fie fra Mertimes 1665 till Witsonday 1667 .... • 24 • 01 • –

The 6 off June 1667 to John Lowrie at the mill off Pennycooke –
47–06–8: 1 The 18 off Aprill 1667 we got 1 boll of barle to sawe at Neubiging 05–06–08
26–10–0: 2 For a making off malt made in Marche 1667 02–18–00
83–12–6: 3 For a making off malt made the 6 June 1667 .... 02–18–00 • 11 • 02 • 08

02–05–4: The 14 off June 1667 to Alexander Ogilvie ane off the collector deputs
07–14–0: off a taxation grantit to his Majestie in Agust 1665 – 55–2–2d. as the
24–01–0: second terms taxt off the personage off Pennycooke fra Witsonday 1666
11–02–8: till Witsonday – 1667 on his discharge date – the 14 off June 1667 John
55–02–2: Clerk peyit this be my order .... • 55 • 02 • 02
24–00–0: The 13 off June 1667 to Mr Thomas Baird advocat on[e] off the shireff
281–14–4 deputs in Edinburgh – 24 lib. Scots – as the second terms payment off
a taxation – imposd be the convention off estats in Agust 1665 for my
twelve pound lands of Pennycooke – Cookeing and the Halls – and that
fra Witsonday 1666 till Witsonday 1667 – on his discharge date the –
13 off June 1667 – John Clerk – peyit this be my order...................... • 24 • 00 • –

all above on this syde is .... • 281 • 14 • 04

11 June 1667 John Clerk disbursit at Edinburg for the particullars underwreatten –

1. for the gray horse charges 00–04–00
2. for a pair off whyt 4 threid hose for my self 03–03–00
3. to Mr Thomas Baird for a charge of horneing he sent me 01–10–00
4. for 12 catechisms & 2 proverbs for the bairns.............................. 00–09–00

06–09–0. 5. for 1 pound off great raisings.. 00–11–00

23–10–6. 6. for some small expensis for himselff – – 12s. .... 00–12–00 • 06 • 09 • –

02–18–0. more he disbursit at Edinburgh the said day for

03–07–6. 1– for a barkit horse hyde 02–10–00

09–14–6. 2– for a gray curried & barkit cows hyde 07–00–00

45–19–6. 3– for halff a blak cows hyde curried... 02–10–00

281–14–4. 4– for halff ane Irish hyde – off bend soll leather 10–11–06

327–13–10. 5– for a pound off steill hemp 00–15–00

6– for a pound off ruset .... 00–04–00 • 23 • 10 • 06

On Wedensday the 19 off June 1667 – given to Sarah Broun a rex dolor for 14 days – shoe stayd at our howsse shoe wes recommendit to our services be David Boyds wyffe bot shoe wes not pleasd to stay any longer & so went away .... • 02 • 18 • –

Given to Margaret Clerk which shoe disbursit 03–07–06

1 for eygs 01–04–02

2– copres & gals some lit 00–10–04

3– pound off butter 00–09–00

4– to Helen Patersone at 2 tymes 00–09–00

5– to David Clerk – 3s. 4d. to Margaret Hopkirk to give the millers ~~~
5s. to the good wyffe off the mill for ale – 6s. 8– is in all – 15s. ~~~
they got when they grand the 16 bols of oats wes got fra W: houses .... 00–15–00 • 03 • 07 • 06

Munday 24 June William Stewart boght in Carnwath fair which cost ~~

1– 4 corne sleds cost – 3 lib. 11s. .... 03–11–00 • 16

2– 3 fir teathers .... 00–05–00 • 03 • 00 • –[44]

3– for his charges– & 2 horse .... • 00 • 07 • –

20 June John Clerk peyit to Isobell Fermer – 5–11–6 – in full of ane accompt for blind nails on hir discharge at the fit off the compt off the said date .... • 05 • 11 • 06

• 09 • 14 • 06

The disbursments above in June 1667 is.................................... • 327 • 13 • 10

[57]

The disbursments on the other syde in June 1667 is – 327–13–10 .... • 327 • 13 • 10

John Clerk disbursit at Edinburgh the 19 off June 1667 ~ ~

1– for a girdle 02–12–00

2– for half a pound off leaff tobaco 00–08–00

3– to David Hume for dying a pair off hose for my self blak 00–06–00

4– for horse charges – 6s. & 2d. with James Adamsone..................... 00–08–00 • 03 • 14 • –

The 29 June 1667 to Helen Patersone for 2 small tennor bow saws –16s.
&– ane long yrne driller – 4s. – is 20s. –& 4s. 10d. for ale & breid wes
oweing – for the bairns – is in all – 24s.–10d. 01–04–10

4 ell of small lining at – 18s. the ell 03–12–00

1– spyndle off whyt whiling – worset .... 02–00–00 • 06 • 16 • 10

29 June 1667 Jo– Clerk disbursit at Edinburgh ~ ~

327–13–10 1– for twa half barels of herings........... cost – 8 lib. 08–00–00

.3–14– 0 2– ane achtindaill off soap .... 5–10.......................... 05–10–00

.6–16–10 3– for bringing bak Jack – 3s. – corne to him – 2s. – for carying the

14–19– 0 sope & hering to John Lowries...6s. – for the gray naig – 2s. –

.8–11– 0 with Merchestoun – 12s. – for carying thair coffers –& books –

361–14– 8 to William Hamiltons – new housse – 4s. is in all.....29s. .... 01–09–00 • 14 • 19 • –

[44] It is clear Clerk made a mistake when entering this sum and sought to correct it by adding the 16 shillings directly above.

1– for fresh beiff 02–04–00
2– 1 milk laiglen.......... 00–12–00
3– 15 June to John Rob for 1 quart off oyll for wooll.......... 01–12–00
4– 1 pair off cards for cairding woll.......... 01–04–00
5– 15 June to John Broun for 10 hanks of virginel strings.......... 00–10–00
6– 3 June to James Peirie for drink money – in making 8 bols off malt 9s.
7– to David Clerk to tak off a making off malt – 3s.– 4d. – to dry 16 bols off oats – 3 pynts off ale – 5s. is 00–08–04
8– to Mage Blak – & Tom Kede for weiding the gairden......8s.– 4d. for Jacks expensse when he tooke in Nans Trumble – 3s. 4d. is 00–11–08
9– for whyt breid in the month off June.......... 01–09–00 • 08 • 11 • –

The end off June 1667 The disbursments in June 1667.......... • 361 • 14 • 08

Jully – 1667 The disbursments in Jully 1667..........

Teusday 16 Jully 1667

1– to William Thomson gairner at Craigmiller.......... 00–12–00
2– to David Sheils gairner at Bruntstaine.......... 00–12–00
3– to Alexander French gairner at Pinkie 00–12–00
4– spent other ways the said day 01–04–00
5– to Wallace for a whyt hand creill .... 00–04–00 • 03 • 04 • –

The 19 off Jully 1667 to William Simpsone in Easter Ravensneuk – 27 lib. which – he disbursit in anno 1665 & peyit to Charles Campbel and Androw Blaikie millers for biging the dweling howsse off Easter Ravensneuk fra the foundation – and for timbering the vault............ • 27 • 00 • –

John Clerk disbursit be my order at Edinburgh the 10 off Jully 1667 as follows –

1 A pair of whyt 4 threid stockings for my self 03–00–00

2 A pair off whyt 4 threid stokings for himself .... 03–00–00[45]

3 To William Hamiltoun to compleit James Clerks boord fra the – 24 of Aprill – 1667 to the 13 off Jully 1667 that he returnt to Newbiging..... 18–10–05

4 For a last for my own fit – 9s. 00–09–00

5 He peyit to William Hamiltoun to compleit his own boord to the 1 off May 1667.. 04–00–00

6 1 suger loaffe weying – 3 lb 4 once off suger at 16s. 6d. the pound 02–13–06

7 To William Hamiltoun – 6s. for a beir glasse James Clerk brak 00–06–00

8 To Arche Gib 2s. with William Hamiltoun 4s.–6d. horse meat 8s. with Merchistoun – 15s. – to a woman for weiving a pair off strong stokings for John Clerk to weir in the contrie – 14s. to on[e] for carying a letter to Silver burne – 2s. to William Hamiltouns woman in drink money – 12s. is in all....... 02–17–06 • 34 • 16 • 05

Fryday 5 Jully – sent with John Rob seald in a peper – 7– 6–8d. to be delivert to Mistress Jean Gray for 11 ell off round he: lining at a merk the ell.. 07–06–08

45 While there have been other examples earlier in the accounts, this line and the one immediately preceding illustrate well Clerk's idiosyncratic spelling. In particular, using the words 'of' and 'off' interchangeably and spelling the word 'stocking' with and without the letter 'c'.

The 27 Jully to John Rob for what is under wreatten which he boght –
1– pound off steill hemp.................................... 15s.
2– 6 pair off timber heill....................................6s. 01–07–00
3– 2 pair off jumps ....6s.
For fresh herings – 2 tyms....................................9s. .... 00–09–00 • 09 • 02 • –

The 23 off Jully 1667 – John Clerk be my order peyit to John Cooke locksmith – 4 lib. 8s. in full off ane accompt on his discharge at the fit theroff and all uther accompts preseiding the said 23 Jully 1667 – & 4s. for the gray horse .... • 04 • 12 • –

The 29 Jully 1667 – to Charles Maitland merchant in full off ane accompt on his discharge off the said date for whyt lead – horne & box wood combs – 9 lib. is .... • 09 • 01 • –

3–04–0. Whyt breid in the month off Jully 1667.. • 01 • 04 • –
27–00–0. The end off Jully 1667 The disbursments in Jully 1667......... • 88 • 19 • 05

34–16–5.
9–. 2–0.
4–12–0.
9–. 1–0.
1–. 4–0.
88–19–4[46]

[58]

Agust 1667 The disbursments in Agust 1667...

On Munday 29 off Jully John Clerk disbursit at Edinburgh –
1: for 2 boxes off lamb blek... 00–06–00

2– 2 gray bonets for the bairns	00–14–00		
3– for himselff and the horse a night	00–18–00	•	01 • 18 • –
To James Austin for mending sives & ridles	00–05–06		
+ 2 Agust – David Clerk boght at Edinburg – 3 bols of meill at 4 lib. 5s. 4d. the boll – is 12–16	12–16–00		
6 hooks at 5s. the peice..........1–10s. – charges allowed him – 3s.	01–13–00	•	14 • 14 • 06
Fryday the 2 off Agust Cristian Ramsay in Braidwood wes mairied – John Clerk James Clerk; Marie & Margaret Clerks given every ane – off them – 16s. to pay thair lawing – at the said brydel........is		•	03 • 04 • –
The 3 off Agust 1667 to Thomas Rob – for making shoone 19 ½ days – at 6s. in the day – with his meat is		•	05 • 17 • –
The 10 of Agust 1667 to John Stinsone waker in Edinburgh – in full of ane accompt – 23 lib. 6s. on his discharge off the said date		•	23 • 06 • –
The 10 off Agust 1667 to Thomas Sandelands on his discharge – 28 lib. 16s. for 48 dails at 12s. the peice	28–16–00		
100 fresh herings	01–00–00		
2 douzan off ram horne spoons	00–16–00		
1– coll ridle	00–05–00		
2 new hooks	00–07–00	•	31 • 04 • –
7 Agust Jo: Clerk disbursit at Edinburgh –			
1– 2 ell off blak cloth to be a sute of cloths for my selff at 8 lib.–14s. the ell	17–08–00		

[46] Clerk's sum in the margin does not match with the sum at the end of the page. The third entry in the margin, '34–16–5', makes obvious Clerk's error.

1–18–0. 2– 1 ½ once off blak and sad cullort silk at 24s. the once 01–16–00
14–14–6. 3– 8 douzane off blak breist buttons 01–00–00
3–04–0. 4– 8 once off leaff tobaco 00–08–00
5–17–0. 5– his own expense 20s. – for the horse 6s. .... 01–06–00 • 21 • 18 • –
23–06–0. 12 Agust to John Tait for yrne in full off ane accompt 13–03–00
31–04–0. 14 Agust to Hew Macculloch for 3 months cesse – Aprill. May. June.
21–18–0. 1667 on his discharge off the said date 83–12–08
202–15–0. 14 Agust to John Gray off Crichie in full off ane accompt on his
7–03–0. discharge date the said 14 off Agust 1667 83–09–04
8–03–2. 1 whyt yrne box – painted with blak & whyt 01–00–00
320–02–8. 6 fadome off tows 00–10–00
For peirs for the bairns 01–00–00
96–00–0. 14 Agust to Sir John Smith – 20 lib. to mak up a yeirs interest of a band
12–15–8. off – 7000 lib. the interest – 4 yeir being – 1680 lib. this – 20 lib. made
48–00–0. it up 1700 lib. for which – 1700 lib. he ane his 2 sons gave me their band
111–10–2. payable at Candlemes 1668 interest frie – this 1680 lib. wes the interest off
1–10–6. a band off 7000 lib. fra Candlemes 1663 till Candlemes 1667 .... 20– 00–00 • 202 • 15 • –
269–16–4. 17 Agust to John Dows wyffe for 2 French wyne pomshons 02–18–00
21 Agust 2 whyt wand baskits 02–00–00
2 peper off prins 00–08–00
1 whyt yrne baskit 00–09–00
1– whyt lame dish 00–08–00
1– brush to wash the walls 00–08–00
16 pincels .... 00–12–00 • 07 • 03 • –

For registrating Blacadars discharge off 400 lib. Scots – 2 extracts 03–06–08
320–02–8. 22 Agust to John Gray in Leith for 1000 taks 01–09–00
269–16–4. 5 fadom off tows for rigwides 00–15–00
589–19–0. 5 fadom off great tows for rigwides 01–04–00
2 barels off lamb blaik 00–02–00
11 ½ once off tailyeurs threid .... 00–16–06 • 08 • 03 • 2

The 15 off Agust 1667 to Thomas Sandelands wright 8 lib. sterlin – which I delivert to him in my brothers chamber to pay for 40 firgeists – which he boght fra my Lord Lithgow for my usse to be geists to the new – housse at the great outter gate – I tooke no discharge nor recept off him for – this 8 lib. sterlin – thir 40 geists at 48s. Scots the peice is .... • 96 • 00 • –

To John Gedes for binding a litle booke in 12° 00–15–01
24 Agust to Margaret Clerk for small disbursments about the housse 03–08–08
28 Agust 1 rubber with a fir handle for washing fleurs 01–00–00
1 barel off lamb bleck 00–06–00
28 Agust to Robert Weir for 2 tin chopin stoups –& 1 tin pynt stoup in full off his accompt .... 07–16–00 • 12 • 15 • 8

The 26 of Agust 1667 peyit to Mr Robert Alisone minister at Glencorse 48 lib. as my proportion off his stipend for the lands off Cooking fra Witsonday 1666 till Witsonday 1667 on his discharge date – the 2 off Jully 1667 .... • 48 • 00 • –

31 Agust 1667 to Hew Macculloch collector – 111–10–2d. for 4 months cesse – to wit Jully. Agust. September 1667 and October

1667 on his discharge date the 31 off Agust 1667 for my lands in
Pennycooke & Glencorse paroishes.. • 111 • 10 • 2
For whyt breid in Agust 1667.. • 01 • 10 • 6
The end off Agust 1667: The disbursments in Agust: 1667........ • 589 • 19 • –

[59]

September 1667

The disbursments in September – 1667 ~~~~

On Wedensday – 4 September to William Stewart 20 lib. 10s. which he peyit – four [sic] a broun ox he boght in Skirling fare for the plough off – 5 yeir old – and a grot for William Stewart to drink is............... 20–14–00

6 September to John Rob which he peyit to Thomas Waterstoun in Leith – for 23 pynts off brande – at 20s. the pynt – is 23 lib. I have Thomas Waterstouns recept of the same.. 23–00–00 • 43 • 14 • –

1 peice off fresh beiff 00–06–06
2 cunings.. 00–09–06
For carets 00–02–00
To a couper for girding looms.. 01–17–06
For halff a hundreth herings .... 00–10–00 • 03 • 05 • 6

19 September disbursit at Edinburgh –

1– to George Still for making 4 stikit caps the calico my own........... 01–16–08
2– 1 pound off leaff tobaco 00–16–00
3– 1 draper – boght fra Sande Reuls wyffe.. 00–04–00
4– to Alexander Simpsons woman .... 00–13–04 • 03 • 10 • –

	+ 16 September for 6 firlots of salt – William Stewart boght at Prestoun –		
	pans cost – 4 lib. – 8d. off customs is	04–00–08	
	8 oxen bows William Stewart boght at Skirling fare cost – 2 merk &–		
	20d. for carying them to Newbiging is – 28s. 4d.	01–08–04	
43–14–0	18 September – William Stewart peyit for 3 bols off meill he boght		
03– .5–6	in Edinburgh mercat cost – 4–6–8d. the boll is..................................	13–00–00	
03–10–0	The said day a firlot off great salt he boght in Leith............................	02–00–00	
22– .6–0	Charges be William Stewart – 3s. 4d. – Mr Jo: Clerk for the horse –		
20–00–0	3s. – my selff off charges......................30s. 8d.	01–17–00	• 22 • 06 • –
01–10–0	26 September 1667 – to Androu Hepburn for weiving 24 ell of narow		
94– .5–6	cloth for the bairns sarks at 20d. the ell is	02–00–00	
	To Bessie Whyt in all – for a yeirs fie fra Mertimes 1666 till Mertimes		
	1667 – the 27 off September peyit to hir	15–00–00	
	To Margaret Clerk for severall small disbursments	03–00–00	• 20 • 00 • –
	For wheat bread in the month off September – 1– 10..........................		• 01 • 10 • –
	The end of September 1667; The disbursments in September 1667		• 94 • 05 • 06
October –	The disbursments in October 1667		
1667	1 October – to Isobel Grays nourish in drink money 1 dolor	02–18–00	
	Said day to hir woman in drink money..	01–09–00	
	6 douzane off oynions..	00–14–06	
	3 October to James Cockburne for a pynt of lintseid oyll..................	01–12–00	
	3 pound of candle for my chamber	00–13–06	
	To John Cooke for a litle bordert lock for a kist................................	01–04–00	

6 ½ douzane off peirs.............. 12s–
4 once off leaff tobaco............. 06s–
4 once of juss of reglis............. 06s– .... 01–04–00 • 09 • 15 • –

5 October 1667 – to Dame Geils Smith for 12 ell off teyking at 33s. 4d.
the ell.. • 20 • 00 • –

The 12 off October to James Ramsay for 12 ston – 3 lb of cheis at 30s.
the ston is.. 18–00–00
09–15–0. To him for 2 ston off wooll David Clerk got fra him at 4 lib. the
20–00–0. ston .... 08–00–00 • 26 • 00 • –

26–00–0. 10 October 1667 to William Steill in Newhall for 22 laid of cols 05–00–00
13–09–0. 15 October to Robert Dewer for 23 pynts off ale wes goten fra his wyffe
10–07–0. in harvest when the corne gate corn wes shorne in Pennycooke 01–18–08
79–11–0. 4 lb off small candle John Rob boght in Edinburgh 00–17–04
11 of October – to John Rob for his harvest fie in harvest 1667 –
1– in money for his fie – 4 lib. in money for his supper mail –
20s. is 05–00–00
8 October to Wille Steuart when he went for the tarr –& 7s. when –
he went to Dalkeith fare to sell – 5 beasts is – 13s. .... 00–13–00 • 13 • 09 • –

22 October – to James Frizel in the Carlips for girsing a meir staig wes –
sent to him the 15 off May 1667 – 40s. & 7s. 6d. for 1 peck of beir
is... 02–07–06
26 October for a spyndle off whyt twynd worsit............................. 02–04–00
26 October to William Thomsone in Pennycooke for 12 ½ ell off
hemp twidlt cloth at – 7s. the ell – is 04–07–06

For whyt breid in – the month off October .... 01–08–00 • 10 • 07 • –

The end off October 1667; The disbursments in October 1667 is .... • 79 • 11 • –

[60]

November 1667

The disbursments in November 1667 –

The 5 off November 1667 – to Jean Steuart for hir fie fra Witsonday – 1667 till Mertimes 1667.....5 lib. & 18s. to buy hir shoone is 05–18–00

The 11 off November to John Gray for his fie fra Witsonday 1667 til – Mertimes 1667 – 5 lib. and 9s. to buy his shoone is – 5– 9s. 05–09–00

The 6 off November – to John Reids wyffe for haws –& sloe thorns – & some holin seid shoe gathered.. 01–10–00

The 7 off November – to Alexander Falcons wyffe – 20s. for hir supper maill – in harvest 1667 01–00–00

The 9 off November to John Broun bedel for 6 broome busoms .... 00–03–00 • 14 • 00 • –

Archbald Gib:

Teusday morning – the 22 of October 1667 – Archbald Gib began to wirk at the hedging & planting betwixt the gairners housse & the corne yard and went away on Saturday the 9 off November – is 16 days he wroght at the said hedging for – which I gave him – 2 dolors with his meat is 05–16–00

To Patrik Dryburgh for wirking – 12 days at the said hedging 03–10–00

For 6 quarts off ale I gave them when they wer[e] wirking................ 01–00–00

For by the help off Alexander Falcon – Alexander Hastie – Wille Clerk ~~
John Reid and our own men .... • 10 • 06 • –

Will & Alex[r] Clerks — Munday the 11 off November 1667 being Mertimes day enter William & Alexander Clerk in boording in Mr William Hamiltouns minister in Pennycook and – peyit them for thair boord – 14 dolors is 40 lib. 12s. fra the 11 of November 1667 to the 11 off February 1668 is 20 lib. 6s. for ilk ane off them 40–12–00
To thair woman Mairion Blaiklaw in drink money 30s. .... 01–10–00 • 42 • 02 • –

2: — The 15 off November 1667 – to Jennet Shanks for 3 months fie fra Lames 1667 till Mertimes 1667 1 dolor and a halff..........is.......... 04–07–00

Sows libit ~~~~ — The 15 off November to Patrik Corstoun who dwels in Langhermistoun under Alexander Bethun 24s. for libing 2 sows .... 01–04–00 • 05 • 11 • –

disbursit at Edinburgh in November 1667 — A B

1 To Alexander Simpson – for my chamber maill fra Witsonday 1666 till wi [sic] Mertimes 1667 12 lib. on his discharge date the 21 November 1667 12–00–00

2 The 23 off November – to William Hamiltoun merchant for 3 months boord – for John Clerk fra the 23 off November 1667 to the 23 off February 1668 – 40 lib. 40–00–00

3 The 19 off November to Thomas Pringle in my own chamber for a barrell off tarr William Steuart our hynd I got fra him .... 16–18–00 • 68 • 18 • –

4 To William Reid for a timber wey balk 03–12–00

14–00–0 3 pair off wooll sheirs for cliping sheip at 12s. the pair 01–16–00

10–06–0 1 whyt yrne box with divisions .... 00–09–00 • 05 • 17 • –

42–02–0	To George Still for making a blew tabein caip	00–12–00	
5–11–0	To John Rob for – 2 pecks off pan cratch for the ovens	00–08–00	
68–18–0	To Abraham Clerk for a peice off Virginia wood 6s. & 2s.	00–08–00	
.5–17–0	To Mr Alexander Cameron for extracting my wyffs age	00–12–00	
.5– .6–8	20 November to my brother – Jo: Andersone to cause registrat a discharge –		
.7–18–0	for Jo: Byres off Coitts – being – 2 extracts	03–06–08	• 05 • 06 • 08
67– .8–6	To John Cooke for ane yrne box for Alexander Clerk	00–18–00	
227– .7–2	For 3 pair off bair[n]s – gloves	00–12–00	
4– .5–0	For a soll off leather to a shewd coishon	00–12–00	
231–12–2.	22 November to Alisone Troup for 12 ell of sprangd bed plaids at 10s. the ell – 00 – I say 12 ell some what braid sprangd – course thick plaids	05–16–00	• 07 • 18 • –
			A · B:

The accompt off 23 dolors being – 66–14s. which I delivert to Marie Clerk – The [blank] of October 1667 – when shoe went to hir ante [sic] Isobell Grays housse –

1	6 stone off butter at – 3 lib. 6s. the ston	• 19 • 16 • –
2	pair off shoone for hirselff at 35s. the pair is	• 03 • 10 • –
3	1 brasse pan weying – 5 pound at 18s. the pound	• 04 • 10 • –
4	9 ½ ell off harden to be James Clerk – 3 shirts at 10s. the ell	• 04 • 15 • –
5	1 ell and halff a quarter off Holland to be bands for John Clerk at – 4–6–8 the ell	• 04 • 17 • 06
6	1 ell off Holland to be James Clerk bands	• 03 • 00 • –
7	5 quarters off drogit – at 12s. the ell	• 00 • 15 • –

8 1 pound off ginger.. 00–07–00
9 For mater[i]als for litting 00–13–00
10 1 pair off gloves for hir selff 01–08–00
11 For threid and some small things... 00–08–00 • 02 • 16 • –
12 4 stone and a halff off lint at – 4–16s. 8d. the stone............................. 21–15–00 • 21 • 15 • –
13 – halff a pound off balling.. 00–16–00
14 – 2 ell off stenting... 00–18–00 • 01 • 14 • –

67– 8 – 6~~~~ Somma of hir disbursments........is ..... • 67 • 08 • 06

Accompt off charges spent at Morphit when Prestoun Grainge gave me –
5 or 6 skore ashes & elms for as good agane ~~~~
1: November 1667 when I went first to sie them to Alexander Mitchel
gairner 6s. more spent 12s. is 00–18–00
29 November when I got them to Alexander Mitchel gairner............ 01–04–00
For corne & stroe to our horse 00–11–08
For a gallon off ale.. 00–13–04
For meit to the gairner & uther men to William Braikenrigs royffe
for it .... 00–18–00 • 04 • 05 • –

231– 12 – 2 The disbursments in November 1667 on this syde is ...... • 231 • 12 • 02

[61]
The disbursments in November 1667 is – 231–12–2.......................... • 231 • 12 • –[47]

14 November to John Rob for – 4 lb off small candle 00–17–00
15 November to John Reid couper in Bigger – for 17 girds................ 00–14–00

		Entry	Amount	Total
		18 November for a horse hyre to James Adamsone when cam out –		
231–12–0.		to see the turnpyke head	00–18–00	
2–16–8.		25 November – to Thomas Andersone – when they went to the mill		
1– .9–0.		with 10 ½ bols off oats – to grind	00–03–04	
235–17–8.		28 November to Arche Craig – for Jacks meet [sic] when he went to the –		
		town for Anna Irving	00–04–00	• 02 • 16 • 08
		For whyt breid in the month off November – 1– 9s.		• 01 • 09 • –
		The end off November 1667 The disbursments in November 1667 ..		• 235 • 17 • 08
December		The disbursments in the month off December 1667		
1667		The 2 off December to Margaret Clerk for some small disbursments ..		• 03 • 00 • –
		Teusday 3 December 1667 I went to Edinburgh & disbursit as follows –		
	1	2 souters knyves for sneding treis	00–06–00	
	2	To John Geddes for binding *Mariana* in octava	00–09–00	
	3	The 5 off December to John Mein for a staff for Alexander Leslie	02–18–00	
	4	To him the said day for a staff for my selff	02–18–00	
	5	7 December for a Barbadas [sic] suger loaff weying – 14 lb weying –		
		13 lb 14 once at – 12s. the pound	08–06–08	
	6	– 1– quair off bleu peper	00–08–00	
	7	– 1 Falding knyffe and a stamp off brasse	00–09–00	• 15 • 14 • 08
		The 7 off December 1667 – accompt peyit to Isobell Gray off some things shoe disbursit for me – which compt I have lying by me ~~~		

[47] Clerk made an error in leaving out the 2 pence from the final sum.

1. for working 22 ell off stuffe at 5s. the ell 05–10–00
2. for sowing warping & drink money 00–15–00
3– 8 toungs at 5s. the peice 02–00–00
4– 21 ½ ell off bed plaids narrow sprangd at – 12s. 6d. the ell 13–08–09
5– 1 ell off rubens for – Mar[y] Cl[erk] shoes 00–05–00
6– 1 ½ ell off blak louping for a lace 00–04–00
7– for whale bon[e]– & boosts for Margaret Clerk .... 00–06–00 • 22 • 08 • 09

7 once off jusse off reglis 00–07–00
9 December to David Boyd in full off ane accompt on his discharge –
for cloth & furnishing to be a cot for James Clerk 07–01–00
4 ½ fadome off tows 00–07–06
1 lb off cut & dry – 8 once off leaffe tobaco 01–06–00
1– pair off wooll sheirs for cliping off sheip 00–12–00
10 December to William Reid for 3 suger loaffs weying – 7 lb
7 once at – 13s. the pound 04–17–06
For wreatting James Clerks indentor – 58s. to his man in drink money –
12s. is 03–10–00
To Thomas Wyllie for severall small things 02–04–00
To David Boyds nourish in drink money 02–18
To David Boyds servant woman in drink money .... 02–18 .... 05–16–00 • 26 • 01 • 04

To Mr – John: Clerk

17 December 1667 delivert to John Clerk
1– off drink money to give William Hamiltouns woman 01–04–00
2– off drink money to give William Hamiltons[48] nourish 01–16–00
3– to him to give the meassers 02–18–00

4– to pay for 4 pound off candle 00–18–00

5– to him to pay for 2 laid off cols.. 01–04–00

6– to him to drink with the meassers .... 00–16–00 • 08 • 16 • –

2 lb off raisings for the bairns .... 14s.~~

03–00–0 For r: chasnuts –& walnuts for them .... 12s.~~ 01–06–00

15–14–8 18 December to William Deans my brothers man in drink money 00–13–04

22–. 8–9 18 December – to Alexander Simpsons woman in drink money 00–13–04

26–. 1–4 1 miroir in a blak frame.. 5 lib.–

08–16–0 1 lesser miroir in a blak frame.................................. 4 lib.–.............. 09–00–00 • 11 • 02 • 08

11–12–8 The 27 off December – I say the – 23 off December 1667 to Margaret

87–13–5 Hopkirk for hir fie fra – Witsonday 1666 till Mertimes 1667 is –

6–. 2–6 1 ½ yeir ....

93: 15 – 11 1– in money for 1 ½ yeir at 16 lib. in the yeir is................................ 24–00–00

2– to hir for 3 pair off shoone at 25s. the pair at 2 pair ilk yeir .... 03–15–00 • 27 • 15 • –

2 December to John Reid to give the gairner in Morphit – 12s.

To John Reid himselff– 6s. 06s. 00–18–00

To John Rob for pirns & haiks – 2 tymes 00–16–00

2 peices off fresh beiff 00–18–00

25 December – to James Chisholms woman in drink money............... 01–09–00

26 December – to Thomas Andersone when he wes at the mill........... 00–06–08

23 December to Margaret Hopkirk for a pair off shoone 00–18–00

[48] This is one of the rare occasions where Clerk spelled ‘Hamilton’ without a ‘u’.

To Wille Lishman for carying hir kist to Leswaid 00–06–08
26 December – sent with Arche Craig to the ministers wyffe –
10s. 2d. for some things wes got to the bairne Arche .... 00–10–02 • 06 • 02 • 06
93–15–11d. The disbursments above in December – 1667 is .... • 93 • 15 • 11

[62]

The disbursments in December 1667– on the other syde is .... • 93 • 15 • 11
The 28 off December 1667 – William Stewart be my order peyit to Robert
Cleghorne in Dalkeith for – 7 ston off candle off severall sorts – 17 lib.
17s. – with – 25 lb off sheip tallon –& 15 lb ox tallon – is 40 lb in both acording –
to a letter resavet fra Robert Cleghorne date the 28 of December 1667 • 17 • 17 • –
93–15–11 The 28 off December to James Frizel in the Carlips for – 50 laid off cols –
17–17–0 wharoff he rebated 4 laid rests 46 laid at – 4s. the laid .... • 09 • 04 • –
09–04–0 The 30 off December 1667 to John Rob to get twa firikins off soape –
16–06–4 fra Robert Dowglas in Leith – 15 lib. & 1s. for customs is 15–01–00
137–03–3 For wheat breid in December 1667 .... 01–05–04 • 16 • 06 • 04
The end off December 1667 The disbursments in December 1667 • 137 • 03 • 03

1: Januar 1667 333–03–10
2: February 1667 532–03–00
3: Marche 1667 278–01–10
4: Aprill 1667 2088–12–10
5: May 1667 152–17–02

6: June 1667 361–14–08
7: Jully 1667 088–19–05
8: Agust 1667 589–19–00
9: September 1667 094–05–06
10: October 1667 079–11–00
11: November 1667 235–17–08
12: December 1667 137–03–03

The disbursments in the yeir of God 1667 – fra the 1 off January 1667 to the last day off December 1667 – which yeir wes a most sad & fatall yeir to me – in the losse off my dear & well beloved dochter Elizabeth Clerk who dyed the –27 off Januar 1667 and in the losse off my dear & weell beloved wyffe who dyed – the 17 off Aprill 1667– 4972–09–02 •4972 • 09 • 02

John: Clerk

[63]

January 1668– The disbursments in January – 1668 ....

For a wirt laiglen for the brewhousse 00–12–00
1 thorn for the fatt 00–06–00
2 pigs to tak mysse in the gairden 00–05–00
2 horne spoons for bairns 00–03–00

1 brasse pan for the brewhousse weying 4 lb 5 once–
17s. the lb 03–13–06
To Robert Dewer for putting a bowll thairtoo 00–10–06 04–04–00
To William Reid for a ston – 8 lb – 4 lb – 2 lb – 1 lb is 31 lb ~ ~ ~ ~
in all is a sute off wechts for which I peyit – 4 lib. 7s. 04–07–00
13–07–8 – · 2 douzane off pack neidles 00–06–00
. 3–07–0 – · 1 sawe all 00–01–08
59–00–0 – · 1 visorne 00–05–00
75–14–8 – To Richard Smiths wyffe for a leather botle...1 – dolor – I am to give hir
it bak agane – iff shoe rander me the dolor betwixt & 1 off May
1668 .... 02–18–00 • 13 • 07 • 08
4 key rings 00–06–08
12 corks for bottels 00–03–04
1 pound off ginger 00–07–00
14 litle horne spoons for childring 00–14–00
4 large horne spoons 00–06–00
4 loch litches – 6s. 00–06–00
8 once off whyt suger candie 00–12–00
4 January 1668 to Alexander Simpsons woman in drink money .... 00–12–00 • 03 • 07 • –
The 1 off January 1668 to Sir Robert Sinclair off Longformacus ~~ ~~ ~~ ~~
1. A peice off gold coynd be the earle off Mortoun when he wes regent
King James the 6: his pourtraict [sic] on the on[e] syde – and a Lyon
on the other worth – 45 lib. 45–00–00
2. 1 fyne Bible in octava – bound in Maroquin – with gilt in a plain grein

	velvit bag – very netlie [sic] made at Paris both worth 14 lib. at leist	14–00–00	• 59 • 00 • –
	Fra the 1 off January 1668 to Saturday the 4 off January 1668 – I disbursit all above mentioned which doth amount to – 75–14–08		• 75 • 14 • 08
	====================~~ ~~ ~~ ~~~~ ~~ ~~ ~~ ~~ ~~ ~~ ~~====================		
1	To John Clerk – 2 new Inglish crowns	06–00–00	
2	To James Clerk a 40s. peice	02–00–00	• 08 • 00 • –
1	To Marie Clerk – 3 rex dolors – 8–14–1 steill key ring – 1–10–1 curious litle horne ink horne – 6s. is in all	10–10–00	
2	To Margaret Clerk – 2 rex dolors – 1 curious steill key ring – 1–10s. – 1 fyne litle horne ink horne – 6s. is in all	07–12–00	
3	To Agnes Clerk – 1 rex dolor – 2–18–1 fyne curious steil key ring – 1–10– 1 fyne litle horne ink horne – 6s. is in all	04–14–00	
4	To Marie Douglas ane new halff crown	01–10–00	• 24 • 06 • –
	To the bairns in turnors among them – 16s. –& other things worth – 24s.	02–00–00	
	To John Rob 6s.	00–06–00	
	To Alexander Falcon for some cow rash bands	00–04–00	
	To John Brown – bedel – 12s.	00–12–00	
	To George Reid – 6s. 8d. to Helen Reid – 3s. is	00–09–08	• 03 • 11 • 08
1	To Anna Irving – 36s.	01–16–00	
2	To Jennet Lamb – 1 pair off new shoone worth –24s.	01–04–00	
3	To Jennet Shanks – 18s.	00–18–00	
4	To Bessie Whyt – 1 merk and a grot	00–17–04	

	5	To Jean Stewart – 9s.	00–09–00	• 05 • 04 • 04
	1	To David Clerk……18s.	00–18–00	
	2	To John Clerk…..12s.	00–12–00	
8–00–0	3	To John Sibbald – 9s. –& 12s. for mending the bairns shoone is	01–01–00	
24–06–0	4	To Arche Craig – 9s.	00–09–00	
. 3–11–8	5	To John Dicksone – 9s.	00–09–00	
. 5– .4–4	6	To Thomas Andersone –		• 03 • 09 • –
. 3– .9–0		The 10 of January to John Ramsay for – 30 mure fowls I wes oweing		
. 9– .0–0		him at 6s. the peice is – 9 lib.		• 09 • 00 • –
. 4– .8–6		The 2 off December 1667 – delivered to Margaret Clerk – 3 lib. which		
. 4– .1–6		shoe debursit – on small things – includit 40s. shoe peyit to the webster		
62–01–0		in Braidwood for weiving 40 ell off plaiding shoe gave me ane accompt		
75–14–8		off the said 3 lib. the 16 January1668	03–00–00	
137–15–8		4 pynt bikers at 30d. the peice	00–10–00	
		1 douzane off ram horne spoons	00–06–00	
		3 whyt caps	00–04–06	
		16 January to To: Andersone – 40d. to dry 2 kill full off oats		
		1 quart ale	00–03–04	
		20 – to To: Andersone to get 3 pynts of ale when they wer at the mill:		
		with – 19 bolls off oats	00–05–00	• 04 • 08 • 06
		25 Januar – for 1 firlot of great salt Jo: Rob boght in Leith	02–16–00	
		2 douzane off oynions	00–03–06	
		For whyt breid in January	01–02–00	• 04 • 01 • 06
		The disbursments in Januar 1668 on this syde is…….		• 137 • 15 • 08

[64]

The disbursments in Januar 1668 on the other syde is .... • 137 • 15 • 08

Thursday 24 January 1668 to Edoward Adamsone 25 lib. to –
give to James Telfeir in Bigger for ane ox I boght fra him to slay
at Silver burne the said day being the – 24 off January 1668 .... • 25 • 00 • –

Fresh beiff 00–12–00

10 Januar to John Thomson to get 4 pynts and 1 mutchkin off –
waters in the water of Leith at 18s. the pynt........................ 03–16–06

137–15–8 17 Januar to Jo: Donaldsone – my brothers man when he broght a –
25–00–0 lyge off – Berwick veill [sic] 00–12–00
6–01–6 18 Januar to John Reid Roslings [sic] man for 30 gein standerts he
168–17–2 broght.. 00–12–00

2 bolts off knitings.. 00–09–00 • 06 • 01 • 06

The end off January 1668 – The disbursments in Januar 1668............. • 168 • 17 • 02

Februar 1668 The disbursments in February 1668 ~~ ~~

The 4 off February 1668 to David Boyd merchant 600 lib. and retird
my ticket fra him off the lyke soume – which I canceld and hath lying
by me which wes for James Clerks prentize fie– who entert home prentize
to him the 11 off December 1667 – and is bound 5 yeirs to him fra the
date off the – indentors – which indentors ar date the said 11 off December
1667: and – his 5 yeirs expyrs the 11 off December 1672; my said ticket off
600 lib. wes date the said 11 of December ~~1672~~ 1667 – payable the 10 of Februar
1668 .... • 600 • 00 • –

The 3 off February to James Adamsone customer at the West Port 29s.
for my – small customs fra the 1 off January 1668 till the 1 Januar
1669 01–09–00
The 6 February to Jo: Andersone which he gave Margaret Clerk to buy
a pair off shoone 01–16–00
To Mary Clerk which shoe gave for halff a pound of spyce 00–09–00
1 blaid for Alexander Clerks knyffe 00–06–00
1 lock for William Clerks kist 01–10–00
For great weyr .... 02–00–00 • 07 • 10 • –
The 6 January 1668 – sent to Mr John Clerk – 8 rex dolors which he
gave to Isobell Gray 23–04–00
6 February 1668 given to hir my selff when I resavet the plaids .... 01–03–06 • 24 • 07 • 06
For the which– 24–7–6d. – shoe boght fra John Gray agent –
and delivert to me the said 6 off February 1668 – 37 ½ ell off bed
plaids – sprangd a litle braid with grein at 13s. the ell is ~~
24–7s.–6d. ....
6 Februar to John Fergusone cordoner for 1 pair off shoone for James
Clerk 01–04–00
Given him to buy a pen knyffe 00–12–00
600–00–0 Given him 1 pair off gloves cost 00–12–00
. . 7–10–0 Given him a horne combe– cost 6s. 00–06–00
. 24–. 7–6 6 Februar to Isobell Fermer for – 300 double flourings –
. . 5–12–0 at – 19s. 4d. the – 100th .... 02–18–00 • 05 • 12 • –
11–09–0 1 brasse pan of a quart weying 1 lb 15 once at 17s. the lb 01–13–00

42–00–0	For ingredients to be ink	00–15–00	
40–00–0	1 grosse off blak..........		
. . 7–11–6	1 grosse sad minim....... is 24 douzane at 2s. the douzane	02–08–0–	
738–10 –:	3 quair off peper blak on the edg at 6s. the quair	00–18–00	
15–. 8 –:	1 pound off leaff tobaco	00–16–00	
753–18 –:	15 Februar to William Jack for mending a pad &c	01–04–00	
	12 ½ pound off fygs at 6s. the pound	03–15–00	• 11 • 09 • –
Lint –	The 13 off Februar 1668 to Isobell Gray which shoe disbursit for me for		
Isobell –	3 stone off knok lint at – 7–13–4d. the stone	23–00–00	
Gray	Said day to Francis Hendersone for a short French carabin –		
	12 lib. with a Scots pistol cost me – 7 lib. 4s. is	19–04–00	• 42 • 00[49] • –
	The 14 off February 1668 to William Hamiltoun merchant for John Clerks		
	boord fra the – 23 off February 1668 to the 23 off May 1668 – his first –		
	3 month expyrd the 23 off February 1668.........................40 lib.		• 40 • 00 • –
	20 lb off plume dames at 2s. the pound	02–00–00	
	10 lb off great raisings at 6s. the pound	03–00–00	
	10 lb off currents at 5s. the pound	02–10–00	
	To a porter for carying them	00–01–06	• 07 • 11 • 06
	all above in Februar 1668		• 738 • 10 • –
	1 ell off stenting	00–10–00	
	1 pair off gloves	00–13–04	
	1 grosse off blak breist buttons – 30s. – for change in 1 grosse 5s.	01–15–00	

49 Not clear why Clerk omitted the 4s. from his sum in the margin.

To William Shaws widow for gairden seids.. 03–10–00
1 lb off whyt suger candie 01–03–00
22 February to John Andersone to give Mr John Clerk – 42s. to pay –
ane accompt off small things he debursit for himselff the compt markit –
A B 02–02–00
6 February to Androw Pourdie for weiving – 26 ell off linze winze 01–09–00
3 February to William Stewart to go to the pans for 1 ½ boll off whyt –
salt – cost customs excyse and all – 4–2–8d. 04–02–08
For the gray horse when Marie Clerk went to the town .... 00–03–00 • 15 • 08 • –
The disbursments in Februar 1668 on this syde is........ • 753 • 18 • –

[65]
The disbursments in February 1668 on the other syde.............is .... • 753 • 18 • –
Thursday the 27 off Februar sent William Stewart to the Queens Ferrie to
Archebald Wilsone bailyie thair – who got fra him a barel off seck which –
conteind – 32 pynts at 20s. the pynt is 32 lib. – which 32 lib. William Stewart
753–18 delivered to Archebald Wilsons wyffe – Archebald Wilsone said the barel
32– .8 wold contein – 34 pynts – bot that he wold tak bot for 32 pynts 32–00–00
2–14–8 For the horse & mans charges & a shoe to the horse .... 00–08–00 • 32 • 08 • –
789–00–8 26 February sent George Reid to Mussilburgh with a letter to Patrik
Widerspoons – given him – 6s. to drink with – P: W –& a grot to give
for graffs 00–10–00
Fresh beiff in this month.. 01–06–08

	Whyt breid in this month	00–18–00	• 02 • 14 • 08
	The end of February 1668 The disbursments in Februar 1668		• 789 • 00 • 08
Marche	The disbursments in Marche 1668		
1668 :	The 4 off Marche to John Tait on his discharge for – 5 ston 5 ½ pound off yrne at 29s. the ston		• 07 • 15 • –
	The 9 off Marche 1668 – peyit to James Ramsay in the Halls – 60 lib. for 21 ews – sold be him to me as being with lamb – for 60 lib. Scots		• 60 • 00 • –
	The 10 off Marche 1668 to John Hunter in Straiton for making 12 ½ bols off beer in malt thair wes – 13 ½ bols off malt	05–00–00	
	To his man George Scot in drink money	00–12–00	
Malt	To the men to drink that broght the malt	00–04–00	• 05 • 16 • –
	The 11 Marche to a chapman for 10 ell –off ell braid lining at – 18s. the ell – & to him – 3s. more amongst all the 10 ell	09–03–00	
	1 pair off gloves for Helen – 2s. – whill bands – 1s. is – 3s.	00–03–00	• 09 • 06 • –
Archbald Clerk	The 13 off Marche 1668 to Archbald Craig in the Towr for his wyffs nourishing Archebald Clerk fra the – 8 off June 1667 to the 8 off December 1667– is – 6 month at 12 lib. ilk 3 month is – 24 lib.	24–00–00	
	The said day to him – 4–16– 8d. to buy a ston of bounteth lint for – his wyffe	04–16–08	• 28 • 16 • 08
	Disbursit at Edinburgh – when I wes thair on Teusday 17 Marche 1668 –		
	5 pair off bairns shoone at 10s. the pair	02–10–00	
	To James Grhame for – 2 rim off peper at 4 lib. the rim	08–00–00	

2 sand ridles at – 7s. the peice 00–14–00
17 ½ ell off secking at 7s. the ell........ 06–02–06
2 pound of pack threid at 8s. the pound........ 00–16–00
1 bolt off cords fyne........ 00–03–06
2 hair cods................at 2s. 6d. the peice........ 00–05–00
To John Salomon for a wooll hatt 4–16 .... 04–16–00 • 23 • 07 • –

James Clerk — 21 February 1668 for a hatt to James Clerk............ 2–18
To him for mending his shoone........................ 0–10........ 03–08–00
20 Marche to Robert Hamiltoun merchant on his discharge
in full of acompt........ 26–14–00
20 Marche – to John Gray off Crichie in full off ane accompt 10–17–06
20 Marche to Margaret Tam for a pair of whyt 4 threid hose for
my selff........ 03–00–00
21 Marche to David Boyd for – 3 ½ ell off musk cullort Dutch serge
to be a cot for my selff at 58s. the ell........ 10–03–00
6 douzane off musk cullort mandel buttons yairtoo at 5s. the
douzane 01–10–00
1 once off round musk cullort silk........ 01–00–00
16 pound off great raisings at – 6s. the pound........ 04–16–00
4 pound off feygs at 4s. the pound........ 00–16–00
T[o] John Broun for 2 pen knyves........ 00–19–00 • 63 • 03 • 06

Vinaigre — 21 Marche to [blank] Dick in Leith for 11 pynts off vinaigre at 8s. the
pynt is – 4 lib. 8s. – 1 litle halff anker barel to put it in 9s. is both........ 04–17–00
Mr John–Clerk~~ — 23 Marche to Robert Hamiltoun Merchant – on his discharge for 2 ¼

07–15–0 ell off blak cloth to be Mr Jo: Clerk a blak cot at 9–18s. the ell 22–05–06
60–00–0 22 Marche to Archebald Teinder tailyeur on his discharge for making
. 5–16–0 the said cot and furnishing thairtoo 04–03–04
. 9–06–0 25 Marche to John Reid for 3 thorns for a masking fatt .... 00–18–00 • 32 • 03 • 10
28–16–8 27 Marche 1668 to Isobell Hamiltoun for – I say to Isobell Gray for –
23–07–0 1– 33 ell off braid bed plaids braid sprangd at 24s. the ell 39–12–00
63–03–6 2– 5 ell off sad cullort stuff at – 20s. the ell 05–00–00
32–03–10 3– 8 ell of licht cullort stuff at 22s. the ell .... 08–16–00 • 53 • 08 • –
53–08–0 Fresh beiff in Marche 1668 02–08–00
283–16–0 Whyt breid in Marche 1668 .... 01–03–00 • 03 • 11 • –
03–11–0 The end off Marche 1668–
287–07–0 The disbursments in Marche 1668 ...... • 287 • 07 • –

[66]

Aprill The disbursments in Aprill 1668 ~~

1668 The 1 off Aprill 1668 to John Sibbald for his fie fra the 2 off Jully 1667 to
Mertimes 1667.............06–13–04 06–13–04
More to him the said day for his fie fra Mertimes 1667 till Witsonday
1668 – 9 lib. I peyit him this befor the terme – Witsonday 1668 .... 09–00–00 • 15 • 13 • 04
The 16 off Marche 1668 given John Reid to go to Craigmiller to get
some small things for the yard – 1 merk to give the gairner –& 6s. to
drink is.. 00–19–04

Brande – The 3 off off [sic] Aprill to Robert Hamiltoun in full of ane acompt
for brande 15–03–06

Mary Clerk The 10 of Aprill 1668 to James Boe tailyeur for making –& furnishing –
to a goun off Marie Clerks off blak ferandin .... 12–00–00 • 28 • 02 • 10

The 6 off Aprill to David Boyd for – 2 ell off cloth to be Ja:
Clerks cloth 08–00–00
3 quarters off stenting – at 8s. the ell 00–06–00
James– 2 ¾ ell off twidle for lying doublet & breiks at – 9s. the ell 01–04–09
Clerk 4 douzane off buttons at – 30 penies [sic] the douzane 00–10–00
11 Aprill to Archbald Teinder tailyeur on his discharge for making –
his cloths and some furnishing thairtoo .... 02–02–00 • 12 • 02 • 09

12 Aprill – to Mr Alexander Cameron when I looked Ja: Flem: age.... 00–12–00
13 small cords at 18d. the peice 00–19–06
4 once off leaff tobaco 00–06–00
12 Aprill to Patrik Murrays man when he gave the cut & dry tobaco... 01–09–00
12 Aprill to John Whyt for 4 pair off bairns shoone at 18s. the pair 03–12–00
7 once off juss off reglis 00–07–00
6 unshod shools at –10s. the peice 03–00–00
To John Fergusone for 1 pair off shoone for my selff 40s. to his man –
2s. .... 02–02–00 • 12 • 07 • 06

Mr John Clerk.. The 10 off Aprill 1668 to Alexander Leslie for the 2 yeir Mr John –
Clerk wes in his chamber – fra the 1 off November 1667 to the 1 off
November 1668....23 dolors .... • 66 • 14 • –

The 9 off Aprill 1668 to Isobell Grey – which shoe disbursit for me –

Isobell Gray 1– for 3 ¼ ell off Holland to be Marie Clerk a peticot at 2 merk the ell 04–06–08

2– for a pound off whyt & blew stiffing .... 00–06–00 • 04 • 12 • 08

To Alexander Ogilvie on his discharge date the 6 off Aprill 1668 – ane off the sub collectors: 55 lib. 2s. 2d. – as the thrid [sic] terms peyment off – the taxation imposd be the convention off estats in Agust 1665 – for the personage off Pennycooke – in which discharge he discharged – me off the twa former terms taxations which discharge is date the 6 off Aprill 1668 – I neidit not to have peyit it till Witsonday 1668 – not the lesse I peyit him the same befor the tyme .... • 55 • 02 • 02

Mr Thomas Baird The 11 off Aprill 1668 – to Mr Thomas Baird ane of the shireff deputs off Edinburgh – 24 lib. Scots as the thrid [sic] terms peyment of the – taxation imposd be the convention off estats in Agust 1665 and – lykewyse off the twa former terms taxations peyit be me formerlie for my – 12 // for my 12 pound land lying within the paroish off Pennycooke and for Cookeing in Glencorse paroish all the said 3 terms is compleitlie peyit till – Witsonday 1668 – acording to the said Mr Thomas Baird his discharge date – the 11 off Aprill.......1668 .... • 24 • 00 • –

Robert Dewer The 14 off Aprill 1668 to Robert Dewer for

1. for a boll of oats 03–13–04
2. for 2 pecks off beir .... 00–13–04 • 04 • 06 • 08

which compleits his boll fra Witsonday 1667 till Witsonday 1668:

Ro: Dewer 15–13–04 The 14 off Aprill 1668 to Robert Dewer for 10 thraive 3 shaivs lesse of beir stroe at – 4s. the thraive .... • 02 • 00 • –

28–02–10 4 Aprill to Storie webster in Braidwood for weiving
12–02–09 34 ell off cloth – 6 quarter braid for courtins at 18d. the ell 02–11–00
12–07–00 21 ell off cloth – 6 quarter braid at 2s. the ell– for blankets 02–02–00
66–14–00 and 3 lib. Margaret Clerk disbursit in small disbursments Januar February
04–12–08 Marche .... 03–00–00 • 07 • 13 • –
55–02–02 Fryday 24 Aprill 1668 – sent to my brother seald in a peper to be given to –
24–00–00 Mr John Clerk – acording to a compt he sent me therof of his disbursments –
04–06–08 for himself –
02–00–00 1. for mending my shoes 00–10–00
07–13–00 2. to John Fergusone for a pair off shoone 02–00–00
232–14–05 3. 1 pair of blak stokings 02–08–00
06–14–06 4. for ane pound off candle 00–04–06
11–04–06 5. for dying my hatt 00–02–00
250–13–05 6. 6 quair of peper at 5s. the quair .... 01–10–00 • 06 • 14 • 06
AB: Mr AB;
John Clerk Accompt off a Yorkshyre cloth clok for James Clerk –
1– 24 Aprill to David Boyd for 11 quarters of cloth at 4 lib. the ell 11–00–00
James 2– 1 neck button .... 00–04–06 • 11 • 04 • 06
Clerk Thomas Andersone peyit to David Boyd this – 11–04–6d.

Soma off the disbursments above in–
Aprill 1668 .... • 250 • 13 • 05

[67]

Margin	Entry	Amount	Total
	The disbursments in Aprill on the other syde....................................		• 250 • 13 • 05
1. barell hering:	The 24 off Aprill 1668 to William Stewart 9 lib. which he peyit for a– barell off Lews hering in Leith..	09–00–00	
	His & the horse charges & custome	00–06–00	• 09 • 06 • –
	24 Aprill – 4 ell off peirling for bairns mutches at 4s. the ell................	00–16–00	
	18 ell off whyt worsit stringing at – 4d. the ell	00–06–00	
	25 Aprill to John Broun to buy a pen knyffe	00–10–00	
Couper –	29 Aprill to Jo Davisone couper in Linton for seting on 17 long girds & 14 shorter girds in all – 24s.	01–04–00	
Webster	29 Aprill to Androw Pourdie for weiving 35 ell off round lining.........	01–14–00	• 04 • 10 • –
250–13–5	27 Aprill for the bairns–		
9–06–0	1– 1 pynt of clairet wyne..	00–18–00	
4–10–0	2– 6 limons	00–11–00	
2–4–4	3– man & horse expensis	00–06–00	
5–3–0	4– 2 lb off fresh butter...	00–09–04	• 02 • 04 • 04
0–11–8	For fresh beiff in the month off Aprill..	04–02–00	
272–8–5	For whyt breid in the month off Aprill...	01–01–00	• 05 • 03 • –
Mill..... Kill	24 Aprill thair wes taken to the mill – 18 bolls 4 pecks off oats to be meill – Margret Clerk gave David Clerk – 6s. 8d. to get ale when they dryed the corne I gave Thomas Andersone – 5s. to get 3 pynts off ale when they mild [sic] the said corne is – 11s. 8d.		• 00 • 11 • 08
	The end off Aprill 1668 The disbursments in Aprill 1668 is		• 272 • 08 • 05

May 1668: The disbursments in May – 1668 ....

At Archebald Clerks buriell who wes buried the 1 off May 1668 –

1: to John Dewer for making his kist the timber wes my own 02–08–0
2: to John Broun bedel for making the graffe 01–10–0
3: to Helen Thomsone for a barell of ale 02–02–8
4: 6 great loaffs – 21s. 01–01–0
5: 2 pound off cut & dry tobaco 01–12–0
6: 3 douzane off comon tobaco pyps 00–04–6
7: to John Rob for going to Edinburgh 00–08–0
8: to George Reid for going to Mont Lothian &c .... 00–04–0 • 09 • 10 • 02

Thomas Mein — The 1 off May 1668 – to Thomas Mein for 8 bolls off oats at 3–13–4d. the boll is – 29–6–8d. 7 bolls theroff for Jo: Reids boll –& 1 boll for our own horse .... • 29 • 06 • 08

Jo: Reid — The 4 off May to John Reid for 6 firlots off beir to sawe on the beir land at 5–: 6–8..........the boll .... • 08 • 00 • –

Robert–Dewer– — The 4 off May 1668 – put by ane accompt off a sheit off peper off – 135–11–8 which I have peyit to Robert Dewer smith in Pennycooke for severall – yrne wark I have resaivit fra him fra the 7 off December 1665 untill the 4 off May 1668 amonting to – 135–11–8 .... • 135 • 11 • 08

Jo: Clerk — As apears on the 34 leaffe off the booke whair the servants fies is wreatten doun – peyit to John Clerk 28 lib. for his fie fra Witsonday 1666 till Witsonday 1667 28–00–00

Bessie Whyt	The 16 off May 1668 to Bessie Whyt for hir fie fra Mertimes 1667 till Witsonday 1668	07–10–00	
	To Arche Andersone at 3 tyms for trouts	00–13–00	
	For a pynt off clairet wyne for the bairns when they wer sick	00–16–00	
	The gray horse charges 3 severall tymes	00–09–00	
	The 12 off May to Isobell Gray 3– 9s. shoe peyit out in the toun for – a stone off salt butter for our usse	03–09–00	
Nicol – gairner	The 13 off May to George Reid 12s. to give John Nicoll gairner in Temple for some things for our yard – to George Reid 4s. –& 20d. is in all	00–17–08	• 41 • 14 • 08
Ja: Frizel	The 19 off May 1668 to James Frizel for 44 laid off cols whairoff he rebated 4 laid at: rests 40 laid at – 4s. the laid is 8 lib.	08–00–00	
Wm Johnstoun tinkler	23:[50] 21 May to William Johnstoun tincler in Trenent for mending: the litle coper ketle the coper wes my own – for solding a chopin: stoup for a yetling pot bottom –& for mending a brasse pan –:	00–10–00	
Bee skaipes	23 May to George Bell for – 2 bee skaips he boght for me in Leswaid–:	01–00–00	• 09 • 10 • –
David Clerk	The 26 off May to David Clerk for his fie fra Mertimes 1667 till Witsonday – 1668– 18–14–8d. as it is particullarlie set doun on the booke whair servants – fies is wreatten on the 1 page theroff	18–14–08	
Lining — fra Lady Bagillo	27 May 1668 – fra William Ramsay servitor to the Lady Bagillo –		
	1– 17 ell off lining at 14s. the ell ... 11–18–00		
	2– 15 ell off lining at– 15s. the ell ... 11–05–00		

[50] Clerk mistakenly began to note the date of this entry as 23 May but corrected it to 21 May.

3– 16 ell of round lining at 10s. the ell................ 08–00–00
4– 10 ½ ell off lining at – 17s. the ell.................... 08–18–06
To William Ramsay to drink .... 00–03–04............. 40–04–10 • 58 • 19 • 06

Soma off the disbursments above –
in May 1658 [sic]....292–12–8 .... • 292 • 12 • 08

[68]

The disbursments on the other syde in May 1668 .... • 292 • 12 • 08

Archbald 27 off May to Archbald Craig – 24 lib. for his fie fra Mertimes 1666
Craig till Witsonday 1668 is a yeir and a halff at 16 lib. in the yeir 24–00–00
1 salmond boght at Edinburgh cost 20s. 01–00–00
20 May to John Rob for – 3 pecks off pan cratch.............................. 00–12–00
292.12.8 30 May to Alexander Hastie 34s. for 1 ½ ell off gray for 2 saidle
28.8.4 cloths.. 01–14–00
6.17.4. To Arche Andersone at 2 tyms for trouts 00–08–00
1.8.0 To a chapman for severall things –12s. –& 6 cogs & pails – 4s. 00–04–00
329.6.4 26 off May to David Clerk to kill – 11 bolls 4 pecks off oats 00–03–04
28 May – for the gray horse when Tibe Hamiltoun cam out –& to Jo:
Rob – 4s. for his horse– the said day to bring out Will Hamiltoun is... 00–07–00 • 28 • 08 • 04

For fresh beiff in the month off May.......06–17–04.......................... • 06 • 17 • 04
For whyt breid in the month off May..................28s. .... • 01 • 08 • –
The end off May 1668: The disbursments in May 1668......... • 329 • 06 • 04

June: The disbursments in June 1668 ....

1668: *Halls: Marche*

Rydeing ~~~~

Upon Munday the 1 off June 1668 – I with John Lowrie at the mill: James – Lowrie in Dyke Neuke: James Ramsay in the Halls Edowart Adamsone in – Silver burne; did meet at the Walltowr – Walter Scot in name of my Lord Rosse who broght with him Androw Lawther at Melen Mill – 2 tenents off – Sir John Nicolsons – the on[e] callit [blank] Turnbull the other Alexander – Lawther –& James Simpsone in Pendrich – and did visit ryde & consider – the marches betwixt my Lord Rosse – and the Halls –& efterward went & dynd at the Walltowr – whair I peyit 1 dolor for our dinner – 20s. for a chopin off brande is – 3–18s. – I wold have peyit all willinglie bot Walter Scot bailyie for my Lord Rosse & indweller in Leswaid wold not suffer me – so that they peyit divers mutchkins off brande amongst them – thair wes present also David Hislop in over Mosse Housses Thomas Ramsay in the Walltowr –& all the tenants off this nether Mosse Housses we did alter nothing conclude nothing – bot left it to the tenents off my Lord Rosse above mentioned & James Ramsay in the Halls to consider the – bussynes weell –& see iff they could agrie amongst them selvs which they promist to doe –& not with thair folie & wickednesse to bring my Lord Rosse & me in a contraversie all togither need lesse & all that wes present thoght fit it sould be so: & so we partit all – good friends – Long may it continow so .... • 03 • 18 • –

The rydeing of the Halls marches

2 ky –	Teusday 2 June 1668 – peyit to Thomas Trequair 36 lib. to himselff – 9s. for 2 – young blak ky & 2 calffs which his master William Russell fe. off the Sliperfeild [sic] sent to me with him the said day– which 36 lib. is to be delivert be him – to his said master William Russell off Slipperfeild		• 36 • 09 • –
	4 June to Alexander Leslie for wreating – FF: & M: C: contract	05–16–00	
	To William Russel in drink money	01–09–00	
	For a band off relieff for my brothers cautionrie anent the testament	00–11–00	
	For wreating ane assignation to my brother to Hermistouns band	00–11–00	• 08 • 07 • –
Mr Robert Alisone	The 8 off June 1668 to Mr Robert Alisone minister at Glencorse kirk – 48 lib. for his stipend for the lands off Cookeing – fra Witsonday 1667 till Witsonday 1668 – on his discharge date the – 8 off June 1668		• 48 • 00 • –
Jenet Lamb	The 8 off June 1668 to Jennet Lamb for hir yeirs fie fra Witsonday 1667 till – Witsonday 1668.....17 lib.	17–00–00	
yrne	The 3 off June 1668 to John Tait merchant on his discharge the said day in full off ane accompt for – 20 stone 9 lb yrne at 28s. the ston	28–16–00	
Mary Clerk	3 June 1668 to David Boyd in full of ane accompt on his discharge the said day for a ferandin goun &c for Marie Clerk	58–18–00	
	To John Cooke for a key to my wyffs studie dore	00–16–00	
	Halff a pownd off leaffe tobaco	00–12–00	
	To Margaret Tam for a pair off whyt 4 threid stokings	03–06–08	

	1 litle brush – 5s.	00–05–00	
	For fliting my chamber 30s. for taking doun & puting up my bed – 12 which I peyit to Patrik Thomsone wright is 42s.	02–02–00	• 111 • 15 • 08
Isobel Gray Mary Clerk	5 June to Isobell Gray for 9 ell off Holland at 4 lib. the ell and 6 quarters of the said Holland to be Marie Clerk 2 pair off hand cuffs at 4 lib. the ell is 10 ½ ell – at 4 lib. the ell is – 42 lib. I have William Bell merchants discharge of this – not the lesse that I peyit the money to Isobell Gray	42–00–00	
Isobel Gray	5 June to Isobell Gray for 6 ell off the Lady Bagillos lining at 15s. – the ell is – 4–10s. – whairoff I rebated 15s. for inlaike off the – measur off former lining cloth I boght fra Isobell Gray – rests	03–15–00	• 45 • 15 • –

3–18–00
36–09–00
8–07–00
48–00–00
111–15–08
45–15–00
254–04–08

The disbursments in June on this syde is	• 254 • 04 • 08

[69]

The disbursments in June on the other syde amounts to...254–04–08 .. • 254 • 04 • 08

Lady Bagillo: For– lining round & small & tuidling — round & small

Upon the 19 June 1668 resavit fra William Grigorie servitor to the – Lady Bagillo the particullars under wreatten to wit –

1– 6 ell off small lining callit Scots Holland at – 30s. the ell 09–00–00
2– 15 ell off twidling at – 12s. the ell 09–00–00
3– 20 ell off lining in 2 peices at – 10s. the ell 10–00–00
4– 12 ell off twidling at – 8s. the ell 04–16–00
5– 4 ell off twidling at 7s. the ell .... 01–08–00 • 34 • 04 • –

Which 34 lib. – 4s. I delivert to the said William Grigorie the said 19 June – 1668 to wit 11 dolors – 31–18s. & 46s. is– 34–4s. I wreat to the Lady Bagillo bot keiped [sic] not the copie off the letter I wreat to hir...................

Thomas Sandelands

The 20 of June 1668 to Thomas Sandelands wright – on his discharge off the said date – 140 lib. Scots – for furnishing oake to be a roofe to the turnpyke head bewest the great new gate – for furnishing dails to sark it and for the warkmanship off all – 140 lib. Scots .... • 140 • 00 • –

John Andersone

22 June 1668 – sent to my brother John Andersone – 6–4s. which he debursit to wit to Mr Jo: Clerk – 6 lib. and 4s. he spent with Androw Haliburton Newtoun Kers man – sent to my brother the said day – 9s. sterlin and a grot – and a shilling – Androw Haliburton gave him – to drawe out Robert Kers principall band out of the register – which shilling I sent to Newtoun Kerr the 22 of June 1668 – becaus the principall band could not be got out off the register..............................

Mr John: Clerk

The copie off Mr Jo: Clerks compt with his recept off – 6 lib. at the fitt yairoff

	1– for ane hatt	03–11–00	
	2– to John Donaldsone for going to Leith 2 severall tymes	00–06–00	
	3– for mending my shoes	00–08–00	
	4– for 3 ell off morning rubens	00–15–00	
	5– spent with Mr John Lyon –& Mr John Leslie	01–00–00	• 06 • 00 • –
Margaret	The 23 off June to Margaret Hopekirk for – 13 ell off lining – to be cod		
Hopekirk	wairs at 20s. the ell is – 13 lib.		• 13 • 00 • –
John	The 27 off June 1668 to John Stinsone waker in full off ane accompt		
Stinsone–	on his discharge date the the [sic] said 27 off June 1668 & off all		
waker –	accompts preseiding the – said 27 of June 1668		• 16 • 10 • 04
254–04–8	6 June for 2 peices off fresh beiff	01–01–06	
34–04–0	15 June to John Reid for the lyge off a calff	00–12–00	
140–00–0	For a quart off barme	00–04–00	
06–00–0	10 June for 4 lb off steill hemp John Rob boght at 8s. the pound	01–12–00	
13–00–0	To Arche Andersone for trouts – 4 tyms	00–15–00	
16–10–4	To a couper for girds	00–06–08	
5–11–2	1 June to David Clerk 40d. till – for ale to mill – 11 bols 1 firlot		
6–16–0	of oats	00–03–04	
476–06–2	23 June to Margaret Hopekirk for 1 quart ale 3s. 4d. and 3 douzane		
	off eygs for the bairns – 5s. is 8s. 4d.	00–08–04	
	26 June to the meassons for – 5 pynts of ale Anna Irving got	00–08–04	• 05 • 11 • 02
	19 June – at Satir seyk at Jennet Lambs brydel – for myselff Marie Gray –		
	I say – Jean Gray and Marie Clerk is – 3– at 1 merk the peice to the		
	pyper 4s.	02–04–00	

26 June at William Telfeir younger his brydel at the – 9 Myle Burne
For myselff – James Adamsone – Marie & Margaret Clerks at 13s. 4d.
the peice for 4 – and 6s. 8d. to the pypers – is 03–00–00
For breid whyt breid in the month off June .... 01–12–00 • 06 • 16 • –
The end off June 1668 – The disbursments in June 1668 .... • 476 • 06 • 02

Jully 1668: The disbursments in the month of Jully 1668 ....

James - Adamsone — The 4 off Jully 1668 – to James Adamsone plumber – 234–10: 6d. on his discharge off the said date; and off all former accompts preseiding the said day – for lead & warkmanship – for theyking the turnpyke head off the new howsse bewest the great gate – as we enter into that close – I have the particullar accompt theroff wreatten above the said discharge ...... • 234 • 10 • 06

Robert Ritchesone — The 7 off Jully 1668 – boght fra Robert Ritchesone in Leith –
1– 300 dails at – 48 lib. the hundreth 144–00–00
2– 40 double treis at – 25s. the peice 50–00–00
dails 3– 40 single treis at 12s. the peice 24–00–00
treis 4– 20 dails for Robert Sands at 8s. the peice .... 08–00–00 • 226 • 00 • –

I gave the said Robert Ritchesone a bill on my brother John Andersone – date the said 7 Jully 1668 – for the said 226 lib. payable on demand I have the copie off the said bill on my brothers accompt ....

oake — The 7 Jully 1668 to John Trotter servitor to Robert Ra for –
1– 1 peice off oak for the warkhousse chimney 01–15–00
2– 1 peice oak to be a muller for the great gate .... 01–15–00 • 03 • 10 • –

Jo: Mein Sklaitter – To John Mein sklaiter for theyking the new housse bewest the new great yeat 39–00–00

234–10–6 To him for a yard maill in Leith the sklaits lay in 02–18–00
226–00–0 To his men in drink money .... 01–10–00 • 43 • 08 • –
3–10–0 For which I have his discharge date the 10 Jullу 1668 ....
43–08–0 The disbursments above in Jully 1668 is – 507–08–6 .... • 507 • 08 • 06
507–08–6

[70]

The disbursments in Jully on the other syde is........507–08–6 .... • 507 • 08 • 06

beir — The 14 Jully 1668 to James A. Simpsone in Bruntsaine for – 3 bols 3 firlots off beir – wes got in beirseid tyme 1668 – at 5 lib. the boll is ..... 15 • – • 18 • 00 • –

Hew Mack–Culloch — The 25 off Jully 1668 to Hew Mackculloch on his discharge of the said date – 55–15–2d. for 2 months cesse – November & December 1667 for my lands – in Pennycooke & Glencorse paroish – which compleits the 12 months cesse imposd be the act off convention of estats in January 1667 .... • 55 • 12 • 02

Isobell Gray. — 14 Jully 1668 sent to Isobel Gray – 3 ell off braid spraingd bed plaids at 24s. the ell so much I peyit to hir for the same is .... 03–12s. ~
The way shoe peyit me the said 3 lib. 12s. –
1– shoe peyit 30s. for 1 pair off shoone for Marie Clerk .. 01–10–
2– the 24 of April – resavit fra Isobell Gray – 42s. .... 02–02–: is.. • 03 • 12 • –

1 whyt curple 00–08–00
2 cordoners dropers cost 00–13–04
4 gray bonets for the bairns 01–02–06

	To Abraham Clark for turning 2 globs	00–08–00	
	For some peices off rushie leather	00–03–00	• 02 • 14 • 10
Ed: Cleghorn	24 Jully 1668 to Edowart Cleghorne goldsmith for a cadel – coup with –		
Newhall	a covert weying – 15 once 4 drope at 3–8s. the once which I gave to –		
	Alexander Pennycooke off Newhall for some pains he tooke on my		
	childring		• 51 • 17 • –
John:	24 Jully 1668 to John Cooke for		
Cooke	2 pair off bands for a presse		
	1 bordert lock for the presse		
	2 check sneks		
	2 braid yrne poynts for the chek sneks		
	And nails to put all those things on ... peyit for all		• 04 • 07 • –
	27 Jully 1668 – to William Jack saidler for mending a saidle &c	01–09–00	
	To Robert Watsone in Berwick for a whyt hamper with a lock	02–08–00	
	28 Jully to John Whyt for 4 pair off bairns shoone at 16s. a pair	03–04–00	
	25 Jully to Marie Clerk to buy spyceries	02–18–00	
	To William Meik for – 8 lb 2 once off glew at 7s. the lb	02–16–10	
	29 Jully to John Fergusone for – 1 pair off shoone for James Clerk	01–07–04	• 14 • 03 • 02
Alexander	29 Jully 1668 to Alexander Simpsone 12 lib. on his discharge date 29		
Simpsone	Jully 1668 – for a chamber maill fra Mertimes 1667 till Witsonday 1668 –		
	that I flited out off the said chamber		• 12 • 00 • –
John	29 Jully 1668 to John Hamiltoun merchant in the Bow in full off ane		
Hamiltoun	accompt on his discharge at the fit theroff date 29 Jully 1668	16–07–06	• 16 • 07 • 06
Isobell –	The 27 off Jully 1668– to Isobell Gray which shoe peyit to Alexander –		

Gray –	Bain webster for weiving – to wit –		
Alexander	17 ell off braid lining at – 4s. 6d. the ell	03–16–06	
Bain–	26 ell off lining at 3s. the ell	03–18–00	
webster	for warping ale – 12s.: for sowing 7s. is	00–19–00	• 08 • 13 • 06
Robert	The 28 Jully 1668 to Robert Ritchesons wyffe in ready money for –		
Ritchesone	which I peyit befor Alexander Pitcairne – John Andersone & John Steuart		
	1– 25 double treis at 24s. the peice	30–00–00	
	2– 10 single treis at – 10s. the peice	05–00–00	• 35 • 00 • –
Thomas	The 30 off Jully 1668 to Thomas Sandelands wright for – 40 double		
Sandelands	treis & 40 single treis – 60 lib. on his discharge off the said date		• 60 • 00 • –
Mr John	29 Jully 1668 to William Hamiltoun for Mr John Clerks boord fra the		
Clerk –:	23 off May 1668 till Munday – 3 Agust 1668 is – 2 month – 10 days at		
	40 lib. – in the 3 month 31–03–04		• 31 • 03 • 4
	19 ½ ell off round twidlt harden for palliases at 5s. 6d. the ell	05–07–03	
507–08–6	30 Jully 1668 to Ard More for – 8 short knapel at 12s. the peice –		
.18–15–0	is – 4–16– for cairiage fra Leith to Leith wynd – 4s. 4d. – 2 off		
.55–15–2	them sawen – 2 drachts milk on – 2–8d. is 7s. in all	05–03–00	• 10 • 07 • 6
.03–12–0	22 Jully to John Rob for a seyth	01–05–00	
.02–14–10	22 Jully to John Pennycooke for biging – 52 rude of fald dykes at 2s. –		
.51–17–0	a rude	05–00–00	
.04–07–0	Munday 13 Jully to Sir John Nicolsons meassons – 36s.	01–16–00	
.14–03–2	To Arche Andersone for trouts at 4 severall tyms	01–00–00	
.12–00–0	For the gray horse his charges severall tyms	00–06–00	
.16–07–6	18 Jully to William Oustin for bottoming – 2 ridls	00–09–00	

.08–13–6	7 Jully to Anna Irving to get oyll.......................... 10s.		
.35–00–0	11 Jully to John Rob for a pynt off oyll .... 12s.		
.60–00–0	23 Jully – 1 quart off oyll .... 20s.	02–02–00	
.31–03–4	For hering 4s.	00–04–00	
.10–07–6	Whyt breid in the month off Jully	01–10–00	• 13 • 12 • –
.13–12–0	The end off Jully 1668;		
845–16–6	The disbursments in Jully 1668		• 845 • 16 • 6

[71]

Agust 1668–	The disbursments in Agust 1668–		
	T[51] 1 Agust to William Brouns woman – whair I have my chamber	00–12–00	
	For sad louping to my cloths	00–15–00	
	1 Agust to my brother Jo: Andersone – for mending James		
	Clerks shoone	00–10–00	
	For 6 New Testaments whyt print at 17s. the peice	05–02–00	• 06 • 19 • –
Roᵗ Rae – :	1 Agust 1668 to Robert Rae on his discharge date the 1 off Agust 1668 –		
dails –	96 lib. for – 200 dails at – 48 lib. the hundreth		• 96 • 00 • –
200th....	Wedensday 5 Agust 1668 to Rachel Rutherfoord Alexander Clerks mamie		
Alexander	1– given hir a stone off wooll worth – 4 lib	04–00–00	
Clerks Mamie	2– given hir a shilling	00–12–00	• 04 • 12 • –
Couper	The 5 off Agust 1668 – to John Davisone couper – for girding severall looms		
	26s.	01–06–00	
	10 Agust to Marie Clerk to buy blew & whyt stiffing	01–09–00	

	10 Agust to my brother John Andersone – for 6 halff pounds of whyt		
	confections – coriander & carv[i]e at 12s. the pound is	01–16–00	
	11 Agust to John Walker smith for a litle bordert lock &c	01–05–04	• 05 • 16 • 4
Armes for	Leith the 7 off Agust 1668 peyit to Alexander Mill merchant in –		
the Militia	Lithgow for – [blank] on F[r]yday – 7 Agust 1668 –		
	4 muskets at 6 lib. the peice	24–00–00	
	4 pair off bandelirs at – 24s. the pair	04–16–00	
	4 picks at 48s. the peice	09–12–00	• 38 • 08 • –
	In Edinburgh – Saturday the 8 off Agust 1668 to the said Alexander –		
	mill for a pair off pistols – and a pair off hulsters 12 lib. 12s.		• 12 • 12 • –
Militia	Charges in Leith – 7 Agust 1668 – when I boght the said armes –		
	1– for a tow cairiage & pack threid	00–10–00	
	2– spent severall ways	02–06–00	• 02 • 16 • –
	[blank in the original manuscript]		
divets	The 12 off Agust 1668 to John Nilsone for – 7000 divets for sarking the		
	new howsses is to be theyked with heather – at 12s. the 1000 is – 4–4s.		
	bot I peyit him bot 4 lib.	04–00–00	
Patrik Craig	18 off Agust to Patrik Craig – 3–13–4d. for a boll off oats David		
James Frizel	Clerk got fra him the 18 off February 1668 for the fowls	03–13–04	
cols	18 Agust to James Frizel for – 22 laid off cols	04–00–00	• 11 • 13 • 4

[51] Clerk began this entry with a 'T' (likely to write 'The') then changed his mind and entered the date.

Agnes Clerk	18 Agust to Agnes Clerk 3–10s. to buy a hood off taffatie..................	03–10–00	
pouder	18 Agust to John Rob for – halff a pound off powder	00–08–00	
blitching	22 Agust to Agnes Clerk to give Jennet [blank] for being 30 days –		
cloth	about the housse – blitching cloth at 1s. a day and hir meit................	01–10–00	
George bell	22 Agust Saturday at night to George Bell for ale & eygs		
	to the bairns	00–14–10	
	22 Ag[ust] to Helen Clerk to give William Steuarts wyffe for – 4		
	douzane eygs..	00–06–08	
	22 Ag[ust] to Tho: Andersone for thee gray horse when Mistre Haml:		
	cam out..	00–01–06	• 06 • 11 • –
.6–19–0	To Arche Andersone for salmond trouts	00–10–08	
96–00–0	20 Agust to Montlothians in [sic] woman in drink money James		
.4–12–0	Chisholms...	01–09–00	
.5–16–4	Said day to Mr Kintors quarier – 6s. – at Walltowr – 3s. 4d. is	00–09–04	
38–.8–0	26 Agust to George Clerk webster in Leswaid for warping ale	00–12–00	
12–12–0	29 Agust to John Rob for 1 pair off hervest gloves for David Clerk.....	00–04–06	
.2–16–0	To Arche Andersone for a salmond trout...	00–03–00	
11–13–4	For whyt breid in the month off Agust...	01–03–06	• 04 • 12 • –
.6–11–0	The end off Agust 1668		
.4–12–0	The disbursments in Agust 1668.....		• 189 • 19 • 8
189–19–8			

[72]

September 1668	The disbursements in September 1668		
A bull	F[r]yday – 4 of September– to William Stewart– 5–6–8 to give to James Russell in Draiwa for a blak bull he got fra him for our usse of a yeir old........		• 05 • 06 • 08
3 Bols of Leith meil	5 September – to Cudbert Kyll in Lintoun for peirs	02–02–04	
	4 September Will Stewart & Anna Irving boght at Leith – 3 bols off – meill at 4 lib. 8s. the boll........ls. 8d. off custom is	13–05–08	
	2 ell off stenting at 6s. 4d. the ell	00–12–08	• 16 • 02 • 08
	To Arche Andersone for trouts & pleting rash cords..........................	00–09–00	
	4 September to Anna Irving 11s. shoe gave to Nathaniel Thomsone For mending the bairns shoone	00–11–00	
	To John Rob for – 2 pecks off salt	00–08–00	
	11 off September to William Storie for weiving 32 ell off hardn	01–12–00	• 03 • 00 • –
	The 21 Jully to Agnes Clerk for small disbursments	03–00–00	
	1 ell and a halff a quarter off grein peropris......................................	02–08–00	
	4 once off tobaco	00–06–00	
	To John Whyt for – 4 pair off shoone for William & Alexander Clerks	03–12–00	
	3 lb off candle for my chamber in Edinburgh	00–12–00	
	2 lb off Spanish broun	01–08–00	
	1 crooked hunting horne...	01–04–00	
	2 sown sivs	00–05–00	
	1 litle yvorie box	00–06–00	• 12 • 01 • –

Margaret Clerk	24 September to Thomas Mackie tailyeur in full off ane accompt on his discharge – for making 2 gouns &c & furnishing for Margaret Clerk	21–01–04	
Margaret Clerk	23 September to David Boyd in full of ane accompt on his discharge for tabein be Margaret Clerk a goun	43–12–06	
John Cooke	23 September to John Cooke in full off ane accompt on his discharge	15–10–11	
peuter	29 September to Robert Weir peuterer for some new peuter and changing of old peuter on his compt markit – A B	10–04–00	• 90 • 08 • 09
dails – 60	26 September in Leith–		
	1– to Thomas Youngs man for – 60 dails	33–00–00	
	2– 2 pair off peper corns	00–12–00	
	3– to Robert Ritchesone for 20 hizle sticks for mattock shafts and – 5 girth stings for gads	~ ~ ~ 01–05–00	• 34 • 17 • –
	26 of September to James Stewart for a sand glasse off 3 hours	01–04–08	
	For dressing a powder horne	00–06–00	
	Peyit for a tin chamber pot	01–16–00	
	28 September to John Cooke for a stock lock	02–13–04	
	To William Broun for – 4 skins to be poutches	01–04–00	
Fleuring nails	25 September to Isobell Fermer in John Dows housse for 2000 ~ ~ fleuring nails – 11–10s.	11–10–00	
A saidle for my	29 September – to Alexander Dobsone for a pad saidle with a covert – off calff skins – blak – I furnisht the rushie leather my selff &–		

selff	got it fra Archebald More –		
	I got not furnishing at all to it bot the bare saidle	08–14–00	• 27 • 08 • –
Mistresse	24 September to Mistresse Hamiltoun for these things –		
Hamiltoun	1– 5 ½ quarters off Holland at 2 merk ane ell to be Marie Clerk a		
Marie &	waistcot	01–16–08	
Margaret	2– 1 pair off shoone for Margaret Clerk	01–00–00	
Clerks	3– and a dolor shoe gave Marie Clerk to go to a brydel	02–18–00	• 06 • 14 • 08
	To John Mackenzie for stocking a musket	01–16–00	
	To Francis Hendersone for making a dog head to a pistol	01–00–00	
	25 off September to James Clerk – a dolor to ly by him to –		
	pay out for any small thing he neids	02–18–00	
	To Mage Wade for – 2 pecks off salt	00–08–00	
	For – 3 quarters off a hundreth off herings	00–15–00	
	For – whyt breid in September	01–04–00	• 08 • 01 • –
	05–06–8 –: The disbursments in September 1668		• 203 • 19 • 09
	16–02–8 –: The end off September:		
	03–00–0 : 1668		
	12–01–0 :		
	90–08–9 :		
	34–17–0 :		
	27–08–0 :		
	.6–14–8 :		
	.8–01–0 :		
	203–19–9 –		

[73]

October

1668 The disbursments in October 1668 ~ ~ ~:

candles The 3 off October 1668 – to John Rob – 12 lib. which he gave to Robert
Hendrie candl[e] maker for – 4 stone off small candle at 3 lib. the
stone 12–00–00

To [sic] 9 of October to John Reid for – 12 ½ days – that his sone George
Georg Reid did sheir in harvest 1668 01–18–00

1 ston off picked cords for sowing on heather on west syde
of the barn 04–06–08

1 pynt off lint seid oyll .... 01–10–00 • 19 • 14 • 08

at Roslin – 9 October 1668 –

1– for a douzane of trinchers 01–06–08

2– to John Lowrie for – 9 turnt staff heads 00–18–00

3– 1 bolt off whyt knitings 00–04–06

4– 2 trumps 00–02–08

5– to Adam Gate foster off the wood who cutit 24 staiks for the
byre 12s. and 1 quart ale is .... 00–15–04 • 03 • 07 • 02

Mr Jo: Clerk The 17 off October 1668 to James Ramsay in the Halls – 7 lib. 4s. for
Ja[mes] Ramsay 16 days Mr John Clerk wes in his howsse at – 9s. ilk day 07–04–00

To Arche Andersone for salmond trouts 00–06–00

Pan cratch To John Rob for a firlot off pan cratch for Skobie well 00–16–00

14 October to John Rob for 2 pecks off salt 00–08–00

19 October to Arche Paton in Newhall for making a plough 00–13–04

	21 October to Wille Burton for 10 pynts & a chopin of ale	00–17–06	• 10 • 04 • 10
James Fergus tailyeour	23 October to James Fergus tailyeur for 4 days he wroght at Newbiging in shewing bed plaids & helping to mak 2 cots for Will & Alexander Clerk	00–18–00	
Ja– Frizel for cols	24 October to James Frile Frizel[52] in Carlips for – 14 laid of cols whair off he rebated 2 rests – 12 at 4s. the laid & 14 turnors to the bearers is	02–10–04	
John Rob Hervest fie	14 October to John Rob for his hervest fie in anno 1668 – 4 lib. 7s. and for his supper meill 20s. is	05–07–00	• 08 • 15 • 04
Great salt	28 October to John Rob for – 6 pecks off sa: great salt he got at Leith the said day for salting beiff at 12s. the peck	03–12–00	
George Whyt for theyking 3 howsses &c with heather	Fryday – at night – 30 October – to George Whyt indweller at Newland kirk for 43 days – he wes in theyking with heather – the wark howsse – the cow byre – the hen howsse – and laying a new fleis – off heather on all the bak off the barne at 10s. in the day with his – meit is – 21 lib. 10s. bot he rebated me 3 days – so I peyit him bot for 40 days – at 10s. in the day – is – 20 lib.	20–00–00	• 23 • 12 • –
small whyt salt 19 – 14 – .8	31 October to William Stewart who went to the pans and broght 6 firlots off whyt salt fra John Fossys relict – for the salt he peyit 3–16–8d. and for custom & excyse given him – 1 chopin off ale to drink is	03–17–06	

[52] It is unclear if Clerk made a spelling error here and then continued. In the original, he did not cross out the first attempt.

.3 – .7 – .2	To John Rob for – 4 douzane off oynions – 4s. and – 4s. for a		
10 – .4 – 10	haik to a whill.........is 8s.	00–08–00	
.8 –15 – .4	For whyt breid in the month of October	01–07–06	• 05 • 05 • –
23 –12 – .0	The end off October 1668 The disbursments in October 1668		• 70 • 19 • –
.5 – .5 – .0			
70 – 19 – .0			
November	The disbursments in the month off November 1668		
1668	The 3 off November 1668 to George Clerk webster in Leswaid for		
Georg Clerk	weiving 32 ell off cloth – 6 quarter braid for courtings at 2s. the ell	03–04–00	
webster	For poping	00–08–00	• 03 • 12 • –
William	On Wedensday – 28 of October 1668 William & Agnes[53] & Alexander Clerks		
Alexander	entert in boording in George Bels in Pennycooke and on the – 3 off November –		
Jennet	1668 I payit to Margaret Hopkirk – 40 lib. for the boord of the said 3 –		
Clerks	thrie month – fra the 28 of ~~N~~ October 1668 to the 28 of January		
boording	1669 – is acording to 13 lib. 6s. 8d. for ilk ane off them ilk 3 month		• 40 • 00 • –
Androw	3 November 1668 peyit the hird Androw Marshals fie –		
Marshall	The said day to his goodmother Nans Potter................	03–13–04	
hird	He wes absent seik 2 month for which I rebated onlie	01–06–08	
	Given hir for his shoone................	00–09–00	• 05 • 09 • –
Jo:	11 November 1668 to John Sibbald 10 lib. & 12s. for his shoone for his		
Sibbald	his [sic] fie fra Witsonday 1668 till Mertimes 1668	10–12–00	• 10 • 12 • –
Mr John	Accompt which Mr Jo: Clerk disbursit at Edinburg [sic] the 7 of September		
Clerk	1668 – being – 37s. 6d. which I deliverit to him—:		
	1– 5 leather belts	00–16–06	

2– 2 pound off Spanish broun 00–08–00
3– for Jacks meit during the night he wes in toun 00–08–00
4– his own expense .... 00–05–00 • 01 • 17 • 06

03–12.0
40–00.0 The disbursments above in November 1668 ...... • 61 • 10 • 06
05–09–0
10–12–0
01–17–6
61–10–6

[74]

The disbursments on the other syde in November 1668 is.......... • 61 • 10 • 06

Ane accompt of 8 lib. 4s. which I peyit to Mr Jo: Clerk in November 1668 –

Mr John Clerk

1– for dipping his stuff clok 00–12–00
2– to Archbald Teinder for shewing severall things to me 00–06–00
3– for dressing 2 hatts 00–08–00
4– for fitting – 2 pair of stokings 01–04–00
5– for mending my shoes 00–08–00
6– for my dyet– for the space off 3 days 01–04–00
7– to David Gray for a pair of waxt shoone 01–14–00

[53] Clerk listed William, Alexander, and Jennet Clerk in the margin. However, the account makes clear that the payment for boarding was for Agnes, and not Jennet, Clerk.

Margin	Entry	Amount	Total
	8– to William Carmichel for ane pair off leather hose	01–04–00	
	9– spent at the Halls – 24s. – he wes 16 days thair by & attour for which I peyit James Ramsay acording to 9s. ilk day is – 7– 4s.	01–04–00	• 08 • 04 • –
4 No^v^	To George Clerk webster in Leswaid for warping ale	00–09–00	
	Said day to Agnes Clerk for ane once of sene	00–13–04	
	5 November – to Gilbert Pennycooks dochter for skuls – that shoe said Wille Stewart got in summer – & 3 off them I got fra hir my selff	00–07–00	
	11 November to Isobell Scot for a leyg off youn[g] beiff	02–00–00	
	To John Rob – for oynions he boght at 2 tymes	00–06–00	• 03 • 15 • 04
Thomas Andersone	The 24 off November 1668– compleited & peyit to Thomas Andersone – 54 lib. Scots as ane yeir and ane halff yeirs fie at 36 lib. yeirlie and that fra Witsonday 1667 till Mertimes 1668		• 54 • 00 • –
	25 November to Alexander Hastie for 4 litle baskits – 13s. 4d. & 1 large baskit or mand to hold the horse corn – 6s. 8d. is.....20s.	01–00–00	
candles	27 November to John Rob for – 1 ston 2 lb off small candle he got fra Robert Cleghorne in Dalkeith – at 3 lib. 2s. the ston is	03–10–00	
61–10–6.	To John Rob – for going twyse to Dalkeith	00–09–04	
08–04–0.	For whyt breid in the month off November	01–04–08	• 06 • 04 • –
03–15–4.			
54–00–0.	The end off November 1668: The disbursments in November 1668 ...		• 133 • 13 • 10
06–04–0.			
133–13–10.			

December 1668:	The debursments in December 1668	
silver wark	The 2 off December to Edowart Cleghorne goldsmith for a silver tanker – and a silver dish – 108–13s. 6d. in full off his accompt on his discharge – date the said – 2 off December 1668	• 108 • 13 • 06
John Gray smith in north Leith	The 2 off December to John Gray smith in north Leith – 213–2–8 in full off ane accompt on his discharge date the said 2 off December 1668 in full off this accompt & all uthers preseiding the said day – for 4 new bosse – windows – 3 new chimneys –& for mending ane old chimney –& for 1000 – small takits – 213–2–8	• 213 • 02 • 08
David Pringle apothecar	The 9 off December 1668 to David Pringle apothecarie – 13–17– 6 in full off ane accompt on his discharge date the said 9 off December and off all former accompts preseiding the said day	• 13 • 17 • 06
Brande	3 December to Robert Hamilton – 26 lib. 8s. on his discharge date the said day for 22 pynts off brande – at 24s. the pynt	• 26 • 08 • –
Chamber maill	To William Broun – 12 lib. on his discharge date the 2 off December 1668 – for my chamber maill fra Witsonday 1668 till Mertimes 1668	• 12 • 00 • –
John Tod	2 off December to John Tod locksmith – 13–16–8 for bell nails in full off ane accompt on his discharge off all things generallie whatsoever preseiding the said 2 off December 1668	• 13 • 16 • 08
Mr John Clerks boord	1 December 1668 to William Hamilton merchant for Mr John Clerks boord – fra Teusday the 24 off November 1668 that he entert home to his housse – till the 24 off off [sic] February 1669 is 3 month 40 lib	• 40 • 00 • –
	4 December to John Whyt for 2 pair off bairns shoone 01–16–00	
	6 peper off prins at 4s. the peper 01–04–00	

108–13–06	1 dark lantern	16s.–		
213–02–08	1 larger dark lantern	22s.–		
.13–17–06	1 larger dark lantern	30s.–	03–08–00	
.26–08–00	8 December to John Gedd[e]s for binding 6 Neu Testaments		02–10–00	• 08 • 18 • –
.12–00–00	To John Broun for a large kitching knyffe		00–17–00	
.13–16–08	To Thomas Wedel for tining 2 drappers		00–02–00	
.40–00–00	2 pound off ginger		00–12–00	
.08–18–00	4 once off leafe tobaco		00–06–00	
.09–10–00	2 packits off tows		01–00–00	
446–06–04	6 Inglis shod shools		04–12–00	
.03–00–00	8 December to William Brouns woman in drink money		00–12–00	
449–06–04	12 *catechise* –& 4 *proverbs* 6s.		00–10–00	
	For making a blaik muff.................of a dogs skin		00–17–00	• 09 • 10 • –
	1 grosse of long broun leather poynts		00–14–00	
	1 grosse of short broun poynts		00–07–00	
	1 hare broome for swiping chambers		00–15–00	
	To Adam Darlins wyffe for mending a perewick		01–04–00	• 03 • 00 • –
	The disbursments above in December 1668			• 449 • 06 • 04

[75]

The disbursments in December on the other syde amonts to	• 449 • 06 • 04
4 lb of Spanish broun at 4s. the pound	• 00 • 16 • –
8 yrne girds for tubs	• 01 • 07 • –

	For severall toys for the bairns for hansel Munday		• 02 • 15 • –
	11 December to Robert Hamilton for 4 ½ ell off gray tanton serg – 30s. the ell		• 06 • 15 • –
Lint whill	Saturday – 5 December to John Rob – 2 dolors to pay for a lint whill in – Dalkeith		• 05 • 16 • –
	17–09–00//		• 17 • 09 • –
	8 December 1668 to Androw Ker for gloves for the bairns:		
Bairns gloves	8 pair off gloves at 13s. 4d. the pair	05–06–08	
	2 pair off gloves at 3s. 8d. the pair	00–13–04	
	5 pair off gloves at 3s. 8d. the pair	00–18–04	
	2 pair off gloves	00–06–00	
	4 pair off gloves	00–16–00	• 08 • 00 • 04
John... Cooke...	5 December 1668 to John Cooke for		
	1 plait 1 handle and a lifter for the great turn pyke dore	01–16–00	
	30 halff sneks & 30 nails thairtoo	02–18–00	
	For making a lock go easie and making a gaird to it	00–10–00	• 05 • 04 • –
	The 3 of October 1668 delivert to Marie Clerk 7 dolors	20–06–00	
	10 December 1668 delivert to Isobell Gray – 9 lib. 14s.	09–14–00	
		30–00–00	
Marie Clerk	Which 30 lib. wes disbursit as follows–		
	7 ston off butter at 3 lib. 2s. the stone	21–14–00	
	For cairying it fra the weyhowsse	00–03–00	
Isobell Gray	For fieing a woman – 6s. – to the woman in earnest – 3s.	00–09–00	
	1 pair off shoes for Marie Clerk	01–10–00	

For 6 quarters off serge for Marie Clerk at 48s. the ell 03–12–00
For making the waistcot 01–10–00
1 pair off gloves for Marie Clerk .... 01–04–00 • 30 • 02 • –
I have acompt of all this

Marie – Accompt of 5 dolors my brother gave to Marie Clerk – 6 November 1668 –
Clerk – and how it wes imployed –
Isobel– 8 ell off dornick at 10s. the ell.................................. 04–00–00
Gray– 6 ell of 5 quarter braid lining at 24s. the ell.............. 07–04–00.......... 11–04–00 • 11 • 04 • –
10 December Isobell Gray randert me...................... 03–06–00
James– 14–10–00
Clerk– 10 December to William Lorimer on his discharge 11 lib. 11s. for 7
449–06–04 quarters – off cloth at 6 lib. 12s. the ell to be James Clerk a cot 11–11–00
17–09–00 To James Clerk on his recept at the fit off ane particullar –
08–04–00 accompt 03–01–08 to pay for furnishing thertoo .... 03–01–08 • 14 • 12 • 08
05–04–00 I went to Edinburgh on Teusday the 1 off December 1668 –& returnt to
30–02–00 Newbiging on Saturday the 12 off the said month off December 1668 –
11–04–00 during the which 12 days I disbursit – fra the 1 off December to the 12
14–12–08 off the said month – 536 lib. 2s. – as it is particullarlie set doun how I –
536–02–00 disbursit the samin.. • 536 • 02 • –
Orknay 1 December to John Rob to get Orknay butter for the smeiring the rest
butter off the sheip.........................he got 15 trose pound for – 40s. 02–00–00
John Clerks 15 December to John Clerk – 42 lib. for a yeir and half a yeirs –
fie 1 ½ yeir Fie fra Witsonday 1667 till Mertimes 1668 at 28 lib. yeirlie .... 42–00–00 • 44 • 00 •

George Clerk webster –	The 12 off December 1668 to Anna Irving which shoe peyit to Georg[e] Clerk webster.			
	12 ell off stuff at 2s. the ell	01–04–00		
	18 ell off plain cloth at 18d. the ell	01–07–00		
	18 ell off plaiding at 1s. the ell	00–18–00	03–09–00	
Jean– Stewarts fie	The 23 of December to William Stewart for his dochter Jean Stewart her fie fra Mertimes 1667 till Mertimes 1668 is acording		02–00–00	
	to – 8 lib. for ilk halff yeir		16–00–00	
William– Stewart	The said day to William Stewart for – 7 pecks off cutings off oats wes got for our horse a long tyme ago – at 3s. the peck		01–01–00	• 20 • 10 • –
	For oynions		00–06–08	
Mill –	17 December to the millers for drying 26 bols off oats		00–06–08	
Kill –	21 December to Thomas Andersone when he went grind them		00–06–08	
	On Wedensday at night – 16 December – to Thomas Andersone – when he went to Edinburgh with the gray horse to bring out – Marie Clerk and stayd a night in the toun his & horse charges		00–12–00	
James – Peirsie– maltman	23 off December to James Peirsie maltman for making 3 steips – off mal[t] 2 in the end off anno 1667 and 1 in December 1668 6s. – 8d. for ilk steip in drink money		01–00–00	• 02 • 12 • –

536–02–00
44–00–00
20–10–00
02–12–00
603–04–00

The disbursment in December 1668 on this syde and the other is – 603–04–00 .... • 603 • 04 • –

[76]

The disbursments on the other 2 syds in December 1668 is .... • 603 • 04 • –

24 December to Agnes Clerk to give hir sister Margaret for spindls 00–04–00

24 December – 2 cunings – 19s. 1 rumple peice off beiff 11s. 6d.
both .... 01–10–06 • 01 • 14 • 6

Bessie Whyt 23 December 1668 to Bessie Whyt for hir fie fra Witsonday –
hir fie 1668 till Mertimes 1668 – 8–14s. .... 08–14–00 • 08 • 14 • –

28 December to a chapman for severall small things 00–14–00

The accompt off a dolor given to James Clerk – 25 September 1668

James 1– for mending his shoone 00–10–00
Clerk 2– 3 douzan off silk breist buttons at 2s. the douzane 00–06–00
3– 3 douzan off silk mandill buttons at 4s. the douzane .. 00–12–00
4– 1 pair off gray waxed leather shoes 01–06–08
5– 6 neidls and a timber caisse .... 00–03–04 ... 02–18–00 • 03 • 12 • –

30 December to Anna Irving.......19–05–06...which shoe waird at
Edinburgh for:

Lint....... 1– 4 ston – 4 lb of lint at 4 lib. 6s. the ston 18–05–06
2– 1 pair off shoone for Agnes Clerk 00–14–00
3– 1 string off clasps –& eyes...6s I say –3s. 00–03–00
603–04–00 4– for the gray horse his expense .... 00–03–00 • 19 • 05 • 6

01–14–06 For whyt breid in the month of December .... • 01 • 06 • –

08–14–00 The end off December 1668 The disbursments in December 1668...... • 637 • 16 • –

03–12–00

19–05–06
01–06–00
637–16–00

1: January	1668	168–17–02
2: Februar	1668	789–00–08
3: Marche	1668	287–07–00
4: Aprill	1668	272–08–05
5: May	1668	329–06–04
6: June	1668	476–06–02
7: Jully	1668	845–16–06
8: Agust	1668	189–19–08
9: September	1668	203–19–09
10: October	1668	070–19–00
11: November	1668	133–13–10
12: December	1668	637–16–00

The disbursments fra the 1 off January 1668 to the last day off December 1668 is............... 4405 lib. 10s. 6d. .... •4405 • 10 • 06

John: Clerk

[77]

January 1669 The disbursments in January – 1669

To Marie Clerk – 4 dolors 11–12s. 1 box – 6s. 11–18–00
To Margaret Clerk – 3 dolors – 1 box – 6s. 09–00–00

To Agnes Clerk which wes my dear and weell beloved –
dochters Elizabeth Clerks ....

2 dolors and a halff 07–05–00
1 36s. peices 01–16–00
1 thick swams 18s. peice 00–18–00
1 merk peice 00–13–04
1–5 sols peice 00–06–08
1–3 pence and 1 whyt pennie .... 00–04–00 .... 11–03–00 • 32 • 01 • –

More to Agnes Clerk – which wes hir dear sisters Elizabeth Clerks
1 – round box silvert & painted with grein ....
1 – venize litle fiol with a skrewing on silver head ....
1 – round yvorie box with a handle for keiping musk ....
1 – spreklt yvorie pick tooth caisse with a whisle ....
1 – litle shewd silk purse with a si:[54] cristel stamp ....
1 – large cut wark band made for a man ....
1 – box lyke Maries & Margarets cost 6s. ....

To Mr John Clerk 08–14–00
32–01–00 To James Clerk 02–00–00
14–14–00 To the younger bairns – 40s. off turnors – with divers small toys 02–00–00
05–01–00 To Marie Dowglas a – 40s. peice .... 02–00–00 • 14 • 14 • –
04–13–00 To Thomas Andersone 01–09–00
03–06–00 To David Clerk 00–18–00
06–01–06 To John Clerk 00–12–00
326–00–00 To John Sibbald for mending the bairns –

20–00–00 shoone –& for hansell 01–04–00
23–05–00 To Arche Craig – 9s. 00–09–00
08–09–00 To John Dicksone.. 00–09–00.......... • 05 • 01 • –
443–10–06 To Anna Irving 01–16–00
To Jennet Shanks.. 00–18–00
To Nans Johnstoun.. 00–18–00
To Isobell Waker kitchin woman 00–12–00
To Jean Stewart byre woman .... 00–09–00.......... • 04 • 13 • –
To John Broun schoolmaster ane
pair off gray stokings worth 36s. 01–16–00
To John Rob 6s. 00–06–00
To John Broun bedel 00–12–00
To Sande Stewart 00–02–00
To George Reid 00–06–08
To his sister.....................[blank] Reid.................. 00–03–04.......... • 03 • 06 • –
3 January – to John Crawford when he cam to Newbiging to put in –
a cauter in Jennet Clerks neck Newhals man – 30s. 01–10–00
Mill – Kill 7 Januar to David Clerk for milling & killing 24 bols of [o]ats 00–13–04
11 January to Edowart Thomsone for a haire 00–06–08
To Jo Rob for 2 douzane oynions & 6 hadocks.. 00–09–02
Herings – 16 Januar to John Rob for halff a hundreth salt hering 00–13–04
Kipper – 18 Januar to John Rob for 2 kipper 01–06–08 & 6s. 4d. to: G. Bell

[54] It is unclear what Clerk was trying to write here before he changed his mind and wrote the word ‘cristel’. The error was left as found.

	for carying them to Edinburgh.........is – 33s.	01–13–00	
	18 January to Alisone Craig for a hair	00–06–00	
	18 January to Edowart Thomsone for 2 perdriks	00–10–00	• 06 • 01 • 06
Mr William Hamilton	The 21 off January 1669 to Mr William Hamiltoun minister at – Pennicooke [sic] – 322 lib. as his yeirs stipend fra Mertimes 1667 – till Mertimes 1668 –& 4 lib. for his grasse for the said yeir – is both 326 lib. which is conteind in a discharge he gave me date the – 21 off January 1669		• 326 • 00 • –
John Broun schoole – master –	The 23 off January 1669 to John Broun schoolemaster in Pennycooke – 20 lib. for his stipend fra Candlemes 1668 till Candlemes 1669 – on his discharge date the said 23 January 1669		• 20 • 00 • –
Alexander[55] Cleghorne Candlemaker in Dalkeith	The 23 off January 1669 to Robert Cleghorne candlemaker in Dalkeith – 23 lib. 5s. – for 7 ½ ston off candle small on[e]s all at 3 lib. 2s. the stone – on his discharge at the fit off his accompt off the said date – which accompt is markit – AB		• 23 • 05 • –
	For – haddocks – 5 – 6d. to Sande Hairtie for sweiping – 2 chimneys – 4s. – To Edowart – Thomson for a hare 6s.	00–15–06	
	For whyt breid in Januar – 1669	01–10–00	
	For fresh beiff in Januar – 1669	06–03–06	• 08 • 09 • –
	The end off January 1669 — The disbursment in Januar 1669		• 443 • 10 • 06

[78]

February	The disbursments in February – 1669		
1669 oters skin	1 – off Februar: to John Ramsay for ane otters skin he took in Ravens Hauch – burne – 40s.	02–00–00	
Couper:	2 – February to John Davisone couper in Lintoun – for girding severall looms	01–16–00	
Marie Clerk	The 20 off February to Adam Patersone 18s. for a horse hyre Mr Jo: Clerk cam out on – with his sister Marie Clerk on Thursday the –	00–00–00	
	17 off December 1668 – when shoe cam to Newbiging	00–18–00	• 04 • 14 • –
	I went to Edinburgh the 10 of February 1669 being on a Wedensday and disbursit as fellows [sic]		
William Stewart hynd.....	The 11 of Februar – to John Hamiltoun merchant in the Bow 57s. which our hynd – William Stewart gave me to pay him – for halff a ston off lint the said William Stewart wes resting unto the said John Hamiltoun....	02–17–00	
William Beck for secking & twidlt hardn	To William Beck merchant for 10 February 1669 ~		
	1– 31 ell of twidlt hardn at 5s. the ell........................	07–15–00	
	2– 12 ell off braid secking at 8s. the ell........................	04–16–00	
	3– 25 ell off narow secking at 6s. 8d. the ell	08–06–08	
	4– 14 ½ ell more off narow secking at 6s. 8d. the ell	04–16–08	
	5– 2 ½ ell off secking to be a poik for holding great nails at 6s. 8d. the ell	00–16–08	• 26 • 09 • –
	2 lb off whyt suger candie at 20s. the pound........................	02–00–00	

[55] Clerk made an error, either in the margin or the body of the account, when identifying the candlemaker.

	4 lb off whyt stiffing at 3s. 4d. the pound	00–13–04	
	4 once off blew stiffing	00–03–04	
	3– bolt off whyt twidlt knitings	01–09–00	
	2– wooden dishes –& – 2 litle trinchers	00–12–00	
	To Androu Ker for – changeing 8 pair off bairns gloves	01–00–00	
	15 February to my brothers man – William Deans	01–04–00	• 07 • 01 • 08
Ro: Walker	The 11 off February 1669 to Robert Walker on his discharge off the		
smith –	said date for 400 great diamant headit nails at – 7 lib. 10s. the 100	30–00–00	
William	The 11 off February 1669 to William Seaton on his discharge of	–00–00	
Seatoun	The said date – for making 2 cloth cots for James Clerk	02–18–00	
	For Mr Androw Grays booke for Alexander Clerk	00–16–00	
	2 douzane off buttons for Robert Sands clok	00–09–00	• 34 • 03 • –
	To Mr Robert Swintoun for lookeing out Largos registrat band	00–12–00	
	1 pound off diapalma	00–18–00	
	For waxt cloth for cauters	00–03–00	
	2 dandre combs	00–14–00	
John Tod	15 February to John Tod for 300 small bell nails at 40s. the 100	06–00–06	
1 small	15 February to John Crichtoun for 1 fyne small meil sive	03–07–04	
meill sive	1 fyne wyde sive	00–10–00	
	For – 12 fyne trinchers to him	01–10–00	• 13 • 04 • 04
	1 – chopin glasse botle	00–08–00	
	8 once off broun suger candie	00–07–00	
	4 once off whyt candie	00–05–00	
	1 once off almond oyll in a glasse	00–09–00	

	To Androw Ker for dressing 2 hart hyds	01–04–00	
	To John Fergusone – for 1 pair off pantons	01–15–00	• 04 • 08 • –
Bend leather	The 15 off February to John Fumertoun cordoner for halff ane Irish		
	hyde off bend leather weying – 20 lb wecht at 10s. the pound	10–00–00	
Mr Jo: Clerk	The 16 off February 1669 to William Hamiltoun for Mr John –		
	Clerks boord fra the 24 off February 1669 to the 24 off May 1669	40–00–00	
tyking	18 February to Thomas Reid for 12 ell off fyne tyking at 20s. the ell	12–00–00	
John	16 of Februar to John Cooke for a fyne bordert lock with a – –		
Cooke –	gard on its bak – it cheks in with a half cast 4 nails to put it –		
04–14–00	on 1 crosse sheild with 4 takits to put it on 8s. sterlin	04–16–00	• 66 • 16 • –
26–09–00	18 February to John Handisyde for – 4 suger loaffs – weying 8 lb 11		
07–01–08	once at – 12s. the pound	05–04–06	
34–03–00	8 lb off fygs at 4s. the pound	01–12–00	
13–14–04	1 chopin of hony for the bees – 20s. – 1 pig to put it in	01–02–00	
04–08–00	3 box wood combs	00–10–00	
66–16–00	5 litle glasse botls	00–16–00	
11–05–10	6 pound off raisings at 6s. the pound	01–16–00	
18–00–00	4 key rings at 16d. the peice	00–05–04	• 11 • 05 • 10
186–11–10	Fryday 19 February 1669 to Stephen Bruntfield in his own howsse –		
Soape	1– for 2 firikins off soape at 6 lib. 15s. the firkin	13–10–00	
herings	2– halff a barell off Lews hering	04–10–00	• 18 • 00 • –
	all above on this syde		• 186 • 11 • 10
Jo: Lowrie	The 25 off February 1669 to John Lowrie at the mill – 58s. for a making –		
at the mill	a steip off malt – in December – 1668	02–18–00	

1 making of malt........ And for a boll of malt I say for a boll of whyt resavet in ~ December 1668 .... 06–00–00 • 08 • 18 •

1 boll of whyt

186–11–10:
8–18–00: The disbursments on this syde in ~
195–09–10: February 1669 .... • 195 • 09 • 10

[79]

Mr John – Clerk

The disbursments in Februar on the other syde is .... • 195 • 09 • 10

Ane accompt off 14–17–6 – which my brother John Andersone furnished the money theroff to him –& repeyit my brother the same on the 17 of Februar 1669 – I mean he furnished the money to Mr John Clerk the compt is lying by me markit on the bak.........AB ....

1. to Androw [blank] for weiving 6 ell off cloth to be a winter syde cot at – 2s. the ell 00–12–00
2. to John Stinsone for warking it on his discharge 00–15–00
3. (1 pair shoone) the 1 off November 1668 to David Gray for 1 pair waxt shoone.... 01–12–00
4. 3 lb off candle at 4s. 6d. the lb 00–13–06
5. (1 rim peper) 1 rim off peper 04–00–00
6. (700 pens–) 700 pens for my father at 6s. the 100 02–02–00
7. for washing my blak cot 00–06–00
8. to William Hamiltons women in drink money 01–10–00
9. (1 pair shoone) 20 January 1669 to Jo: Fergusone for 1 pair shoone 01–12–00

cols	10. 3 load off cols at 10s. the laid	01–10–00	
	11. for jews ear to my fathers sore throt	00–05–00	
	21 January 1669 – my brother gave James Clerk to mend his	14–17–06	
	shoone – 13s. 4d. which I repeyit to my brother 17 off Februar 1669	00–13–04	• 15 • 10 • 10
cols James Frizel	The 27 off February 1669 to James Frizel for – 70 laid of cols whairof he re [sic] rebated 10 laid so thair rests 60 laid at 4s. the laid is 12 lib. and 10s. I gave him to pay the cairiers at 2d. ilk cairiage		• 12 • 10 • –
kill – – –	3 Februar to David Clerk to kill – 16 bols & 1 firlot off oats	00–05–00	
mill – – –	5 February to him to mill the same	00–05–00	
herings– – –	100 hering – 25s.	01–05–00	
	8 once off whyt suger candie	00–11–00	
Jo: Ramsay	8 February to John Ramsay for 20 perdriks	06–00–00	
	12 ell off whyt worsit at 6d. the ell	00–06–00	
	25 Februar to Arche Andersone for 8 broome boosoms	00–03–04	
	16 February 1669 to David Clerk to drink when he took to the – Lone head 12 bols off beir – to Sander Cutle to be malt – to drink – with the men that helpit him to cary the said beir	00–08–00	• 09 • 03 • 04
	For fresh beiff in the month off February – 33s. and – 13s. 4d. & 59s. ....is	07–05–08	
	For whyt breid in the month of February – 24s.	01–04–00	• 08 • 09 • 08
	The end of February 1669 The disbursments in February 1669 ...		• 241 • 02 • 10

Marche	The disbursments in the month of Marche 1669		
1669	The 2 off Marche 1669 compleited Archebald Craig his fie fra Witsonday		
	1668 till Mertimes 1668 to wit in money – 8 lib. and 20s. for 2 pair		
Arche –	off single sold shoone fra mertimes 1667 till Mertimes 1668 is –		
Craig	acording to a pair off single sold shoone ilk halff yeir with 8 lib. off –		
	– money ilk halff yeir	09–00–00	
seid peys	The 3 off Marche 1669 to James Bothwels wyffe for – 6 firlots		
James	off peys at 4 lib. the boll – whair off 1 boll for seid and halff a		
Bothwell	boll for boylling	06–00–00	
	3 Marche 1669 Anna Irving went to Edinburgh –& waird as folows		
Anna – –	1– 10 ell of stenting at –7s. the ell 03–10–00		
Irving –	2– 8 drop off clovs... 00–07–00		
boght in –	3– 8 once off baling 00–10–00		
Edinburgh	4– 1 pair off shoone for Margaret Clerk .... 01–03–00..........	05–10–00	• 20 • 10 • –
	Accompt of moneys disbursit at my going to Edinburgh which wes		
	on the 5 off March 1669 –		
Jo: Gray	To John Gray smith in north Leith in full of ane accompt the –		
smith in Leith	9 off Marche 1669	10–03–00	
tows	4 lb off small tows at 10s. the lb	02–00–00	
ginger	2 lb off ginger at 6s. the lb..	00–12–00	
	4 lb off fygs.............at 4s. the lb	00–16–00	
clovs	1 once off clovs..	00–11–00	
tows	To John Hamiltoun for 2 packit tows weying 3 lb 12 once		

	at 4s. 6d. the lb	00–17–00	• 14 • 19 • –
	2 once off small whyt threid	00–16–00	
hemp	2 lb off steill hemp.......at 8s. the lb	00–16–00	
	2 lb of other hemp at 7s. the lb	00–14–00	
hardn	To John Whyt for 2 pair of shoone for William & Alexander Clerks	01–16–00	
bleitcht	To William Lawsone for 17 ell of bleitcht hardn at 7s. 4d. the ell	06–05–00	
tows	To John Hamiltoun for 19 fadom of great tows for thets weying 9 – pound at 4s. 6d. the pound	02–00–06	
	1 ell and a halff a quarter of bed plaids	00–14–06	• 13 • 02 • –
hardn	To Thomas Reid for 38 ell of hardn in 3 peices at 4s. 6d. the ell	08–11–00	
Marie Clerk	9 Marche to Isobell Gray to give Marie Clerk to buy a hoode	03–10–00	
	To John Hamiltoun for 10 fadom off tows	00–12–00	
	8 once off whyt candie	00–10–00	
James Clerk	To James Clerk to buy a pair of shoone	01–09–00	
	3 once flour off Brunstaine at 4s. the once	00–12–00	
	12 Marche to my brother for 8 lb of carv[i]e & coriander 10s. the lb	04–00–00	• 19 • 04 • –
	The disbursments above in Marche 1669 – 67–15–0		• 67 • 15 • –

[80]

	The disbursments in Marche 1669 on the other syde is		• 67 • 15 • –
oake planks	11 Marche to Ro: Ritchesone for 7 oaken planks at 24s. the peice	08–08–00	
oyll barels	To Archbald Campbell for 3 cardails oyll treis 18s. a peice	02–14–00	
	2 half cardails oyll treis at 12s. a peice	01–04–00	

Brande –	11 Marche to James Fisse couper in Leith for 24 pynts off brande –		
	at 20s. the pynt	24–00–00	
	To him for a barel to hold the same	01–00–00	
David –	12 Marche to David Pringle in full of ane accompt........	08–00–00	
Pringle	which accompt is markit – DP – I tooke no recept of it	00–00–00	• 45 • 06 • –
	11 Marche 1669 to my brother John Andersone which he gave to Mr		
Mr John:	John Clerk – 3–12s. to buy........		
Clerk	To give Archebald Teinder for making his cot	01–04–00	
	To buy a pair of blak stokings	02–08–00	• 03 • 12 • –
Sanders –	The 8 of Marche 1669 to David Clerk to pay Sanders Cutle in Loanhead		
Cutle 1 steip	– 5 lib. 2s. for making a steip off malt off – 12 bols........	05–02–00	
off malt –	To David Clerk – 3s. 4d. to drink with the men helpit to cary it........	00–03–04	• 05 • 05 • 04
Anna Irvings	The 23 off Marche 1669 compleited Anna Irving a yeirs fie to Witsonday –		
fie 1 yeir	fra Mertimes 1667 till Mertimes 1668 – being 40 merks in the said yeir		
	and 30s. I gave hir the said day to buy a pair off shoone more nor I –		
George	promist hir is in all for the said yeir which I peyit to hir –28–3–4d.		• 28 • 03 • 04
Stewart;	The 26 off Marche 1669 given to George:		
George	Stewart mussitian – twentie thrie dolors		
Thomson	is 66 – 14s.		• 66 • 14 • –
I say George	The said day given to the said George Stewart a fyne new mandor with –		
Stewart	5 strings – cost in Paris – 9 livers [sic]........		• 09 • 00 • –
John	The 30 off Marche 1669 boght fra John Hogens;		
Hogens	10 ell..........		
stuffs	16 ell..........		

	3 ell...............is 29 ell of stuff at 8s. the ell 11–12–00		
	4 ell off twynd stuff at 12s. the ell............................ 02–08–00..........	14–00–00	
	10 ½ ell of bed plaids wit[h] braid sprangs at 12s. the ell	06–06–00	
small grein	22 ell.....		
hardn	20 ell.........is 42 ell of grein small hardn at 7 lib. 15s. the skore is.........	16–05–06	• 36 • 11 • 06
Rachel	Boght fra Rachel Kinneir relict off umquhill Thomas Clirtle merchant in –		
Kinneir	Edinburgh the 3 11: off Marche 1669 whairoff I have a discharge at the fitt of		
	acompt theroff ~ ~ ~:		
seck...	1– 24 pynts off seck at 18s. the pynt	21–12–00	
tent...	2– a barel to put it in	01–00–00	
raisings...	3– 10 pynts off tent at 33s. 4d. the pynt	16–13–04	
2 barels...	4– 1 barel to put it in	00–12–00	
67–15–00	5– 16 pound off raisings at 5s. the lb...	04–00–00	• 43 • 17 • 04
45–06–00	// 43–17–04 //		
03–12–00	29 Marche to Arche Andersone for 2 skuls	00–06–00	
05–05–04	12 Marche to John Pourdie webster – fo[r] warping ale &c................	00–05–00	
28–03–04	For fresh beiff in Marche	02–04–00	
66–14–00	For whyt breid in Marche...........24s.	01–04–00	• 03 • 19 • –
09–00–00	The end of Marche The disbursments in Marche 1669		• 310 • 03 • 06
36–11–06	1669 ~ ~		
43–17–04			
03–19–00			
310–03–06:			

Aprill		
1669	The disbursments in Aprill – 1669	
William	The 6 off Aprill 1669 – to Margaret Hopekirk – 40 lib. for William Alexander &	
Alexander	Jennet Clerks boord fra the 28 off January 1669 to the 28 off Aprill 1669	
Jennet Clerks	is – 3 month is 13–6–8d. in 3 month for ilk ane off thair boord..........	• 40 • 00 • –
Isobell	The 14 of Aprill – peyit to Isobell Fermer in full off ane accompt markit –	
Fermer	A B for nails –39–05–10	• 39 • 05 • 10
Jean	The 14 off Aprill 1669 to Jean Gilles relict off umquhill John Dow merchant –	
Gilles	in Edinburgh in full off ane accompt markit CD and hir discharge at the –	
	fit theroff – for 28 ell and 1 quarter off tanton serge in – 4 remnants of 34s.	
	the ell – 48 lib. 6d. Scots..	• 48 • 00 • 06
	The 14 off Aprill 1669 – peyit and compleited to my brother John –	
A howsse	Andersone – 5 lib. 6s. 8d. sterlin – for a howsse clok Anthonie Storie	
striking clok	merchant in London – boght and sent him for my usse according to ane	
	accompt I have lying by me – markit on the bak – 333....is in –	
	Scots money –: 64 lib.	• 64 • 00 • –

40–00–00		
39–05–10	The disbursments in Aprill 1669 –	
48–00–06	on this syde is....................................	• 191 • 06 • 04
64–00–00		
191–06–04		

[81]

	The disbursments in Aprill 1669 on the other syde amonts to		• 191 • 06 • 04
	The 15 off Aprill at Dalry to Walter Cheislies meassons & wrights		
	in drink money – 30s.	01–10–00	
For barking	16 off Aprill – to David Lindsay for barking 2 ox hyds	05–16–00	
2 ox hyds	The said day to John Hamilton for 8 lb off tows at 4s. 6d. the lb	01–16–00	
	To him for 2 cords	00–04–00	
	The said day to James Lidel for a remnant of serge	03–10–00	
	The said day to Hary Stewart for a douzane of band strings	02–08–00	• 15 • 04 • –
	20 Aprill to Sanders Miller – for a great earthen hollands can – with		
Alexander	a tin lid wroght without with flowrs holds – 9 pynts & a chopin.........	03–08–00	
Clerk for	To Alexander Clerk for a fyne gun – the ratch wroght with – –		
a gun with	silver – with a musket wark & snap wark – to him the 23 of Aprill		
musket &	for the same – 18 lib.	18–00–00	
snap wark	To him for a tin mustard pot	01–06–08	
	To him for a blew & whyt lame pot with a covert	00–03–00	
191–06–04	To my brother the said day for a pictur............	00–18–00	• 23 • 15 • 08
15–04–00	To Mungo Hinsha for 1 deat[h]s head on a round	01–16–00	
23–15–08	To him for 9 taile douces	01–00–00	
09–18–00	To Thomas Fisher for 4 douzane off mandel buttons for my cot.........	00–18–00	
25–02–00	1 chopin botle	00–07–00	
265–06–00	1 chopin off blak wyne	00–12–00	
	4 lb off plum dames Deip plum dames	00–12–00	

	24 Aprill to James Steuart drogist in full of ane accompt – on his discharge	04–13–00	• 09 • 18 • –
John Stinsone waker	The 26 off Aprill – to John Stinsone waker –13–17–4d. in full off ane accompt on his discharge and off all uther accompt preseiding the said – 26 off Aprill 1669	13–17–00	
gairden seids	The 20 off Aprill 1669 to George Reid –2–16s. 6d. whiche peyit to Widow Shaw for gairden seids according to the accompt – markit – 334	02–16–06	
	To Arche Andersone for trouts – 2 tymes	00–08–06	
	1 quart off barme	00–04–00	
	For fresh beiff in the month of Aprill	06–10–00	
	For whyt breid in the month of April	01–06–00	• 25 • 02 • –
	The end of Aprill 1669 The disbursments in Aprill 1669		• 265 • 06 • –
May 1669	The disbursments in May – 1669:		
Jo: Clerks fie	The 4 off May 1669 to John Clerk for his fie fra Mertimes 1668 till Witsonday 1669	14–00–00	
John Andersone Marie Clerk	Fryday 7 May 1669 sent with John Rob to be delivert to my – brother John Andersone four dollors whiche he gave Marie – Clerk to buy a pair off plaids	11–12–00	• 25 • 12 • –
John Andersone	The said 7 off May 1669 sent with John Rob to be delivert to my said brother John Andersone – 36 lib. 18s. 2d. which he gave to Mr John Clerk to – compleit & pay off all his accompts off his cloths & turk clok &c is	36–18–02	

	8 May 1669 – to John Broun – for 10 hanks off virginel strings..........	00–08–00	
Master John Clerk	On Saturday the 8 off May 1669 I resavet ane accompt fra Mr John Clerk – off – 142–00–02d. which I peyit out for him – for 1– a sute off cloths – 2 – a turk clok – 3 – ane whatt – 4. a pair of silk stokings – 5. a peice off blak rubens – for making & furnishing to his cloths and divers other necessars – according as it is particullarized in the said accompt at Newbiging this – 8 day off May 1669..	142–00–02	• 142 • 08 • 02
James Clerk	The 24 off Aprill 1669 – delivert to my brother John Anderson – 23–18–3d. which he disbursit for James Clerk to wit – for cloth to be him dowblet & breiks – for 1: new hatt – 1 pair off new stokings for making & furnishing to his cloths &c..		• 23 • 18 • 03
Isobell Wakers fie half yeir	The 12 off May 1669 – delivert to Agnes Clerk seald in a peper to pay – Isobell Waker hir fie fra Mertimes 1668 till Witsonday 1669 to wit 7ll. for hir fie ane halff a croun for hir shoone is 8ll. 10s. thair wes in the peper 2 ½ dolors is 7–5s.– & 2s. sterlin & 12d. is 8 lib. 10s		• 08 • 10 • –
Nans Johnstouns fie: 1 yeir	The 12 off May 1669 – delivert to Agnes Clerk to pay Nans Johnstoun hir fie seald in a peper – fra Witsonday 1668 till Witsonday 1669 for the yeirs fie – 16 lib. for 2 pair off shoone – 3 lib. is – 19 lib. in all – thair wes in – the peper – 5 dolors – 14–10s. and halff a crown is 16 lib. the 27 off Februar 1669 I gave hir 3 lib. to buy hir shoone is in all for 1 yeir		• 19 • 00 • –
John Mein sklater	The 20 off May 1669 to John Mein sklaitter on his discharge – date the 20 off May 1669 – for theyking the brewhowsse – be east the great yeat – 24 lib. 12s. to buy 1 pair off gloves 12s. to give –		

	Sanders Slowan who helpit him to theyk the same & 12s. to –		
	give his 2 service men is in all – 25–16s.		• 25 • 16 • –
	The disbursments in May 1669 on this syde is		• 245 • 04 • 05

[82]

	The disbursments in May 1669 on the other syde–245–04–05		• 245 • 04 • 05
	1 pynt of lint seid oyll..........	01–04–00	
Mill & kill	6 May to David Clerk for killing & milling 13 bols of oats	00–06–08	
	To Arche Andersone for trouts – 3 tyms..........	00–10–00	
	To a chapman for knitings –&c	00–08–00	
	To 2 – severall coupers..........	00–13–00	
	11 May to Edowart Ander: [sic] Adamsone to drink when he went to –		
	John Watsone in Diels mill to obtein his license to pow heather..........	00–06–08	• 03 • 08 • 04
Richard	20 May to Richard Twidie in Daufingtoun[56] head for cutting the gray		
Twidie horse	meir off the cords and for blooding my brothers pownie 1 dolor		• 02 • 18 •
phisitian	For fresh beiff in the month of May	04–16–00	
	For whyt breid in the month of May..........	01–03–00	• 05 • 19 • –
	The end of May 1669 – The disbursments in May 1669		• 257 • 09 • 09

June 1669	The disbursments in June 1669..........		
Alexander Ogilvie	The 1 off June 1669 to Alexander Ogilvie – ane off the collector deputs off a – taxation – grantit to his Majestie in Agust 1665 – 55–2–2d. on his discharge –		

Taxation	date the said 1 off June 1669 for the personage off Pennycooke and that – fra Witsonday 1668 till Witsonday 1669 which is the fourth terms – taxt and payment off the said taxation	• 55 • 02 • 02
Mr Robert Alisone	The 7 off June 1669 to Mr Robert Alisone minister at the kirk of Glencorse 48 lib. Scots – as my proportion off his stipend for the lanes off Cookeing lying in Glencorse paroish & that fra Witsonday 1668 till Witsonday – 1669 which discharge is date the said [blank] off June 1669................	• 48 • 00 • –
Wm Rouen in Wrights Housses tenent	The 5 off June 1669 to William Rowen tenent in Wrights howsses – 6–13–4d. on his discharge date the said day which is lying amongst Wrights howsses – discharges off victuall – for 2 bol off peys – which Patrik and Archbald – Craigs resavet fra him the – 29 off December 1668 for my usse	• 06 • 13 • 04
James Adamsone plumber	The 18 off May 1669 to James Adamsone plumber on his discharge date the said 28 off May 1669 for 8 ston 11 lb off lead for runing off bats – at – 24s. the stone is – 14–11s.	• 14 • 11 • –
William Broun chamber mail	The 1 off June 1669 to William Broun skinner 12 lib. for a terms maill off a chamber – fra Mertimes 1668 till Witsonday 1669 which discharge is date the 1 off June 1669..	• 12 • 00 • –
1 pair off cairt whils:	The 29 off May 1669 to James Bell wright in Leith for a pair off cairt whils which he says is all elme – except the spaiks which is off oake – peyit to him. The said day in John Stewarts howsse for the same – 10 lib. befor Thomas Lyll cairter – Mathiew Birsbane and my brother John Andersone.. 10–00–00	

[56] Dolphinton.

James Bell — The said day before the said James Bell wrights the said –
wright — Mathiew Birsbane & John Andersone delivert to the said – Thomas Lyll
cairter above nominat – 16 lib. 10s. to be delivert be him to William
William — Hopekirk smith – for 6 ston 3 pound off – yrne wark furnished be him to
Hopekirk — the said cairt whils – at 4 merks the stone – Thomas Lyle promist to deliver
smith — the said 16–10s. to the said William Hopkirk smith .... 16–10–00 • 16 • 10 • –

27 May May [sic] 1669 – 1669 to John Crichtouns wyffe for –
trinchers — 1– 3 douzane of trinchers at 30s. the douzane 04–10–00
sand ridls — 2– 2 litle baskets 00–06–00
baskits — 3– 1 large baskit 00–06–00
4– 2 sand ridls .... 00–15–00 • 05 • 17 • –

whyt Holland — 27 May 1669 to Mathiew Birsbains wyffe for – 3 caips off Holland –
stikit caips — stikit with cades at –24s. the peice –3–12: 1 caip stikit with cades off Scots –
lining –18s. is 04–10–00
1 horne combe in a caisse 00–06–00
To Edowart Cleghorne for mounting a nit with silver with a–
skrewhead weying – 6 drop .... 01–17–04 • 06 • 13 • 04

Fra William — The 28 day off May to William Reid for–
Reid — 2 large holland cans 02–18–00
Hollands — 2 lesser holland cans 01–16–00
pigs –&c — 2 lesser holland cans 01–00–00
3 Spanish boosoms 00–18–00 06–12–00
31 May to Wil: Alexander Clerk for –
1 Hollands pestilen pot blew & whyt with a covert .. 02–10–00

2 Rainish wyne glasses painted at –7s. the peice .... 00–14–00 .... 03–04–00 • 09 • 16 • –

Jo: Cooke The 3 off June 1669 to John: Cooke for
for a large 1 fyne large bordert lock – opens on both syds – 1 crosse sheild with a –
bordert covert – 4 nails to put on the lock – 4 taks to put on the crosse sheild –
lock –&c: for the first chamber dore – above the new vault on the west syde off
the great yeat 10–12–04
55–02–02 1 crosse sheild for the last dore off the new howsse 00–10–00
48–00–00 To John Kirk in drink money .... 00–05–00 • 11 • 07 • 04
06–13–04 The disbursments above in the month off June 1669 and some in –
14–11–00 the month off May – amonts to .... • 186 • 10 • 02
12–00–00
16–10–00
05–17–00
06–13–04
09–16–00
11–07–04
186–10–02

[83]

The disbursments in June 1669 as is mentioned on the other syde is .... • 186 • 10 • 02
1 June – to Henry Santinell painter for a pictur with 2 fish 02–08–00
5 ½ quarters off hardn 00–06–08
1 ½ douzane off corks 00–05–06
To James Stewart for – 2 – pigs 00–10–00
To Alexander Pitcairns nourish ....1 June 02–18–00

	1 June to William Brouns woman – whair I have my chamber	00–12–00	• 07 • 00 • 02
	To William Reid for 2 lb 4 once castel soap at 12s. the pound	01–07–00	
whyt lead	To Hew Broun for grein –& yellow – cire cloth for cauters	00–18–00	
	3 June to James Stewart for 4 lb off whyt lead at 4s. 6d. the lb............	02–14–00	
James Cromie	To Robert Hamiltoun – for 1 ell off blak serge	01–08–00	
webster – for	5 June to James Cromie webster for 4 ell 3 quarters off strypt —		
hingings	hingings – 2 ell and halff a quarter braid for a skringe at – 3:		
	6s. 8d. the ell –15–16–8d. – I did pay him bot for the same	15–00–00	• 21 • 07 • –
Mr John Clerks	The 5 off June 1669 to William Hamiltouns wyffe for Mr John –		
boord in Wm	Clerks boord – 2 month acording to – 40 lib. in the 3 month – fra		
Hamiltons	the 24 off May 1669 to the 24 off Jully 1669 is 2 months is		• 26 • 13 • 04
Marie Clerk	3 June for a pair off shoone for Marie Clerk............ 01–09–00		
	1 pair off gloves for hir.. 01–09–00..........	02–18–00	
Margaret Clerk	For Margaret Clerk 1 taffatie skerff 08–08–00		
	1 taffatie hood .... 03–08–00..........	11–16–00	• 14 • 14 • –
Helen	Agnes –& Helen Clerks 2 pair off shoone for ilk ane off them		
Clerk	is 4 pair	02–18–00	
Agnes	For Agnes Clerk –		
Clerk	1– a taffatie skerff..05–04–00		
	2– a gaze hood 00–18–00		
	3– 1 sute off ribens contining [sic] 5 ell at 7s. the ell.....01–15–00		
	4– 1 ell off ribens for tying 00–01–00		
	5– 2 ell off ribens for 2 skerffs 00–04–00	08–02–00	• 11 • 00 •
Isobell: Gray	3 June to Isobell Gray when I peyit out the last 2 articles above ane		

to a webster	off 14 –14 the other off 11 lib. to Isobell Gray the said day – for weiving		
	21 ell off twynd stuffe – to be ryding cloths –& mantls to the lasses		
	at 4s. the ell	04–04–00	
Loch litches	To Agnes Clerk – for 8 loch leitches – 8s. to George Clerk webster –		
Warping aill	for warping ail – 8s. –& some other small disbursments in all	01–01–00	• 05 • 05 • –
272–11–06;	Soma off all above disbursments in June 1669 till this 7 off June 1669		• 272 • 11 • 06
Jo: Ramsay	12 June 1669 to John Ramsay for 21 mure fowls –& perdriks	06–00–00	
Ja: Frizel –	17 June 1669 to James Frizel in the Carlips for – 22 laid off cols		
cols	at 4s. the laid for which I peyit him 03–16s. –& 3s. 4d. I gave him		
	to give to the bearers is 03–19–04 is 3 laid he rebated	03–19–04	
David	Fryday – 18 June to W: David Livingstoun – lint whill wright in		
Livingstoun –	Dalkeith for 3 litle round pictur frames off peir trie at 18s. the peice		
in Dalkeith –	is 54s. – 1 off them for a mort head 1 off them for a horse head –		
lint whill	1 off them for a lyons head – both the last 2 ar[e] done in reid killevyne –		
Wright	be my Lord Kerr off Neubattle	02–14–00	• 12 • 13 • 04
	18 June 1669 to the gairner in Stonie Hill for showeing me the yards		
	and d[o]vcat – 12s. – said day spent at Fisher Rave severall ways when		
	I went to buy timber thair 40s. is – both	02–02–00	
	Teusday 15 June at Arche Andersons brydel	02–04–00	• 04 • 06 • –
John	The 22 June 1669 boght fra John Hogens		
Hogens	1– 44 ell off sad cullort twynd stuff at 15s. –3d. the ell	33–11–00	
	2– 16 ell off grein lining at 8s. the ell	06–08–00	
	3– 8 ell off gray stuff at 7s. 6d. the ell	03–00–00	
		42–19–00	

	The 6 off May 1669 peyit to John Hogens – 12 lib.	12–00–00	
	The 22 off June 1669 peyit to the said John Hogens	30–11–00[57]	• 42 • 19 • –
Mill–kill	7 June to David Clerk for killing 18 bols oats – 3s. 4d. –& the 12 off		
Lint seid oyll	June to him – 3s. 4d. for milling the same is	00–06–08	
	25 June – 1 pynt off lint seid oyll	01–04–00	
	To Arche Andersone for trouts	00–03–04	
	To a chapman – for a bolt of knitings	00–04–00	
Bee skaips	14 June – to George Reid for 2 – top swarme bee skaips	01–00–00	
	22 June – 2 pynts off fish oyll for creishing wooll	01–00–00	
	28 June to Nathaniel Thomson for mending shoone	00–14–00	• 04 • 12 • –
4 birk sleds	24 June William Stewart boght in Carnwath faire –		
272–11–06	4 birk sleds at 18s. 6d. the peice	03–14–00	
12–13–04	4 firr teathers	00–07–00	
04–06–00	To William Stewart	00–02–00	• 04 • 03 • –
42–19–00	Wedensday 25 June – to David Clerk – 5s. to get 3 pynts off ale – when he –		
04–12–00	went to Lonhead with 12 bols beir – to Sanders Cutle to be malt	00–05–00	
04–03–00	Whyt breid in the month of June	01–14–00	
07–16–00	Fresh beiff in the month of June	05–17–00	• 07 • 16 • –
349–00–10	The end of June 1669 The disbursments in June 1669		• 349 • 00 • 10

[84]

Jully 1669 The disbursments in the month off Jully 1669 ~~

Gallow sheils –	The 1 Jully to George Gibsone in Muslbrugh [sic] for 1 boll off whyt salt		• 03 • 01 • 08
fare for custome–	Gallowsheils fare wes on Munday 28 June 1669 for the custome off 11 – young catel and 60 sheip – 34s.	01–14–00	
	For William Stewarts – Jo: Clerks –& Tomas Andersons expense	01–06–00	• 03 • 00 • –
John:..... Stinsone waker	12 Jully to John Falcon in name of his master John: Stinsone waker for litting 20 ell off grograin to be the bairns – hoods & rydeing cloths at 3s. 4d. the ell –3–6–8– and a grot to himselff is –3–10–8– I have ane order fra John Stinsone to pay the same to the said John Falcon	03–10–08	
Alexander Cutle – maltman	13 Jully to Sanders Cutle maltman in Lonhead for making – 12 – bols off beir in malt – thair cam home agane 13 ½ bolls off dry – malt – I peyit him my selff 5 lib. for the same as I went through the Lonhead the said day when I wes going to the Fisherrave	05–00–00	• 08 • 10 • 08
	Fryday – 16 Jully 1669 sent in with John Rob seald in a peper to be delivert to Marie Clerk		
	1– 1 ½ ell off gimp lace at 22s. the ell		
Agnes Clerk	2– 3 lib. 17s. to pay for 3 ½ ell off the said gimp lace at 22s. the ell – for Agnes Clerks petticot	03–17–00	
	3 Jully to William Reid for ~~		
	1– 1 large brasse frying pan	02–08–00	
	2– 6 earthen Hollands botls at 18s. the peice	05–08–00	

[57] It is unclear whether this is an error in recording what was paid to John Hogens or if Clerk was noting here that he paid out a lesser amount at that time.

3– 1 French etuis with sheirs & 1 botkin 00–10–00

Yrne wechts 4– 1 sut off yrne wechts – to wit – 1 ston – 8 lb – 4lb – 2 lb – 1 lb
is in all – 31 lb for which I peyit him .... 04–07–00 • 16 • 10 • –

3 lb off small pack threid 01–08–00

4 ¾ ell off hardn for 2 crosse wallets at 7s. the ell 01–13–00

3 ½ off secking at 7s. the ell 01–04–06

1 cain with a yvorie head I gave to William Russel wreatter 03–02–00

2 picturs To Henrie Sentinelle painter for a pictur – a chyl leaning on a deaths
head on – cloth 05–02–00

To him for the Countesse D' Feghein on wood 01–10–00

1 peice of cork .... 00–10–06 • 14 • 10 • –

Mr William Wallace – the 4th terms taxt

The 3 off Jully 1669 to Mr William Wallace advocat shireff depute off Edinburgh – 24 lib. Scots – as the fourth terms peyment off the taxation imposd be the convention off estats in Agust 1665 for my 12 pound lands – in Pennycooke paroish –& Cookeing in Glencorse paroish – and that fra Witsonday 1668 till Witsonday 1669 – I offert this to Mr Thomas Baird – shireff deput to whom I peyit the 3 preseiding terms taxt – bot he refused to tak it –& desyrd me to payit to the said Mr William Wallace –& said it wes on[e] and the same thing as if I peyit it to him – Mr William Wallace gave me a discharge off the said 24 lib. being the 4th terms taxt date the 3 off Jully 1669 .... • 24 • 00 • –

Thomas Rob:

The 7 Jully 1669 Thomas Rob cordoner boght the particullars and under wreatten – – – –

1– 1 horse hyde 03–10–00

Leather	2– 1 gray cows hyde 06–06–08	
	3– halff a blak cows hyde 02–16–00	
	4– 4 lb off roset 00–08–00	
	5– 2 lasts for Nans & Margaret Clerks 00–12–00	
	6– 6 pair off timber healls .... 00–06–00..........	• 13 • 18 • 08
220 portage	The 14 off Jully 1669 to William Lawsone indweller in Leith then in	
dails	the Fisher Rave herbrie for 220 portage dails is thirtein skore at 48 lib.	
	the hundreth is	• 104 • 00 • –
66–10–00	The 13 Jully 1669 – boght fra George Smart in the Fisher Rave	
27–00–00	1– 30 double treis for geists to the staible & byre –	
92–00–00	2– 40 double treis for the rooffe of the staible: is 70 at 19s. the peice	• 66 • 10 • –
44–10–00	3– 60 single treis at 9s. the peice	• 27 • 00 • –
230–00–00	4– 202 dails at 46 lib. the hundreth	• 92 • 00 • –
19–00–00	For the cairiage to Newbiging the said 70 double treis – 60 single treis –	
26–13–04	and – 202 dails...............44–10s.	• 44 • 10 • –
275–13–04	all above	• 230 • 00 • –
George	More – 10 off the said double treis for geists –:	
Smart –	More – 10 off the said double treis for the rooffe –: is – 20 treis at 19s.	
	the peice..	• 19 • 00 • –
double treis	More 26–13–04 – for cairiage off the said 20 treis –& the 220 portage –	
single treis	dails boght fra William Lawsone to Newbiging acording to agriement	• 26 • 13 • 04
dails	Soma off all resting to George Smart is – 275–13–4...........................	• 275 • 13 • 04
	The which 275–13–4d. I peyit to the said George Smart the 17 off Jully 1669	
	and hath his discharge theroff at the fitt off his accompt	

03–01–08
03–00–00
08–10–08
16–10–00
14–10–00
24–00–00
13–18–08
104–00–00
275–13–04
463–04–04

Soma off the disbursments in the month off Jully on this syde above is .... • 463 • 04 • 04

[85]

The disbursments in the month off Jully 1669 on the other syde is...... • 463 • 04 • 04

Disbursments be Agnes Clerk – in Jully 1669 –

1 to George Clark for warping ale 00–08–00
8 Jully to Margaret Hopkirk for ale & eygs to the bairns 00–08–00
For a pig 00–02–08
webster 9 Jully to George Clark for weiving 27 ell of lining at – 3s. the ell 04–01–00
16 Jully to a chapman for 2 ell off lining to be aprons for
Agnes Clerk Agnes Clerk at 17s. the ell.......... 01–14–00 • 06 • 13 • 08
webster 1 Jully to Androw Pourdie for weiving 14 ell of small hardn 00–14–00
19 Jully to Isobell Scot for 49 pynts and 1 chopin off beir the men got

	when they powed ten skore & nyne thraive off heather for the staible		
Powing off	at 2s. the pynt is	04–19–00	
heather for	20 Jully to James Lowrie for powing heather 4 days	01–06–08	
the staible	21 Jully for 3 chopins off barme	00–03–00	
	22 Jully to Arche Andersone for trouts	00–05–00	• 07 • 07 • 08
Jo: Andersone	Jully to my brother John Andersone – 12s. which he gave to James		
Ja: Clerk	Clerk for mending his hose & shoon –& 10s. 6d. he spent be my order		
	with Mathiew Wood Coits tenent is 22s. 6d.	01–02–06	
Abram Clerk	27 Jully to Abraham Clerk for mending a chek reill	01–14–00	
John Cooke	Said day to John Cooke for a stock lock	02–08–00	
	Said day to Hary Stewart for 4 rim off peper off a small seyse [sic] at		
	31s. the rim	06–04–00	• 11 • 08 • 06
John Crichton –	27 Jully to John Crichtoun for –		
sive wright	1– 3 sand ridls		
	2– 3 coll ridls		
	3– 1 milchesir		
	4– 4 earthen pigs		
	5– 4 hizle handls for mattoks ... for all		• 02 • 13 • 04
William Reid –	27 Jully to William Reid for ~		
merchant	1– 1 large yrne frying pan ... 02–08–00		
	2– 3 lb off small brasse wechts ... 04–04–00		
	3– 6 suger loaffs weying 20 lb at 11s. the lb ... 11–00–00		• 17 • 12 • –

	27 Jully to Henrie Sentinelle painter for ~		
picturs	1– Mr Alexander Hendersons pictur –		
	2– 2 drumaderies on a brod	02–18–00	
	3– 1 mort head	02–13–04	• 05 • 11 • 04
Isobell Gray	27 Jully – to Isobell Gray which shoe peyit to a webster for weiving 36 ell off braid round lining for sheits at 4s. the ell is 7–4s. for warping ale and – 36 ell off sowing &c: 31s. – is 8 lib. 15s	08–15–00	
	To James Stewart for – 7 lb of Spanish broun	01–06–08	
John Cooke	To John Cooke for a handle & snek &c: for the staible dore	01–16–00	
	For mounting ane Indian nit with silver	01–09–00	
John Clerk	30 Jully to John Herreis wright for a fir presse for Mr John Clerk – to keip his cloths in	09–00–00	• 22 • 06 • 08
463–04–04			
06–13–08	1 lb off leaff tobaco	00–15–00	
07–07–08	8 once off whyt candie	00–10–00	
11–08–06	To Alexander Andersone copersmith for a coper skoope	01–16–00	
02–13–04	For fresh & salt beiff in the month off Jully	02–11–00	
17–12–00	For whyt breid in the month off Jully	01–13–00	• 07 • 05 • –
05–11–04			
22–06–08			
07–05–00			
544–02–06	The end off Jully 1669 The disbursments in Julllly 1669 is		• 544 • 02 • 06

Agust	The disbursments in the month off Agust 1669 ~:		
1669	5 Agust 1669 to Anna Irving which shoe peyit out to George Clerk – webster		
webster…..	in Leswaid for weiving – 36 ell off small hardn at 1s. the ell – and 20d. wes –		
George Clerk	given him more because it wes weill wroght is	01–17–08	
	To Arche Andersone for trouts severall tyms	00–17–00	
Fald dyks	16 Agust to John Pennycooke in Ravenshauch for biging 3 fald		
Jo: Pennycooke	dyks – being eight skore & 2 rude at 2s. the rude	16–00–00	
Jenet Spalding –	Said day to Jennet Spalding for – 42 days shoe wes bleitching –		
blitching cloth	cloth at 1s. ilk – day and hir meit	02–02–00	• 20 • 16 • 08
	12 off Agust to Alexander Keith for 2 days wark	00–10–00	
	14 Agust to Androw Dog for a skabert to the bakit sowrd [sic]	01–06–08	
hooks	15 Agust to John Rob for 6 serp hooks at 4s. the peice	01–04–00	
	1 pair off sheiring gloves for David Clerk to bind with	00–05–00	
20–16–08	7 Agust 1 peice off fresh beiff – 10s.	00–10–00	• 03 • 15 • 08
03–15–08	The 16 off Agust 1669 completed to Robert Dewer smith in Pennycooke		
163–14–00	a compt off – 163 lib. 14s. merkit – 333 for severall sort of wark –		
188–06–04	fra the 30 off May 1668 till the 16 off Agust 1669		• 163 • 14 • –
Robert Dewer	The disbursments above in Agust 1669		• 188 • 06 • 04

[86]

The disbursments on the other syde in Agust 1669 –188–06–04 .... • 188 • 06 • 04

17 Agust to John Rob for – 31 heren 00–10–00

24 Agust to Margaret Hopkirk for a gallon off ale the bairns got – 13–4d. & a douzane of eygs............2s. is.......... 00–15–04

19 Agust to Arche Craig for 1 boll off oats he got fra James Frizel in Baivlawe for Jack.......... 03–13–04

22 Agust to John Reid to give Richard Twidie in Daufintoun for doeing some thing to Jack – 30s. –& 6s. to John Reid who went with him.......... 01–16–00

19 Agust to John Davisone couper in Lintoun for –
33 girds at 10d. the peice 01–07–06
& 43 smaller girds at –7d. the peice is.......... 01–05–01 .... 02–12–07 • 09 • 07 • 03

Munday 23 Agust to Mr William Caderwood minister in Dalkeith his woman 29s. & 6s. to his man –& 6s. to Mr William Hamiltouns man is – 41s. 02–01–00

on Munday – 23 Agust to Thomas Andersone when he went to the rande vous [sic] in the links off Muslburgh – whair he wes 2 days togither.......... 01–16–00

Tam – Rob cordoner — 25 Agust to Thomas Rob cordoner for 32 days he wroght at Newbiging making bairns shoone – at 6s. ilk day with his meit is – 09–12.......... 09–12–00

John[58] Thomsone – — The 28 of Agust 1669 to James Thomsone glaisier in full of ane – accompt on his discharge date the 28 off Agust 1669 – 28 lib. 17s. 6d. and his discharge off all uther accompts preseiding –

glaisier	the said day for glaising the new howsse be west the great gate & doeing some other small things	28–17–06	• 42 • 06 • 06
	31 Agust 1669 boght fra George Blaikie in Gallowshiels –		
George	9 ell off lining at –18s. 6d. the ell	08–06–06	
Blaikie –	12 ell at 16s. 6d. the ell	09–18–00	
lining	10 ell at 13s. 6d. the ell	06–15–00	
cloth	3 ell off small lining at 28s. the ell	04–04–00	
	40 ell off lining in 5 peices at 14s. 6d. the ell ilk peice conteind – 8 ell Scots	29–00–00	
	6 pair off leather poutches	00–18–00	
	2 bolt off narow knitings	00–07–00	
	3 large kitching knyves	00–11–00	• 59 • 19 • 06
	Whyt breid in the month off Agust	32s.	• 01 • 12 • –
	The end off Agust 1669 The disbursments in Agust 1669		• 301 • 11 • 07

Septem[r] 1669	The disbursments in September 1669		
Mr John Clerk	On Fryday 10 September 1669 – sent with John Rob to be delivert to my brother John Andersone – 40 lib. seald in a peper to be delivert to William Hamiltoun for Mr Jo: Clerk boord 3 month fra the 24 off Jully 1669 till the 24 off October 1669		• 40 • 00 • –
	3 September – 1 pynt of lintseid oyll	01–04–00	
	8 once off whyt suger candie	00–10–00	

58 Clerk has 'John Thomson' listed in the margins, but he named 'James Thomson' in the body of the account.

	60 hering	00–12–00	
	4 September custome off 11 catel in Skirling fare – 7s. 4d. William		
	Stewarts – charges – 4s. 6d. is	00–11–10	• 02 • 17 • 10
A blak	Thee [sic] 13 off September 1669 to John Lowrie in Logan housse 40 lib.		
bull stot	For –:		
A sore brown	1– a young blak bull stot of a yeir old	05–00–00	
staig	2– a young sore broun staig wes fole in anno 1666 –		
	off – 3 yeir old going in his fourt[h] yeir – 35 lib.	35–00–00	• 40 • 00 • –
Jo: Cooke	The 21 off September 1669 to John Cooke lock smith on his discharge in –		
	full off ane accompt – – 10–2s.		• 10 • 02 • –
Jo: Walker	15 September to John Walker locksmith in Caldtoun in full off ane		
	accompt for yrne wark to the knok caisse on his discharge	04–07–00	
Thomas	On Wedensday 15 September 1669 for a booke in quarto wreatten		
Crauford –	be Moyse Amyraut callit *Discours de Liestat des ames fidelles*		
a booke	*apres la mort* – at Alexander Leslies stare fitt peyit to Thomas Crauford		
	merchant – 45s. which booke wes sent to him fra Paris be –		
	Francis Kinloch merchant thair for me	02–05–00	
	2 lb off whyt suger candie....at 20s. the pound	02–00–00	
40–00–00	4 box wood combs	00–13–04	
02–17–10	1 moyer – 3s.	00–03–00	
40–00–00	For changing a tin quart stoup	00–12–00	
10–02–00	To James Clerk for 3 gilt brushes – 36s. – 2 tobaco boxes 4s. is	02–00–00	
18–17–08	1 thrie squair fyll – 6s.	00–06–00	
111–17–06	8 once off diapalma	00–08–00	

	6 ½ pound off steill hemp at 8s. the pound	02–12–00	
	2 whyt lame baisins at 12s. the peice	01–04–00	
	3 lb of gun powder at 11s. the lb	01–13–00	
	4 once off whyt candie	00–05–00	
	To John Geddes for binding a booke for Alexander Clerk	00–09–04	
		18–17–08	• 18 • 17 • 08
	The disbursments in September on this syde		• 111 • 17 • 06

[87]

	The disbursments in September 1669 on the other syde is		• 111 • 17 • 06
James Clerk	20 September to my brother John Andersone 29s. which he gave to – James Clerk to buy a pair off shoone	01–09–00	
	24 September – to James Clerk to buy 1 pair off stokings	01–10–00	
Margaret Clerk	24 September to Margaret Clerk to buy a halff plaid	06–06–08	
	To hir for 2 ell off small lining for hand cuffs at 22s. the ell	02–04–00	
	21 September to Alexander Pennycooke off New hall for severall – drogs he furnished to us	09–02–00	• 20 • 11 • 08
Isobell Gray – lining bed plaids	The 20 off September – to Isobell Gray for –		
	10 ell off braid – braid sprangd bed plaids at – 19s. the ell	09–10–00	
	5 ell off lining at 12s. the ell	03–00–00	
	2 ell off lining at – 22s. the ell	02–04–00	
	20 ell off lining in – 2 peices at 15s. the ell	15–00–00	• 29 • 14 • –

Alexr Leslie	The 25 off September 1669 to Alexander Leslie for Mr John Clerk his		
Mr John Clerk	roume in his chamber – the thrid yeir 66–14		• 66 • 14 • –
	8 lb off pick	01–00–00	
	4 lb off bruntstaine at 4s. the pound..	00–16–00	
	For chalk..	00–02–06	
jeans – breid	To William Hamiltoun for a great jeans breid	04–07–00	
	For oynions..	00–06–00	
2 sled saidls	22 September to William Jack for – 2 sled saidls at 55s. a peice	05–10–00	
tobaco pyps	Fryday 18 September to Patrik Crawford in the Potter raw[59] – for		
	1 grosse –& six off his best tobaco pyps he gav the six to them...........	01–00–00	• 13 • 01 • 06
	25 September 1669 to Alexander Leslie for wreating ane assignation		
	to Sir John – Mr Robert –& Mr John Smiths thair band off the principall		AB.
Alexander	soume off – 7000 lib. –& for wreating ane assignation to a securitie off		
Leslie:	20 000 lib. on the lands off Barntoun –& for wreating ane assignation		
	to a securitie off 22 400 merks on the lands off Roslin for all – 3 dolors		• 08 • 14 • –
Alisone	25 off September to Alisone Troup Ladie Crichie for –		
Troup – stuffs	11 ½ ell......		
	10 ell.......... is – 21 ½ ell off twyne sad cullort stuff at 19s. the ell is		• 20 • 02 • –
	AB: to Mr John Leslie for wreating – 1 off the above mentioned		
	assignations –& to Mr Jo: Clerk for wreating on[e] off them.............		• 02 • 18 • –
Wm Stewart	The 14 off September 1669 William Stewart boght in Athelstoun fare		
1 large ox	a blak large beld ox cost	35–00–00	
2 large stots	And in Lithgow fare – he boght the –21 off September –		
	1 brandit stot of – 3 yeir old going in his four yeir – cost...................	20–00–00	

	1 blak beld tagit stot 4 yeir old going in his fyft yeir	19–10–00	
	Given him 18s. for his charges in the said twa fairs	00–18–00	• 75 • 08 • –
	29 September for – 7 douzane off long whyt laisses	00–13–00	
	To John Rob for a pynt of ale – oyll	00–12–00	
	21 September to George Clark for warping ale	00–08–00	
	For breid whyt breid	02–05–00	• 03 • 18 • –
	The end off September – 1669: the disbursments in September 1669		• 352 • 18 • 02

October 1669	The disbursments in the month off October 1669 –:		
	The 2 off October to Margaret Andersone – Isobell Grays woman in drink money – 29s.	01–09–00	
Margaret Clerk	5 October 1669 for 3 ½ ell off whyt serge to be Margaret Clerk a peticot at – 22s. the ell	03–17–00	
1 barel off tarr	The 6 off October – William Stewart peyit to Elspeth Mure for a barel off tarr – 12 lib. – custom at the port – 3s. 12d. off cassow maill –12d. to William Stewart is		
	For corne to the horse...........2s.	12–07–00	• 17 • 13 • –
Agnes Clerk	7 October to Agnes Clerk – 2 ell off small lining to be 3 or 4 pair off hand cuffs – cost 22s. the ell	02–04–00	
Cairnhill stable at Newbiging	14 October to Edowart Thomson – for – 9 days he wes theyking– Cairnhill howsse with heather at 9s. ilk day & his meat is	04–01–00	

59 Potter Row in Edinburgh.

theykit with	The said day to him – for theyking the new staible at Newbiging		
heather	with heather – he being 22 days on the same at 9s. a day & his meat	09–18–00	• 16 • 03 • –
	19 October 1669 sent with Jo: Rob to be given to my brother John		
Mr John	Andersone & be him to be given to Mr John Clerk to pay thir particullars		
Clerk	in acompt he sent me – 2 lb off candle..................00..........................	00–09–00	
	For mending his shoes severall tymes..	00–08–00	
17–13–00	For dressing a hatt	00–06–00	
16–03–00	To John Meason for binding Stairs *Practicks*	01–10–00	• 02 • 13 • –
02–13–00	The disbursments above in October 1669 is		• 36 • 09 • –
36–09–00			

[88]

	The disbursments on the other syde in October 1669 is		• 36 • 09 • –
	21 October for alming ane oters skin	00–16–00	
	1 whyt yrne bowet	00–18–08	
	21 October to Jenet Hardie Isobel Grays woman	01–04–00	
	15 October to Jenet Shanks to go to Leswaid to warp........................	00–08–00	
...cols	16 October to Arche Craig for 2 laid of cols he got in Lonhead..........	00–14–04	
great salt	18 October to John Rob for 6 pecks of great salt at 10s. 6d. the pek	03–05–00	
couper	23 October to John Davisone couper in Lintoun	01–16–08	• 09 • 02 • 08
Isobel Gray....	24 September 1669 delivert to Isobel Gray to buy butter	18–00–00	
	5 October 1669 sent with John Rob to hir to buy lint – 12 dolors	34–16–00	
	Fryday 8 October – sent to hir with John Rob...........3 dolors............	08–14–00	
		61–10–00	

	Whairof shoe disbursit as follows........................		
butter	7 October – for 6 ston of butter at 3 lib. the ston	18–00–00	
bound lint	8 October – for 4 ston off bound lint at 4 lib. the ston	16–00–00	
knok lint	& 3 ston off knok lint at –5–13–4d. the ston	17–00–00	
	For cairying the butter from the weyhousse	00–02–00	
Margaret	1 gaze hood for Margaret Clerk	01–00–00	
Clerk	1 pair off gloves for Margaret Clerk...	00–16–00	• 52 • 18 • –
	So that thair is yet resting – 8 – 12s. unwaird which is the remainder –		which 8 – 12
	off the 61–10– abovementioned	8–12–OF [sic]	Isobel Gray did
			hold compt y^{r}off
	On Teusday 26 off October 1669 sent to my brother John Andersone –		
Mr John	with John Rob – 40 lib. to be given be him to William Hamiltoun for –		
Clerk	Mr John Clerks boord fra the 24 of October – 1669 to the 24 off –		
	January 1670..		• 40 • 00 • –
William –	On Munday 18 October 1669 William – Alexander – & Jennet Clerks –		
Alexander –	entert in boording in George Bels measson in Pennycooke and on –		
Jennet –	Munday – 25 off October 1669 – I peyit to his wyffe Margaret Hopkirk		
Clerk –	for the boord off the said 3 bairns fra the – 18 off October 1669		
	to the 18 off January – 1670 – for the thrie I peyit hir 40 lib. is –		
36–09–00	acording to – 20 merks for ilk on[e] – ilk – 3 month		• 40 • 00 • –
09–02–08	4 once of blak spyce..	00–05–00	
52–18–00	2 douzane off oynions...	00–04–00	

40–00–00	27 October to William Stewart to pay for making a plough	00–13–04	
40–00–00	For whyt breid in the month of October	01–04–04	• 02 • 06 • 04
02–06–04	The end off October 1669: the disbursments in October 1669		• 180 • 16 • –
180–16–00			

November 1669			
	The disbursments in November 1669		
cols	The 1 of November 1669 to James Frizel for 34 laid of cols at		
peyit	4s. 2d. the laid is – 7–01–8	07–01–08	
	The 2 of November 1669 delivert to George Bell thrie merk		
George	peices to be given to Margaret Dow William Clerks widow in –		
Clerk	Pennycooke for 4 or 5 month hir sone George Clerk wes at		
	Neubiging in sum[m]er – 1669	02–00–00	• 09 • 01 • 08
small whyt –	The 3 off November 1669 William Steuart boght fra Widow Fossy –		
salt	6 firlots off whyt salt	03–15–00	
	1 pynt ale 4d. stroe custom 2d. is	00–02–02	• 03 • 17 • 02
106 young	The 2 off November 1669 John Reid & Thomas Andersone –		
ashes which	went to Craigmiller & boght fra William Thomson gairner		
wes plantit	at Craigmiller – six skore & six young ashes for which –		
in November	they peyit – 6–13–4d.	06–13–04	
1669	Thair own & the horse – charges	00–10–08	• 07 • 04 • –
	The 3 of November 1669 – John Sibbald went to the Lonhead & broght –		
	2 off our own horse .... 2 laid		

Cols broght fra the Lonhead	The mill James Lowrie............ 2 laid			
	Tam Abernethie .... 2 laid			
	William Thomson .... 1 laid			
	David Ramsay........................ 1 laid			
	Robert Dewer .... 2 laid	For which he peyit 3 lib.		
	John Clerk .... 2 laid	for all –& 18d. is in all.........		• 03 • 01 • 06
	09–01–08			
	03–17–02	The disbursments in November		
	07–04–00	on this syde above..................		• 19 • 04 • 04
	03–01–06			
	19–04–04			

[89]

	The disbursments in November on the other syde is		• 19 • 04 • 04
Jean Steuart	The 4 off November 1669 completed Jean Stewart a yeirs fie being – 16 lib. fra Mertimes 1668 till Mertimes 1669......................................	16–00–00	
John Sibbald	The 4 off November 1669 completed John Sibbald 21 lib. 4s. for – a yeirs fie to wit fra Mertimes 1668 till Mertimes 1669.......................	21–04–00	• 37 • 04 • –
Ashes.... Elms Plains –	Saturday the 6 of November 1669 John Reid & Thomas Andersone – went to Craigmiller –& boght fra William Thomson gairner thair – 80 young treis for planting – to wit ashes – elms –& plains all cost – 4 lib. 2s. 4d.	04–02–04	
	Expensis – 5 pynts of ale	00–08–04	• 04 • 10 • 08

Munday – 8 November 1669 John Sibbald went to the Lonhead with
some off the tenents horse & broght cols to wit –

17 laid of	1 – our own horse – 2 laid....... 2			
cols out	2 – David Dryburgh 2	is in all – 17 laid – ilk laid 5 burthen – whairof		
off the Lon –	3 – James Ramsay 2	4 laid small col at 3s. 4d. the laid	00–13–04	
head	4 – William Simsone............... 2	13 laid great col at 6s. 8d. the laid...	04–06–08	
	5 – Patrik Craig 2	For the cairiers – 17 turnors is........	00–02–10	• 05 • 02 • 10
	6 – Archbald Craig 2			
	7 – Coits 2			
	8 – Edouart Clerk.................... 2			
	9 – John Thomson.................. 1			

James	9 November 1669 to James Abernethie –5–9s. for his fie fra me:		
Abernethie	Witsonday 1669 till Mertimes 1669 for keiping the catel.....................	05–09–00	• 05 • 09 • –
	Disbursments at Edinburgh the 10 of November 1669		
	10 November to Androw Doig for dichting a sowrd [sic] staff............	00–12–00	
James Clerk	Said day to my brother John Andersone – 14s. which he gave at –		
	twa tymes to James Clerk to mend his shoone	00–14–00	
Blak spyce	2 lb of blak spyce at – 15s. the lb..	01–10–00	
....	For a pictur to give my brother for ane on parchement he gave me	01–00–00	
	4 douzane off courtin rings at 3s. the douzane	00–12–00	
	2 gray bonets for William & Alexander Clerks..................................	00–12–00	• 05 • 00 • –
1 gray horse	The 17 off November to Alexander Sharp who dwels neir Dundas for		
cost	a gray horse about 10 yeir old – 42 lib. – for custome – & bookeing 5s.		
42 lib. 12s.	to William Steuart – 3s. – 1 pynt ale – 2s. – 2s. to Sanders Sharps man –		

	1s. – 12s. off charges is in all – 42 lib. 12s. – I got onlie a Scots brydle		
	in his head		• 42 • 12 • –
To Mr Willm	The 15 off November to Mr William Wallace advocat shireff depute		
Wallace 3 lib.	off Edinburgh – 3 lib. for the blanche dewtie off the Halls – being a pair		
for a yeirs blanche	off gloves yeirlie estimat to 3 lib. and that fra the 1 off January 1669 –		
dewtie of the	to the 1 off January 1670 of which he gave me a discharge date the –		
Halls till the 1	15 off November 1669 so that all the yeirlie blanche dewtie of the Halls		
off January 1670	is peyit till the 1 off January 1670		• 03 • 00 • –
	18 November to Thomas Fisher for 18 douzane off cullort breist buttons		
	at 2s. 6d. the douzane	02–05–00	
	1 once of round silk of the same cullor	01–00–00	
4 stikit	Said day to Mistresse Birsbane – for 4 Holland stikit caips with cades –		
whyt caips	at 24s. the peice	04–16–00	
	1 bolt off body worset	01–02–00	
	4 counterfit pearlt neck laisses	00–14–08	• 09 • 17 • 08
To David	25 November to David Lindsay merchant for causing bark......2 ox		
Lindsay for	hyds and a bulls hyde	08–00–00	
barking of	1 brasse pen – 3s. 6 whyt yrne pennets 3s. – 2 fill off –		
3 hyds 8 lib.	reid boxes – 2s. 1 whyt wood box 8s. is in all	00–16–00	
	4 fill off painted boxes with skrews	01–04–00	
	1 horne call with a brasse pype	00–06–00	
	4 cords –7s.	00–07–00	
	27 of November to Mr William Clerks nourish 1 dolor	02–18–00	• 13 • 13 • –

John Cooke –	26 of November to John Cooke for 6 handls –& sneks with all that		
locksmith	belongs thairtoo – at 33s. 4d. the peice is	10–00–00	
	1 lock with a sprent band & staipl for a French tronk	03–01–00	• 13 • 01 • –
	Fryday 26 November 1669 to Sanders Andersone gairner in Intherleith for –		
Plumb	60 plumb – standerts..	02–18–00	
standerts;	80 plumb standerts not so good	01–09–00	
	For ale & breid	00–09–00	
	2 plum imps		
	1 chirrie imp.....................		
	Some grosert bushes	00–00–00:	• 04 • 16 • –
	163–10–06: All the disbursments in November on this syde is		• 163 • 10 • 06

[90]

The disbursments on the other syde in November 1669 is..................		• 163 • 10 • 06
18 November to David Clerk for kill ale..	00–06–08	
23 November to Thomas Andersone when he went to the mill..........	00–05–00	
To Agnes Clerk for small disbursments – 13s. and 20s. shoe		
lost or did let it be stoln fra hir is	01–13–00	
5 November to John Rob to bring out Marie Douglas.......................	00–04–00	
For wheat breid in the month off November	01–00–04	• 03 • 09 • –
The end of November 1669 The disbursments in November 1669 is ..		• 166 • 19 • 06

December 1669

The disbursments in December 1669 ....

Marie Clerk

Margaret Clerk

3 December – 3 ell of whyt serge to be a peticot for Marie Clerk
at 22s. the ell 03–06–00
Said day – 2 ell lining to be Margaret Clerk – naipkins 14s. the ell ...... 01–08–00 • 04 • 14 • –

Accompt of peys boght and resavet fra William Rolland tenent in Wrights howsses:

11 bols of peys fra: Willm Rolland in wrights howsses

1 On Teusday 7 December David Dryburgh broght – 1 boll –
on Wedensday the 8 off December these tenents broght
to Newbiging ....
2 William Thomsone.................. 1 boll
3 Helen Thomsone..................... 1 boll
4 Coits..................................... 1 boll
5 Tam Abernethie .... 1 boll
6 John Clerk .... 1 boll
He broght 2 halff bols on 2 hors.
7 John Penycooke malt man......... 1 boll
8 John Thomsone....................... 1 boll is 10 bols........10 bols......is in all 11 bols
9 Edouart Clark .... 1 boll of peys at 3 lib.
10 Patrik Craig .... 1 boll 3s. 4d. the boll • 34 • 16 • 08
11 Robert Dewer .... 1 boll The way how I peyit the 11 bols of peys –

3 December 1669 sent with John Rob which he delivert to William
Rolland.. 30–00–00

Of which I have his discharge date the 10 off

7 December 1669 sent with John Rob which he delivert to his wyffe 01–13–04

10 December 1669 sent with John Rob which he delivert to [blank] ... 03–03–04

34–16–08

Nota on Wedensday – 8 December 1669 – William Thomsone in Pennycooke broght fra the said William Rolland – a boll off peys for Robert Dewer smith in Pennycooke 1 boll off peys for which he peyit in readie money 3–3s. 4d.

---

7 December to David Clerk when he went to sie 11 bols of peys dicht at W[rights]–housses 00–06–00

Tow cards — 11 December to John Rob for a pair off tow cairds 00–18–00

1 ston off candle — 13 December to John Rob for 1 ston of candle he got at Dalkeith .... 02–16–00 • 04 • 00 • –

W. Broun – skinner — The 16 off December 1669 to William Broun skinner 12 lib. for my chamber maill fra Witsonday 1669 till Mertimes 1669 on his discharge date the said 16 off December 1669 12–00–00

5 firlots of wheat — Teusday 14 December to William Rolland tenent in Wrights housses – for 5 firlots off new wheat at – 7 lib. the boll .... 08–14–00 • 20 • 14 • –

Boght fra James Clerk — 15 December 1669 to James Clerk for –

1– 1 box wood comb 00–08–00

2– 1 rubber with a turnt handle 00–09–00

3– 1 brush with a long turnt handle for dichting picturs 01–00–00

4– 1 reid caisse conteining a glasse –& a horn comb .... 01–00–00 • 02 • 17 • –

1 spyce mill	To William Reid for ane yrne spyce mill	02–00–00	
	2 ships bells	00–08–00	
	5 hair cods	00–12–06	
	1 quair off gray peper	00–03–00	
	1 once off measses	00–13–04	
	1 lb off whyt confiturs	00–12–00	• 04 • 08 • 10
04–14–00	1 blew and whyt salt	00–15–00	
34–16–08	To Jhon Crichtoun for 3 whyt drinking caps	00–12–00	
04–00–00	2 large whyt yrne sawe alls	00–07–00	
20–14–00	2 lb off leaffe tobaco	01–10–00	
02–17–00	1 thing for laying and hot yrn on it for drying off cloths	00–04–06	
04–08–10	To David Home litster for dying – 2 pair stokings blak	00–12–00	• 04 • 00 • 06
04–00–06	21 December to James Corser for a peruque	11–12–00	
24–03–08	22 December to Margaret Tam for 1 pair off whyt – four		
99–14–08	threid stokings	04–00–00	
	21 December to John Cooke for perfyting 5 handls & sneks	03–11–00	
	28 skinners neidls	00–06–08	
	8 once of broun candie	00–07–00	
	23 December to Harie Stewart for a rim of peper	04–07–00	• 24 • 03 • 08
	The disbursments on this syde in December 1669 is		• 99 • 14 • 08

[91]

	The disbursments in December 1669 on the other syde is		• 99 • 14 • 08
Mr. John Clark[60] – a blak cot	The 20 off December 1669 to Robert Hamiltoun – merchant – in full off ane accompt on his discharge for blak cloth and serge to be a cot for Mr Jhon Clerk & uther necessars he furnished thairtoo according to the accompt – 29–15–6d.	29–15–06	
	20 December to Alexander Weir tailyeur be his accompt & his discharge at the fit theroff for making the said cot &c	03–16–00	
	29 December to Mr Jhon: Clerk to pay for 1 pair of shoone	01–12–00	
	To Patrik Rainie for solling 1 pair shoone for my selff	00–16–00	• 35 • 19 • 06
Alexander Leslie	22 December 1669 to Alexander Leslie for 2 doubls off a contract 3 assignations –& a procutrie off resignation – 6 dolors	17–08–00	
	To his man Mr John Leslie a dolor and a halff	04–07–00	• 21 • 15 • –
	23 December to Helen Cadel – William Brouns woman..........	00–12–00	
	The 28 December to Tam Wolff my brothers man	01–06–08	• 01 • 18 • 08
99–14–08	Agnes Clerk gave to go to the kill	00–06–08	
35–19–06	Shoe gave to go to the mill..........	00–06–08	
21–15–00	3 laid off cols out off Clarkingtoun	00–18–06	
01–18–08	Uther small disbursments..........	00–08–02	
03–00–00	For whyt breid in December 1669	01–00–00	• 03 • 00 • –
162–07–10	The end off December 1669 — The disbursments in December 1669..........		• 162 • 07 • 10

1: Januar............................ 1669...		443–10–06
2: Februar .... 1669...		241–02–10
3: Marche........................... 1669...		310–03–06
4: Aprill .... 1669...		265–06–00
5: May................................ 1669...		257–09–09
6: June .... 1669...		349–00–10
7: Jully .... 1669...		544–02–06
8: Agust .... 1669...		301–11–07
9: September .... 1669...		352–18–02
10: October......................... 1669...		180–16–00
11: November .... 1669...		166–19–06
12: December...................... 1669...		162–07–10

1669 Soma off the haill disbursments fra the 1 of Januar
till the last day off December 1669 is 3575–09–00

John: Clerk

[92]

Januar 1670 The disbursments in Januar – 1670

1 to Mr Jhon Clerk.. 08–14–00
2 to James Clerk – a 3 lib. peice.............................. 03–00–00.......... • 11 • 14 • –

[60] Clerk used both 'Clark' and 'Clerk' in this entry.

To William Clark...

1– a fyne horn inkhorne cost .... 10s. ....
1– horn skraiching call cost................................. 06s. ....
1– brasse killevyn pen cost.................................. 04s. ....
1– pair of gloves cost .... 06s. ....
1– turnt skrewd painted box cost .... 03s. ....
1– new halff merk peice .... 06s. 8d. ....
1– pire cost .... 01s. ....
1– box cost 6d. with – 18 turnors.......................... 03s. 6d. ....
1– box with whyt confections............................... 03s. 10 .... • 02 • 04 • –

To Alexander Clerk...

1– reid gilt caisse with a miroir glasse in it
and a tortl[e] shell combe cost – 20s. .... 20s. ....
1– brasse killevyn pen cost................. 4s. .... 04s. ....
1– turnt painted skrewd box .... 3s. .... 03s. ....
1– halff merk peice.. 06s. 8d. ....
1– 1 box 6d. – 3s. of turnors in it .... 03s. 6d. ....
1– pire .... 01s. ....
1– pair gloves cost .... 06s. ....
1– 1 box with whyt confections in it .... 03s. 10d. .... • 02 • 08 • –

To Robert Clerk...

1– turnt skrewd painted box .... 03s. ....
6– turnors.. 00s. 6d. ....
1– painted box with whyt confections.................... 03s. 6d. .... • 00 • 07 • –

To Marie Clerk		
To Margaret Clerk		
To Agnes Clerk....		
1– pearle neck laisse	03s. 8d.	
1– whyt yrne neidl caisse	01s. 4d.	
1– large painted skrewd turnt box	04s.	
1– dolor 2 lib. 18s.	058s.	
1– pair of gloves	12s.	
1– box with whyt confections	04s.	• 04 • 03 • –
To Helen Clerk...		
1– pearle neck laisse	03s. 8d.	
1– 1 whyt yrne neidle caisse	01s. 4d.	
1– turnt painted skrewd box	03s.	
in turnors	06s.	
1– new halff merk peice	06s. 8d.	
1– pair off gloves	07s. 4d.	
1– box wit[h] whyt confections	03s.	• 01 • 11 • –
To Jennet Clerk...		
1– pearle neck laisse	03s. 8d.	
1– whyt yrne neidle caisse	01s. 4d.	
1– turnt painted skrewd box	02s. 0d.	
17–turnors	03s. 0d.	
1– box with whyt confections	03s.	• 00 • 11 • –

Item	Amount	Total
Katherin Clerk...		
1– pearle neck laisse	03s. 8d.	
1– whyt yrne needle caisse	01s. 4d.	
1– turnt skrewd painted box	02s.–0	
18 turnors	03s.–0	
1– box with whyt confections	02s.–0	• 00 • 12 • –
To Marie Dowglas...		
1– 40s. peice	40s.	
1– pair of gloves	12s.	
1– turnt painted skrewd box	04s.	
1– whyt yrne neidle caisse	01s.	• 02 • 17 • –
1– to Anna Irving	01–16–00	
2– to Jennet Shanks	00–18–00	
3– to Jennet Thomson byre woman	00–12–00	
4– to Nans Frizel	00–12–00	
5– to Marion Rob	00–12–00	• 04 • 10 • –
1– to Thomas Andersone	01–09–00	
2– to David Clerk	00–18–00	
3– to Jhon Clerk	00–12–00	
4– to Edowart Thomson	00–12–00	
5– to Arche Craig	00–09–00	
6– to John Dicksone	00–09–00	
7– to William Stewart to buy a caip	00–18–00	• 05 • 07 • –
The disbursments above in January 1670		• 36 • 04 • –

[93]

	The disbursments in Januar – 1670 on the other syde is		• 36 • 04 • –
	1– to Jhon Rob 00–06–00		
	2– to George Reid...00–06–00		
	3– to Jhon Broun bedel 00–12–00		
	4– to Sande Stewart...00–02–00		
	5– to Jhon Broun schoole master 1 pair off blak worsit stokings cost 01–16–00		• 03 • 02 • –
	On Munday – being hansel Munday the 3 off January 1670 the disbursments on the other syde & this above amounts to...		• 39 • 06 • –
	4 Januar – to Arche Adersone for a hair	00–06–00	
cols – Lonhead	7 Januar to Jhon Clerk to pay – 3 laid off cols at Lonhead..................	01–00–06	
	7 Januar to Edowart Thomsone to buy cols at Clarkingtoun.		
	1– our own hor[s]e................. 2		
Clerkingtoun –	2– the mill horse 2		
cols	3– Jhon Clerk 2		
	4– Thomas Abernethie 2		
	5– David Ramsay................... 2		
	6– William Thomson 1		
	7– William Simsone 1		
	8– Halls 2		
	9– David Dryburgh................ 2 ......is 16 laid cost	04–18–08	• 06 • 05 • 02

Archbald	The 15 off Januar 1670 – to Archbald Craig for his fie fra Mertimes 1668			
Craig his fie	till Witsonday 1669 – to wit 8 lib. & 12s. to buy 1 pair off shoone		08–12–00	
Caps	17 Januar to William Clarks for whyt caps –&c		02–08–00	• 11 • 00 • –
	Disbursments at Edinburgh the 19 off January 1670 – I went to Edinburgh			
06–05–00	1 rouch old mans head		00–14–00	
11–00–00	4 litle pad locks at 5s. the peice		01–00–00	
19–04–04	1 brasse killevyn pen – 4s.		00–04–00	
08–08–00	2 suger loaffs weying – 6 lb 4 once at 10s. 6d. the lb		03–05–06	
53–12–06	2 pepers off whyt confiturs....10s.		00–10–00	
04–14–00	For caps –& trinchers –&c –26s. 10d.		01–06–10	
104–11–04	1 whyt wand baskit	18s.	00–18–00	
207–15–04	1 bell	24s.	01–04–00	
	24 yrne nuik bands for a kist	24s.	01–04–00	
	For skinners threid	4s.	00–04–00	
	1 sive for the horse corne	9s.	00–09–00	
	3 braid whisks	9s.	00–09–00	
	6 fadome off tows for a coffer	8s.	00–08–00	
	To David Gray for a Scots hatt		03–02–00	
	To Piter Maill for a cudbek hatt		04–00–00	
	For a horne catt or skraicher		00–06–00	• 19 • 04 • 04
James	20 Januar – to Patrik Rainie for 1 pair off shoone for James Clerk		01–10–00	
Clerk	21 Januar to him – to get 6 quarters off Holland for 12 bands at 3–8s. ell		05–02–00	
	27 Januar to him to pay for 2 stikit night caps for himselff		01–10–00	

	Said day to him to pay for mending 2 pair off stokins........................	00–06–00	• 08 • 08 • –
Marie Clerk	24 Januar to Isobell Gray 4 dolors to buy a laistband for Marie Clerk	11–12–00	
Isobel Fermer for nails	25 Januar to Isobel Fermer 36–16s. in full of ane accompt for nails......	36–16–00	
	20 Januar to Patrik Rainie for a pair off shoone for my selff...............	01–18–06	
	For mending a lint whill	01–16–00	
	2 pair whyt spektakls – 6s. – 4 pair grein spektakls – 24s. is	01–10–00	• 53 • 12 • 06
	28 Januar 1670 to John Cooke for...............		
	1 second key for a new firr presse & 4 skrew nails.....		
	For making 19 coper virols		
	1 bordert lock – 2 keys – 4 – skrew nails –& 1 sheild for ane other new firr presse		
	For lynthning 2 litle keys for the knok caisse .... all....................		• 04 • 14 • –
Marie Clerk Marg Clerk	The 21 off Januar 1670 to David Boyd in full of ane accompt on his discharge..	43–18–04	
	The said day to Robert Hamiltoun in full off ane accompt on his discharge...	60–13–00	
	Thir 2 accompts wes for the usse off Marie –& Margaret Clerks for mourning when the registers ladie dyed....................................		• 104 • 11 • 04
	The disbursments on the other syde and this in the month off January 1670 – amonts to		• 247 • 01 • 04

[94]

	The 25 off January 1670 boght fra – [blank] Sandersone off		
A young gelding cost 142 lib. 4s.	Tillrlygen[61] in Ireland a young large gelding going in his fourt[h] yeir will be 5 yeir old come May 1670 –// he is off a bad cullor some what whytish on the head and neck –& begining to mix with gray hairs everie whair – so that iff he live & thryve he will be a sad gray cullor –		
	cost 140 lib. Scots	140–00–00	
	To his man in drink money	000–12–00	
	To Jhon Campbel staibler for helping me to buy him	001–09–00	
	Charges	000–03–00	• 142 • 04 • –
	I got onlie with him		
	1– a colt halter		
	2– a sheit		
	3– a howsin girth		

Mr John Clerk	25 Januar 1670 – to Mr Jhon Clerk in full off ane accompt off some disbursments he peyit out for him selff 05–16	05–16–00	
	said day to him which he gave William Hamiltouns women – to thair hansel	01–16–00	• 07 • 12 • –
Clarkingtoun	Whyt breid in the month off Januar 1670		• 01 • – • –
10 laid cols	23 Januar 10 laid off cols got at Clarkingtoun – 6s. 2d. the laid	03–01–08	
	To Agnes Clerk for some small disbursments	01–08–00	• 04 • 09 • 08

		This accompt off charges occasioned at my mariage with Elizabeth Jhonstoun – being maried on Thursday the 27 off Januar 1670 in the colledg kirk off – Edinburgh be Mr William Hamiltoun minister at Pennycooke		ABC;
	1	22 Februar my brother Jhon Andersone delivert to hir off my money	18–00–00	
	2	25 Februar to him a dolor	02–18–00	• 20 • 18 • –
	1	21 Januar 1670 to Mr Robert Smith to give to Cramond box	02–18–00	
	2	And halff a dolor to give the clark off the session	01–09–00	
	3	To Mr Jhon Smith to give the bellman	00–12–00	• 04 • 19 • –
	1	27 off Januar to the treasurer off the colledg kirk whair we wes maried	02–18–00	
	2	To the bedel of the colledg kirk	02–14–08	• 05 • 12 • 08
	1	28 January to the drumers	01–09–00	
20–18–00	2	30 January on a Sunday a voyage to Leith in a cotch[62] cost	05–16–00	
04–19–00	3	Munday 30 January to hir 2 halff crouns	03–00–00	• 10 • 05 • –
05–12–08		22 January to hir to pay for 35 pair off gloves at 30s. the pair	52–10–00	• 52 • 10 • –
10–05–00		The 5 off February 1670 –		
52–10–00	1	To the box off Pennycooke	08–14–00	
10–15–00	2	To Jhon Broun schoole master & clark to the session	01–09–00	
21–00–00	3	To Jhon Broun bedel	00–12–00	• 10 • 15 • –

61 Possibly Tullylagan, Co. Tyrone (Ir: *Tulaigh Lagáin*).

62 A coach.

06–05–00 Drink money shoe gave in Edinburgh –

132–04–08 1 To Sir Jhon Smiths servants – 1 ½ dolor ....

2 To Mr Robert Smiths servants – 1 dolor.................

3 To Mr Jhon Smiths woman – 1 dolor ....

4 To the Lady Grays women – 1 dolor.......................

5 To Isobell Grays servants.................1 dolor.............

6 To Geils Dowglas woman – 2 dolors...... is 7 ½ lyg dolors – at 56s. the peice • 21 • 00 • –

3 Marche 1670 when we cam to Neubiging – drink money to our own servants –

1 To Anna Irving..0...... 01–09

2 To Jennet Shanks.. 00–12

3 To Nans Frizel... 00–12

4 To Marion Rob 00–18

5 To Jenet Thomson... 00–12

6 To Thomas Andersone 01–04

7 To Jhon Reid .... 00–18 .... • 06 • 05 • –

Soma off the disbursments betwixt ABC & this is 132–04–08 .... • 132 • 04 • 08

The names off those to whom gloves wes given –

1– Dame Geils Smith.............. 1 pair

2– Geils Gray .... 1 pair

3– Katherin Gray .... 1 pair

4– Helen Gray........................ 1 pair

5– Mistress Jean Gray .... 1 pair

6– Isobell Gray 1 pair [sic] ...... 1 pair

7– Marie Clerk........................ 1 pair
8– Margaret Clerk.................. 1 pair
9– Mr Jhon Clerk.................... 1 pair
10– James Clerk........................ 1 pair
11– Agnes Clerk....................... 1 pair
12– Marie Douglas .... 1 pair
13– Jhon Andersone .... 1 pair
14– Robert Johnstoun .... 1 pair
15– 1 sister in London............. 1 pair
16– 1 other sister in London..... 1 pair
17– Geils Douglas.................... 1 pair
18– Jenet Dowglas................... 1 pair
19– Mr Jhon Smith.................. 1 pair
20– Mr Jhon Smiths wyffe .... 1 pair
21– Sir John Smith .... 1 pair
22– Mr Robert Smith .... 1 pair
23– his lady .... 1 pair
24– Southfields dochter .... 1 pair
25– ane other off his dochters .. 1 pair
26– Lady Bagillo...................... 1 pair
27– Mr William Grays wyffe.... 1 pair
28– minister off Cramond........ 1 pair
29– Mistresse Primrose in –
Cramond.......................... 1 pair

30– minister of Penycooke .... 1 pair
32– his wyffe .... 2 pair
33– Mr Jhon Smiths wyffs –
sister .... 1 pair
34– ane other off his wyffs –
sisters .... 1 pair[63]

Is in all 35 pair off gloves cost as is above
52–10s.

The disbursments in Januar 1670 on this syde.................................... 287–10–04
The disbursments in Januar 1670 on the former 2 sydes 247–01–04
all the disbursments in Januar 1670 is .... 534–11–08 • 534 • 11 • 08

[95]

Februar 1670 Mr Jhon Clerk — The disbursments in Februar – 1670 –
The 1 off February – to William Hamiltoun merchant 40 lib. for
Mr Jhon Clerks boord fra the 24 off Januar 1670 till the 24 off
Aprill 1670 is – 3 month.. • 40 • 00 • –

George Clerk – webster — The 3 off Februar 1670 to George Clerk webster for weiving –
1– 30 ell of 6 quarter braid blanketing at 2s. the ell............................ 03–00–00
2– 24 ell of braid blanketing at 1s. the ell 01–04–00

	3– 31 ell off b[raid] courser blanketing at 1s. the ell	01–11–00	
	4 for popeing ale	00–08–00	• 06 • 03 • –
	4 Februar – to Jhon Davisone couper for 2 handes and seting on a girth on a tub	00–13–06	
Jhon Broun schoole master	5– Februar 1670 to Jhon Broun schoole master at Penycooke 20 lib. for his stipend fra Candelmes 1669 till candlemes 1670 on discharge date the said 5 off February 1670	20–00–00	• 20 • 13 • 06
	5 Februar to Jhon Rob – for a pirn to a lint whill	00–02–00	
mending the bairns shoon	To Arche Andersone – 15 Februar for mending & helping the bairns shoone in Penycooke at divers tymes	00–10–00	
	16 Februar to Jhon Rob for 3 peices of bacon	00–17–00	
Ja Pirsie for making 8 bolls off malt	The 16 off Februar to James Pirsie for making 8 bols off malt; 1– for making the said 8 bolls off malt ... 03–00–00 2– to him in drink money as his due ... 00–06–08 3– to him 1 pynt ails [sic] pryce more nor his due ... 00–01–08	03–08–04	• 04 • 17 • 04
8 laid Clark–ingtouns cols	The 25 & 28 off Februar – 8 laid off cols out off Clarkingtoun at 6s. 2d. the laid	02–09–04	
	For fresh beiff	01–06–00	
20 cogs	To William Clerk 12 cogs at 20d. the peice – 1 lib. – 8 cogs at 16d. the peice – 10s. 8d. 1 whyt cap – 2s. 6d. is in all	01–13–02	
Breid	For breid in Februar	01–00–00	
	To Agnes Clerk for disbursments when I wes in Edinburgh	01–00–00	• 07 • 08 • 06

[63] The list jumps from 30 to 32 in the original.

Whyt threid	26 Februar – to James Arbukls wyffe for –		
knitings	1– 1 once 4 drop off small whyt threid at 14s. the once	00–17–06	
plane &	2– 1 once 12 drop whyt threid at 7s. the once	00–12–02	
twidlt	3– 3 bolt twidle knitings at – 9s. 6d. the bolt	01–08–06	
balin	4– 2 bolt off plane knitings at 6s. the bolt	00–12–00	
	5– 1 bolt plane knitings	00–04–00	
	6– 1 lb 8 once 10 drop off balling at 20s. the lb	01–10–08	• 05 • 04 • 10
	26 February 1670 – to William Reid for –		
rysse.....	4 lb off rysse at 5s. the lb	01–00–00	
casnet suger	4 lb off casnet suger at 6s. the lb	01–04–00	
raisings	2 lb of raisings at 6s. the pound	00–12–00	
pruns	2 lb of pruns at 3s. the pound	00–06–00	
canel	1 once off canel	00–13–04	
confiturs	3 baist off confeits	00–18–00	• 04 • 13 • 04
Marie & Margaret Clerks	The 25 off Februar – to Thomas Mackie tailyeur for making a blak taffatie gown for Margaret Clerk & furnishing thairtoo & for doeing some things for Marie Clerk on his discharge on the fitt off his accompt........15 lib.		• 15 • 00 • –
James Clerk	22 Februar – to my brother Jhon Andersone 42s. which he gave to James Clerk for buying some necessars & 10s. to James Clerk for helping his cloths is	02–12–00	
	2 horne spatulas	00–06–00	• 02 • 18 • –
40–00–00	The end off Februar 1670 the disbursments in Februar 1670........		• 106 • 18 • 06
06–03–00			
20–13–06			

04–17–04
07–08–06
05–04–10
04–13–04
15–00–00
02–18–00
106–18–06

[96]

Marche 1670 — The disbursments in Marche 1670.........:

1 young horse 45 lib. — The 8 off Marche – to Cristian Ramsay in Braidwood for a large lyert staig off 5 yeir old...45 lib. .... • 45 • 00 • –

The 8 off Marche 1670 to Robert Cleghorne candle maker in Dalkeith for 8 ston off candle at 4 merk the ston is 32 merk............................ 21–06–08

8 stone off candle fra Robert Cleghorne — The way how I peyit him the same –
1– The 11 off December 1669 sent to him with William Stewart 3 ston tron wecht off sheep & oxen talon at 40s. the ston................ 06–00–00
2– The said 8 off Marche 1670 peyit to himselff at Newbiging .... 15–06–08 • 21 • 06 • 08

23 mure fowls...... — The 10 Marche 1670 – to Jhon Ramsay for 23 mure fowls at 6s. the peice – is 6–12s. he gave me on the skore.. 06–12–00 • 06 • 12 • –

Marie & Margaret Clerks — Disburset for Marie & Margaret Clerks as follows............................
1 3 ell off gimp lace for Marie Clerks dyed tabie peticot at 48s. the ell.. 07–04–00
2 1 pair off shoone for Marie Clerk 01–10–00

3 1 laiced hood for Marie Clerk 03–00–00
4 For making Marie Clerks tabein peticot 00–09–00
5 For liting Marie Clerks tabein peticot 03–00–00
6 1 pair off [....] gloves for Marie Clerk 00–16–00
7 12 once off baling 00–15–00
8 For liting 3 ½ ell off whyt serge for a peticot for Margaret Clerk 01–00–00
9 3 ell of gimp lace for Margaret Clerks serge peticot 34s. the ell 05–02–00
10 For making Margaret Clerks peticot 00–06–00
11 1 pair off shoone for Margaret Clerk 01–10–00
12 6 spindls 00–03–04
13 For making a night waistcot for Margaret Clerk .... 01–12–00 • 26 • 07 • 04

Disbursit for Marie and Margaret Clerks as follows –

Marie & Margaret Clerks

1 2 pair off blak shoone for them 03–00–00
2 For making 2 blak peticots 00–12–00
3 Drink money to the tailyeurs man 00–06–00
4 2 loote string hoods for them 06–16–00
5 1 tiffinie band 04–16–00
6 1 pair off shooes 01–10–00
7 4 ell off Holland for hand cuffs to them at 36s. the ell .... 07–04–00 • 24 • 04 • –

They made usse off severall off these things befor the registers ladys sicknes & efter hir death which wes about the midle [sic] off December 1669 .....

Great salt...

5 Marche to Jhon Rob for a peck off great salt 00–13–04
7 Marche to Jhon Rob for bringing out my wyffs coffer 00–06–08
10 Marche to Anna Irving to give William Jhonstoun tinkler – for mending

	a holl [sic] in a pot bottome	00–04–00	
1 calff	12 Marche to Edouart Adamsone for a calff he boght for our usse	02–10–00	
Isobell Gray	16 Marche to Jhon Rob to pay Isobell Gray for 2 baps with raisins –&c cam out to Newbiging the 1 off Marche	02–08–00	
	16 Marche to Jhon Rob for halff a mutchkin off rose water – 3s. for oyll & chalk to skour plaits – 3s. 6d. is	00–06–06	• 06 • 08 • 04
Half a barel of hering......	The 16 off Marche 1670 – to William Stewart 8 merks who got halff a barell off hering in Leith for the same –5–6–8– for fixing a shoe on the horse 1s.–6d. To William Stewart – 1s. 8d. to get a pynt ale	05–09–10	
	16 Marche to Wille Mihi for 26 ell off whyt wirsit at 5d. the ell	00–10–10	
gals	23 Marche – 1 pound off gals	00–10–00	
copres	1 pound off copres	00–02–00	
plum dames	1 ston off plumb dames	01–04–00	
tulip	1 tulip	00–02–00	
rudiments 4–13–4 Ja: Clerk....	25 Marche within a letter sent with Jhon Rob to be left at my brothers chamber for James Clerk for 4 rudiments for William & Alexander Cler[k]s 1 merk for the 4 rudiments & 6s. 8d. for James Clerk for binding them	01–00–00	• 08 • 18 • 08

The 24 off Marche 1670 George Reid peyit to James Stewart drogist for these gairden seeds undermentioned to wit –

24 Marche 1670	1– 4 once off liks[64] [sic]	00–10–00
	2– 4 once off carrets	00–16–00

[64] Leeks.

gairden seids	3– 4 once off sybous	00–10–00	
cost 3–14s.	4– 1 once off parsnips	00–05–00	
	5– 2 once off turnips	00–08–00	
	6– 1 once off letus [sic]	00–04–00	
	7– 2 once off rifarts	00–08–00	
	8– 1 once once [sic] off purpe	00–06–00	
	9– 1 drop off mergelin	00–01–00	
	10 1 drop off gille flours	00–06–00	• 03 • 14 • –
D. Glendining 3 bols off seid oats	The 25 Marche 1670 peyit to David Glendining 3 bolls off oats grew in Cookeing which wes to sawe in Newbiging at 4 lib. the boll at 4 lib. the boll		• 12 • 00 • –
	25 Marche – to James Bothwel his women in drink money	01–16–00	
	31 Marche – to Robert Cleghorne for 1 quarter peck off mustard	00–13–04	
	My voyage to Dalkeith the said day	00–16–00	
	Fresh beiff in the month off Marche	04–05–00	
	Whyt breid in the month off Marche	01–06–08	• 08 • 17 • –
	30 Marche 2 oranges –& 2 limons	00–08–06	
	To Arche Craig when he went in with Geils Dowglas 18 Marche	00–03–00	• 00 • 11 • 06
	The end off Marche 1670: the disbursments in Marche 1670		• 163 • 19 • 06

[97]

Marche 1670	I say Aprill 1670	The disbursments in Aprill 1670:
carlip cols	1 Aprill – to James Frizel – for 26 laid off colls which he gave for 24	

	laid at 4s. the laid is 4–16–& 4s. to the cairiers is	05–00–00	
lint seid oyll	Said day to Jhon Rob to get a pynt off lint seid oyll	01–04–00	
Marion Robs fies	The 6 off Aprill 1670 compleited Marion Rob 7 lib. 10s. for hir fie fra Witsonday 1669 till Mertimes 1669	07–10–00	• 13 • 14 • –
	Disbursit at Edinburgh 8 Aprill 1670		
	1 lb off pack thread	00–07–00	
copres	2 lb off copres at 2s. the lb	00–04–00	
galls	2 ½ lb off gals at 10s. the lb	01–05–00	
	4 once off leaffe tobacco	00–05–00	
anis seids	To William Reid for 2 lb off annis seids at 9s. the lb	00–18–00	
pils	Halff a box of Doctor Andersons pils	01–13–04	
neidles	To Geils Dowglas for six skore & 5 neidls of divers sorts	01–05–00	• 05 • 17 • 04
400 bell nails	The 8 off Aprill to Jhon Tod on his discharge for 400 bell nails at 4 lib. the hundredth	16–00–00	
11 ell Yorkshyre cloth	The 9 off Aprill to Umphrey Clark for 11 ell of sad cullort Yorkshyre cloth at 5–6–8d. the ell on his discharge of the said date	58–13–04	
James Adamsone plumber	12 Aprill to James Adamsone for 4 peices off oake for axiltreis – for hurle barrows – 17s. 6d. and for 2 peices off squair lead 20 lb 13 once at 40s. the ston 2–2s. is both 3–10s.	03–10–00	
2 firkins sope	Thursday 14 Aprill 1670 – to Archbald Cambel in his chamber in the sope wark 13 lib. for 2 firikins [sic] off sope at 6 lib. 10s. the firkin	13–00–00	
Alexander Simpsone – for ane yrne pot	The 12 off Aprill 1670 to Alexander Simsone for ane yrne pot with ane holl [sic] in it to hold peck– 42s. on the conditions under wreatten –1– for 2 brasse pins –& a ring of brasse he giftit me for a glasse – 2		

	that I sould quyt him a miroir glasse he brak in my chamber –		
	So we wes both content all bygans being close betwixt us preseiding		
brande	the said 12 Aprill 1670........	02–02–00	
8 pynts off	13 Aprill– to Thomas Wilsone for 8 pynts brande at 24s. the pynt.......	09–12–00	• 102 • 17 • 04
John Cooke	13 Aprill to Jhon Cooke– for a bosse lock –& a sprent band with		
for making	shorne headit nails to put it on –55s.	02–15–00	
a plough	20 Aprill to William Stewart – to give Ard Paton for making a		
	plough	00–13–04	• 03 • 08 • 04
	The 8 off Aprill 1670 – to William Russell wreatter in Edinburgh on		
For taking	his discharge off the said date 30–05–4– which he disbursit for me in		
infeftment of	taking infeftment off 2 lu chops in the Luken Booths to wit –		
2 chops	1– to Mr James Ruchheid toun clerk for the seasine & registration		
in the Lukn	off the procutrie off reg: resignation granted be Elizabeth Jhonstoun		
booths	in favors off – Jhon Clerk off Pennycooke for the said seasine – 7		
	rex dolors........	20–06–00	
	2– to the officers at the taking off the seasine & instrument money ...	02–02–00	
	3– to Henry Lyon the clerks depute	06–13–04	
	4– off drink money to his servant	01–04–00	• 30 • 05 • 04
William	The 20 off Aprill 1670 to Margaret Hopkirk 40 lib. for William –		
Alex[r]	Alexander and Jenet Clerk their boord fra the 18 off January 1670 to		
Jenet Clerks	the 18 off Aprill 1670 is 3 month		• 40 • 00 • –
boords;			
Small lining	The 22 off Aprill 1670 boght fra George Blaikie chapman 24 ell off small		
cloth	lining in 3 peices – 8 ell in everie peice at 2: at 17s. 6d. the ell.............		• 21 • 00 • –

4 coverings	The 23 off Aprill 1670 – to William Watsone webster in Dalkeith for weiving		
weiving 4 lib.	4 blak & whyt coverings for servants beds at 20s. the peice	04–00–00	
Jhon Reid 2	26 Aprill to Jhon Reid for 2 peks off beir he gave Anna Irving –		
peks of beir	for knoking at 6 lib. the boll is 15s.	00–15–00	
	26 Aprill 1670 – to Alexander Haistie for 8 saltit codlings –18s.	00–18–00	• 05 • 13 • –
Mr Samuell	Wednesday the 27 off Aprill 1670 to Mr Samuel Colvin five rex dolors –		
Colvin – a	W: for a booke in wreat covert with reid leather – a litle gilt anent the		
booke 14 lib.	combat betwixt Generall Daliell & the West Contrie men –&c		• 14 • 10 • –
10s.			
	The 21 off Aprill to a webster for warping ale..................................	00–06–00	
	1 once off whyt thread 7s.	00–07–00	
13–14–00	1 peice off narow whyt knitings	00–04–00	
05–17–04	23 Aprill my wyffe payit Jhon Reid for a calff..................................	01–16–00	
102–17–04	1 pound off kitchin suger..	00–06–00	
03–08–04	Halff ane once off whyt aple	00–04–00	
30–05–04	7 Aprill at Thomas Marshalls dochters brydel in Silver burn – their		
40–00–00	being 4 persons –2–13–04 to fidlers & pypers 7s. 6d. is......................	03–00–10	
21–00–00	Neidls	00–01–06	
05–13–00	1 blak silk lace for a gown	00–05–00	
14–10–00	For bairns...	00–04–00	
07–03–06	Uther small disbursments...	00–09–02	• 07 • 03 • 06
05–08–04	3 Aprill – half a mutchkin off rose water	00–03–00	
249–17–02	To Jhon Rob –& Arche Andersone for trouts	00–10–00	

27 off Aprill to James Persie in drink money for making 2 stips
malt 00–13–04
6 douzane off egs [sic] in Aprill 00–10–00
Fresh beiff in Aprill 03–02–00
Whyt breid in Aprill with sour[e]d breid off our own .... 00–10–00 • 05 • 08 • 04
The end of Aprill 1670 – the disbursments in Aprill 1670.......... • 249 • 17 • 02

[98]

May 1670 The disbursments in May 1670 ....

The 2 off May – 1670 to Alexander Etkin in Welstain – for 6 bolls of oats –
6 bols oats Jhon Reid got fra him – 21 Januar 1670 – in part off his boll at 3–6–8d.
the boll is 20–00–00

Jo: Andersone 3 May sent with Jhon Rob to my brother Jhon Andersone – 48s. which he
gave James Clerk to buy buttons & silk for my clok 02–08–00

2 steips off malt 5 May 1670 to Widow Lowrie at the mill for making 2 steip off
malt .... 05–16–00 • 31 • 10 • 08

8 thraive peys stroe 8 thraive oat stroe got at Clarkingtoun The accompt off oate & peys stroe resavet at Clarkingtoun or Nicolsone
in the month off April 1670...which stroe David Clerk – peyit the 4 off
May 1670 – Wedensday I gave him money to pay it –
1– 8 thraive off peys stroe at 20s. the thraive 08–00–00
2– 8 thraive off oat stroe at 13s. 4d. the thraive.......... 05–06–08 • 13 • 06 • 08

Teusday 10 May 1670 sent within a letter to my brother Jhon Anderson –
James Clerk 34s. which he gave James Clerk to buy a pair off shoone.......... 01–14–00

1 ston butter	11 May for 1 ston of salt butter	03–06–00	
	7 quarters of hardn for a crosse wallet 5s. ...ell	00–08–10	• 05 • 08 • 10
	The 11 off May 1670 – Mr John Clerk peyit to William Hamiltoun –		
Mr Jhon	which my brother gave him to pay –& I sent it bak to my brother on Fryday –		
Clerk – his	13 May with Jhon Rob for 17 days he wes in his house fra 24 off		
boord to	Aprill 1670 till Thursday 12 May 1670 acording to 40 lib. in 3		
William	month	06–13–04[65]	
Hamiltoun &	16s. he spent with William Hamiltoun becaus he wold tak		
&c	nothing for the od[d] 2 days more nor the halff month	00–16–00	• 07 • 09 • 04
	1: pair off shoone for Mr Jhon Clerk	02–00–00	
	For the gray horse charges	00–03–04	• 02 • 03 • 04
	Thir – 2 last articles is 9–12–8d. which my brother gave to Mr Jhon Clerk & I sent to my brother with Jhon Rob the said 9–12–8d. on Fryday the 13 off May 1670 seald within a letter		
	Thir 3 last articles is		• 15 • 01 • 06
William	The 16 off May to William Andersone waker for		
Andersone –	48 ell off course bed plaids for skowring ilk ell therof 6d. is	01–04–00	
waker	25 ell off braid freisd blanketing at 3s. the ell...............is	03–15–00	• 04 • 19 • –
	Thursday 19 May a voyage to Dalkeith	01–08–06	
	Said day to Roslins meassons 12s.	00–12–00	
	To Mathew Mitchels sone for some herbs to set in the yard	00–06–08	

65 As in other places in the account book, Clerk alternated in how he spelled the name 'John' in this entry.

123 peices off small silver cost 4–10–8

The 20 off May 1670 – John Clerk casting truffs in the mure of Newbiging –
fand [sic] 123 litle small peices of old silver which weyed 5 once 6 drop –
for which I gave 7s. sterlin & to Wille Stewart 6s. 8d. wes casting truffs –
with him...............is 04–10–08d. .... 04–10–08 • 16 • 17 • 10

For casting divets to Al: Grays house

15 May – to James Bruntoun for casting divets to Alexander Grays
howsse in anno 1669 which wer all lost 12s. & for casting divets over
agane in anno 1670 for the said housse to him – 20s. is in all................ 01–12–00

Jenet Shanks fie 2 ½ yeirs

The 24 off May 1670 – to Jennet Shanks fie fra Mertimes 1667 till
Witsonday 1670 being 2 yeirs and a halff at 8 lib. ilk halff yeir and
30s. for a pair off shoone ilk halff yeir is – 9–10s. ilk halff yeir is fra
Mertimes 1667 till Witsonday 1670.. 47–10–00

John Clerks fie.............

24 May – to John Clerk for his fie – fra Witsonday 1669 till Witsonday
1670 is a yeir........28 lib. .... 28–00–00 • 77 • 02 • –

3 oxen and a stot boght – fra the Ladie Newhall the 23 off May 1670 for – 92 lib.

23 May 1670 boght fra the Ladie Newhall – –
1– 2 oxen off 5 yeirs old the peice....
2– 1 other ox not so good...............thir 3 oxen at 40 merks
the peice on[e] with ane other ... 80–00–00
3– 1 stot off 2 yeir old beld in the face estimat to 12 lib. .... 12–00–00 • 92 • 00 • –
The said day to the Lady Newhall in earnest a rex dolor..................... 02–18–00
On Fryday 27 off May 1670 sent with William Stewart –
to the Lady Newhall seald in a peper when he resavet fra hir the said
3 oxen & – stot above mentioned – –
1– 30 rex dolors 87–00–00

	2– 3s. sterlin and six pence	02–02–00	
		is 92–00–00	
2 bee skaips	Thursday 26 May to Androw Howisone for 2 top swarme skaips 24s. and a pynt ale is	01–05–08	
40 ashes..... plains & plumb standerts Mathew Mitchel in Dalkeith	The said day – to Mathew Michel gairner in Dalkeith for 40 young treis which I am to choy[s]e out amongst all he hath in his yard to wit – off ashes plains & plumb standerts 40s. Scots I advanced him the said 40s. & he is to deliver me the said treis in the season off the yeir when it is fit to lift them – about Mertimes 1670	02–00–00	• 03 • 05 • 08
rouch almonds	7 May – 1 lb of rouch almonds	00–08–00	
rose water...	Half a mutchkin off rose water	00–03–00	
	To Mage Wade for 2 douzane off eygs	00–03–04	
	To Arche Andersone for trouts	00–09–00	
	To Margaret Hopekirk for mending the bairns shoone 3s. & 2s. 6d. for my selff	00–05–06	
	Munday 23 May to Mathew Mitchel gairner in Dalkeith when he cam to Neubiging	00–12–00	
	23 off May to David Clerk to kill 15 bolls off oats	00–06–08	• 02 • 07 • 06
	The disbursments on this syde in May 1670		• 246 • 10 • 10

[99]

The disbursmens in May 1670 on the other syde is .... • 246 • 10 • 10

David Livingstoun — 26 May 1670 – to David Livingstoun in Dalkeith for 5 turnt handls for feather boosoms – 36s. and of quart ale is 01–19–04

To a cuper [sic] in Roslin for a litle cap off wood bind trie spent at Roslin the said day 1 pynt off bier & a quart ale with the old laird ...... 00–05–04 • 02 • 04 • 08

Peyit for the said litle coup off wood bind above mentioned 4s. 6d. ... • 00 • 04 • 06

Soma off – all that is above on this syde is...........240–00–00 .... • 249 • 00 • 00

26 May 1670 — On Thursday 26 May 1670 I went to A: Dalkeith with William & Alexander Clerks to the schoole of Dalkeith

William & Alexr Clerks boord 3 month & schoole – master & uther – charges – &c — On Thursday 19 May 1670 I peyit to Abraham Makmillen in Dalkeith – fiftie merks for William & Alexander Clerks boord for 3 month bot they entert not home to his howsse till Thursday 26 May 1670 – fra the 26 off May 1670 to the 26 off Agust 1670 – is 33–06–8d. is 3 months so so [sic] that he is peyit for – 3 month till the 26 off Agust 1670 33–06–08

To Mr John Bower[66] schoolemaster for 3 months for the 2 youts [sic] fra the 26 off May 1670 to the 26 off Agust 1670 04–00–00

To his doctor[67] – [blank] for the said 3 month for them both............. 01–16–00

To Abraham Mackmillens dochter – 5 quarters off lining at 17s. the ell... 01–01–03

To Abraham Mackmillens woman 12s. 00–12–00

To Alexander Clerk 6s. to buy ink & 2s. for themselves to buy any litle thing with –is 8s. – I desyred him to give it to the good man to keip for them 00–08–00

	To Abraham Mackmillen 8s. 8d. to give them – 2 turnors ilk Sonday for 26 weiks is fra 26 May 1670 halff a yeir to come	00–08–08	
	For my own charges & horse charges thrie horse	01–10–00	
	43–02–07	43–02–07	• 43 • 02 • 07
John Dicksone his fie –	Saturday 28 off May 1670 to John Dicksone it being the remainder off his fie for 3 yeir fra Witsonday 1667 till Witsonday 1670 as apears on the booke whair 28 servants feis on the 18 page thereof	21–08–00	
John Davisone couper –	28 May to John Davisone – couper in Lintoun –		
	1– 2 milk laiglins 01–00–00		
	2– 16 girds at 10d. the peice 00–13–08		
	3– 12 girds at 9d. the peice 00–09–00		
	4– 17 girds at 6d. the peice 00–08–06	02–11–02	• 23 • 19 • 02
Boght – 1 gelding 1 coy 1 stot fra the Lady Newhall –	The 30 off May 1670 on a Munday boght fra the Lady Newhall		
	1– a gelding off 3 yeir old wes a bull beld in the forheid	16–00–00	
	2– a blak stot off a yeir old	06–00–00	
	3– a blak coy off 2 yeir old broun bakit	11–00–00	• 33 • 00 • –
	The way how I peyit hir		
	1– the said 30 off May I peyit to hir at Newhall		
	1– 31 lib. 31–00–00		

[66] Clerk refers to the schoolmaster as John Bowie on [105].

[67] See below, [105].

2– 2– and 3 merks peices I sent with hir with
William Stewart on Teusday 31 off May 02–00–00

33–00–00

Marion Robs — 31 May 1670 – to Marion Rob – 7 lib. 10s. for hir fie
fie – fra Mertimes 1669 till Witsonday 1670 07–10–00

Michel – The 3 off June 1670 – resavet I say I peyit to Michel Lowrie in Cairnhill
1 young swyne — 6 lib. for a young swyne 06–00–00

Lowrie — 31 May – to William Johnstoun tinkler for mending a litle coper
kaitle .... 00–06–08 • 13 • 16 • 08

E–J ; My wyffs disbursments in May 1670

1– port off a letter fra England 00–03–00

a cok – 2– a cok 00–04–00

barme – 3– for barme 00–04–00

salmon – 2–[68]cuts off salmon 00–08–00

ox gall – 3– ane ox gall 00–01–04

webster – 4– to the webster in Leswaid for wirking 24 ell of lining cloth 3s.
[the] ell 03–12–00

5– to him for weiving 18 ell off hardn at 1s. the ell 00–18–00

mill ale – 6– to David Clerk to go to the mill – 4 pynts off ale 00–06–08

2 pigs – 7– 2 pigs 00–04–00

whyt breid 8– 2 whyt breid 00–04–00

20 douzane — 9– 20 douzane off eygs at 20d. the douzane .... 01–13–04 • 08 • 01 • –

of eygs — 1– for fresh beiff in May 04–10–00

fresh beiff –	2– for 4 cuts off salmon	00–18–00	
salmon –	3– for whyt breid in May	02–14–08	• 08 • 02 • 08
whyt breid –	246–10–10 The end off May 1670		
	02–09–02	The disbursments	
	43–02–07	in May 1670	• 385 • 02 • 01
	29–19–02		
	33–00–00		
	13–16–08		
	08–01–00		
	08–02–08		
	385–02–01		

[100]

June 1670	The disbursments in June 1670 –	
William Alexr & Jenet Clerks	William Alexander & Jenet Clerks wes in George Bels fra the 18 off Aprill – 1670 till Munday 21 May 1670 is a month – is 13–6–8 bot Jenet Clerk wes – absent 14 days – is 2–6–8 which being rebated rests 11 lib. which 11 lib. I delivert to James Blaikie tailyeur on Fryday 3 June to be given be him to hir being 7 halff crouns & 10s. is 11 lib.	• 11 • 00 • –
Thomas Andersons	Saturday 4 June 1670 to Thomas Andersone for his fie a yeir and a halff – fra Mertimes 1668 till Witsonday 1670 at 136 lib. yeirlie is	• 54 • 00 • –

[68] It is unclear why Clerk chose to number this list in this way.

fie –	The 3 of June Fryday – at Alexander Pennycooke in Satir Seyk his dochters		
brydel in	brydell with [blank] Marshall – Agnes Clerk and my selff 2 merk to		
Satire syke	a fidler 3–4d. uther charges – 13s. is	02–03 –	
	1 June Mr John Clerk & the horse when he went to Edinburgh	00–06 –	
	3 June 1670 sent with John Rob – to John Rob – to pay John Davisone		
3 pair off	for 3 pair off woll sheirs for cliping sheip at 10s. the pair & 2s for		
wooll sheirs	sharping – 2 pair off old sheirs..	01–12–00	• 04 • 01 • –
Tam Abernethie	The 4 off June 1670 to Thomas Abernethie for –		
3 bolls beir	1– 3 bolls of beir – 1 boll for seid – 2 bolls for knoking wes got the		
6 thraive	25 off Aprill at 6 lib. the boll	18–00–00	
off beir stroe	2– the 11 & 12 off Aprill for 6 thraive off beir stroe at 8s.		
	the thraive	02–08–00	• 20 • 08 • –
A gray meir	Wedensday the 8 off June 1670 – Mr John Clerk & William Stewart –		
cost 38 lib.	went to Edinburgh –& boght a gray meir off 6 yeir old cost 38 lib.	38–00–00	
16s......	Custom.................................. 00–01–00		
	2 pynts off ale.......................... 00–04–00		
2 hatts for	Horse grasse & stable male 00–04–00		
Alexander	Mr Jo – Clerks dinner.............. 00–04–00		
& William	To Wille Stewart .... 00–03–00 .... 00–16–00..........	38–16–00	
Clerks......	2 gray hatts – Mr Jo: Clerk boght for William & Alexander Clerks.....	01–16–00	• 40 • 12 • –
John Clerks	At John Clerk & Jannet[69] Shanks brydel in Silver burne Thursday 9 June 1670 –		
brydel in	1– my self – 2 my wyffe – 3 Mr John: Marie – Margaret & Agnes		
Silver Burn	Clerks is in all – 6 at a merk the peice is	04–00–00	
	2 off extreordiners & to the pyper	00–16–00	• 04 • 16 • –

lock litches	10 June to Helen Williamson in Hadingtoun for 3 ½ douzane off loch leitches – shoe dwelt in Hadingtoun	00–13–04	
chessirs –	10 June to John Cochran for 5 chessirs	02–05–00	
1 barel ale	10 June to John Pennycooke for 1 barel off ale for Jennet Shanks brydel	02–02–08	• 05 • 01 • –
21 ews & 21 lambs cost 70–02–0 cam att Fairlihope	Munday 13 June 1670 to William Broun off Stinsone for 20 ews & 20 lambs off Fairlie hope – 23 rex dolors is 66–14–00 more to him for ane other ew and a lamb off the same sort – a lyge dolor 2–16s. is in all– 21 ews & 21 lambs – for which I peyit the said day in all	69–10–00	
	Expense is the said day in Silver burne & Froste holl	00–12–00	• 70 • 02 • –
Anna Irvings fie 1 ½ yeir	On Teusday [sic] 14 June 1670 – Anna Irving went away to whom I peyit the said day fiftie merk peices for hir fie fra Witsonday 1669 till Witsonday 1670	33–06–08	
	The 22 off Aprill 1670 – I completed Anna Irving hir fie – fra Mertimes 1668 till Witsonday 1669	13–06–08	• 46 • 13 • 04
Cochron... tinkler...	15 June 1670 – to Michel Cochron tinkler in the Potter raw – for seting a clout on the bottom of a yetlin brasse pot	00–05–00	
George... Reid....	15 June – to George Reid to drink with the gairner at Bruntstain – 1 pynt at – Stones hill – a pynt at Dalhowssie – 2 pynts & to bring me some elm seid – fra John Reid gairner at Dalhowssie......is 4 pynts	00–06–08	

69 This is one of the only occasions where Clerk spelled this name this way. In most entries, he spelled her name 'Jennet Shanks'.

A brydell	Fryday – 17 June at James Frizels brydel in Pennycooke 13s. 4d. – a grot		
in Penycooke	to the pypers....extraordiners......7s. 8d. is in all	01–05–00	
Nicolsone	Munday 20 June – to Sir John Nicolsons meassons...halff a dolor	01–09–00	• 03 • 05 • 08
	259–11–00 All above on this syde................		• 259 • 11 • –
Eliz[t] Lowries	Teusday 21 June – at Elizabeth Lowries brydell at the mill my selff –		
brydell	13s. 4d. – my wyffe Marie & Margaret Clerks is 3 at 12s. the peice –		
	36s. to pypers 6s. – extreordiners– 9s. 8d. is in all – 3 lib. 5s	03–05–00:	
Small salt	22 June 1670 to Alexander Haistie for a boll and a halff & 2 – pecks		
	off small salt – 4 lib. 10s. it cost him at Preston pans – 3 lib. 15s. so		
	I gave him off proffeit & for cairiage –15s.	04–10–00:	
Dalkeith	24 June – Margaret Hopkirk went to Dalkeith to see the bairns for –		
bairns......	a horse – 6s. ale 4s. 2d. – 12 whit bands – 2s. breid – 3s. ...is 17s.	00–17–00	
	For barme...........4s. – to Arche Andersone for trouts – 3s. 4d. is	00–07–04	
	William Stewart & Edowart Thomson – wes 17s. off charges in selling		
	3 oxen I boght fra Lady Newhall	00–17–00	• 09 • 16 • 04
Pynt coigs	28 June to William Clark for 14 pynt timber coigs at 2s. 3d.		
	the peice..	01–11–06	
1 pynt stoup	1 timber – pynt stoup	00–07–00	
12 lib. for	17 June 1670 – Mr John Clerk peyit to William Broun skinner –		
chamber maill	12 lib. Scots for my d: chamber maill fra ~~Mertimes 1670 on~~		
	Mertimes 1669 till Witsonday ~~17~~ 1670 date – 17 June 1670.................	12–00–00	
	Mr John Clerks disbur[s]ing at Edinburgh		
	The 16 & 17 off June – 1670;		
Glew	8 lb off glew at 7s. the pound	03–016–	• 16 • 14 • 06

Also his disbur[s]ments at Edinburgh – 16 & 17 June 1670 –

For alming – a gray cafs skin	00–05–00	
ane old Bible in octava – for Helen Clerk	00–14–00	
1 – vocables for the bairns	00–02–00	
12 – lint whill whill [sic] bands	00–04–06	
12 douzane clasps & eyes for womens & bairns cloths	00–04–06	• 01 • 10 • –
The disbursments in June – 1670 on this syde is		• 287 • 11 • 10

[101]

	The disbursments in June 1670 on the other syde is		• 287 • 11 • 10
Alexander Ogilvie 55–2–2	The 16 off June 1670 – Mr John Clerk peyit to Alexander Ogilvie ane off – the collector deputs off the taxation grantit to his Maiestie in Agust 1665 55–2–2d. as the 5th & last terms payment off the personage of Pennycooke – whairoff he gave a discharge date the said – 16 off June 1670 – I say 55 lib. 2s. 2d.	55–02–02	
Mr William Wallace 24 lib.	The 16 off June 1670 – Mr John Clerk peyit to Mr William Walace advocat shireff depute off Edinburgh 24 lib. Scots as the 5th & last terms payment off the taxation imposd be the convention off estats – in Agust 1665 for my 12 lib. lands in the paroishes off Pennycooke & Glencorse & that fra Witsonday 1669 till Witsonday 1670 off which I have his discharge date the said – 16 off June 1670	24–00–00	• 79 • 02 • 02
	Thir 2 discharges bears registration ~:		

	Mr John Clerks disbursing at Edinburgh – 23 June 1670			
2 cows hyds	To William Hils at the West Port for 1 blak cows hyde 5–10 & for a gray			
hors hyds	cows hyde 5–10s. – both the hyds……11		11–00–00	
bend leather	A horse hyde and a halff tand [sic]		04–06–00	
	To James Grahame[70] for 11 lb 2 once off Inglis bend leather			
	at 14s. the lb		07–15–06	
roset……	2 lb of roset at 2s. the pound	00–04–00		
hemp……	2 lb 2 once off steill hemp at 8s. 6d. the lb	00–18–00		
lasts……	2 lasts for women	00–12–00		
timber heils	12 pair off timber heils	01–04–00	01–18–00	• 24 • 19 • 06
Mr John	Mr John Clerks charges &c who went to Edinburgh 15 June 1670 – & returnt			
Clerk……..	on Saturday the 25 June 1670 –			
1– sowrd [sic]	1. for mending his shoes		00–04–00	
1– bodeleir	2. for skouring & diping ane old worset turk clok		00–06–00	
his expensis	3. for dying a pair off stokings blak		00–06–00	
&c	4. for 4 fadom off cords at 10d. the fadom		00–03–04	
	5. to David Howisone for a sowrd		06–12–00	
	6. for ane sowrd belt		07–00–00	
	7. for his dyet –& uther expensis fra Wedensday 15 June 1670 –			
	till Saturday 25 June 1670		06–09–00	• 21 • 00 • 04
190–rude off	To John Pennycooke in Ravens Hauch for biging 4 fald dyks being nyne skore			
fald dyks at	& ten rude at 2s. the rude is……19		19–00–00	
2s. the rude	28 May 1670 peyit to him	10–00–00		
19 lib.	2 Jully 1670 peyit to him 9 lib.	09–00–00	19–00–00	• 19 • 00 • –

Will Stewart	4 Jully 1670 to William Stewart for 7 firlots off beir wes got fra him –			
7 firlots off	The 16 off October 1669 for knoking at 5–14s. the boll		09–19–06	
beir..........	25 June to John Rob for a pynt of oyll – 12s. –& 1s. for grasse to the			
fish oyll	horse when he went to the toun		00–13–00	• 10 • 12 • 06
E J	Wyffs disbursments be my wyffe –			
For the bairns	1– to Margaret Hopkirke for ale & eygs to the bairns		00–08–08	
Jenet Shanks	2– 3 loaffs for Jennet Shanks mariage [sic]	00–012–08		
mariage	3– 2 peices off beiff thairtoo	01–01–00		
shooe strings	4– 1 pair off worstit shoe strings	00–02–08	01–12–04	
4 laid cols	5– 4 laid off cols at 6s. 2d. the laid	01–04–08		
for the bairns	6– 5 pynts of ale to the childring	00–06–08		
14 ½ do[ze]n eygs	7– 14 ½ douzane off eygs at 20d. the dou[ze]n	01–05–00	02–16–04	• 05 • 01 • 04
Fresh beiff	For fresh beiff in the month off May.......I say in the month of June –			
Whyt breid	I say for fresh beiff		03–13–00	
	For whyt breid in the month of June		01–07–00	• 05 • 00 • –

287–11–10		
79–02–02	The end off Ju[n]e 1670 the disbursments in June 1670	• 452 • 07 • 08
24–19–06		
21–00–04		
19–00–00		
10–12–06		

70 In this instance, Clerk did not omit the first 'a' when he spelled 'Graham'.

05–01–04
05–00–00
452–07–08

Jully 1670	The disbursments in Jully 1670		
A gray meir boght in Bigar fare	The 1 off Jully 1670 Fryday at Biger fare peyit for a gray meir off 7 or 8 yeir old 33–13–04 expensis at the faire in going & cuming –&c......2–6–8	36–00–00	
Mr Robert Alisons Stipend	The 1 off Jully to Mr Robert Alisone minister for his stipend for the – lands off Cookeing fra Witsonday 1669 till Witsonday 1670 on his discharge date 1 Jully 1670	48–00–00	
4 laid cols	The 4 & 9 off Jully to Edouart Thomson to get 4 laid off cols	01–04–08	
John Ramsays Brydel	Mr John Clerk spent at John Ramsays br[y]del 1– his dener ....00–13–04 2– to the fidler ....00–04–00 3– 1 pynt off wyne ....01–00–00 4– grasse to the horse 00–02–00	01–19–04	
	The disbursments above in Jully 1670		• 87 • 04 • –

[102]

	The disbursments in Jully on the other syde	• 87 • 04 • –
Webster in Leswaid	The 9 off Jully to George Clerks wyffe webster in Leswaid for weiving 33 ell off lining at 3s. ...the ell is	• 04 • 19 • –

	To hir the said day to buy 2 lb off soape & warping ale		• 00 • 15 • –
			• 05 • 14 • –
Agnes Clerk 1 hood	Saturday 9 Jully to my brother John Andersone 3 lib. – 6s. which he gave Agnes Clerk to buy a hoode	03–06–00	
3 Brasse pans	Agnes Clerk boght 3 brasse pans weying 4 lb wecht at 17s. – 6d. the pound	03–10–00	
5 laid of Stobhill cols	The 11 off Jully to George Blaikie in West Howsses for 5 seck laid off Stobhill cols at 9s. the laid 45s. & 3s. 4d. to drink is	02–08–04	
5 laid Stobhill cols	Teusday 12 Jully to George Blaikie for 5 laid off Stobhill cols – in seck laids – at 9s. the laid – 45s. & 3s. 4d. to drink is	02–08–04	• 11 • 12 • 08
5 laid Stobhill cols	22 Jully – to George Blaikie for 5 laid of Stobhill cols at 9s. the laid & 3s. 4d. to drink	02–08–04	
Small salt	22 Jully to Samuel Burne for 26 pecks off small salt at 3s. 4d. the peck is	04–06–08	
	27 Jully – to webster in Leswaid warping ale	00–06–08	
	To Margaret Hopkirk to give the bairns in Dalkeith	00–06–00	
	14 Jully – a voyage to Dalkeith	01–13–00	
beiff	16 Jully – 1 peice off beiff	00–09–00	
wyne	16 Jully – 1 mutchkin off clairet wyne	00–05–00	
	1 quart off barme	00–03–04	
eygs	5 douzane off eygs	00–08–04	

stifing	23 Jully – 1 pound whyt stiffing – 3s. 4d. 1 once off blew[71] – 10d.		00–04–02	
	29 Jully to Alexander Gray when he went to Fisher Rave		00–06–00	
hering	For hering at – 3 severall tymes		01–07–00	
trouts	For trouts at severall tymes to Arche Andersone		01–00–00	• 12 • 17 • 06
	The 29 Jully 1670 boght fra the Lady Bagillo – lining round & harden round			
35–08–00	1– 12 ell round harden at 6s. the ell		03–12–00	
38–19–00	2– 12 ell round lining at 11s. the ell		06–12–00	
10–00–00	3– 12 ell round lining			
84–07–00	4– 10 ell round lining	32 ½ shoe rebated the 2 ½ ell		
	5– 10 ½ ell round lining	rests– 30 ell at 8s. the ell	12–00–00	
	6– 12 ell round lining			
29 Jully	7– 12 ell round lining	is 24 ell at 11s. the ell	13–04–00	• 35 • 08 • –
1670	Twidling small & round –			
Boght fra	1– 12 ell.....			
the Lady	2– 12 ell.....	24 ell at 16s. the ell	19–04–00	
Bagillo	3– 11 ell.....			
1 – lining	4– 08 ell ¾..	19 ¾ ell at 10s. the ell	10–00–00	
2 – tuidling	5– 13 ell in 2 peices			
3 – blak serge	6– 13 ell in 2 peices	is 26 ell in 4 peices at 7s. 6d.	09–15–00	• 38 • 19 • –
	10 ell off blak serge in 2 peices at 20s. the ell			• 10 • 00 • –
Bagillo	Somas off all boght fra the Lady Bagillo is		84–07–00	• 84 • 07 • –

	The said 29 Jully 167[0] to the Lady Bagillo 4 lib. and halff –		
	ane ell off sad broun stuff cost 10s. which I gave hir for 7s. is both	04–07–00	
	Brother at sight pay to the Lady Bagillo – four skore pounds Scots		
87–04–00	for so much I rest hir for round lining – twidling & blak serge & place		
05–14–00	the same to my accompt at Neubiging this 29 Jully 1670 Jo: Clerk......	80–00–00	
11–12–08	For his loveing – brother John Andersone merchant in Edinburgh –		
12–17–06		84–07–00	
84–07–00			
01–10–00	For whyt breid in Jully 1670..		• 01 • 10 • –
203–05–02	The end off Jully 1670 The disbursments in Jully 1670		• 203 • 05 • 02
Agust	The disbursments in Agust 1670 –:		
1670	1– peice of fresh beiff	00–06–00	
	For trouts..	00–03–04	
	For hering – 6s.	00–06–00	
	4 Agust to John Davisone couper for – 16 girds..............................	00–09–00	
	4 Agust to the meassons for 5 pynts & 1 mutchkin of ale wes		
	got for the usse off the howsse	00–10–06	• 01 • 14 • 10
	Munday 25 Jully 1670 – Mr John Clerk spent at the randevous [sic] –		
	1– a pynt of wyne with the officers...	01–00–00	
	2– horse charges..	00–10–00	
	3– he gave the bairns at Dalkeith	00–06–00	• 01 • 16 • –

[71] This likely refers to zaffer, a blue pigment obtained by roasting cobalt ore.

	9 Agust to Margaret Hopekirk for the bairns for 5 weiks –		
	1– 2 douzane & 4 eygs	00–04–00	
	2– 13 pynts off ale & milk	01–01–08	• 01 • 05 • 08
	The disbursments in Agust on this syde		• 04 • 16 • 06

[103]

2 cows –	The disbursments in Agust on the other syde is		• 04 • 16 • 06
hyds gray	3 Agust 1670 Thomas Rob – boght these things I gave him money to pay them –		
roset –	1– 2 gray cows hyds	11–04–00	
Jumps	2– 2 lb of roset	00–04–00	
2 botkins	3– 2 botkins with box wood handls	00–06–00	
	4– 6 pair off jumps	01–00–00	• 12 • 14 • –
lint seid oyll	10 Agust – 1 pynt of lint seid oyll John Rob broght out	01–04–00	
2 chessirs	11 Agust 1670 to John Cochran in Rossling [sic] for a large chessire to hold 8 lb & a lesser	01–00–00	
Jennet Spalding – blitching cloth	12 Agust to Jenet Spalding for 5 weiks 3 days shoe wes bleithing cloth at – 1s. and hir meit in the day – shoe comptit 33 days in all the said 5 weiks & 3 da[y]s is 33s.	01–13–00	
	8 Agust given to pay 4 ½ douzan off eygs 7s. 6d. – oynions – 6d.	00–08–00	
	13 Agust to Will Stewart to give Brunstains hir for keiping ship	00–04–00	
	Said day to a couper for 6 girds	00–05–00	
	William Stewart & Edowart Thomson Carnwath fare		

Carnwath	1– 6 firr teathers	10s.		
fare	2– custome of 5 catel and a horse Logan Housse	06s.		
	3– thair charges	05s. ....21s.	01–01–00	• 05 • 15 • –
	Boght fra George Smart in Fisher Rave – Saturday the 30 of Jully as follows			
Boght fra				
George Smart	1– 312 dails is auchtein skore & 12 at 46 lib. the 100th he gave – the			
in Fisher Rave	12 to the 300 & comptit them at 48 lib. the 100th is		144–00–00	
the 30 Jully	2– 12 double treis at 19s. the peice		11–08–00	
1670 –	3– 73 single treis at 10s. the peice		36–10–00	
	4– 30 hizle stiks for mattok – shafts – then efterward he promist me			
1 – dails	10 more is 40 in all		01–00–00	
2 – double	Alexander Gray		192–18–00	
treis –	For Alexander Gray –			
3 – single	1– 30 dails	12–00–00		
treis	2– 2 single treis	01–00–00	13–00–00	
4 – hizle	is		205–18–00	
stiks	The said day peyit to George Smart		AB 5–18–00	
	So thair rests	200–00–00		
For Cookeing	18 Jully 1670 he delivert to Alexander Meygit for –			
housse –	Cookeing howsse – 4 double treis at 17s the peice	003–08–00		
	so rests in all	203–08–00		
	More 11 Agust 1670 boght fra him 14 single treis			
	For sleds at 7s. the peice	004–18–00		

So rests in all – 208–8s. bot in the compt thair wes
bot 208–2s. – I wold not after the compt so I gave
him – 6 pence out off my pokit so rests onlie 208–02–00

Robert Sands– More I am content to pay him for Robert Sands wright the –
particullars under wreatten which he resavet fra the said
George Smarts father in the month off June or Jully 1670
1– 30 dails 12–00–00
2– 2 single treis..................... 01–00–00 13–00–00

Soma off all above resting is .... 221–02–00 .... • 221 • 02 • –

Brother at sight heeroff pay to George Smart in Fisher Rave – AB & 5–18
Twa hundreth twentie ane pounds twa shilling Scots in full – peyit as is above • 05 • 18 • –
and compleit payment off this above wreatten accompt and all for timber
uthers that ever wes betwixt him & me preseiding the date – all above........ • 227 • 00 • –
heer off – tak his recept on the bak heer off and place it to my
accompt – at Fisher Rave Thursday the 11 off Agust 1670 –
For his loveing brother..................................; John: Clerk
John Andersone merchant in Edinburgh;
This is the copie off the bill I drew on –
my brother – at the fitt off the above –
wreatten accompt.....................

04–16–06 The accompt what I peyit to John Cairingtoun cairter for cairying the
12–14–00 said dails & treis – the 19 off Agust 1670 –
05–15–00 1 For cairiage off 312 dails being 18 skore & 12 in all 23 lib. ilk cairt

227–00–00		broght 40 dails thair wes 9 cairts that cairied them – ilk cairt stood		
52–01–04		2–11–1d. is for the said 9 cairts	23–00–00	
302–06–10	2	Then for cairiage off 73 single treis I boght at first & 12 double treis &14 single treis I boght efterward at 7s. the peice & for Sande Grays 30 dails & 2 single treis & for 40 hizle cuts for mattok shafts all thir tooke 10 cairts to cairy them is 51s. 1d. for ilk cairt according to the		
Cairiage		pryce off the dails is	25–11–00	
of timber			48–11–00	
be John	3	The said day peyit him 12s. for cariage of the od 12 dails and 1		
Cro:		od single trie	00–12–00	
	4	Peyit him for the custome off 19 cairts at 1s. 4d. the peice	01–05–04	
Cairing–	5	Peyit for ale to them at severall tyms	01–05–00	
toun	6	For cairying a long ston out of the quarel to Newbiging	00–08–00	
		The disbursments in Agust 1670		
		on this syde is – 302–06–10; in all peyit to John Cairingtoun	52–01–04	• 52 • 01 • 04

[104]

		The disbursments in Agust on the other syde is........		• 302 • 06 • 10
Voyage to		The Munday 15 Agust 1670 when I went to Cranstoun to meet with		
Cranstoun		Sir William Kerr –		
to Sir Will[m]	1–	for aples & peirs – 35s. and for a creill to hold them 5s. is........	02–00–00	
Kerr –	2–	for my own charges & Mr John Clerks & Edowart Adamsons:		
		& 3– horse being a night in Dalkeith & 2 days out	03–16–00	• 05 • 16 • –

Cheise	22 Agust to David Hislop for 15 cheise weying 5 ston at 30s. the		
	ston is 7–10	07–10–00	
	The 6 off Agust 1670 my brother John Andersone peyit to David		
	Murray customer in Leith – for my accompt on his discharge date		
	the said 6 off Agust 1670 for the particullars under wreatten –		
Tent -	1– 16 pynts of tent at 2 merk the pynt	21–06–08	
Brande –	2– 10 pynts off brande at 20s. the pynt	10–00–00	• 38 • 16 • 08
Helen Gray	27 Agust 1670 to Helen Gray for 10 ell off sad cullort twynd stuff –		
10 ell stuff	at 26–8d. the ell	13–06–08	
	24 Agust to John Cochran for a turnt bottom for a great 9 pynt can	00–06–00	
	15 Agust 100 hering – 29s.	01–09–00	
	25 Agust 63 hering	00–12–00	
	15 Agust to get a quart off barme	00–04–00	
	Said day to David Clerk to buy a pair off gloves for binding	00–04–00	
Isobel Gray	16 Agust to Isobell Gray for a pair off wooll cairds...24s.	00–24s.–00	
	18 Agust to the meassons for 3 pynts 3 mutchkins off ale	00–06–06	
George Clerk	25 Agust 1670 to George Clerk for weiving –		
webster –	28 ell....		
	22 ell.... is 50 ell at 1s. the ell	02–10–00	• 20 • 02 • 02
Sir William	Wedensday 24 off Agust 1670 to Sir William Murray off Neutown 6		
Murray	lyg dolors and a shilling is 17–8s. – to give George Smart in the Fisher		
	Rave for 8 great geists at 44s. the peice is 4s. lesse amongst the 8 then		
	44s. the peice – Sir William tooke the money when we wes on horse bak –		
George –	convoying me out off Mussilburgh –& said he sould cause the said George		

Smart–	Smart be content – thair with which it seims [sic] he wes since he sent me			
	the said treis		17–08–00	
8 great firr	On Saturday 27 off Agust 1670 to John Cairingtoun cairter for bringing			
geists –	the said –8 geists to Neubiging – on 2 cairts with 6 horse ilk cairt cost			
at 44s. the	51s. 1d. – is	05–02–02		
peice –	For the custom of ilk cairt 16d.	00–02–08		
6 rex dolors –	Given him to drink	00–03–04		
	My voyage to Fisher Rave said 24 of Agust cost	02–00–00	07–08–02	• 24 • 16 • 02
	Saturday 27 Agust 1670 boght fra George Blaikie chapman.....			
	in Gallowsheils off lining cloth off divers sorts for which I peyit			
	him –;			
George –	1– 8 ell at 13s. 6d. the ell		05–08–00	
Blaikie –	2– 8 ell at 14s. 6d. the ell		05–16–00	
lining cloth	3– 9 ell at 10s. the ell		04–10–00	
off divers	4– 10 ell at 10s. the ell		05–00–00	
sorts &c:	5– 2 ell at a merk the ell		01–06–08	
	6– 12 ell at 14s. the ell		08–08–00	
	7– 9 ell at 10s. the ell at 10s. the ell		04–10–00	
	8– 8 ell at 20s. the ell		08–00–00	
	9– 10 ell at 20s. the ell		10–00–00	
	halff a grosse off broun poynts		00–07–00	
	For narow whyt kniting –& cullort threid		00–12–00	
Geils			53–17–08	• 53 • 17 • 08

Dowglas – The accompt off 7 peice off dornick and a peice off lining which
Geils Dowglas – relict off umquhill Mr Thomas Young sent to
7 peice off Newbiging the 16 off Agust 1670 –
dornick 1– 8 ell off dornick at 15s. the ell.............................06–00–00
& – 2– 9 ell off dornick at 8s. the ell 03–12–00
1– peice off 3– 22 ell of dornick at 8s. the ell............................08–16–00
lining cloth 4– 20 ell off dornick at 11s. the ell 11–00–00
5– 22 ell off dornick at 11s. the ell 12–02–00
6– 20 ell off dornick at 16s. the ell 16–00–00
7– 13 ell off dornick at 26s. the ell 16–18–00
8– 13 ell and a halff of lining at 17s. 74–08–00
302–06–10 the ell is.. 11–09–06 – 85–17–06 • 85 • 17 • 06
05–16–00 Brother at sight heeroff pay to Geils Dowglas relict off umquhill Mr Thomas
38–16–08 Young – four skore fyve pounds seventein shillings six pennys Scots in
20–02–02 full & compleit payment off the above wreatten accompt – tak hir recept
24–16–02 at the 20 off Agust 1670 – for his loveing brother John Andersone –
53–17–08 merchant in – Edinburgh –
85–17–06 The 26 off Agust 1670 – my brother – peyit to the said Geils Dowglas –
531–13–00 the said –85–17–6d. & tooke hir discharge theroff at the fit off the accompt
& sent me the same..

1– syde X X X X X XX	04–16–06	The disbursments in Agust	
2– syde – – – – – – – – –	302–06–10	1670 on this syde is...	• 229 • 06 • 02
3– syde being this..........	229–06–02	All the former disbursments in	
	531–13–00	Agust 1670 hithertoo is...	• 531 • 13 • –

[105]

All the former disbursments in Agust 1670 on the first second and thrid [sic] syde is – 531–13 .... • 531 • 13 • –

James – Clerk for cloths &c–

The accompt off severall disbursments for cloths & uther necessars for James Clark – according to thrie compts which I have lying by me – particullarlie mentioning the same – all the money off the said 3 accompts wes be my order delivered be my brother John Andersone to James Clerk to pay the said 3 accompts ....

65–10–8d.

1– to David Boyd on his discharge date 25 Agust 1670 which discharge is at the fitt off his accompt 38–05–02

2– James Clerk his recept off 20–16–6 fra my brother John Andersone at the fit off ane accompt date the – 25 off Agust 1670 20–16–06

3– Alexander Weir tailyeur his discharge at the fit of his accompt date 26 off Agust 1670 – off –6–9s. .... 06–09–00 • 65 • 10 • 08

John – Hogens – unbleitcht – round lining

The 30 off Agust 1670 boght fra John Hogens which wes delivert – to me be Elspeth Herrin Sande Haisties wyffe – unbleitcht round lining –

1– 21 ell and a halff at 10s. the ell 10–15–00

2– 16 ell–
12 ell– is 28 ell at 9s. the ell is.......... 12–12–00 is in all..... • 23 • 07 • –

Delivert to Elspeth Herrin the said day –

8 rex dolors 23–04–00

In turnors.......... 00–03–00 23–07–00

Agnes Clerk	1– pair off gloves for Agnes Clerk 1 pair off gloves – 13–4d.		
4 laid of	& – 3s.	00–16–04	
Newhall cols–	2– 29 Agust – 4 laid off Newhall cols at 5s. 2d. the laid	01–00–08	
Barme....	31 Agust for barme	00–04–00	
hering....	Said day halff a hundreth hering..	00–11–06	
	Said day to George Bell for eygs & ale the bairns got	00–10–08	
Marg^t Hopkirk	For whyt breid in the month off Agust.........38s.	01–18–00	• 05 • 01 • 02
	The end off Agust 1670 – The disbursments in Agust 1670.......		• 625 • 11 • 10

September	The disbursments in September 1670 –.................................1670.....		
1670 –	2 September to John Rob 40s. for 2 lb off leaff tobaco he got fra –		
Leaff Tobaco	Robert Selkrig at 20s. the pound is	02–00–00	
Ro^t Finlasone	3 September 1670 to Robert Donaldsone[72] in Prestoun pans		
Small salt	for 1 boll 2 pecks off small salt at 4 merk the boll	03–00–00	
Isobel Gray	Fryday 19 Agust 1670 sent to Isobell Gray with John Rob six lyg dolors		
6–ston off –	to buy 6 ston off butter and on Saturday the 3 off September 1670 my		
butter at 56s.	good mother Dame Geils Smith sent out with John Rob the said six ston		
the ston.....	off butter –& 1 lb more in 2 round lumps at 56s. the ston is	16–16–00	• 21 • 16 • –
William &	Teusday the 6 off September 1670 William & Alexander Clerks entert		
Alexander	in boording in Archibald Gemls in Dalkeith....................................		
Clerks.....	To Archbald Gemle the said day for thair boord for 6 month – 72 lib. –		
	fra the 6 off September 1670 to the 6 off Marche 1671 is according to		
Archbald	36 lib. for them both ilk 3 month 72–00–00		
Gemle –	To him the said day 2 ston off cheis for the said 6		

	month	03–00–00		
Mr John	Said day to Archbald Gemls dochter	00–13–04	75–13–04	
Bowie –	Said day to Archbald Gemls wyffe seald in a peper 12 merk peices			
Schoole master	is 8 lib. to give to Mr John Bowie – schoole master – for 6 month			
	to come to wit fra the 6 off September 1670 to the 6 off Marche			
	1671 is according to 4 lib. for them both ilk			
Mr Hew –	3 month	08–00–00		
Gray –	Given to the doctor Mr Hew Gray said day for 6 month			
doctor –	to come fra the 6 off September 1670 to the 6 off			
	Marche 1671 6s. sterlin – is according to 36s. ilk 3 month –			
	For them both	03–12–00	11–12–00	• 87 • 05 • 04
Tam Rob –	The 9 off September 1670 to Thomas Rob for 55 ½ days he made			
for making –	shoone at Newbiging at 5s. 6d. ilk day with his meit & bed –			
off shoone –	which wes – too much he being bot a faking rascall		15–05–00	
Skirling–	Munday 5 September 1670 William Stewart went to Skirlin far[e] –			
Fare–	with 2 stots wes got fra Thomas Mein –& 2 coys off our own –&			
	Logan Housse staig – sold nothing at all – custome 7s. and 4s.			
	off charges is –11s.		00–11–00	• 15 • 16 • –
3 peices off	Accompt off Holland cloth resavet fra Geils Dowglas 8 September 1670 –			
Holland –	1: 6 ell and 1 quarter at 50s. the ell		15–12–06	
cloth boght–	2: 17 ell at 3 lib. 4s. the ell		54–08–00	
fra Geils –	3: 19 ell and a halff at 32s. the ell		31–04–00	• 101 • 04 • 06

72 Clerk named Robert Finlasone in the margin but 'Robert Donaldsone' in the main body of the account.

Dowglas – 16 September 1670 sent to hir seald in a peper with John Rob............. 01–04–06
amonting – Brother at sight heiroff pay to Geils Dowglas relict off umquhill Mr Thomas
to Young ane hundreth pound Scots in full & compleit payment off the above
101–04–06 wreatten accompt tak hir recept– thairoff on the bak heiroff –& place
the same to my accompt – at Newbiging – the 16 off September
1670 100–00–00
To his loveing brother John Andersone merchant in Edinburgh..........................
.... 101–04–06

Dame Geils – Smith for– Teusday 20 September sent to my mother in lawe Dame Geils Smith with John Rob
14 1/2 ell off seald within a letter – I wreat to hir said day for 15 ell off dornick without inches
dornick which wes 14 ½ ell with inches – at hir own pryce at 18s. the ell the said 14 ½ ell
13 lib. 1s. at 18s. the ell – com[e]s to 13 lib. 1s. sent hir 4 rex dolors 11–12s. & halff
a rex dolor – is 29s. is both 13 lib. 1s. .... • 13 • 01 • –

The disbursments in September 1670 on this syde .... • 239 • 02 • 10

[106]

The disbursments in September 1670 on the other syde is.................. • 239 • 02 • 10

eygs– 1 September for 8 douzane eygs ....
9 September for 4 douzane eygs...........is 12 douzane eygs 01–00–00
fish oyll – 24 September – to John Rob for a pynt off fish oyll........................... 00–10–00
For wooll – Said day 1 quart off barme 4–0
To Alexander Hastie for swiping 2 chimneys 6–8

To Al: Clerk for helping to sow W. & Alexander Clerks coits 4–0 00–14–08

1 – syth.... 14 September – to Wille Stewart for a syth 01–05–00

couper – 7 September – to David Gibsone for 9 girds off several sorts .... 00–05–04 • 03 • 15 • –

1 – litle stak off hay 13–2s. The 26 off September – to John Dicksone in Ancre lawe for a hay ruck or litle stak the said day to him 20s. in earnest & in part off payment – 20s. 01–00–00

Teusday 26 September – I say on Teusday – 27 September to him in Nicolsone fare – 12 lib. & 2s. to his wyffe to buy hir fare is .... 12–02–00 • 13 • 02 • –

2 – peice off narow – dornick – fra Geils– Dowglas – cost – 19 lib. 6d.

On Fryday 30 September 1670 sent to Geils Dowglas with John Rob seald in a peper – for twa peices off narow dornick shoe sent me to wit – –

1. 20 ell off dornick narow at 10s. the ell 10–00–00
2. 19 ell off narow dornick at 9s. 6d. the ell .... 09–00–06 • 19 • 00 • 06

The especies I sent wes –

1– 6 lyg dolors at 56s. a peice 16–16–00
2– halff a croun 01–10–00
3– a six pence 00–08–00
4– 2 grots 00–08–00
5– 3 turnors 00–00–06 19–00–06

To James Bowie to get 2 once off tailyeurs thread 00–03–04

A. To him for halff a lippe off oats for the horse 00–01–04

A. 28 off September for the gray horse stayd 1 night & almost 2 days in Edinburgh waiting on Isobel Gray 8s. 00–08–00

haws	28 off September – to George Reid for 2 peks off haws	01–04–00	
2 peks off –	30 September – 61 hering	01–04–00	• 03 • 00 • 08
61 hering –	For breid in the month off September		• 01 • 12 • –
	The end of September 1670 The disbursments in September 1670…		• 279 • 13 • –

October –	The disbursments in October 1670.....		
1670	Halff a pound off pig taill tobaco	00–06–00	
Webster....	1 October – to George Clark webster in Leswaid for weiving 25 ell – off plaiding 25s. & 5s. wes oweing him for butter is 30s.	01–10–00	
	7 October – to Archbald Andersone for taking the bairns kist to Dalkeith	00–06–00	
	2 once off liquores 3s. for reid centurie 2s. for Helen Clark	00–05–00	• 02 • 06 • –
webster	6 October – to George Clerks wyffe webster in Leswaid for weiving 11 ell off plaiding at 16d. the ell is 15s. 8d. – warping ale 1s. 18d. – to hir man 1s. 8d. is	00–19–00	
oynions	2 douzane off oynions	00–03–04	
eygs	10 douzane & a halff off eygs at 20d. the douzane	00–17–06	
couper	To a couper for 7 girds	00–05–08	
Jenet Spalding	To Jennet Spalding for 12 days bleitching & hir meat	00–12–00	
18– lb off small candle	Fryday the 7 off October 1670 – sent to Dalkeith with Archebald Andersone 3–7–6d. who boght for [sic] fra Robert Cleghorne for the same – 18 lb off small candle at 3 lib. the stone is	03–07–06	• 06 • 05 • –
2 peks haws	11 October the expense off 2 horse going in with Isobell Gray	00–04–00	
John Robs	8 October – to Georg Blaikie in West Housses for 2 peks of haws	00–13–00	

harvest fie	12 October – to Margaret Hopekirk for all eygs & milk to the bairns.. 00–06–08		
for Anno–	The 12 October 1670 to John Rob for –		
1669 –	1– his harvest fie in harvest 1669 04–07–		
&	for his supper maill in harvest 1669.................. 01–00–	05–07–00	
Anno 1670	2– and for his fie in harvest 1670 04–07–		
is – 2 yeir	and for his supper maill in harvest 1670............ 01–00–	05–07–00	• 11 • 17 • 18
Helen Gray	Fryday 14 October 1670 sent with John Rob within a letter for Helen –		
2 gourds	Gray 48s. for 2 pair off whyt stokings for women at 24s. the pair	02–08–00	
Geils Dowglas	Said day to Roslins man – when he broght 2 gourds....to drink	00–09–00	
4 ell off –	The 12 off October at Newbiging peyit to Geils Dowglas – 3 lib. 6s. 8d.		
strong dornik	for 4 ell off strong dornick to be 2 towels at 16s. 8d. the ell is – 3 lib. –		
	6s. 8d.	03–06–08	• 06 • 03 • 08
8 – bolls	Fryday 14 October 1670 – sent William Stewart & Edowart Thomsone		
of Leith	to Leith who boght fra Robert Lermond – 8 bolls off meill & peyit for		
meill;	the same 8 bolls off meill at 4 lib. 8s. the boll	35–04–00	
	Halff a peck off oats to the horse	00–04–00	
	Custome for the said meill	00–03–04	
	1 pynt off barme 2s. & 1 pynt of ale for them selves	00–04–00	
	1 botle off stroe for the horse	00–01–00	• 35 • 16 • 04
	15 October – to George Reid for 2 skulls & a round mand handle....	00–13–04	
	Teusday 18 October sent with John Rob within a letter seald to my –		
John –	brother John Andersone 20s. to give John Dows wyffe for oynions he		
Andersone –	sent me fra hir & 6s. for himselff he peyit for part of a letter		
	to borrow brig for the Lady Grhames is 26s.	01–06–00	

	The 18 off October 1670 to Sanders Lillie sone to Robert Lillie –		
pecks off	gairner in Elphistoun for [blank] pecks of haws which –		
haws......	William Steill causd him bring on his own horse to Neubiging..........	02–08–00	
	17 October to South fields gairner who broght a few aples	00–09–00	
18 lib. 10s.	The 21 off October 1670 to Jennet Meurs for ane ox off 7 yeir –		
to Jennet	old ar: 18 lib. 4s. & 6s. wes given in earnest – 18–10s.	18–10–00	• 23 • 06 • 04
Meurs for	The disbursments above in October 1670................		• 85 • 15 • –
ane ox –			

[107]

lint seid oyll	The disbursments on the other syde in October 1670		• 85 • 15 • –
Ja: Broun –	22 October to John Rob for a pynt off lint seid oyll he broght me		• 01 • 04 • –
for barking	The 22 October – to John Rob 5 lib. Scots which he peyit to James Brown		
2 ox hyds –	tanner at the West Port for barking 2 ox hyds as apears on a long compt		
	booke with 3 brasse clasps on the 64 page theroff		• 05 • 00 • –
James Clerk	Munday 24 off October 1670 sent within a letter off my brothers –		
3 lb lickres	15s. Scots to be given to James Clerk for 3 lb off grein lickres he sent		
	me at 5s. the pound..	00–15–00	
A voyage	On Munday 24 October 1670 I went to Mr Robert Smiths –		
to Cramond	off Southfield in Cramond whair I wes all night on Munday the		
24 Octobre –	24 off October in geting severall things out of his yard – –		
1670 – for	1 to his gairner for 13 imps of plumbs – peirs – chirries and		
baren treis –	aples...	06–06–00	

&c –	2 to thair stewart in drink money......3 merk peices	02–00–00	
	3 to thair gairner – David Reid – in drink money for helping to drawe some barren treis &c...24s.	01–04–00	
	4 to the tenents men that cam to that place to carie [sic] the treis to Neubiging – to drink	00–06–08	• 10 • 11 • 08
Jennet – Thomsons – fie	The last off October 1670 to Jennet Thomsone byre woman 8 lib for hir fie fra Mertimes 1669 till Witsonday 1670	08–00–00	
	26 October – to John Rob for reid centurie 3s. –1 once off anet seids – 1s. is 4s. to be a drink to Helen Clerk	00–03–00	
Marie Clerk stuff to be a goun – cam to – 13–06–08	31 October – to Marie Clerk to be a goun – 10 ell off sad cullort stuff boght fra Helen Gray cost 26s. 8d. the ell is	13–06–08	
	Given the good wyffe to pay 8 douzane off eygs	00–13–04	
	For whyt breid in the month off October 1670	01–09–00	• 23 • 12 • –
	The end off October 1670. The disbursments in October 1670.....is ...		• 126 • 02 • 08

November 1670 –	The disbursments in the month of November 1670 –:	
E Johnstoun	The 5 off November 3 ½ ell and a halff a quarter off canell cullort serge boght fra Crichie at 2 merk the ell to be lady mistresse madame a petticot is	04–16–08
Robert – Cleghorne	The 16 off November 1670 to Robert Cleghorne candlemaker in Dalkeith on his discharge the said day for 8 ston off candle at four merks the	

8 – ston of candle –& 1 pair off creils

ston –21–06–08d. 21–06–08
To him for a pair off creils to cary [sic] candle in – 40s. 02–00–00
23–06–08

The way how I peyit the said 23–6–8d.
1– 29 ½ pound off oxen talon............29 ½ lb –
2– 21 ½ pound off sheips talon..........21 ½ lb – is is [sic] 51 lb
tross wecht is 2 ston & a halff & 1 pound tron wecht at 40s.
the ston.. 05–02–00
The 16 off November.....1670 peyit to him in money 18–04–08
23–06–08

To his man in drink money 3s.–4
To him selff – 4s. for 2 peices off tows & cords to
bind the creils .... 4s.–0 .... 00–07–04 • 28 • 10 • 08

Mathew – Mitchel in – Dalkeith – barren treis– & imps &c

The 16 off November 1670 – to Mathew Mitchel in Dalkeith for –
1– 40 treis – ashes plains & plumb standerts 02–00–00
2– to his sone in drink money 00–12–08
3– for an quinch trie.. 00–09–04
4– for ane aple imp off 6 or 7 yeir old the long Lidingtoun aple......... 00–19–04 • 04 • 01 • 04
To Patrik Logan in Dalkeith for 1 chirrie imp 00–13–04
1 – ash raik shaft .... 00–04–00 • 00 • 17 • 04

William & Alexander Clerks –

The 16 off November 1670 – to Archebald Gemls wyffe which shoe
disbursit for William & Alexander Clerk ....
1– for candle to them in the schoole all winter 00–16–00
2– for mending thair shoone.. 00–07–06

	3– for mending thair hose	00–02–08	
Dalkeith	4– spent in Archebald Gemls howsse	01–13–04	
& c	5– to his dochter in drink money	00–13–04	
	6– peyit for 2 horse expense	01–00–00	
	7– expense with bailyie Scot & uthers	03–08–02	• 08 • 01 • –
	To John Rob for 3 mutchkins off oyll	00–07–06	
	To George Reid for 4 litle mands	00–16–00	
	To a couper for girds	00–13–08	
George Clerk – webster –	To George Clerk for weiving 16 ell off drogit at 16d. the ell – & his bounteth & for cloth wes wroght befor &c	01–13–08	• 03 • 10 • 10
2... websters	The 16 off November to George Clerk wobster for working 8 ell of cloth to be Mr John Clerk a shag cot at 2s. the ell – for warping ale & for paping 14s. is in all 30–22 nor to Wille Storie for warping ale of some – course blankits – 3s. 4d. is in all to the said 2 we[b]sters – 33s. 4d.	01–13–04	
Agnes Clerk[73]	22 November – to Agnes Reid for 2 wand creils or baskits George Reid made for hir – 12s.	00–12–00	• 02 • 05 • 04
	The disbursments on this syde in November 1670 is		• 47 • 06 • 06

[73] Clerk wrote 'Agnes Clerk' in the margin, but he wrote 'Agnes Reid' in the main entry.

[108]

Margin	Entry	Amount	Total
	The disbursments in November 1670 on the other syde is 47–6–6		• 47 • 06 • 06
	On Teusday 22 November 1670 peyit to George Bell measson in		
Helen &	Pennycooke – 26–13–4d. for Helen & Jennet Clerks boord fra –		
Jennet Clerk	the 18 off October – 1670 that they entert home till – the 18 off January		
	1671 is – 3 month.		• 26 • 13 • 04
Beatrix –	21 November 1670 – to Beatrix Thomsone for hir fie fra Witsonday		
Thomsons fie –	1670 till Mertimes 1670 – 9 lib.	09–00–00	
Alexr Patersons	21 November 1670 – to Alexander Patersone for his fie fra Witsonday		
fie –	1670 till Mertimes 1670 – 7 lib.	07–00–00	
David –	The 23 off November 1670 I compleited David Clark – 106 lib. for		
Clarks fie	3 yeirs fie fra Mertimes 1667 till Mertimes 1670 is according – to		
3 yeir –	35–6–8d. – ilk yeir this appears on a booke whair I set doun servants		
	fies on the 1 page theroff	106–00–00	• 122 • 00 • –
1 ston – 9	At Silver burne – Wedensday 23 November 1670 – to Androw Wilsone		
lb off butter –	for 1 ston 9 lb off butter at 56s. the ston is	04–07–04	
David Gray –	On Saturday 26 November 1670 sent to David Gray cordoner with		
	John Rob seald in a peper – 4 lib. 12s. David Clerk wes oweing him		
	which I keiped in my hand for him when I peyit David Clerk his fie		
	above mentioned	00–00–00	
	24 November – to Findlay Macknab for 2 douzane off oynions	00–05–00	
Archbald	On Munday the 26 of September 1670 – Archebald Gib gairner cam to		
Gib –	Neubiging whair he wes till Munday the 27 off November 1670 – he		
gairner –	wes at Neubiging all the said tyme except 4 days at on[e] tyme & 2 or		

14 lib. 6s.	3 days that he could not wirk for rain and frost helping to level the gairden –& set a thorn hedg in the gairden & a thorn summer howsse therin –& in helping to mak a ramble hedg be south the gairden and helping to plant baren treis within the said hedg for which I gave him with his dyet 3 rex dolors 8–14 & 2 lyge dolors 5–12s. is in all	14–06–00	• 14 • 11 • –
A young cow to – kill – cost 9 lib. –	Teusday the 29 off November 1670 William Stewart boght at the Howsse off Mure a young cow off 4 yeir old to kill for 9 lib. Scots – David Glendining peyit out the 9 lib. for the same and I am to repay the said David Glendining – the said nyne pounds		• 09 • 00 • –
Mill –& kill –	25 November – to Edowart Thomsone to dry 14 bolls off oats 6s. 8d. & to him 5s. when he went to grind the same is 11s. 8d. to get 7 pynts ale	00–11–08	
	For whyt breid in the month off November	01–12–04	• 02 • 04 • –
	The end off November 1670 – the disbursments in November 1670....		• 221 • 14 • 10
December 1670 –	The disbursments in December 1670 –		
E – John[n] =	The 1 off December 1670 3 ell of lining to be toys pour la femme cost 13s. 6d. the ell	02–00–00	
	1 December – to John Rob for whyt threid 6s. 6d. for cake – 4d. is	00–06–10	
8 douzane – of eygs...	1 December given 13s. 4d. to buy to pay 8 douzane off eygs – to which wes got in November for – from severall persons	00–13–04	• 03 • 06 • 06
	I went to Edinburgh the 2 off December 1670 –		
Chamber – maill –	The 6 off December 1670 – to William Broun skinner on his discharge date – the 6 off December 1670 – 12 lib. for my chamber maill – fra Witsonday 1670 till Mertimes 1670	12–00–00	

James –	To James Adamsone plumber in full off ane accompt on his discharge			
Adamsone –	date the 5 off December 1670		06–00–00	
John – Cooke	To John Cooke locksmith in full off ane accompt on his discharge			
	date the 5 off December 1670		06–06–00	
Will: Stewart	The 3 off December 1670 to Alexander Simpsone on his discharge			
Alexr Simsone	4–10s. – for ane yrne pot William Stewart wes oweing him – William			
ane yrne pot	Stewart gave me this 4–10s. to give him		00–00–00	• 24 • 00 • –
	The 10 off December 1670 – to James Clerk in full off ane accompt			
	for severall things I boght fra him on his discharge theroff date –			
	the 10 off December 1670 – 36–04–08		36–04–08	
	Peyit to my brother John Andersone the 9 off December 1670 –			
	which he lent to James Clerk for his usse			
	1– for mending 2 pair off shoone	01–00–00		
	2– for a pair off new shoone	01–18–00		
	3– 4 douzane off breist buttons	00–08–00	03–06–00	• 39 • 10 • 08
suger almonds	4 lb off suger almonds at 12s. the pound		02–08–00	
danre combs	2– danre combs off boxwood		00–12–00	
	3– key rings		00–06–00	
	1– peice off coper to be 2 round bord things for the bee housse		00–07–00	
	1– pound off suger breid		00–13–04	
Alexr Dobsone	To Alexander Dobsone for mending a saidle		00–13–04	
saidler	1 whyt woven worsit night cap		00–18–00	
	For mending 2 tin stoups		00–06–00	
	3 300 and a hallf off chestins		01–10–00	

2– once off nitmugs .... 00–10–00 • 08 • 03 • 04

The disbursments above in December 1670 is .... • 75 • 00 • 06

[109]

The disbursments in December 1670 on the other syde is 75–00–06 .... • 75 • 00 • 06

The 5 off December to William Reid for –

Margin	Item	Amount	Total
Things –	1 lame quart botle	00–18–00	
Boght fra	1 pynt glasse botle	00–14–00	
William	1 chopin glasse botle	00–07–00	
Reid	1 pound of blak spyce	00–13–04	
	2 suger loaffs weying 5 lb 11 once at 0–10–6d. the pound	02–19–06	
	1 pound off ginger	00–10–00	
	2 once nit mugs	00–10–00	• 06 • 11 • 10
Thomas	The 6 off December 1670 boght fra Thomas Wedell –		
Wedell –	2– pair off stirp yrns at 17s. the pair	01–14–00	
horse –	3– pair yellow stirp leathers at 12s. the pair	01–16–00	
graith –	3– yellow colt helters at 16s. 8d. the peice	02–10–00	
	2– yellow head stails and rains at 17s. the peice	01–14–00	
	1– fyne great large bitt	05–00–00	
	5 great cords 12 fadom long the peice	00–18–00	• 03 • 12 • –
Alexander	The 6 off December 1670 – to Alexander Clark merchant in full		
Clark –	off ane accompt on his discharge date the said 6 off December 1670		
	for severall things he boght in Holland for me	55–02–02	

Inglish forrest –	6 December – to George Swintoun for the *Inglish Forrest* and *Calendarium*		
5 lib 16s	*Hortense* in folio bound togither	05–16–00	• 60 • 18 • 02
	The accompt off charges peyit out when I wes made burges & gild		
	which wes on Wedensday the 7 off December 1670		
	1– libertie & watchings	02–17–04	
Charges in	2– for armes	26–00–00	
Entring –	3– to Pauls in wark – for the poore thair	02–18–00	
Burges –	4– to the poors box	02–08–00	
& gild	5– for the burges ticket	05–16–00	
Brother	6– to John Kniblo – dean off gilds officer	02–18–00	
which wes	Off extreordiner charges –	42–17–04	
53–19–04	1– for gold to gild the great letters	02–18–00	
	2– to William Bell for wreating & gilding the ticket	04–07–00	
	3– spent at twa tymes anent that bussynes	03–17–00	
		53–19–04	• 53 • 19 • 04
Jo: Crichton	The 8 off December 1670 to John Crichtoun for –		
sive wright	3 hony sives at 8s. the peice	01–04–00	
	1 whyt turnt coich	00–05–00	
	6– coks & pails	00–04–00	
	1– great large turnt cap	00–14–00	
	4– pigs	00–04–00	
Spanish –	4 pound off Spanish broun at 4s the pound	00–16–00	
broun –	1 boxwood combe for a horse with a water sponge	00–06–00	
	1 horne skraicher lyke a cat – to Thomas Wyllie for it	00–06–08	• 03 • 19 • 08

William –	8 December 1670 boght fra William Stinsone –		
Stinsone –	6 litle trinchers	00–08–00	
sive wright	2 douzane coks & pails at 10s. the douzane	01–00–00	
	2 wirt dishes with long handls at 8s. the peice	00–16–00	
canel water –	1 great large timber cap – 13s. 4d.	00–13–04	
	8 December – to Jennet Gray for 5 mutchkins off canel water –		
	at 3 lib. the pynt	03–15–00	• 06 • 12 • 04
mandell –	The 12 off December 1670 to Thomas Fisher for –		
buttons –	5 grosse off mandel buttons at 3s. 4d. the douzane	10–00–00	
breist buttons –	6 grosse 7 ½ douzane off breist buttons at 2s. the douzane	07–16–00	• 17 • 16 • –
Isobell Gray –	8 December 1670 to Isobell Gray for 2 ston off knok lint		
knok lint	at 3–16s. the stone		• 07 • 12 • –
	2 gray bonets for William & Alexander Clerks	00–13–00	
	1 ring for a carabin	00–05–00	
	To James Clerk for 1 ½ pound cullort threid at 26s. the lb.	01–19–00	
	2 blew & whyt gally pots	00–07–00	
	2 pound 5 ½ once off reid threid at 20s. the pound	02–06–06	
	1 hamper	00–09–00	
	23 fadome off small cords	00–10–00	
	2 ½ pound off leaffe tobaco at 20s. the pound	02–10–00	• 08 • 19 • 06
	15 December 1670 to James Stewart for –		
	4 lame pots ... 00–16–00		
	1 gally pot ... 00–02–00		
	1 whyt box ... 00–09–00	01–07–00	

Margin	Entry	Amount	Total
	6 ell off hardn at 5s. the ell	01–10–00	
shod shools –	6 shod shools at 15s. the peice	01–10–00	
	12 lyne cords – 29s.	01–09–00	
saffron.....	12 drop off safrin at 3 lib. the once	02–04–00	
	4 once off leaff tobaco	00–05–00	
	3 lyne cords	00–07–06	• 08 • 12 • 06
	The disbursments in December 1670 on this syde & the other		• 257 • 02 • –

[110]

Margin	Entry	Amount	Total
Tows.......	The disbursments in December 1670 on the other syde		• 257 • 02 • –
	2 bundle off tows weying 6 ½ lb at 4s. 6d. the pound	01–08–04	
	15 ½ fadom off tows	01–02–00	
Braid plane knitings.....–	16 December – to Alexander Clerk for 12 peice off braid plan[e]d knitings	02–10–00	• 05 • 00 • 04
Lady – Neuhall 8 – laid cols. –	13 December 1670 to the Lady Newhall for 8 laid off cols at 5s. the laid which we got befor Robert Robisone cam	02–00–00	
To John...– Ramsay – 2 13s–4d for skoreing me – out off a – Registrat – horning –	The 13 off December to John Ramsay for skoreing me out off a registrat horneing done be a messinger – a fals knave I belevd callit Wat – who uses about the castell who not onlie use a fals[e] indorsation against my selff bot also against above 40 noble & gentlmen heritors off the shyre off Midlothian for alledging they did not compeir before or – at the head courts – not the lesse that they did hold blanche off the king[74]	02–13–04	• 04 • 13 • 04

Plane – knitings	4 bolt off narow plane comon knitings at 3s. 6d. the bolt	00–14–00	
	3 bolt off verie fyne verie narow plane knitings at 6s. the bolt	00–18–00	• 01 • 12 • –
Dame Geils Smith 20 – ell of lining	The 19 off December 1670 – to my mother in lawe Dame Geils Smith for – 10 ell............& 10 ell................. is 20 ell off verie good lining for – 2 pair off sheits at 20s. the ell is	20–00–00	
E Vert– 31 ell off – lining......	The 19 off December 1670 to Elizabeth Vert for 31 ell off – lining to be 3 pair off sheits at 12s. 6d. the ell	19–07–06	• 39 • 07 • 06
drink – money –	The 19 off December 1670 given in drink money –		
	1– to Thomas Wolff 01–06–08		
	2– to William Browns woman 00–13–04		
	3– to Margaret Andersone 01–09–00		
	4– to John Gibsons nourish........ 00–12–00		• 04 • 01 • –
Isobell – Gray –	Accompt off severall small things which Isobell Gray boght for me –		
	3 pound off whyt stiffing at 3s. 4d. the pound 00–10–00		
	2 once off blew indigo.......1s. 6d. 00–01–06		
	1 pound off galls – 10s. 00–10–00		
	1 pound off copres – 2s. 4d. 00–02–04		
	1 pound off currents – 8s. 00–08–00		
	1 once off canel – 12s. 00–12–00		
	2 once off wyne ston – 2s. 00–02–00		
	12 ell off grein worsit at 10d. the ell......... 10s. 00–10–00		

[74] Blanch holding was the nominal payment to a superior in acknowledgement of their superiority.

E.J 1 pair off sad cullort gloves – 7s. .... for the good wyffe
E.J 1 pair off cut fingert whyt gloves – 3–4.................... 00–11–04 03–07–02
2 lb off raisings at 8s. the pound 00–16–00
Mary – 1 pair off gloves for Marie Clerk 00–16–00
Clerk – 1 pair off shoone for Marie Clerk 01–10–00
2 pair off gloves for the bairns 00–09–00
2 once off nitmugs at 4s. 6d. the once 00–09–00
6 bolt off whyt narow knitings at 4s. the bolt........... 01–04–00
2 taffatie hoods for Helen & Jennet Clerks 04–16–00
E.J 6 ell off strypit stuff to be a mantle for the good
wyffe at 30s. the ell 09–00–00
E.J 6 ell off strypit rubens to ty [sic] it – at 3s. the ell ..... 00–18–00 .... 19–18–00 • 23 • 05 • 02
The way how I peyit Isobell Gray this – 23–05–2d.
1– The 5 off December 1670 given hir 12 merk
peices 08–00–00
2– The 17 off December given hir.......................... 15–05–02 .... 23–0–5–2[75]
E.J: The 13 off December 1670 to Mr John Smiths wyffe for a lute string
hood cam out off London – for the good wyffe 03–16–00
Nicolsone – The 30 off September 1670 I say the 30 off December 1670 – John Reid
1 boll of got at Nicolsone fra James Jack – a boll off peys whairoff a part off
peis.......... them wes made usse off for the pot...............cost............................. 04–06–08
In December at my being in Edinburgh Mr Jo: C: disbursit off small
Archebald things 14s. and a grot I gave to Archebald Gemls man is 18s. 00–18–00
Gib – The 29 off December – to Archebald Gib 1 lyg dollor for about 16 or

gairner –	17 days he wes helping to set the rest of the barren treis with his meat – by & attour 14 lib. 6s. being 5 dolors I peyit to him formerlie as it is mentioned in the end off November 1670	02–16–00	• 11 • 16 • 08
	The good wyffe disbursit when I went to Edinburgh the 2 off December – & stayed 19 days		
6 – douzan	1– 6 douzane off eygs at 20d. the douzane	00–10–10	
of eygs	2– to the mill & kill	00–11–08	
	3– uther small disbursments	00–05–06	• 01 • 08 • –
	I disbursit my selff in December for breid	01–05–00	
	The good wyffe said shoe disbursit for 10 broun breid at 1s. 8d. the peice – the 19 days I wes in the toun.....is	00–16–08	• 02 • 01 • 08
	The end off December 167[0] The disbursments on thir 3 sydes in December 1670 is		• 350 • 07 • 08

[111]

The haill disbursments fra the – 1 off January 1670 to the last day off December 1670 – everie month off the said yeir being soumd up be it selff –

75 This is how Clerk noted the tally in the original. He did not provide one in the margin.

1 January – 1670........................ 534–11–08
2 February 106–18–06
3 Marche 163–19–06
4 Aprill 249–17–02
5 May 385–02–01
6 June 452–07–08
7 Jully 203–05–02
8 Agust 625–11–10
9 September 279–13–00
10 October 126–02–08
11 November 221–14–10
12 December– 1670 350–07–08
..........3699–11–09

The haill disbursments fra the 1 off Januar 1670 to the last of December 1670 is.............. •3699 • 11 • 09

John: Clerk

This booke off yeirlie disbursments wes begun the 1 off Januar 1663 – fra the 1 off Januar 1663 to the 1 off January 1671 – is 8 yeirs – everie yeirs expensis & disbursments is as follows

1 in anno...1663........................3699–10–11
2 in anno...1664........................2006–15–09
3 in anno...1665........................2183–18–02
4 in anno...1666........................2581–03–03
5 in anno...1667 which wes the dysmall
yeir for me – that me twa dear angels

dyed – my dear & weell beloved wyffe
& my dear & weell beloved daughter[76]
Elizabeth Clerk 4972–09–02
6 in anno...1668........................4405–10–06
7 in anno...1669........................3575–09–00
8 in anno...1670........................3699–11–09
Disbursit in the said 8 yeirs tyme
fra the 1 of January 1663 to
the 1 off January 1671 the
soume off 27 124 lib. 8s. 6d. ....27124–08–06.................................... •27124 • 08 • 06

John: Clerk *John: Clerk*

[112]

Januar 1671 The disbursments in Januar – 1671 –

1– to Mr John Clerk – 3 dolors 08–14–00
2– to James Clerk..03–00–00
3– to William Clerk 00–13–04
4– to Alexander Clerk...00–13–04
5– to Robert Clerk...00–03–00.......... • 13 • 03 • 08

[76] Clerk began to use this spelling more frequently from this point on in this book.

Item	Amount	Total
To Mary Clerk –		
1– 4 rex dolors	11–12–00	
2– 1 pair off ritch [sic] perfumd plane – Spanish cordevans of the best sort	08–08–00	• 20 • 00 • –
To Margaret Clerk – 2 rex dolors		• 05 • 16 • –
To Agnes Clerk –		
1– a rex dolor	02–18–00	
2– a silver peice Francis & Maria	00–12–00	
3– a gilt French etuise	00–18–00	• 03 • 16 • –
To Helen Clerk –		
1– a hood cost – 48s.	02–08–00	
2– a pair off gloves 5s.	00–05–00	
3– a French etuise sheirs & botkin	00–09–00	
4– a painted box – 3s. conteining	00–03–00	
5– a new halff croun – 30s.	01–10–00	
6– a new halff merk peice	00–06–08	
7– turnors – 4s.	00–04–00	• 05 • 05 • 08
To[77] Jennet Clerk –		
1– a blak taffatie hood cost – 48s.	02–08–00	
2– a French etuise sheirs & botkin	00–09–00	
3– 1 painted box – 3s. conteining	00–03–00	
4– ane old 15s. peice	00–15–00	
5– 3s. in turnors	00–03–00	• 03 • 18 • –

	To Katherin Clerk –		
13–03–08	1– a pair of gloves	00–05–00	
20–00–00	2– a new halff merk peice	00–06–08	
05–16–00	3– turnors.....2s.	00–02–00	
03–16–00	4– a litle painted box.....2s.	00–02–00	• 00 • 15 • 08
05–05–08	To Mary Dowglas – ane old 40s. peice		
03–18–00	To men servants –		
00–15–08	1– to Edowart Thomson	00–18–00	
02–17–08	2– to Archebald Craig	00–13–04	
03–16–00	3– to James Bowie tailyeur	00–13–04	
00–18–00	4– to James Beir	00–09–00	
01–16–00	5– to Sande Steuart	00–04–00	• 02 • 17 • 08
62–02–08	To women servants –		
03–18–00	1– to Jennet Hay	01–16–00	
22–13–04	2– to Margaret Shanks	00–13–04	
03–18–02	3– to Margaret Blak	00–13–04	
92–12–02	4– to Jennet Thomson	00–13–04	• 03 • 16 • –
	To John Brown bedel	00–12–00	
	To John Rob	00–06–00	• 00 • 18 • –
	To John Brown schoole master – 1–36s. peice		• 01 • 16 • –
		all above	• 62 • 02 • 08

[77] A portion of the first few letters/numbers on this (and the next seven) line(s) are partially obscured.

Brande	7 Januar – to John Rob for 5 chopins off brande at 30s. the pynt	03–15–00	
	to him for toothing ane old haik – 1s. and 2s. for a pirn – is	00–03–00	• 03 • 18 • –
4 ston off	Teusday the 3 off January 1671 – sent to Mary Clerk with John Rob seald		
knok lint	in a peper for 4 ston off knok lint which John Rob broght out Saturday		
at 5 lib 13s 4d	the 31 off December 1671 – at 5 lib. 13s. 4d. the stone –		
the ston–	1– 8 lyg dolors at 56s. the peice	22–08–00	
is 22–13–04	2– 10 turnors & a 4s. 6d. peice..	00–05–4d.	• 22 • 13 • 04
9 mure	Thursday 5 January – to John Ramsay for 9 mure fowls at –		
fowls–	6s. the peice..	02–14–00	
	11 Januar to Wille Steuart to seik oats in Calder mure	00–08–00	
	14 Januar to John Rob for a great Scots pig to hold hony...................	00–06–02	
	13 Januar to Edowart Thomson to dry 10 bolls 4 pecks of		
	oats – 5s. – & 5s. to mill the same is both	00–10–00	• 03 • 18 • 02
	The disbursments in January 1671 on this syde		• 92 • 12 • 02

[113]

	The disbursments on the other syde in Januar 1671 – is		• 92 • 12 • 02
Fra John	The 13 off December 1670 to John Clerk officer in the head of the		
Clark–	Canegate for 10 pynts off vinaigre at – 7s. the pynt –3–10s. on Wedensday		
officer– –	the 4 off Januar 1671 – John Rob did tak in a litle barel to resave the said		
11 pynts	vinaigre which barel did hold a pynt more nor I had peyit him for – John		
of vinaigre	Rob did pay him 7s. for the od pynt is in all elevin pynts at 7s.		
	the pynt is	03–17–00	

Margin	Entry	Amount	Total
8 peks off peys – – in Dalkeith	6 Januar – to John Hodg for halff a boll of peys he boght in Dalkeith – 40s.	02–00–00	
webster–	Said day to George Clerk for warping ale off 2 bits off webs the on[e] whyt tamein – the other gray	00–06–00	• 06 • 03 • –
Isobell – Gray – E. J. –	Teusday 10 Januar – sent in with John Rob seald in a peper to be delivert to Isobell Gray – it wes within a letter I wreat to hir – 3 lib. 12s. for 4 ell off serge shoe sent out at 18s. the ell to lyne the good wyffs spangaried mantle	03–12–00	
Isobell – Gray –11– ell off – bustian –	On Wedensday the 18 off January sent in to my brother Mr John Andersone with Mr John Clerk 7–6–8d. seald in a peper which he gave to James Clerk to give Isobell Gray for 11 ell off bustian – at a merk the ell	07–06–08	• 10 • 16 • –
	18 Januar – to William Austen for a coll ridle 3s for ane sowin sive – 3s. for monting a beir ridle in ane old rim – 6s. – is	00–12–00	
	Wedensday 18 Januar for the gray horse when Mr Jo: C. – went to toun	00–03–00	
Margret – Clerk – –	19 Januar – 1 ell and halff a quarter off Holland to be Margaret Clerk 2 bands at 3 lib. 4s. the ell is	03–12–00	• 04 • 07 • –
Nans – Frizels fie – 3 halff yeirs –	As apears on the 48 page off the booke whar servants feis – ar wreatten doun on the 25 off January 1671 payit to Nans Frizell – 24 lib. for 3 halff yeirs fie fra Witsonday 1669 – till Mertimes 1670 at 8 lib. ilk half yeirs is 24 lib.		• 24 • 00 • –
William –& Alexander	Wedensday 25 January 1671 – to the minister off Pennycooke seald in a peper with a letter to them – to be sent to William & Alexander Clerks		

Clerks – 4 lib.	in Dalkeith – 6 merk peices to be given at Candlemes – to wit – 4 merks		
to be given at –	to thair master & 2 merks to thair doctor..	04–00–00	• 04[78]• 00 • –
Candlemes –	On Thursday 26 Januar 1671 – William Barclay maltman in Ormstoun		
David Maither–	broght me fra David Maither in Ormstoun hall – 6 plumb trie coichs –		
in Ormstoun	which cam to 8 lib. 6s. as is undermention – the said day I delivert to –		
hall –	the said William Barclay 8 lib. 6s. to be delivert be him to the said David		
6 plumb trie	Maither for the said 6 coichs – 12 merk peices and a six pence I delivert		
coichs–	to William Barclay befor Rober[t] Dewer smith and James Lowrie at the mill		
	–& wreat a letter with William Barclay to David Maither that I had resavit		
	the said 6 coichs and delivert to William Barclay 8–6s. to be given to him.........		
	1– 1 coich.......37s. 01–17–00		
	2– 1 coich.......32s. 01–12–00		
	3– 1 coich.......28s. 01–08–00		
	4– 1 coich.......27s. 01–07–00		
	5– 1 coich.......22s. 01–02–00		
	6– 1 coich.......20s. .... 01–00–00...........		• 08 • 06 • –
1– libed	Thursday 26 January – given to William Stewart 8 pound which he		
sow fra–	delivert to William Johnstouns wyffe in Newhall for a libit sow he		
William–	resavit fra hir –& broght to Newbiging the said day this wes the		
Johnstoun–	pryce I agried for with hir for the said sow with the said William –		
8 lib–	Johnstoun	08–00–00	
couper –	27 Januar to a lame couper for 14 large girds at 10d. the		
Thomas –	peice 11–8		
Mosey –	12 litle girds at 6d. the peice 06–0	00–18–00	

waker in –	27 Januar to Thomas Mozes wyffe waker in Roslin for –			
Rosling	1– for skouring 17 ell off plaiding at 6d. the ell	00–08–06		
	2– for skouring & whytining [sic] 10 ell plaiding at 1s. the ell	00–10–00		
	3– for waking & shaging 6 ell off sad cullort shage to be my selff & Mr John 2 coits at 2s. the ell	00–12–00	01–10–06	
	27 Januar – 20d. to tak a cow to Brunstaine bull		00–01–08	
	26 Januar – for the gray horse when he went in w[ith] for Isobell Gray		00–03–00	• 10 • 13 • 02
whyt–	The last of January 1671 to Isobell Gray being at Newbiging for –			
knitings–	1– 1 peice off knitings	00–14–00		
&–	2– 1 peice off knitings	00–11–00		
twidlt &–	3– 2 peice off knitings	01–00–00		
whyt threid–	4– 2 peice of knitings	00–16–00		
Isobell–	5– 1 once 1 drop off threid	01–01–04		
Gray–	6– 9 drop off threid	00–15–10		
	7– for rolls & weirs	00–03–00		
	8– 1 douzane off spindles	00–06–00		
	9– 6 whorls	00–01–00	05–07–02	• 05 • 07 • 02
	24 January to John Rob for taking in to William Brown – 48 skins		00–06–00	
	For fresh beiff in January		03–01–06	

[78] The sum is obscured by a panel inserted onto the tally section of this page.

	For whyt breid in January	01–19–02	
	30 January – for the gray horse when he went in for Isobell Gray	00–02–00	• 05 • 02 • 08
	The end off January 1671 the disbursments in Januar 1671		• 167 • 07 • 02

[114]

Februar	The disbursments in February 1671–		
1671–	Fryday 3 Februar– sent with John Rob to be delivert to Mr John Clerk		
300 pens–	20s. for 300 goosse pens at 6s. 8d. the douzane	01–00–00	
A fowlling	The 3 off February to Monsieur Sochon for a fowling gun –		
gun–	4 rex dolors– 11–12s.	11–12–00	
John Reid	Fryday 3 off February 1671– to John Reid for 7 bolls of oats we		
7 bolls of	sould pay him yeirlie at 4 lib. the boll – 28 lib. we wes –		
oats–	skarce of oats this yeir & so gave him money for the same	28–00–00	• 40 • 12 • –
25 ell of–	Teusday 7 February – William Stewart boght at the 9 Myll Burn for		
secking–	me 25 ell off seking at 7s. 4d. the ell – it wes ell braid	09–03–04	
	He spent 3 chopins off off [sic] ale in buying it	00–02–06	
	4 Februar to John Rob for 1 haik and 2 pirns	00–08–00	
	10 Februar – to Adam Elleis wyff for a hen	00–06–08	• 10 • 00 • 06
4 bolls of	Saturday 4 Februar – to John Penycooke [sic] in Ravens Hauch for		
seid oats–	4 bolls off seid oats at 4 lib. 10s. the boll	18–00–00	
John Hogens	Fryday 10 February 1671 – boght fra John Hogens		
59 ell of–	1– 28 ell		
grein lining–	2– 17 ell		

	3– 14 ell.................. is 59 ell off round grein lining at 8s. 6d. the ell..	25–01–06	• 43 • 01 • 06
brande–	11 Februar – to John Rob for 5 chopins off brande he got fra John Crauford at 30s. the pynt	03–15–00	
webster–	The said day to John Storie webster for weiving 30 ell of course – blanketing – 30s. for bountith –&c 9s.	01-19-00	
Isobell Gray– for peirling– 28s. –	Teusday 14 Februar – wreatten to Isobell Gray & sent hir with in a letter with John Rob – 28s. for peirling shoe sent out for cudy – G – C[79] mutches to wit – 2 ell at 10s. the ell is – 20s. – 1 ell– 8s. is in all	01–08–00	• 08 • 00 • –
13 ½ bolls off Leith meill– 60–4. s–	Munday 13 Februar – William Stewart & Edowart Adamsone went to Leith & boght 13 ½ bolls off meill – out off Robert Lermonds celler at 4 lib. 8s. the boll	59–08–00	
	Custom – 6s. stable fie –& stroe – 3s. – halff a peck off oats for the horse 4s. – 3 chopin off ale –3s. is in all off charges – 16s.	00–16–00	• 60 • 04 • –
Disbursments for Mr John– Clerks usse–	Mr John Clerk went to Edinburgh Wedensday 18 January 1671 – and returnd on Wedensday the 15 off February 1671 and boght – for him selff as follows with money I gave him with him		
	For mending his spurs 10s.	00–10–00	
	For a leather litle valize..	02–14–00	
Mr Jo: Clerk–	To David Gray for a pair off boots for him selff	06–12–00	
	To David Boyd for 4 ½ ell off hemp cloth at 24s. the ell – to be breiks to put above his cloth breiks..	05–08–00	

[79] This is likely 'George Clerk'.

	For dressing a hatt which my brother gave him	00–14–00	
	For transporting his firr presse out of William Hamiltons to –		
	his Ants [sic] housse Isobell Grays	00–06–00	
	For his expense – fra Wedensday 18 Januar till Wedensday –		
Disbursments	18: till Wedensday 15 Februar waiting to end the bussynes with		
for– I say be–	Mr William Kintor – 17–8s.	17–08–00	• 33 • 12 •
Mr John	At the said tyme when he wes in Edinburgh – he boght & disbursit		
Clerk–	for me – for which I gave him money to pay for the same –:		
for my usse–	To William Lawsone for 8 lb off tobaco in a row at 9s. the lb	03–12–00	
	1 pound off candle for his usse in the chamber	00–03–04	
	1 horn – brod for Robert Clerk – ABC	00–02–00	
	For virginell strings – 12s.	00–12–00	
	For corne –& stroe to the gray horse	00–03–00	
wreating–	1 rim off peper 03–16–00		
peper–	1 rim off peper 03–06–08 07–02–08	07–02–08	• 11 • 15 • –
George–	17 February – to George Clerk webster –;		
Clerk–	For weiving 8 ½ ell off tamein at 4s. the ell	01–14–00	
webster–	For 9 ½ ell of gray plaiding at 16d. the ell	00–12–00	
	For poping for both the webs – 6s.	00–06–00	• 02 • 12 • –
Edouart Adam–	The 15 off February 1671 – to Edowart Adamsone for 16 ell off hardn		
sone 16 ell	he boght for me – I say – 16 ell – off secking at 7s. 6d. the ell	06–00–00	
secking	25 February – to Arche Andersone for trouts 2 tymes	00–05–00	
Trouts– 2– mure	Said day to Nicol Ramsay for 2 mure fowls	00–12–00	
fowls	14 February – to John Clerk in Braidwood for 8 thraive off oat stroe		

8 thraive of oat stroe	at 10s. the thraive	04–00–00	• 10 • 17 • –
For making & furnishing a goun to Mary Clerk	The 21 off February sent to Mary Clerk with John Rob seald in a peper 8 lib. 2s. – to pay for making –& furnishing to a sad cullort stuff goun which wes boght fra Helen Gray being 10 ell theroff at 2 merk the ell which 8 lib. – 2s. wes peyit to [blank] Mackie tailyeur according to his discharge theroff at the fit off his accompt – date – the 25 off February 1671	08–02–00	
	15 Februar to James Bowie to go & mend the bairns cloths – at Dalkeith	00–06–08	• 08 • 08 • 08
	21 Februar – to John Rob 6s. to bring out Mary Clerk on his horsse ...		• 00 • 06 • –
	The disbursments above in February 1671		• 229 • 14 • 02

[115]

The disbursments in Marche on the other syde amonts too	[80]	• 237 • 13 • 02
To James Hamiltoun in the Bow for – I have his discharge for this......	63–18–09	
27 ½ ell 07 ell – 03 ell – is 37 ½ ell of hare stuff at 20s. the ell........	37–10–00	
12 ½ ell off grein serge at 24s. the ell........	15–00–00	
2 remnants off skarlet serge........	03–00–00	
16 ½ ell off skarlet............. 21 – ell off silk and silver... is 37 ½ ell off rubens at 4s. 6d. the ell	08–08–09	• 63 • 18 • 09

[80] In the original, the sum entered at the top of this page differs from the sum entered at the bottom of the previous page.

	More to the said James Hamiltoun for the 10 off Marche 1671 –		
	60 ell off 8d. skarlet and silk and silver rubens at 4s. the ell	12–00–00	
	144 ell off small rubens some off them gold & silk – some silk and		
	silver –& some satyne off divers cullors thair being 34 ell comptit to		
	ilk peice – is – 4 peice –& 8 ell more at 40s. the peice is......................	08–09–04	• 20 • 09 • 04
	15 Marche to Elizabeth Vert for 20 ell off whyt stuff or tamen which		
	being lited Margaret Clerk is to have a goun theroff at 16s.		
	the ell is..	16–00–00	
	21 Marche – to James Arbukles for 30 ell off Scots turk at 3 at –		
	16s. the ell	24–00–00	
	The said day – to Widow Dow for........		
	10 ell of strypit Scots cloth at 24s. the ell	12–00–00	
	15 ell off strypit worsit stuff at 24s. the ell	18–00–00	
	Said day – to William Beks wyffe for 7 ¾ ell off tanton serge at		
	32s. [the] ell...	12–08–00	
	Halff a pound off leaffe tobaco..	00–10–00	
	22 Marche – to Androw Wernards wyffe for 16 ½ ell off gray serge –		
	at 33s. 6d. the ell is..	27–12–09	
	1– hank off small cords...	00–02–06	• 110 • 13 • 03
Lady Crichie	The 25 off Marche 1671 – boght fra Isobell Gray which did belong to		
round grein	the Lady Crichie –		
lining– 38 ell &	1– 38 ell off unblitcht lining at 14s. 6d. the ell is................................	27–11–00	
11– ell–	2– 11 ell off unblitcht hardn at 8s. 6d. the ell	04–13–06	• 32 • 04 • 06

The 21 off Marche 1671 – to Mr John Nasmith 10 lib. Scots – which he gave me – for a blak meir and a foll in Biger fare in anno 1670 – I randert him the said – 10 lib. because the meir dyed within 23 days efter I sold hir – and hir foll – dyed shortlie there efter – he knows verie well I wes in no sort oblidged to doe this – however I thoght fitt to rander the gentlman his money bak agane .... • 10 • 00 • –

The 11 off Marche 1671 – to Edowart Cleghorne 2 old silver spoons with some – brok[e]n silver weying 7 once 9 drope at 3 lib. the once is.. 22–14–00
The said day to him in money 07–16–06
is 30–10–06

For which I resavet fra him the said day – 4 silver spoons weying 9 once – 4 drop at 3–6s. the once is 30–10–06 .... • 30 • 10 • 06

The 20 off Marche 1671 – to Hew Macculloch on his discharge off the said – date 61–17–6 for the new supplie mending off hy ways – drums & trumpeters
1– part off new supplie.. 55–15–02
1– part off reparing hy ways 03–07–00
1– part off trumpeters & drums .... 02–15–04.......... • 61 • 17 • 06

Isobell– Fermer

Wedensday 15 Marche 1671 – peyit to Isobell Fermer for –
1– 2000 headit windows at 32d. the 100th 02–13–04
2– 1000 headit plenchins at 6s. the 100th 03–00–00
3– 1500 blind floorings at 10 [blank] the 100th......... 07–02–06
4– 3000 headit flooreings at 10s. the 100th............... 14–10–00.......... • 27 • 05 • 10

To the good wyffe efter my return fra Edinburgh which wes on the –
25 off Marche 1671 –

1– 2 pynts off ale 03–4d
2– to old Jon Broun &c 02–4–
3– for great prins 01–0–
4– to a woman for carding 2 days 02–0–
5– for 8 douzane off eygs 13–4–
6– halff a mutchkin off seck 04–6– 01–06–06

3 Marche 1671 – at William Slowans brydell in the Marche well 02–05–00
To Arche Andersone for trouts 00–05–06
22 Marche 1671 – to Widow Borthwick at the mill for making –
3 makings off malt – 8 lib. 14s. 08–14–00
To James Peirsie in drink money .... 01–00–00 .... 09–14–00 • 13 • 11 • –

For whyt breid in the month off Marche 01–08–04
For fresh beiff in the month off Marche .... 05–17–08 • 07 • 08 • –

The end off the month – off Marche – 1671 – The disbursments in the month off Marche 1671 – on the other syde and this .... • 615 • 11 • 10

[blank][81]

Marche 1671– William– Jhonstoun

The disbursments in Marche 1671–

Wedensday the 18 off January 1671 accompt off victuall boght fra
William Johnstoun in Newhall –

1– on Saturday the 28 off Januar– resavet 2 bolls off wheat at 6 lib.

2 bolls wheat–		6s. 8d. the boll	12–13–04	
12 bols peys–	2–	on Teusday the 21 off February 1671– resavet 12 bolls off seid		
12 bols–oats		oats at 4–6–8d. the boll	52–00–00	
all	3–	on Munday 27 off February resavet 8 ½ bols of peys – is 12 bolls off peys		
112–13–04	4–	on the 4 off Marche resavet 3 ½ bolls off peys.......... – at 4 lib. the boll is –		
		48 lib.	48–00–00	
		is in all –	112–13–04	
		The 18 off January 1671– given him in earnest	00–13–04	
		Munday 6 Marche 1671 – to the said William Jhonstoun–		
	1–	38 rex dolors at 58s. the peice 110–04– 00		
	2–	and 3s. sterlin– is .... 001–16–00 is	112–00–00	• 112 • 13 • 04
3– bolls–		Munday 6 Marche 1671– sent William Stewart to Prestounpans who–		
off whyt–		broght home 3 bols off salt cost 6–18s.	6–18–00	
salt–		charges and customs –&c	0–07–08	• 07 • 05 • 08
		On Teusday 7 Marche 1671 I went to Edinburgh –& disbursit as follows –		
		8 Marche 1671 to William Reid for –		
		2 lb off brown candie at 12s. the pound	01–04–00	
		1 once off nutmegs	00–05–00	
		3 peper off prins at 4s. the peper	00–12–00	
		4 lb off raisings at 8s. the pound	01–12–00	
		2 suger loaffs weying 6 lb 1 once at 10s. 6d. the pound	03–03–08	• 06 • 16 • 08

[81] This page was not numbered in the original. It falls between the pages numbered 115 and 116.

10 Marche to William Robertsone for 8 brasse pans weying 15 lb
3 ½ once at 17s. the pound is 12–19–00
14 Marche to Adam Tait for ane yrn pot off 4 quarts........................ 03–00–00
To Jo Hamiltons wyffe for 7 hanks off Inglis tows weying 1 ston 12 –
pound at 3 lib. 16s. the ston is.. 05–16–00
6 small hanks off cords– 12s. 00–12–00
10 lb 15 once off steill hemp at 8s. the pound is 04–08–00
To John Hamiltouns wyffe for a ston off Bourdeaux pruns .... 01–12–00 • 28 • 07 • –
2 grosse off short brown poynts 00–14–00
2 grosse off long broun Dumblane poynts at 15s. the grosse............... 01–10–00
2 large comon knyves 5s. 00–05–00
Peyit to Jo: Fergusons wyffe for braid whyt threid knitings............... 01–04–00
1 pound off candle for my chamber 00–03–04
To James Stewart for 6 mutchkin glasse bot[l]s at 4s. the peice........... 01–04–00
8 key rings at 18d. the peice.. 00–12–00
25 Marche to Alexander Clerk for a brasse round pomp .... 01–16–00 • 07 • 08 • 04
For William & James Clerks....
2 severall 4 parts off gramer [sic] .... 8s.
2 *Colloquie* Erasmus .... 4s.
2 Ciceros *epistles* .... 6s.
2 Ovids *epistles* .... 12s.
1 *Act off Regulation the Courts of Justice* .... 10s.
1 Lauderdails *Act of his Second Session* 10s. 02–10–00
To John Waker for binding the 8 books for the bairns 01–04–00

For shewing a pair of gloves	00–04–00	
To John Sands for 10 peices off oak and a peice of ash	02–00–00	• 05 • 18 • –
20 Jan: Marche 1671 to my brother John Andersone: on his I say on James Clerk his recept – date 20 February 1671 –		
1– for severall necessars for James Clerk 01–15–00		
2– 2 pair off gloves for Margaret & Agnes Clerks.... 01–07–00	03–02–00	
To John Fergusone on his discharge date 24 March 1671 for 22 pynts off brande at 29s. the pynt	31–18–00	
The 22 off Marche 1671– to David Pringle on his discharge in full off all accompts preseiding the said 22 off Marche 1671	11–06–00	• 46 • 06 • –
16 Marche to Jo: Cooke for –		
1 – litle bordert lock for the drawer of a table .... 1–4 –		
For mending a large bordert lock 0–12	01–16–00	
1 roll & 1 pair off weirs for Jennet Clerk	00–04–00	
Halff a box Doctor Andersons pills	01–13–04	
1 grosse off sand cullor breist buttons	01–04–00	
1 once off round silk thertoo	01–00–00	
12 threid laces	00–03–06	
6 ell off grein worset at 6d. the ell	00–03–00	
14 Marche– to James Abercrombie for 2 large geins breid	10–00–00	• 16 • 03 • 10
15 Marche to James Stewart for –		
1 rose water trie	00–12–00	
4 once off pomgranat skins at 2s. the once	00–08–00	
To him for gairden seids according to the accompt	02–05–04	

To him for ane old firr box 00–03–00

EJ: 4 ½ ell off clov cullort taffatie rubens for Luckie at 4s. 6d. ell 00–19–00

24 Marche to Jean Forret William Brouns woman 00–12–00

Said day to Sir Lawrens Scots meassons 00–12–00

Said day to Monsieur Sochon for 4 lb off small lead shot 00–12–00

To his men in drink money–6–8d. ale & brande 4–6d. .... 00–11–00 • 06 • 14 • 04

The disbursments in Marche on this syde • 237 • 13 • 02

[116]

Aprill — The disbursments in Aprill 1671 –

1671– — 30 Marche– 3 ell off linings for 12 naipkins cost 14s. the ell 02–02–00

James Clerk – — 2 ¼ ell off twidle for a pair off lynings at 10s. the ell 01–02–06

3 ell off whyt wirseting for the lyneings .... 00–01–06 • 03 • 06 • –

Mr William – Hamiltoun – his– stipend — The 24 off Marche 1671 – to Mr William Hamiltoun – minister at Pennycooke – 322 lib. for his stipend fra Mertimes 1669 till Mertimes 1670 and 4 lib. for – his grasse for the said yeir– is in all 326 lib. on his discharge date the 24 off Marche 1671 .... • 326 • 00 • –

Lining–cloth– Isobell Gray Lady Bagillo 20 ell– — The Teusday – 4 Aprill 1671 – sent with John Rob seald in a letter– to be delivert to Isobell Gray for lining cloth shoe sent me which – did belong to the Lady Bagillo to wit –
10 ell in on[e] peice – –
10 ell in ane other peice – is 20 ell at a merk the ell – is 13–6–8d. – I sent as said is – 20 merk peices seald in a letter for the said cloth is .... • 13 • 06 • 08

halff a barell	The 16 off Marche 1671– to William Stewart for halff a barell off hering		
off hering–	he got at Leith 6 lib. and 7s. 6d. for custom and charges......................		• 06 • 07 • 06
Lint seid oyll–	7 Marche 1671 left with Mr Jo: Clerk – 24s. for which John Rob got a		
Mr John Clerk–	pynt off lintseid oyll	01–04–00	
1– pair off	To Mr John Clerk.......		
shoone –&c	1– at 2 Sondays in Pennycooke..	00–10–00	
	2– at Lintoun with the schoolemaster when he went thair	00–16–00	
	To Mr John Clerk to get a pair off shoone	01–06–08	• 03 • 16 • 08
Arche Craigs	The 11 off June 1670– to Arche Craig for his fie fra Witsonday 1669		
fie fra Witsonday	till Witsonday 1670 17 lib.	17–00–00	
1669 till	The 8 off Aprill 1671 to the said Arche Craig for his fie fra Witsonday		
Witsonday 1671	1670 till Witsonday 1671 – 17 lib.	17–00–00	• 34 • 00 • –
Isobel Scot	The 8 off Aprill 1671 boght fra Isobell Scot at Silver burne –		
28 ell off–	which shoe is to cause bleitch on hir own charges		
unblitcht–	1– 16 ell..................................		
lining–	2– 12 ell..................................is 28 ell off unbleitcht lining to be –		
	sarks to my selff at 12s. the ell is.......		• 16 • 16 • –
Marg Clerk–	The 11 off Aprill – to Margaret Clerk to buy a pair off shone –		
Marg Clerk	when shoe went to the toun to cause mak a tamen goun – 24s.	01–04–00	
lace for a–	The 14 off Aprill 1671 – being Fryday sent to Margaret Clerk seald		
peticot–	in a peper with John Rob– 4 lib. 19s. to buy 2 ell 3 quarters.....off lace		
	to put about a tabein peticot at 36s. the ell	04–19–00	• 06 • 03 • –
Adam–	The 12 off Aprill 1671– to Adam Buckls couper–		
Bukls–	1– 40 large girds at 10 [d.] the peice..	01–13–04	

couper– –	2– 16 lesser girds at 8d. the peice	00–10–08	
	3– given him 6s. because he altert and put in the –		
	bottoms in 2 tubs	00–06–00	• 02 • 10 • –
Hay –&	The 2 off Aprill to William Stewart whiche peyit to John Dobie in		
stroe –	Grein lawe for hay and stroe		
	1– for halff a litle ruck off hay	08–13–04	
	2– twa thraive off oat stroe	01–06–08	• 10 • 00 • –
George–	15 Aprill to George Clerks wyffe for weiving 21 ell of round –		
Clerk–	lining at 2s. the ell to be my selff sarks as wes said with –		
webster–	warping ale – soape – soweing halff a peck off meill to the spyndle –		
	&c all 3 lib. 12s.		• 03 • 12 • –
Kill: Mill–	15 Aprill to John Rob for causeing mend Nans Clerks shoone	00–06–00	
barme–	Said day to Edowart Thomsone off ale for a making –		
Agnes– Clerk	off malt for kill & mill off 6 bolls 12 pecks off oats all	00–13–04	
whyt–	15 Aprill to William Gray – for 59 ell off whyt worsit strings	01–04–00	
worsit–	15 Aprill to James Bowie to get barme	00–04–00	• 02 • 01 • 04
5– thraive	The 16 off Aprill 1671 – to Robert Burnet in Montlothian 50s. for –		
of oat stroe–	5 thraive off oat stroe – William Stewart got fra him the 20 off Marche –		
William–	1671 at 10s. the thraive	02–10–00	
Johnstoun–	The 17 off Aprill 1671 peyit to William Johnstoun in Newhall for......		
10– thraive	1– For 10 thraive off oat stroe got at 3 severall tyms in the month off		
off oat stroe–	Marche 1671 out off Swanstoun – at 12s. the thraive	06–00–00	
20– thraive	2– For 20 thraive off peys stroe got at severall tyms out off Swanstoun –		
off peys–	at severall tyms in the end off Marche & the begining off Aprill –		

stroe–	1671 – at 20s. the thraive	20–00–00	• 28 • 10 • –
3 top–	I gave William Johnstoun the said day – nyne rex dolors		
swarme–	The 19 off Aprill 1671 – to Androw Howisone in Leswaid Loanhead		
bee–	for 3 bee skaips top swarms at 10s. the peice		
skapis–	He hath promist the same against the 20 off May 1671	01–10–00	
	Given him 20d. for a pynt ale – he said belong to him –		
	More given him – 20d. to get ane other pynt ale is	00–03–04	• 01 • 13 • 04
	The disbursments in Aprill above is		• 455 • 00 • –

[117]

19–	The disbursments in Aprill 1671 on the other syd[e] is		• 455 • 00 • –
19– Aprill 1671– To– Archebald Gemls wyffe 80 lib. for– William and Alexr. Clerks boord 6 months– boord fra the 6 off Marche 1671– to the 6 off September 1671	On Wedensday the 19 off A[prill] 1671 – to Archebald Gemls wyffe – for William & Alexander Clerks boord fra the 6 off Marche 1671 – to the 6 off September 1671 is 6 month – 80 lib. is – acording to 40 lib. for ilk ane off them the said 6 month & is acording to 20 lib. for ilk ane off them ilk 3 month – the first 6 month I peyit bot 72 lib. for them both –& 2 ston off cheis ilk 6 month wes 36 lib. for ilk ane off them the said 6 month and wes 18 lib. for ilk ane off them everie 3 month – bot at this tyme shoe wold have 8 lib. more for them both in the said 6 month because shoe alledgit meill & everie thing els wes dear at present – shoe soght some wooll bot wold promisse hir non – also I told hir I wold give hir – no cheise – because shoe had highted – them 8 lib. this 6 month	80–00–00	
	To his daughter in drink money – 24s.	01–04–00	• 81 • 04 • –

To the schoole	The 18 off Aprill 1671 – to Mr John Bowie schoole master in Dalkeith –		
master for the	for 6 months quarter payment fra the 6 off Marche 1671 to the 6 off		
said 6 month fra	September 1671 – 8 lib. is according to 4 lib. for ilk ane off them everie		
the 6 off Marche	3 month and acording to 40s. for ilk ane off them – ilk 3 month	08–00–00	
1671– to the 6 off			
September 1671–			
	To Mr Hew Gray doctor – for William & Alexander Clerks for the		
& to the doctor–	said – 6 months – 6s. sterlin is.	03–12–00	• 03 • 12 • –
	The said 18 off Aprill 1671 – to Archebald Gemls wyffe for some –		
for mending–	small things shoe disbursit for them –		
thair cloths–	1 for mending thair shoone	01–00–00	
	2– for mending thair cloths –& stokings	00–11–00	
	3– for a part off a sand glasse & to the wrights in drink money	00–03–00	• 01 • 14 • –
Expensis &c	18 Aprill 1671 – to Patrik Logan gairner for some turnt handls –&c	00–06–00	
in Dalkeith–	I spent on my voyage to Dalkeith the said 18 off Aprill 1671 for my		
the said day–	own expenses horse meat and severall other occasions	03–14–00	• 03 • 14 • –
	Soma off all the disbursments on the other syde & this in the month		
	off Aprill 1671 is...............545–04		• 545 • 04 • –
	The 18 off Aprill 1671 – to Robert Cleghorne candle maker in Dalkeith		
candle–	for the change some creish being – 13 trose pound with small		
	candle – 15s.	00–15–00	
drink money–	17 Aprill – to the good wyffe to give Mr William Hamiltouns nourish –		
	in drink money – 36s.	01–16–00	
John Broun–	19 Aprill – to John Brown schoole master in Pennycooke for a yeirs		

schoole master in Pennycooke–	stipend fra Candlemes 1670 till Candelmes 1671 .... 20 lib. on his discharge date the said 19 off Aprill 1671	20–00–00	• 22 • 11 • –
Mr John– Clerk– anent Mr– Kintors– bussynes–	The 6 off Aprill 1671 – sent Mr John Clerk to the toun anent my – bussynes with Mr William Kintor who wes thair 5 days waiting – on the same –& cost as efter follows for his expense the said 5 days – 3 lib. horse expense.....9	03–09–00	
	To the cairier off Newcastell who went with James Clerk	00–12–00	• 04 • 01 • –
Isobel Gray E·J –	On Teusday the 25 off Aprill 1671 – sent with Mr John Clerk seald in a peper to be delivert to Isobell Gray – 3 lib. 3s. for 3 ½ ell of whyt serge shoe sent out to be the litle rumple – G – C – 2 whyt coits at 18s. the ell is – 3 lib. 3s.	03–03–00	
David Hislop– 3 ½ lb of fresh butter–	The 20 off Aprill – to David Hislop seald in a peper to give to his wyffe – for 3 ½ lb off fresh butter – 15s. 6d. this I gave him at the Halls – the said day befor David Hi: I say before James Ramsay and do [sic] James Lowrie in Dyke Neuke	00–15–06	
cardus seid– Jews ear– & reid centurie–	22 Aprill to John Rob for 1 once off cardus seid – 4s. for Jews ear and reid centurie 3s. – is– 7s.	00–07–00	• 04 • 02 • 06
Ro Johnstoun– E·J–	Teusday 28 Marche 1671 – given to Luckie the good woman – 6–4s.–4d. – when shoe went to the toun whair shoe stayed – 8 days – giveing clisters –& seisik to hir to the wysse brother Robert Johnstoun	06–04–04	
Helen and– Jenet Clerks boord 3– months–	The 26 off Aprill 1671– to Margaret Hopekirk for Helen & Jennet Clerks – 3 month – to witt fra the 18 off January 1671 to the 18 off Aprill 1671 is – 3 months boord for the said 2 – is – 13–6–8d. for ilk ane off them 3 month	26–13–04	• 32 • 17 • 08

Mr John– Clerk– a voyage to the toun–

Teusday 25 off Aprill Mr Jo: Clerk went to the toun & stayed a night – & 2 days broght out his sister Margret & spok to Isobell Gray and my brother anent the bussynes betwixt Dauf: & his sister Marie C. expensis for him selff and the horse 36s. 01–16–00

To John– Ramsay for 8 mure fowls–

Saturday 29 off Aprill 1671 – to John Ramsay for 2 perdricks resavet fra him – neir Freirtoun on the mure – and for 6 mure fowls resavet on – Saturday the 29 off Aprill 1671 – is 8 in all at 6s. the peice .... • 02 • 08 • –

The disbursments in Aprill on the other syde and this is .... • 591 • 04 • 02

[118]

James– Lowrie at– the mill– his brydel–

The disbursments in Aprill 1671 on the other 2 syds is........ [82] • 591 • 04 • –

Fryday – 28 Aprill 1671 – James Lowrie at the mill off Penycooke – wes mairied on a widow – Margaret Thomsone – William Thomsons dochter in the Kirktoun – it wes a frie brydel – 1– to John Cranstoun Mr Houshold – 1 merk peice – to Robert Poter cooke halff a merk to Jo: Robisone pyper – 6s. is in all – 26s. 01–06–00

plew [sic] yrns– 25 Aprill – to William Stewart for laying the plew yrne twyse........ 00–03–04

trouts– 25 Aprill – to Archebald Andersone for trouts severall tyms 00–10–00

barme– 28 Aprill – to James Bowie to get barme .... 00–04–00 • 02 • 03 • 05

3 bolls off beir for seid & horse.......

The 22 off Aprill 1671 – to William Stewart to pay for 3 bols off beir – wes got fra Androw Marshall – tenent in Lamyrs at 5 lib. 13s. 4d. the boll – is 17 lib. whairoff 1 boll off it wes sawn –& 2 bolls theroff keeped to boyll to the horse – is 13 lib. 17–00–00

beiff–	For fresh beiff in Aprill	08–02–00	
breid–	For whyt breid in Aprill..	01–10–00	• 26 • 12 • –
	The end off Aprill 1671 The disbursments in Aprill 1671 is		• 619 • 19 • 04
May 1671–	The disbursments in May 1671–		
	Teusday 2 May 1671 – sent to Isobell Gray seald in a letter with –		
	John Rob 4s. 6d. for a quarter off whyt fingering wes lost or stoln		
	be the way when it wes sent out		
	which – 4s. 6d. shoe sent bak to me the 3 off May 167[1]	00–04–06	
Isobell Gray	Fryday 5 May 1671 – sent with John Rob to Isobell Gray seald in a letter		
William–	9 lib. Scots which shoe peyit to William Dowglas litster – on the 28 off		
Dowglas	Aprill 1671 – in full of ane accompt on his discharge date 28 Aprill 1671		
litster–	which compt & discharge I have – which wes for liting –		
	1– 20 ell off grograin boght fra Elizabeth Vert sand cullor – 4s. ell.....	04–00–00	
	2– 14 ell off grein stuff for aprons at 5s. the ell..............................	03–10–00	
	3– 8 ell off sad cullort clov grograin at 4s. the ell.............................	01–12–00	• 09 • 00 • –
Alexander Adam	Wedensday 3 May 1671 John Rob broght out a pair off mony cords which –		
1– pair off	Alexander Adam in the Canegate made thir pryce wes 16 lib. the way how –		
mony cords–	I peyit the same		
	1– the 9 of [sic] off Marche 1671 – to Alexander Adam in part off		
	peyment when I bespok the mony cords 4 lib.	04–00–00	

82 In the original, the sum entered at the top of this page differs from the sum entered at the bottom of the previous page.

	2– the 13 off Marche 1671 left with my brother Jo: Anderson 12 lib. seald in a peper which he delivert to Alexander Adam when he broght the mony cords to his chamber	12–00–00	• 16 • 00 • –
pan–cratch oyster–shels	5 May to Arche Andersone for a peck off pan cratch 4s. & for bringing a laid off oyster shels........8s. is.....12s.	00–12–00	
Isobell Gray Mary Clerk– Margaret– Clerk	Teusday 9 May 1671 wreatten to Isobell Gray –& sent to hir with John Rob seald in a packit – 23 lib. to be peyit to James Telfeir tailyeur in the head of the Canegate for making –& furnishing a clov cullort grograin goun for Margaret Clerk & for reforming a poudesoy goun & for 5 ½ quarters off poudesoy for Mary Clerk & for doeing some other things for Mary Clerk – I have James Telfeirs discharge off the said accompt markit on the bak ABC........	23–00–00	• 23 • 12 • –
Mr Patrik Sibalds– daughters–	The 8 off May to Agnes & Katherin Sibbalds daughters to umquhyll Mr Patrik Sibbald sometyme minister at the kirk of Pennycooke – 4 lyg dolors	11–04–00	
Mr John – Nasmith	The 9 off May – to Mr John Nasmith in the Drock hill his nourish in drink money – halff a rex dolor	01–09–00	
1– Blak coy 1– Blak bull stot–	9 May – to Thomas Denholme hynd in the Stinsone – 5 lib. for a blak coy off a yeir old	05–00–00	
	9 May – to John Dicksone – hird in Stinsone for a blak bull stot off a yeir old off a good kynd 2 lyg dolors –& a mark [sic] peice is	06–05–04	• 23 • 18 • 04
Wm Johnstoun– 9 thraive of– oat stroe–	The 15 off May 1671 – peyit to William Johnstoun for nyne thrave and a halff off oat stroe – he gave doun the halff thraive and wold have no lesse then 12s. sterlin is 7–4s. for the 9 thraive – is about – I say it is just –		

	16s. the thraive is – for 9 thraive		• 07 • 04 • –
Jumps–	The 12 off May to James Duncan cordoner 16s. to buy for me –		
timber heils–	1– 6 pair off timber heils.......................................4s.		
2 cows hyds–	2– 5 pair of jumps .... 12s.	00–16–00	
1 horse hyde–	12 May sent with John Rob to David Gray cordoner to buy for me		
for to–	15 lib for which he boght......		
mak shoon–	1– 2 gray cows hyds – curried – 10–00–00.............. 10–00–00		
	2– 1 horse hyde .... 04–04s................. 04–04–00..........	14–04–00	• 15 • 00 • –
Wm Johnstoun–	Munday 22 May to William Johnstoun for 15 thraive off peys stroe		
15 thraive of–	at 18s. the thraive..		• 13 • 10 • –
peys stroe	The disbursments in May		
	above mentioned..............................		• 108 • 04 • 04

[119]

	The disbursments in May on the other syde is.......... 108–04–04		• 108 • 04 • 04
	The 24 off May – boght fra James Sterlin – chapman in Dalkeith –		
girding–	1– 5 ell off whyt girding at 2s. 2d. the ell..	00–10–10	
grein worsit–	2– 9 ell off grein worsit at 8d. the ell	00–06–00	
why[t] worsit–	3– 48 ell off whyt worsit at 6d. the ell	01–04–00	• 02 • 00 • 10
Alexr– Leslie	The 26 off May 1671 – to Alexander Leslie on his discharge off the said		
Mr William–	date –14 lib. 18s. for himselff and 2 rex dolors for his men – is 20 lib.		
Kintor–	14s. which – Mr William Kintor – desyrd me to pay him the said Mr		
	Kintor allowed me the same when we comptit togither	20–14–00	• 20 • 14 • –

Mathew–	26 off May 1671 – to Mathew Mure in Leith Wynd for –		
Mure for–	6 ½ pound off weir at 10s. the pound	03–05–00	
hooks & eys–	1 grosse off hooks & eys for mens breiks	00–12–00	
clasps –& eys	4 grosse off hooks of clasps & eys for bairns cloths at 4s. a grosse	00–16–00	
for bairns cloths	2 grosse off best hooks –& eys for mens breiks at 16s. the grosse	01–12–00	• 06 • 05 • –
shoone–	27 May – to David Gray for a pair off shoone for my selff	01–16–00	
tobaco–	2 lb cut & dry tobaco at 15s. the pound	01–10–00	
glew–	8 lb off glew at 6s. 8d. the pound	02–13–04	
blak spyce–	1 lb off blak spyce	02–13–04	
roset–	6 lb off roset at 2s. the pound	00–12–00	
pick–	4 lb off pick at 3s. 6d. the pound	00–14–00	
muthkin [sic] stoup	To William Crystie for mending a tin moutchkin [sic] stoup	00–07–00	
1– litl barell	To James Stewart for a litle barell	00–06–08	• 08 • 12 • 04
galls–	1 ell off galls for the bairns	00–16–00	
balin–	2 lb off balin at 24s. the pound	02–08–00	
1 ty–	1– blak ty	00–18–00	
2 yellow curpl–	2– yellow curpls at 7s. 6d. the peice	00–15–00	
crooked oake–	To Androw Colm – for a peice off crooked oake to be a frame for the auvall dovc: window off the dovcat	00–16–00	
hizle stiks–	To James Finlasone– for 40 hizle sticks to be handls for mattoks &		
For binding–	hows &c	00–10–00	
ane old bible–	To John Waker – for binding & claspeing ane old Bible in 8° for		
in octava–	Agnes Clerk with the New Psalms added thairtoo	00–18–00	
For mending ane	To John Ritchie saidler at the West Port for mending ane old saidle –		

old saidle–	with a new blak calff skin covert thairtoo	02–04–00	• 09 • 05 • –
2 firikins off–	The 30 off May 1671 to Archebald Campbell on his discharge		
soape–	for 2 firikins off soape at 6–5s. the firikin is	13–10–00	
7 blew	7 blew turkie stons with a printed peper for the		
turkie stons	eys –&c	00–09–00	
1 steill k[e]y band	1 larg steill key band to hold many keys	00–05–00	
Trouts	To Arche Andersone for trouts at severall tymes	00–10–00	
salt butter	To John Rob for 4 lb off salt butter	00–19–00	
2 skait	To him for 2 skait	00–04–00	
barme	To James Bowie to get barme	00–04–00	
threid laces	8 threid laces	00–07–08	
9 douz. eygs	To pay for 9 douzane off eygs at 20d. the douzane	00–15–00	
1 milk tub	For a milk tub in Peibls [sic] fare	00–14–00	• 17 • 17 • 08
whyt breid	For whyt breid in the month of May	01–08–00	
fresh beiff	For fresh beiff in the month of May	03–11–00	• 04 • 19 • –
	The end off the month off May 1671 — the disbursments in the month of May 1671.....		• 178 • 07 • 04

June 1671	The disbursments in the month off June 1671 –:	
gray serge	The 1 off June 1671 – to Thomas Clunes for 15 ell of gray serge in –	
15 ell–	3 remnants acording to his accompt at 32s. the ell	24–00–00
2 stikit caps	To Mistresse Birsbane – for 2 stikit Holland caps........	02–08–00
rushe leather	To Arche Mores wyffe for divers peices off rushie leather........	01–07–00
Spanish brown	To James Cokburne for 8 lb of Spanish broun – 4s. the lb........	01–12–00

Margin	Entry	Item	Total
8– key bands	8 key bands at 20d. the peice	00–13–04	
pouder– horne–	For putting a bottom – in a large powder horne which William Home gave me	00–08–00	• 30 • 08 • 04
Arche– More 12 knapell	The 5 off June 1671 – to Archbald More for 10 great knapel at 25s. the peice is 12 lib. 10s. on his discharge off all things – whatsoever preseiding the said 5 off June 1671		• 12 • 10 • –
Brande 32 pynts 2– French wyne hogs heads– 2– barels to hold brande–	The 5 off June 1671 – to William Home merchant on his discharge off the said date for –		
	1– 32 pynts of brand[e] at 22s. the pynt	35–04–00	
	2– 2– 2 gallon barels to hold the same 18s. the peice	01–16–00	
	3– 2– French hogs heads – to be 4 tubs at 20s. a peice	02–00–00	• 39 • 00 • –
30–08–04 12–10–00 39–00–00 81–18–04	The disbursments in June on this syde is		• 81 • 18 • 04

[120]

Margin	Entry	Total
Chamber maill –	The disbursments in June on the other syde is	• 81 • 18 • 04
William Broun	The 15 off June 1671 – to William Brown skinner on his discharge off the said date – 12 lib. for my chamber maill – fra Mertimes 1670 till Witsonday 1671	• 12 • 00 • –
New suplie Hew Mack culloch–	The 3 off June 1671 – peyit to Hew Macculloch 30–18–10d. for the second part off the new supplie which wes payable the 1 off May 1671	• 30 • 18 • 10

33–00–0	A	The 12 off June 1671 peyit to Edowart Thomsone – 33 lib. in full and		
08–10–00		compleit payment off all fies I wes resting him till and preseiding		
07–18–00		Witsonday 1671 as apears [sic] on the booke markit 347 whair servants		
16–00–00		feis is wreatten doun on the 43 page theroff	33–00–00	
17–00–00		The 16 off June 1671 – to James Beir for his fie fra Mertimes 1670		
17–04–00	X	till Witsonday 1671	08–10–00	
Servants feis–		The 15 off May 1671 – to William Stewart for his sone Sande Stewarts		
fra A–		fie fra Witsonday 1670 till Witsonday 1671 – 7 lib & 18s. for 2 pair		
above–		off shoone is – 7–18s.	07–18–00	
till B–		The 16 off June 1671 – to Jennet Thomsone 8 lib. in compleit payment		
heirunder–		off a yeirs fie at 16 lib. in the yeir and that fra Witsonday 1670 till		
X..		Witsonday 1671	16–00–00	
99–12–00		The 16 off June 1671 – to Margaret Blak for hir fie fra Witsonday 1670		
		till Witsonday 1671 – 17 lib.	17–00–00	
		The 16 off June 1671 – to Margaret Shanks for hir fie fra Witsonday –		
	A.	1670 till Witsonday 1671	17–04–00	
		The 6 articl[e]s above off servants feis	99–12–00	• 99 • 12 • –
Mary Clerk–		27 May Mr Jo: Clerk gave his si[s]ter Mary to pay for 1 pair		
		off shoo[n]e	01–04–00	
Mr Jo: Clerk–		Said day to Mr Jo: Clerk 10s. he spent at Silver burne with kirk wrd ..	00–10–00	
Mr Jo: Clerk–		Mr Jo – Clerk disbursit when he went to Edinburgh – 16 June 1671 –		
Irish horse		on a Fryday for persewing Michel Lowrie –		
mending–		1– to Robert Crichtoun for sureing the Irish horse. 02–08–00		
&c		2– he spent with him & Nicoll Campell [sic] 00–05–00		

	3– to Nicol Campbell for the horse dyet – 3 nights & 3 days	01–16–00		
	4– for his own dyet 3 nights & 3 days he wes in toun	02–08–00	06–17–00	• 08 • 11 • –
Lint seid oyll	26 May 1671 – to Mr John Clerk which he gave to John Rob – 24s. for which he got a pynt off lint seid oyll		01–04–00	
Fish oyll– Marg Hopkirk	To John Robisone for 1 quart and a mutchkin off fish oyll for creishing wooll at 9s. the pynt is 20s. 3d.		01–00–03	
10 ell off round lining	The 16 off June 1671 – to Margaret Hopkirk for 10 ell off round lining at 11s. the ell		05–12– 00	
Webster Alexander Wederburn	23 of June – to Sanders Wederburne webster for weiving 22 ell of hardn at 1s. the ell with the rest of the harre graith all togither		01– 15– 04	
Edowart Thomsons brydel	Thursday 22 June 1671 Edowart Thomsone wes mairied – my self – Agnes & Helen Clerks at a merk the peice – 3 chopins off wyne 27s. – & 1 quart ale is – 30s. 4d. is		03–10–04	• 13 • 01 • 11
Fald dyks	The 24 off June 1671 – to John Pennycooke in Ravens Hauch for biging six skore –& 12 rud[e]s off fald dyks at 2s. the rude is 13–4s.		13–04–00	
William Simpsone 2 ruks of hay–	The 27 off June 1671 peyit to William Simpsone in Easter Ravens Neuk for 2 litle ruks of hay – resavet fra him the 7 off October 1670..			
	1– ruck of hay	12–00–00		
	1– lesser ruck of hay	10–00–00	22–00–00	• 35 • 04 • –
round– hardn–	28 June boght at Silver burne fra cairier – 12 ell of bleitcht hardn at 6s. the ell.......ell is		03–12–00	

8 bolls– of Leith– meill–	9 ell off whyt worsiting cost...... Thursday 29 June 1671 – sent William Stewart & James Patersone to Leith for meill with money to pay for meill which wes boght fra Adam Leslie ...... 8 bolls off meill at 5–6s.–10d. the boll is......	00–04–04 44–16–00	• 48 • 12 • 04
Rosline– 5 bolls– of Bay– salt	The last off June 1671 – to James Sinclair off Rosline – 24–10s. for 5 bols off bay salt at 4–18s. the boll which William Stewart resavit out off Bailyie Curries celler in Leith on the 22 off September 1670 off which I have Rosline his discharge date the 3 off June 1671 bot he wes mistaken off the date off the discharge – it sould have been dated the last off June 1671 bot it is a mater indifferent......		• 24 • 10 • –
Mr William Wallace– 2 yeirs– blanche dewtie– of the Halls being 6 lib. –	The 15 off June 1671 – to Mr William Wallace advocat shireff deput off Edinburgh – 6 lib. Scots at the pryce off 2 pair off gloves for the blanche dewtie off the Halls for 2 yeir fra the 1 of January 1670 till the 1 off January 1672 for which 6 lib. I gat [sic] his discharge date the said 15 off June 1671......		• 06 • 00 • –
	360–8–5 All the former disbursments in the month of June 1671...... is......		• 360 • 08 • 05

[121]

George	The disbursments in June on the other syde is..................................		• 360 • 08 • 05
Clerk–	The 6 off May 1671 – to Lu[c]kie peyit with my money to George Clark		
webster	webster for weiving – 29 ell off small lining at 8s. the ell –		
Warping–	I say at 4s. the ell without bounteth..	05–16–00	
ale–	More to George Clark for warping ale	00–06–00	
Barme–	For barme	00–04–00	
all theis de–	For 8 douzane and 8 douzane and a halff off eygs..............................	00–04–02	• 07 • 06 • 02
bursit be–			
E·J–	Mor[e] – Lukie disbursit in other small things	00–16–00 [83]	
	For beiff 3 tymes in the month of June...	01–11–00	
	To Arche Andersone for trouts severall tyms	00–08–00	
	Whyt breid in the month of June	01–18–00	• 03 • 17 • –
	The end off the month off June 1671 – The disbursments in June 1671		• 371 • 11 • 07
Jully	The disbursments in the month of Jully 1671 –		
1671–	The 1 Jully 1671 – boght fra the Lady Bagillo –		
69 ell off	1– 11 ell..........		
lining–	2– 12 ell.......... is 23 ell off lining at 12s. the ell	07–16–00	
Boght fra	3– 11 ell..........		
the Lady–	4– 11 ell..........		
Bagillo–	5– 10 ell..........		
1– pair off	6– 14 ell.......... is 46 ell off lining at 8s. the ell is............................	18–08–00	• 32 • 04 • –

boots for	The 3 off Jully – to David Gray for		
my selff–	1 pair off gray boots for my selff..	07–00–00	• 07 • 00 • –
32 ell off	On Fryday the last of June 1671 – the Lady Bagillo sent out to Newbiging		
lining–	the 3 peices off lining eftermentioned all the 3 markit with – 555 to wit –		
boght fra–	1– 12 ell at 12s. the ell – markit 555	07–04–00	
the Lady–	2– 11 ell narower [sic]...		
Bagillo–	3– 09 ell narower.......... is 20 ell at 8s. the ell both markit– 555........	08–00–00	
being–	15–04–00– is......................	15–04–00	• 15 • 04 • –
3 peices–	The way how I peyit hir the said – 15 lib. 4s. –		
ilk peice–	1– On Fryday the 7 off Jully 1671 – sent to Isobell Gray with John Rob –		
markit–	to be delivert to the Lady Bagillo seald in a peper.........................	05–04–00	
555	2– The 12 off Jully 1671 – sent to the toun with John Rob – to be delivert		
	to the Lady Bagillo 3 stain off wooll at 5 merk the ston is	10–00–00	
36– rude of		15–04–00	
fald dyks–	The 27 off June – to William Elphistou[n] for biging 36 rude off		
in Penycooke	a fald dyke in Penycooke in the roume callit the grein fit at 2s. the rude		
Edowart	is 03–12s. – to which roume Edowart Thomsone enter at Witsonday 1671 –		
Thomsone–	I thoght once to have labort the said roume my selff which wes the cause		
	that I caused big the said fald dyks – bot Edowart Thomsone entring to the		
	said roume he must repay me the said – 03–12s.		• 03 • 12 • –

[83] The original makes clear that Clerk added these additional charges later. Clerk's sum of 07–06–02 incorporated those charges.

1– stobo hop	Wedesnday 5 Jully 1671 – William Stewart boght fra Alexander Dicksone		
young blak	in Stobo Hopehead for my usse ane blak young cow for my usse with		
cow– cost–	calff as the said Alexander Dicksone – said off 3 yeir old for which I		
16–13–04	peyit – 16–13s.–4d.		• 16 • 13 • 04
Wm Thomson	The 24 Jully 1671 – to William Thomsone now in the Towr –		
1– blax [sic] ox	for a blak ox to teather & kill – 18 lib.	18–00–00	• 18 • 00 • –
to kill–	The 27 off Jully 1671 – to Cristian Ramsay in Braidwood for –		
Cristian Ramsay	1– for 16 thraive off st: oat stroe – at 10s. the thraive which wes resavet		
16 thraive of oat	fra hir the 8 off Marche 1671	08–00–00	
stroe– 8– peks	2– and for halff a boll off beir – Edowart Thomsone resavet fra hir –		
off rouch beir	the 30 off Marche 1671 for knoking..........	02–13–04	• 10 • 13 • 04
Georg[e] Clerk	27 Jully 1671 – to George Clerk for weiving 18 ell off small hardn for		
webster–	sheits at 2s. the ell – 1–16s. –& 3s. 4d. off warping ale is 39s. 4d	01–19–04	
James–	Munday the 31 Jully 1671 – compleited James Bowie – 23 lib. for his		
Bowies–	fie fra Witsonday 1670 till Lammes 1671 is 15 month – which day		
fie–	he went away	23–00–00	• 24 • 19 • 04
Aloes–siccotrin	1 once off aloes siccotrin for the Irish horse	00–14–00	
1– boll barley	22 Jully – to John Rob to get a boll off barley for knoking 8 lib. – to hier [sic]		
for knoking–	pains in bringing it home – 8s. is	08–08–00	
	For 3 quarts off – barme in Jully 12s. – 20 Jully – 32 hering – 10s. –		
	1 bairns last 1s. 4d. – trouts – 3s. 4d. is	01–03–04[84]	
	Whyt breid in the month off Jully..........	01–05–08	• 11 • 11 • –
	The end off Jully 1671 — The disbursments in the month off Jully 1671 is		• 139 • 17 • –

[122]

Agust– 1671	The disbursments in the month off Agust 1671 –	
8 cheis– weying– 6– ston– – – at– 36s the ston–	Teusday the 8 off Agust 1671 – sent William Stewart to Robert Hope in the Spittels who broght me 8 great cheis weying –; 6 stone wecht at 40s. the ston – is 12 lib. William Stewart – peyit him 9 lib. 10s. and on the [blank] off Agust 1671 – I gave his sone Robert Hope 28s. is in all – 12 lib ...... 12–00–00 is in all I peyit – bot 10 lib. 18s. –	• 12 • 00 • –
James Broun tanner– for barking & currying– 4 hyds–	On Wedensday the 9 off Agust 1671 – sent with John Rob seald in a peper which he delivert to James Broun tanner at the West Port 9 lib. barking 4 hyds whair off 2 off them wes curried & made blak for shoone – off which 9 lib. he broght me the said James Broun his discharge – these 4 hyds is wreatten on a long comptbooke with 3 brasse clasps on the 64 page theroff..........	• 09 • 00 • –
Things boght in Carnwath faire –& charges– &c	Thursday 10 off Agust 1671 – William Steuart boght at Carnwath faire – 1– a douzane off hooks .... 02–00–00 2– 6 firr teathers .... 00–07–00 3– the custom off 8 beasts young and old .... 00–05–04 4– William Stewart & Arche Craigs charges 00–10–08	• 03 • 03 • –
Mr Robert Alisone – his stipend– 48 lib.	Munday 14 Agust 1671 – to Mr Robert Alisone minister at Glencorse – 48 lib. as a part off his stipend for the lands off Cookeing lying in Glencorse Paroish on his discharge date the thretie [sic] day off June 1671 – I say & that for a yeirs stipend fra Witsonday 1670 till Witsonday 1671	• 48 • 00 • –

[84] I have transcribed Clerk's tally as found in the original.

24– loch leitches–	The 19 off Agust 1671 – to Jennet Hall who dwels in Oxenhim water in Tividaill – under the earle off Lothian – for 2 douzan off loch leitches at 8s. the douzane is	00–16–00	• 00 • 16 • –
Thomas– Woulff– 2 merks	Teusday 22 Agust 1671 – sent in with my brother seald in a letter adrest to his man – Thomas Woulfe – 2 merk peices for his pains in going eirands [sic] for me & to be carefull to deliver such letters of myne as coms to his hands	01–06–08	
	5 Agust for 60 horns – 12s.	00–12–00	
	6 douzane of Duns poynts whyt 10s.	00–10–00	
	100 peirs........7s. ....7s.	00–07–00	
2 ston hair	16 Agust to John Rob for 2 ston off hair for plaistering	00–16–00	
	1 once of indigo – 4s. to himselff to drink – 2s. is	00–06–00	
	19 Agust – to John Rob to drink when he broght out some lead for the dovcat –& to him for 8 Dunbar hering – 2s. 8d. is	00–07–08	
1– plough	14 Agust to William Stewart – to get a plough at Dalry	04–04–00	
	To Arche Andersone for trouts	00–07–04	• 08 • 16 • 08
4– bolls of Leith meill– 27–4s	Teusday 22 Agust 1671 – sent William Stewart to Leith who boght 4 bolls of meill at 6 lib. 16s the boll – is 27 lib. 4s. – 2s. custom &c	27–04–00	• 27 • 04 • –
peirs.......	23 Agust to Cudbert Kyll for 14 douzane of peirs at 16d. a do[ze]n	00–18–08	
James Louri[e] 3 days mawing–	Said day to James Lourie for maweing [sic] the hay off Cairnhill – 3 days & some other hay with Adam Lowrie– at 6s. 8d. in the day and his meat	01–00–00	
David Garwin– knok mender	23 Agust – to David Garwin for comeing out 3 tymes to looke on the knok and help to set up the knok	01–10–00	

Margin	Entry	Amount	Total
61 hering & 2 douzan of oynions	25 Agust – to John Steill for 61 hering – 12s. & 2 douzane off oynions 2s. 8d. is 14s. 8d.	00–14–08	• 04 • 03 • 04
Margaret– Hopkirk–	The 25 off Agust – to George Bell to give to his wyffe Margaret Hopkirk – 3 lib. for 10 ell off narow unblitcht – som ell harden narow for towels..	03–00–00	
Heather– powers for the barne–	In Agust 1671 peyit to get drink and some money peyit to those that helpit to pow 5 skore & thretein thraive off heather to theyk the east syde off the barne	02–10–00	
For theyking– Braidwood– howsse–	The 1 off September 1671 – to Edowart Thomsone for theyking the housse off Braidwood with heather he said he wes 16 days in theyking it – the good wyffe gave him his meat at noon – at 8s. ilk day	06–08–00	• 11 • 08 • –
Jenet Spalding– for blitching– cloth–	The 2 off September 1671 – to Jenet Spalding for bleitching cloth 24 days at 1s. in the day with hir meat – this wes for bleitching unbleitcht cloth I boght my selff		• 01 • 04 • –
William –& Alexander– Clerks cam– out of Dalkeith–	To Arche Andersone for trouts – 8s. & 8s. for going to Dalkeith for the bairns kist is	00–16–00	
	To John Rob at twyse for 62 hering at 2 tyms	00–12–08	
	To James Patersone to get barme 4s.	00–04–00	• 01 • 12 • 08
Thursday– 31 Agust 1671– Archbald– Gemle– charges thair– &c Dalkeith	William & Alexander Clarks cam out off Dalkeith schoole to Pennycooke schoole Thursday – last off Agust 1671 –		
	1– the said day – sent to William Borthwick chirugien – for helping the bairns some tyms – 1 rex dolor	02–18–00	
	2– to Archbald Gemls wyffe for causing mend thair cloths & shoone – 6 month	03–00–00	

	3– expensis the said day for men & horse	02–04–00	• 08 • 02 • –
	For whyt breid in Agust		• 01 • 10 • –
	The end off Agust 1671– — The disbursments in Agust 1671 is		• 133 • 09 • 08

[123]

September	The disbursments in September 1671 –		
1671			
Lint– seid	Teusday 5 September – to John Rob to get a pynt off lint seid oyll		
oyle–	24s.	01–04–00	
webster –	8 September – to Thomas Burn webster for weiving 18 ell of hardn –		
in Carlips–	18s. 1 ½ pek off meill – 12s. – warping ale 3s. 4d. is	01–13–04	
James–	Saturday the 9 off September 1671 – payit to James Duncan cordoner –		
Duncan–	at the West Port for making shoone at Neubiging – 56 days and a halff		
cordoner–	at 5s. 6d. ilk day with his meat within the houssse [sic] 15–10–09d.	15–10–09	• 18 • 08 • 01
1– boll–	Teusday 19 September 1671 – sent William Steuart to Leith with money –		
7– firlets [sic]–	who boght at Leith –		
off meill–	1– 7 firlots off new meill at 8–5s.–4d. the boll is	14–09–04	
28–19s	2– 2 bolls off old meill at – 7–4s. the boll	14–08–00	
4d–	3– custome	00–01–08	
	4– peys stroe for the horse	00–00–04	• 28 • 19 • 04
herings–	For hering in September 1671	03–15–00	
barme–	For 2 quarts off barme in September 1671	00–08–00	

Wm Russel– Mary– Dowglas	18 September – to William Russell 36s. to pay his hors[e] when he cam out with Mr Kintor to clos our bussynes	01–16–00	
	23 September – to Mary Dowglas 2 merk peices which the good wyffe Lukie borowed fra hir	01–06–08	• 07 • 05 • 08
2– bolls off malt–	Munday 2 October 1671 – given William Steuart money who went to Straiton & boght fra John Hunter thair 2 bols of malt at 7 lib. the boll is – 14 lib & a pynt [of] ale it cost him is	14–01–08	
	For whyt breid in the month off September 1671	01–09–04	• 15 • 11 • –
	The end off September 1671 – The disbursments in September 1671		• 70 • 04 • 01

October 1671–	The disbursments in October 1671 –		
1– barell– off tarr– 10–10s.–	The 2 off October 1671 – to William Stewart 10 lib. 4s. & 6s. off my money he gave formerlie in earnest off a barell of tar to John Thomson at the West Port is – 10 – 10s. for the said barell off tar		• 10 • 10 • –
William– Alexander– & Robert Clerks boord to– George Bell– 6– month–	On Munday the 2 off October 1671– to George Bell measson in Pennycooke – four skore pounds Scotts [sic] for William Alexander & Robert Clerks boord – 6 month – to wit fra Thursday the 5 off October 1671 that they entert to his housse till the 5 off Aprill 1672 is 6 month – a: is acording to 20 merks for ilk ane off them – everie thrie month..........	80–00–00	• 80 • 00 • –
William–	On Teusday the 3 off October 1671 – to Mr Robert Broun schoole master at Pennnycooke [sic] – 4 rex dolors for William & Alexander		

Alexander– & Robert Clerks quarter–	Clerks ~~boo:~~ quarter payment – 6 month – to wit fra the 5 off October 1671 that they entert to the schoole till the 5 off Aprill 1672 is 6 month – is according to a rex dolor for ilk ane off them everie 3 month is	11–12–00	
payment to Mr– Robert Broun– 6– month	The said 3 off October 1671 – to the said Mr Robert Broun – 48s. for Robert Clerks quarter payment – 6 month to wit fra the 5 off October 1671 that he entert to the schoole till the 5 of Aprill 1672 is 6 month – is according to 24s. for ilk 3 month is........	02–08–00	• 14 • 00 • –
Ja: Lowrie sheiring 3 ½ days– –	The 3 of October 1671 – to James Lowrie in Silver burne for sheiring 3 ½ days with his meat at 5s. ilk day........	00–18–00	
	4 October 1671 – John Rob boght with my money I gave him		
Leaff tobaco	1– 1 pound off leaff tobaco........	01–00–00	
2 gray bonets	2– 2 gray bonets for William & Alexander Clerks........	00–14–00	
1 rudiment–	3– 1 rudiments &c for Alexander Clerk........	00–00–00	• 02 • 12 • –
William– Stewart–	To William Stewart the 4 off October – for 3 fadom off tows when he went for a barel off tar the said day at 16d. the fadom – is......4s. –& 20d. off custom – 20d. is & 8d. for the horse is in all – 6s. 4d.	00–06–04	
James– Thomsone– glaisen wright	The 5 off October 1671 – to James Thomsone glaisen wright – 5 lib. 8s. on his discharge off the said date for ane auvall glasse – and a tirlesse for ane auvall frame – for the dovcat........	05–08–00	• 05 • 14 • 04
	The disbursments above in October 1671........		• 112 • 06 • 04

[124]

	The disbursments on the other syde in October 1671 is	• 112 • 06 • 04
Robert Dewer– smith– 174–11–8d	The 3 off October 1671 – compleited Robert Dewer smith in Pennycooke ane compt off – 174–11–8d. for severall sorts off yrne wark he furnished me fra the 27 off September 1669 to the 3 off October 1671 is some more nor 2 yeir	• 174 • 11 • 08
4 bolls– of meill–	Fryday 6 October 1671 – sent William Stewart to Edinburgh with money who boght 4 bolls off meill new meill at 6 lib. 3s. the boll is 24 lib. 12s. and off chargs – 5s. for man horse –&c is	• 24 • 17 • –
1– ston off butter–	Saturday 7 October – given John Rob 54s. with whiche he boght a ston off candle I say a ston off butter cost – 54s.	• 02 • 14 • –
1– brown– horse cost– 40 lib.–	Teusday 10 October 1671 – Mr John Clerk & William Steuart boght in Dalkeith fare – a sad broun horse off 6 yeir old come Beltoun – 1672 cost 40 lib.	• 40 • 00 • –
Archbald– More– 60 Knapel 18 rushie leather chyrs– 2–	Wedensday the 11 off October 1671 – drawen on my brother John Andersone 158 lib. 8s. payable to Archbald More in Leith Wynd wright & chyre maker at sight for the particullars under wreatin to wit – 1– 60 long large knapel at 24s. the peice .... 72–00–00 18 rushie leather chyrs at 4 lib. 16s. a peice is 86–08–00	• 158 • 08 • –
Thomas Burne– webster–	The 21 off October 1671 – to Thomas Burne webster in the Carlips for weiving 21 ell off plaiding all sort of harre graith comptit – 32s.........	• 01 • 12 • –

3– ston off butter– for smeiring– sheip	21 October – to John Rob for 3 stone off butter he boght for 3 stone of butter he boght[85] for smeiring the sheip at 4 merk the ston is 8 lib. & 12d. for weying it is	08–01–00	
barme–	For 1 quart off barme	00–04–00	
pirns & haiks	For pirns & haiks	00–06–00	
kill– & mill	21 off October – to Adam Lourie for drying 8 bolls of oats 3s. 4d. –& for for milling the said oats– 3s. 4d. is	00–06–08	• 08 • 17 • 08

Marie Douglas– brydell– which wes on Thursday the 12 off October– 1671 at Newbiging	The accompt off disbursments peyit out when John Hunter wes mairied on Marie Dowglas – which wes on the 12 off October 1671 they were mairied at the kirk off Pennycooke the said 12 of October 1671 – be Mr William Hamiltoun minister thair –		
	1– for 2 young pownie hens	04–00–00	
	2– 2 rumple peices off beiff	00–13–00	
	3– 12 pair off dovs	01–10–00	
	4– 4 pair off cunings	02–10–00	
	5– 1 pound off caipres	00–16–00	on the 9 of October
	6– 1 mutchkin off olives	00–12–00	1671 – I sent with
	7– 1 pound off great raisings	00–07–00	John Rob which he
	8– 31 prins off virginel strings	00–03–00	delivert to Geils
	9– 12 pound off butter	00–06–00	Douglas 5 rex dolors
	10– 1 pound off great raisings	00–07–00	& halff a croun is 16
15–12–04	11– 1 pound off currents	00–07–00	lib. – AB.....
02–00–00	12– 1 bust off carvie	00–07–00	
10–10–08	13– 2 douzane off rolls	00–16–00	AB: shoe disbursit

32–00–00	14– 2 whyt loaffs	00–08–00	therof 15–12–04 &	
03–06–00	15– 2 geisse	01–04–00	randert me 7s. 8d. is	
63–09–00	16– 1 once off clovs	00–12–00	16ll. – I say is 16 lib.	
	17– for a loaffe	00–03–04	as is above mentioned	
	18– for a peck off flour	00–18–00	15–12–04	• 15 • 12 • 04
63–09–00	On Saturday 7 October 1671 – given John Rob 40s. 8d. who boght these things			
16–11–00	– 1 once off canel 14s.		00–14–00	
80–00–00	– 1 once off maces		00–12–00	
	– 1 pound off currents		00–08–00	
	– 2 pound off plumb dames		00–06–00	
	– 3 for cake		00–.08 [86]	• 02 • 00 • –
	On Munday 9 October 1671 – I boght at Silver burne a young fat coy cost 17s. sterlin		10–04–00	
	Said day to John Rob – for going to Leith for 2 – 16 pynt barels of wyne		00–06–08	• 10 • 10 • 08
	The 13 off October 1671 – to Rober[t] Douglas as merchant in Leith – 32 lib. off which I have his charge on his accompt for –			
	1– 16 pynts off seck at 22s. the pynt		17–12–00	
	2– 16 pynts clairet wyne at 15s. the pynt is		12–00–00	
	3– 2 – 16 pynt litle barels to hold the same		02–08–00	• 32 • 00 • –
	1 great suger loaffe weying 6 lib. at 11s. the pound			• 03 • 06 • –

[85] Clerk erroneously repeated 'for 3 stone off butter he boght'.

[86] Clerk's entry of 00–.08 for cakes was not included in the final sum for this section.

The disbursmens anent Marie Dowglas brydell as it is –
above mentioned beginning at ABC – is to ABC heir is.................... • 63 • 09 • –

For by off our own –

3– weathers	estimat to 16 –11s............................	• 16 • 11 • –
1– hamme	suma off all the disbursments at hir brydell	• 80 • 00 • –
colle....................................		
candle	all the disbursments fra the beginning off –	
ale &c..................................	October 1671 – till the end of this syde is...	• 603 • 06 • 08

[125]

The disbursments since the beginning off October 1671 as it is
mentioned on the uther 2 syds is – 603–06–08.................................. • 603 • 06 • 08

On Fryday the 20 off October 1671 – Mr Alexander Gibsone now laird off Pentland hils or utherways St Katherin off the Hopes did meet me – at a hauch belongs to the roume off Welstaine callit the Plea Hauch – and at a litle but off land hard by a litle burne syde which lyes to the westard off the burne syde hard by & nixt to the said Mr Alexander Gibsons land – this litle but off land belongs to the Braid wood – Welstaine & Braid wood belongs to me – on James Portois now dwelling in the west syde – tenent at present to the said Mr Alexander Gibsone – 1– he wold have causd his master beleve [sic] that the said litle but off land did belong to him – so that the said James Portois did til & save the said but off land in anno 1671 & when the corne theroff wes rype in harvest being in September 1671 – I causd Cristian Ramsay who then had the Braid wood as tenent thairoff sheir the corne grew on the said but and tak it home to Braid wood thair wes 2... stuks thairoff – –

2 – and as for the Grein Hauch comonlie callit the Plea Hauch which belongs to a roume off myne callit Welstaine – 1– he spok[e] to his master to see iff I wold set the said hauch to him for payment –& when his master spok to me in James Portois name I refused absolutlie to doe any such thing – 2 when he did see that he could not prevail that way the said Portois offert a peece [sic] off the end off mucks rig – for the said Plea Hauch which I also refused to doe no treking off such bussynes – then the said Portois wold have been at the devyding off the said hauch or parting it the an halff thairoff for Welstaine the other for the west syde belonging to the said Mr Alexander Gibsone which I refused absolutelie to do – –

The said Mr Alexander Gibsone did bring with him the said day

1– on[e] Mr Alexander Gibsone bouffe[87] his brother a friend off his own –;

2– Thomas Borthwick a tenent off his own in Kirktoun –;

3– John Lawrie a tenent off his own in Logan housse –;

4– & his own man did ryde with him –;

And I had with me at the said meeting –

1– my sone Mr John Clerk– – – – – – – – – – – .

2– James Simpsone in Brantstaine – – – – – – .

3– Alexander Pennycooke in Satirsyke– – – – .

87 http://www.dsl.ac.uk 'Bouff(e)': 'A dull big person'.

4– William Thomsone then tenent in the – – – .
Towr off Pennycooke– – – – – – – – – – – – .

And when the said Mr Alexander Gibsone had tryed all he could hear or learnt at his own and my men above mentioned anent these differences occasioned by that covetous fellow James Portois whairoff never a tenent that dwelt in the west syde before – ever aimd nor spok off any such thing in end at my desyre on the said 20 off October 1671 – the said Mr Alexander Gibsone tooke the pains to go doune to Bruntstaine – to informe him selff at John Simsone the old bailyie a very honest man off 86 yeirs off age who all his days had dwelt thair & thair about –& had the Braid wood himselff many yeirs for maill paying – he stayd above halff ane hour with the said John Simpsone trying & informing himselff anent the 2 particullars above mentioned fra whom he resavet great cleirnes –& satisfaction in in [sic] both these particullars – it is to be rememberit that about 70 or 80 yeirs ago thair wes a great plea about that hauch – thair being 2 men kild then whairfor ever since it wes callit the Plea Hauch – Pentland Hils belongd then to the lairds off Rosline –& Weltstaine belongd then to Crichtoun – Bruntstaine –& since these 2 men wer kild thair wes never a word off it till now & ever since the said 70 or 80 yeirs ago – Roslins tenent in the west syde –& Crichtons tenent off Bruntstaine who had Welstaine for maill paying & thair successors did put ther catel [sic] on the said hauch & eatit promiscououslie [sic] throgh uther as occasion offert & since the said 70 or 80 yeirs ago thair wes never a word off it till this covetous crocadaill James Portois wold stur it up agane – And efter all this past the said 20 of October 1671 it seemd be his cairage which wes very discreit & peacable that he wes not pleasd with the said James Portois– Go to: ABC on the other syde –:

[126]

ABC I intreadted him & his cousin to go & stay all night with me – which he wold not grant to doe – then I desyrd him earnestlie to go & dyne with me – which he also refused alledging he wold be too late & that he behoved to be in the toun that night – then I desyred him to go to Silver burne & to tak such refreshment thair as we could gate [sic] which he granted – so we went to Silver burne & got what the[y] could afford – it is to be remarkit –

That the said James Portois went alongst to Silver burne with his master & before Mr Gibsone went to the howsse – he cald Jams Portois a syde & spok a good whyll to him – then the said Portois slipt away home very blunt & discontented lyke – in a word the said Mr Alexander Gibsone – with his cousine & my selff &c past 2 hours verie weell –& sindert very good friends & said we sould tak a chopin off wyne at Edinburgh – so that be all apearance he wes ill satisfied with the said Portois who most unjustlie wold have set him and me in a contraversie togither – at Newbiging Fryday this 20 off October 1671 –

At Silver burne the said day.. • 04 • 10 • –

John Clerk

William– Watsone– his fie– On Teusday 24 October 1671 – peyit to William Watsone 7 lib. for his fie fra Witsonday 1671 til Mertimes 1671 he wes our hynd the said halff yeir.................................07–00–00 .... • 07 • 00 • –

Mr John– Clerk a– sute off– Ane accompt fra Mr John Clerk – which he disbursit in June & Jully 1671 – off 117–2s. – 1– for cloths & uther necessars to himselff 50–2s. AB – 2– for severall uther disbursments – 52–04–04 – and spent at severall tymes.....5–7s. –& disbursit in

cloths– perseuing Michel Lowrie – 6–14s. all which coms to 117ll. 2s. – he wes a month
&c– in Edinburgh at this tyme thair is a compt wreatten with my own hand in which
compt is conteind all the particullars wes peyit out for the said 117 lib.–2s. this
compt is markit on the bak – No. 333–.. • 117 • 02 • –

Mr John Ane other accompt off Mr John Clerks disbursit he went to Dalkeith for the
Clerk bairns –& when he went to the toun with John Hunter to see Marie Douglas
contract wreatten whair he wes 3 days with the gray horse – this compt is markit
on the bak – No. 334 .... • 07 • 15 • –

Alexander Al[88] The 25 October 1671 – peyit to William Steuart for his sone Sande
Steuarts– Steuarts fie fra Witsonday 1671 till Mertimes 1671 – 4ll. & 9s. to buy a pair
fie– off shoone is...............4 lib. 9s. 04–09–00

webster– The 15 off November 1671 – to Thomas Burne webster for weiving – 6 ell
off braid plaiding– at 2s. the ell .... 00–12–00 • 05 • 01 • –

Isobell Fermer The 3 off November 1671 – to Isobell Fermer – 4–10s. for 500 double
fleurings I got fra hir in Februar 1671 04–10–00
2 pair off gloves at 11s. the pair..
3 pair off gloves for Will – Alexander – & Robert Clerks....12s. 01–14–00
E·J 1 peper off prins 00–04–06
1 pair off gloves for Luckie.. 00–07–00
For changing a chamber pot.. 00–11–00
To James Duncan cordoner for 6 pair off timber heils .... 00–06–00 • 07 • 12 • 06

1 sute off– In a compt off 16 lib. 6s. 4d. sterlin resavet fra James Clerk which I have
cloths for lying by me he sets doun for his brother Mr John his usse – 3 ½ ell of mixt
Mr John– Spanish cloth – cost 16s. 6d. the ell is – 2–17–9 pence at 15s. the testin – is

Clerk– 43 lib. 6s. Scots – I think this wes to be a cot & breiks for Mr Jo: Clerk...43–6s.
93–6s. & 50–^{2}4s.–[...]d. on this syde above markit AB[89] is both – 93–8s. for his
cloths at this tyme and becaus the 50 lib. 2s. wes set doun alreadie above –
I have onlie set doun at present 43 lib. 6s. .... • 43 • 06 • –

This compt off James Clerks is date in June 1671 ....

Mary– In the said accompt off James Clerks he furnished at his own hand without
Clerk– my order – to his sister Marie Clerk –
603–06–08 2 ell off midlin lustre taffatie for a skairffe................ 13s. 4d.
04–10–00 1 lustord hood cost – 4s. 6d. .... 04s. 6d. .. is .... 17s 10d. • 10 • 14 • –

07–00–00 Turne over – All the disbursments fra the begining of October
117–02–00 1671 – till present is – 806–07–02d. .... • 806 • 07 • 02

07–15–00
05–01–00
07–12–06
43–06–00
10–14–00
806–07–02

88 This line begins with a mistake. Having started to write the name Alexander, Clerk changed his mind and entered the date.

89 It is not clear why Clerk added the superscript '2' when he wrote '50–^{2}4s.–[...]d.' in this section. There is also an inkblot which makes part of the tally illegible. However, 'on this side above marked AB' suggests that the entry should probably be 50–2s. and not 50–4s.

[127]

The disbursments on the other 4 syds since the begining off October
1671 is – 806–07–02d. .... • 806 • 07 • 02

James Clerk a sute off– cloths &c 60 lib.–

In James Clerk his said accompt – date June 1671 – he at his own hand
unacquainting me – sets doun for a sute off cloths for himselff – stokins –
shoes – felt and other necessars – 5 lib. sterlin and this 5 lib. he tooke att
the first & readiest – off 15 lib. sterlin – I furnished him when he went to
London in summer 1671 – which wes a bold impertinent thriftles
baisse trick in him.......... • 60 • 00 • –

For wheat breid in October 1671 .... • 01 • 18 • 08

The end off October 1671 – The disbursments in October 1671 is...... • 868 • 05 • 10

November 1671 Liting– materials Stifing– blew –& blew indigo &c of divers sorts–

The disbursments in November 1671 – as follows –

The 1 off November 1671 – to Margaret Boig in the Bow for –

1– 4 lb off whyt stiffing at 3s. the pound.......... 00–12–00
2– 4 once off bleu stiffing – 2s. 00–02–00
3– 4 once off bleu indigo at 3s. the once 00–12–00
4– 2 pound off alume 00–06–00
5– 2 pound off wald 00–06–08
6– 1 pound off gals 00–09–00
7– 4 once off reid brizel.......... 00–05–00
8– 4 once off wyne ston –.......... 00–04–00

Not the lesse off what I boght as is above mentioned Luckie caused
John n.[90] Rob bring out of the toun – 3s. worth of alme & wald .... 00–04–00 • 03 • 00 • 08

spyceries–	More fra the said Margaret Boig the said day –		
gele graith	1– 4 lb off Dieppe plumb dames	00–11–00–0	
&c –	2– 1 lb off ginger	00–09–00–0	
	3– 2 lb off Bourdeaux pruns	00–04–00–0	
	4– 1 lb off currents – 7s.	00–07–00–0	
	5– 1 lb off great raisings – 6–8d.	00–06–08–0	
	6– 1 once off canel – 13s. 4d.	00–13–04–0	• 01 • 11 • –[91]
For chamber maill – 12 lib.	The 15 off November 1671 – to William Broun skinner on his discharge off the said date – for my chamber maill fra Witsonday 1671 till Mertimes 1671 – 12 lib.	12–00–00	
	To his woman the said day	00–06–00	• 12 • 06 • –
Tobaco –	2 pound off leaff tobaco at 20s. the lb.	02–00–00	
&c–	1 pound cut & dry tobaco	00–16–00	
1 weir tirles	1 pound off pack threid	00–09–00	
for dovcat	1 November – to James Thomsone – 42s. for a 4 squair weir tirles – for the inner syde off the dovcat window	02–02–00	
1 dry seat pan off brasse –	The said day to Alexander Andersone copersmith for a brasse pan for a dry seat weying – 7 lb 12 once at 22s. the pound	08–11–08	
John Cooke	The 2 off November 1671– to John Cooke locksmith on his discharge in full off ane accompt	05–16–00	• 19 • 14 • 08

90 I suspect that the 'n.' was a mistake that Clerk did not cross out before proceeding to write Rob's surname.

91 The tallies and sum are incorrect. It appears that Clerk did not include the last two entries in his sum which should probably read '2–11–'.

James Clerk–	1– to James Clerk for a grosse off whyt threid buttons	00–12–00	
1 suger–	2– to him for 8 skore & 12 made pens	00–15–00	
loaffe–	3– 1 suger loaffe weying – 3 lb 5 once at 9s. the pound	01–10–00	• 02 • 17 • –
Hew– Macculoch– 61–17–08	The 2 off November 1671 – to Hew MacCulloch on his discharge off the said date – 61–17–8d. for the thrid & last part off the new supplie & for my proportion off a yeirs pay – for the trompets & drums –& 10s. upon the 100 lib. off valued rent for mending the hie ways for my lands in Pennycooke & Glencorse paroishes date the 2 off November 1671		• 61 • 17 • 08
Arch More– 6 knapel– takits–	The 3 off November 1671 – to Archbald More on his discharge for 6 knapell – at 20s. the peice is – 6 lib. to wit 4 beitch knapel & 2 wainscot knapel is both – six	06–00–00	
	Said day to his wyffe for 1000 small takits	00–16–00	
spektakls–	For 3 pair off spektakls mountit in blak horne at 6s. a pair	00–18–00	
oynions–	For a poikfull off great oynions	01–04–00	
	5 whyt round litle boxes	00–06–08	
Bound lint– 4 ston off–	The 7 off November – to Isobell Gray for 6 ston – 3 pound off bound lint at 3–16s. the stone is	24–04–06	
salt butter	To Jennet Weill who boght 4 ston off salt butter for the usse of the housse at 56s. the stone is	11–04–00	
	The 9 off November 1671 – to Helen Gray for 16 ell off whyt mild linze winze at – 12s. the ell is 9–12s. – bot I gave hir for it onlie 9 lib.	09–00–00	
	For 5 pound off whyt confections at 11s. the pound is	02–15–00	
	400 chestins	01–04–00	• 48 • 07 • 06

Jo Reid–	14 November to Jo– Reid for 6 thraive off beir stroe he said we got		
6 thraive of–	in winter 1670 at 6s. the thraive is	01–16–00	
beir stro–	To him for 2 douzane of peirs his sone sent out off Hamiltoun..........	00–06–08	
peirs–	18 November – to John Rob for 2 pynts – 3 mutchkins of brande at		
brande–	30s. the the pynt is	04–02–06	• 06 • 05 • 02
	The disbursments in November on this syde is		• 155 • 19 • 08

[128]

	The disbursments in November on the other syde is		• 155 • 19 • 08
Mr George Barclay–	The 4 off November 1671 – to Mr George Barclay in the Queens ferrie for		
7– suger loafs	1– 7 suger loaffs weying 27 lb 15 once at 9s. 6d. the pound	13–05–06	
whyt candie	2– 4 pound off whyt candie at 17s. the pound....................	03–08–00	
broun candie–	3– 2 pound off broun candie	01–04–00	• 17 • 17 • 06
Holland–	The 6 off November 1671 – more to the said Mr George Barclay for –		
strypit taftit–	1– 17 ½ ell off Holland at 46s. the ell....................	40–05–00	
Holland–	2– 17 ½ ell off Holland at 3 lib. 6s. the ell	57–15–00	
taftit–	3– 10 ell off whyt strypit taftit Holland at 24s. the ell......................	12–00–00	
Holland–	4– 14 ell off taftit Holland at 11s. the ell	07–14–00	• 117 • 14 • –
James– Patersons– fie–	The 20 off November 1671 – to James Patersone for his fie fra Witsonday 1671 till Mertimes 1671 – 10 pound and 12s. to buy his shoone – is – 10–12s.		• 10 • 12 • –
5 firlots of malt–	The 20 of November 1671 – to William Stewart – 8–15s. for 5 firlots off malt at 7 lib. the boll which he boght fra John Hunter in Straiton toun		• 08 • 15 • –

Jo – Robs harvest fie–	The 22 November 1671 – to John Rob for his harvest fie in anno – I say in harvest 1671 –		
	1– in money for his fie	04–07–00	
	2– for his super maill	01–00–00	
	3– for bringing out off the toun 2 creils with 17 glasse botls in them	00–06–00	• 05 • 13 • –
Jennet– Barclays fie–	The 23 off November 1671– to Jennet Barclay for hir fie fra Witsonday 1671 till Mertimes 1671 – 9 lib.		• 09 • 00 • –
Margaret Hopkirk– 17 ell lining– 10 lib 4s	Saturday 25 November 1671 – to George Bell for 17 ell sharp off lining cloth which his wyffe broght to Neubiging – at 12s. the ell is – 10 lib. 4s. given him the said day – 15 merk peices and a grot is – 10–4s.		• 10 • 04 • –
Brande–	28 November 1671 – to Isobell Scot 10s. for a mutchkin off brande I got when I had the gravell	00–10–00	
Mill– Kill	27 November to Adam Lowrie for killing & milling 18 bolls – 12 peks off field oats	00–10–00	
	To John Rob for mending a Scots brydle	00–01–00	
	For whyt breid in the month off November	01–19–08	• 03 • 00 • 08
	The end off November 1671– The disbursments in November 1671		• 340 • 15 • 10

December	The disbursments in December 1671 –		
1671– 1 boll 4 pecks off malt–	Saturday 2 December 1671 – to Isobell Scot 8 lib. 10s. for 5 firlots off old malt wes got fra hir when I wes in Edinburgh in the begining off November 1671	08–10–00	

Lint seid oyll–	Said day to John Rob for a pynt off lint seid oyll	01–04–00	
Couper–	4 December – to John Davisone couper for 18 girds great & small	00–11–08	
Couper–	7 December – to Adam Buckls for girds he set on about Lammes 1671	00–18–04	• 11 • 04 • –
5 firlots– off malt–	The 7 off December 1671 – to William Stewart 8 lib. 15s. for 5 firlots off malt he got fra John Hunter in Straiton at 7 lib. the boll	08–15–00	
Adam– Lowries fie– 17–10s	Witsonday wes on the 11 off June 1671 – Adam Lowrie entert not hame till Fryday at night – 23 off the said month – the 9 off December 1671 being Saturday I peyit him 15 lib. for his fie fra Witsonday 1671 till Mertimes 1671 and for staying fra Mertimes 11 November 1671 till Saturday the 9 off December 1671 which wes 28 days – I owe him 50s. – is in all I peyit him fra the 23 June 1671 till the 9 off December 1671 is is [sic] 5 month & 16 days for which I peyit him the said 9 December 1671	17–10–00	• 26 • 05 • –
Jo Rob sold– 42 skins– for 13 lib. 14s.	The 14 December – to John Rob for his pains & horse hyre in selling – 1– 13 dracht ewes grein skins – 2– 9 shorl in weathers skins – soon slain efter the cling – 3– 18 good dry weaters slaughter skins – is in all off thir above 40 skins –& 2 weathers skins new slaine is – 42 in all which he sold for 13–14s. I gave him for his pains & horse hyre to Edinburgh – 13s. 8d.	00–13–08	
Edowart– Thomson– for theyking the east syde–	Saturday 16 December 1671 to Edowart Thomsone – 6–16s. for theyking with heather the east syde off the barne he said he wes 17 days wirking at it at 8s. ilk day with his meat bot it wes in the winter tyme he theykit it off which 6–16s. I rebated 3–12s. he wes resting me for 36 rude off fald		

off the barne– dyke I caried big on the grein fitt roume in Pennycooke at Witsonday 1671
when Edowart Thomson entert to the said roume off grein fitt it wes to Wille
Elphistoun to whom I peyit the said – 3 lib.–12s. .... 06–16 • 07 • 09 • 08

The disbursments on this syde in
December 1671 is .... • 44 • 18 • 04

[129]

The disbursments on the other syde in December 1671 is ....[92] • 44 • 18 • 08

William Burell plaiding — 19 December to William Burels wyff for 6 ell off 5 quarter braid plaiding
at 10s. the ell 03–00–00

4 botls– — Said day to hir to hir [sic] for 2 Hollands earthern pynt botls – 1 litl
earthen Hollands botle more then – a mutchkin – 1 glasse chopin botle
is 4 in all for which I payit hir 26s. .... 01–06–00 • 04 • 06 • –

Lady Bagillo — 21 December – to the Lady Bagillo for 13 ell off lining at 20s.
the ell.. 13–00–00
7 quarters off lining at 16s. the ell... 01–08–00
2 lame poringers 00–08–00
18 fadome off small tows at 14d. the fadome................................. 01–01–00
2 pound off knok lint to be threid......8s. 6d. the pound 00–17–00

James Clerk — To James Clerk for a grosse off braid whyt threid buttons .... 00–08–00 • 17 • 02 • –

brasse laidles — 28 December to Alexander Andersone for 3 brasse mouths off laidls –
weying 4 lb 14 once at 24s. the pound is.. 04–13–00

E·J.	25 December to Jhon Galloway for 11 ell off sand cullort tamen to be Luckie a goun – cost 18s. the ell is	09–18–00	
Isobell Gray	26 December to Isobell Gray for – 1– 20 ell– 2– 02 ell– is 22 ell off small hardn at 8s. the ell is	09–00–00	
Arch– More	The 27 off December 1671 – to Archebald More on his discharge 6 lib. for 2 wainscot knapel – 40s. –& for a rushie hyd weying 4 lib. at 20s. the pound is 4 lib. is – both 6 lib.	06–00–00	
	6 lb of Spanish broun at 4s. the pound 1–04–		
	1 small neckit glasse botle........ 0–06–		
corks–	5 douzane off corks great & small for botls 1–17–	03–07–00	
brande–	6 December – to Jhon Rob for 2 pynts & 1 chopin of brand[e] at 30s. the pynt	03–15–00	
E J.	20 December to Luckie wes given for heren........	00–13–03	
	Said day 1 ell off lining to be G. Clerk mutches	00–18–00	
	For breid in the month off December........	02–10–08	
		40–15–00	• 40 • 15 • –
	The end off December 1671 — The disbursments in December 1671 is		• 103 • 01 • 08

92 I have transcribed the sum as found in the original. It is unclear why Clerk wrote 44–18–8 on this page when the sum at the bottom of the preceding page reads 44–18–4.

[130]

The disbursments in January 1672 –

Accompt what I gave on the 1 Munday of January 1672 –

1– to Mr John Clerk..
2– to James Clerk... 03–00–00
3– to William Clerk 00–16–08
4– to Alexander Clerk....................................... 00–16–08
5– to Robert Clerk.. 00–08–08 ....

1– to Mary Clerk ....
2– to Margaret Clerk..
3– to hir in money off severall sorts &c 06–10–00
4– to Helen Clerk off severall sorts &c 03–00–00
5– to Jenet Clerk......39s. 01–19–00
6– to Katherin Clerk .... 01–04–00 ....

Men servants –

1– to Arche Craig the 8 Aprill 1672 00–12–0–

[blank space for a number of lines]

Women servants –

1– to Jennet Hay– 36s. 01–16–00

[blank space for a number of lines]

	1– to Mr Robert Broun schoole master	01–16–00	
	2– to John Broun bedel 12s.	00–06–00[93]	
	3– to John Rob – 6s.	00–06–00	
	4– to Sand[e] Stewart	00–04–00	• 02 • 18 • –

[131]

	The disbursments in January 1672 on the other syde is			
	1 Januar to Thomas Wolffe 1–6–8	1–06–8		
	To Bessie Gibsone William Brouns woman 0–13–4		02–00–00	
pills –	Halff a box off Doctor Andersons pils		01–13–04	
	1 reid horne spoone		00–04–00	
David Pringle –	5 January to David Pringle in full of ane accompt on his discharge		13–02–06	
Robert Sands–	Said day to Robert Sands in full off ane accompt on his discharge		06–19–08	• 23 • 19 • 06
Robt Walker–	8 Januar – to Robert Walker smith in Caldtoun in full off ane accompt on his discharge for bell nails & lozen headit nails		24–19–04	
	2 pound off candle for my chamber		00–08–00	
	5 once off tobaco – 6s.		00–06–00	
watch–mender	To Jhon Alexander for stringing a great monter & mending it		04–03–00	
	To Jhon Crichtoun – for 2 beir ris[94]		01–04–00	

93 Clerk made an error in the initial entry but corrected it for the sum in the margin. I have transcribed both as they are found in the original.

94 Rice.

	To James Mackcalzien – for making a blaid to a knyffe &c.................	00–08–00	
fir seid–	To Capiten [sic] Jhon Farsyth for 2 once off firr seid	05–14–00	
horse – medicin[e]	To Jhon Crichtoun – for 2 drinks he gave the Braid wood horse – 36s.		
	–& for his dyet – 3 nights & 3 days – 18s. is	02–14–00	
peper –	To Thomas Allen in the Bow for 2 rim off peper	07–10–00	• 47 • 06 • 04
	16 Januar – to Jo: Falconer servitor to James Steuart on his recept for		
	some drogs for George Clerk	01–07–00	
	20 Januar – to [blank] Garvin for a pair off knok strings....................	00–15–00	
	To James Clerk for a litle studie or enclume..	00–12–00	
	23 Januar – to Mr Jo: Clerk for some expense he wes at in pulling up		
	treis in Roslin wood & – setting them	03–05–08	
eygs – &c	2 douzane eygs – 3s.– 4d. – cantarides – 2s. – 2 pirns 4s. – is	00–09–04	
mill & kill	To Luckie – 24 Januar shoe peyit for mill & kill	00–14–06	
2 firikins–	On Fryday – 19 January to Archbald Campbell in my chamber for 1		
off soape –	firikin sueit soap – 7ll. 1 firikin blak soap – 6 lib. which 2 firikins Jhon		
	Rob broght fra Leith to Neubiging on Wedensday 24 Januar 1672....I		
	tooke no recept off this– 13 lib.	13–00–00	
Sir George –	The 11 off January 1672 –	20–03–06	• 20 • 03 • 06
Lockhart –	1– Sir George Lockhart wes for my Lord Balmerino		
for Balmerino –	2– Sir Robert Sinclair wes for me anent the setling off a securitie for		
Sir Robert	10000 lib. for ane appryseing which expyrd the 4 off February 1672		
Sinclair for me	on all Balmerinos lands on the south syde off forth – I peyit the		
on a consultation	consultation to Sir Robert Sinclair onlie – to wit –		
anent a securitie	1 to himselff 15 lib. 15–00–00		

on Barntoun &c–	To his man Hary [sic] Sinclair	02–18–00	
for 20000 lib.	To his man that keeps the doors	01–09–00	• 19 • 07 • –
& 10000 lib.			
Ane other – consultation with Sir Robert Sinclair ane the securitie off Barntoun &c as is above mentioned	On the 18 off January 1672 I had ane other consultation – my selff alon[g] with Sir Robert Sinclair anent the securitie off Barntoun &c above mentioned for which I peyit –		
	1– to himselff	15–00–00	
	2– to his man [blank] who did wreat the consultation	02–18–00	• 17 • 18 • –
Dolphing – toun to– Alex[r] Leslie– For wreating– 4–13–4	The 18 off Januar – to Alexander Leslie wreatter –		
	1– for wreating a band off 1915 lib. granted to Daufingtoun payable at Candlemes 1673 –& for ane assignation to the laird off Innes band off 2 sheet – to the principall soume off 3800 lib. granted to Daufingtoun also	03–06–08	
	2– to his men in drink money	01–06–08	• 04 • 13 • 04
James Broun gairner in the shank for – some busses– 18s.	Wedensday 24 Januar – to William Burrell to given [sic] to William Burrell – 18s. to be given be him to James Broun gairner in the shank for 6 dwerff aples – some glob grossiers – same [sic] rezer busses & may rolt & a slip off a vyne trie	00–18–00	
	29 January to James Mackcalien – for sharping 4 razoirs & 2 corne knyves– 8s.	00–08–00	

31 Januar to Mr Archebald Cameron for lookeing out Balmerinos
age........ 00–12–00
2– on Saturday – 20 Januar for fresh beiff........ 00–10–00
23 January to Wille Steuart to get barme 00–04–00
25 January – to James Peirie in drink money for making 2 makings –
off malt........ 00–13–04 • 03 • 05 • 04

[2 consultations on Barntoun &c Sir Ro Sinclair]
26 Januar 1672 to Sir Robert Sinclair and his man 17–08–00
29 Januar 1672 to Sir Robert Sinclair & his man .... 17–08–00 .... • 34 • 16 • –

[20 ston 6 lb off yrne at 32s. the ston......]
The 29 Januar 1672 – to John Thomsone merchant neir the West Port on
his discharge for 20 ston 6 lb off yrne at 32s. the ston – is 32–12s. .... • 32 • 12 • –

[brande – 5 chopins....]
To Jo: Fergusone for 5 chopins off brande – 1 ½ gill lesse which he
reated at 28s. the pynt 03–10–00
To Joh[n] Walker for binding a French psalme booke in octava .... 01–00–00 • 04 • 10 • –

1 The disbursments in Januar 1672
on this syde and the other is .... • 208 • 11 • –

[132]
All former disbursments in Januar 1672 amonts to........ • 208 • 11 • –

[Charges – disbursit for Mr Jo. Smith]
The 31 Januar: to Mr Archbald Cameron for ane extract off the master
of Balmerinos age........ 00–12–00
Said day to Mr James Scot for: shireff Clerk for lookeing that particullar

anent Barntoun	register off inhibitions	01–08–00	
&c–	Said day to David Piter – for lookeing the register off seasins [sic] fra		
	1640 till 1653– 29s. & 18s.	02–07–00	• 04 • 07 • –
1	For breid in January 1672 1–14s.	01–14–00	
	[blank space for a number of lines]		
February	The 2 off Februar 1672 to William Russell for lookeing the register of		
1672 –	inhibitions appryseings & seasins fra – 1640 till 1658	05–16–00	
Charges disbursit	The said day to John Ramsay 1 ½ dolor is – 4–7– & 18s. to his man is		
for Sir John	5–5s. for lookeing the register of inhibitions against Sir John Smith &		
Smith anent	his sone Mr Robert – more to his man 12s. for for [sic] lookeing it over		
Barntoun &c	agane anent a particullar against Sir John & Mr Robert Smiths – is in		
	all to John Ramsay & his man – 5–17s.	05–17–00	• 11 • 13 • –
1 table cloth – 2	The 3 off Februar 1672 – 84 lib. 9s. 6d. on his discharge off the said date –		
douzane servits	I say I peyit to John Hunter merchant the said day for a dames table cloth		
off dames	–& 2 douzane off dames servits all new – never made usse off		
2 peices off –	And 2 peices off course dornick	84–09–06	
cours[e] dornick –	The 10 off Februar 1672 – to John Cooke locksmith in the Canegate		
John Cooke –	in full off ane accompt on his discharge – 17 lib.	17–00–00	
locksmith–			

To Jenet Gray– for a horse –	The 8 off February 1672 – to Janet[95] Gray in the Canegate on hir recept off the said date – for a sad broun horse off 6 yeir old 5–10s. sterlin	66–00–00	
Mr William – Clarks 2 – nourshes [sic]	The 6 off Februar – to Mr William Clerks 2 nourishes – 2 lyg dolors	05–12–00	• 173 • 01 • 06
	4 once off leaffe tobaco	00–05–00	
	1 booke callit *A Sainct indeed*[96]	00–12–00	
	4 box wood combs at 4s. the peice	00–16–00	
32 once whyt worsit –	14 Februar to Marion Thomson for 32 once off whyt worsit 4 threid & thrie threid at 3s. 6d. the once	05–08–00	• 07 • 01 • –
To James – Clerk 8 lib.	16 Februar 1672 to James Clerk for –		
	1– 3 douzane off silk laces at 32s. the douzane	04–16–00	
	2– 2 peice off cullort cades tape at 32s. the peice	03–04–00	• 08 • 00 • –
peper– steill hemp –	16 Februar 1672 to William Lawsone for –		
	1 rim and a halff off peper at 4 lib. the rim	06–00–00	
	8 lb off steill hemp at 8s. 6d. the pound	03–08–00	• 09 • 08 • –
For cuting 20 ston – 6 lb of yrne	22 Februar to Robert Deuer– for cuting 8 gads off yrne 8s. and 1 quart of ale– 4s. is	00–12–00	
2 bolls of peys – –	The 14 off February William Steuart boght 2 bolls off peys cost 7 lib. the boll – 14 lib.	14–00–00	
	& for custome & charges off the peys	00–03–00	
	To the bairns for cok money	00–06–00	

	To Mr John Clerk for expenses – 2 Sundays	00–11–04	• 15 • 12 • –
To the good wyffe at the mill for– William Steuart 7 bolls of oats –	The 22 off Februar 1672 to the good wyffe at the mill for 7 bolls off oats craft oats at 5 lib. the boll which shoe delivert to William Steuart in part off payment off 8 bolls off oats which I sould pay him yeirlie is 35 lib.	35–00–00	
	He got them about – I say he got them – on Fryday the 26 January 1672 14 February for barme – 4s. – to Robert Crichtoun for drawing blood off the Dalkeith horse– horse & powder for his eyes – 10s. for the horse 2 night when he went in with Luckie to sie the Lady – 16s. & Alexander Clerks expensse 2 days – 9s. – is in all	01–19–00	• 36 • 19 • –
	The disbursments above in February 1672		• 261 • 14 • 06

[133]

Mr William Hamiltoun to him – 326 lib.	The disbursments on the other syde in February 1672 is	• 261 • 14 • 06
	The 23 off February 1672 – peyit to Mr William Hamiltoun minister at Pennycooke – 322 lib. Scots as a yeirs stipend for my lands lying within the paroish off Pennycooke and that fra Mertimes 1670 till Mertimes 1671 –& 4 lib. for his grasse fra Mertimes 1670 till Mertimes 1671 is both 326 lib. includit in a discharge I got fra him – date the 3 off Februar 1672	• 326 • 00 • –

95 Clerk used a different spelling of her name in the margin. I transcribed them both as found in the original.
96 J. Flavel, *A Saint indeed* (London, 1668).

E – J	2 pound off tow to be threid	00–10–00	
Harregraith	Halff a pound off casnet suger	00–03–00	
	Halff a pound off plumb dames	00–01–04	
	Halff a pound of feygs	00–02–04	
	1 once off broun suger – cand[i]e	00–01–06	• 03 • 05 • 04
A goun &	The 27 off Februar 1672 – to Agnes Clerk for a goun & peticot – 10 ell		
peticot for	off canell cullort tamen – cost 20s. the ell	10–00–00	
Agnes Clerk	4 ell off skarlet serge de challon – very fyne cost 3–10s. the ell........	14–00–00	
	3 quarters off reid serge for a band to the peticot cost........	01–04–00	• 31 • 00 • –
	For fresh beiff in the month off Februar– 6–2–10	06–02–10	
	For whyt breid in the month off February........	01–08–04	• 07 • 11 • 02
	The end of February 1672 The disbursments in Februar 1672		• 672 • 04 • 02

March 1672 –	The disbursments in the month of Marche 1672 –		
James Brunt–	The 6 off Marche 1672 to James Bruntoun – 3 lib. and his meet for thrashing		
touns fie –	in the barne efter Adam Lowrie went away fra the 14 off December 1671		
	the 2 off Februar 1672 that John Hamiltoun cam home is 6 weiks		• 03 • 00 • –
Gairden seids	The 5 off Marche 1672 to William Burrel – 3–7s. which he peyit the		
cost 3–7s.	said day – to Robert Mein for gairden seids according to the said		
	Robert Meins compt – markit on the bak – 333	03–07–00	
John Stewart	Fryday the 8 off Marche 1672 – sent with John Rob to be delivert to my –		
in the loch of	brother John Andersone and be him to be sent to John Stewart in the Lock [sic]		
Balfour for 3	off Balfour – 1 packit conteining seald compleitlie –		
once off –	1– 2 litle harden purses in which he sent about 3 once off firr seid		

firr seid	2– 5s. sterlin for gathering the firr seid		
3 lib. 8s.	3– 2 grots to pay the ports off letters – is in all sent him 3–8s.		
	4– 1 letter in the said packit off halff a sheit on 1 syde	03–08–00	• 06 • 15 • –

Robert – Clerghorne in Dalkeith 6 stone – 6 ½ pound off talon – trose weht [sic]	On Fryday the 15 off December 1671 – I sent with William Steuart who delivert the same to Robert Cleghorne candlemaker in Dalkeith –		
	1 off sheep talon – 4 stone 4 pound.......................... 4 ston – 4 pound		
	2 off oxen talon – 2 ston 8 once .... 2 ston – 8 once		
	Is 5 skore 2 pound and a halff is off trose wecht – 6 stone 6 ½ pound		
	And be his accompt off the 23 off January 1672 – he wreats that he had sent me – 6 ston off candle according to my order – and that he had resavet off talon – 5 ston – 2 pound off talon – tron wecht – and that I wold be resting to him – 14 pound off candle – and the change off – 5 ston 2 pound off talon –		
	1– the 2 pound off I say the 14 pound off candle com[e]s to	02–11–02	
6 ston – off candle	2– the change off the 5 ston– 2 pound off talon at a merk the stone com[e]s to 3 lib.–8–4d.	03–08–04–	
		05–18–06	• 05 • 18 • 06

And on the 23 off February 1672 – I delivert to Mr William Hamiltoun minister at Pennycooke the said – 5–18–6 to be delivert to the said Robert Cleghorne –& to get some rebated iff he could and on the 7 off Marche 1672 the said Mr William went to the presbiterie in Dalkeith – being on a Thursday –& peyit to Robert Cleghorne 5 lib. 12s. – who rebated only 6s. 6d. which 6s. 6d. he sent to me with John Rob with Robert Cleghorns accompt I gave him – with him –

2 halff barels – off hering –	Saturday 9 Marche 1672 to John Rob 12 lib. which he delivert to William Lawsone merchant in the Bow for 2 halff barell off salmond he causd come out of Glasgow for me	12–00–00	
brande –	To John Rob for changeing a chamber pot	00–10–00	
changing a– chamber pot	To John Rob – for 3 pynts halff a mutchkin lesse off brande at 28s. the pynt	04–00–06	
2 bolls off seid beir –	The 9 off Marche 1672 – 16 merk which he peyit to Archbald Hamiltoun in the Grainge for 2 bols off seid beir at 5 lib. 6s. 8d. the boll	10–13–04	• 27 • 09 • 04
Alexander – Hastie –	The 9 off Marche – to Alexander Hastie for a skaip to sawe the corne and a litle skaip to give the horse thair corne in – both	00–09–00	
barme –	Barme – 2 tyms	00–08–00	
salmond –	5 Marche to George Bell for a salmond	00–12–00	
dovs –	To Mr John Clerk when he went to seik dovs	00–10–00	
Findlay –	To Findlay Macknab for a lyne cord – 22 Marche	00–03–00	• 02 • 02 • –
	The disburs in Marche above is		• 45 • 04 • 10

[134]

1 cow for	The disbursments in Marche on the other syde is	• 45 • 04 • 10
Mary – Clerks – brydell –	The 20 off Marche 1672 – to William Steuart 23–16 which he peyit to Alexander Hamiltoun in the Cowdcot for a full cow to kill to – Mary Clerks brydell	• 23 • 16 • –
Jennet – Lowries –	The 20 off Marche 1672 – peyit to Jennet Lowrie hir [sic] for hir – fie fra Witsonday 1671 till Witsonday comeing 1672 –	

Fie –	1– for yeirs fie	16–00–00	
	2– & for 2 pair off single sold shoone the said yeir	01–00–00	• 17 • 00 • –
John – Rob –	To John Rob – when he went in for Marie C – 2s. 8d. for the hors[e] – 4s. to him selff is – 6s.–8d. to him for bringing out the hering – 4s.– 6d. to the man helpit him on with them – 3s. for the horse is – 7s. 6d. is in all	00–14–02	
Nicol Ramsay –	26 Marche to Nicol Ramsay – for a wyld draik & a duck	00–13–04	
	Thursday the 28 off Marche 1672 – sent with Mage Tot to be delivert to		
Jo Broun – 3 chopins off brande cost – 40s.	John Broun schoolemaster in Prestoun pans –		
	1– a Hollands botle in which he sent 3 chopins off brande		
	2– a letter to him in which wes – 3 merks for the said 3 chopins off brande – it wes seald within the letter	02–00–00	
	3– to Mage Tot – 2s.	00–02–00	• 03 • 09 • 06
Jo Pennycooke maltman for ale & halff a peck off malt	The 29 Marche 1672 – to John Pennycooke maltman for –		
	1– 3 barels off ale got the 8 December 1671 – 1 barell – 25 December 1671 – 1 barell – 26 Februar 1672 – 1 barell is – 3 barels at 42s. 8d. the barell	06–08–00	
	12 off November 1671 – a litle barel off 23 pynty [sic] at 16d. the pynts is 1–10–8	01–10–08	
	1 peck off malt got at 2 tyms – to be 2 masks for gray horse	00–09–00	
	3 pynts off ale Wille Steuart & Jo: Hamiltoun got when they tooth the harrows & 1 pynt Jo: Hamiltoun got some peys & beir to dry for grots	00–06–08	• 08 • 14 • 04

Mr Robert – Broun – schoole master –	Mr Robert Broun schoole master – entert home to the kirk off Pennycooke at Witsonday 1671 and on the 30 of Marche 1672 – I peyit to him 20 lib. as my proportion off his stipend fra Witsonday 1671 till Witsonday 1672 on his discharge date the 30 off Marche 1672 – I advanced him the yeirs stipend befor it wes due	20–00–00	• 20 • 00 • –
George – Clerks – nourishing – 14 month – &c 63–13–4d.	As apears on a long compt booke with 3 brasse clasps: on the 67 page theroff peyit for George Clerks nourishing –		
	1– to William Steuarts wyffe for 6 month & halff a ston off lint – 50s.	26–10–00	
	2– to Thomas Burns wyffe webster in the Carlips for 8 month & halff a ston off lint – 50s. is both........	37–03–04	• 63 • 13 • 04
	For fresh beiff in Marche 1672........	08–08–02	
	For whyt breid in Marche 1672	01–16–08	• 10 • 04 • 10
	The end of Marche 1672 — The disbursments in Marche 1672		• 192 • 02 • 04
April 1672 William Burrel got things in Hatoun for the yard	The disbursments in Aprill – 1672 The 3 off Aprill 1672 – William Burrell went to Hatoun & broght a sack full – 4 severall ussefull things for the yard – according to a memor I have off the same – I gave 31s. to pay for the same – he said he gave the gairner 24s. and spent 7s. with him & his men – is 31s.		• 01 • 11 • –
To Jo Clerk for 7 bolls off oats for Willm	The 4 off Aprill 1672 peyit to John Clerk in Pennycooke 7 bolls off oats at 5 lib. the boll is – 35 lib. which he delivert to William Burrell our gairner on the 12 off Februar 1672 for his boll fra Mertimes 1671		

Burrell	that he entert to Neubiging till Mertimes 1672		• 35 • 00 • –
To a –	The 5 off Marche[97] 1672 to William Findlay chapman for –		
Chapman	1– 6 pair off litl French cizers...	00–16–00	
	2– 17 ell off blak & whyt worsit at 7d. the ell..	00–09–11	
	3– 1 knyff for Wille Steuart	00–02–08	
	4– 2 boxwood combs..	00–03–00	
	5– 6 once off threid – 10s.	00–10–00	• 02 • 01 • 07
pan – cratch	3 Aprill – to Jo: Rob for halff a peck off pan cratch............................	00–02–06	
barme –	1 quart off barme...	00–04–00	
worseting –	For grein & whyt worseting...	00–08–00	
Jo: Rob p–horn	3 Aprill to John Rob for a powder horne	00–06–00	
drying oats –	6 Aprill to Arche Craig to dry 6 bolls off oats.....................................	00–03–04	
maces –	6 Aprill – to John Robe [sic] for halff ane once off maces	00–09–00	• 01 • 12 • 10
	The disbursments in Aprill on this syde....		• 40 • 05 • 05

[135]

Archbald	The disbursments in Aprill 1672 on the other syde is 40–05–05		• 40 • 05 • 05
Craig – a yeirs fie	The 8 off Aprill 1672 – to Arche Craig for a yeirs fie fra Witsonday 1671 till Witsonday 1672 – 20 lib. & 20s. I gave him which he allegit I promist him to buy 2 pair off single sold shoone for the said yeir is in all 21 lib.	21–00–00	• 21 • 00 • 00

[97] Unless this entry was already on this page before Clerk began entering information for the new month, he likely meant to write April and not March.

Jean – Steuarts fie – 1 yeir

The 8 off Aprill 1672 – to Jean Steuart hir selff 16 lib. as a yeirs fie fra Witsonday 1671 till Witsonday 1672 which fals on the 26 off May 1672 16–00–00

Sande Steuarts – fie –

The 9 off Aprill – to William Steuart for his sone Sande his fie fra Mertimes 1671 till Witsonday 1672........ 05–09–00 • 21 • 09 • –

George – Clerks buriell on Wedensday – 10 Aprill 1672

George Clerk dyed on Wedensday morning the 10th of Aprill 1672 betwixt 3 & 4 hours in the morning & wes buried the said day about 7 hours at night at the kirk off Pennycooke in the quire under the fitt gaing off the Halls seat disbursit at his buriell........

1– 6 quarters off lining for his winding sheit at 12s. the ell – I say 2 ½ ell at 12s. the ell 01–10–00

2– to John Broun for making the graff 00–18–00

3– 4 whyt breid........ 00–13–04

4– 2 pound cutt & dry tobaco 01–08–00

5– 4 douzane off tobaco pyps........ 00–05–04

6– 5 chopins off brande at 29s. the pynt........ 03–12–06

7– for corne to the horse 00–02–00

8– to John Rob – for going to the town expresslie........ 00–06–10

9– to Alexander Gray – for making the kist........ 00–12–00

10– for drink to some men at Pennycooke said day........ 00–12–00

11– 2 once lickeresse 00–02–00

13–[98] for blak chirrie water........ 00–06–00

14– 2 once broun candie........ 00–02–00 .... 00–10–00 • 10 • 10 • –

secking &	The 9 off Aprill 1672 – given William Steuart money who went to		
grein lining	Lanerik fare the said day & boght – to wit –		
	1– 16 ell off secking at 6s. 8d. the ell	05–06–08	
boght at	2– 6 ½ ell of secking at 6s. the ell	01–19–00	
Lanerik fare	3– 12 ell unblitcht lining at 6s. the ell	03–12–00	
	4– 14 ½ ell off unblitcht lining at 7s. – 2d. the ell	05–04–00	
	5– 3 milk quart – bikers	00–12–00	
	6– he wes off charges for him selff & the horse 8s. and 2s. I gave		
	him to drink is – 10s.	00–10–00	• 17 • 03 • 08
4 mure fowls	10 April – to Nicoll Ramsay for 4 mure fowls	01–04–00	
Roslin dovs	11 Aprill to Roslins man – who broght 22 pair off young dovs for the		
Drink money	dovcat	00–12–00	
16 pynts ale	15 Aprill – to Isobell Scot for 16 pynts off ale wes got the 27 off		
to Isobell Scot	December 1671 at 20d. the pynt – 26s. 8d.	01–06–08	
Couper...	17 Aprill – to [blank] Davisone couper for putting on severall girds ...	00–16–00	
Chalk....	Said day to John Rob – for 12 lb off chalks	00–05–06	
Trouts...	Said day to Jo: Rob for – 3 douzane off trouts	00–04–00	• 04 • 08 • 02
Agnes & Helen	On Munday 22 Aprill 1672 – sent with John Rob to be delivert to Mr John		
Clerk for a dyet	Clerk – 2 rex dolors to pay Hew Broun apothecar ane accompt off 5 lib.		
drink – peyit to	16s. for a bag off severall things to be Agnes and Helen Clerk a sort off		
Hew Broun –	dyet – drink for some thing troublt them & for Helens sore toe off		
apothecarie...	which I have the said Hew Broun his accompt with his discharge at		

[98] Clerk skipped over the number 12 in this list in the original.

3 chopins	the fit theroff	05–16–00	
whyt wyne	22 Aprill 1672 – to John Rob to get 3 chopins off whyt wyn to steip		
	thair bag above mentioned in	01–07–00	• 07 • 03 • –
William	Munday 22 Aprill 1672 – to William Andersone waker		
Stinsone –	For shaging & waking 11 ell off cloth for winter cots at 2s. a ell	01–02–00	
waker in	For waking and freizing 5 ell off plaiding at 1s. the ell	00–05–00	
Edinburgh	28 Marche 1671 – for waking 19 ell off blankets at 6d. the ell	00–09–06	
	For dresseing – waking & pressing 7 ell off mixt stuff – 7s. the ell	00–07–00	• 02 • 03 • 06
3 bolls off	Munday 22 off Aprill 1672 – I sent William Steuart who boght fra Hew		
seid beir –	Johnstoun 3 bolls off beir at 5–14s. the boll is 17 lib. 2s. to sawe a part		
cost – 17–2s.	of it & knok a part of it	17–02–00	
	8 Aprill – to John Hamiltoun for milling 6 bolls off oats	00–03–04	
	26 off Aprill to a chapman for some small things	00–13–08	
8 lb butter	27 Aprill to John Rob for halff a stone off salt butter	01–12–00	
	Said day to him for printed *Declarations anent war with*		
	Hollanders	00–03–04	
	19 ell of whyt worsiting at 6d. the ell	00–09–06	• 20 • 03 • 10
1 boll off beir	3 May 1672 – to William Steuart to pay to Hew Johnstoun for a boll off		
for Hew –	the said beir for knoking to the pot – 5–14s.		• 05 • 14 • –
Johnstoun for knoking to the pot	The disbursments in Aprill 1672 on this and the other syde is		• 150 • 00 • 02

[136]

The disbursments in Aprill 1672 on the uther 2 syds is........................ • 150 • 00 • 02

About the end off A[99] Marche 1672 we got off dovs to plenish our dovcat fra these under mentioned to wit –

Thomas – Cosh – for – plenish the dovcat –

1– fra the Laird off Rosling.................................. 22 pair
2– fra the Bailyie Johnstoun off Polton .... 22 pair
3– fra Mr William Hamiltoun.............................. 04 pair
4– fra Dolphintoun .... 08 pair
5– in our own litle dovcat in the south gavel off the staible & about the neidle holls in the house.................................. 12 pair .... is 68 pair –

is....................... 68 pair –

Whairoff thair dyed off them – efter they cam to Neubiging – 14 pair

So thair restit 54 pair which wes learnt to eat & fend for them selves .... 54 pair –

The 27 off April 1672 peyit to Thomas Cosh who wes about Neubiging 20 days in learning & feiding the said dovs till they could shift for themselves–

Thomas – Cosh –

The 1 off Aprill 1672 given him at Pennycoke 01–04–00
The 22 off Januar 1672 given him in arles... 00–06–08
The 8 off Aprill 1672 given him – 3 lib. 03–00–00
The 1 off Aprill given him – 12s. to pay his expensis for seiking dovs in the contrie.. 00–12–00

[99] Clerk had started to write 'April' before writing 'Marche 1672'. He did not cross out his mistake.

	The 27 off Aprill given him 9–16s.	09–16–00	
	The said day given him for a blak & whyt whelp	00–09–00	
	The said day given him to drink	00–03–04	• 15 • 11 • –
Disbursments for James Clerk in – tyme off his sicknes off a – rheumatisme	In a compt markit on the bak – 567 – which I resavet fra Mr John Clerk – whairin is conteind the moneys he disbursit for his brother James Clerk – in tyme off his sicknes which wes a rheumatisme –		
	1– 2 off Marche 1672 to Doctor Hendersone – 4 dolors	11–12–00	
	2– the 25 off Marche 1672 to Doctor Hendersone– 6 dolors & his man 1 dolor is 70 [sic] dolors – is	20–06–00	
	3– 2 lb off suger at 15s. the lb is	01–12–00	
	4– 12 limons for him – 12s.	00–12–00	
James Clerk	5– for a night cap to him – 11s.	00–11–00	
	6– for a chopin off Rainish wyne for him	01–04–00	
	7– to 2 women who waked him – 20 days	02–18–00	
	8– to Duncan Milcolme who waited on him constantlie in the day – tyme dureing his sickness – 30s.	01–10–00	
	9– more for 6 limons for him – 6s.	00–06–00	
	10– to John Bogie for a sedan with 2 horse & 2 men to tak him – to Neubiging – 11s. sterlin	06–12–00	
	11– for meat to the horse – 6s. 4d.	00–06–04	
	47–09–04		• 47 • 09 • 04
James – Clerk – David –	Peyit to David Pringle apothecarrie in full off ane accompt for drogs – blodding &c– he furnished & did to James Clerk in the tyme of his sicknes above mentioned – 37–17–8 bot it is wreatten doun efter ward		

Pringle –	on this booke in February 1673 I mean the said 37–17–8 so that it must not be set doun heir also	• 00 • 00 • –
disbursments be Mr John – Clerk – in on[e] of his – compts – markit – n°– 567 –	Ane accompt off disbursements be the said Mr John Clerk of I say in the month off Marche 1672 – which is conteind in the said accompt off 636 – 14s. Scots ballanced markit on the bak – No– 567........	
	1– 7 Marche 1672 – to Richard Hislop for a rim off fyne peper 05–16–00	
	2– said day 2 corderivs for Will & Sande........ 00–06–00	
	3– to Thomas Wedel for tinning 3 litle things........ 00–06–00	
	4– for the *Declaration against the Hollandes & tolleration* 00–02–00	
	5– spent with Mr Piter Patersone at severall tyms 00–15–00	
	6– for his dyet fra the 5 off Marche 1672 till the 27 off the said Month being 22 days at – 13s. 4d. a day........ 13–04–00	
	20–09–00	• 20 • 09 • –
disbursments – be Mr John – Clerk in ane – other compt – markit – n°– 222 – which compts ar both put togither amongit the other compts in the drawer	In ane other accompt off Mr John Clerks date 6 Aprill 1672 off 101 lib. 14s. 10d. ballanced markit on the bak – 222–	
	1– to James Broun for 10 ½ ell off serge to lyne 3 mantls for Helen Jennet & Kathein [sic] Cler[k]s at 15s. the ell 07–17–06	
	2– 1 pound off leaf tobaco 01–04–00	
	3– to Thomas Clerk tailyeur when given over efter he wes fied......... 00–12–00	
	4– the horse Thursday 11 Aprill........ 00–06–00	
	5– for his dyet fra 6 till 14 Aprill........3–12–0........ 03–12–00	
	6– for a sowrd in place off that he lost when he fell........ 06–12–00	
	7– spent with Glencorse 00–13–00	
	8– spent with Sir Jo: Nicolsone at Dalkeith & horse meit........ 01–04–00	

	9– for his dyet fra the 20 till 25 Aprill	03–12–00	
	10– for 3 horse 2 nights they wer in toun	02–08–00	• 28 • 00 • 06
	The disbursments in Aprill 1672 on this syde 261–10–00		• 261 • 10 • –

[137]

	The disbursments in Aprill 1672 on the former syds is		
William & Alexr & Rob Clerks quarter payments till the 5 off October 1672 is 6 months	On Saturday 27 Aprill 1672 to Mr Robert Broun schoole master – 1– for William & Alexander Clerks quarter payments for 6 months fra the 5 off Aprill 1672 to the 5 off October 1672 – 11 lib. 12s. is acording to a rex dolor for ilk ane off them ilk 3 month	11–12–00	
	2– and to him for Robert Clerk – fra the 5 off Aprill 1672 to the – to the [sic] 5 off October 1672 is 6 month – 48s. is acording to – 24s. ilk quarter	02–08–00	• 14 • 00 • –
	For fresh beiff in Aprill 1672	03–12–00	
	For whyt breid in Aprill 1672	01–15–00	• 05 • 07 • –
	The end off Aprill 1672 – The disbursments in Aprill 1672 is		
May 1672	The disbursments in May 1672		
22 ½ ell off whyt grograine	7 May 1672 to – [blank] Wederburne webster in the Firth for 22 ½ ell off wyt [sic] whyt grograine at 12s. the ell	13–10–00	
1 pynt oyll	8 May 1672 to John Rob for 1 pynt of oyl for crishing [sic] wooll	00–18–00	
Brande	8 May – to John Rob for 2 pynts 3 ½ mutchkins of brande at 29s. the pynt............4–4–0	04–04–00	• 18 • 12 • –

James Peirsie drink money for malt making	14 May 1672 to James Peirsie in drink money for making the last 2 makings off malt – 13s. 4d. ....the first 2 makings I peyit him formerlie the drink money theroff	00–13–04	
Tho – Burne webster in – the Carlips – horse girding –	The 6 off May 1672 – to Thomas Burne webster in the Carlips – 1– for 23 ell off horse girding at 1s. the ell .... 01–03–00 2– for weiving 19 ell off lining to be sarks at 3s. 4d. the ell .... 03–02–00 3– for warping ale for the same 00–03–04	04–08–04	• 05 • 01 • 08
4 ell off gals – for the bain – for the bairns –	The 28 May 1672 sent to my brother John Andersone with John Rob in a letter to be delivert to James Clerk 3 lib. for 4 ell off gals he boght for the bairns to sheu on at 15s. the ell	03–00–00	
5 top swarme bee skaips –	23 off May 1672 delivert to William Burrell – 50s. & 3s. 4d. for 2 pynts off ale which he peyit to Androw Howisone in Leswaid for 5 top swarme be[e] skaips at 10s. the peice	02–13–04	
Richard Twidie in Daufingtoun for helping – the bleu – gray horse	Wedensday 29 May 1672 to John Rob 3 pynts halff a mutchkin lesse off brande fra John Fergusone at 29s. the pynt is	04–03–04	
	22 Marche 1672 to Richard Twidie in Daufintoun – 12s. & the 10 off May 1672 to Mr John Clerk 36s. when he went to Daufingtoun to give the said Richard Twidie is both 48s. for helping the bleu gray old horse when it wes thoght he had the fairsie	02–08–00	
kill – mill –	20 May 1672 to John Hamiltoun for killing 14 ½ bolls off oats & 6s. 8d. & for milling them – 4s. 4d. is.............11s.	00–11–00	• 12 • 15 • 08
Accompt – E·J –	Wedensday 22 May 1672 to Lucki[e] – E·J· – 5–2–8 in full off ane accompt which shoe said shoe had peyit out in January & Februar		

	1672 when I wes in Edinburgh which accompt is amongst the rest of the peyit accompts	05–02–08	
	2 drop off mercusus dulcis for Helen Clerks to [blank]	00–04–00	
butter –	22 May to John Rob for 4 lb off butter to creish wooll	00–14–00	
	For the gray horse – horse his expense	00–03–00	
loch litches –	23 May to Helen Williamsone in Hadingtoun for 27 loch litches	00–10–00	
barm[e]....	27 May to Alexander Clark[100] [...] for a quart off barme – 4s. & a quart formerlie	00–08–00	
	27 May to Alexander Clerk – 3s. 4d. for a pynt off ale he gave Richard Twidie when he tooke the Dalkeith horse to him anent the fairsie	00–03–04d.	
Tam Wolff	29 May – to Thomas Wolff for bringing me a letter fraw my [...][101] said day	00–06–08	• 07 • 11 • 08
4 ½ lb off tobaco	30 May 1672 – to Edouart Adamsone for 7 ½[102] pound of row tobaco at 11s. the pound which he boght in Prestoun pans for me the said day	04–16–06	
James Peirse his brydell	Fryday 31 May 1672 at James Peirse his brydel – my selff & Agnes Clerk at 1 merk the peice – 1–6–8 – to the pypers 4s. 4d. – 1 quart off beir 3s. 4d.	01–14–04	
3 mure fouls	1 June 1672 – to Nicol Ramsay for 3 mure fowlls 6s. the peice	00–18–00	• 07 • 08 • 10
	For whyt breid in the month off May 01–16–04		
	For fresh beiff in the month off May 05–02–00	06–18–04	• 06 • 18 • 04
	The end off May 1672 – The disbursments in May – is		• 58 • 08 • 02

June 1672	The disbursments in the month off June 1672 –		
	30 May 1672 Mr Jo: Clerk went to Edinburgh to delyver – 5000 pound to my Lord Register and disbursit as follows		
	1– to on[e] that cairied the money to my Lord Registers housse	00–04–00	
	2– to Robert Crichton for blooding & cureing the horse boght fra Widow Campbell of the blak jandise as he said	01–06–08	
	3– for his charges – 3 days in the toun.........36s.	01–16–00	• 03 • 06 • 08
4 – June	To Jennet Lourie for a turnt cap shoe boght at Peibls [sic]	00–04–06	
5 – June	To a woman for horn spoons & threie [sic] knitings	00–14–00	
4 – makings off malt	The 8 off June 1672 to Margaret Borthwick good wyffe – at the mill for 4 makings off malt till this 8 June 1672 – at 58s. the making is – 11–12s.	11–12–00	• 12 • 00 • –
	The disbursments in June on this syde is		• 15 • 06 • 08

100 The spelling of 'Clark' here is not a mistake. This Alexander Clark was employed by Clerk and is not to be mistaken for Clerk's son, Alexander, mentioned in the next line.

101 An inkblot obscures the word on the original manuscript.

102 There is a discrepancy between the amount of tobacco listed in the margin and the amount of tobacco listed in the body of the account. I have transcribed the amounts as found in the original.

[138]

The disbursments in June on the other syde is.................................. • 15 • 06 • 08

Fyve – servants – fies –

1 27 off May 1672 to John Hamiltoun for 1 quarter of a yeirs fie fra Candlemes 1672 till Mertimes till – I say Witsonday 1672 which fell on the 26 off May 1672 – 7–10.. 07–10–00

2 3 June 1672 to Jenet Hay 30 lib. for 1 ½ yeirs fie fra Mertimes 1670 till Witsonday 1672 at 10 lib. for ilk halff yeir is 30–00–00

3 June 1672 to Nans Gourlay for halff a yeirs fie fra Mertimes 1671 till Witsonday 1672 – 7 lib. 07–00–00

4 3 June 1672 to Bessie Whyt – 17 lib. for 1 yeirs service fra Witsonday 1671 till Witsonday 1672 is acording to 8–10 ilk halff year 17–00–00

5 3 June 1672 to Alexander Clark for halff a yeirs fie fra Mertimes 1671 till Witsonday 1672 – 10 lib. .... 10–00–00 • 71 • 10 • –

14 ½ ell lead cullort grograin

The 11 off June – to Alexander Wederburne webster for 14 ½ ell of lead cullort grograine at 11s. 6d. the ell is.. 08–06–09

Scots – waters

12 June – to John Rob for 5 chopins off Scots waters at 18s. the pynt is 45s. 02–05–00

Mr Robert Alisone – his stipend 48 lib.

The 13 off June 1672 – to Mr Robert Alisone minister at the kirk – off Glencorse kirk – 48 lib. as his stipend for the lands off Cooking lying in Glencorse paroish and that fra Witsonday 1671 till Witsonday 1672 off which 48 lib. I resavet his discharge date the said 13 off June 1672 .... 48–00–00 • 58 • 11 • 09

William Andersone –

Fryday 14 June 1672 – to William Andersone waker for –

1– for liting 15 ell off linze winze at 3s. 4d. the ell is 02–10–00

waker	2– for skouring & waking 5 ell off braid plaiding at 6d. the ell..........	00–02–06	• 02 • 12 • 06
Jo – Hogens	The 17 off June 1672 – boght fra John Hogens in Pennycooke –		
1 – grograin	1– 7 ell off whyt fangrin at 13s. the ell..	04–11–00	
2 – fingrin [sic]	2– 9 ¾ ell off stenting at 7s. 6d. the ell	03–13–01	
3 – stenting	3– 25 ell off whyt blitcht lining at 12s. 6d. the ell...........................	15–12–06	
4 – whyt lining	4– 21 ell off grein lining at 9s. 6d. the ell	09–19–06	
	5– 19 ell off cullort worsit grograin – the warp twynd – double worsit at 12s. 8d. the ell	12–00–08	• 45 • 16 • 09
Edouart – Thomson for – ane ox.......	The 20 off June 1672 – peyit to Edowart Thomson in Pennycooke – a blak ox to leather & kill pryce – made and peyit the said 19 lib.	19–00–00	• 19 • 00 • –
Jenet Lowrie – brydell – 5–2–8	George Pennycooke & Jennet Lourie wes mairied at the kirk off Pennycooke on Fryday 21 June 1672 – spent at the said brydell.........		
	1– my selff & Mr Jo: Clerk – 2 merk – Luckie – Helen Gray – Helen Clark – Nans Clerk – is 4 at 12s. the peice is – 48s. is in all for – 6	03–14–08	
	2– my selff in uther companie – 28s.	01–08–00	• 05 • 02 • 08
Phisick for Robert – Clerk – 22s. –	22 June 1672 – peyit to John Rob – for some drogs to be Robin Clerk a purge efter he had the guilso...		
	1 once off manna 00–12–00		
	4 drop off reubarb.. 00–05–06		
	1 mutchkin off clairet wyne to steipit in 00–04–06		• 01 • 02 • –
John – Hogens 6 ½ ell grograin	24 June 1672 – peyit to John Hogens for 6 ½ ell off light gray grograine the warp twynd at 12s. 8d. the ell is I say – is 4–02–04	04–02–04	• 04 • 02 • 04

William – Steuart – boght in – Carnwath – fare –

On Munday 24 June 1672 boght at Biger[103] [sic] fare with my money –
1– 1 corne sled of birk 00–14–00
2– 1 other corne sled off birk 00–13–04
3– 6 firr teathers at 16d. the peice 00–08–00
4– 2 seyths at 24s. the peice 02–08–00
5– 1 pair of hizle hems 00–01–08
6– his charges for him selff & horse 00–05–00
7– given him to get a pynt ale – 20d. .... 00–01–08 • 04 • 11 • 08

couper

25 June 1672 – to Jo: Davisone for 10 girds to set on ale barels at 10d.
I say at 8d. the peice 00–06–08

Thomas – Burne – webster – 4–06–8d.

27 June 1672 to Marion Hendersone spous to Thomas Burne webster
in the Carlips 00–00–00
for weiving –
1– 19 ell & uther ....
2– 19 ell .... is 2 peices conteining 38 ell off round
lining at 2s. the ell is 03–16–00
3– for 2 warping ails for the 2 peices – 6s. 8d. 00–06–08
given hir a grot more since shoe complaind .... 00–04–00 • 04 • 13 • 04

strae berries

29 June – to Lize Reid for great strae berri[e]s – 9s. – 1 litle whyt mand
shoe broght them 6s. & 2s. to hir selff is in all 17s. 00–17–00

Richard Twidie a horse

28 June to Richard Twidie for some drogrie he used & girnt a sad broun
horse – wes boght at Dalkeith fare in anno – he broght home the
horse on Fryday 28 June & he dyed on Saturday – 29 June 02–00–00

Robert	Peyit for kill to – kill the sheip.................5s.	00–05–00	
Adamsons	On Fryday 28 June 1672 – Robert Adamsone wes mairied the brydell wes		
brydell.....	at Silver burne – Luckie – Agnes & Helen Clerks & Helen Gray – 48s.		
	my selff & Mr Jo: Clerk – 2 merks is – 3–14–8d. & 35s. 4d. in extreordiners		
5–10–0	the said day is in all – 5–10 – On Saturday 29 June I returnt whairit cost me		
3–00–0	for my selff & 3 meassons is 4 at 4s. the peice our dinner is – 16s. – to the		
1–06–8	pyper – 5s. & extraordiners the said day – 39s. is in all – 3 lib. – I gave to		
9–16–8	ilk ane off these – the first day to help to pay thair brydell laveing – 6s. 8d.		
	to wit Alexander Clerk – William Steuart – Jo Rob – & James Meygit –		
	is 2 merks – is in all this brydell cost me..	09–16–08	
	For whyt breid in the month off June 33s.	01–13–04	• 14 • 12 • –
	The end off June 1672 The disbursments in June 1672		• 247 • 01 • 08

[139]

Jully – 1672	The disbursments in Jully 1672 –		
Wil–Thomson	1 Jully 1672 – peyit to William Thomsone in the Towr for 3 bolls off		
3 bolls of seid	seid oats William Steuart resavet fra him the 4 off Marche 1672 at 5		
oats.........	lib. 13s. 4d. the boll is – 17 lib.	17–00–00	
Brande	To John Rob for 5 chopins & a mutchkin off brande at 30s. the pynt		
	is 4–2–6d.	04–02–06	• 21 • 15 • 10

103 Clerk wrote Carnwath 'fare' in the margins but 'Biger fare' in the main entry.

William –	The 4 off Jully 1672 – to William Storie in Braidwood webster for weiving –		
Storie – webster	1– 35 ell off round hardn for servants sheits at 12d. the ell	01–15–00	
in Braid wood 2–	2 ½ pecks off meill for bounteth at 6s. 8d. the peck	00–17–00	
	3– for warping ale	00–03–04	• 02 • 15 • 04
George Reid	The 4 off Jully – to George Reid at Foull foord for 3 whyt wand creils		
3 whyt wand	with handls at 6s. the peice – 18s. and 6s. for stroe berries & reim we		
creils &c–	got to our 4 hours Mr William Hamiltoun being with me is – 24s.	01–04–00	
Trouts –	Said day to Arche Andersone for 3 ½ douzane off trouts	00–05–04	• 01 • 09 • 04
Cristian –	Jennet Simpsone – daughter to Cristian Ramsay in Braid wood wes		
Ramsay in	maried on Thursday the 4 off Jully 1672 at the kirk of Pennycooke		
Braid wood hir	be Mr William Hamiltoun it wes a frie brydell at the 4 myll housse –		
daughters	1– to John Reid Mr Cooke – 12s.	00–12–00	
brydell –	2– to the pyper	00–10–00	
	3– at Silver burne for brande the said day	00–05–00	• 01 • 07 • –
William –	On Saturday 6 Jully 1672 – peyit to Margaret Hopkirk – 40 lib. for		
Alexander &	William Alexander & Robert Clerks boord fra the 5 off Aprill 1672		
Robert Clerks	to the 5 off Jully 1672 is according to – 13–6–8d. for ilk ane off them		
boord – 3 months	ilk 3 month is 40 lib. I peyit hir for the said quarter off a yeir – for		
	the said 3 bairns		• 40 • 00 • –
small salt	The 10 off Jully 1672 – to Samuel Young for 7 firlets & a peck off		
	whyt salt at 4–10s. 8d. the boll is	08–04–04	
Lady Bagillo	Fryday 12 Jully 1672 – sent with John Rob in a seald packit –		
for 14 ell	direct to Mr Jo: Clerk – 2 lyg dolors seald in a peper to be given be		
off twidle	him to the Lady Bagillo for 14 ell of twidle at 8s. the ell is 5–12s.		

	which shoe sent to Neubiging with John Rob on Wedensday 10 Jully 1672	05–12–00	• 13 • 16 • 04
Fra a chapman	The 16 off Jully – to a chap[m]an callit Thomas Stirk for severall small – necessar thin[g]s – 3–18s.	03–18–00	
Wm Broun chamber maill 12 lib.	On the 10 off Jully 1672 – be my order and with my money – Mr John Clerk did pay to William Broun skinner in Edinburgh – 12 lib. Scots for my chamber maill fra Mertimes 1671 till Witsonday 1672 off which I have his discharge date the 10 off Jully 1672	12–00–00	• 15 • 18 • –
Brande	Fryday 19 Jully 1672 – to John Rob for 3 pynts off brande 1 mutchkin lesse at 30s the pynt is	04–02–06	
Midltoun –	Saturday 20 Jully 1672 to [blank] Midltoun who cald hirself Francis Midltouns daughter and said shoe wes going to be maried on a cooke callit Peuterer who dwels at the Cresse off Edinburgh – I say given hir the said 5 rex dolors	14–10–00	• 18 • 12 • 06
168 rude of fald dyks	The 25 off Jully 1672 – peyit to John Pennycooke in Ravenshauch for biging eight skore and eight rude off fald dyks at 2s. the rude thair being 6 ell to the rude is – 16–16–0	16–16–00	
Tho–Burne webster...	The 30 off Jully 1672 – to Androu Burn webster 1– for weiving 15 ell off hardn for sheits at 1s. the ell .... 00–15–00 2– 6s. 8d. for 1 peck off meill .... 00–06–08 3– 3 chopins off ale 00–02–06	01–04–02	• 18 • 00 • 02

Fresh hering	Fresh hering at divers tyms in the month off Jully	01–01–02	
Trouts –	To Arche Andersone for trouts 3 tyms & a salmond trout	00–12–08	
fish oyll –	10 Jully to Jo: Rob to get a pynt off fish oyll for the wooll	00–13–04	
	To Jo Rob 5 Jully to pay for the horse when he went in with Mr Jo: C.	00–02–00	
	29 Jully to a chap[m]an for severall necessar things	01–00–00	
	31 Jully to Alexander Clerk to get a quart of barme	00–04–00	
drink money	2 Jully given to the good wyffe –		
to Mr Wm	1– to give the ministers wyffs midwyff 01–09–00		
Hamiltons –	2– 18 Jully to hir to give thair nourish ...... 01–09–00 is	02–18–00	
nourish–	For whyt breid in the month off Jully	01–07–10	• 07 • 19 • –
	The end off Jully 1672 The disbursments in Jully 1672		• 141 • 13 • 06

21–15–10
02–15–04
01–09–04
01–07–00
40–00–00
13–16–04
15–18–00
18–12–06
18–00–02
07–19–00
141–13–06

[140]

Agust 1672	The disbursments in Agust 1672 –			
	6 Agust for fresh hering		00–02–06	
	8 Agust to a couper for setting on 12 girds off severall seyses		00–10–00	
	10 Agust to John Rob for a pound off whyt stiffing		00–05–00	
Brande	To him the said day for 2 pynts 3 mutchkins of brande 18s. a pynt		03–17–00	
eygs…	10 Agust for 4 ½ douzane off eygs……20d. a douzane		00–07–08	
Lady Brae	10 Agust to Lady Brae for fieing Jennet Gourlay		00–10–00	
Will Steuart Carnwath fare the 10 of Agust 1672	The 10 off Agust 1672 – William Steuart boght at Carnwath fare			
	1– 4 ell off narow secking to be a seck all the 4 ell cost	01–03–00		
	2– 5 pynt cogs – cost 9s. 4d.	00–09–04		
	3– Will Steuart & Arche Craigs expense 4s. custome of 2 oxen – 1s. 4d. – grasse to the horse 4d. is – 5s. 8d.	00–05–08	01–18–00	• 07 • 10 • 02
fish oyll	[…] Agust to John Rob for 2 pynts off fish oyll for crishing wooll		01–02–00	
Barme	To John Rob – for a quart off barme		00–04–00	
Trouts	14 Agust to Arche Andersone for 6 trouts & mending bairns shoon		00–04–00	
hooks for shiring	15 Agust to Mary Adamsone for 13 hooks 48s. and a grot to hirself – is 52s.		02–12–00	
Brydell at Jo – Louries in the	Fryday 16 Agust 1672 at a brydell off John Louries daughter – I in the Log[a]n housse – 1– brydell laveing for my selff only 13–4 – 2– to			

Logan housse	pypers & fidlers – 7s. – with some gentlmen for extraordiners – 32s. 8d. is in all – 2–13s.	02–13–00	• 06 • 15 • –
Harvest gloves	The 28 off Agust 1672 to John Rob for –		
2 lasts....	1– 1 pair of harvest gloves for James Meygit 00–04–00		
	2– 2 lasts to mak shoone on 00–13–04		
Brande	3– 3 pynts 1 mutchkin lesse of brande at 30s the pynt 04–02–06	04–19–10	• 04 • 19 • 10
	Whyt breid in the month off Agust 1672 – 34s.		• 01 • 14 • –
	The end off Agust 1672 – The disbursments in Agust 1672		• 20 • 19 • –
September 1672	The disbursments in September 1672 –		
	30 hering	00–04–06	
	1 quart off barme	00–04–00	
Hislop – David 5 stone – of cheis	3 September – to Alexander Clerk 7–5s. which he peyit to David Hislop for 5 ston off cheis – litle ons off divers bignes at 29s. the ston	07–05–00	
	4 September – to Jo: Rob for a laid off lyme he got at Esperstoun – for washing the walls – 6s. to himselff for carying it – 4s. 6d.	00–10–06	• 08 • 04 • –
Skirling – fare –	Wedensday 4 September – Mr Jo: Clerk and William Steuart went to Skirlin fare with Widow Campbels horse & a gray pownie I had fra Thomas Mein to sell – they sold nothing – thair charges & the 2 horse	00–16–00	
3000 – divets	To Arche Andersone – 39s. in part of payment off 3000 divets he did cast for the housses – Alexander Falcon –& Alexander Hastie		

	dwelt in	01–19–00	
James Duncan cordoner – 4–13–6	On Saturday at night 7 September to James Duncan cordoner for 17 days at 5s. 6d. ilk day with his meit in which 17 days he made onlie 7 pair off new shoone off divers seyses & mend it – shoone all the rest of these days is – 4–13–6	04–13–06	• 07 • 08 • 06
Hew – Macculloch 90–6–8	On the penult day off Agust 1672 – my brother John Andersone peyit to Hew Macculloch for my accompt – 90–6–8 for the thrie months new supplie that wes payable at Lammes 1672 & for the second & thrid yeir for the 10s. upon the 100 lib. off valued rent for repairing the hie ways whairoff I have his discharge dat[e] the penult day off Agust 1672 & is markit on the bak – 1		• 90 • 06 • 08
Jo – Anderson	Fryday 13 September 1672 – delivert to John Rob 1 packit seald to be delivert to my brother John Andersone conteining –		
Jo – Colvin cordoner	1– six pound 8s. to be delivert to John Colvin cordoner in full off his accompt for shoone &c he furnisht to Marie Clerk befor shoe wes maried	06–08–00	
	2– and 6–12s. to be delivert to James Clerk to pay for a blak skairf & 2 ell off ribens he boght for hir when shoe wes going to Prestoun – pans to the schoole	06–12–00	
Jo – Andersone	3– & 6s. for him selff he spent with Hew Macculloch	00–06–00	• 13 • 06 • –
	On Teusday the 10 off September 1672 I gave John Rob money to pay & buy the particullars efter mentioned to wit –		

Diapanti 1– 4 once off diapanti at 5s. the once 01–00–00

John Rob 2– to himselff – for carying in to James a blak ox hyde I boght fra – Edowart Adamsone 4s. 00–04–00

To George – Bain webster 10–11–4 3– to George Bain webster – for weiving 69 ell of lining at 3s. the ell bot he gave 1 to the skore & comptit bot 66 ell is......09–18–00
To the said George Bain for soweing ....00–13–04 ..... 10–11–04 • 11 • 15 • 04

peirs – To William Baird for 8 douzane off peirs 00–08–00

Jo – Hunter John – Hunter Fryday 13 September wreatten to John Hunter & sent him – 5s. 4d. for a gallie lame pot which he sent me with a few cucumbers his letter wes under covert off James Clerk & James Clerks letter under covert off a letter I wreat to my brother the said day 00–05–04

Alexander Wedderburn webster – 20 September – to Alexander Wederburn webster in the Firth for weiving 10 ell off linze winze at 18d. the ell....................................
To him to buy a pynt ale – 20d. .... 00–16–08 • 01 • 10 • –

Disbursments in September on this syde 104

[141]

Mr John Clerk a voyage to Edinburgh – The disbursments in September on the other syde is ....

Fryday the 5 off Jully 1672 – Mr John Clerk went to Edinburgh anent the bussynes with my Lord Balmerino – Sir John – Mr Robert Smiths and me – & stayed thair till Thursday 8 Agust 1672 being 33 days – heir follows the accompt he gave me off severall disbursments & his own expensis dureing

Mr John –	the said tyme –&c..		
Clerk	1– a sand glasse for the measson to buy which they gave me 12s.	00–12–00	
	2– a pound of baline..	02–00–00	
	3– at Marie Midltouns mariage	03–04–00	
	4– 1 lb off candle...	00–04–00	
	5– 1 lb off leaffe tobaco – for my selff..	01–04–00	
	6– 2 *Confessions off Faith* at 8s. the peice.	00–16–00	
Go – to AB	7– 2 catechises – ABC..	00–01–00	
Mr John	8– for the Act off Retention	00–01–00	
Clerk for	9– for 4 lb off lead at 3s. 8d. the lb..	00–14–08	
his own usse	10– for the horse – 5s.	00–05–00	
	11– 22 Jully 1672 – to Sir Hary Sinclair – Sir Robert Sinclairs man when the provest off Edinburghs summones wes given him	02–18–00	• 11 • 19 • 08
	Accompt he gave up for things – he gave – hi: for himselff		
AB	1– to William Andersone for diping & washing		
11–19–8	a blak cot..	00–12–00	
11–06–0	2– 1 pair off stokings	02–18–00	
19–16–0	3– 1 pair off shoes	01–16–00	
43–01–8	4– 1 hatt..	06–00–00	• 11 • 06 • –
	For 33 days he wes in Edinburgh fra the 5 off Jully to the 8 off Agust 1672 at 12s. ilk day – is – 19–16s.		• 19 • 16 • –

104 Clerk did not tally the sums on this page or carry that sum over onto the next page in the original.

He gave me in his accompt off the said 43–01–08d. – on the 5 Jully 1672 when he went to the toun – I gave him with him 40 lib. –& on the 24 September 1672 I gave him in the od money being 3–1–8d. ....

The last 3 articles above is 43–01–08

James – Helen Clerks – gimp lace........ On Saturday 28 September – sent with John Rob to be delivert to my brother John Andersone & be him to be delivert to James Clerk – 36s. seald in to pay for 2 ell 3 quarters off gimp lace for Helen Clerk g gray serge peticot when shoe went to the schoole to Prestoun – pans 01–16–00

Marg – Hopkirk 5 ell off lining 20 September 1672 given to my sone – Sande Clerk – 30s. to give to Margaret Hopkirk for – ell[105] off round lining at 30s. the ell which shoe sent to Neubiging with the said Sande the said day 01–10–00

Mr – John Smiths wyffe 12 ell of small lining 24s. the ell 14–08–00 On Teusday the 24 off September 1672 delivert to our good on Teusday // Elizabeth Johnstoun seald in a peper – 14–8s. to wit 3 rex dolors – 8–14s. & a lyg dolors is – 2–16s. is as is already said – 14–8s. to be sent to Mr John Smiths wyffe for 12 ell off small lining at 24s. the ell is 14–8 which shoe delivert to John Rob the said day to be delivert to the said Mr John Smiths wyffe .... 14–08–00 • 17 • 14 • –

Mr John – Clerk for buying – 100 dails – The 24 & 25 off September 1672 – Mr John Clerk went [to] Edinburgh & Leith and boght fra James Dicksone – 100 dails being six skore for 46 lib. Scots – his expensis in going about the buying off the same ..... 1– to the gairner in Gray crooke 00–09–00

at Leith	2– for nails to nail the dails	00–01–00	
	3– to a wark man that helpit to cast & big the dails	00–02–00	
	4– the horse charges at Edinburgh & Leith	00–09–00	
	5– his own expense at Edinburgh & Leith	01–01–00	• 02 • 02 • –
	28 September to David Clark for 2 hollands cans	00–12–00	
	To a chap–man for 2 ink horns	00–06–08	
	1 October 1672 to William Steuart for 44 fresh herin[g]	00–05–08	
	12 September to Alexander Clerk a grot to get barme	00–04–00	
	24 September to Robert Burnet for 2 lb off butter	00–08–00	
	For whyt breid in the month off September	01–06–08	• 03 • 03 • –
	The end off September 1672 the disbursments in September 1672		
October – 1672	The disbursments in October 1672 –		
	2 October at Roslin – to John Cochran for a milchesir & 10 boulls to put on the poynts off the hart hart [sic] horns	00–12–08	
Leaff tobaco	4 October – to John Rob for 1 pound off leaff tobaco	01–04–00	
Brande...	Said day to him for 3 pynts off brande 1 mutchkin lesse at 30s. the pynt	04–02–06	• 05 • 19 • 02
Mr Jo Smiths wyffe – 10 ell off lining at 27s. the ell 13–10s.	Fryday 4 October 1672 – sent with John Rob seald in a peper to be delivert to Mr John Smiths wyffe – 13–10s. for 10 ell off lining at 27s. the ell which wes rat & spoyld with rain water		• 13 • 10 • –
	The disbursments in October on this syde is		• 19 • 09 • 02

105 Clerk did not identify here how many ell of round lining he received from Margaret Hopkirk. The price paid suggests that it was for a single ell.

[142]

Edouart	The disbursments in October on the other syde is		• 19 • 09 • 02
Adamsone	The 15 of October – to Edowart Adamsone for a blak ox hyde which I		
1 – blak	boght fra him the 10 off September 1672 – this ox had ane incurable		
ox hyde	disease & he behoved to kill him..	04–06–08[106]	
small – salt	The 15 off October – to John Patersone for 14 pecks off small		
	salt at 7s. the peck – is	04–18–00	• 09 • 04 • –
Will Alexr	On the 15 off October 1672 – peyit to Mr Robert Brown schoole master		
& Robert –	in Pennycooke – for William Alexander & Robert Clerks quarter payments		
Clerks –	for 6 months – to wit fra the 5 off October 1672 untill the 5 off Aprill 1673		
quarter –	is 6 month is – 14 lib. – to wit for William & Alexander Clerks – for 6 months		
payments –	4 rex dolors is – 11–12–00 & for Robert Clerk for the said 6 months – 48s.		
	is in all for the 3 till the 5 off Aprill 1673 – 14 pounds........................		• 14 • 00 • –
Jo Smith in	Fryday the 18 off October 1672 boght fra John Smith in Achnouns hill		
Achnouns – hill	the meir and horse under wreatten – to wit –		
1 – horse	1– a gray horse for the ston sled which cald 7 yeir come May 1673 –		
1 – meir	for which I peyit him in money – 35 lib. Scots 35–00–00		
	And a gray stond staig I had fra Thomas Mein cost...15–00–00	50 lib.	
	More boght fra the said John Smith the said day –		
	1– a sad gray cullort young meir off 4 yeir old com[e]		
50–00–00	the 3 off May 1673 – for which I peyit him in		
89–05–00	money.. 23–00–05		
139–05–00	And a blak horse – I boght fra Jennet Gray Widow –		
	Campbell in the Canegat cost me – 66 lib. 66–00–00	89 lib. 5s.[107]	

	Peyit to the said John Smith – for the horse & meir above mentioned		• 139 • 05 • –
James – Adamsone plumber 122 lib. 4s.	The 19 off October 1672 – compleited & peyit to James Adamsone the full peyment off ane accompt off 122–10s. for furnishing lead for the top off the dovcat & for the warkmanship theroff –& for some other lead I got for some other usses – which lead wes employed & layd on the dovcat in the begining off November 1671 – according to ane accompt which I have markit – 339 – on which accompt is the said James Adamsone his discharge off the said 122–4s. & off all uther accompts generallie whatsomever that ever wes betwixt the said James Adamsone & me preseiding the said 19 off October 1672 which accompt is lying amongst uther lead compts in a peper bag – in a reid box lyke a booke which – box is lying in the yrne tronk		• 122 • 04 • –
	19 October – to Alexander Clerk to get barme – 4s.	00–04–00	
	To Jo Rob – 2s. for a lipe off oats for the gray horse	00–02–00	
	22 October – to Jo Rob when he went to Prestounpans with Helen Clerks cloths & coffer – 2s. for the horse & a grot to drink	00–06–00	
	21 October – to Androw Mackgie couper for girds great & small & for girding severall looms pontions & barells great & small	02–06–04	
	To Will Lishman for 2 douzane off eygs for the gray horse	00–03–04	
	To Alexander Clark to get barme for baiking	03–03–04	• 03 • 05 • –

[106] Clerk did not enter the 8 pence from this entry in the sum in the margin.
[107] It appears that Clerk made an error in tallying 89 lib. 5s. when his entries add up to 89–00–05.

William –	The 27 off October 1672 – to Wille Watsone 11 lib. which compleits		
Watsons –	him 2 halff yeirs fie is a yeir and that fra Mertim[e]s 1671 till Mertimes		
fie for a yeir	1672 according to 7 lib. off fie & 9s. for a pair off shoone ilk halff yeir		
	is 14 lib 18s. in the said haill year		• 14 • 18 • –
Helen –	On Thursday the 24 off October 1672 – Helen Clerk entert in boording		
Clerks	in the housse off Katherin Sinclair in Prestoun pans to whom I peyit		
boord to	the said day – 40 lib. for hir boord for 6 months – to wit fra the 24 off		
Katherin –	October 1672 untill the 24 off Aprill 1673 is according to 20 lib. ilk 3		
Sinclair –	month..	40–00–00	
in Prestoun –	To hir woman in drink money – callit Geils Gray	01–09–00	
pans –	My own charges & Alexander Clarks and 2 horse being 2 days & a		
	night in Prestounpans	03–11–00	• 45 • 00 • –
Dalkeith	The 26 off October 1672 to Robert Hardie in Dalkeith for –	ABC	
ashes –	1– 66 ashes whairoff 2 plains in all – 66.................. 03–00–00		
plains –	2– 10 aple imps......................		
imps &c	3– 3 chirrie imps		
as is under	4– 1 peir imp........................		
mentioned	5– 1 aple stock......................		
	6– 1 plumb stock..................		
	7– 3 box litle treis................. for all these		
	I peyit..................... 07–06–00	10–06–00	• 10 • 06 • –
	Said day to Patrik Logan – for 1 peis trie – 1 aple off paradysse –		
	1 yellow rose – 1 hundreth leaf rose – 1 muslrien trie bears a purp[l]e		
	flowr smels lyke civit – 1 handle for a sneding knyffe – 1 handle off a		

	gemlit – 1 handle off a hooke without teith for cutting & cleiring hashrie about the roots off busses &c & for helping to pow the barren treis boght fra Robert Hardie 20s.	01–00–00	
	To Mathew Michel for some small things I got fra him	00–06–08	
	I wes a day & 1 night at Dalkeith my selff Alexander Clark & 2 horse which wes off charges	02–10–04	
	At Waleys foord to Patrik Widerspoons – 13–4d. & for drink – to the meassons & barrow men – & wrights – 8s. 8d.	01–02–00	
	Fra ABC to this A: ABC........4–19s.	04–19–00	• 04 • 19 • –
	The disbursments in October on the other syde & this is 382–10–2		• 382 • 10 • 02

[143]

	The disbursments in October on the other syde & this is 382–10–2		• 382 • 10 • 02
goosse pens	24 October for 400 goose pens at Prestoun pans	00–12–00	
Mr – Jo Clerk –	26 October – to Mr Jo – Clerk for a voyage to Achinouns Hill – 15s. & for gathering ashe & holin seid – 6s. & a pynt ale at Androw Burns when he went to sie a gray horse	01–02–08	
barme	29 October for barme	00–04–00	
Dalkeith –	Said day Alexander Clerk – to Jo: Rob & 2 horse went to Dalkeith to bring home barren treis & imps &c boght thair – thair charges	00–16–00	
kill mill	To James Meygit for kill & mill – 5 bolls & 1 firlet off oats	00–03–04	• 02 • 18 • –

William Stewart	Wedensday 30 October 1672 – William Stewart went to the toun & boght with my money			
	1– 3 ston off butter for smeiring sheip at 55s. the stone		08–05–00	
butter –	2– 3 ston off butter for the usse off the housse at 56s. a ston		08–08–00	
butter –	3– for oynions – 7s. 4	00–07–04		
&c–	4– for his own & horse charges – 4s.	00–04–00		
	5– custom ... 4d.	00–00–04		
	6– for weying 6 ston off butter ...4s.	00–04–00	00–15–08	• 18 • 08 • 08
	Whyt breid in the month off October ... 26s.			• 01 • 06 • –
	The end off October 1672: The disbursments in October 1672 ... 405–02–10			• 405 • 02 • 10
November 1672	The disbursments in November 1672 –			
John Robs harvest fie	1 November – to John Rob for his harvest fie 1672 – 1 ½ dolor – 04–07s.& 20s. for his supper 20s. is in all		05–07–00	
12 – oxen – bows – 36s.	Hallow fare – Wille Stewart boght 12 oxen ash bows at 3s. the peice		01–16–00	
dunce [sic] laces –	2 November – 30 duns laces		00–04–00	
Scots grograine	1 November – 7 ¾ ell off double Scots grograine to be dyed a cloth – cullor at 12s. the ell is 4–13 with a litle blew in it		04–13–00	• 16 • 07 • –
Jenet Hays fie –	The 9 off November 1672 – to Jennet Hay for hir fie fra Witsonday 1672 till Mertimes 1672 – 3 rex dolors shoe wes the halff off this halff yeir at Aire & seik at Neubiging not the lesse I gave hir the said		08–14–00	

aples – 8 November to John Steill for 5 douzane off great aples – 25s. and a
hering – douzane off fresh hering – 2s. is 01–07–00
8 whyt – mand 11– a November – to George Reid for.................8 whyt wand mands
baskits – at 6s. the peice with whyt hands – all off whyt wands .... 02–08–00 • 12 • 09 • –
George Reid

AB – On Munday the 11 off November 1672 – sent with John Rob seald in a
Mr John peper which he deliver to Mr John Smiths wyffe to pay the particullars –
Smiths – under wreatten which shoe boght fra Robert Handesyde for my usse to witt [sic] –
wyffe – for 1– 5 ston off bound lint at 4 lib. 10s. the ston is....... 22–10
lint fra 2– 1 pair off tow cairds 00–18 23–08–00
Robert – I have Robert Handesyds compt with his discharge
Handsyde– theron for the said 23 lib 8s. –
&c– More on Teusday the 12 off November 1672 wreatten to Mr John
Smiths wyffe & sent hir seald in a litle pakit 4–17–6d. to pay the
under wreatten particullars which shoe got fra the said Robert
Handesyde and sent out with John Rob the said day ....
1– ane other ston off the said bound lint 04–10–00
23–08–00 2– 1 pound off beirded tow at 6 lib. the stone......... 00–07–06 04–17–06
04–17–06 And on the said 11 off November 1672 sent hir when I sent the 23 lib.
00–09–08 8s. above mentioned – I sent hir also the said day for the particullars
28–15–02 under mentioned 9s. 8d. 00–09–08
1– for spinels being 7.. 3–4d.
2– 4 whorls 1–4

3– for arles to a woman – Steuart........................... 3–0
4– for arles to a woman –Cooke 2–0 00–09–08–
all above fra AB – to this AB is.......... 28–15–02 • 28 • 15 • 02

Alexander & Katherin Clerks – sick– I–nesse off the fever–

12 November 1672 – John Rob went to the toun & boght thes[e] things
when Alexander & Katherin Clerks had the fever –
2 lb off Deip pruns 00–06–00
2– halff ane once off maisses 00–08–00
3– 1 chopin off clairet wyne .... 00–09–00 ....
4– A ~~rots~~ grots worth off tamarins .... 00–04–00.......... 01–07–00

George Clerk webster

13 November to George Clerk webster for weiving 6 ell of plaiding
at 18d. the ell.. 00–09–00

Patrik.... Dicksone – 46–00–00 for 100th dails

On Munday the 11 off November 1672 – Mr John Clerk went to
Edinburg to whom I delivert 46 lib. seald in a peper with which he
peyit to Patrik Dicksone merchant ane accompt off the lyke soume
off 46 lib. for 100 dails Mr Jo: Clerk boght fra him the 25 off September
1672 according to his discharge at the fitt off the said accompt date 13
off November 1672.. 46–00–00 • 47 • 16 • –

The disbursments on this syde in November 1672 is .... • 105 • 07 • 02

[144]

To William – Home – 33–16–8

The disbursments on the other syde in November 1672 is.................. • 105 • 07 • 02
The 14 off November 1672 – Mr John Clerk having money off myne in
his hands & be my order peyit to Agnes Peacok spous to William Home

for 2 gallons off seck & 2 gallons off clairet – 33–16–8	merchant in Edinburgh – 33–16–8d. in full off ane accompt for ane gallon off sek & a gallon off clairet wyne – I say for 2 gallons off seck & 2 gallons off clairet wyne resavet – the 9 off Aprill 1672 – according to hir discharge theroff on the said accompt date the date the 14 off November 1672 – on the said accompt William Home subscryved ane warrant to pay hir the said – 33–16–8		• 33 • 16 • 08
oynions –	3 douzane off oynions........	00–04–06	
Dalkeith aples–	15 November 1672 Alexander Clerk gave for 5 douzane off aples in Dalkeith – 10s. .... 10–0 For corne for the gray horse........ 02–0 For 1 pynt ale he tooke 01–8	00–13–08	• 00 • 18 • 02
Robert – Cleghorne in Dalkeith – 18–13–4	On Munday the 11 off November 1672 – I sent William Stewart to Dalkeith who broght fra Robert Cleghorne candle maker in Dalkeith 7 ston off candle off divers sorts – at 4 merk the ston is	18–13–04	
for 7 ston off candle at 4 merk the ston is – 18–13–4	I sent him off our own talon the said day with William Steuart 1– a ston & eleven pound off oxen talon........	1 ston 11 pound	
	2– off sheip talon – a ston and 17 pound........	1 ston 17 pound	
	Is 3 ston 8 lb in all tron wecht........	3 ston 8 pound	
	For the said 3 ston 8 lb off talon tron wecht he allowed & rebated onlie	06–17–06	
Robert Cleghorn – in Dalkeith –	The 15 off November sent Alexander Clerk to Dalkeith & gave him 11–15–10d. which he payit to the said Robert Cleghorne the said 11–15–10 & tooke his discharge on his accompt for the same	11–15–10	
		is 18–13–04	• 18 • 13 • 04

George Clerk	18 November – to George Clerk webster for 8 ½ ell off canel cullort		
8 ½ ell – canell	cloth about 3 ½ quarter braid at 25s. the ell is – 17s. sterlin & 8 pence		
cullort cloth –	is 10–12s.	10–12–00	• 10 • 12 • –
George Reid 3	19 November – to George Reid for 3 whyt wand creils	01–10–00	
whyt wand creils	On the 30 off October 1672 – I resavet a letter fra James Clerk with a		
James Clerk	compt on it off 16–12–6 he had disbursit for divers necessars for		
16–12–6	himselff & on Teusday 19 November 1672 I wreat to him & sent him		
for divers	with John Rob seald in a peper the said 16–12–6	16–12–06	• 18 • 02 • 06
necessars			
Robert	On Teusday the 19 off November 1672 – I sent William Burrell to Dalkeith		
Cleghorne	who resavet fra Robert Cleghorne candle maker thair & peyit him with my		
8 peir &	money for the same to wit –		
aple imps	1– 4 peire imps at 30s. the peice	06–00–00	
cost 9 lib.	2– 3 aple imps and a lesser peir imp	03–00–00	• 09 • 00 • –
	William Burrels & the horse charges wes 5s. 10d. when he went to Dalkeith		
	for the imps above mentioned	00–05–10	
Jean Stewarts	The 14 off November 1672 peyit to Jean Stewart for hir fie fra Witsonday		
fie halff	1672 till Mertimes 1672 shoe went away to Mathew Woods		
a yeir	at Mertimes 1672	08–00–00	• 08 • 05 • 10
Alex^r Grays	16 November – to Alexander Grays wyffe for helping to dicht lint –		
wyffe	6 days	00–06–00	
barme...	1 quart off barme	00–04–00	
hering...	32 hering	00–04–00	

stiffing & 2 pirns &c...	18 November – to John Rob for 1 lb of whyt stiffin – 4s. 1 once off blew stiffings – is – 2 pirns 4s. is in all – 9s.	00–09–00	• 01 • 03 • –
Archbald Craig his fie for a yeir – fra Witsonday 1672 till Witsonday 1673	On the 9 off November 1672 – peyit to Archbald Craig 20 lib. for a yeirs fie fra Witsonday 1672 till Witsonday 1673 I advanced him this money before hand – I wes not obliged to pay him till Witsonday 1673 bot at his earnest desyre I advanced him the said 20 lib. becaus he said he wes hard craved be on fra whom he had boght some hogs & he could not get in his own whair it wes oweing him to pay the same with	20–00–00	
21 lib. –	The 21 off November 1672 – given him 20s. to buy 2 pair off single sold shoone for 2 halff yeirs fra Witsonday 1672 till Witsonday 1673	01–00–00	• 21 • 00 • –
William Broun 12 lib. for – chamber maill fra Witsonday 1672 till Mertimes 1672	On the 12 off November 1672 – sent with John Rob seald in a peper which he delivert to Mr John Clerk – 12 lib. Scots he peyit the same to William Broun for my chamber maill fra Witsonday 1672 till Mertimes 1672 and sent Mr William Brouns discharge off the same date the 20 off November 1672		• 12 • 00 • –
Jennet Gourlays fie	The 23 off November 1672 – to Jennet Gourlay for hir fie fra Witsonday 1672 till Mertimes 1672 – 7 lib.		• 07 • 00 • –
Bessie de – Vaitch fie	The 23 November 1672 – to Besse Vaitch – 8 lib.[108] for hir fra Witsonday 1672 till Mertimes 1672		• 08 • 10 • –

[108] Clerk added another entry for Besse Vaitch for 10s. at the bottom of the page. He added that 10s. to the sum here.

Soma off all the disbursments in November 1672
on the other syde & this...is........ • 254 • 08 • 08

Said 23 November to Bessie Vaitch
for a pair off single sold shoone..........10s. –

[145]

Alex[r]– Gray	The disbursments on the other 2 syds in November 1654[109] is..............................254–08–08..		• 254 • 08 • 08
11 ½ ell of plaiding	The 23 off November 1672 to Alexander Gray for 11 ½ ell off whyt plaiding at 6s. the ell	03–09	
John Rob 1 horse hyde	23 November 1672 – to John Rob for 1 ane horse hyde he boght fra James Broun 03–00–00		
reubarb –	Halff ane once off reubarb 00–09–00		
1 chopin – clairet wyne–	½ chopin off clairet wyne 00–09–00	03–18	
James Clerk – 9 ell off serge –	On Munday the 25 off November 1672 – sent to James Clerk with John Rob – 6 lib. Scots seald in a peper to pay 9 ell off sad cullort serge he sent out to Newbiging to lyne 2 mantls to his sister – Margaret & Agnes Clerks – at 13s. 4d. the ell	06–00–00	• 13 • 07 • –
Tomas Burne – webster 20 ell off – plaiding –	The 25 off November 1672 to Thomas Burne webster for weiving 20 ell off plaiding with reid and yellow sprangs at the syds at 20d. the ell is	01–13–04	
	For warping ale – 3s. 4d.	00–03–04	

Alexander Wederburn – 38 ell off – whyt serge –	26 November – to Alexander Wederburne weiver for 38 ell off whyt serge at 12s. the ell – I boght it fra him on Teusday the 26 off November 1672 – is – 22–16s.	22–16–00	
3 pynts of Scots waters	The 27 off November – to Isobell Scot for 3 pynts off waters – a gill lesse at 20s. the pynt – I drank the gill my selff....................................	03–00–00	• 27 • 12 • 08
	For whyt breid in the month off November – 36s. 8d.		• 01 • 16 • 08
	The end off November 1672 — The disbursments in the month off November 1672 is – 297–05..............		• 297 • 05 • –

December 1672	The disbursments in the month of December 1672 –		
D: Glendining 7 – great cheis weing [sic] – 8 ston wecht	Munday the 2 off December 1672 – boght fra David Glendining – 7 great cheis – made in Fingland – hard be Hakshawe – about 21 myll fra Newbiging which 7 cheis weyd 8 ston wecht....at 38s. the ston...........	15–04–00	
3 bols off beir fra Patrick Craig 15–5s.	On Munday 9 December 1672 to Patrik Craig in the Towr for 3 bols off beir – William Stewart & James Meygit resavet fra him the 9 off November 1672 at 5 lib. 1s. 8d. the boll – is 15 lib. 5s. – 1 boll sent to the mill – 1 boll given for knoking & the thrid boll wes layd in the new housse – is in all – 3 bolls	15–05–	• 30 • 09 • –
To John – Thomson – for a barrell off	On the 1 off November 1672 – William Steuart boght fra John Thomsone neir the West Port – a barrell off tarr – for 10 lib. and gave 6s. in earnest theroff and on Fryday the 13 off December 1672 – I delivert		

109 It is unclear why Clerk wrote '1654' instead of '1672' in this entry. The sum here matches the sum at the bottom of the previous page.

tarr – 10 lib. to John Rob 9 lib. 14s. to be delivert be him to the said John Thomson
which compleits 10 lib. for the said barrell off tarr 10–00–00

E•J• 7 & 2 is 9 ell off lining

The 10 off December 1672 taken att for lang Luck[i]e –
1– 2 ell off small lining for [blank] pair hand cuffs at 20s.
the ell is 2 lib. 2–00–00
2– 7 ell lining to be [blank] aprons at 13s. 4d.
the ell.. 4–13–04 06–13–04

Margaret Agnes – Clerks in tyme of thair sicknes in the fever

Fryday 13 December 1672 – to John Rob for –
1– a chopin off clairet wyne.................................. 00–09–00
2– a chopin off seck.. 00–18–00
3– 1 once off tamarins 00–03–00
4– [blank] lb off Bordeaux pruns .... 00–06–06.......... 01–16–06 • 18 • 09 • 10

Thomas Burne webster 38s.

Saturday 21 December 1672 – to Thomas Burne webster for
1– weiving 24 ell off blanketing with reid sprainges at the
selvidg at 1s. the ell.. 01–04–00
2– for 1 ½ peck off meill.. 00–10–00
3– for warping ale .... 00–04–00 • 01 • 18 • –

James Brown tanner 17 Decem[r] 1672

The 17 off December 1672 – compleited James Broun tanner at the
West Port and accompt off 17 lib. 10s. bot I must set doun only heir
bot 9 lib. 10s. for tanning 2 oxen hyds – 5 lib. & for taning & currieing
2 cows hyds – 4 lib. 10s. is – 9 lib. 10s. – for the 8 lib. to mak up the
17 – 10s. it is all ready set doun on this booke – too wit for a blak cows
hyde tand – & curried – 5 lib. & for a tand horse hyde – 3 lib. is – 8 lib – –
I have his accompt off the said 17–10s. with his discharge at the fit thairoff

date 17 December 1672 – bot for the reason above mentioned – I set only
doun heir – 9–10s. .... • 09 • 10 • –

A voyage to Prestoun pans to see Helen Clerk

On Thursday the 26 off December 1672 – I went to Prestoun pans to see my dear litle daughter – Helen Clerk – & tooke with me Mr William Hamiltoun minister & Edowart Adamsone –:

1– our expensse off men & horse – &c 05–19–00
2– for 10 douzane off aples 01–01–08
3– to a servant woman of Katherin Sinclairs wher Helen Clerk was boordit – a merk peice .... 00–13–04 • 07 • 14 • –

The disbursments above in December 1672 .... • 68 • 00 • 10

68–00–10d.

[146]

The disbursments in December – 1672 – on the other syde is .... • 68 • 00 • 10

George Clerk webster

The 30 off December 1672 – to George Clerk webster for weiving –
1– 28 ell off plaiding at 12d. the ell 01–08–00
2– for 1 ½ peck off meill 00–10–00
3– for warping ale .... 00–03–04 • 01 • 01 • 04

kill – mill

5 December – to James Meygit for killing – & milling – 26 bolls off oats 00–16–08

leaffe tobaco

23 December – to Jo: Rob for 2 lb off leaffe tobaco 02–08–00

pruns.... 3 ½ lib.

30 December – to Jo: Rob for 3 ½ lb off pruns 00–09–04

30 December I sent Sanders Clerk to Prestoun pans – to tak Helen

Clerks measur to mak hir a mourning sute & see how shoe wes in hir
healt – his & the horse charges wes ....
Whyt breid in the month off December – 2–5s. .... 01–00–00 • 04 • 14 • –

68–00–10 All the disbursments on the other syde & on this
01–01–04 syde above in December 1672 – 73–16–2 .... • 73 • 16 • 02
04–14–00
73–16–2

On Fryday the 20 off December 1672 – my dear & weell beloved daughter
(& blissed angel) Agnes Clerk – departed out of this vaile off miserie –
about 10 hours in the morning the said day – A B:

The 17 off December 1672 – to Doctor Hendersone –
1– to himselff – 12 rex dolors 34–16–00
2– to his man – 2 rex dolors .... 05–16–00 • 40 • 12 • –

To Robert Dewer for yrne wark to the kist –
1– 3 pair off handles ....
2– 18 nooke bands ....
3– six skore shorne headit nails ....
4– 12 skrew nails ....all.......... • 05 • 06 • –

For 5 ½ ell off fyne tich small lining at 20s. the ell .... • 05 • 10 • –

The [blank] off [blank] 1673[110] – to Robert Douglas for –
11 pynts off seck at 24s. the pynt 13–04–00
10 pynts off brande at 29s. the pynt .... 14–10–00 • 27 • 14 • –

James Clerk disbursit at Edinburgh with the money I gave him –
1– 2 back seyse off beiff 02–16–00

Item	Amount	Total
2– 4 douzane off rolls at 8s. the douzane	01–12–00	
3– 8 great whyt loaffs at 6s. the peece [sic]	02–08–00	
4– 10 douzane off tobaco pyps at 18d. a douzane	00–15–00	
5– a creill to cary them in	00–04–06	• 07 • 15 • 06
1– halff ane once off olium rhodium	01–16–00	
2– 2 once off oyll off aspeck	00–08–00	
3– halff a pound off cuming seed	00–06–00	
4– 2 glasses to put the oyls in	00–02–00	
5– 2 barrels to put the seck & brande in	01–08–00	• 04 • 00 • –
1– 4 lb off tobaco cut & dry at 18s. the pound	03–12–00	
2– 2 lb cut & dry tobaco at 14s. the pound	01–08–00	
3– for expensse off men & horse	02–02–08	• 07 • 02 • 08
24 December 1672 – to Helen Patersone for 2 barels of ale	04–05–00	
For severall expresses sent to the toun & with letters – for the buriell	03–12–08	• 07 • 17 • 08
The day the buriell wes on – Teusday the 24 December 1672 –		
1– for the mort cloth – a rex dolor	02–18–00	
2– to the – B: – 2 rex dolors	05–16–00	
3– to Jo: Brown – bedel for making the graffe	01–09–00	
4– to Alexander Falcon for helping to mak the graffe	00–12–00	• 10 • 15 • –

110 Unclear if this entry was added later or if he mis-wrote 1673. There is nothing in the original to guide the reader.

On Thursday 27 December 1672 – to Doctor Hendersone when he cam to Newbiging to see Jennet & Katherin Clerks – the said day I went my selff to Prestoun pans with Edowart Adamsone to see Helen Clerk – and in my absence – Mr John Clerk gave the said day to – gave to
Doctor Hendersone – 9 rex dolors 26–02–00
And to his man – a rex dolor .... 02–18–00 • 29 • 00 • –

On Teusday the 31 off December 1672 when Mr Jo: Clerk went to Edinburgh –& the said day I gave him the 29 lib. above mentioned which he gave to doctor Hendersone –& his man ....

Soma off all above fra AB to
this AB is – 145–12–10 .... • 145 • 12 • 10
Turn over;

[147]

The disbursments in December 1672 at this on the other syde is .... • 73 • 16 • 02

James Duncan cordoner – for 24 days

The disbursments on the other syde in December 1672 – fra AB up by to AB doun by at the end off the syde is – 145–12–10 .... • 145 • 12 • 10

On Teusday – 3 December 1672 – to James Duncan cordoner for 12 days he wroght with his meat at 5s. 6d. ilk day 03–06–00
On Saturday 14 December 1672 – to the said James – for 12 days wark more at 5s. 6d. ilk day .... 03–06–00 • 06 • 12 • –

Thomas –

In December 1673[111] – thair wes ane accompt off severall things got fra

Margin note	Entry		Amount
Hendersone – apothecary 30–01–00	Thomas Hendersone apothecarrie when the bairns wes sick off the fever which accompt did amont to 30 lib. 1s. Scots which 30–01 – Mr John Clerk did pay (with my money) to the said Thomas Hendersone apothecarie – according to his discharge at the fit of the said compt date the 2 off January 1673		• 30 • 01 • –
Hew Brown apothecarie – 7–18–0	On Teusday 21 January 1672[112] – sent with John Rob seald in a peper – 7–18s. to be delivert to Mr John Clerk to pay Hew Browns compt – apothecarie off the lyke soume off 7–18s. for drogs got fra him for Agnes Clerk		• 07 • 18 • –
Margaret Clerks – mourning gown &c for hir dear sister – Agnes Clerk	The accompt off a mourneing gown &c wes taken att for Margaret Clerk which accompt wes date the 17 off January 1673 – I have the accompt lying by me with James Clerk his recept or discharge at the fitt theroff – off – 49–05–06		
	1– 15 ell off blak wirsit grograin at 24s. the ell	18–00–00	
	2– halff ane ell of blak serge	00–07–00	
	3– 4 ½ ell off blak rubens at 5s. the ell	01–02–06	
	4– ane love band	03–12–00	
	5– ane pair off love cuffs	03–12–00	
	6– ane pair off taffatie cuffs	02–08–00	
	7– ane love hood	03–00–00	
	8– ane lustert hood	03–12–00	

111 This is likely a dating error. I have transcribed it as found in the original.

112 This is likely a dating error. I have transcribed it as found in the original.

9– 7 ell off love ribens at 3s. the ell 01–01–00
10– a pair off mourning gloves 00–18–00
11– a blak neck lace 00–05–00
12– peyit to Patrik Telfeir tailyeur in full off his compt
on his discharge at the fitt thairoff 07–08–00

45–05–06 is 45–05–06

A ston off almonds — A ston off almonds at 5s. the pound which wes set doun at the fitt
off the said accompt 04–00–00

all this compt .... 49–05–06 • 49 • 05 • 06

On Teusday the 21 off Januar 1673 – sent to James Clerk with John
Rob in a bygirdle – 17 rex dolors – is – 49–06 to pay the above
wreatten compt with 49–06–00
I have the accompt above mentioned with James Clerks – –
recept at the fitt thairoff – off– 49–05–06 date 22 Januar 1673

Helen Clerks – mourning gown for hir dear sister – — Ane accompt off a blak mourning gown & petticot & uther necessars belonging
thairtoo – for Helen Clerk which James Clerk tooke att be my order – the 30
off December 1672 –
1– 13 ell off blak worsit grograin at 21s. the ell 13–13–00
2– 3 ell of blak waltings at 30d. the ell 00–07–06
Agnes Clerk — 3– 3 ell off firritin ribens at 30d. the ell 00–07–06
4– 1 pair off blak worsit stokings 01–00–00
5– 1 pair off love cuffs 03–08–00
6– 1 love band 03–08–00
7– 1 pair off taffatie cuffs 02–04–00

8– 1 neck lace – 4s. 6d. – 1 box 6d. 00–05–00
9– 1 pair off blak gloves 00–14–00
10– halff a pound off balling 00–14–00
11– the 11 off January 1673 – to Patrik Telfeir tailyeur – for making the gown &c & some furnitur thairtoo – on his discharge thairon date the 11 off January 1673 at the fitt off his compt 06–18–00
12– a love hoode 02–08–00
13– 5 ell off love ribens at 4s. the ell 01–00–00

36–07–0 Helens compt .... 36–07–00 –

36–07–00 1– a prognostication 00–00–06
02–15–06 2– 2 blak bonets for Will & Alexander
39–02–06 Clerks for which I tooke 7 batons brunt wax 01–10–00
3– 1 blak bonet for Rob Clerk 00–13–00
4– 3 pair off gloves for the 3 boys 00–12–00 02–15–06

is .... 39–02–06 • 39 • 02 • 06

Fra the begining off December 1672 to this – A – is .... • 352 • 08 • –

[148]

The disbursments in the monthe off December 1672 on the other syde • 352 • 08 • –

I have ane accompt fra James Clerk off Helen Clerks mourning gown – amonting to 36–07–00 & 2–15–6d. is both 39–02–6d. with his discharge at the fitt off the said accompt ....

[blank the rest of the page]

[149]

Anno 1673 — The disbursments in the month off January –: 1673

Whyt – wand baskits	1 Januar 1673 – to John Wallace indweller at Foull foord for 4 whyt baskits with handles – 2 larger –& 2 lesser		• 00 • 15 • 04
William Stewart – 2 bols off peys in Dalkeith	Thursday the 16 off January 1673 sent William Stewart to Dalkeith with money – who boght –		
	1– 5 firlots off peys at 4–17s. the boll is	06–01–00	
	2– 3 firlots off peys at 4–12s. the boll is	03–08–02	
	1 long ry breid 00–02–04		
	3 litle whyt breid for the bairns 00–02–02	00–04–06	
	Wille Stewarts & 2 horse charges – 4s. 4d. for custom is	00–04–04	• 09 • 18 • –
7 ell – whyt fingering	The 21 off January – to Androw – to Thomas Burne webster for 8 ell off whyt fingering at – 7s. 3d. the ell is	02–18–00	
Thomas Burne –			
William Yeiltoun a boll of malt	On Teusday the 21 off January – to James Yeiltoun William Yeiltoun –: his brother for a boll off malt to try v: how prowes – 6 lib.	06–00–00	• 09 • 06 • –
Dalkeith	Thursday 23 Januar 1673 – sent William Stewart to Dalkeith //	all above	

1 boll off – seid peys &c–	who boght for me with my own money – – –		AA	• 19 • 19 • 04
	1– a boll off seed peys – 5–8s.	05–08–00		
	2– 2 long ry breid – 4–8d.	00–04–08		
	3– 6 litle whyt breid – 4–4d.	00–04–04		
	4– for himselff the horse & custom	00–03–00	06–00–02	
	4 Januar to John Rob for going to Prestoun pans with Alexander Clerk to bring home Helen Clerk	00–10–00		
	8 Januar – to Arche Andersone for smeiring a day	00–04–00		
	10 Januar – to William Thomsone for 8 once fygs for Jennet Clerk	00–02–06		
	11 Januar to Jo: Rob for causeing sole a pynt stoup	00–06–00		
....	14 Januar – to Jo: Rob for going to the toun with Margaret Clerk	00–07–00		
piklt oysters	22 Januar to John Bowie in Prestoun pans for 2 litle – barels off pick[l]t oysters at 14s. the barell	01–08–00	02–17–06	
28 ell off secking	The 28 off Januar – boght fra ane Anndaill man – – – At Silver burne – 26 ell[113] off secking at 6s. 8d. the ell – He said it wes made off hemp	–	08–13–04	
Richard Twidie	21 Januar 1673 – to Richard Twidie in Dauffingtoun when he cam to see the young Achnnouns Hill mare who wes elphshot – 24s. & ane off David Hislops cheese		01–04–00	

[113] Clerk wrote '26 ells' in the body of the account, but wrote '28 ells' in the margin. The tally suggests that 26 ells is correct.

3 ¾ ell off	The last off Janur [sic] to William Stewart for 3 ¾ ell off minim shag –	
minim shge	to be a cott for my selff at 2 merk the ell	05–00–00
E•J• Dauff	The 21 off January to E–J – to Luckie when shoe went to Dauffingtoun	
	2 halff dolors – 58s.	02–18–00
oynions	1 douzane oynions	00–01–06
duerf aples	21 January – to James Brown gairner in the shank for 2 dwerf aple treis	
19–19–4	& 14 aples & peirs	00–06–08
25–00–00	For fresh beiff in the month off January	02–08–00
44–19–4	For whyt breid in the month off January	01–10–08
	Soma fra the 2– AA – to this	25–00–00
	The end off January 1673 — The disbursments in January 1673......is	44–19–04
		• 44 • 19 • 04

February 1673	The disbursments in February 1673 –	
Mr Robert	Munday 3 February – to Alexander Clerk to give his master Mr Robert	
Brown	Brown – off blize money – 3 lib. to wit 24s. for William Clerk – 24s.	
blize money	for Alexander Clerk & 12s. for Robert Clerk is – 3 lib.	03–00–00
Samuel Young	The 4 off February – to Samuel Wood for – to Samuell Young – I	
2 bolls off smal	say – for 2 bolls off whyt salt at 4–10s. 8d. the boll is 5s. 8d. the	
salt	bolpeck [sic] the 2 bolls is.......... 09–00 1s. – 4d.	09–01–04
	The 6 off February to Isobel Scot for –	
	1– 3 eirnings or reids shoe boght fra Wille Baird..... 12s.	
	2– 13 pynts off ale for the usse off the howsse......... 21s. 8d.	01–01–08

Margin	Entry	Amount	Total
Isobell – Fermer – for nails 14–18	The 28 off January 1673 – Mr John Clerk peyit to Isobell Fermer ane accompt off nails off – 14–18s. & tooke hir discharge at the fit off the compt off the same –& the said Mr Jo: Clerk being at Newbiging on the 6 off February 1673 – I peyit him the said 14–18s.	14–18–00	• 15 • 19 • 08
Mr William Hamiltouns stipend fra Mertimes 1671 till Mertimes 1672	The 5 off February 1673 peyit to Mr William Hamiltoun minister at Pennycooke – 326 lib. for his stipend fra Mertimes 1671 till Mertimes 1672 – for my lands lying within the paroish off Pennycooke to wit the Baronie off Pennycooke – Easter Ravensneuk – and the Halls for which I have his discharge date the said 5th off February 1673		• 326 • 00 • –
	The disbursments above in February 1673		• 354 • 01 • –

[150]

Margin	Entry	Amount	Total
	The disbursments in February on the other syde is............................		• 354 • 01 • –
2 highland durks –	The 11 off February to Charles Machelen for 1 long highland durk [sic] and a short highland durk......both – 7s. sterlin	04–00–04	
Margaret Andersone 2–18–00	Said day to Margaret Andersone when shoe went to the toun with Will: Hamiltoun – a rex dolor – 58s.	02–18–00	
	6 February – to Arche Craig when he went in for James Clerk and his 2 sisters 2 horse & himselff	00–06–00	
	11 February to Alexander Clerk to give the bairns at the seting doun off thair 3 coqs to feight [sic]..	00–06–00	
E: J-	14 February to the wyffe to pay Wille Stewarts wyffe a douzane off eygs........20d.	00–01–08	• 07 • 12 • –

	For fresh beiff in the month off February	03–11–06	
	For whyt breid in the month off February	01–08–06	• 05 • 00 • –
	The end off February 1673......................... .... The disbursments in February 1673........		• 366 • 13 • –
	RS;		

Marche 1673 February 1673	The disbursments in the rest off February 1673 – I went to the toun on Fryday the 14 off February 1673 – and returnt not to Newbiging till Saturday the 22 off Marche 1673 – is – 5 weiks I wes in the toun at this tyme – follows the disbursments made in the toun – fra the 14 off February to the end off February 1673		ABC;
Small hinging locks	1 round hinging lock	00–04–00	
	1– triangle hinging lock – 9s.	00–09–00	
	2– long large hinging locks ilk ane off the heips tyed to the locks with a peice off weir at 13s. 4d. the peice	01–06–08	• 01 • 19 • 08
8 ell of hardn peper corns – 2 pair........	The 20 off February 1673 – to Thomas Reid for 85 ell off hardn – in 3 peices at 4s. 4d. the ell..	18–02–08	
	2 pair off peper corns at 7s. 6d. the pair	00–15–00	• 18 • 17 • 08
David Pringle – apothecarie	The 15 off February 1673 – to David Pringle apothecarie in full off ane accompt on his discharge & off all uther accompts preseiding the said 15 off February 1673 – 37–17–8 – This compt wes for James Clerk when he wes sick off a rheumatisme on his joynts..	37–17–08	
David Gray cordoner	The 18 off February 1673 – to David Gray cordoner on his discharge off the said date..............3–16	03–16–00	• 41 • 13 • 08

Archbald More – in Leith wynd	The 18 off February 1673 – to Archebald More in Leith Wynd for –		
	1 peice rushie leather to be a bag	00–16–04	
	1 ½ hundreth large brasse nails	00–10–08	
	200 and 1 quarter large brasse nails	00–14–00	
	16 old garron nails	00–01–04	• 02 • 02 • 04
whyt yrn pots –	The 18 off February 1673 –		
	To Thomas Laing for 3 whyt yrne pots for holding pincils	01–10–00	
James Brown tanner –	To James Brown tanner for 13 horns	00–15–04	
Mr Jo Smiths – wyff for 3 peuter plaits –	The said day to Mr John Smiths wyffe for 3 pewter plaits weying 12 pound wecht at 12s. the pound	07–04–00	
	5 lb off small pack threid consisting in 10 halff pounds at 9s. the pound	02–05–00	
2 yrns for – gooseing cloths –	2 yrns for goosseing – linings	02–08–00	• 14 • 02 • 04
2 pair sheirs –	The 20 off February 1673 – for –		
	2 pair off large sisers boght in the Parlament housse	00–14–00	
lignum wite – boxes – 2	2 round lignum wite boxes at 10s. a peice	01–00–00	
secking –	To Widow Dow – for 12 ell off narow secking 4s 8d. the ell	02–16–00	• 04 • 10 • –
Thom Wedel for horse graith	21 February 1673 to Thomas Wedell spur maker for –		
	1– for mending a large brydle bit	00–10–00	
	3 pair off yellow stirp leathers at – 12s. the pair	01–16–00	
	3 pair off yellow brydel rains at – 12s. the pair	01–16–00	• 04 • 02 • –
Mistresse Conrad	The 21 off February 1673 – to Mistress Conrad for –		
	1 yrne chimney with a braid yrne plait under it	06–13–04	

	For severall uther small trifling things	05–13–00	
	1 litle long booke off taile douces	01–04–00	• 13 • 10 • 04
James –	The 21 off February 1673 to James Stewart drogist for –		
Stewart –	10 douzane off small corks		
drogist –	1 round reid vernicht box.........lyne with –		
	in with marbert peper – 13–4d.	00–13–04	
	1 great antique hak bell	00–02–00	• 02 • 03 • 04
	The last disbursments in February 1673 begining at ABC –		
	above on this syde till this – ABC is		• 103 • 01 • –
	Turn over to the rest of the disbursments in the month off February 1673		

[151]

	The last disbursments on the other syde in February 1673 – fra		
	ABC: to ABC at the end off the syde amonts to – 103–01–00		• 103 • 01 • –
John–	The 21 off February 1673 to John Crichtoun for –		
Crichtoun –	1 wyde sive............		
sives –	1 oate sive............	01–04–00	
ridls –	4 strong coll ridls	01–03–00	
caps –	6 litle trinchers 00–06–00		
coichs –	For mending ane lym ridle............03–00............	00–09–00	
&c –	1 large whyt cap.......12s.		
	1 drinking coichs......24s. 00–12–00		

	1 whyt turnt drinking cap	01–04–00	all thir 4 artickls is	
	1 larg strong turnt dish	00–00–00	wrong wreatten – –	00–00–00
	1 large strong turnt dish	00–12–00		
	2 drinking coichs	01–04–00		
	1 whyt turnt drinking cap	00–05–00		02–01–00
				MA
	In all to John Crichtoun	04–17–00		• 04 • 17 • –
James – Clerk –	The 21 off February 1673 to James Clerk on his discharge in full off ane accompt the said day – on his discharge for severall small ussefull things – 6–10–6	06–10–06		
Half a barrel of hering –	22 February – to Donald Mackeys wyffe at the head off the Cowgate – for halff a barell off Glasgow hering	05–00–00		
	4 once off leaffe tobaco	00–06–00		• 11 • 16 • 06
James – Childers saidler –	25 February 1673 – to James Childers saidler – in the Cowgate head – 2 sled saidles at 4 merk the peice	05–06–08		
	1 – 1 coller for porter	00–12–00		
	For cutting Jacks hyde in targets	01–04–00		• 07 • 02 • 08
Monsieur Sochon	The 26 off February 1673 to Monseur Sochon – For stocking a hand bell			
	For making a skrew for a vyce			
	whch [sic] Conrads wyffe sold me			
	To his man Androw to drink 6s.			• 02 • 02 • –
John – Cooke –	The 24 of February 1673 to John Cooke for – 2 – bosse locks for kists with thair pertinents at 34s. a peice	03–08–00		

1 – fyne stock lock with a handsome key for the yard doore
goes att the clos 02–13–04
1 pair off glaiks off – 14 rings .... 00–00–00 • 06 • 01 • 04

The 24 off February 1673 to John Armstrang for –
18 pack neidls 7–6d. 00–07–06
6 earthen – brem 1– handlt pigs at 18d. the peice........ 00–09–00
4 fadom off whip cord and ane Hollands lyne about 34 fadome both
cost – 18s. 00–18–00
To Thomas Wedel – for a bolt off whip cords 10s. 00–10–00
To Thomas Crichtoun for 6 peice off fyne small whip cord........ 01–19–06
2 round whyt yrne moyers – cost 9s. 00–09–00
To Widow Dunlap in the Bow – for a severall small ussefull –
things for the usse off the housse according to hir accompt as
whyt & blew stiffing strae wald – alme – copres – galls –
birnstoun –&c .... 03–01–00 • 04 • 02 • –

Widow Dow for – The 25 off February 1673 to Widow Dow: in full off hir accompt –
57 ell off Irish – on hir discharge on the said accompt date the said 25 off February 1673
serges – 29s. 6d. For 3 severall peeces [sic] off Irish serges cullort at 29s. 6d. the ell –
the ell – 1 peece sad cullort the other 2 peeces light gray is – 84–13–6 .... • 84 • 13 • 06

Hew Mackculloch To Hew Macculloch – 90–06–8 on his discharge date the 25 off
90–06–08 February 1673 as the second 3 months off the 12 months new supplie –
second 3 months – according to the Act of Parlament off the 5 off Jully 1672 & payable at
pay Candlemes 1673 – off which soume I resavet Hew Maccullochs –
discharge date the said 25 off February 1673........ • 90 • 06 • 08

Ro Dowglas – for seck & brande	The 25 off February 1673 – peyit to Robert Dowglas in Leith on his discharge date the said 25 off February 1673 – 27–14s. for seck & brande resavet fra him when Agnes Clerk wes buried........................		• 27 • 14 • –
James – Mackcalzien – cutler 3–10s.	2 large whyt yrne moyers..	00–09–00	
	28 February 1673 – to James Mackcalzien cutler for sharping & polishing a great many knyves – razoirs & corne knyves – pen knyves –&c & for a sheith to a long durk – 16s. all I peyit him for all..	03–10–00	• 03 • 19 • –
246–06–08	1 The disbursments in February above fra MA on this sy[d]e is.........		• 246 • 06 • 08
366–13–00	2– The disbursments fra the begining off February till – RS is..........		• 366 • 13 • –
103–01–00	3– The disbursments in February fra ABC till ABC........................		• 103 • 01 • –
716–00–08	The end off February 1673 All the disbursments in February 1673......		• 716 • 00 • 08

[152]

Marche 1673 –	The disbursments in Marche 1673 fra the 14 off February 1673 to the 22 off Marche 1673 that I returnt to Newbiging which wes 5 weiks I wes in Edinburgh at this tyme – bot I begin and compts heir – my disbursments – fra the 1 off Marche 1673 till the 22 off Marche 1673 that I returnt to Newbiging –	
	The 1 off Marche 1673 – to Abraham Clerk for turnig [sic] some small things...	00–15–04
	3 blew & whyt lame pots – litle ons with coverts	00–12–00
	4 whyt yrne spyce boxes at 4s. the peice...	00–16–00

1 ½ pound off fyas[114] at 6s. the pound	00–09–00	
2 pair off womens gloves – 24s. 1 pair tand gloves for my selff 10s. is	01–14–00	• 04 • 06 • 04
The 3 off Marche 1673 to William Blaikwood for 5 once 10 drop off light cullort silk off divers light cullors at 19s. the once	05–09–00	
6 pound 7 once off fygs at 6s. the pound	01–18–08	• 07 • 07 • 08
The 3 off Marche 1673 – to James Stewart drogist for	–	
2 pound off gum arabique at 15s. the pound	01–10–00	
14 gray Hollands pots with 1 handle at all cost – 40s.	02–00–00	
1 whyt firr box ... 8s.	00–08–00	
1 other whyt firr box	00–06–06	
2 horns for bowets	00–02–00	
To him for garlick	00–04–00	
In the Bow – for 12 fadom off tows for theats	01–04–00	• 05 • 14 • 06
The 3 off Marche 1673 to Eusten Nisbit for 5 ½ ell off Diepe fringe & 38 ell off narow fringe orange minim & light gray all weying 23 ½ once at 22s. the once is 25–17s. thir fringes wes for a new bed off gray drap de berrie		• 25 • 17 • –
The 4 off Marche 1673 to James Clerk in full off ane accompt markit on the bak – ABC as silk buttons great & small fyne cullort threid 1 lute string hood &c – 41–01–0 on his discharge – on the said accompt – the lute string hood cost – 4–14s.		• 41 • 01 • –
The 5 off Marche 1673 – peyit to Duncan Semple on his discharge – at [t]he fitt off the compt – the compt is markit on the bak MA;		

1– 16 pynts off juniper waters at 20s. the pynt 16–00–00
2– 14 pynts off comon waters at 16s. the pynt.................................. 11–04–00
3– 3 douzane off litle birk – knaps for – knaps to lids off boxes –& lids off Hollands pigs at 4s. the douzane...................... 00–12–00 • 27 • 16 • –

Leith – The 6 off Marche 1673 –

1– to James Campel for 2 firikins off soape at 8 lib. the firikin acording to his accompt markit on the bak – LM and his recept at the fitt theroff the said – 16 lib. .... • 16 • 00 • –

2– in in [sic] Leith the 6 off Marche 1673 – to Robert Sandelands in full off his accompt with his discharge off – 50–12–8 at the fitt theroff – which accompt is markit on the bak HA – for –
18 ½ pynts off brande at 29s. the pynt 26–16–06
17 pynts & a mutchkin off seck at 26s. the pynt........................... 22–08–06
2 barels to hold the same .... 01–07–08 • 50 • 12 • 08

3– in Leith the 6 off Marche 1673 – to Patrik Smith couper in Leith in full off his accompt with his discharge at the fitt theroff – off – 6–09–00 – which accompt is markit on the bak – OP – for – ....
1– 4 bundls off French girds conteining 65 girds ilk bundell – is – 2 hundreth and a halff thair being six skore comptit to ilk hundreth at 30s. the hundreth 03–15–00
2– ane bundle off Inglish pinks conteining 200th girds – at – 18s. the 100th is 01–16–00

114 Based on the context, and an entry 4 lines down, this is likely meant to read 'fygs'.

3– ane bundle off Inglish halff pinks conteining 100th 00–18–00
6 – bundls in all – conteining 500 ½th cost .... 06–09–00 • 06 • 09 • –

7 Marche 1673 – to John Armestrang for –
1– 9 painted fyne twidlt bags which did come home with gairden
seids – cost 7s. the peice 03–03–00
2– 10 cords at 18d. the peice.. 00–15–00
3– 1 ½ pound off claiver seid at 10s. the pound 00–15–00
4– 2 once off cromock seid 01–00–00
5– to James Clerk for a blak clock bouton 00–08–00
6– to him for a peper off prins 00–05–00
7– 3 douzane off litle birk knaps at 4s. the douzane........................... 00–12–00
8– 2 once off tobaco – cut & dry 00–04–00
9– 4 once off pomgranat skins at 2s. the once.................................... 00–08–00
10– 12 Marche 1673 – to Alexander Andersone –
coper smith – for 2 coper skoops – to put up
gairden seids &c in litle poiks 02–02–00
11– 1 inkhorne for Robert Clerk.. 00–05–00 • 09 • 17 • –

The disbursments on this syde in –
Marche 1673 is............................. ....195–01–02 • 195 • 01 • 02

[153]

The disbursments in Marche 1673 on the other syde is – 195–01–02.... • 195 • 01 • 02

Saturday the 15 off Marche 1673 –

	5 ½ pound off knok lint at 10s. the pound	02–10–	
	2 rows & 2 weirs for Jennet & Katherin Clerks	00–17–	
	2 single catechise	00–01–	
	The said day to James Hamiltouns nourish – a rex dolor....58s.	02–18–	
	The 18 off Marche 1673 to Hew Broun for ane ascraboutique purgeing bag.......3–15	03–15–	
	The said day – for a Westfalia hame [sic] weying 7 ½ pound at 9s. the pound	04–11–06	• 14 • 12 • 06
	On Teusday the 18 off Marche 1673 – to Sir Robert Sinclair – for a consultation anent Balmerinos bussynes – 15 lib. and to his man Hary Sinclair – a rex dolor – 2–18 is both		• 17 • 18 • –
	4 once leaffe tobaco	00–06–00	
	21 Marche – to William Brouns 2 women – 3 merk peices in drink money – is – 2 lib.	02–00–00	
	21 Marche – to Widow Dow for 6 douzane & 5 ell off whyt worsit at 4s. 6d. the douzane is	01–08–08	• 03 • 14 • 08
To William Russell – wreatter 35–4s.	The 13 off Marche 1673 – peyit to William Russell wreater in Edinburg in full off ane accompt with his discharge on the bak – theroff – 35–4s. which accompt is markit on the bak.....ABC – and it is the first accompt betwixt me & him		• 35 • 04 • –
Jo Rob – for disbursments – 20s.	The 27 off Marche to John Rob which he disbursit – 1– 2 whill bands 6s. ....00–06–00 2– for corne & stroe to the hors when – he went to Leith for soap brande &c 00–08–00		

	3– for a quart off barme	00–04–00		
	4– custome at Leith	00–02–00 20s.	01–00–00	
George Clerk for 40 ell off plaiding	The 24 off Marche to George Clerk for weiving – 40 ell off plaiding – at 2s. the ell		04–00–00	
	For paping ale		00–06–08	• 05 • 06 • 08
To the good wyffe at the mill for 8 bolls off oats – A 3	The 27 off Marche 1673 – to the good wyffe at the mill for 8 bolls off oats at 4 lib. the boll which William Stewart resavart [sic] resavet fra hir the 7 off Februar 1673 which compleited the said William Stewart his boll fra Witsonday 1672 till Witsonday 1673		32–00–00	
3 steips off malt – 41–14–00	The said 27 off Marche 1673 to the said good wyffe at the mill – for making 3 steips off malt – 8 bols in everie steip – at 58s. ilk steip	08–14–00		
	And 20s. off drinking money for the – said 3 steips	01–00–00	09–14–00	• 41 • 14 • –
beiff –	For whyt breid in Marche	01–12–00		
bread –	For fresh beiff in Marche	06–03–00	07–15–00	• 07 • 15 • –

[blank space fills the last half of this page]

[154]
[blank space fills the first third of this page]

Aprill 1673	The disbursments in Aprill 1673 – Aprill 1673 –	
Alexander Meygit for 6 bolls off – seid oats –	The 18 off Aprill to Alexander Meygit in Cookein[g] – 30 lib for – 6 bolls off seid oats at 5 lib. the boll which William Stewart – resavet fra him – the 27 off fra him the 27[115] of February 1673............	• 30 • 00 • –
10–16s. to Mr John Smiths – wyfe – to pay a webster – 10–16	The 18 off Aprill 1673 – wreatten to Mr John Smiths wyffe & sent to hir with John Rob – the said day seald in a litle packit 10–16s. to pay to James Lawsone webster – for weiving 35 ell off dornick at 6s. the ell is – 10–10s. & 6s. to his man is 10–16s. – according to a compt I have off his..	• 10 • 16 • –
Mr Jo Smiths – wyffe – 15 ell of lining at 24s. the ell is – 18 lib.	On Wedensday 23 off Aprill 1673....sent with John Rob to Edinburgh to be delivert to Mr John Smiths wyffe – a litle packit seald conteining six rex dolors and a shilling – is – 18 lib. for 15 ell off unblicht lining shoe sent out to me with John Rob on Saturday the 19 off Aprill 1673 at 24s. the ell is – 18 lib.	• 04 • 02 • –
	The 2 off Aprill – to John Rob – for gairden seids according to ane accompt he broght fra Robert Mein theroff.................................... 02–10–08 Said day to him for v[e]rsis catechise for Alexander Clerk................. 00–02–00 Said day – to him for 8 weirs for the bairns to weive stokings with ..... 00–01–06 21 Aprill to Jo: Austin for botto[m]ing a ridle.................................. 00–06–00 Said day to John Clerk for bringing half a barel off hering out of toun 00–06–00	• 03 • 06 • 02

[115] Clerk repeated himself here.

On Fryday the 11 off Aprill 1673 – at John Reid his brydel in Foull foord to his eldest daughter – 29s. to John Cranstouns brother – 4s. is.......... 01–13–00

The 9 off Aprill 1673 – to Helen Clerk – 30s. which shoe peyit to a couper – the 17 off February 1673 when I wes in the toun 01–10–00

The 4 off Aprill 1673 – for milling & killing 26 bolls off oats & 13 bolls is 39 bolls...31s. 01–11–00

The 3 off Aprill 1673 – being at Silver burne – to Edowart Adamsone for a naughtie cows hyde – 30s. – at leist I gave him the wort[h] off 30s. in severall small usse full things .... 01–10–00 • 06 • 01 • –

William – Morisone – cordoner – in Borthwick

The 28 off Aprill 1673 – to William Morisone cordoner who dwels in Borthwick – for mending severall shoone to the bairns &c 2 ½ days he furnished threid & ruset himselff and I furnished the leather..........22s. .... • 01 • 02 • –

The 26 off Aprill – to John Rob for 1 lb off Bourdeaux pruns 00–02–06

& to him for fish the said day 00–04–00

To William Burrel – 23 Aprill to get box wood at Darne hall .... 00–01–08 • 00 • 08 • 02

For fresh beiff in Aprill 1673 08–04–00

For whyt breid in Aprill 1673 – 01–13–04 .... 01–13–04 • 09 • 17 • 04

The end off Aprill 1673 – The disbursments in Aprill 1673 .... • 79 • 10 • 08

May 1673 The disbursments in the – month off May 1673 – ....

Follows the accompt off tocher peyit to Mary Clerk – & accompts peyit for hir brydell cloths & other occasions & disbursments peyit out – upon that occasion – all amonting to........6766–08–5 – this sould have been booked on I say in the month off Aprill 1672 – becaus Mr Androw Brown off Dolphintoun & Mary Clerk wes mairied at the kirk off Pennycooke be Mr William Hamiltoun minister thair on Fryday the 12 off Aprill 1672 bot could not till this month off May 1673 – becaus thair wes severall reasons why I could not get it booked in Aprill 1672 nor sooner then this month off May 1673......

1. On the 22 off February 1673 – I peyit to Mr Androw Brown off Dolphintoun – 1915 lib. & retird my band off the lyke soume with his recept on the back theroff off the said 1915 lib. the said day – this band off myne wes date the 17 off January 1672 – payable at Candlemes 1673 .... •1915 • 00 • –

On the 19 off Marche 1673 – the laird off Innes younger peyit to Mr Androw Brown off Dolphintoun – the principall soume off [crossed out] lib. Scots – I say ....

2. I say the principall soume conteind in Innes & cautioners band wes 3800–00–00
And the interest theroff – fra Mertimes 1671 till Candlemes – 1672 is 15 month is – 285–00–00... 285–00–00
is – 4085–00–00– principall & interest theroff at Candlemes 1673 .... 4085 lib. •4085 • 00 • –
Be my assignation made to the said Mr Androw Brown date; is........ •6000 • 00 • –

the 17 off January 1672 – whairoff I have the copie – I –:
assignd him to the laird off Innes his band with certane –:

Marie Clerk hir tocher & uther expensis all amonting to 6766–08–05 –

cautioners – thairin mentioned conteining the principall soume off 3800 lib. and to the anuel rent theroff – fra Mertimes 1671 till Candlemes 1673 – which did amont to the said – 4085 lib. –

The accompt off merchants & tailyeurs accompts – being – 10 in nomber – peyit for Marie Clerk when shoe wes mairied –

who wes – maried on Fryday – the 12 off – Aprill 1672

Thir 10 underwreatten accompts wes all peyit in the month off Marche – 1672 according as thair several discharges bears mentioning the – day off the month off Marche 1672 – when they wer peyit – –

1– to David Boyd merchant in full off ane accompt according to his discharge theron 231–04–00
2– to William Blackwood in full off ane accompt 098–05–02
3– to John Hunter merchant in full off ane accompt 057–08–00
4– to Alexander Carshore merchant in full off ane accompt 020–18–09
5– to Hew Trotter merchant in full off ane accompt 018–03–00
6– to Lilias Campbel in full off ane accompt 012–11–06
7– to Robert Hamiltoun merchant in full off ane accompt 008–04–00
8– to ante [sic] Isobell Gray in full off ane accompt 57–00–06 which ~ ~ ~ ~ wes peyit to hir the 28 off February & the 25 off Marche 1672 057–00–06
9– to James Clerk in full off ane accompt 010–06–00
10– to Patrick Tailyeur in full off ane accompt 068–04–06

Thir – 10 compts amonts to 582–05–05 is .... 582–05–05 • 582 • 05 • 05

Thair is a discharge on ilk ane off these 10 compts ....

I have a sheit off peper markit on the back – 999 – on which sheit off peper – all this bussynes is wreatten at great lynth which sheit off peper is lying with uther pepers anent this bussyness in a litle tykeing [sic] bag – in which bag – a double off the contract off mariage past betwixt the said Mr Androw Brown & Marie Clerk – which teyking bag is lying in the top off the yrne tronk – thair is also a seasine [sic] off the lands off Dolphinstoun be which the said Marie Clerk is infeft in the lands off Dolphintoun for 1000 lib. Scots yeirlie –

On the above mentioned sheit off peper markit on the back 999 – thair is wreatten on the 1 syde theroff –

1– on the first syde theroff 9000 merks off tocher 6000–00–00

2– on the same first syde – 10 accompts amonting to.......................... 582–05–05

3– on the second syde off the said sheit off peper markit 999 – severall accompts amonting to................................ 184–03–00

The tocher & expensis that I peyit out on this – 6766–08–05–
matrimoniall bussynes – extends in all to sevin –
I say to six thousand sevin hundreth thrie–skore
six pounds – 8s. – 5d. Scots................................ •6766 • 08 • 05

John Clerk

Go to ABC on the other syde –

[156]

May – The disbursments in May 1673 –

1673 The 19 off Marche 1673 when the laird off Innes younger – I peyit to Mr Androw Brown off Dolphintoun the 3800 & bygon anuel rents

ABC... he wes assignd too – thair wes 6–8s. off charges Dolphintoun disbursit Innes wold not peyit & Dolphintoun wold have it – so that I peyit the said – 6–8s. to put a close to the bussynes rather then to hear such fangling for such ane inconsiderable thing – so I gave the 6 lib. 8s. to Dolphintoun – to wit to pay –

1– William Russel got for registrating Innes band letters off horneing & signeting them –& for chargeing with horneing in the north 05–16–00

2– a shilling to get Innes principall band out off the register............. 00–12–00 • 06 • 08 • –

The other syde amonts to 6766–08–05 .... •6766 • 08 • 05

Soma off all on the other syde & this tocher & uther charges peyit out at Marie Clerk hir brydell which wes on the 12 off Aprill 1672 is – 6772–16–5 I say .... •6772 • 16 • 05

John Clerk

Memento –

Thair is lying in the yrne tronk a litle packit in a new teyking bag mad in forme off a port letter with a parchement shewd on it mentioning what is within the same – to wit –

1– a contract off mariage betwixt Mr Androu Brown off Dolphintoun & Marie Clerk – date at Newbiging the 8 off December 1671 ....

2– seasine in favors off the said Marie Clerk off ane yeirlie anuel rent off 1000 lib. Scots to be uplifted furth off the lands of Dolphintoun –

3– accomp how hir – tocher being 9000 merks wes peyit & uther disbursments on hir cloths & brydell being 772–16–5 in all 6772–16s. 5 this accompt is markit on the bak – 999 ....

4– divers marchants [sic] accompts & a tailyeurs compt wes peyit out for hir with discharges on the backs off them they wer all peyit in Marche 1672

5– divers uther memors pepers – accompts &c off severall sorts – relateing to that mariage ....

The seasine above mentioned is date the 11 off Aprill 1672 and registrat the 14 off May 1672 ....

6– ane canceld band off myne off – 1915 lib. Scots date the 17 Januar 1672 which 1915 lib. I peyit to Dolphintoun the 22 off February 1673 & retird my band & canceld it with Dolphintoun – his recept on the bak off the said band off the said – 1915 lib. Scots –

7– copie off ane assignation made to the said Mr Androw Broun date the 17 off January 1672 to a band off Sir Robert Innes off that ilk – off the principall soume off 3800 lib. & to the anuel rents – wes peyit be the laird off Innes younger to Dolphintoun the 19 off Marche 1673 ....

Marie Clerk hir tocher and uther expensis all amonting to 6772–16–5 .... •6772 • 16 • 05

who wes maried on Fryday
the 12 off Aprill 1672

John: Clerk

Turn over to the month off May 1673 –

[157]

May	The disbursments in May 1673 –		
1673	In the end of Aprill & begining off May 1673		
13 thraive off oat stroe –	To William Stewart – to pay Thomas Straitoun in Pentland for 13 thraive off oat stroe – at 8s. the thraive	05–04–00	
	2 May – to Arche Andersone for 19 great trouts	00–03–04	
	3 May – to Charles Campbell for puting a head on a plough	00–04–00	
James Park – for mending a plough –	The 7 off May 1673 to James Park for puting a head on a plough & for mending the plough in December 1672 – this William Stewart said – so I gave him the said 10s. the said day	00–10–00	• 06 • 01 • 04
Will Broun – 12 lib. for my chamber maill	The 22 off May 1673 – to William Brown skinner – 12 lib. for my chamber maill fra Mertimes 1672 till Witsonday 1673 on his discharge date the said 22 off May 1673		• 12 • 00 • –
Gairner of Glencorse	The 10 off May 1673 – to the gairner off Glencorse for some grein sege & potatos	00–04–00	

To John Meurs in Lintoun for a pair off pomps	The 10 off May 1673 to Dan[i]el Whyt to deliver to John Meurs cordoner in Lintoun for a pair off pomps – I desyrd him to mak for me and to send them to Silver burne for me so soone as could be – 18s.	00–18–00
Ja: Clerk 24 ½ do^n neidls	The 12 off May 1673 – to James Clerk for 24 ½ douzane off neidls off divers seyses at 2s. the douzane	02–09–00

Anuites – Anuites –	Ane accompt what I peyit to James now earle off Lowdoun for a disposition to the anuites – being 500 lib. Scots and uther charges disbursit anent that bussynes as follows –		
Accompt for anuites & a disposition thairtoo and charges as is under wreatten – amonts to – 537–08–00	Ane extract off a disposition on parchement granted be James now earle off Lowdoun – to John Clerk off Pennycooke to the anuities off his lands lying in the paroishes off Pennycooke & Glencorse and that for all tyme by gain anuities & in all tyme to come – for the soume off fyve hundreth pound Scots date the 13 off Marche 1673 & registrat on the 17 day off – the said month off Marche 1673 – I say –& registrat on the 17 day off the said month off Marche 1673 with divers other pepers memors & accompts &c relateing to that bussynes which ar all in a litle tyking bag – markit ON the back – 29.......which bag is lying in the yrne tronk –		
	The said 500 lib. wes peyit to Mr William Nimmo in name off James now earle off Lowdoun – as his depute anent the anuities to wit –		
	1– on the 8 off Marche 1673 – peyit to the said Mr William Nimmo 500 merks	333–06–08	
	2– on the said I say on the 20 off Marche 1673 peyit to the said Mr William Nimmo – 250 merks is	166–13–04	• 500 • 00 • –

Anuites – Follows the accompt off disbursments anent that bussynes of the anuities

Anuites – 1– to Mr William Hamiltoun for wreating the disposition to the
anuities – 2 rex dolors 05–16
to his man.......12s. 00–12 06–08–00

2– to my Lord Register – for registrating the disposition 17–08–00

3– to David Piter for his pains.. 02–18–00

4– for parchment & to the wreatter theroff 01–00–00

5– to David Piter – (befor the granting off the disposition) to looke the registers – whither or not Sir John Prestoun off Airdrie who wes proprietar off the lands off Pennycooke & Glencorse had boght the anuities off the lands off Pennycooke as he did the anuities off the lands off Glencorse 02–18–00

6– to Mr James Hendersons sone who keeps the minuts off the register off anuities iff any persone had boght the anuities off the lands off Pennycooke.. 01–09–00

7– to John Mackronell – servitor to Mr Jo: Elleis for presenting the bill off suspension & grounds theroff to the clerk of the exchequer & for procureing the pepers out off the clarks hands agane & to get that charge off horneing against Pennycooke anent the anuities suspendit....... 02–18–00

8– to William Russell – for draweing up & wreating the bill of supension at Pennycooks instance against the earle of Lowdoun suspendit anent the anuities.. 02–09–00

The accompt off the charges as is above amonts to .... 37–08–00 • 37 • 08 • –

	The accompt off all above anent the annuities – 500 lib. for the disposition & 37–8 for the charges amonts to	• 537 • 08 • –
06–01–0 12–00–0 500–00–0 37–08–0 555–09–0	The disbursments on this syde is .... in May 1673 is 555–09–0	• 555 • 09 • –

[158]

	The disbursments in May 1673 on the other syde is		• 555 • 09 • –
Archbald – Craig for 7 bolls off – oats – 4 lib. – 28 –	On the 17 off May 1673 – peyit to Archebald Craig for 7 bols off oats at 4 lib. the boll is – 28 lib. ....whairoff thair wes 6 bolls –I say whairoff thair wes 6 bolls off them William Burrel resavet – and on[e] boll off seid oats which which [sic] William Burrell – I say which William Stewart resavet & did saw in the northcroft		
William – Burrell –	This boll off seid oats that I got wes for a boll off seid oats which William Burrel borowed fra me in Marche 1672 which is 7 bolls off oats which wes resavet on the William – on the accompt off – William Burrrels accompt which compleits his maill fra: I say which compleits his boll fra Mertimes 1672 till Mertimes 1673..		• 28 • 00 • –
2 mure fouls –	24 off May to Nicoll Ramsay wyffe for 2 mure fowls.........................	00–12–00	
To Tomas – Lowrie for 2 bolls of seid oats – 8 lib.	On Teusday the 27 off May 1673 peyit to Thomas Lowrie at 1erst [sic] allowed in compt to him – for 2 bolls off seid oats which William Stewart resavet fra his deceast mother Margaret Borthwick at the mill off Pennycooke on the 29 off Marche 1673......at 4 lib. the boll	08–00–00	• 08 • 12 • –

Boght fra Lady – Newhall – 4 young oxen – 2 – cows with 2 calffs – all the six – 114 lib.

On Teusday the 27 off May 1673 – boght & resavet fra the Lady Newhall be William Stewart & James Mey[g]it the said day –

1– four young oxen off 4 yeir old the peice at 18 lib. the peice all blak exept on a litle whyt on thier [sic] womb 72–00–00

2– blak cow with a calff off 6 or 7 yeir old.. 21–00–00

3– ane other brown cow with a calff off 4 yeir old also .... 21–00–00 • 114 • 00 • –

I peyit this – 114 lib. to the Lady Newhall at Newhall the 19 off May 1673 – ....

1– 39 rex dolors at 58s. the peice 113–02–00

2– & 18s. .... 000–18–00 114 lib.

John: Clerk

Marg – Grisone Marion – Herbersone Cristian Wade Jennet – Thomsone – To these 4 – women – 40 lib.

The accompt off 4 women servants fies payit at Witsonday 1673 – which fell on the 18 day off May 1673 –

The 23 off May 1673 – to Margaret Grisone for hir fie fra Mertimes 1672 till Witsonday 1673 .... 8 lib. 08–00–00

The 28 off May 1673 – to Marion Herbersone for hir fie fra Mertimes 1672 till Witsonday 1673 .... 8 lib. 08–00–00

The 23 off May 1673 – to Cristian Wade for a yeirs fie fra Witsonday 1672 till Witsonday 1673 .... 16 lib. 16–00–00

The 27 off May 1673 – to Jennet Thomsone for hir fie – Mertimes 1672 till Witsonday 1673 – 8 lib. 08–00–00

Thair 4 feis above mentioned amonts to 40 lib. .... • 40 • 00 • –

kill & mill – 14 14 bolls oats –

17 May – to James Meygit to kill & mill – 14 bolls off oats... 00–06–08

leaffe – tobaco	17 May to John Rob for a pound off leaffe tobaco	01–04–00	
lintseid oyll –	24 May to John Rob for a pynt off lint seid oyll	01–10–00	
	20 May to Alexander Clerk to get barme at 2 tyms	00–08–00	
	Teusday 20 off May to Wille Stewart when he went to sell the 2 Slipper – field cows & 2 calffs in the toun	00–12–00	
	24 off May to Sande Gray – to go to Fisher Rav[e] & Leith to looke for some single treis & dails....absent 2 days	00–12–00	
	28 off May to Nicoll Ramsays wyffe for 2 mure fowls	00–12–00	
James – Clerk 5–19.....	The 30 off May 1673 – to James Clark 5–19 in full off ane – ane [sic] accompt on his discharge date 30 May 1673 for a peice yellow 2d. ruben & 14 sticks off reid & blak brunt wax	05–19–00	
John Broun Prestoun pans –	The 30 off May 1673 to John Brown in Prestoun pans – 12s. to buy a pen knyffe for making my pens & 12s. to pay a days horse hyre	01–04–00	
Jo. Andersone – for Jo: Stewart for – 3 once a drop lesse off firr seid 2–16–8	Fryday 30 May 1673 sent to my brother John Andersone seald in a letter a 4 merk peice to send to John Stewart in the loch off Balfour for 3 once a drop lesse off firr seid & a 40d. peice – to the post that broght it to my brother is – 2–16–8	02–16–08	
		15–04–04	• 15 • 04 • 04
	For whyt breid in the month off May 01–11–08		
	For fresh beiff in the month off May 06–07–00		• 07 • 18 • 08
	7 May to John Rob for 2 skait		• 00 • 04 • –
	The end off May 1673............The disbursments in May 1673 is		• 769 • 08 • –

[159]

June – 1673 –	The disbursments in June 1673 –		
Dalkeith – 2 bolls off barley for knoking – &c – William – Stewart –	Thursday 5 June 1673 to William Stewart for William Stewart for twa bolls off barley beir for knoking at 6 lib. 8s. the boll which he boght at Dalkeith the said day	12–16–00	
	He peyit for a quart off barme..	00–03–04	
	For 2 horse & custome..	00–03–00	
	For a ry fadge..	00–01–04	
	To Wille Stewart for a chopin of ale..	00–00–10	• 13 • 04 • 06
drink money	Munday 2 June 1673 – to Ha[w]thorndons women in drink money....	01–09–00	
George Bells – housse –	9 June to Androw Wilsone for casting 1500 divets for Georg Bells housse	00–18–00	
D: G Smith & the	1 strong long double Leith trie to be a rooffe trie for his howsse	01–16–00	
Lady Bra – earnest shoe – they gave to 2 servant women –	11 June to Lady Bra: 6s. shoe gave in earnest to Helen Aikinhead to Helen Aikenhead Stewart befor Witsonday 1673..............................	00–06–00	
	12 June – sent to my good mother with Jo – Rob – a grot shoe gave to Mairzere Wood kitchen woman before Witsonday 1673....................	00–04–00	• 02 • 13 • –

James Brown – tanner – for a cows hyde of his own – 5 lib. & for barking ane ox hyde off my –	On Fryday 13 June 1673 sent to James Brown tanner with John Rob who broght me his recept off the same (8 lib.) which recept is lying amongst the rest off the recepts & discharges the particullars under mentioned to wit – 1– for a blak cows hyde off his own – blak leather curried & ready for cuting to be shoone to the bairns..........5 lib.: 2 for barking a large ox hyde off my own to be soll leather which is the first

own – 3 lib. is both – 8 lib. on his recept – off the said 8 lib.	hyde on the compt is at present betwixt the said James Brown & me – for barking the same – 3 lib. is both 8 lib. which ox hyde I boght fra Edowart Adamsone the 10 off September 1672 – cost – 4–6–8d. as it appears on a long compt booke with 3 brasse clasps on the 64 page theroff – I mean the compt betwixt James Brown & me is on the 64 page off the said booke	08–00–00	
To Mr Robert Brown the – 3 lads quarter peyment till – the 5 off – Jully 1673–	On Wedensday 18 June 1673 – sent to Mr Robert Brown schoole master with my sone Alexander Clerk seald in a peper – 7 lib. Scots – being 2 rex dolors & 2s. sterlin is 7 lib. 2 rex dollors being for William & Alexander Clerks for 3 months and the 2s. sterlin for Robert Clerk for 3 month – to wit fra the 5 off Aprill 1673 till the 5 off Jully 1673	07–00–00	• 15 • 00 • –
	all above	30–17–06	• 30 • 17 • 06
To George – Broun litster – 23–09 in full off ane acompt on his discharge – date – 13 June 1673 –	Fryday 13 June 1673 – delivert to James Clerk......19 lib. which he peyit to George Broun litster in full off ane accompt for liting severall things stuffs his accompt wes 23–09 and I wold give bot 19 lib. and it wes ynough – I have his accompt – with a discharge theron off the said 23–9s. & off all uther accompts what so ever preseiding the date off the said discharge which –discharge is date the 13 off June 1673	19–00–00	
barme – trouts –	19 June to Arche Andersone for trouts.................... 4s. Said day to Alexander Clark for barme he broght..............4s.	00–08–00	• 19 • 08 • –
James Clerk – 5 lib. 5s. in –	The 13 off June 1673 – I sent James Clerk to Edinburgh to doe some litle bussynes thair heir follows the accompt he gave me in off expensis		

full of ane accompt –	it cost him – thair being 5–5s. which I peyit him the 27 June 1673 & hath his recept thairoff on his compt date 27 June 1673		
	1– for my dyet being 9 days	03–10–00	
	2– spent with James Mackalien & John Scot wright	00–03–00	
	3– peyit for a Bible for Jennet Clerk.....28s.	01–08–00	
	4– for the horse expensse	00–04–00	• 05 • 05 • –
Alexr Clerk – ane accompt off 5 lib. tailyeur	Ane accompt off 5 lib. which Alexander Clerk spent the 2 & 5 off January 1673 when he went to Prestoun pans for Helen Clerk & then tooke hir to Edinburgh – it wes efter the death off hir dear sister Agnes Clerk who dyed the 20 off December 1672 which accompt is markit ABC	05–00–00	
41: loch leitches	The 28 off June – to James Kelte & Katherin Dicksone his wyffe who dwels within 3 quarters off Hadingtoun for 3 douzane & 5 loch litches....15s.	00–15–00	
Ja – Lawsone webster – 40 ell off lining at 3s. the ell 6–10–00	The 24 off June 1673 – sent to Mr Jo: Clerk with John Rob seald in a peper 6–10s. – who peyit the same to James Laweson webster for weiving 40 ell off lining at 3s. the ell is 6 lib. for ale 4s. drink money 6s. is 6–10s. – I have James Lawsons compt theroff with his discharge at the fitt theroff	06–10–00	• 12 • 05 • –
	To Arche Andersone for powing thrisles – 5 days	01–04–00	
	1 pig to hold hony for the bees – 2–8 – 1 pig to hold eirning is 8d. is	00–04–04	
	To James Clerk for 6 litle horne spoons	00–06–08	
	To a horner for 6 ram horn spoons & 6 ox horne spoons	00–09–00	• 02 • 04 • –

	For whyt breid in the month off June		• 01 • 10 • –
	The end off June 1673 – The disbursments in June 1673		• 71 • 09 • 06

[160]

Jully – 1673 Mr John Clerk –	The disbursments in Jully 1673 –		
	Saturday 21 June 1673 – delivert to Mr John Clerk when he went to Edinburgh which he disbursit as follows to wit – I delivert him – 12 lib. –		
	1 whyt yrne box to keep new clein [sic] pincels in	00–18–00	
	For horse meat	00–10–00	
	For his dyet fra the 21 off June to the 29	05–08–00	• 06 • 16 • –
		06–16–00	
	The 3 off Jully – he rendert me – 5 lib. 4s. which maks up the 12 lib.	05–04–00	
		12–00–00	
9 skore & 12 rude of fald dyks at 2s. the rude – 19–4	The 5 off Jully 1673 – peyit to James Bruntoun for biging 9 skore & 12 rude off fald dyks at 2s. the rude is........19–4s.		• 19 • 04 • –
Jo: Cokburne [sic] 12 silver spoons weying 25 once at 5 merk the once 83–06–08	The 1 off Jully 1673 – James – I say Mr John Clerk – peyit to James Cockburne 83–6s. –8d. for 12 silver spoons weying – 25 once at 3–6–8d. the once – is – 83–6–8 which 83–6–8 I delivert to Mr John Clerk the 2 off Jully 1673 according to the said James Cockburne his accompt with his discharge at the fit theroff date the 1 off Jully 1673		• 83 • 06 • 08

Margin	Entry		
Mr Robert – Alisone his – his stipend fra Witsonday 1672 till Witsonday 1673 – 48 lib.	The 2 off Jully 1673 – peyit to Mr Robert Alisone minister minister [sic] at the kirk off Glencorse – 48 lib. for his stipend off the lands off Cookeing lying within the la:[116] within the paroish off Glencorse –& that fra Witsonday 1672 till Witsonday 1673 on his discharge date the 2 off Jully 1673 which I delivert to his man Alexander Findlasone according to his letter		• 48 • 00 • –
To Mr Robert – Broun for 3 months quarter payment – 7 lib.	Munday the 7 off Jully 1673 – to Mr Robert Brown schoole master 7 lib. for the 3 bairns quarter payment for 3 month to wit fra the 5 off Jully 1673 – till the 5 off October 1673 – 1 rex dolor for W.C. 1 rex dolor for A.C[117]: & 24s. for Robert Clerk is in all – 7 lib. fra 5 Jully 1673 till the 5 off October 1673		• 07 • 00 • –
3 Jully 1673 voyage to – Prestoun pans with Jennet – Clerk	Disbursit at Prestoun pans on Thursday the 3 off Jully 1673 when I went thair with Jennet Clerk to John Brounns [sic] schoole –		
	1– to John Tait for 4 lb off Brizill tobaco at 16s. the pound is	03–04–00	
	2– 1 great whyt loaffe – 4s. 12 dry fish – 5s. is	00–09–00	
	3– charges on that voyage my selff – Edowart Adamsone & his horse Jo: Rob & his horse –& my own horse – 2 days & a night	05–07–00	• 09 • 00 • –
E–J	A B C: ~ ~ ~		
	Isobell Clerk wes born Thursday 12 June 1673 – baptized Saturday the 14 off June 1673		ABC;
Isobell – Clerk – Baptized – Saturday –	Helen Carmichel midwyffe cam to Newbiging on the 29 off May & returnt on Munday the 16 June 1673 to whom I gave 6 rex dolors........	17–08–00	
	To Mr Robert Broun schoolemaster	01–09–00	
	To Alexander Gray bedell.....12s.	00–12–00	• 19 • 09 • –

14 June 1673 – To William Mitchel baxter for 2 pecks off short breid on his discharge 02–04–00
7–40d. whyt loaffs 01–03–04
1 once off canel 00–14–00
1 litle whyt yrne pan 00–05–00
2 once off sirop off violets ....
Halff ane once off oyll off almonds 23s. 01–03–00
6 drop off safron – cost 2 merks 01–06–08
For a pape glasse which my good mother boght for E·J – 8d. – which I sent to hir with John Rob on Fryday 20 June 1673 .... 00–08–00 • 07 • 04 • –
1 pynt & halff a mutchkin off whyt wyne at 24s. the pynt 01–07–00
6 pynts off seck cost – 30s. the pynt 09–00–00
2 pynts off brande cost 30s. the pynt 03–00–00
1 very large suger loaffe – 1 lesser suger loaffe both weying 8 pound cost – 15s. the pound .... 06–00–00 • 19 • 07 • –
ABC
Fra ABC above to this is 46 pound 46–00–00

06–16–06 All above on this syde is – 219–06–08 .... • 219 • 06 • 08
19–04–00 8 Jully to John Rob – for a pynt off oyll for crishing wooll 00–12–00
83–06–08 10 Jully to a cadger – for a pynt off oyll for crishing wooll 00–09–00
48–00–00 Munday 14 Jully – to Roslins man who broght 6 litle salmond
07–00–00 trouts 00–13–04

116 Clerk likely began to write 'lands' but changed his mind. He did not cross out 'la:' before proceeding to write the rest of the entry.
117 The context makes clear that the initials W.C. and A.C. stand for William and Alexander Clerk.

09–00–00 For 31 Glasgow hering fresh 00–09–00

46–00–00 Tuesday 15 Jully 1673 – to Thomas Leys saidler who dwels neir

219–06–08 Dalmene doun at the sea syde at the Halls for – mending saidls & pads in the housse – 3 days with his meat in the housse at – 8s. ilk day is........ 00–01–04 • 03 • 03 • 04

Thomas Leys – saidler 219–06–08
3–03–04
222–10–00

The disbursments on this syd in Jully 1673 is – 222–10........ • 222 • 10 • –

[161]

James – Aikinhead– in Rougla– 60 ell off – lining – amonts to – 40–18s.

The disbursments on the other syde in Jully 1673 is – 222–10–00........ • 222 • 10 • –

Teusday – Jully 1673 boght fra a chapman dwels in Rougla in the Weste Contrie ....

1– 11 ell off lining at 15s. 6d. the ell 08–10–06
2– 17 ell off lining at 15–6 the ell .... 13–03–06........ 21–14–00
3– 12 ell
4– 10 ell
5– 10 ell is 32 ell off lining in 3 peices at 12s. the ell is 19–04–00

60 ell in all amonts to .... 40–18–00 • 40 • 18 • –

James Beir a yeirs fie – 21–04–00

On Wedensday 16 Jully 1673 – to James Beir – 20 lib. & 24s. for 2 pair off single sold shoone is 21–4s. for his yeirs fie fra Witsonday 1672 till – Witsonday last by past 1673 – 1673 .... 21–04–00 • 21 • 04 • –

10 lib. sterlin is 120 lib. for a bay – brown Inglish – mear	On the 18 off Jully 1673 – Mr John Clerk peyit to Richard Glover for a bay brown Inglish mear [sic]..............10 lib. sterlin is 120 lib. off which – 120 lib. I have Mr Glover his discharge – this 120 lib. wes a part off – 220 lib. the said Mr Jo: Clerk....resavet fra Thirlstains man the 14 off Jully 1673 as ane yeirs interest off 4000 lib. fra Witsonday 1672 till Witsonday 1673 the on[e] halff yeir at 6 per cent. The other halff yeir at 6 percent is 220 lib. I mean Thirlstains anuel rent off 4000 lib. for the said yeir..	• 120 • 00 • –
04–05–04 To Mr John – Smiths wyffe for causeing – bleitch the 3 particullars – under wreatten	To Mr John Smiths wyffe for causeing – bleitch – 1– 34 ell off dornick at 8 turnors the ell is.. 02–05–04 2– 15 ell off lining at 2s. 4d. the ell .... 01–15–00 3– for taking out the spots off 10 ell off lining................................ 00–05–00 Newbiging – Teusday 22 off Jully 1673 to Mr Jo: Smiths wyffe mistresse resave fra John Rob seald in a peper 4–5–4d. which the layd out for causeing bleich the 3 particullars according to the compt above mentioned cast up the compt above I think it is right iff it come to more it shalle be sent you – the 15 ell off lining wes not weell bleitched at all – nor ticht nor cleinlie bot it is no mater – I am sorie I sould have troubled you & thanks you for the pains the have been at & rests your h: S – J C..	• 04 • 05 • 04
Richard Twidie in Dauffintoun	To Richard Twidie in Dauffingtoun – for droging and tampering on with the brown Inglish meir above mentioned cost 10 lib. sterlin – on hir 4 feit – wes all wrong – & a knot on hir ribs 40s. 02–00–00	
Robert Hope 6 greit cheis–	Teusday the 22 off Jully 1673 peyit to Robert Hope younger in the – Spittel for 6 great cheis weying 6 ston – 4 lb lesse at 32s. the ston is	

	9 lib. 4s. which I peyit to him the said day	09–04–00	
barme –	19 Jully – to him for a quart of barme..........	00–04–00	
vinaigre–	23 Jully – to him for a mutchkin off vinaigre	00–02–06	
fresh Hering–	1 quarter – 100th fresh hering..........	00–07–06	• 11 • 18 • –
E–J...	24 Jully to E·J to give Mr William Hamiltons wooms [sic] 29s.	01–09–00	
Jo: Andersone	Fryday 25 Jully – wreatten to Daniell Whyt and sent him within the		
18s. –	letter 18s. – to give to his master John Andersone – for so much he		
A: Johnstoun –	spent with D·H	00–18–00	
for 5 firlots	Saturday 26 Jully 1673 – to Androw Johnstoun in the Halls – 4 lib.		
off oats – 4 lib.	for 5 firlots off horse corne – all 4 lib. which William Stewart resavet		
To James –	fra him the 7 off May 1673	04–00–00	
Broun tanner	Saturday 26 Jully 1673 – sent with John Rob 7 lib. 10s. which he delivert		
7–10 for	to James Brown tanner & broght me his compt & recept off the same for		
dressing 3 –	the particullars under mentioned to wit –		
hyds –	1– for barking ane ox hyde 2–10–00		
7–10–00	2– for barking ane other ox hyde 2–10–00		
	3– for tanning & currying a cows hyde off George Bels.......... 2–10–00..........	07–10–00	• 13 • 17 • –
George Clerk –	The 28 Jully – to George Clerk for weiving – 18 ell off lining at 3s.		
webster – 18	the ell – is – 54s. & 2s. for warping ale is – 56s. peyit to him the said		
ell off lining	day..........Georg Clerk webster	02–16–00	
herings –	Peyit at 2 tymes for 47 fresh hering..........	00–10–00	
trouts –	Last Jully – to Arche Andersone for trouts..........	00–02–06	
whyt breid –	For breid in the month off Jully – whyt breid..........	01–12–00	• 05 • 00 • 06

	The end off Jully 1673 The disbursments in Jully 1673 – amonts to – 439–12–10		• 439 • 12 • 10

	[162]		
Agust – 1673 –	The disbursments in Agust 1673;		
Mr John Clerk – a compt off disbursments off – 7–14–0 in Jully – 1673 –	Ane accompt off some small things Mr John Clerk boght & sent me at divers tymes in the month off Jully 1673 – according to his accompt & his recept at the fitt theroff dat the last off Jully 1673 off 7–14s. markit AB		
	1– ane ell off reid & whyt strypit Indian stuff 18s.	00–18–00	
	2– 2 Indian napkins off strypit lining & silk....................	01–16–00	
	3– for mending a pair of spurs	00–09–00	
	4– for the laton tirles for the pond being 8 foot of measur........	03–00–00	
	5– for 2 yrne rods thairtoo....................................	00–18–00	
	6– disparitors gramer for William Clerk........................	00–09–00	
	7– 2 onces off turpentin in a pot	00–04–06[118]	• 07 • 14 • 06
To Alexr Grays – wyffe–	The 16 off June 1673 – delivert to Alexander Grays wyffe in Pennycooke to bleitch lining cloth &c		

[118] Clerk noted above, and in the margin, that the disbursement amounted to 7–14–0. It is clear by this last entry, and the sum in the margin, that it should be 7–14–06.

for bleitching–	1– 21 ell is 34 ell off cloth I boght my selff		
136 ell off –	2– 13 ell unbleitched	34 ell –	
cloth	Delivert hir also to bleitch off cloth wes made within the housse –		
	1– 21 ell		
	2– 21 ell		
	3– 21 ell is......63 ell &		
	1– 19 ell		
	2– 20 ell is......39 ell is 102 ells	102 ell –	
	is in all	136 ell –	
	Is in all 136 ells at 1s. the ell.........is............6–16	06–16–00	
	For 3 pecks off meill at 5s. the peck	00–15–00	
	This 7 lib. 11s. I peyit hir on Saturday 2 Agust 1673	07–11–00	
	And on the 16 off June 1673 I gave hir – 28s. shoe said it wes to buy soap	01–08–00	• 08 • 19 • –
Mr John Clerk – 18s.	On Wedensday 6 Agust 1673 – wreatten to Mr John Clerk & sent him seald with in a letter – 18s. which wes sent with Alexander Clerk tailyeur the said day for 1 once off canel he sent me – cost 14s. and a pound off plum dames – is both 18s.	00–18–00	
Helen Patersone 20 ell of lining cloth – 9 lib.	The 8 off Agust 1673 – to Helen Patersone for 20 ell off lining cloth at 9s. the ell is	09–00–00	• 09 • 18 • –
11 Agust – 1673 – William –	On Munday 11 Agust 1673 – William Stewart – Arche Craig & Alexander Clerk went to Carnwath fare & sold the 4 oxen under mentioned to wit –		
	1– 1 ox got fra David Dryburgh cost 20 lib. sold for 20 lib.	20–00–00	

Stewart – sold at – Carnwath fare

2– 2 stots off 4 yeir old boght fra Newhalls Lady for 36ll. sold for 40–00–00
3– 1 brandit ox boght at Lithgow in a stot off 4 yeir old cost 19 lib.
sold for 26–6–8d 26–06–08

86–06–08

Charges peyit out –
For William Steuart – Patrik Craig & Alexander Clerk the first night fixing on a horse shoe & grasse to the horse......& 2s. off luck money..... 14s. 2d. for thair dinner in comeing home 6s. – custome off 5 oxens whair off 4 sold 3s. 4d. at Silver burn – 4 pynts – 4 pynts off ale is in all off charges....30s. 2d. which being rebated off – 86–06–08 – thair rests off frie money for the 4 oxen .... 84–16–8d.

stenting – The said 11 off Agust 1673 – Alexander Clerk boght with money I gave him 20 ell off stenting at 6s. the ell is.....6 lib. 06–00–00

fir – teathers – The said day – William Stewart – boght with my money I gave him to buy them – 6 firr teathers at........18d. the peice........................ 00–09–00 lib. s. • 06 • 09 • –

Hew Mackulloch 90–6–8 The thrid 3 months payment of the 12 months new [supplie] – The 6 off Agust 1673 – peyit to Hew MacCulloch – 90–06–08 on his discharge date the said day at the thrie – 3 months off the 12 months – new supplie imposed the 5 off Jully 1672 for my lands in Pennycooke & Glencorse paaroishes [sic] and my proportion that I fall to pay now – is included in the said soume above mentioned.
For mending the high ways – Mr Jo. Clerk peyit him the said 90–6–8 the said day – out – off 213 lib. he resavet fra Kimerghome for my accompt as the anuel rent off – 3550 lib. fra Mertimes 1671 till Mertimes 1672...... • 90 • 06 • 08

herin.... 6 Agust 1 quart off barme 00–04–00

ane yrning 12 Agust to Joyfull John for 31 oynions & 10 oynions........................ 00–06–00

a couper	Said day to Jo: Hogens for ane yrning	00–05–00	
	13 Agust to [blank] Davisone couper for setting on 62 girds		
vinaigre	16 Agust Saturday to Jo: Rob for –		
	1 mutchkin off vinaigre..........2s. 6d.		
leaffe tobaco	8 once off leaffe tobaco.........12s.	00–14–06	
hering	19 Agust to Alexander Clerk for hering he disbursit	00–05–00	
Jennet	Said day – to Jennet Spalding for 18 days shoe wes bleitching some		
Spalding	cloth at 12d. in the day – hir meat	00–18–00	
barme	20 Agust – to Jo: Rob for a quart off barme got at Gorge mill	00–06–00	• 03 • 07 • 06
	The disbursments on this syde – in Agust 1673............................		• 126 • 14 • 08
	126–14–8		

[163]

	The disbursments in Agust 1673 on the other syde is......126–14–8......		• 126 • 14 • 08
	20 Agust 1673 – to [blank] Pourdy webster in the Towr for weiving		
	14 ell off plaiding for the young gluton rumple 00–14–00		
	3 – 4 parts off meill – 4s. 6d. 1 pynt ales pryce – 20d. is		
E • J	6s. 2d. ....00–06–02..........	01–00–02	
13 ell off mixt –	23 Agust – to Mr William Hamiltons wyffe – for 13 ell off mixt		
grograine at 13s.	grograin at 13s. the ell is....................................08–09–00..........	08–09–00	
the ell	The 23 Agust – to Jo: Rob for 1 once off flour off Brunstaine	00–04–00	
Thomas Vaitch	The 25 Agust 1673 to Thomas Vaitch for 9 cheis weying 4 ston –		
4 ston 7 lb. cheis	7 lb at 30s. the ston is ....06–14s.	06–14–00	

at 30s. the ston
6–14

To a chapman – 1–12–0	25 Agust – to a chapman fo[r] 6 horn combs – 3 boxwood combs – 12 ell off small whyt knitings – 11 ell off worsetting – 1 knyffe for Sanders Clerk minor – 4 douzane & 8 duns poynts	01–12–00	• 17 • 19 • 02
Mr John Clerk his recept & disbursments off 243 lib. 16s. in Jully & Agust 1673	The accompt off moneys delivert to Mr John Clerk & that which he resavet for my accompt – to wit –		
	1– on the 2 off Jully 1673 delivert to him – 11 lyg dolors	30–16–00	
	2– on Thursday 7 Agust – Robert Home off Kimerghein peyit to him for my accompt – 213 lib. as ane yeirs interest off 3550 lib. fra Mertimes 1671 till Mertimes 1672 on my discharge date the 11 off Marche 1673	213–00–00	
	Ane accompt off his debursements off the said 1– – 243–16s. –		• 243 • 16 • –
	1– on Munday 11 Agust 1673 peyit be him to Hew MacCulloch on his discharge 90–06–08 as the thrid 3 months payment of the new supplie	90–06–08	
	2– the 1 off Agust to William Russel at 3 severall tymes for instrument money when the simulat consigation wes made be Sir John Smith	00–12–00	
	3– the 8 off Jully to Sir Robert Sinclair for consulting anent Balmerinos recognition – Mr Robert Smith gave as much	08–14–00	
	4– to Sir Jo: Dal: nourish	02–16–00	

5– 19 Agust – to James Clark glasser for making a laton tirles for the pond – the upmost pond – 4 lib. & for the yrne rods thairtoo – 26s. is........ 05–06–00

Mr John Clerk

6– 28 Jully – to Mr James Deans – anent the obteining off 2 decreits against costs –& Wrights Housses tenents........ 05–16–00

7– for ane pound off tarpentine........ 00–04–00

8– for his dyet – fra the 21 off June to the 21 off Agust as he comptit – 36 lib......... 36–00–00

10 [sic] for horse meat at 3 severall tymes........ 00–09–00

The disbursments above........ 150–03–08 • 150 • 03 • 08

The 28 off Agust 1673 – resavet fra Mr Jo: Clerk for the ballance off this accompt........ 93–12–04........ 93–12–04

243–16–00

On Munday the 14 off Jully 1673 – Mr John Clerk resavet fra the laird off Thirlstaine his man – 220 lib. Scots as the anuel rent off – 4000 lib. fra Witsonday 1672 till Witsonday 1673 the one – 6 month theroff being at 6 percent the other 6 month theroff being at 5 per cent........ 220 lib.

The way how he dibursit the said 220 lib. ....

Mr John Clerk his disbursment off

1– he peyit to Richard Glower the 18 Jully 1673 – 10 lib. sterlin for ane Inglish brown meir bot shoe is booked heer on this booke in the month off Jully 1673 – on the second page backward & is not to be comptit at this tyme agane bot only to be wreatten doun – to let know how this – 220 lib. wes disbursit........ 120–00–00

2– the 28 off Agust 1673 Mr Jo: Clerk peyit to Sir John Fowls at my

220 lib. Scots — desyre – 100 lib. Scots – for which 100 lib. he assigned Mr Jo: Clerk to a band off Archebald Teinders tailyeur off 158 lib. Mr Jo: Clerk wes caution – for this – 158 lib. to William Fowls – Sir John his brother – so he got this band off – 158 lib. for 100 lib. – bot a foole by being caution will find him selff cheated be a rascall – will never recover a penny off the said 158 lib. – I will set doun only heer bot this 100 lib. because the mear wes set doun on this booke befor .... 100–00–00 • 100 • 00 • –

220–00–00

John Clerk –

Alex[r] or Sande Stewarts fies preseiding Mertimes 1673 — As it apears on a booke covert with parchement whair servants fies is wreatten doun markit on the syde – 347 – on the 29 off Agust 1673 – peyit William Stewart for his sone Sande Stewart his fie – fra Witsonday 1672 till Mertimes 1673 is 3 halff yeirs according to – 5 lib. ilk halff yeir – and a pair off single sold shoone is in money – 15 lib. & for his shoone 28s. is in all – 16–8s. which I peyit to William Stewart the said 29 off Agust 1673 – in full off all his fies till & preseiding the terme off Mertimes 1673 16–08–00

souding a stoup — 27 Agust – to Jo: Rob – for sowding a pynt stoup 00–04–00

barme — To him for 1 quart off barme 00–04–00

Salustius – — 2 *Salustius* for Will & Alexander Clerks – 18s. .... 00–18–00.......... 01–06–00 • 17 • 14 • –

Whyt breid in the month of Agust – 40s. .... • 02 • 00 • –

This syde is – 287–16–8 126–14–8 414–11–4 — The end off Agust 1673 The disbursments in Agust 1673 is ..... • 414 • 11 • 04

[164]

September	The disbursments in September 1673 –		
1673	On the 1 off September 1673 – peyit to Arche Craig – 10 lib. & 10s.		
Arch: Craigs	for a pair off single sold shoone for his fie – fra Witsonday 1673 till		
6 months fie	Mertimes 1673 is – 10–10s. for the said haill yeir	10–10–00	
Helen – Gray	On Teusday – 2 September 1673 – sent to Helen Gray with John Rob		
14 ell plaiding –	seald in a peper – 5 lib. 12s. for 14 ell off plaiding at 8s. the ell – cam		
5–12s.	fra the Lady Bagillo......is	05–12–00	
26 rude of	1 September 1673 – to James Bruntoun for biging a litle fald for –		
fald dyks	the lambs – being 26 rude at 2s. the rude is.....52s.	02–12–00	• 18 • 14 • –
To a chapman	3 September – to a chapman – for 2 ½ ell off lining at – 16s. the ell –		
56s.	40s. & for divers other small things – 16s. is	02–16–00	• 02 • 16 • –
4 September	On Thursday the 4 off October 1673 – I say the 4 off September 1673		
1673	William Stewart & Arche Craig – tooke to Skirlin fare to sell – 1. 2 oxen –		
catel sold	2. a cow – 3. 3 stirks is – 6 in all – whairoff he sold only – as follows –		
in Skirlin fare	1– a blak gelding ox – boght fra James Russell a bull stot cost 8 merk –		
for – 50–13–4	I sold for 25–06–08	25–06–08	
being –	2– a rown bakit ox off our own breiding sold for: off – 12 yeir old –		
2 oxen	sold for 25.............25–06–08 also	25–06–08	
	50–13–04	50–13–04	
	Charges – luck penny –& custom – which I compt & sets doun only on		
	this booke....................13s. 8d.		• 00 • 13 • 08
John – Rob	Saturday 6 September 1673 – to John Rob for all the particullars under		
	wreatten – to wit –		

wool cairds –	1– 1 pair off wooll cairds he got fra James Hamiltoun	01–04–00	
tobaco pyps –	2– 4 douzane off tobaco pyps castel mark at 20d. the douzane	00–06–08	
oynion heads	3– for oynion heads	00–04–00	
fresh beiff –	4– 1 rumple peece off beeff	00–08–00	
peirs – plumbs	The said day – to Cudbert Kyll – for Carnok peirs & plumbs	02–01–00	
Marg – Hopkirk	4 September – to Margaret Hopkirk shoe disbursit for the bairns		
for the bairns –	1. for a gallon off ale – 13s. 4d. – for 2 lb off butter – 8s. – 3 – for		
23s. – 10d.	eygs – 2s. 6d. is in all – 23s. 10d.	01–03–10	• 05 • 07 • 06
Helen Gray –	On Teusday – 9 September 1673 – wreatten to Helen Gray & sent hir with		
whyt worsit –	William Blackwood merchant – a packit be itselff seald conteining – 5 lib.		
5 lib. – 2s.	2s. for 2 pound – 2 once off whyt worsit to be stokins – at –3s. the once –		
	I sent with him the letter also the said day	05–02–00	
James –	Saturday the 19 off September 1673 – to James Lawsone tailyeur four		
Lawsone –	merks – for 16 days he wroght at Newbiging with his meat at 3s. 4d.		
tailyeur	a day – is – 2–13–4d. & halff a merk I gave him to drink is in all	03–00–00	• 08 • 02 • –
John Rob –	10 September 1673 – to Jo: Rob for 1 quart off barme 4s. – halff a hundreth		
James Meygit –	hering – 6s. 8d.	00–10–08	
harvest gloves	10 September – to James Meygit – to buy a pair off harvest gloves	00–06–00	
Androw –	The 12 off September 1673 – to Androw Burn webster – for weiving		
Burne	27 ell off cloth – made off grounds to be sheits at 12d. the ell – is –		
webster –	01–07–00 –& 14 ell off cloth to be sheits to the bair: to be sarks to the		
3–11–00	bairns at 2s. the ell……&–		
	& for meill & warping ale &c – 16s. is in all	03–11–00	• 04 • 07 • 08

Elvinstoun – Thursday 18 September 1673 – I went to Elvinstoun in East Lothian – cam
to that place about 10 hours – stayd 2 nights thair – & returnt homeward on
Nunland – Saturday the 20 off September about 10 or 11 hours – I tooke Edowart
Adamsone to ryde with me ....

Prestoun – pans
1– to ane old wyffe wes the ladys mame
3 halff rex dolors 04–07–00
2– to the meassons halff a rex dolor &–
6s. 8d. for halff a gallon off ale is 01–15–08
3– to the gairner.. 01–04–00
Dalkeith 4– to 2 men servants with aprons .... 01–10–08.......... 08–17–04 • 08 • 17 • 04

To Mr John Dowgals woman off Nunland who keiped his youngest chyld –
newly spaind – a rex dolor & to his man – 13s. 4d. is 03–11–04
2– it cost me at Prestoun pans 01–04–08
3– to John Tait for 4 lb off bizel row tobaco....58s. 02–18–00
4– it cost me at Dalkeith in going and at my returning..................... 02–08–00 • 10 • 12 • –

John Rob 13 September to John Rob – for 1 soum sive – 2s. 4d. – 1 peice of fresh
beiff – 7s. – 60 fresh herings – 10s. 2d. is 00–19–06
24 September – 100 fresh hering – boght at Newbiging..................... 00–13–04 • 01 • 12 • 10

The disbursments in September 1673 on
this syde above is – 61–03–00 .... • 61 • 03 • –

[165]

	The disbursments on the other syde in September 1673 is –61–03–00			• 61 • 03 • –
Sold at	William Stewart & Arche Craig went to Athelstoun fare on Munday			
Athelston fare	the 15 off September 1673 & sold the catel – under mentioned			
18–16–8	to wit			
	1– a brandit stot	05–01–08		
	2– a tagit coy	05–01–08		
	3– a blak stot	04–13–04		
	4– a coy off a yeir old	04–00–00	18–16–08	
oxen	William Stewarts charges &c	00–06–08		
bows	4 oxen bows – cost	00–12–08	19s. 4d.	• 00 • 19 • 04
David	The 24 off September 1673 to David Glendining			
Glendining	1– 2 young toops for breiding Wille Stewart resavet fra			
2 toops –	him – at – 46s. the peice		04–12–00	
11 ston off –	2– 6 great cheis weying 6 stain wecht at 38s. the ston		11–08–00	
cheis –	3– 10 lesser cheis off thair own making weying 5 ston wecht at			
24 lib.	32s. the ston is 8 lib.		08–00–00	• 24 • 00 • –
harvest	1 pair off harvest gloves for Alexander Clerk tailyeur...4s.		00–04–00	
gloves –	Saturday morneing the 27 off September 1673 – to James Duncan			
James Duncan –	cordoner for – 47 days he wroght at Newbiging at 5s. 6d. ilk day with			
cordoner	his meat dayly is		12–18–06	• 13 • 02 • 06
John Rob....	27 September – to Jo: Rob for 1 peice off beiff – 7s. 6d. – 1 quart of barme			
	4s. – for the horse charges – Mr Jo: Clerk took in 4s. – custom off 4 ½ ston			
	off wooll – Jo: Rob took in for the Lady Bagillo – 1s. is in all		01–01–06	• 01 • 01 • 06

Newhall ingredients – for a shortnes of the braith – & a sore breast	On Saturday 27 off September 1673 at Newhals desyre & according to a memor he gave me to use for the shortnes off the braith – his sone John Pennycooke helpit John Rob to buy them & John Rob peyit for them with my money.........		
	1– halff a pound off fygs..	00–03–06	
	2– a pound of blew raisings	00–06–00	
	3– halff a pound off finkle seid..............................	00–10–00	
	4– 3 ½ onces of oyntment off marsh–mallows..	00–15–10.......... 35s. 4d.	• 01 • 15 • 04
hering –	100 herings......13s. 4d.	00–13–04	
barme –	1 pynt off barme..	00–02–00	
fresh beiff –	1 peice off fresh beiff	00–07–00	
whyt breid –	Whyt breid in the mont[h] off September	01–10–08	• 02 • 13 • –
	The end off September 1673 The disbursments in September 1673		• 00 • 14 • –
	104–14–08		• 104 • 14 • 08

October	The disbursments in October 1673 –		
1673 – Jo Robs harvest fie & super maill	Munday 6 October 1673 – peyit to John Rob for his harvest fie 1673 a rex dolor and a halff is 4–7s. & 20s. for his harvest super 1673 – is 5 lib. 7s. is	05–07–00	
G. Clerks harvest super maill	The said day to George Clerk for his harvest super 1673....................	01–00–00	• 06 • 07 • –
Jennet Clerk hir going to	On Thursday in the afternoone – being the 9 off October 1673 – I sent John Rob & Alexander Clerk with 2 horse to Prestoun pans with Jennet		

Margin	Entry	Amount	Total
Prestoun pans	Clerk – to John Brouns schoole who entert home in boording in Katherin Sinclair hir housse on Fryday the 10 off October 1673		
Dalkeith fare on Fryday the 10 October 1673	Thair expense in going to Prestoun pans – 1. for the 2 horse on Thursday at night – 16s. – for thair supper 8s. is................................	01–04–00	
	At Dalkeith fare which wes on th[e] Fryday – 10 October 1673 – severall expensis & charges –it cost me – 3 lib. Jo: Rob – peyit for oynions – 4s. is	03–04–00	• 04 • 08 • –
W: Steuart a brandit coy – 10 lib.	10 October 1673 at Dalkeith fare boght fra William Steuart – a brandit coy off 3 yeir old weill hornt for which I peyit him – 10 lib. Scots	10–00–00	
	11 October – to Jo: Rob for 1 peice off fresh beiff............................	00–07–06	
	1 quart off barme..	00–04–00	
	1 pynt off fish oyll	00–11–00	
	15 October to him for 2 douzane off oynions...................................	00–04–00	
	18 October to him for 5 mutchkins brande at – 28[s.] the pynt	01–15–00	• 12 • 04 • 06
	The disbursments in October 1673 on this syde is..............................		• 23 • 03 • 06

[166]

Margin	Entry	Amount	Total
	The disbursments in October 1673 on the other syde is		• 23 • 03 • 06
4 ston – off butter 11–16–00	Wedensday 22 October 1673 – William Stewart boght at Silver burne – 4 ston off butter at 59s. the staine is – 11 lib. 16s. – 2 ston thairoff for helping to smeir the sheip the uther 2 stain for the usse off the housse		• 11 • 16 • –
ridls – & sives John	23 October 1673 to Jo – Austin in Cairingtoun for – 1 ridle for ridling corne...	00–06–08	

Austin	1 sive for the sanding off stuffe	00–06–08	• 00 • 00 • –
	1 barn wyd ridle	00–05–00	• 00 • 18 • 04
vinaigre	1 pynt off vinaigre	00–09–00	
webster	25 October to Adam Elleis for weiving 9 ell off hardn at 1s. the ell	00–09–00	
	And 3s. 4d. for harregraith – thairtoo	00–04–04	
barme	25 October – 1 quart off barme	00–04–00	• 01 • 06 • 04
Housse – off Mure – 12 ews at 28s. the peice is – 16–16	Teusday 28 October 1673 – sent with William Stewart to the Housse off Mure to be sold – 12 dracht ews who sold the said – 12 ews at 28s. the peice – is – 16–16–00 – I peyit him 3s. 8d. off custome & bought maill	16–00–00	
Will Alex[r] Ro: Clerks boord in 3 month	30 October 1673 to Margret Hopkirk – 40 lib. for William Alexander & Robert Clerks boord fra the 22 off October 1673 till the 22 off January 1674 is 3 month – is according to 20 merks in the quarter for ilk ane off them		• 40 • 00 • –
Thair quarter payments 6 month till the 5 off Januar 1674	30 October 1673 – to Mr Robert Broun – 14 lib. for William Alexander & Robert Clerks quarter payments – 6 month fra the 5 Jully 1673 till the 5 off January 1664[119] is halff a yeir at 1 rex dolor in the quarter for ilk ane off the 2 eldest & 24s. in the quarter for Robert Clerk....is	14–00–00	• 14 • 00 • –
	31 October – 5 chopins off brande at 28s. the pyynt [sic]	01–15–00	
	For whyt breid in October	01–11–00	
	1 peice off fresh beiff	00–06–00	• 03 • 06 • –
	The end off October 1673 – All the disbursments in October 1673 is – 94–14–02		• 94 • 14 • 02

November 1673	The disbursments in November 1673 –	
	The 4 off November 1673 to Margaret Heren for hir fie – fra Witsonday 1673 till Mertimes 1673 – 8 lib.	• 08 • 00 • –
	The 4 off November 1673 to Helen Aikinhead Stewart 8 lib. & 30s. for a pair off shoone is – 9–10s. for hir fie fra Witsonday 1673 till Mertimes 1673 is........9–10	• 09 • 10 • –
4: servants fies	The 4 off November 1673 peyit to James Beir – 10 lib. 12s. for his fie fra Witsonday 1673 till Mertimes 1673	• 10 • 12 • –
2 men – 2 women –	The 4 off November 1673 to William Watsone hird for a yeirs fie fra Mertimes 1672 till Mertimes 1673 with his shoone	• 15 • 01 • 08

George Reid imp lawrels bays &c.	The 5 off November 1673 to George Reid gairner in the Bill for 13 or 14 fyne young imps off aples & chirrie – rose mary – with the roots a good qu[a]ntite theroff – lawrels – bays &c all – ver[y] prettie – young on[e]s for which I peyit him 14s. sterlin is	• 08 • 08 • –
mouton	6 November – Alexander Clerk to give Isobell Scot for 2 peices mouton 00–16–00	
whyt wyne ry breid	At Dalkeith said day – Will: Stewart boght 1 pynt of whyt wyne – 24s. – 2 ry anker stoks – 2s. 8d. is 01–06–08	• 02 • 02 • 08
James Clerk	Sunday 8 November 1673 sent with Arche Craig seald in peper adrest to Mr Jo: Clerk & be him to be delivert to his brother James Clerk – 27s.	

[119] Clerk mistakenly wrote 1664 instead of 1674 in the original.

27s.	for 2 bellum gramatical[120] is – 9s. & 8 douzane off gray flat buttons – 18s. is 27s.	• 01 • 07 • –
14 whyt wand baskits	10 November 1673 to John Wallace for – 14 whyt wand hand baskit off divers bignes whairof 3 off them with lids	• 03 • 10 • –
	The disbursments in November on this syde is	• 58 • 00 • 04

[167]

	The disbursments in November 1673 on the other syde	• 58 • 00 • 04
Mr John Clerk – Accompt off	Accompt off 12–9s. disbursit be Mr John Clerk at Edinburgh – 7 September 1673 which I peyit him on his recept on the compt the 5 off November 1673	
	1– drink money at Jennet Dowglas brydell	• 02 • 16 • –
12 lib.	2– for his dyet fra 27 September till the 3 off October	• 04 • 10 • –
9s.	3– for the horse 3s. & for oynions – 20s. is	• 01 • 03 • –
	4– for his dyet fra Munday – 20 October till Thursday – 23 off October – 36s. & for the horse wes keeped 3 days – 18s.	• 02 • 14 • –
	1– a currie combe 00–12–	
	2– a timber combe & water spungue 00–04–	
	3– a rubber – 4s. ..... 00–04– is – 20s.	• 01 • 00 • –
		• 12 • 09 • –
Jennet Spalding	The 11 off November 1673 to Jennet Spaldings doghter [sic] for spining wooll 26 days 2 merk and halff a merk I gave hir over & above to hir selff friely is – 33s. 4d. 01–13–04	

Margin	Entry	Amount	Total
Edowart Adamsone 1 – ane ox hyd 2 – 14 lb. off talon	Thursday 13 November 1673 – peyit to Edowart Adamsone for –		
	1– ane ox hyde off a hurlie ox	04–00–00	
	A loffe off his talon weying 14 lb wecht	01–19–00	• 07 • 12 • 04
1 ½ boll off whyt salt.... cost – 6 lib.	Saturday 15 November 1673 William Stewart went to Preston pans & boght 1 ½ boll off whyt salt at 4 lib. the boll – is – 6 lib. & for his horse charges 6s. is	06–06–00	
whyt wand baskits	10 November – to Jo: Wallace for 14 whyt wand baskits off severall sorts & bignes [sic]	03–10–00	
Marzere Woods fie	20 November 1673 to Marzere Wood – 8 lib. for hir fie fra Witsonday 1673 till Mertimes 1673	08–00–00	
quart stoup	To Jo: Rob – 19 November – for mending a lid off a quart stoup	08–00–00	
baling	For a pound off baling – 1–6–8d.	01–06–08	
horse charges	To Arche Craig for severall horse charges	01–00–00	
brande....	To John Rob – for 5 chopins off brande	01–15–00	
fresh beiff	3 peices off fresh beiff – 20s. 8d.	01–00–08	
		17–00–04	• 17 • 00 • 04
	Whyt breid in November 1673		• 01 • 08 • –
	The end of November 1673		
	The disbursments in November 1673		• 30 • 09 • 08

120 See E. Butler, *The bellum grammaticale and the rise of European literature* (London, 2016).

December 1673 –	The disbursments in December 1673[121] –		
Jennet Clerks boord 3 – month is 20 lib.	The 12 off December 1673 – Alexander Clerk went to Preston pans – and peyit to Katherin Sinclair – 20 lib. for Jenet Clerks boord fra the 3 off December 1673 till the 3 off Marche 1674 and tooke hir recept off the same date – 12 December 1673 – he got this 20 lib. fra Helen Patersone in part off payment off hir maill shoe wes resting me		• 20 • 00 • –
Fra Edward Cleghorn 12 silver spoons cost 89–18–06	The 4 of December 1673 boght fra Edward[122] Cleghorn goldsmith twelve silver spoons weing 27 ounces 4 drop at 3 lib. 6s. the ounce is	89–18–06	
	For which I gave him of old silver 18 ounce 4 drop at 3 lib. the ounce is	54–15–00	
	And in money	35–03–06 is –	• 89 • 18 • 06
John Rob	To John Rob for wheyt bread fra the 24 of November 1673 till the 24 of December 1673	01–18–2d.	
	More to him for severall uther disbursements the said month	02–07–8d.	• 04 • 05 • 10
Tho: Wodcok for a coach	24 December 1673 to Thomas Woodcok for a coach and four horses to Newbiging 8–14s. & to his man 13s. 8d. is		• 09 • 07 • 04
	The disbursments above in December 1673		• 123 • 11 • 08

[168]

	The disbursments on the other syde in December 1673 –		• 123 • 11 • 08
Margaret Clerk	28 of November 1673 to Mistres[s] Brand on her discharge in full of her accompt – 82–12–10d. for a gown and petticot to Margaret Clerk	82–12–10	

	To Patrik Telfer tayleor for making & furnishing	09–05–02	• 91 • 18 • –
yrne	20 November 1673 to John Thomsone on his discharge in full of his accompt for 21 stone 10 pounds of yrne at 33s. 4d. the stone is	35–14–08	• 35 • 14 • 08
Mr Jo: & James Clerks	To Mr Jo: Clerk in full of his compt for black cloths date 20 November 1672	41–13–04	
	To James Clerk in full of his compt for black cloths date 21 December 1672	75–17–10	• 117 • 11 • 02
lint & Coat of Armes	To James Hammiltone 3 December 1673 in full of his accompt on his discharge for 6 stone 4 lb of lint	28–15–00	
	Payed of all charges for a cott [sic] of armes	21–00–00	• 49 • 15 • –
Mr Jo: Clerk cloths	9 December 1673 to Mr Jo: Clerk on his recept for a suit of cullord cloths Baylie Drummond furnished him	59–01–00	• 59 • 01 • –
			• 353 • 19 • 10
	3 gray bonnets for the bairns	00–17–00	
	4 pair of gloves for them	00–15–00	
	To Jo: Morison for showing 3 pair of triple poynted Inglish cordovans	01–00–00	• 02 • 12 • –
John Cook	1 December 1673 to John Cooke for a bosse lock with two keys & a sprent band and making a litle key to a bitt of ane old box lock	02–13–04	• 02 • 13 • 04

[121] There is a change in the handwriting on the last nine pages of the original manuscript (167–175). Though never explicitly stated in this section of the original, it is likely that Clerk's son, John, took over when Clerk's failing health prevented him from maintaining the account from this point until his death in April 1674.

[122] The change in spelling of this name can be explained by the fact that someone other than Clerk was now maintaining the book of disbursements.

3 stone butter	3 December 1673 payed for 3 stone of butter at 58s. the stone	08–14–00	
stiffing & litts	Payed to Widow Jollie for stiffing things for litting &c: accordin to accompt	04–06–11	• 13 • 10 • 11
teyking	15 December 1673 to Widow Dow for 18 els of tyking at 10s. the ell	09–00–00	
hatt press	13 December 1673 Mr Jo: Clerk payed to Widow Adamsone 1 hatt press weying 20 lb. at 4 merk the stone	03–06–00	• 12 • 06 • –
silver mustard box –	1 silver mustard box with a silver spoone weying 5 onces 3 drop at 3 lib. the once is 15–12s. for making theroff 58s. is		• 18 • 10 • –
	To John Crichton for girding all now & mending 2 large 3 longed coichs wes gagsned [sic] & all in staps[123]	01–04–00	
	1 new pewter plaitt	02–06–00	
	To Daufington for a bras morter	04–00–00	• 07 • 10 • –
	Payed to Robert Richisone for dry confections	03–00–00	
	5 December 1673 to David Gray for a pair of pantons	01–10–00	• 04 • 10 • –
	The 31 December 1673 accompt of 110 lib. payed to Mr John Clerk on his discharge	110–00–00	
	1– whereof to Sir Robert Sinclair & his man	17–06–00	
	2– for making & furnishing a suit of cloths to Mr Jo: Clerk	05–17–00	
	3– for Mr Jo: Clerks expenses in 50 dayes	30–00–00	
	4– for the loan of a mourning clok for Mr Jo: Clerk	00–12–00	
	Thir four particulars is	56–05–00	
	The remainder wes debursed for James Clerk to – doctors &c: in his great seekness in a fever extending to	53–15–00	

		110–00–00	• 110 • 00 • –
	Summa of all above in December 1673		• 648 • 03 • 09
Alex[r] Clerks accompt	24 December 1673 Alexander Clerk gave up the accompt folowing –		
	To Alexander Hastie for sweeping the hems	00–06–08	
	13 December he spent at the pans	00–10–00	
	To James Meggett quhen he recovered the lost swyne	00–12–00	
	To the bairns at 4 severall Sundays	00–11–00	
	9 December 1674 quhen James Meggett went with 24 bols of oats to the mill	01–00–00	
	16 December to Alexander Grays wyfe for dressing lint	00–06–00	
	24 December for horse meat & my own	00–18–00	• 40 • 03 • 08

[169]
The disbursments in Decemberr 1673 on the other two syds

[blank for the rest of this page]

123 'to gang all to staps' is a phrase used to convey that something was falling to pieces.

[170]

The debursments in Januar 1674 –

ANNO 1674

1 boll of seed	1 Januar 1674 William Stewart boght at Dalkeith one boll of seed		
peys &	peys	06–02–00	
1 boll of pott	2– a boll of pott peys	06–09–02	
peys	is both 12–11–2d.		• 12 • 11 • 02
61 ells off	1 Januar 1674 to Thomas Richeson for 61 ells of secking in four		
secking	peices at 7s. the ell is	21–07–00[124]	• 21 • 00 • –
brande	1 Januar 1674 for 5 mutchkins of brande at 28s. [the] pynt is	01–15–00	• 01 • 15 • –
Mr Ro: Brown	5 Januar 1674 to Mr Robert Broun 20 lib. Scots as his stipend fra		
20 lib. Scots	Witsonday 1673 till Witsonday 1674 I resaved his discharge		
	yairof		• 20 • 00 • –
	3 Januar 1674 William Stewart went to Dalkeith & boght & payed for –		
peys	1– a boll of peys and beans mixed	05–16–08d.	
wyne	2– for a pynt of wheit [sic] wyne	01–00–00d.	
candle	3– to Robert Cleghorn candlemaker in full of his accompt		
	on his discharges	14–10–00d.	• 21 • 06 • 08
	3 Januar 1674 payed to John Rob for –		
vinaigre	1– a pynt of vineger [sic]	00–09–00	
beefe	2– a peice of beefe	00–10–00	
bread	3– for bread	00–05–00	
	4– for a cows reed	00–04–00	

	5– for ane almanak	00–00–06	• 01 • 08 • 06
13 els [sic] of plaiden	3 Januar 1674 to Andrew Purdie webster for weaving 13 els of plaiden to be blankets to the hirds 19s.		• 00 • 19 • –
Jo: Robs accompt	10 Januar 1674 John Rob went to the toun & debursed as folows –		
	To Thomas Henrysone for 4 ounces of sennie	01–08–00	
	For half ane ounce of cannell	00–06–08	
	culebs cardamus lefser zedwarie galanga an: 1 dram[125]	00–05–00	
	4 lb almonds at 9s. the lb is	01–16–00	
	Half pound of liquorish	00–06–08	
	12 aples	00–02–00	
	For berm	00–04–00	
	Whyte iron mutchkin pan	00–04–00	
	For solding the salt fatt	00–02–00	
	For 5 mutchkins of brande	01–15–00	• 06 • 08 • 08
Mr Wil: Hammiltons stipend 326	27 Januar 1674 to Mr William Hammiltone for his stipend fra Mertimes 1672 till Mertimes 1673 326 lib. according to his discharge of the said date		• 326 • 00 • –
Ja: Brown tanner	28 Januar 1674 to James Broun tanner on his discharge 5 lib. Scots – which Jo: Rob payed him in full of all accompts preceiding the said 28 Januar		• 05 • 00 • –

124 The sum entered in the margin incorrectly states 21–00–00 where it should probably state 21–07–00.

125 See E. Turner, *Elements of Chemistry: Including the Actual State and Prevalent Doctrines of the Science* (London, 1847), 1134.

Ro: Adamsone 8 bols oats	7 Januar 1674[126] payed to Edward Adamsone I say Robert Adamsone in the Nyne Mill Burn for 8 bols of oats his brother Edward deliverd to me in his name at 4 lib. the boll is 32 lib.		• 32 • 00 • –
Rob Johnstouns funerals gown to E: Johnstone	27 Januar 1674 payed to James Clerk conform to ane accompt given in be him and his recept at the foott yairof –		
	1– for Robert Johnstons funerals being	63–12–10	
	2– for ane gown to my wyfe E: Jo:	33–12–00	• 97 • 04 • 10
	The debursments in Januar 1674 on this syde is		• 545 • 13 • 10

[171]

	The debursments in Januar 1674 in the other syde are........................		• 545 • 13 • 10
Tho: Henrysons accompt	27 of Januar 1674 payed to Thomas Henriesone apothocarie conform to his discharged accompt of the said date...		
	For my fathers accompt	08–17–00	
	For my sister Helens accompt	06–16–00	
	For James Clerk when he wes seek [sic]	70–19–08 is	• 86 • 12 • 08
James Meggett	6 Januar 1674 to James Meggett for killing &c: 20 bols of oats	13s.	
	And for the horse charges to him for 2 days quhen E: Jo: went to the toun..	16s.	• 01 • 09 • –
John Rob	16 Januar 1674 to John Rob for breid at severall tymes	02–00–00	
	& for beef at severall tymes	01–07–00	
	To him for 1 quart & 1 mutchkin of brande at 28s. the pynt is	03–03–00	
	For 2 lb of cutt & dry tobacco at 18s. the lb is	01–16–00	

	For the horse	00–08–00	
	For 10 dusan [sic] of pyps	00–05–00	
	For 1 quart 1 mutchkin of brande	03–03–00	• 12 • 02 • 00
Wil Megett	To him 12 lib. for Isobel Clerk boord fra 11 Januar to 11 Aprill		• 12 • 00 • –
	To Sir Jo: Fouls 150		• 150 • 00 • –
My own debt	To Mr Wil: Clerk		• 200 • 00 • –
	To Mr Campbell		• 100 • 00 • –

[The rest of this page is blank]

[172]

Februar	The debursements in Febuar 1674		
Ed: Thomsone	5 Februar 1674 boght fra Edward Thomsone 7 bolls of oats which William Burrell gatt for his boll at 4 lib. 4s. the boll is –29–08–00 which 29–08s. I payed to the said Edward the said day		• 29 • 08 • –
Ge: Clerk webster	12 Februar 1674 payed to George Clerk webster for weaving 15 els of wollen cloth at 30d. the ell is	01–17–06	
	For warping ale 3–4d. for paping 5s. is	00–08–04	• 02 • 05 • 10
John Rob brande	John Rob gave in ane accompt of 16–7s. the 12 Februar 1674 which wes payed to him the said day marked A..........16–7s.		• 16 • 07 • –

126 The date entered on this line is 7 January 1674 in the original. It is possible that this is a mistake and the writer meant to write 27 January 1674; however, it is also possible that the receipt was entered late (as has been seen in earlier accounts).

Lead fra Mr Andr: Rosse	9 Februar 1674 payed to John Maigue quho wes sent be Mr Andrew Ross to me with with [sic] 14 stone 3 lb at 32s. the stone is 22–14s. which wes payed to the said John according to John I say according to Mr Andrew Ross his order		• 22 • 14 • –
John Rob	16 Februar 1674 payed to John Rob conform to ane accompt given in by him the said day	05–15–00	
	17 Februar 1674 to him conform to ane other accompt	02–19–00	• 08 • 14 • –
James Park	17 Februar 1674 to James Park for a plough	03–00–00	
	4 Februar to John Rob for 2 loaves 5s. & 1 peice of beif 11s.	00–16–00	• 03 • 16 • –
Wil: Stew	To Wil: Stewart for goeing to Clerkingtoun for blankets 16 Februar		• 00 • 06 • 08
Mr Jo: Clerk	To him for 1 pair of verie lairge Leith wynde waked stokins – 5 merk		• 03 • 06 • 08
calf	To Wil: Stewart to pay Thomas Burne for a veall – 21 Februar	03–06–08	• 03 • 06 • 08
Jo: Rob brande	24 Februar to John Rob 16 lib. to be delivered to Jannet Taitt for 11 pynts & 1 chopin of brande		• 16 • 00 • 00
John Rob	20 Februar 1674 John Rob gave in ane accompt of 6–9s. & receaved itt		• 09 • 02 • –
	30 Februar John Rob gave in ane accompt of 12–19s. & receaved it		• 12 • 19 • –
Ja: M^c^allien	19 Februar 1674 to James Mackallien for 2 large sneding knyves	05–08s.	• 05 • 08 • –
Wil: Russell for 2 contracts	To William Russell 24 Februar 1674 for wreiting Mr John & Margaret Clerks contract there being 3 doubles of each of them 30 sheett	26–02–00d.	
	& to his man 1 rex dolor	02–18–00d.	• 29 • 00 • –
D: Young	To Doctor Young 25 Februar 1674 quhen he consulted the second tyme with D: Henriesone & Newhall anent my fathers health 1 guinie cost 21s. 6d. ster:		• 12 • 18 • –

Rob: Dewer	To Robert Dewer 2 March 1674 conform to his accompt – 22–15–8d. which is sett doun in a sheett of paper.....by it self		• 22 • 15 • 08
D: Young	My father gave himself out of his own hands to D: Young 18 Februar 1674 – 8 rex dolors is		• 23 • 04 • –
Nicoll Ramsay	4 March to Nicoll Ramsay for for [sic] 7 wyld fowl	02–02–00	
	30 Februar for 24 dusan of egs [sic]	02–08–00	
	24 Februar to Ja: Alexander for goeing to Preston for Jennett	00–06–00	
	25 Februar for barm	00–04–00	• 05 • 00 • –
	For ale at severall tymes out of Helen Thomson	00–15–00	
	For horse hyre at severall tymes the said moneth [sic]	04–00–00[127]	

[173]

	The debursements in Februar 1674 –	
John Rob	The debursements in March 1674 – 5 March 1674 John Rob gave in ane accompt of 5–2–8d. & receaved it	• 05 • 02 • 08
Will: Blaikwood	12 March 1674 to William Blaikwood for ane stamped callico gown for my father 12 lib.	• 12 • 00 • –
Jo: Rob brande seck &c	9 & 12 of March 1673 John Rob gave in ane accompt for 11 ½ pynts of brande & 11 ½ pynts of seck &c: which he booked in the blew book & for which he payed 40–04–4d.	• 40 • 04 • 04

127 No sum in the margin in the original.

Margin	Entry	Amount	Total
	ditto		
	For 4 sugar loaves weighing 14 lb 2 ounces at 11d. ½ lb is	08–02–06	
	For 2 lb of sugar candie	02–00–00	
	For 4 ounces of the Ladie Inglistoun pectorall syrop	00–18–00	
	To James Meggett for goeing to Dalkeith at 3 tymes	00–06–08	
	To him for milling & killing 17 bols of oats	00–12–00	
	For barm 4s. & 7 dusan of egs 14s. is	01–03–00	
	To Nicoll Ramsay for 4 wyld fowls	01–04–00	
	To Wil: Stewart 4 March for for [sic] a calf fra Jo: Harrper	04–04–00	• 18 • 09 • 04
James Persie malt	To James Persie 17 March 1674 for making 8 bols of bear [sic] in malt		• 03 • 06 • 08
Wil: Steill	23 March 1674 to Wil: Steill: for 80 loads of coals at 4 lib. 40d. the load		• 16 • 03 • 04
Wil: Wilsone girds	27 of March to William Wilsone for putting on 25 girds at 4d. the gird		• 00 • 08 • –
Helen Clerks gown	26 March 1674 to Helen Clerk to buy her a gown 100 merks Scots is ..		• 66 • 13 • 04
John Rob	14 March John Rob debursed conform to his accompt written on the blew book 2–5–4d. & on the 18 of March 5–12–4d. on the 25 of March 3–05–00 is		• 11 • 02 • 08
27 March James Lawsone tayler	To him for 7 days work at 4s. a day is		• 01 • 08 • –
	16 March quhen Wil: Stewart went in for D: Henriesone & his wyfe – –		
	3 lib. of tobacco cutt & drie [sic]	02–08–00	

	Barm	00–04–00	
	2 loaves	00–08–00	
	For a gross of pypes	00–14–00	
	For a veill	03–06–08	
	For beef	02–06–00	
	Horse hyred	01–06–08	
	To D: Nisbitt 10 I gave & 4 my father gave is	40–12–00	
	To D: Henriesons mane	02–18–00	
	To Kenneth Jacksone for horse hyre	06–02–08	
	18 March to Prestons man quhen he broght the load of ale	02–18–00	
	For egs [sic]	01–00–00	• 64 • 04 • 00
Ge: Clerk webster	To him 18 March for weaving 20 els of plaiding 1 lib. & warping ale 2s. is		• 01 • 02 • –
Tho: Henrieson	28 March to him quhen he stayed 4 days on my father	12–00–00	• 12 • 00 • –
Alex^{r} Gray	28 March to him for making ane cover for the horse & furnishing 2 dowls		• 05 • 00 • –
To Wil: Stewart	For a stirk 1 Aprile 1674 5 lib. Scots		• 05 • 00 • –
Tho: Henriesone man	To Mr Josias his man quhen he stayed heer 2 dayes	05–16–00	
To the Ladie	The said day 30 March to her for her own use	05–16–00	
	& to her for the young rump & her self 6 els of ~~Holland~~ lining & 4 of twidle		
	For 2 muir fowls	00–12–00	• 12 • 04 • –

[174]

	The debursements of March 1674 in the other page		
seck	1 Aprile 1674 to Jo: Rob to gait at Leith 11 ½ pynts of seck at 36 the pynt		• 20 • 18 • –
brande	11 ½ pynts of brande at 2 merk the pynt is		• 15 • 06 • 08
soap	2 quarterdales of soap		• 07 • 10 • –
herrine	For a half barrell of herring		• 05 • 10 • –
Mr Ro: Ehot	Ditto to him quhen he came at severall tymes to see my father...18 lib. gold		• 18 • 00 • –
Wil: Megget	To him for Isobel Clerks boord fra 11 Aprile till 11 Julie [sic]		• 12 • 00 • –
Robert Dewer	To him in full of all preceiding 22 Aprile 1674 be whatsomever manor of way & his boll for Witsonday 1674	33–10–00	• 33 • 10 • –
	June 1674 to Jo: Pennycook for 128 rude of dyks 2s. the rude		• 12 • 16 • –

May 1674

3 bols of meall for the use of the house fra Leith	18–00–00
William Eastouns accompt for making my sisters &c: cloths	44–00–00
To Mr Scougall for my wyfes picture & myne	58–00–00
To Sir Ge: McKennie in consulting anent Balmerino	15–19–00
Jo Cook for my fathers iron work to his dead chest	08–08–00
For ane pair of boots	16–06–08
A pair of shoes 1–16s. & mending spurs 12s. is	02–08–00
To Mrs London fo[r] Lises accompt	17–00–00

Mr Will: Clerk	To Mr Wil: Clerk in full of all I wes owing him	20–00–00	
	To Edward Thomsone to awe & keep the gray meer	11–18–00	
	To Childers for Lises sadle	36–00–00	• 247 • 19 • 08
	To Thomas Henriesone for my fathers drogs &c: befor his death	215–00–00	• 215 • 00 • –

---

10 Aprile 1674 my father dyed	The accompt of my fathers funerals quho dyed 10 Aprile 1674 –	
	To Jo: Scott for ane wainscot chest 200 & to Alexander Gray for a fir one 12 lib. for making it	212–00–00
	To Tho: Henriesone for a shier cloth &c & for drogs during his secknes	208–09–00
	For ane terce of wyne 68 lib. 3 gallons 1 pynt of sek 33–6–8 22 pynts brandie at 2 merk 8 lb tobacco 08 lib. is	140–10–08[128]
	For meat 100	100–00–00
	For 27 els of black cloth for the seat in the kirk &c: at 22	022–00–00
	To the scolemaster [sic]	005–16–00
	To Mr Stacie the painter for the armes	058–00–00
	To the grave makers	004–00–00
	To Margaret Clerk which wes given to the poore folk	021–12–00
	// Summa	770–17–08
	Payed to Mrs Campbell I wes owing her	123–00–00

[128] There appears to be a miscalculation or an error in the cost of each item in this entry. I have transcribed it as found in the original.

[175]

Accompt of legacies my father left which I payed

Mr Will: Hammilton

My father gave out of his own hands 1 Aprile 1674 fyve 20s. peices
of gold to Mr William Hammiltone minister he left in legacie to him
2 also 100 lib. which I payed 20 Aprile 1674 ....

[The rest of this page is blank]

[Additional pages]

[On the last few pages, Clerk created entries that were kept separate from the rest of the account book. They are unpaginated, but they appear here in the order found in the original.]

A memor off suger delivert for the usse off the howsse since the 1 off
Marche 1670..
1 1 suger loaffe smallest seysse.................................... 1–:
2 1 suger loaffe of the greatest seyse .... 1–: as mikle as – 2
3 1 suger loaffe off smallest seyse................................ 1–:
4 lb casnet suger....................... //
1 lb casnet suger....................... // is 5 lb .... 5 lb:
4 1– suger loaffe off the smallest seyse delivert
on Munday the 4 Jully 1670............................... 1–:
5 On Thursday – 18 Agust 1– suger loaffe –
off a midling seyse – when Sir George Mack & Mr –

L: Char: wes heir.. 1–:

6 Saturday – 26 November 1670 – 1 suger loafe........... 1–:

7 Munday – 23 ~~November~~; January 1671
1 – great suger loaffe.. 1.

8 Fryday – 3 Marche 1671 1 suger loaffe .... 1.

9 Thursday – 8 June 1671 – 1 suger loaffe .... 1.

10 Fryday – 28 Jully 1671 – 1 suger loaf[fe] .... 1.

Memor – on Munday – 27 May 1672 halff a
suger loaffe.. ½ a on[e] –

On Munday – 15 July 1672 – halff a suger
loaffe... ½ a on[e] – .... 1 loaffe

Is in all off suger loaffe above – 13 suger loaffs
till this – 15 off Jully – 1672 .... 13 loafs

[The rest of this page is blank]

A memor off some things off divers sorts: done a – Sir Jo: Da: & sa dona – begun Anno 1673:

S: J: D:

N° 1 The 27 off January 1673 – Mr John Clerk delivert these things ....

N° 28 1– blew gilt leather caisse with 12 handsome large knyves with round charrm–crosse handls.......No. 28 ....

2– 8 cheis made at Newbiging...

---

2 The 29 off Agust 1673 – sent with Alexander Clerk to N: Lis: with the 5 particullars under wreatten – to wit..

N° 22 1 large charrm cross marber – morter with marbre pistol ....

8 cheis off 72 – off – 1673 made at Newbiging ....

1– blak turnt ebene[129] dask [sic] – to lay a booke – on for reading.....

1– handsome kain with a marbert yvorie head with a knyffe in the head of the kain...

1– yvorie coup for casting dysse off it with 6 dysse ....

---

3 The things under wreatten betwixt this – ABC – and the lyke 3 letters wreatten doun towards the fitt off this syde – I did delyver them my selff at Edinburgh the – [blank] off November 1673 –

1– a very large fyne tortle shell combe ....

2– a very curious yvorie combe – small tootht.................................

3– a ne[a]t steill key ring ....

4– a curious carnation plane velvit purse with a round bottom lynd with sea grein satyne ordert about with gold threid – with gold knops the strings cramosie – silk mixt with gold threid – brand new – never usse ....

1– a long calsidon – litle botle with a silver head & skrew – ....

2– a curious turnt plane yvorie penneth ....

3– a litle curious turnt penneth I say – a brasse siring weell gilt – to drawe up – sueit essence in it – or any li[q]uid thing with a very fyne grein etuis – gilt with small flour de luces ....

4 curious litle boxes –

1– a litle turnt round tortle shell box...

2– a net litle box turnt with a skrew in the head yairoff of blak ebene.

3– a net litle box off a sea horse tooth – with a small skrew in its top.

4– a net box off ebene – & off a sea horse tooth – a handsome litle on[e] ....

5– ane yvorie totum ....

1– a fyne squair handsome litle standish off broun Virginia wood the standish – drew out off a squair caisse off Virginia wood with a gilt brasse knop – the standish conteins a box holding ink –& a box for – holding sand – I did put in [sic] into the said standish..................

2– any yvorie ply letter ....

3– 2 round batons off best brunt wax – 1 stick round – 1 marbert......

4– 1 pen knyffe with a grein handle.......................

[129] Ebony.

5– 1 pen knyffe with a broun handle .... both Thoulouze[130] pen knyves –
6– 1 verie litle broun ha[n]dsome horne penneth for the pokit..........

N° 34 1– large gray pan velvit bag – lynd with handsome whyt leather – with great silk strings –& great handsome silk knaps handsomlie wroght about the edges with gray silk ....

N° 36 1– large grein flourd velvit bag off uncut vilthe raze lyne with handsome whyt leather with great grein silk strings with great handsome grein silk knaps handsomlie wroght about the edges with silk..

ABC ~ ~ ~ ~ *John: Clerk* ~ ~ ~ ~ ABC; ~ ~

[second last page]
A memor off such sort of skins as may be sent to William Brown skinner to be almed whyt this 12 off Januar 1670

1 horse hyds off any sorts..
2 calff skins off any age..
3 hudron skins of 1 yeir 1 ½ yeir or two yeir old.........
4 any litle kows [sic] hyde ....
5 sheips skins – callit – shorlin[g] skins......................

Any of these being almed & weill drest they ar verie fitting for – horse graith – or any uther ussefull thing about a howsse –:

garden seids –

Accompt off gairden seids George Reid boght fra James Stewart drogist the 24 off Marche – 1670 –[131]

1– 4 once off liks ....

1– 4 once of liks 00–10–00
2– 2 once of carrets 00–16–00
3– 4 once off sybows 00–10–00
Garden seids – 4– 1 once off parsnips 00–05–00
5– 2 once off turnips 00–08–00
6– 1 once off letus 00–04–00
7– 2 once off rifarts 00–08–00
8– 1 once off purpe 00–06–00
9– 1 drope of mergelin 00–01–00
10– 1 drop off gille flours .... 00–06–00.......... • 03 • 14 • –

03–14–00

[130] Toulouse.
[131] This set of entries also appears on [96] above.

William Broun skinner

William –
Broun –

In anno – 1670 – whair I have my chamber neir the castel hill –
did alme & dresse for me – the particullars under wreatten for which –
he wold tak no money – not the lesse that I did earnestlie desyre him –
to tak payment for the same – bot he said he wold have nothing for –
doeing off the same ....

1– a horse hyd – which he almed – it wes Jacks hyde – the hyd of the –
best horse ever I had – or – will have in my lyffe tyme – poore Jack –
good Jack – the best horse ever a man crost.................................

2– and 3 calff skins he almed for which he wold have nothing..........
I thoght fit to remark and wreat doun this to the end I might –
remember the same – in cace [sic] –he spok off it efter ward – to the end
I might remember how much – I wes obliged to him ....

John: Clerk ....

~~Munday the 28 off Marche 1670 – 10 lyge dollors at 56s. the peice~~[132]
is... • 28 • 00 • –
~~Saturday – 23 Aprill 1670 – 10 rex dolors is – 29 lib.~~ .... • 29 • 00 • –
~~Thursday – 1 off June 1671 – 4 rex dolors~~.. • 11 • 12 • –
~~Wedensday – 4 off October – 7 rex dolors – 20 lib. 6s.~~ .... trois anes • 20 • 06 • –
~~• 88 • 18 • –~~

William

Edinburgh – Saturday – 16 Marche 1672 fra Mr Jo: Clerk

Home wyn: Merchant

David Nisbet William Home his man will b[e] found at Robert Bowies the coupers neer the soape wark or soape howsse – in Leith – or at William Hom[e]s celler neer the weyhowsse –

[Strip added over top of the struck out entry above]
A recept fra Jo – Broun schoole master to mak some more nor a pynt of ink –

1–	8 once off galls	00–06–00
2–	4 once off copres	00–01–00
3–	2 once off pomegranat skins	00–04–00
4–	2 once off gum arabik – at 3s. the once	00–06–00
		00–17–00

[132] This section is crossed out in the original. Clerk placed a strip over the top of this section with a receipt from John Broun schoolmaster. See below this section.

[Back Cover][133]

The 5 off October 1669 – given to Mr William Clerk at Neubiging, Mr William Clark off Howstoun – advocat –: Go to – MA

M A 1 A fyne velvit cap that draws doun about on[e]s neck lynd with pan with buttons doun before – new never worn – worth ....

2 A fyne chasse brod off Indian wood and boxwood wood with 32 box wood – chasse men blak and yellow cost..

3 1 boxwood butter knyffe ....

4 1 horne filler...

5 1 fyne whyt yrne extinguisher .... [134]

In December 1669 resavet fra Mr George Eidingtoun – [obscured by a small square patch]

1– cok ....

2– hens .... great fowls......go to AB;

AB The 29 off December 1669 wreatten to the said Mr Georg Edingtoun – that I had left at William Brouns housse the particullars under wreatten to be sent him & desyrd him to send me some verses off 2 sorts that he told over me my chamber – – –

1 2 cheisse of the bigest chessire –

2 1 horn filler ....

3 1 plenisht whyt yrne extinguisher ....

4 1 boxwood butter knyffe ....

5 The copie of *A Barrons court* in print .... ;

Fryday 30 September 1670 at Newbiging given to Sir John Nicolsons lady –;

1 1 fynd ticht can with ane long yvorie head ....

1 gray marber morter with nogs – with 1 marbert pistoll ....
1 litle round gray marber morter plain with a marber pistoll ....
1 fyne pearl dish well hold about a mutchkin....................................
2 pearle spoons with plaine silver handls both worth.........................
To hir cousin Mistresse Amelie – 1 pearle spoone with a pearle handle

---

[133] This entry is on the hardback cover of the account book.
[134] Although there is a small patch covering a portion of this page, from what is visible, Clerk did not provide a sum for these items.

GLOSSARY

In constructing this glossary I have endeavoured to provide the meaning of those words, terms, or items which might prove most problematic, are obscure, or are of a specialised nature. It is by no means comprehensive; for the glossary to cover the full extent of the range of items mentioned in this account book would require considerable space. I have also included different variants of spelling, reflecting both what was contemporary practice and also somewhat idiosyncratic to John Clerk. I have split the glossary into two sections: subjects and places. Many of the definitions below have been adopted from the *Dictionary of Scots Language* online, the *Oxford English Dictionary* online, and *A Scots Dialect Dictionary comprising the words in use from the latter part of the 17. century to the present day*.[1]

ague an acute fever.
aller alder.
alme; alm; also, alum(e) alum: an astringent mineral salt that was used in dying, tanning, sizing, and medicine.
alming a tub for use in treating skins with alum.
aloes siccotrin *aloe succotrina*: an aloe found near Cape Town, South Africa.
anet seid dill seed.
anker a liquid measure; sometimes refers also to the barrel containing the liquid.
aquavite; aqua vitae a strong spirit, whisky.
arles payment given for procuring services or for initiating the striking of a bargain.
aspeck; aspick (oyll/oil of) an oil extracted from lavender.
axletree; axiltreis the fixed bar or beam, typically made of wood or iron, on which the opposite wheels of a carriage revolve.
bais; baies; baye(s) baize: plain weave cloth.
ballane; ballen; ballin; balin(e) whalebone, often used in bodices.
bandolir a pocketed belt for carrying ammunition.

1 https://dsl.ac.uk; https://www.oed.com; A. Warrack & W. Grant (comp.), *A Scots Dialect Dictionary comprising the words in use from the latter part of the 17. century to the present day* (Edinburgh, 1911).

barkit; barkitt; barkcat; berkit tanned or hardened; used chiefly with *hide* or *leather*.

barle barley.

barme; berme yeast.

bee skaip; beis skaip beehive.

bicker; biker a small wooden vessel made of staves, with one or two staves prolonged to form lugs.

birk birch.

bistorie; bistouri (*Fr.*) a surgical instrument used to make incisions.

blancheferme; blanchferm; blanche dewtie a nominal quit-rent paid in money or otherwise paid in acknowledgement of superiority.

blechit; bleichit; blitching bleaching.

bolster a long pillow or cushion.

bos(se) lock a type of lock.

bosse window a bow window.

botkin; bodkin a long, thin needle.

boustin; bustiane; bustin fabric made out of cotton.

bout (*v.*) to sift.

bowet; bouet; bowat a hand lantern.

braider soft woollen cloth.

brande brandy.

breiks breeches, trousers.

brizel; brissell; bryssell brazil: a dye-stuff generated from brazil wood; often, blew and rede brissell.

brod a board.

brome; browme; broym; broom a broom plant.

bruntstaine brimstone.

buist a small box used for holding documents, money, small articles.

bukrim buckram: linen or cotton fabric.

burd(e)clath(e); buirdclaith; boord cloth a tablecloth.

bussom(e); bussum; busom; bwsom; busum a besom/broom.

bustian; busstian worsted cloth with a twilled weave.

bygirdle a purse.

cades cotton wool or flock used for padding.

cadger a person that hawks various items, goods.

calsidon chalcedony: a precious stone used in lapidary work.

cambrick cambric: fine white linen originating in Cambray, Flanders.

camlit camlet cloth.

cande candy.

canel; cannell cinnamon or the bark of trees which produce cinnamon.

cap; caup; capp; kap a wooden bowl or cup.

carabin(e) carbine: a firearm shorter than a musket.

cardail; cardaill a hogshead.

cardamus lefser cardamom.

carv(i)e; carwie caraway.
casnet unrefined cane sugar.
cassel; castle (soap) may refer to 'Castile' soap made with olive oil.
cassia fistula a flowering plant native to the Indian subcontinent and adjacent regions of Southeast Asia; used to flavour tobacco, but also as an anti-oxidant, anti-inflammatory, astringent, and purgative.
centurie centaury: an annual, with a yellowish, fibrous, woody root often used to treat indigestion or heartburn.
cesse; sesse a tax raised on the basis of the rental value of land possibly introduced by the English army of the Commonwealth during their occupation of Scotland; maintained to raise money for a variety of purposes.
cheise cheese.
chessire; chessirt a tub for pressing cheese.
chestane; chesten; chestin a chestnut.
chiffron; cheiffroun, chiffrine a glove.
chirageon surgeon: someone who cures diseases and/or injuries by manual operation.
chirrie cherry.
chopin a liquid measure equal to a half (Scottish) pint.
chyre a chair.
cire cloth; cere claith waxed cloth.
cizers scissors.
clow; clowis clove(s).
cod(d) a pillow or cushion.
cog; coge; coig a wooden vessel made of hooped staves.
coll riddle a hay sieve.
cols coal.
confeits sweetmeats or sealed, salted, and preserved meat.
copres copperas: green crystals from hydrated ferrous sulphate used often in making ink or pigment.
corail; curale; curell coral.
cordovans cordovan leather.
corsdesitron; cordisidron lemon peel.
cotta a surplice.
courtin; courting; courtyne curtains.
coy a heifer.
craim; crame a stall or stand for the sale of goods.
crammasy; cram(m)osie crimson.
creill; crele; creel a large wicker basket; or, a wooden box or crate.
creish grease; often used as an emollient in preparing wool for spinning.
cudbek possibly a caudebec hat: a felt hat originating from Caudebec-en-Caux, Normandy.
culebs an aromatic made from the fruit of *piper cubeba*.

cuning; cunning rabbit.
curpl(e); curpal a crupper.
dail; dale a wooden plank.
dale; daill; daile a quantity, number, amount, or portion of some item.
dams; damas; damask; dammask a rich, colourful fabric, often of silk, wool, linen, or cotton, with designs and figures.
diapalma an unguent used to treat sores.
dicht (*v.*) to prepare, put in order.
doghead part of the lock that holds the flint; or, the hammer of a firelock.
dornick; dornock linen cloth originally made at Tournai (Belgium); used especially for tablecloths, serviettes, or towels.
doucat; dovcat dovecote.
dracht a draught, load, or freight.
drap de berrie a woollen cloth originating in Berry, France.
drogs a drug or medicinal substance.
drop one sixteenth of a troy ounce.
druggett; droggit a coarse woollen fabric.
dyst (*adj.*) dyed.
ell a measure of length approximately 37.2 inches.
elphshot a disease, most commonly of cattle, thought to have been inflicted by elves or fairies.
enclume an anvil.
etuis (*Fr. étui*) a small case for scissors.
extinguisher a hollow conical cap for extinguishing the light of a candle.
fadge a flat loaf.
fadom a measure of rope or cord approximately 6 feet in length.
fairsie a disease found in horses, mules, and cows often allied with glanders.
fald dyke a wall enclosing a fold.
fangrin; fing(e)ring; fingram woollen cloth often attributed with plaid or serge.
fasset facet: the small cut and polished face of a diamond.
finkle fennel.
fiol a vessel for holding liquids.
firgeist a fir joist.
firikin; firkin a small cask for liquids or solids equal to a quarter of a barrel or half a 'kilderkin' (16–18 gallons).
firkist a fir chest, box, coffer, or trunk.
foll; fole a foal.
freing a fringe.
gad an iron rod.
galangal refers to several tropical rhizomatous spices.
gally pot gallipot: a small earthenware pot or jar used for ointments or medicines.

gals an outgrowth on trees, galls were largely used to make ink and tannin; also used in dyeing and in medicine.

garron a large broad-pointed nail frequently used to fix the body of a cart to the axle.

gein; geine wild cherry.

gill a measure of capacity for liquids approximating to 1/4 of a mutchkin or pint.

gille flower a gilliflower.

gimp; gymp a narrow ornamental trim used in sewing or embroidery often made of silk, worsted, or cotton twist with a cord or wire running through it.

girds a metal or wooden hoop often used for barrels or tubs.

girn(t) to catch in a 'girn' or a trap.

girs(ing) to feed on grass or to pasture.

girsing; gyrsing pasturage.

glaik; glaikis a puzzle-game consisting of a set of rings, nails, and wire loops.

glob a globe; or, a blob (often a conflation of blob and glob).

graf; graffe a grave or tomb.

graith; graitht; graythe accessories, accoutrements, equipment, or tackle; furnishings of any sort; when used in relation to the webster craft, it can also mean a leaf of heddles for a loom.

gravell kidney stones.

grograin; grogram; grogran fabric made of silk or mohair; a garment made of grogram.

grosert gooseberry.

gryce; gryse a young pig.

gum arabick gum arabic.

handsel; hansell a gift given at the beginning of the year, a birthday, or other special occasion; or, a token of good luck.

hardn; harden coarse cloth, sometimes of linen or the hurds of flax or hemp; sackcloth.

hare stuff stiff cloth woven with a cotton or linen warp and horsehair weft; haircloth.

haws the red fruit of the hawthorn.

hazel; hizel hazel.

haick; haik; heck a rack; or, a slatted framework made of wood or iron fixed to the wall of a stable and used for feeding sheep.

hauch(e); haugh; hawch a haugh: flat alluvial land by the side of a river; river meadow.

headstail; heidstail a headstall: part of a bridle or halter that fits over the horse or draught animal.

hecklt lint that has been combed.

hekil; heckle a hackle for combing out flax or hemp.

herin; heren; heiring; herine herring.
hird a keeper of a hird; e.g. a shepherd.
holin(e) seid seed from a holly-tree.
holt; hout; howt a shortened form of 'knapholt': a wood or copse.
huddron; hudderon; huddro(u)n; hutheron a young heifer or the skin of one.
hynd a skilled agricultural labourer; or, the steward on an estate.
Jew's ear *auricularia auricula-judae*; a type of mushroom.
jump a layer of leather or a 'lift' of which the heel of a shoe is built up.
jupe a loose tunic or jacket; sometimes a woollen undershirt.
jus(se) de reglis; jus de réglisse a licorice extract often used to relieve the symptoms of indigestion.
killavyne; killavein; kilevyne; killevyne a pencil with black lead; or, sometimes, *reid killevyne pen*.
kirn a butter churn.
kist a chest, box, trunk, or coffer.
knap; knapp; knaip an ornamental knob, tassel, or button.
knapel; knapholt; knap(p)ald; knap(p)ell; knap(p)le clapboard.
ky cow.
laft the upper storey of a two-storey building.
laid; lade a load.
laistband the selvage of a piece of fabric.
Lam(m)as; Lammes 1 August: refers to one of the quarter- or term-days; also, ancient festival of ripening of corn.
lame earthenware dishes or crockery.
lancet; lansett a double-edged surgical instrument typically used for bleeding or to make punctures.
lapsters a lobster.
last a mechanical form shaped like a human foot used by shoemakers for manufacturing or mending shoes.
leglin; laiglen a wooden pail, often with a projecting stave for use as a handle.
libing gelding, castrating.
lickeres; licorass; lickres; liquorish; liquores licorice, liquorice.
linen, linings, lineings, lyneing linen.
linze winze linsey-woolsey: a strong, coarse fabric woven from linen and wool.
lip(e); lippie a dry measure equal to roughly a quarter of a peck.
lit (*v.*) to dye, or colour.
litting; liting; litting dyeing.
loffe an amount or portion.
loup a cord or braid consisting of a series of loops used for fastening garments or for ornamentation.
love/lowe a kind of crape or gauze used for mournings.

lozen diamond-shaped.
lug(e) the handle of a jar, cup, jug, etc.
lustart; lusterit; luisterit velveteen or satin cloth; having a lustre or sheen.
lutestring glossy silk fabric.
lyert streaked with two colours; dappled.
lyg(e) dolor; leg-dollo(u)r; lyg(g)-dollar a silver coin of the United Provinces.
lym mortar or cement; lime.
mail(l); mail(e) rent or payment in kind.
male; maile; meal(le); meill meal, typically oatmeal.
mandel(l); mandil(l); mantl; mantil a cloak, cape; a loose, sleeveless cloak or wrap, a mantle.
mandor(e) mandola: an instrument similar to a mandolin.
mand a woven basket, typically made of wicker.
marber(t) marble, marbled; borrowed from the French: *marbre, maubre*.
mashlock; mashloch a mixture of various grains or legumes ground into meal or flour.
mattock a mattock; a hand tool used for digging and chopping, similar to a pickaxe.
meassons a stonemason.
mair; meir a mare.
mercusus dulcis calomel: used as a purgative or fungicide.
mergelin; mergeleine marjoram.
Mertimes Martinmas: the feast of St. Martin, 11 November; one of the term-days or quarter-days.
mezels measles.
minim dark brownish grey (referring to the colour of the robes of the Minim Friars).
monter/mounter a watch.
morter a mortar: the vessel used to hold solids that are pounded into powder with a pestle.
moudewarts a mole.
mountebank a person who sold medicines in public, a charlatan, or sometimes physician.
moyer *Origin and meaning obscure.*
muller a frame or moulding.
mure fowl; muir-foul(l) a red grouse.
mutch a headdress; a close-fitting day cap of white linen or muslin.
mutchkin a measure of capacity for liquids equal to a quarter of a Scottish pint.
naill a Flemish unit of weight of wool, apparently equal to 6 pounds; more commonly, a measure of length of cloth the sixteenth of an ell.
neuk; newk; nuik a corner, angle, or recess.
nitmug nutmeg.

olium rodium oil of rosewort.

once ounce.

ort-dollour a coin valued at a quarter of a dollar.

paisboord pasteboard: a board made by pasting sheets of paper together.

pallias; palliase a straw-filled mattress or under-mattress.

pan cratch; pan-crach(e) precipitate of lime forming on the sides of salt pans; typically used for rendering or harling walls; or, used for filling up joints.

pantons a slipper.

pap; pape; paip a nipple or a breast of a woman.

peirling pearling: a type of lace of thread or silk used to trim garments.

peper; pepper; paper paper.

perdrik; perdrix a partridge.

peropris propolis: a red or brown resinous substance derived from tree buds; commonly used as an ointment to promote healing in minor wounds.

peruque a wig; periwig.

phisik a practitioner of medicine.

pick pitch.

pig tail a twist of chewing tobacco.

pig an earthenware pot or jar used to hold a variety of items.

pirns a small cylinder or spool on which a measure of thread was wound; a reel for thread or yarn.

pistoll; pestell a pestle.

plenchin a flooring nail.

plew a plough.

poik an approximate measure of a commodity, usually less than a sack; sometimes, a small sack or bag.

pomp pump.

pomshon; pontions; puns(c)hio(u)n(e) puncheon: a large barrel or cask often used for fermenting or ageing wine.

poping; pop; pap a sheep-mark made by dipping a stick into the marking substance and applying it on the wool.

porringer; porringer a small bowl or basin with a handle, typically used for soup, stews, or similar dishes.

poudesoy; podesway; poudesay paduasoy: a strong, corded, silk fabric.

pow (*v.*) to pluck, tug, pull.

powny-hen a female turkey.

powny; pouny; pownie pony; *dimin.* – young animal.

prin; prene; prein a pin.

purpie; purpy; purp purslane or *Veronica beccabunga*; often used for salads or medicinal purposes.

quair; quar(e); quhair quire: a measure of a number of sheets of paper amounting to a twentieth of a ream.

quinch; quench; queens a quince.

raising; raisine a raisin; alternatively, a grape or cluster of grapes.
ras; raise; raze a smooth fabric of silk or worsted.
rashe; ras(c)h(e); res(c)h rushes.
reglis; réglisse (*Fr.*) licorice; liquorice.
reim; reyme; ream cream.
ridle; riddl(l)e a mesh sieve.
rigwide rigwiddie: a ridge-band; the band, rope, or chain running across a cart-saddle on a draught-horse supporting the shafts of the cart.
rissart; rizer; resor; rasour redcurrant.
roset; rosit rosin.
rou; row; roll; roulle a piece of parchment or writing paper.
rouche (*adj.*) rough or unrefined.
roume a particular space or area.
row(l); rowle; rou(l) padded support for a gown or petticoat worn around the waist.
rubber a brush or cloth used for 'rubbing', for the purpose of cleaning or polishing.
ruben ribbon.
rude; ruid a measurement of area equal to eighteen-and-one-half feet.
rushie Russia leather; a 'durable leather made of skins impregnated with oil distilled from birch-bark' (*OED*).
rym ream.
saltfat a salt cellar, or salt dish.
sark (*v.*) to furnish with sarkings ('rough boarding nailed on top of rafters to which slates are nailed') (*DSL*).
sark a shirt, undershirt, chemise, or shift.
say; sae; sey a fine cloth similar to serge.
scorling; shorling the skin of a recently shorn sheep.
scull; skull a shallow basket, often made of wicker or wooden laths.
seck sack: a Spanish white wine.
selvidge edging or a border of a garment; 'the edge of a piece of woven material finished in such a manner as to prevent the ravelling out of the weft' (*OED*).
sene; sennie senna: dried leaflets of various species of *Cassia*, used as a purgative or emetic.
serge de challon cloth or frieze originally associated with or produced in Châlons-sur-Marne.
sering; siring a syringe.
seyse; seise size.
seyth a coalfish.
shag; schage (*v.*) to make rough, shaggy; to make rough nap or pile on cloth.
shaive a sheaf of a cereal crop made up after reaping; a rough measure of the yield of a crop.

s(c)shod shool a wooden shovel with a blade edged with metal.
shoe (*pron.*) she, third-person feminine.
shook a set of staves and headings for one hogshead, cask, or barrel.
shool a skin, husk, pod, shell, or membrane.
shoon(e) a shoe.
shotl(e) an inner compartment in a drawer, chest, or cabinet.
sive; sif(f); seve a sieve.
skerf; scarfe; scarf; skarf(f); skairf a scarf or sash.
sklait(t) a slate.
skring a screen.
snek a door or gate latch.
soutar; souter; soutor; soutter; sowter a shoemaker or cobbler.
spangaried the ornamentation on clothes.
spinel; spen(n)el(l) a spindle.
sprangd; spraingit; springed striped.
spreckel; sprekle; sprekkel; spraekle; spraikle (*v.*) to mottle, fleck, or variegate.
sprent a spring or clasp of a lock.
spurier a spur-maker.
stave a staff.
steip a measure (usually of barley) amounting to what would be steeped for the process of making beer.
stiffing; stifting material (starch) used for stiffening (part of) a garment.
sting; stang a wooden pole or stake.
stirp stirrup.
stoop; stoup cup.
stouk a stook; a group of sheaves of grain, oats, peas, etc.
stroe straw.
studie; study; stwdy an anvil.
swingling hards swingle-tree hurds often used to make coarse bagging.
sybous a spring onion.
syde; side pendulous, of a garment.
tab(b)ie; tabin; tabyne tabbie: silk taffeta.
tailsdouce; taileduce; talliduse; taildous a process of engraving on metal using a burin.
tak(e)it; takit a small nail.
tallo(u)n; tallow(e) tallow: the fat of an animal; when melted down and clarified, it was used for a lubricant; also used for candles.
tamein; tameing; tamin tammy: a type of thin woollen cloth, a kind of worsted.
teis; te; tie; tais (*pl.*) a fastener; part of a horse's harness or a side-rein.
tent Malaga wine.
terce; tierce a measure of liquid capacity, equal to a third of a pipe, or 42 gallons (159 litres).

teston; testane; testaine a silver coin of Milanese origin copied by the French and later minted in Scotland. It was valued at four or five shillings. Contextually, it was noted to be of little value.

thet(t); theat; theit the rope attached to a horse's harness by which a plough or carriage is pulled.

theyk; theiking material used for roofing a building or the act of causing a building to be roofed.

thraive; thraiwe; threave a measure of cut grain, oats.

tiffany; tiffenie; tiffinie; tiffeine; tiphanie a thin, transparent material, usually silk, muslin, or lawn.

tiking; ticking; tayking; teyking a durable cotton or linen textile often used for making bed coverings and casings.

timber heil a wooden heel for shoes.

tinkler; tinklar; tincla(i)r an older variant of 'tinker'.

tirlesse a lattice or grating (often used for covering a door or window).

toop a male sheep or ram.

tou; tow(e) flax, jute, or hemp fibre used for spinning.

toung a pair of tongs.

towl cloth used for bathing; also, the cloth used for wiping fingers at the table.

trincher; truncher a trencher.

troy wecht; triose wecht based on the *marc de Troyes*, it is a standard system of weights used for precious metals, precious stones, and medicine.

truff turf, sod; sometimes used for fuel.

trump a mouth harp.

turnor a small copper coin in Scotland valued at one-sixth of an English penny.

twidl(e) a strong, twilled, woollen cloth.

twill a 'woven fabric characterized by parallel diagonal ridges or ribs' (OED).

tyrl(e)is; trillis; tirls a lattice, grille, or grating of wood or metal.

unguent an ointment of salve.

valize a suitcase; or, a travelling bag or saddlebag.

vele; veil; veil a calf intended for food.

venize; venysse a very fine, delicate glass often used to make vials.

vilthe felt.

virginells a virginal: a musical instrument within the harpsichord family.

virol; viral; vyral; wir(r)al(l) a metal band fitted around the end of a wooden rod, implement, or cane to prevent splitting or wear.

visorne a visor.

wairing; waring to utilise or employ a person or an object. It also refers to the action of spending or disbursing monies.

wake; wauke; wauch (*v.*) to full (cloth).

wald *reseda luteola*: also known as 'dyer's rocket', a wild flower used to produce a yellow dye.

waltings; watting; watten selvedge.
walt(ing); wa(u)t(ing) a welt on a show; a strip of leather used to join the sole and upper; leather strip used to decorate garments.
weathers wether: a castrated male sheep.
weir; weyr; wire can refer to a knitting needle; also, wire-thread (cotton thread).
welicot; wel(y)cot(e); wylecot a waistcoat; also, a woman's undershirt or petticoat.
wernicht varnished.
wey balk weigh-bauk: the beam of a pair of scales.
whalt; whatt; walt; watt *see above*, waltings.
whorl a small wheel.
wirt unfermented beer.
worsit turk worsted Turkish cloth.
worstit; wurset; wusert; wutert worsted cloth.
wyne ston a compound found in wine barrels and casks.
yetling items made of cast iron.
zaffre; zaffre a deep-blue pigment obtained by roasting cobalt ore.
zedwarie ginger.

Place-names

As with the glossary of terms, I have tried to include as many as possible of the place-names Clerk referenced in his account book. Again, the list is by no means comprehensive; many of the places mentioned were farms, hamlets, or villages that may no longer exist, have been subsumed into larger entities, or share common or obscure names that cannot be verified.

Ancrelaw (Ankrielaw) Settlement due W of Howgate and N of Mount Lothian.
Auchincorth (Auchencorth) A peatland lying about 13 miles SW of Edinburgh.
Barnbougel The lands, and tower house, were situated on the S shore of the Firth of Forth. Located in the parish of Dalmeny, it is 1 mile SE of South Queensferry. The Primrose family, later earls of Rosebery, purchased Barnbougel in 1662 and made it their family seat.
Bavelaw Located on the northern slopes of Hare Hill in the Pentland Hills. It is 4 miles W of Penicuik and 2 miles S of Balerno. The lands, and castle, of Bavelaw lie on the southern border of Edinburgh. In 1641, Charles I ratified his father's grant of the lands and buildings of 'Easter' and 'Wester' Bavelaw to the Scott family of Harperrig and Clerkingtoun following the resignation of the estate by Sir Walter Dundas of that Ilk.
Bigger (Biggar) A town, and former burgh, approximately 20 miles SW of Penicuik.

Braid Law A hill lying 4 miles SW of Penicuik and 3.5 miles N of Carlops.

Braidwood A small village in South Lanarkshire approximately 1 mile from the River Clyde and 36 miles from Edinburgh.

Brunstoun (Brunstane) A suburb of Edinburgh in the NE part of the city.

Cairnhill The lands of Cairnhill were bounded to the S by Braidwood and Brunstane and to the N by the Loan Burn on the N side of Cairnbank.

Caldtown The lands of Calton (Wester Restalrig) were held by the Elphinstone family in the seventeenth century. The village was situated on the western end of Calton Hill.

Canegate (Canongate) The former burgh of Canongate.

Carlips (Carlops) A small village lying between West Linton and Penicuik.

Carnock A village and parish of Fife about 3.5 miles W of Dunfermline.

Carsewell The lands lie 1.5 miles W of Penicuik and 0.5 miles from the lands of Newbiggin.

Clerkingtoun Located in the parish of Haddington, the lands and castle (now demolished) were in the hands of the Scotts of Harprig from 1628.

Coits (Coates) Previously, lands lying to the W of Edinburgh. It is now a residential area to the W of Haymarket railway station.

Cooking (Cuiken) Lies 2 miles NE of the lands of Newbiggin and 0.5 miles W of Penicuik.

Craigmiller (Craigmillar) The lands of Craigmillar (including the castle) lie approximately 3 miles SE of Edinburgh city centre. In the 1660s, the estate was purchased by Sir John Gilmour, Lord President of the Court of Session (d. 1671).

Cramond A parish in the county of Edinburgh (and partly of Linlithgow) situated on the S shore of the Firth of Forth.

Crawford Moor Lies 20 miles SW of Biggar and 16 miles NW of Moffat. The region was known for extensive mining of gold, silver, and lead.

Darnhall An estate near Eddleston about 4 miles N of Peebles and 9 miles S of Penicuik.

Daufington (Dolphinton) A village and parish in Lanarkshire.

Dieppe A port town in Normandy, France.

Duns A livestock market town lying 15 miles W of Berwick-upon-Tweed.

Dykneuk (Dykeneuk) Lies approximately 1 mile SW of Penicuik at a bend in the Black Burn.

Elvingstone (Elphinstone) A village in East Lothian lying 1.5 miles SW of Tranent.

Esperstoun (Esperston) Lands lying about 3 miles S of Gorebridge in Borthwick Parish.

Glencorse Lies 7 miles S of Edinburgh and is bounded to the NW by Lasswade and to the SW by Penicuik. The barony of Glencorse was in the hands of the Bothwell family until the early nineteenth century.

Hakshawe (Hawkshaw) A village (and estate) lying 2 miles SW of Tweedsmuir in the Scottish borders.

Halls Lands lying a mile S of Penicuik.

Hurlie An area lying on the S bank of the River North Esk, about 1.5 miles SW of Penicuik.

Kimerghein (Kimmerghame) An estate lying 2.5 miles SE of Duns.

Lanerik (Lanark) A royal burgh, and important market town, located 12 miles WNW of Biggar and 16 miles W of Dolphinton.

Langshaw A small border village approximately 2.5 miles NE of Galashiels.

Largo A parish in Fife containing the village of Lower Largo on the N side of the Firth of Forth.

Lesswaid (Lasswade) A village located between Dalkeith to the E and Loanhead to the W, lying on the River North Esk. Situated 9 miles S of Edinburgh, the parish of Lasswade is bounded to the S by Penicuik and the W by Glencorse. It includes the villages of Lasswade, Roslin, and Loanhead, and is notable for Roslin Chapel and Hawthornden Castle.

Libertin (Liberton) A former village and parish of Edinburghshire, it lies 2.5 miles SSE of Edinburgh city centre. Liberton parish is bounded to the S by Lasswade and the W by Colinton. Its principal antiquity is Craigmillar Castle.

Lintoun (West Linton) Known as 'Lintoun' until the nineteenth century, in the seventeenth century the village had a prominent sheep market and was known for silver and lead mining, as well as stone carving.

Loanheid (Loanhead) A town located 5 miles SE of Edinburgh. In the seventeenth century, Loanhead was known for its market, coal mining, and paper making.

Logan House Land lying in a hollow in the Penicuik Hills.

Longformacus A village in Berwickshire lying 6 miles NW of Duns.

Marchestoun (Merchiston) The estate (and castle) lying SW of Edinburgh city centre was the seat of the Napier family from the early fifteenth century.

Mosshouses Arable land lying 2 miles WSW of Mount Lothian.

Mount Lothian (Mo(u)ntlothian) An estate lying 3 miles SE of Penicuik and 1.5 miles ESE of Howgate.

Musselburgh A town on the Firth of Forth about 5 miles E of Edinburgh.

Newhall Lying within the parish of Penicuik, about 1 mile NE of Carlops and 5 miles SW of Penicuik. In the early sixteenth century, the Crichton family owned a castle said to have extended over the whole of the promontory jutting out above the River North Esk. The property was purchased by Dr. Alexander Pennycuick in 1646, staying in the family until it was sold to Sir David Forbes (m. Catherine Clerk) in 1703.

Nunland(s) Lands lying in the (now) civil parish of Foulden in Berwickshire about 7 miles W of Berwick-upon-Tweed.

Nyne (9) Myll Burn (Nine Mile Burn) A hamlet in Midlothian about 1.25 miles NE of Carlops.

Owsenam (Oxnam) A village 4 miles SE of Jedburgh in the Scottish borders.

Pennycook(e)/Penny cook(e) (Penicuik) A town on the W bank of the River North Esk, 7 miles SW of Bonnyrigg and 10 miles S of Edinburgh.

Pinkie (Pinkie House) An historic house located in Musselburgh. In the seventeenth century, it was in the hands of the Setons, earls of Dunfermline.

Preston Pans (Prestonpans) A fishing town 9 miles E of Edinburgh. In the seventeenth century, it was known for its salt and coal industries.

Prestoun Grainge (Prestongrange) Parkland in East Lothian originally granted to the monks of Newbattle Abbey. It lies 3 miles E of Musselburgh and 0.5 miles W of Prestonpans.

Ravensneuk Easter and Wester Ravensneuk formed a part of the barony of Roslin until the end of the seventeenth century. The castle, belonging to the Sinclair family, stood on the S bank of the Esk, on lands bordering the farm of Ravensneuk, 0.5 miles NW of Ravensneuk Farm and 1 mile SSW of Penicuik.

Satir Seik; Satyr Seik; Satir Syke (Saltersyke) Land lying near Braidwood.

Silverburne/Silver burne (Silverburn) An area lying 6 miles N of Carlops and 2 miles W of Penicuik.

Skirling A former burgh of barony at the northern end of Tweeddale, lying 3 miles NE of Biggar. In the seventeenth century, it was renowned for its horse market.

Spittal (Hill) A summit of the Pentland Hills in the W of Midlothian, approximately 2 miles N of Carlops and 4.5 miles WSW of Penicuik.

Stobo A hamlet in Tweeddale, approximately 5 miles W of Peebles.

Straton (Straiton) A village near the River Girvan in South Ayrshire.

Towr (Tower of Penicuik) An area 0.5 miles W of the current church of St. Mungo in Penicuik, situated above the Esk. Before the reformation, the old proprietors of St. Mungo's held these lands. John Clerk (d. 1674) pulled down the Tower to use the stones in the park dyke at Newbiggin.

Trenent (Tranent) A town in East Lothian approximately 9 miles E of Edinburgh.

Uttershill Located 0.5 miles from Penicuik, S of the River North Esk. The lands were purchased by the Clerks in 1702.

Walltower Lands lying 3 miles SE of Penicuik, 8 miles NE of Carlops, and 1.5 miles WNW of Mount Lothian.

Wantonwas; Wanton Wa's; Wantounwallis (Wanton Walls) There is uncertainty about the location of the land Clerk mentions by this name, as it was both 'common' and 'obscure'. It likely refers to a former village close to Musselburgh.[2]

2 N. Dixon, 'The Placenames of Midlothian'. University of Edinburgh Ph.D. thesis, 1947, p. 187.

Welstoun (Walston) A parish in Lanark county, approximately 4 miles NE of Biggar.

Wrights houses (Wrychtishousis) A former village near Bruntsfield Links in Edinburgh.

INDEX OF PERSONAL NAMES

Excluding the glossaries, this index covers the primary parts of the text: the Introduction, main body, and footnotes.

I have indexed the vast majority of personal names that appear in Clerk's book of disbursments. Where individuals appear only once, without any sort of designation (occupational, status, geographical connection), and their appearance in the book is seemingly unremarkable, I have chosen to exclude their names from the index. Where it was possible I also included basic biographical details and attempted to differentiate between individuals that shared a name. If Clerk made note of a servant's role in the house or on the estate, I have included that role beside the person's name; all other servants are identified simply by their service designation. Unnamed individuals who appear in Clerk's book, and who were connected to some other named individual, appear as Clerk recorded them (e.g. Mr Broun's man, Lady Bagillo's woman, etc.)

As I mentioned in the Introduction, Clerk's 'man', John Rob, appears in the book more than any other individual. I chose to index only those entries involving Rob that highlight his range of responsibilities or where his involvement in Clerk's activities was in some way exceptional. Given that Clerk was prone to make the odd mistake when recording names, and did not always include contextual information to differentiate indviduals who shared a name, readers are advised to excercise a degree of caution in their searches and to examine similar entries.

INDEX OF PLACE NAMES

Excluding the glossaries, this index covers the primary parts of the text: the Introduction, main body, and footnotes.

The index offers a list of place names that appear in Clerk's book. Where it was possible to identify accurately the places that Clerk mentions, I modernized the spelling of those place names. Many of these place names also appear in the glossary which highlights the variants in Clerk's spelling of those places. Because of the exceptionally high number of references to Edinburgh in the accounts, I have chosen to index only the entries which mention Clerk, or members of his household, undertaking lengthy stays there or which document activities related to his chambers within the town.

INDEX OF SUBJECTS

Excluding the glossaries, this index covers the primary parts of the text: the Introduction, main body, and footnotes.

Clerk's book of disbursements documented his household expenditures covering the quotidian and mundane necessities to the more unique or extravagant undertakings. It would have been impossible to index every distinct item, service, or transaction. However, care was taken to include in this index the full range of items, services, and transactions that appear in the book, particularly if they were frequent expenditures or of an exceptional nature. As with the Index of Place Names, I have modernised the spelling of most words, but advise readers to look to the glossary for assistance with less familiar items or terms.